THE SS: HITLER'S INSTRUMENT OF TERROR

THE SS: HITLER'S INSTRUMENT OF TERROR

The full story from street fighters to the Waffen-SS

GORDON WILLIAMSON

CHARTWELL
BOOKS, INC.

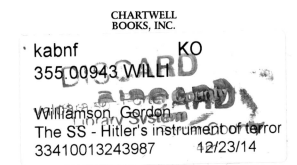

British Library Cataloguing in Publication Data:
A catalogue record for this book is available
from the British Library

This edition published in 2013 by

CHARTWELL BOOKS, INC.
A division of
BOOK SALES, INC.
276 Fifth Avenue Suite 206
New York, New York 10001
USA

The material in the chapter entitled 'SS Biographies' was extracted from
SS: Roll of Infamy by Christopher Ailsby.

ISBN: 978-0-7858-3012-2

Editorial and design by
Amber Books Ltd
74–77 White Lion Street
London
N1 9PF
United Kingdom
www.amberbooks.co.uk
Appstore: itunes.com/apps/amberbooksltd
Facebook: www.facebook.com/amberbooks
Twitter: @amberbooks

Printed in China

AUTHOR'S ACKNOWLEDGEMENTS

In any book like this, one must invariably seek the help and advice of others who have an interest in the subject. Although official archives, such as those held by the Imperial War Museum in London and the German Bundesarchiv, are an excellent source of material, photographs in particular, an amazing amount of unpublished material is still to be found in the hands of private collectors and in the personal albums of surviving veterans. I would like to take the opportunity of thanking the following people for their invaluable help with this book:

Josef Charita, who always seems to come up with fresh photographs, and whose assistance in supplying photographic material has been acknowledged by many authors.

Holger Thor Nielsen, whose enthusiastic willingness to assist is greatly acknowledged.

My friends John White, Erwin Bartmann, Ernst Barkmann and Hein Springer, who were, as always, helpful and supportive.

David Littlejohn, an acknowledged and respected expert on the subject of the Third Reich's military history, who kindly proofread much of the text and offered helpful advice and constructive comments.

Jim Skeldon, who undertook much time-consuming work on my behalf digging out facts and figures from various reference works, and thus ensured that this work met its tight schedule.

CONTENTS

THE BIRTH OF THE SS

In the turmoil that existed in Germany in the years after World War I, new political leaders arose. Among them was Adolf Hitler. The Schutz Staffel (Protection Squad) was first formed to protect him at political meetings. This was the beginning of one of the most infamous organisations in history.

Despite the fact that by the end of World War II the SS was a truly vast organisation, with branches that seemed to reach into almost every sphere of German life, and could boast a field Army of some of the most effective troops the world has ever seen, its beginnings were far from impressive. In its formative years, this most elite of the Nazi formations had been subordinated to, and often humiliatingly treated by, the common street louts of the Sturmabteilung (SA), the Party's Storm Troops. To fully appreciate how the dreaded Schutz Staffel (SS), Protection Squad, came about, as well as its conflict with the SA, it is necessary to go back in time to the years immediately preceding the outbreak of World War I and briefly consider the political situation then prevailing.

By 1914, the Social Democratic Party in Germany was one of the largest political parties in Europe. However, although Germany had a parliament of elected members, it was in reality far from being a parliamentary democracy. The German Reichstag, in which the Social Democratic Party formed a considerable majority, had neither the power nor the influence to overrule the wishes of the Kaiser and his military staff, who ruled very much as they wished.

German troops in action in World War I. Many ex-soldiers became members of Freikorps units after the war, and later went on to join Ernst Röhm's SA.

ABOVE: The Army returns from the front. Disillusioned German soldiers return to Berlin after the end of hostilities in November 1918. The fact that many soldiers believed the Army had not been defeated on the field of battle gave rise to the theory of the 'dolchstoss', the stab in the back. This stated that the Army had been betrayed on the home front by Jews, Social Democrats and profiteers. The Nazis were not responsible for inventing the term, but they exploited it brilliantly to discredit the Weimar Republic and its supporters.

As conflict loomed in August 1914, the Social Democrats protested loudly at the preparations for war and used their influence with the working classes to call for strike action against the Kaiser's military build-up. On the recommendation of his generals, the Kaiser declared martial law and thus rendered parliament impotent, while the threat of strikes quickly evaporated. In any case, the militarists had been conducting an effective propaganda campaign to whip up patriotic fervour among the masses, and the general feeling among the populace was of support for the Kaiser and his armed forces. When war broke out in 1914, the Social Democrats allowed their sense of patriotic duty to outweigh their opposition to the war, and thus the largest of Germany's political forces supported the war effort, albeit grudgingly.

This situation continued while the German Army was successful in its military endeavours, and while shortages on the home front were not excessive. However, as the war dragged on into a virtual stalemate and military actions in the West degenerated into static trench warfare, disillusion set in. Shortages in Germany became acute due to the Allied blockade. The population gradually became aware of the horrific conditions under which the troops were fighting at the front, as well as the horrendous losses, as countless lives were squandered by both sides in fighting for often the most strategically worthless piece of ground.

At the same time there was, on the home front, an increasing black market which the authorities seemed unable, or unwilling, to control. A growing undercurrent of unrest manifested itself as the people railed against the injustice and corruption around them. Black marketeers grew rich while German soldiers died in droves at the front. The trade unions actively considered taking strike action to protest against the situation both at home and at the front, but feared that any workers involved in such protests would find themselves conscripted by the military authorities and sent to the front, where they would face almost certain death (left-wing radical groups like the Spartacists, led by Karl Liebknecht and Rosa Luxemburg, were at this point too weak to mount any sort of meaningful challenge).

Matters were soon to change, however. In Russia in 1917, the February Revolution saw the abdication of Tsar Nicholas II, and the October Revolution brought the Bolsheviks to power, who secured a peace treaty with the Germans in March 1918. Russia, formerly an arch-conservative country, became a revolutionary state.

This situation produced two diametrically opposed sentiments in Germany. First, a wave of left-wing fervour swept the working classes. The Russian people had removed an authoritarian regime to form a new state and end a war. Many felt that the potential existed for German workers to do the same. Support for left-wing radical groups therefore increased dramatically. Conversely, however, the release of so many troops from the Eastern Front raised hopes for a successful offensive in the West, and thus eased the pressure on the Kaiser and his generals.

A near mutiny by the High Seas Fleet in 1917 was suppressed, but radical opposition within the Kaiserliche Marine was not destroyed, merely driven underground. In addition, when the Kaiser failed to implement a number of minor social and political reforms he had promised the

Social Democrat-dominated government in return for its support for the war effort, a potentially devastating strike by munitions workers was barely averted.

The considerable reinforcement of German forces in the West by troops released from combat on the Eastern Front allowed the generals to prepare for a massive new offensive in 1918. The hope of ultimate victory led to an upsurge in patriotism among the populace, which resulted in the home front situation stabilising somewhat.

The March-July 1918 offensives, however, soon ran out of steam, and the Allies counterattacked in August. On the 14th, Ludendorff admitted to the Kaiser that the Imperial Army had shot its bolt. The troops were exhausted, the reserves spent and, worst of all, the general staff was forced to admit to the Kaiser that the Army could no longer guarantee that the anticipated Allied counteroffensive could be successfully halted outside Germany's borders. The situation had become critical.

In October 1918, the commanding admiral of the High Seas Fleet, Admiral Franz von Hipper, decided to take the fleet to sea and force a showdown with the Royal Navy. Hipper undoubtedly knew that this might well result in a defeat for Germany, but considered that even if a defeat ensued, the honour of the Navy would at least be preserved. The sailors who manned the ships, however, were well

BELOW: Freikorps men on the streets of Berlin during the Spartacist uprising, January 1919. The insurrection was put down by a combination of Army and Freikorps units. The Freikorps member and later Nazi, Ernst von Salomon, saluted them in 1930, admiring them for their 'ruthless action against armed or unarmed enemy masses, their limitless contempt for the so-called sanctity of life and their marked disinclination to take prisoners under any circumstances.' It is unsurprising that many ex-Freikorps men joined the SA and SS. The leaders of the Spartacist uprising, Rosa Luxemburg and Karl Liebknecht, were subsequently murdered by right-wing elements. The Freikorps were dissolved in 1921, but their flags were later laid to rest in the Nazi Party's HQ in Munich.

aware of the military situation and had no intention of sacrificing their lives in some meaningless gesture solely to protect the honour of the Kaiserliche Marine. Heavily influenced by the part played by the Russian Navy in the revolution in that country, the sailors refused to put to sea. Once lit, the fires of revolution spread quickly, not only to the principal naval ports but also to the larger cities. Sailors, soldiers and workers councils sprang up everywhere and grasped the reins of power from the civil and military authorities.

The Army returns from the front

In this uneasy situation the Social Democrats saw a chance to make their influence felt. In a move designed to bring pressure to bear, they threatened to withdraw their support and resign from government unless the generals prevailed upon the Kaiser to abdicate, and agreed to peace terms being negotiated with the Allies. Hindenburg and Groener were loathe to agree to these terms, but on 8 November 1918 a call for a general strike was answered by tens of thousands of workers taking to the streets throughout Germany. The generals had no choice but to agree, and by 10 November the Kaiser had abdicated. Friedrich Ebert, the Social Democratic leader, was pronounced chancellor and an armistice with the Allies was quickly agreed.

Promising that revolutionary reforms would now be made, the government appealed for calm and a return to work by those on strike. Elated at the part they had played in toppling the Kaiser and ending the war, the workers readily agreed and a period of relative calm ensued.

The workers councils, however, were quick to realise that many of the changes made were merely cosmetic, and the reforms minor in nature. Admittedly the Kaiser had gone and, theoretically at least, a more democratic type of government was now in power, but many of the major reforms, such as the promised nationalisation of heavy industry, were swept under the carpet. Germany was rapidly polarising: extreme left- and right-wing groups were beginning to proliferate, and the centre-moderates were losing ground. The influence of the powerful industrialists and the militarists on the government seemed hardly affected, while the working classes appeared destined to be dominated by the left. Into this delicate situation, at the end of 1918, was about to enter a major new factor: the returning German armies.

The German Army was to be limited by the terms of the Armistice to a mere 100,000 men. Vast numbers of disaffected and often fully armed soldiers flocked back into Germany to be demobilised, and with them came a growing feeling that the troops at the front had been stabbed in the back by the corrupt machinations of a weak and vacillating government. Indeed, the government was soon to become known as the 'November Criminals'. The economy had been ruined by the war and there were few jobs available for these demobilised soldiers. A number of plots were hatched by senior military figures intent on overthrowing the government, but these were invariably leaked by soldiers whose sympathies were with the left, and they came to nothing.

The birth of the Freikorps

Well aware of the volatility of the situation, senior officers of the Army, now known as the Reichswehr, actively encouraged and often surreptitiously supplied arms to several small groups of right-wing ex-soldiers who were considered sufficiently politically reliable to be called upon to support the Army if circumstances required it. These groups of soldiers, generally referred to as Freikorps, usually banded themselves around a former officer whom they knew and trusted from wartime experience. Whatever official or semi-official title they may have held, they were generally collectively known by the name of their commanding officer. The sense of purpose and comradeship offered by these Freikorps units filled the gap in the lives of many of these men, caused by their demobilisation and subsequent failure to find employment. Many future prominent SS figures were members of the Freikorps during these turbulent times.

Freikorps units sprang up all over Germany. Generally well disciplined, the men of the Freikorps owed their loyalty first and foremost to their unit commander. Many units reached brigade size and were heavily armed, their small arms being supplemented in many cases by heavy machine guns, mortars, artillery, armoured cars and even a few tanks. Over two hundred Freikorps units are thought to have emerged during this period, their strength, if not their organisation and equipment levels, soon rivalling that of the Reichswehr itself. So much so, in fact, that the Freikorps formations became commonly referred to as the 'Black Reichswehr'. The men offered the individual Freikorps lead-

'It is much better to kill some innocent people than let one guilty person escape... You know what to do... shoot them then say that they attacked or were attempting to escape.'
– Major Schultz, Lutzow Freikorps, 1919

LEFT: *The enemies of the Army, the Freikorps, the Nazis and other right-wing elements in Germany: armed left-wing workers. In early 1919, it appeared that Germany was on the brink of a communist revolution, as a host of workers' and soldiers' councils sprang up, and in Munich a Soviet government was established for a few weeks. To many on the right, Hitler included, the troubles in Germany in the years after World War I were all part of a conspiracy: the Jewish-Bolshevik attempt to take over the world, and all other democratic and left-leaning ideas were merely cloaks to mask the grand plan. In 1925 Hitler wrote in* Mein Kampf: *'Now that I realised that the Jews were the leaders of Social Democracy, scales, as it were, began to fall from my eyes. My long mental struggle was over.' The crushing of the left-wing uprisings in 1919 by the Army and Freikorps delighted the right, but discredited the government because it had employed anti-democratic elements to restore democracy. For the right the fear of a Bolshevik takeover never disappeared, and the Army in particular became paranoid about 'subversive' movements. In September 1919, it employed one Adolf Hitler to report on a meeting of a small Bavarian political organisation: The German Workers' Party, based in Munich, which the ex-Army corporal joined as member number 7.*

ers unswerving loyalty, but the loyalty of these individual commanders to the Reichswehr or the government was by no means so unconditional. Some were little more than mercenaries, whose loyalty was bought by the level of arms and assistance offered by the Reichswehr.

This cult of the personality was reflected by the naming of Freikorps units after their commanders. Soon, Brigade *Ehrhardt*, Freikorps *Ritter von Epp*, Freikorps *Mossbach* and many others were to stamp their mark most forcefully on German life.

Most of the Freikorps personnel wore the original Army uniforms in which they had been demobilised, together with an appropriate Freikorps emblem. Swastikas and death's head badges abounded, predating the adoption of the swastika by the Nazis and the death's head by the SS by several years. The death's head badge had been a particularly important symbol in German military heraldry, being the traditional badge of the elite hussar units of the Imperial Army, and also of the flame thrower-equipped assault troops of World War I. Those without uniforms took to wearing a windcheater-type jacket of a more or less military appearance. To many Germans, these Freikorps units represented at least a semblance of order in the chaos that was Germany during the years immediately after the end of the war.

In general, naval units seem to have been affected more deeply by the swing to the left, probably because their home bases were in German ports and not at the front, they were thus more likely to be influenced by events on the home front. Conversely, however, naval Freikorps units such as the notorious Brigade *Ehrhardt* were among the most virulently right wing. From among the more left-wing sailors came the so-called People's Naval Division (interestingly, the communist East German regime of post World War II used a similar title for its navy: the Volksmarine, or People's Navy). When, at one point, the sailors' pay failed to materialise, the division rebelled, surrounded the Chancellery in Berlin and arrested a Social Democrat member. Army officers were incensed and demanded the use of force to oust the rebellious sailors. Chancellor Friedrich Ebert, in a panic, eventually agreed. The Army attack on the rebels, however, was foiled by the appearance on the scene of a large force of armed workers intent on supporting the sailors. Fuming, the Army was forced to withdraw and nurse its humiliation, determined to even the score with the rebels.

Ebert's agreement to the use of force against the rebels enraged many socialists in parliament and several resigned in protest. Political chaos and a dangerous level of instability, in which the Freikorps revelled, ensued. Meanwhile, radical left-wing groups, including the Spartacists, merged to form the Kommunistische

BELOW RIGHT: Adolf Hitler (with moustache on right) as a corporal in the German Army during World War I. During the war he was awarded the Iron Cross First Class for his bravery, and afterwards was employed by Army intelligence. By this stage of his life he already possessed the extreme views on nationalism and anti-semitism that would become the hallmarks of Nazi ideology, and it was perhaps inevitable tha he would be attracted by the policies of the extremist German Workers' Party. Originally, the Sturmabteilung (SA), or Storm Troops, were formed to keep order at the Party's meetings, but Röhm's Brownshirts were not unquestionably loyal to Hitler. The latter needed a force that was prepared to obey him without hesitation. As he later wrote: 'I told myself then that I needed a bodyguard, even a very restricted one, but made up of men who would be enlisted unconditionally, ready even to march against their own brothers. Rather a mere 20 men to a city (on condition that one could count on them absolutely) than an unreliable mass.' Thus was the idea for the SS born. Its first uniform was supposed to be brown shirt, black tie, swastika arm band and black Austrian ski cap with a silver death's head badge. All members were to have healthy physiques, good characters and not be drunkards.

Partei Deutschland (KPD). With the left wing rapidly consolidating its position and the centre parties now very much under the influence of the right, the scene was set for disaster.

The Western Allies, of course, were fully aware that Germany was breaching the conditions of the Treaty of Versailles with the barely concealed support of the Freikorps units by the Reichswehr. The Allies, however, were also worried by the rise of the Bolsheviks in Russia, and saw the aggressive stance of the right in Germany towards the growing influence of the communists as the lesser of two evils, and were thus reluctant to interfere.

The Spartacist revolt

In January 1919, a rather inept move by the government in sacking the Berlin Chief of Police Emil Eichhorn was met by a mass protest by left-wing groups, who occupied the offices of the Social Demo-cratic Party newspaper *Vorwärts*. At first Ebert's government was reluctant to inter-vene, and seemed willing to adopt a con-ciliatory approach and negotiate a peace-ful settlement to the protest. However, a large Freikorps force was assembled on the outskirts of Berlin, and when the rebels refused to evacuate the occupied building, it was unleashed upon them. Bloody street fighting erupted almost immediately as the Freikorps acted against the rebels with unbridled savagery. The struggle raged for several days as the Freikorps took every opportunity to elimi-nate their sworn left-wing enemies. Many

radicals were deliberately shot 'while try-ing to escape', with others disappearing either into hiding or being murdered. Communist leaders Liebknecht and Luxemburg were among those abducted and murdered during these turbulent days.

The government was greatly dismayed by these events and shocked by the brutal-ity of the Freikorps. The latter, however, were schooled in the savagery of war. Death was no stranger to them and they neither gave, nor expected, any quarter. The government, in sanctioning the use of the Freikorps, had opened a Pandora's Box. Once unleashed, the Freikorps became a law unto themselves and were almost impossible to control.

It was not only Berlin which suffered in this manner: Freikorps units went on the rampage throughout Germany. For example, bitter fighting raged in Bremen for several days as Freikorps *Gerstenberg* took action to ensure that a proposed 'Workers Republic' was eliminated before it could take control, and savage reprisals were taken against any leftists that fell into the hands of the Freikorps. The whole of Germany was in turmoil.

One of the many political groups that sprang up during this tempestuous period was the so-called Political Workers' Circle, which had been formed in the autumn of 1918 in Munich by Karl Harrer and Anton Drexler. The group met regularly in a local beer hall to discuss politics, and despite the implications of its title, it was fervently right wing and anti-semitic. Drexler was keen to form a political party proper as opposed to a mere discussion group, and so, in January 1919, the German Workers' Party, Deutsche Arbeiter Partei (DAP), was formed as the political wing of the Workers' Circle.

While the fledgling DAP struggled to gather support in Bavaria, the turmoil that raged throughout Germany continued. A series of strikes by coal miners in the Ruhr, Germany's industrial heartland, took effect. One of the strikers' demands was the disbandment of the hated Freikorps. The government replied by declaring martial law, which was followed by the brutal intervention by Freikorps.

In Berlin, meanwhile, workers' leaders were incensed by the part played by a so-called socialist-dominated government in the savage suppression of their fellow workers. When the factory councils held their next elections, virtually every social democratic representative was ousted. The government reacted by announcing that it would not allow the promised inclusion of the factory councils in the constitution. The left wing reacted predictably as outrage swept the workforce and a general strike seemed imminent. Alarmed, the government backed down and agreed to the strikers' terms if the industrial action was called off. Socialist members of the Reichstag appealed to the workers not to strike.

By now, totally mistrustful of any politicians, the workforce ignored the pleas of the government and took matters into

their own hands. Rioting and looting broke out as workers took to the streets. Defence Minister Gustav Noske assembled various Freikorps units, including Brigade *Ehrhardt*, into a new formation called the Guards Cavalry Rifle Division, and prepared for action against the strikers. Properly entitled 2 Marine Infanterie Brigade, the *Ehrhardt* Brigade had been formed to assist in quelling the mutinous sailors in the naval ports of northern Germany, and was commanded by former naval Korvettenkapitan Hermann Ehrhardt, one of the most fanatically right wing and brutal of all the Freikorps leaders. Ehrhardt was also to become one of the most celebrated Germany nationalists, his fame exceeding that of Adolf Hitler almost up until Hitler took power in 1933.

Martial law was declared, and although workers' leaders called off the strike, it was too late. Freikorps units were unleashed on Berlin once again. Street battles degenerated into a massacre as over 1200 workers were killed. Several of these were executed in revenge for the alleged murder of some 60 Berlin police officers by the rebels. In fact, all but two of the 60 were found to be alive and well. One had been killed in the street fighting, and the other had simply disappeared.

In Bavaria, by mid-1919, the DAP had started its drive to attract members and began to hold public meetings to espouse its extremist views, attracting a great deal

ABOVE: Freikorps soldiers in Berlin during the Kapp Putsch. In February 1920, the Western Allies requested the surrender of 895 Germans as war criminals. This outraged the right in Germany and increased the anger against the socialist government that had signed the peace treaty. The right-wing coup was undertaken by the Freikorps **Ehrhardt** *Brigade, with the tacit support of the Army and the Navy's high command. The soldiers marched on Berlin in the early hours of 13 March and seized control. However, the government, re-sited to Stuttgart, called for a general strike and the factories ground to a halt. Kapp resigned four days after taking office. Ironically, the restored government was forced to turn to the Army and Freikorps to restore order in the Ruhr.*

RIGHT: Ernst Röhm. Leader of the SA and one-time close friend of Hitler, he was one of those responsible for starting off the career of the Führer as an orator. Röhm was employed by the Army in the Munich area to establish weapons and ammunition dumps for right-wing groups and to create a special intelligence unit for the Army. It was this unit that recruited Hitler to investigate the German Workers' Party. From this came the Nazi Party and the creation of the SA. However, Röhm saw his SA as a people's army and replacement for the German Army. Once in power, Hitler became alarmed at Röhm's beliefs. The Führer wanted to keep the support of the Army, industrialists and land owners, whereas Röhm believed that there should be a 'second revolution', and that Hitler had made too many compromises. These irreconcilable differences led to the Night of the Long Knives and to Röhm's execution. Though he had some talents, not least turning the SA into a mass organisation, Röhm was out of place when the Nazis had taken power. In addition, he was a homosexual who used the SA to supply him with lovers – the SA Intelligence Section was tasked with supplying him with young boys. This sort of behaviour outraged both Himmler and the SS, fearing it could damage the reputation of the Party.

of public attention, if not a large number of new members.

At this point the Reichswehr, being restricted officially to a strength of just 100,000 men, was actively investigating such small political groups with overtly right-wing views, with a view to recruiting them to its cause and expanding the 'Black Reichswehr'. To this end, undercover Reichswehr agents attended public meetings held by such groups and reported back on their political reliability. One such undercover agent was a former corporal in the Bavarian Infantry Regiment *List*, one Adolf Hitler, who had recently been discharged from hospital after suffering a poison gas attack in the closing stages of the war. He was seen as a highly reliable type, having been highly decorated for gallantry in action as a regimental runner in the trenches. Hitler, in fact, won the Iron Cross Second and First Classes, as well as other regimental citations for bravery. He was recruited by Hauptmann Karl Mayr of the Reichswehr. Mayr had seen Hitler speaking at political rallies and, recognising his untapped talents, quickly recruited him to the cause. Hitler, for his part, was pleased to have paid employment doing what he liked best: attending and addressing political meetings.

Hitler dutifully attended the DAP meetings, and although he was not particularly impressed by the organisation of this new party, its right-wing, anti-semitic

stance did appeal greatly to him. He joined the party in September 1919 and, in view of his undeniable qualities as an orator, was appointed to the executive committee as propaganda chief. Adolf Hitler's ambitions knew no bounds. He soon arranged for the party to change its name to the Nationalsozialistische Deutsche Arbeiter Partei (National Socialist German Workers' Party, or NSDAP), and pushed for rapid expansion. The astute addition of the words 'national' and 'socialist' to the title was aimed at attracting members from both left and the right.

The Kapp Putsch

Meanwhile, in Berlin, even hard-line Defence Minister Gustav Noske was becoming alarmed at the excesses of the Freikorps. In January 1920, a workers protest rally outside the Reichstag in Berlin was fired upon by Freikorps units under the overall command of General Lüttwitz, resulting in the death or wounding of 147 workers. In a panic, Noske demanded the disbandment of Ehrhardt's notorious brigade. Lüttwitz refused, demanding the resignation of the government for agreeing to Allied demands for the surrender of war criminals. When the politicians refused, Lüttwitz and his troops marched on Berlin, occupying what most Germans still considered the capital of the Reich, despite the government now ruling from Weimar. The government fled and Lüttwitz installed a puppet figure, journalist Wolfgang Kapp, to head the government. The reaction of the workers was swift, and a general strike quickly ensued.

As chaos reigned throughout Germany, the NSDAP grew slowly, but significantly, in its Bavarian power base. Bavaria had long been a stronghold of the political right; indeed, there were some extremists who wanted Bavaria to declare independence from the rest of Germany and become a sovereign state. By this time Hauptmann Mayr had retired and his place had been taken by another Reichswehr officer: Hauptmann Ernst Röhm. Röhm was a brutal, homosexual thug who was responsible to the Reichswehr for the surreptitious arming and supplying of right-wing groups and Freikorps units. He took an active interest in the progress of the NSDAP, and actually joined the movement himself. He recognised in Hitler the qualities of one who could incite the masses with his near hypnotic oratory. Röhm's intent, however, was never to become an acolyte of Hitler but, rather, to use the NSDAP to further his own ambitions for political and military power.

In Berlin, the Kapp Putsch quickly fizzled out when the strikers held firm and Freikorps units began to refuse orders from the new regime. In the strategically vital industrial heartland of Germany, the Ruhr, the left was particularly strong and here, for the first time, armed workers took on and defeated one of the Freikorps, driving off all relief attempts. At one point it is estimated that over 100,000 workers took up arms against their right-wing opponents, and the whole of the Westphalian sector of the Ruhr was eventually cleared of Freikorps elements by the workers.

Kapp himself quickly fled into exile in Sweden. On 20 March 1920, the legitimate government returned to Berlin and called for an end to the strike and a return to law and order. The strike leaders agreed but demanded, and got, the resignation of Defence Minister Noske.

Germany's problems, however, had not by any means been restricted to internal strife. When the war ended the Polish state had been reformed, and no sooner had the Poles been released from Tsarist Russian domination than they invaded the Silesian area of Prussia in an attempt to wrest land from the weakened Germans. The tiny German Army could not cope on its own, and soon the Freikorps were flocking eastwards intent on driving the invaders from German soil. In vicious fighting the Reichswehr and Freikorps brigades swept the Poles out of Germany's eastern provinces.

Farther north, in 1919, Soviet Red Army units had invaded the Baltic state of Latvia. The Latvians had no army to speak of, but a defence force known as the Landwehr was set up by the Germans, who were alarmed by this Bolshevik invasion near their eastern border. The Landwehr was officered by Germans and also had a high proportion of German NCOs. Reinforced by the Freikorps, the Landwehr soon successfully drove out the Soviets. The Latvians, however, were in reality no better off, having merely exchanged Soviet invaders for a swarm of Freikorps freebooters. The Western Allies, relieved that the Soviet invaders had been driven out on the one hand, were on the other more than a little alarmed at what appeared to be no less than a German invasion force taking its place. An Allied control commission duly arrived and set about Latvianising the Landwehr. German officers and NCOs were ousted and replaced, and the Latvian cadres reinforced and given supplies and equipment by the Allies. A British naval force also provided support.

The disgruntled Germans ousted from the Landwehr, together with their Freikorps supporters, joined forces with an anti-communist white Russian force and attempted to take the Latvian capital of Riga. Their attempt was rebuffed with heavy losses, however, and the remnants were set upon by an irate Latvian populace

BELOW: Freikorps and SA men in Munich. The Brownshirts enjoyed a meteoric rise in numbers under the leadership of Röhm: 2000 in 1926, 60,000 in 1930, to nearly three million by the time Hitler became Chancellor in January 1933. However, with the growth in SA numbers came increasing expectations. Influenced by early Nazi thinking, the SA expected a social revolution, and Röhm encouraged the idea that the SA would replace the Army as the true national defence force. His speeches did nothing to reassure his critics. On 6 August 1933 he stated: 'Anyone who thinks that the tasks of the SA have been accomplished will have to get used to the idea that we are here and that we intend to stay here.' Fear of Röhm's and the SA's ambitions would result in an alliance between the Army, the Nazi Party and the SS.

THE SS: HITLER'S INSTRUMENT OF TERROR

BELOW RIGHT: 'Being convinced that there are always circumstances in which elite troops are called for, I created in 1922-23 the "Adolf Hitler Shock Troops". They were made up of men who were ready for revolution and knew that some day things would come to hard knocks.' This is how Hitler later described the genesis of what was to be the SS. He saw very early on in his political career that there would be friction between the SA and the political leadership of the Party. He therefore needed a force that would protect him from external and internal enemies. The Stosstrupp (Shock Troop) Adolf Hitler, created in Munich, is shown here with the man who formed it: Julius Schreck (centre, with moustache), Hitler's bodyguard and chauffeur. The men who were tasked with protecting the life of Hitler included Joseph Berchtold, who ran a stationery business, Ulrich Graf, a butcher and amateur boxer, Emil Maurice, a watchmaker who had been convicted of embezzlement, and Christian Weber, who was a groom. Their uniform is very similar to that of the SA, the only major difference being the black ski caps adorned with death's head badges. The latter had been adopted by Schreck from the Brigade Ehrhardt, of which he had been a member. Hitler described the Stosstrupp as being 'the first group of toughs.'

and all but annihilated. Only the arrival of a further Freikorps force allowed the survivors to withdraw to safety.

With the failure of the Kapp Putsch in May 1920, the Brigade Ehrhardt had been finally disbanded. Ehrhardt himself and many of his most loyal followers remained active, however, in a number of shady right-wing groups and are suspected of involvement in the assassinations of Foreign Minister Walther Rathenau and Finance Minister Mattias Erzberger.

In Munich, meanwhile, the NSDAP went from strength to strength. In December 1920, using secret funding from the Reichswehr, it had purchased the independent newspaper *Völkischer Beobachter* (People's Observer). As the party's official chief of propaganda, Hitler now had his own newspaper with which to spread his particular version of the party line. Hitler was now determined to take over the party and began to work towards the destabilisation of the existing leadership. His first move was to begin undermining the status of Anton Drexler as party leader.

The NSDAP had expanded rapidly, and by 1921 it could boast a dozen branches outside its Munich power base. In February of that year, at the first Party congress, it was announced that membership stood at 3000 and was still growing. Its attempts to recruit from the working classes had as yet failed to bear fruit, however, and in the main the membership was at that point from the middle and lower-middle classes.

Anton Drexler became aware of Hitler's machinations against him and so, in an attempt to force the Party to move away from the Munich area where Hitler's influence was strong, he negotiated for a merger with the German Socialist Party and a new base in Berlin. Hitler reacted immediately, resigning from the Party and calling for a ballot of the membership. He refused to return unless given complete control of the Party. Drexler dearly wanted rid of Hitler, but could not afford to lose the backing of Hitler's personal supporters, some of whom were very affluent and influential. His attempt to eliminate Hitler had merely played straight into Hitler's hands. Drexler knew he was defeated and accepted Hitler's terms. Adolf Hitler was appointed Chairman of the NSDAP on 29 January 1922. He at once put his most trusted followers into all of the party's most important posts, but astutely retained Drexler on the executive of the party so as not to alienate the former leader's supporters outside Hitler's own Munich power base.

Political meetings during these chaotic days would often deteriorate into running battles with opposition hecklers intent on disrupting proceedings. Many of these fights became extremely violent. In order to protect its speakers, the NSDAP formed its so-called Sports and Gymnastics section, from which the toughest members were selected as bodyguards for the orators. Under the tutelage of Ernst Röhm it was developed and expanded under a new title: Sturmabteilung (SA) – Storm Troops – a title which appealed to ex-soldiers because it was associated with the elite assault detachments, or storm troopers, of World War I. Röhm attempted to recruit Ehrhardt into the SA, but Ehrhardt, a former naval officer, was contemptuous of Hitler and refused. He did respect Röhm, however, and assigned him his trusted comrade, Johann Ulrich Klintzsch, to help organise and run the SA.

The Stabswache

As many of the SA's recruits were former Freikorps soldiers accustomed to giving their personal loyalty only to their unit commander, it became clear to Hitler that although he was nominally in command of the party, and by implication the SA, he could not expect the unconditional loyalty of the SA's rank and file.

In May 1923, a special guard element was set up to protect Hitler personally. It was recruited from dependable and trustworthy SA members ready to give their unquestioned loyalty to Hitler. The new unit was known as the Stabswache (Headquarters Guard). The unit was short-lived, however, and was disbanded when Ehrhardt finally broke with Hitler and withdrew his men from the SA. Ehrhardt, even more fanatical than Hitler, had called for a declaration of war on France when French troops occupied the Rhineland. Hitler refused to support Ehrhardt's call and so, in a fit of pique, Ehrhardt withdrew all of his supporters from the SA (Ehrhardt's personal influence in these days was still stronger than Hitler's).

In order to counteract the influence of Ehrhardt's friend Röhm in the SA, Hitler had placed Hermann Göring, his trusted comrade, in command of the party's 'military wing'. It was clear to Hitler that Röhm saw the SA as some sort of private army, but with Göring in command of the SA he could expect to have at least some degree of control. Göring set about organising the SA along military lines, and for this task he was an excellent choice, despite his innate laziness. A highly decorated former soldier, a war hero holder of the coveted *Pour le Mérite* and last commander of the famed Richthofen Squadron, he could thus expect to command the respect of former soldiers within the SA and give it a respectable public image. Most importantly, however, was Göring's undoubted personal loyalty to Hitler.

Göring established a command structure that placed the Oberste SA Führung (Supreme SA Leadership) in overall control. Despite his efforts, however, relations between the party and the SA continued to deteriorate, with many SA men critical of the party leadership and even of Hitler himself. Röhm, who was second-in-command of the SA and in reality, because of Göring's lack of drive, its real moving force, was among the critics.

It was ironic that having established the SA to protect party speakers from attack by their political opponents, it was now considered necessary to form a bodyguard to protect the leadership, and Hitler in particular, from the machinations of the SA. Subsequently, a new bodyguard was formed with two of Hitler's most trusted comrades at the fore – Julius Schreck and Joseph Berchtold. It was known as the *Stosstrupp Adolf Hitler* (Adolf Hitler Shock Troop). It included many who were later to rise to prominence in the Third Reich, men such as Josef 'Sepp' Dietrich, Rudolf Hess and Ulrich Graf.

At the beginning of the 1920s, when the recent success of the Bolshevik Revolution in Russia had many Germans fearing the same would happen in their country, many right-wing paramilitary groups hoped to use the suppression of a communist uprising as a pretext for staging an armed coup, and Hitler was anxious for his NSDAP to play its part in any such struggle. By 1923, however, although the communists in Germany still commanded considerable support, the threat of imminent revolution had passed and the extreme right had missed its chance.

The Beer Hall Putsch

The fragmentation of the various Freikorps led to many of their former members drifting into the SA. Those of the ex-Freikorps who had come from a disciplined military background were often rather contemptuous of their SA comrades, many of whom appeared to have left-wing tendencies. By 1923 Hitler himself had been appointed head of the Association of Bavarian Freikorps units, the Kapfbund, and reckoned that he could count on their support to prevent the nationalistic Bavarians from breaking away from the Reich. Needless to say, though, Ehrhardt, still smarting from Hitler's refusal to support his call for a war with France after the latter's occupation of the Rhineland, refused Hitler his allegiance. Despite this, Hitler still commanded widespread support among the right in Bavaria.

'Swastika on our helmets, Black-white-red armbands, Storm Detachment Hitler Is our name.'

– SA song

'The armed SS originated out of the thought: to create for the Führer a selected, long-service troop for the fulfilment of special missions. It should make it possible for members of the general SS, as well as for volunteers who fulfil the special requirements of the SS, to fight in the battle for the realization of the National Socialist idea...'
– Organization Book of the NSDAP (1937)

Knowing that the leader of the Bavarian government, Gustav Ritter von Kahr, intended addressing a meeting in the Bürgerbräukeller in Munich on 8 November 1923, and suspecting Kahr was about to announce Bavaria's independence, Hitler ordered armed SA and Freikorps men to surround the building once von Kahr and his retinue were inside. Hitler, brandishing a pistol, then burst in with his bodyguard and proclaimed the beginning of the national revolution. Hitler succeeded in gaining the apparent acquiescence of the bemused von Kahr and his supporters with a mixture of threats, cajoling and pleading. In the confusion which followed, however, von Kahr, together with the head of the Bavarian Police and the Bavarian district army commander, were able to leave the building undetected and mobilised police and Army units against Hitler. On the following day, Hitler, now joined by war hero General Ludendorff, learned that Ernst Röhm and one of his Freikorps groups, the Reichskriegsflagge, had occupied the War Ministry in the centre of Munich. He resolved at once to march to his support with a column of some 3000 supporters, including Ludendorff, Hermann Göring and Heinrich Himmler.

The failure of the putsch

Some time after midday on 9 November, the column reached the Lüdwigsbrucke, to find their way barred by armed police. Goring threatened to execute hostages he claimed were being held at the rear of the column unless the police allowed them to pass. The bluff worked and Hitler's column moved on. On reaching the Odeonsplatz near the Feldherrnhalle monument, however, the marchers were once again confronted by armed police. Hitler's bodyguard, Ulrich Graf, stepped forward and shouted to the police not to fire as Ludendorff and Hitler were present. At this point a shot rang out and a police sergeant fell dead. A volley of shots then rang out from the guns of the police and Max Erwin von Scheubert-Richte fell dead, shot through the lungs. His arms had been linked with Hitler's, and as he fell he jerked Hitler down with such force that he dislocated the latter's arm. Ulrich Graf, the faithful bodyguard, then threw himself on Hitler to protect him and was rewarded by being peppered with bullets. Göring was shot in the leg and Joseph Berchtold was also wounded. A total of 14 marchers were killed, with a further two of

Hitler's supporters being killed during the occupation of the War Ministry.

The attempted putsch had been a farcical disaster, but the party now had its first sacred relic: the blood-spattered flag carried at the head of the column and thereafter referred to in Nazi lore as the Blutfahne, or Blood Banner. The flag was thereafter used to consecrate the individual flags and banners of newly formed SA and SS units as they were touched briefly against this revered relic. The party also had its first martyrs.

The SS is born

Hitler was arrested the following day and eventually sentenced to five years for treason. In fact, he served only a few months before being released in December 1924. While Hitler was incarcerated in Landsberg Prison, Ernst Röhm struggled to keep the movement alive as Göring fled into exile and the SA was leaderless. Both the NSDAP and the SA were banned in the wake of the abortive putsch. Hitler nominated Röhm as the new head of the SA and, in order to circumvent the ban on the organisation, Röhm gathered its members into a new movement: the Frontbann.

A number of ex-Freikorps members also adhered to this new paramilitary organisation, bringing their own creed of ruthless brutality with them. Membership soared and had exceeded 30,000 by the time Hitler was released from prison, compared with a pre-putsch SA membership of only some 2000. Hitler was alarmed at the massive increase in Röhm's power, however, and the two soon clashed. As a result, Röhm was relieved of his post and left the SA at the end of April 1925.

Hitler, impressed with the behaviour of his bodyguards during the attempted putsch, now determined to create a dedicated personal bodyguard unit. To form this elite band of loyal comrades he selected his trusted personal chauffeur and comrade, Julius Schreck. Initially only eight men were to be recruited to form the nucleus of this praetorian guard, all of whom were former members of the Stosstrupp Adolf Hitler. Göring, who had returned from exile, is generally credited with suggesting the name Schutz Staffel (Protection Squad). This was a reference to aircraft that flew on escort duties during his period of service with the elite Richthofen squadron. Schreck issued guidelines intended to reinforce the elite status of this new guard unit. The Schutz Staffel, or SS, was to be a select band of no more than 10 men plus an officer in each district, the exception being the capital Berlin, which was permitted an SS unit of twice the normal size. These men were to be specially selected, and only those of sober habit, aged 25 to 35, of good standing with no criminal record, of good health and robust physique would be considered. More importantly, however, each SS recruit would owe his unswerving loyalty not to the Nazi Party but to Adolf Hitler personally.

In April 1926, Joseph Berchtold, now fully recovered from his wounds, took over command of the SS from Julius Schreck. Hitler greatly enhanced the status of the SS by passing into its safekeeping the sacred Blutfahne, a move which the SA resented greatly. The new bearer of the Blutfahne would be Jakob Grimminger of the Munich SS, a tall, lean man with a small Hitler-type moustache.

Hitler then turned his attention to the SA. With Ernst Röhm gone, he appointed Hauptmann Franz Pfeffer von Salomon to command the Sturmabteilung, giving him wide freedom of action to develop the SA along his own lines. As a token gesture to the SA, Hitler placed the SS under the command of the Oberste SA Führung. This was probably a move intended to placate the SA units in the north of Germany away from Hitler's Munich power base, but was no doubt also influenced by his tendency to play off opposing factions against each other.

Resentment of SS elitism by SA men was countered by the rising level of discontentment among SS men at their cavalier treatment by their SA overlords. In 1927, Berchtold resigned his post, dismayed at the alarming growth of the SA while his SS was restricted to a maximum of only 10 per cent of the SA strength in each area, and SS units in any case were only permitted to be raised at all when the SA unit in the area was at full strength. These rules gave the SA the ability to restrict growth of the SS by manipulating the latter's manpower strengths. SS morale fell as the SA delighted in finding the most menial tasks for the SS to perform.

After the departure of Berchtold, control of the SS passed to his deputy, Erhardt Heiden. Heiden's own deputy was a member of the Reichskriegsflagge unit that had marched in the Munich Putsch: Heinrich Himmler.

Heiden was no more able than his predecessor to stand up to the SA, and so the morale of the SS continued to decline. When Heiden also resigned his post, the vacancy automatically passed to his deputy, and the SA smugly assumed that it would have no problem riding roughshod over this quietly-spoken new incumbent with his unprepossessing appearance. The SA was to be very wrong.

'I am a strong believer in the doctrine that, in the end, only good blood can achieve the greatest, enduring things in the world... only good blood, blood that history has proved to be leading and creative and the foundation of every state and all military activities, only Nordic blood, can be considered.'
– Himmler, *Organization and Obligations of the SS and the Police, 1937*

Himmler had been born in Munich in October 1900. His family were highly respected middle-class Catholics, and his father Gebhard Himmler a private tutor whose pupils had included Prince Heinrich of Bavaria. A devoted royalist, Gebhard Himmler had sought, and been granted, royal permission to name his new son after the Royal Prince. Prince Heinrich also graciously consented to becoming godfather to the young Himmler. Heinrich Himmler had two brothers, Gebhard junior and Ernst. Himmler spent a perfectly normal childhood in the bosom of the family. He performed adequately at school, if not exceptionally, and was known as a polite, respectful and considerate child, always ready to help the aged or run errands for neighbours. Brought up with a healthy respect for the concepts of discipline and order, the young Himmler longed for the life of a soldier. Army life was as ordered and disciplined as any, and brought with it the potential to earn glory on the field of battle. His desire to become a soldier was further encouraged by the wave of patriotic fervour that swept the country in the wake of the outbreak of war in August 1914. A growing awareness of the sacrifices being made on the battlefield was furthered by the sight of wounded German soldiers returning from the front, and by Russian prisoners of war being transported to a nearby camp.

Himmler's adolescence

Himmler was determined to do his bit in the service of his country and pleaded with his father to use what influence he had to arrange his acceptance by the military, despite his being under age. Eventually his father succeeded and Himmler joined Infanterie Regiment (bayersiches) Nr 11 *Von der Tann* in late 1917. By 1918 the young Himmler had become an officer cadet, but the war ended before he could be commissioned and see frontline service, much to his chagrin. It can be seen, therefore, that his lack of frontline combat experience cannot be put down to any lack of fighting spirit on his part, but was due entirely to circumstances beyond his control. Nevertheless, it was to be a constant source of discomfiture to Himmler and one which he often sought to conceal.

Himmler certainly felt that his lack of combat experience left a great gap in his life. One aspect of Army life, however, that was to have a profound effect on him was the time he spent as the unit orderly room clerk. Here, Himmler's already

methodical mind became fascinated with keeping tidy and accurate records, with no minutiae too insignificant to escape his notice, or for his mind to retain. His military career prematurely ended, Himmler returned to his academic studies and completed a course in agricultural studies at the University of Munich. Here, another influencing factor appeared as he developed an intense interest in breeding and genetics. At university he joined a number of student bodies and tried in vain to become proficient at athletic and sporting activities. His rather weak physique, however, precluded any great chance of success in this direction and he was regarded with a degree of good humoured amusement by his more athletic colleagues. He did achieve one ambition, however, when his face was marked with a small duelling scar inflicted by an obliging fellow student.

Unable to attain any significant level of physical prowess himself, Himmler became even more fascinated by the heroic figures of Nordic legend and mythology, and his head became filled with bizarre romantic notions of Germanic chivalry and purity of spirit.

Himmler joins the NSDAP

At a gathering of a Munich student duelling group, Himmler had a chance meeting with Ernst Röhm, who attended such meetings regularly, seeking suitable recruits for his right-wing factions. At Röhm's suggestion Himmler joined the Reichskriegsflagge. Himmler approved of the nationalistic and anti-semitic stance of this group, though at this point it would appear that his anti-semitism was not a particularly deeply held belief. Further encouraged by Röhm, Himmler joined the NSDAP in 1923, by which time he had gained his degree from university and found himself a full-time job as a salesman with the firm of Stuckstoff in Schleisheim.

As a member of the Reichskriegsflagge, Himmler took part in the Munich putsch in November 1923, carrying the banner of his organisation at the head of the march. He escaped injury and arrest, but lost his job for taking unauthorised leave to take part in the march. He was untroubled by this, however, and took great pride in his participation in the putsch. Out of work, he busied himself in voluntary work for the NSDAP. His devotion to his duties was quickly noted and he was soon taken on in a full-time capacity as secretary to Gregor Strasser, at that time the NSDAP propaganda chief for lower Bavaria. His sometimes irritating and pedantic attention to detail was offset by a natural organisational flair, his dedication to his work and his eagerness to please his superiors. As a reward he was appointed deputy district organiser for lower Bavaria, a position which brought with it the post of deputy leader of the latest branch of the NSDAP: the SS. A small organisation at this stage, the SS took on Heinrich Himmler as member number 168. When Heiden resigned from the SS in 1929 and Himmler was appointed Reichsführer-SS, the fate of Heinrich Himmler and his SS became inextricably linked.

As newly promoted Reichsführer-SS, Himmler threw himself into his work with great determination. So much so, in fact, that his home life began to suffer. He had married in 1927 and set up a chicken farm business with his wife Marga. His constant absences on SS and NSDAP duties led to eventual estrangement from his wife and the failure of his business. Himmler was genuinely dedicated to his work and was determined to repay the faith his masters had shown in him by appointing him Reichsführer. That this had destroyed his marriage was of secondary importance to Himmler so long as he fulfilled his duties loyally and efficiently.

Himmler persuaded Hitler to agree to the racially pure and elitist lines along which he wished to develop the SS, though it is probable that Hitler was not particularly interested in Himmler's notions at this point, but was prepared to let him have his way so long as the SS was totally loyal to him personally.

From an early age Himmler had been fascinated by the history of the Nordic peoples, and in particular King Heinrich I, also known as Henry the Fowler. Heinrich I had successfully defended the German lands from the invasion attempts of the Slav hordes, and was elected King of the Germans in 919. It has often been suggested that Himmler considered himself the spiritual reincarnation of Heinrich I.

The racial guidelines for the SS

Himmler was also enthralled by the history of the Order of Teutonic Knights. Formed in the late part of the twelfth century, the Order was entrusted with colonising the Slavs under its Grand Master, Hermann von Salza, after whom Himmler was later to name one of his elite panzer units of the Waffen-SS. For almost 200 years, the Teutonic Knights spread German culture and influence throughout eastern Europe. In July 1410, however, a combined Slavic army of Poles, Russians and Lithuanians defeated the Teutons at the Battle of Tannenberg. After the Order had been defeated, the legends of its chivalry lived on. To many Germans, the tales of the gallant deeds of the Teutonic Knights were as much a part of their cultural heritage as were the legends of Arthur and the Knights of the Round Table to the English-speaking world.

His interest in the medieval legends of Teutonic chivalry imbued in Himmler a romanticised view of the history of the Germanic races. Much of the symbolism of German military pageantry stemmed from its medieval past. For example, the design of the Iron

BELOW LEFT: A very rare early photograph of the first SS men, taken in 1925. On his release from Landsberg Hitler had set about forming a new bodyguard, and instructed Julius Schreck to do so. In April 1925 this headquarters guard was renamed Schutz Staffel (SS). Then Schreck set about forming SS units in other German cities, but unlike the SA recruitment was very selective. SS guidelines stated: 'Habitual drunkards, gossip-mongers and other delinquents will not be considered.' These early SS men included such characters as Alois Rosenwink, a section head and the organiser of SS headquarters, who described the unit's task thus: 'We carry the death's head on our black cap as a warning to our enemies and an indication to our Führer that we will sacrifice our lives for his concept.'

RIGHT: The 120-strong Stabswache (Headquarters Guard) assembled on the steps of Munich's Brown House, the Nazi Party headquarters, in 1930. Though they still wear brown shirts, they are adorned with black boots, trousers, ties and caps. Josef 'Sepp' Dietrich is third from the right in the front row. When Hitler became Chancellor in 1933, the Stabswache moved into the former Imperial Cadet barracks on the outskirts of Berlin. During the Nazi Party rally in September 1933, Hitler gave his Stabswache the official title Leibstandarte SS Adolf Hitler *(SS Bodyguard Regiment Adolf Hitler). On 9 November of that year, the men of the* Leibstandarte *swore an oath that bound them unconditionally to Hitler himself. With this act the Führer had created an independent military force – the forerunner of the Waffen-SS.*

Cross, a black cross trimmed with silver, was influenced by the design of the cross used by the Teutonic Order. The colours of the order, black and white, became the colours of Prussia and, later, the SS. Himmler sought to create in his SS a new Teutonic Order to spread his version of Germanic culture throughout Europe. Only the finest of German bloodstock would be accepted into his elite SS, which would celebrate ancient German pagan rites and customs. Ancient runic script was widely used by the SS in its own particular heraldry, the most famous of all being the double Sig-rune of the SS collar patch.

Although Hitler himself was a great admirer of Richard Wagner and the romantic heroes of his operatic works, and admitted to taking great inspiration from them in times of stress, he was by no means as infatuated by the subject as Himmler, and the Führer treated his devoted acolyte's dreams of establishing a race of Nordic warrior heroes with somewhat amused tolerance, initially at least. So long as Himmler provided a totally loyal bodyguard to protect him from the Machiavellian plots of the SA and his other enemies, Hitler was content to allow him to follow the course of his racial theories.

For all Himmler's unimpressive physical appearance, he was a superb organiser and quietly but determinedly set about producing the elite organisation he wished candidate's racial ancestry, respectability, sobriety of habit, physical fitness and, above all, loyalty. Previously, entry into what would have been considered the elite of German society was by wealth, education and family connections. Now a vast new portion of the populace found itself eligible to become a member of Germany's new elite, irrespective of social background. Recruits flooded in, and a number of former Freikorps members applied for membership of the SS. Vast numbers had already drifted into the SA, but were disillusioned by the unruly, undisciplined rabble that the SA had become. To them, the SS appeared a much more attractive proposition.

The resentment of the SA

In addition, many middle-class and professional men who supported the aims of the NSDAP but found the SA crude and uncouth, flocked to the banner of the SS. Membership grew steadily, albeit slowly, for despite the number of prospective candidates coming forward, Himmler was determined to be selective and only accept the very best of the candidates. By the end of 1929 membership of the SS stood at 1000; a year later it had trebled. There was, of course, growing resentment in the SA over the growing power and influence of the SS, as well as its overt elitism, and the SA fought hard to keep Himmler and his SS in its place: subordinate to the SA.

By the end of 1930, Himmler's hard work had begun to pay dividends, as Hitler at long last made the SS independent of the SA. Although still technically controlled by the Oberste SA Führung, Hitler had decreed that no SA commander was empowered to give orders to the SS. It was also at this time that the SS was given its formal sartorial trimmings of black kepi adorned with the death's head, black breeches, black tie and black-trimmed swastika arm band.

The structure of the SS was also totally reorganised, and the old system of a 10-man squad to each district abandoned. A new military style structure virtually identical to that of the SA was introduced, further emphasising to the SA that the SS was now of equal, not subordinate, status.

In his typical style of playing one side off against the other, Hitler forbade the SS to poach members from the SA, but at the same time instructed the SA to make available to the SS any men who wished to come forward of their own volition. Throughout this period Hitler's mistrust of

the SS to become. Discipline was tightened, dubious characters ejected and, from this point on (January 1929), every prospective SS member would be required to produce evidence of his lineage going back over three generations. Together with Nazi ideologist Alfred Rosenberg and crackpot racial theorist Richard Walter Darré, Himmler even introduced marriage rules which gave him the power to veto an SS man's future bride if she could not produce sufficient evidence of Aryan ancestry.

Of course Himmler's rules were not to be applied to himself, and SS members who had served during World War I were also exempt. Himmler's concept of elite was new and was based on a prospective

'On 9th March 1933, members of the SS and SA came to my home in Cologne and destroyed the furniture and my personal records. At that time I was taken to the Brown House in Cologne, where I was tortured, being beaten and kicked for several hours.'
– personal testimony from the Nuremberg Trial

BELOW RIGHT: One of the architects of the Final Solution: Reinhard Tristan Eugen Heydrich. He joined the Nazi Party in 1931 after being dismissed from the Navy for dishonourable conduct towards a young woman. From then on he rose meteorically, becoming chief of the SD and then, in 1941, Protector of Bohemia and Moravia. He organised the the Einsatzgruppen in Eastern Europe and played a key role in the machinery of genocide. Heydrich was certainly one of the most sinister figures of the Hitler's Third Reich.

the SA had increased, and with good reason. The SA had grown too large to be controlled and no longer had any real sense of duty to the NSDAP or to Hitler. Nazism itself was in turmoil: Rosenberg was railing against the Bolsheviks, others such as Gregor Strasser were demanding an alliance with the Soviet Union, and Joseph Göbbels, later to become one of Hitler's most loyal acolytes, was proposing that Hitler be expelled from the Party.

Such were the divisions within the party that the SA commander in Nuremberg was appointed as a full-time trouble-shooter to settle petty and troublesome disputes between senior SA commanders. Hitler, however, was also astute enough to use these internal intrigues to prevent any one faction growing powerful enough to challenge his personal authority while he built up his personal praetorian guard: the SS. Göbbels, correctly assessing that Hitler would emerge unscathed as the dominant figure in the NSDAP, changed his allegiance and became one of Hitler's most loyal subjects. He was dispatched to Berlin as party gauleiter and instructed to weed out any anti-Hitler elements from the SA and NSDAP in Berlin. The huge Berlin SA contingent, however, was still powerful enough to pose a major threat to Hitler's authority, despite the best efforts of Göbbels and the Berlin SS chief Kurt Daluege. A confrontation seemed inevitable, and finally came in August 1930.

The slump in Germany's economy resulted in vast numbers of men becoming

unemployed, many of whom found their way into the SA, including a sizeable criminal element. As a result, the SA became more and more unruly and corrupt, but it was still a powerful force. Knowing that a successful campaign in the elections of September 1930 would be essential to the NSDAP, the SA's deputy commander, Walther Stennes, decided to force a confrontation with Hitler. If the NSDAP expected the support of the SA, he told Hitler, it would have to meet Stennes' demands: a reduction in interference in SA matters by NSDAP gauleiters, the SA to have sole responsibility to provide security at NSDAP meetings, and be well paid for doing so, and for SA commanders to stand as prospective candidates for election to the Reichstag. Hitler refused even to meet with Stennes and discuss his demands, and when the new list of the NSDAP prospective parliamentary candidates was published Stennes had been omitted, a deliberate snub. The Berlin SA rebelled. On 30 August, a mob of SA men broke into the Berlin Gau headquarters building. The intruders smashed the place up and beat up the SS men who were on guard. It took the intervention of the state police to restore order, arresting 25 SA men in the process.

The SA in revolt

Now totally alarmed, Hitler approached Stennes and negotiated an agreement which met most of Stennes' demands. Hitler's conciliatory attitude was a front, however. The SS had shown itself trustworthy and loyal, while he felt the behaviour of the SA was treasonable. He realised that the SA was turning into a movement which owed no true allegiance to National Socialism, Stennes being considered liable to unleash his SA thugs again at any time. Determined to bring the SA to heel, Hitler sacked its leader, Pfeffer von Salomon, and recalled Ernst Röhm. He insisted that all SA men swear an oath of allegiance to him. Stennes was not cowed, however, and rumours of a new rebellion by the SA grew apace.

On 1 April 1931, Röhm received a report from Daluege, the SS chief in Berlin, whose informers had advised him that the SA commanders in Berlin had held a secret meeting and decided to refuse to accept any further orders from Hitler. Stennes' SA men once again occupied the Berlin Gau offices and also took over the offices of the Nazi newspaper *Der Angriff*. SS men went into action against the rebels but were heavily outnumbered. The rebellion spread quickly and soon SA units throughout Germany were declaring for Stennes and against Hitler. The SA rebellion was fatally flawed, however. As SA units rebelled they were expelled from the NSDAP, thus cutting off their source of funding. The rank and file of the NSDAP membership remained loyal to Hitler, as did the SS. The SA, on the other hand, was now generally perceived as a totally undisciplined rabble. Even many of Stennes' own supporters were merely mischief makers who felt no loyalty to him. When the rebels' funds ran out their support melted away, and Hitler was ready to pick up the pieces; Göring was brought in to root out any remaining supporters of Stennes from the fragmented SA.

Once again the SS had remained unswervingly loyal to Hitler, and in return its position as the prime security organ of the NSDAP was firmly established. The SS had begun to collect information on any suspect party member as early as 1925, but now threw itself into this task with a vengeance. The SS had also expanded, and in the year from 1931 to 1932 membership rose from around 2000 to some 30,000. Among these recruits was

one of the most dangerous and sinister men ever to wear the uniform of the SS: the former naval officer Reinhard Heydrich. During his interview for SS membership before Himmler, Heydrich was asked to sketch out a plan for a state security service. Himmler was so impressed with Heydrich's submission that he hired him on the spot and entrusted him with forming a security and intelligence service for the SS – the Sicherheitsdienst (SD) was born. Soon a network of SS spies sprang up throughout Germany as the tentacles of Himmler's secret police network spread into every facet of German life.

The SS was now in the ascendancy and the threat from the SA abated. Soon Hitler, and the SS, would have their day of reckoning with the rebellious SA, whose power would be broken forever.

In seven short years the SS had evolved from a handful of selected tough and reliable men of the Stosstrupp Adolf Hitler into an elite security organisation thousands strong. This, however, was just the beginning. To many the SS represented a vision of respectability and order sadly lacking in the SA. Few suspected that it would grow into one of the most feared organisations the world has ever seen.

ABOVE: On 20 January 1929, Heinrich Himmler (extreme right) became Reichsführer-SS. A business failure and somewhat of a dreamer, his accession to the post of SS leader allowed him to develop and put into practice his rather eccentric racial theories. He started with his own organisation, bringing in the concept of 'racial purity' for membership of the SS. He stated the broad goals of the latter as being the guardian of the German nation, and of the Nordic race as a whole: 'Should we succeed in establishing this Nordic race again from and around Germany...then the world will belong to us. Should Bolshevism win, it will signify the extermination of the Nordic race.'

THE STATE'S TROOPS

Between 1933 and 1939, the power of the SS grew considerably: Ernst Röhm and the SA were dealt with, the armed SS was expanded, and the Gestapo and SD began to round up the enemies of the Reich. For Heinrich Himmler, his SS empire was expanding rapidly.

The growth of the SS closely paralleled the growth of the NSDAP itself during the late 1920s and early 1930s. Although the Party had been slow to gain public recognition and its early membership was predominantly lower middle class, a side effect of the Depression years was to make its manifesto more attractive to manual labourers, particularly agricultural workers (the same was also true for the SS, whereas the Reichswehr recruited mainly from urban areas; this was to have consequences in establishing the fighting qualities of the leading Waffen-SS divisions, as will be discussed later).

The key words in the Party's title, however, were neither 'Socialist' nor 'Workers' but 'National' and 'German': emotive words that appealed to a country which considered itself betrayed in World War I and humiliated by the provisions of the Treaty of Versailles. Similarly, the first two clauses in the Party's 25-point manifesto stressed the need for the unification of all German peoples in a 'Greater Germany', and outright rejection of the Versailles Treaty itself.

The manifesto went on to declare that the state's first responsibility was to uphold the livelihood of its citizens, and that all citizens should have equal rights and responsibilities within the state. It also stated that jobs should

Men of the **Leibstandarte Adolf Hitler** *in full parade dress at Tempelhof airport on 24 March 1934. White belts later became part of the unit's standard parade uniform.*

ABOVE: Hitler and Göring with President Hindenburg, 1933. A veteran of the Prussian wars against Austria and France, elected president in 1925, and re-elected in 1931, Hindenburg showed increasing signs of senility during the last years of his life. He was contemptuous of Hitler and the Nazi Party, referring to the former as a 'Bohemian corporal'. Nevertheless, on the advice of politicians he trusted, notably von Papen, the Deputy Chancellor, who believed the Nazis could be controlled, he was persuaded to appoint Hitler chancellor in January 1933. Hindenburg died on 2 August 1934 and was buried at Tannenburg.

be acquired through merit, not patronage or favouritism; that large businesses should be nationalised, with workers entitled to a share in their profits; and that the state should encourage and support the growth of small businesses. It also called for land reforms (hence its appeal in rural areas), improvements in the education system and in maternity benefits, tougher penalties for criminals, and carried a guarantee of religious freedom, with one ominous exception: no Jew was to be allowed German citizenship. Other clauses included the German people's right to lebensraum (living space), in which the population could expand to fulfil its 'God-given destiny'; that non-citizens should be ineligible for state benefits; and an immediate halt to all non-German immigration.

In the chaos of the 1920s, the rallying cries of 'Germany for the Germans' and 'law and order' were particularly attractive to a large section of the population who wanted nothing more than a return to normality and a chance to get on with their own lives in peace. Nor did the Party's avowed anti-semitism put off potential supporters: many Germans, and indeed Europeans in general, were ill-disposed

towards Jews. It was a rich vein of prejudice Hitler and his supporters could tap, and they intended to do just that.

At the time of his arrest in 1923, power was a distant dream for Hitler and his supporters. The NSDAP numbered 10,000 members at this time – an insignificant number. However, by 1926, two years after he had been released, it had more than doubled, and by 1929, when Himmler became Reichsführer-SS, it had passed 100,000 and the Party had won 12 seats in the Reichstag. At this point membership of the SA stood at 60,000 – a powerful force to be reckoned with – while the SS numbered only 280 men. But the SS was loyal, whereas the SA considered itself the true people's liberation army, independent of the Party, and paying only lip service – if that – to Hitler and his policies. This was a situation that could not endure for long.

Hitler placates the Army

The year 1930 was a turning point in the NSDAP's fortunes. Following the resignation of the last Social Democrat chancellor, Hermann Müller, in March, the Nazi Party approached the September Reichstag elections with confidence. With a paid-up membership of nearly a quarter of a million, the NSDAP succeeded in winning 107 seats, making it the country's second largest party. The Social Democrats were still in front with 143 seats, and the communists third with 77. Another significant point is that the 100,000-strong Reichswehr felt threatened by the rise of the SA (many ex-soldiers joined the latter in the hope it would eventually be absorbed into the Army). Therefore, when three Army officers were tried on charges of spreading Nazism, Hitler himself appeared before the tribunal to assure the generals that the SA posed no threat to them (three years earlier, in 1927, the Army had brought in a rule whereby an individual who was a member of the NSDAP could not join the ranks of the Reichswehr).

In 1931, the ageing President Hindenburg was persuaded to receive Hitler for the first time, and Ernst Röhm was talked into returning from exile and taking over the command of the SA once more. This was a mistake, as Hitler would soon discover, for the portly homosexual had lost none of his earlier ambition. By March 1932 the SA was 400,000 strong, and fears that it might attempt a coup d'etat forced Chancellor Heinrich Brüning to ban all paramilitary groups and prohibit the wearing of political uniforms. SA stormtroopers were feared by the population, and the reasons are not hard to discover: in addition to beating up Jews and people who refused to contribute to Party funds, they regularly disrupted rival political meetings, especially those of the communists, and there were numerous street brawls that resulted in a large number of deaths over the years (the SS itself lost 10 men killed and many others seriously injured in 1932 alone in clashes with the communists).

In January 1932, Reichsführer-SS Himmler was appointed head of security at Nazi Party headquarters in Munich's Brown House. This gave him even more power because he was, in effect, head of the Party police. Shortly afterwards, fresh elections rewarded the NSDAP with 239 seats in the Reichstag, which, due to the German system of proportional representation, made it the largest party, despite the fact that it had only achieved 37 per cent of the overall vote. The Catholic Centre Party politician, Franz von Papen, succeeded Brüning as chancellor. A moderate, he hoped to control the Nazis, and so one of his first acts was to lift the ban on the SA. Meanwhile, Hermann Göring had been appointed Prussian Minister of the Interior, giving him command of the Prussian police force. He then formed the Gestapo, Germany's much-feared secret state police (see Chapter 5). At around the same time, the SA succeeded in persuading the Stahlhelm (Steel Helmet) association of ex-servicemen (whose president was Hindenburg) to merge with it.

The Reichstag fire

Von Papen had only been chancellor for three months when, in November 1932, Defence Minister General Kurt von Schleicher persuaded Hindenburg that the Army had no confidence in von Papen. Schleicher tried to form a coalition with Gregor Strasser, a radical in the Nazi Party, but Hitler and Strasser quarrelled again and Strasser resigned (see Chapter 1). Schleicher's coalition government lasted all of 57 days – Hindenburg dismissed him after he proposed to dissolve the Reichstag – and in January 1933 the aged president invited Hitler to become chancellor, with von Papen as vice-chancellor in a coalition government of the centre and Nazi parties. Hitler had achieved what he had promised on his release from Landsberg: to secure power by constitutional means. However, that power was still far from being absolute, and the constitution would be one of the first things to suffer under Nazi rule.

It soon became apparent that the coalition was not going to work, and so Hitler called for fresh elections in March. Before these took place, however, the Reichstag was set on fire during the night of 27/28 February. Blaming the communists, Hitler rushed through an emergency decree suspending civil liberties and giving the SA and SS police powers. Göring's police, helped by some 25,000 hastily armed SA men and the Berlin SS, led by former Freikorps man Kurt Daluege, poured onto the streets and began rounding up known communists and sympathisers, who were herded into hastily erected concentration camps because the prisons could not cope with the numbers.

It is widely believed, though it has never been proved, that it was the Berlin SS which fired the Reichstag. Whatever the truth, the result was that the NSDAP won 44 per cent of the vote in the March elections. With the support of the smaller Nationalist Party under the wealthy industrialist Alfred Hugenberg, this gave the Nazis a majority in the Reichstag, and Hitler's next step was to declare the communist party illegal. Over the next three months various reasons were found for abolishing all the other political parties, too, the Nationalists being the last to go when Hugenberg resigned on 14 July. For the next 12 years Germany would be a one-party state, while Himmler's SS would grow to become a state within a state.

The first visible symbol of this was the replacement of the traditional Army guard on the Chancellory by a company of SS

BELOW: Hermann Göring, one of the most flamboyant figures of the Third Reich. A hero of World War I, he took part in the abortive Beer Hall Putsch and then fled abroad. He returned to Germany in 1926, rejoined the Nazi Party and was President of the Reichstag from 1932. The creator of the Gestapo, his true nature is perhaps illustrated by a comment he made in February 1933: 'It's not my business to do justice; it's my business to annihilate and exterminate, that's all.' Created Minister of the Economy in 1937, he was named as Hitler's successor in 1939. He planned the Luftwaffe's part in the invasions of Poland, Norway, France and the Soviet Union, but after 1940 his influence declined, largely due to the Luftwaffe's inability to fulfil its tasks. Found guilty on all counts at Nuremberg in 1946, he took poison the day before his execution.

THE SS: HITLER'S INSTRUMENT OF TERROR

RIGHT: An SA parade in Berlin, January 1930. Though undoubtedly useful in the years leading up to Hitler being appointed chancellor, by 1933 the SA was something of a threat to the Party's hierarchy. The SA, understandably, wanted its share of the spoils, specifically what amounted to a second revolution. It could argue that it had more than paid its dues: hundreds of its members had been killed in brawls with the Nazi Party's opponents. A legacy of those turbulent times was the Horst Wessel song, which was written by an SA man of the same name who was killed in a street fight with communists, and which became the Nazi marching song.

men drawn from the earlier Stosstruppe and Stabwache, and commanded by the old street brawler Josef 'Sepp' Dietrich. Then, in September, this Sonderkommando *Zossen* was merged with another company, Sonderkommando *Juterbog*, into a new formation christened the *Leibstandarte Adolf Hitler*. On 9 November 1933 – the tenth anniversary of the Beer Hall Putsch and one of the sacred days in the Nazi calendar – the men of the *Leibstandarte* swore an oath of loyalty to Hitler in front of Munich's Feldherrnhalle.

During 1933, the size of the SS as a whole leaped to 50,000, while the SA, about 500,000 strong at the beginning of the year, grew to nearly three million by its end, as previous waverers jumped on the NSDAP bandwagon. These 'March Violets', as they were known, were generally despised by the old comrades of 1923, who were entitled to wear the Blutorden (Blood Order), one of the highest of several political decorations for service to the Party which Hitler was to introduce. In fact, blood, together with the concept of heroic sacrifice, became an essential component of Nazi ideology, and nowhere was this more true than among the ranks of those who in 1940 would receive the title Waffen-SS.

These concepts aside, the first and most important ingredient of Nazi and SS mythology was race. Hitler, Himmler, Rosenberg, Darré and others, through a mixture of personal prejudice and their readings of such works as the Compte de Gobinau's *Essay on the Inequality of the Human Race*, Houston Stewart Chamberlain's *The Foundation of the Nineteenth Century* and Friedrich Nietzsche's *Man and Superman*, were convinced they all belonged to a superior race – the master race. They called this race 'Aryan', after the writings of the philologist Friedrich Max Müller, who had been dead since 1890, and who would have been appalled to see the Nazi perversion of his theories. These dealt purely with the development of Indo-European languages, and Müller was at pains to point out that they had no relevance to racial differences – a disclaimer which the Nazis conveniently chose to overlook. Rosenberg himself cobbled together many of these earlier ideas and prejudices in his own almost incomprehensible book *The Myth of the Twentieth Century*, which was published in 1930, five years after the first volume of Hitler's rambling *Mein Kampf*, and quickly became the Nazis' second 'bible'.

According to the Nazi 'intelligentsia', who twisted myth and fact to suit their own ends, the 'Aryans' were essentially the German people. They did admit, however, that the people of some other nations – of German extraction living in Czechoslovakia and the Balkans, plus Britons, Dutch and Scandinavians – also qualified as members of the Aryan race, provided they could prove a pedigree 'untainted' by Jewish blood. However, although in the early days of the SS each applicant was supposed to prove his ancestry back a minimum of three generations, Himmler made exceptions to suit himself, as did Darré's RuSHA (Race and Resettlement Office – see Chapter 5). These exceptions grew broader and broader once the war started in 1939, and soon early standards were swept aside in Germany's desperate search for manpower. This trend accelerated after the invasion of Russia in 1941, and, as described in Chapter 6, the SS's ranks became filled with a multitude of nationalities, including Indian and Balkan Moslems, 'Latin' volunteers from France and Italy, Belgians, and even supposedly 'subhuman' Ukrainians, Cossacks and Azerbaijhanis. Similarly, at home many people of power, money and influence, regardless of political allegiance or racial qualifications (so long, of course, as they were not Jewish), were given honorary commissions in the Allgemeine-, or General, SS, though not all appreciated the honour.

SS mysticism

Himmler himself was a firm believer in the 'Aryan master race', but he was also an empire builder, and he was perfectly willing to bend his own rules to achieve greater power and influence. He also indulged in private fantasies, such as his restoration of the ruined castle of Wewelsburg outside Paderborn, in which he had a round table constructed to seat his chosen 'knights' in the manner of Arthurian legend (an idea he got from his favourite composer, Richard Wagner – himself an anti-semite). So intense was his fascination with pagan Nordic and medieval German history, that Himmler created a special research institute, whose study included the meanings of pagan runes – runes that formed the basis of much SS insignia.

Himmler's mystical attitude towards the world was accompanied by a firm belief in the virtues of homeopathic medicine, and he was also, like Hitler, a vegetarian, and these two subjects, in addition to astrology and the occult, soon became

extra subjects of study for the institute – the Ahnenerbe, or Society for the Research and Teaching of Ancestral Heritage. But Himmler's interests were not purely theoretical, they were also pragmatic. For example, he combined the entire German mineral water bottling and distribution system into the highly profitable WVHA, the SS's economic administration department (see Chapter 5).

Himmler was also totally pragmatic in his dealings with the Vatican (which would later help a number of Nazis to escape retribution after the war by providing new identity papers). This was despite his aversion to priests and his largely unsuccessful attempts to stamp out church-going in the SS. Ironically, Himmler did not hesitate to borrow extensively from the Jesuits in the structure and ritual of the SS. With their strict moral code, the Jesuits had been the 'stormtroopers' of the Counter-Revolution, and so close were some of the parallels between the Society of Jesus and Himmler's SS that Hitler called Himmler 'my Ignatius Loyola', after the Society's founder.

Loyalty, discipline and personal honour, as well as a willingness to sacrifice one's own life, became the keynotes of the SS creed. The SS's motto, engraved on the

ABOVE: The remains of the Reichstag after it was gutted by fire in February 1933. Whether it was the work of the Nazis or arsonists remains uncertain, but it resulted in President Hindenburg suspending all civil liberties in the 'Emergency Decrees for the Defence of Nation and State', which became constitutional law in March, giving Hitler dictatorial powers. The subsequent trial organised by Göring, in which the Nazis sought to prove the fire was the work of the communists, was not a success in the eyes of the rest of the world. Nevertheless, it was skilfully presented to the German people to create a sense of shock, and it helped the Nazis to consolidate their power.

ABOVE: Hitler greets the head of the SS Race and Resettlement Office: Obergruppenführer Darré. Note the 1933 service dagger and silver braid cuffband worn by Darré. Something of a crackpot, Darré inspired Himmler with his views on peasant farmers, race and breeding. One of his most 'notable' books was entitled The Farming Community as Life-source of the Nordic Race.

dagger, which was itself part of the overall mystique, is the key to the SS mentality: *Mein Ehre heisst Treue* (Loyalty is my Honour). What made the SS motto so unusual was that the loyalty was to one person alone – Adolf Hitler – rather than to an abstract such as the state or the constitution. This is shown in the SS oath, which in the Waffen-SS was taken after basic military training had been completed as an anwarter (cadet), which was rewarded by the presentation of the SS dagger (which recruits had to pay for themselves), with the oath being taken on 20 April – Hitler's birthday. The oath was as follows:

> *'I swear to thee, Adolf Hitler*
> *As Führer and Chancellor of the*
> *German Reich*
> *Loyalty and bravery.*
> *I vow to thee and to the superiors*
> *Whom thou shall appoint*
> *Obedience unto death*
> *So help me God.'*

Hitler himself did not officially adopt the title 'Führer' (Leader) for himself until he suspended the presidency, following the death of Hindenburg on 2 August 1934, at which time he also made himself commander-in-chief of the armed forces. Before that happened, though, Hitler had been finally forced to take drastic measures to curb Röhm's SA.

Hitler decides to act against the SA

The general membership of the SA was, relatively speaking, more 'socialist' than 'National Socialist', and many of its members had favoured Gregor Strasser as their future leader rather than Hitler. There was also a feeling among the more intelligent members of the SA that the 'revolution' should be a continuous process, and they feared Hitler was too favourably disposed towards the traditional power groups in Germany: the Army, the aristocracy and the industrial and financial magnates. Once he had become chancellor, Hitler decided that the time had come to show the world where the real power lay in Germany, to remove the threat to stability posed by the stormtroopers, and to reassure the armed forces. He had by this time realised that the Army, not the SA, was the real key to maintaining his position. He was also aware that there was a great deal of distrust of the Nazi Party (which, despite its success in the 1933 elections, still did not have a majority mandate), and a dislike of its strong-arm methods. The way to resolve both problems seemed simple: destroy the leadership of the SA and terrorise its membership into subservience, while at the same time casting the blame for all previous excesses on the Brown Shirts.

Although the course of action was obvious, Hitler still dithered because, for all their growing differences of opinion, Röhm had been one of his earlier friends and supporters. It was Victor Lutze, the SA leader in Hamburg, who finally made up his mind for him. Lutze, with an eye for the main chance, reported to Hitler a speech on 28 February 1934 in which Röhm had claimed that the SA was the true army of National Socialism, that the regular Army should be relegated to a training organisation, and that the Ministry of Defence should be reorganised. Although he did not say so, it was obvious that Röhm intended himself to head this new ministry, since he had the allegiance of over three million followers. This, in the eyes of both the Party and the Army, was nothing short of treason.

Yet still Hitler vacillated, and even summoned Röhm to a long conference, held in private on 5 June 1934. The result of the conversation was that the entire SA was given leave for the month of July. Then, as the days of June ticked by, Hitler secretly put the Army on low-level alert, while at the same time accepting Röhm's invitation to attend a conference of high-level SA officers in the Vierjahreszeiten Hotel in Bad Weissee, a spa town outside Munich, on 30 June. Meanwhile, Hitler, together with Himmler, Heydrich, Göring, Lutze and others, compiled a list of SA leaders who were to be executed. Unsurprisingly, it gave the plotters the chance to settle old scores, and both Gregor Strasser and ex-chancellor Kurt von Schleicher were scheduled to be shot without trial.

Night of the Long Knives

Even at this late stage, it is possible that Hitler was trying for a genuine reconciliation, but two factors intervened to make the Night of the Long Knives inevitable. First came a fabricated report from Göbbels that the Berlin SA was to be put on alert instead of being sent on leave. Then came a telephone call from Göring saying that the Munich SA was loading rifles into a number of trucks. The first report was fabricated because Göbbels wanted Röhm out of the way; the second was truthful but distorted. The weapons were indeed being loaded into trucks, but they were old Army rifles from the Freikorps days which were actually being handed over to the Bavarian police.

Nevertheless, manipulated by his comrades, Hitler immediately flew to Munich, arrested the local SA leader at the airport and sent him under SS escort to Stadelheim prison. He and 'Sepp' Dietrich, with an escort provided by the *Leibstandarte*, then drove to Bad Weissee, where he arrested the SA leaders who had gathered for a conference, including Röhm and his boyfriend. The latter was executed on the spot, but the rest were ferried to Stadelheim. At the same time, the Berlin garrison of the *Leibstandarte* immediately began arresting people in the capital and imprisoning them at Bad Lichterfelde.

The *Leibstandarte* was assisted in its task by the men of the SS Totenkopfverbände, the death's head band of guards from the recently created concentration camp at Dachau. They were led by camp commandant Theodor Eicke, who would later command the *Totenkopf* Division. And it was Eicke who, on the afternoon of 1 July, was entrusted with the task of dis-

LEFT: A fine example of an SS honour ring, which is engraved with the death's head design and numerous runic symbols. Himmler accorded great mystical significance to the ring.

posing of Röhm. After a fierce argument with the prison governor, who at first refused to surrender the portly Röhm into Eicke's custody, the former police informer got his way and marched with two of his men to Röhm's cell.

Hitler had ordered that Röhm should be allowed to have the 'honourable way out', and Eicke left a loaded pistol in his cell. After 10 minutes had elapsed without a shot being heard, Eicke went back into the cell and shot Röhm through the head. Eicke's service was rewarded amply when he was promoted to SS-Gruppenführer and made Inspector of Concentration Camps. He was also appointed Führer of SS Guard formations.

The SS consolidates power

Lutze was rewarded for his betrayal of Röhm by being given command of the SA, but it was an emasculated SA whose members knew full well that real power now lay with the SS. How many people died in the Night of the Long Knives has never been established with any certainty. Hitler himself admitted to 77 in a speech to the Reichstag on 13 July 1934, but the true figure was higher – perhaps 1000. Whatever the truth, Hitler now felt more secure, and the instrument of that security was the armed branch of the Schutz Staffel. The latter, in turn, had its own reward when, on 26 July, the Party newspaper *Volkischer Beobachter* was able to announce with satisfaction that 'in consideration of [its] very meritorious service', the SS was elevated to the 'standing of an independent organisation within the NSDAP'.

Almost from the beginning, the SS had been a select body within the hierarchy, an elite embodying Nazi principles. Now it had proved its worth in blood, that most potent Nazi symbol (the Röhm Purge subsequently became known as the 'Blood Purge'). Those who had participated earned themselves a similar position in Nazi mythology to those who had taken part in the Munich Putsch of 1923.

'When the day of seizure of power had finally come, there were 52,000 SS men, who in this spirit bore the revolution in the van, marched into the new state which they began helping to form everywhere, in their stations and positions, in profession and in service, and in all their essential tasks.'
– SS Standartenführer Gunter d'Alquen, *Die SS*, 1939

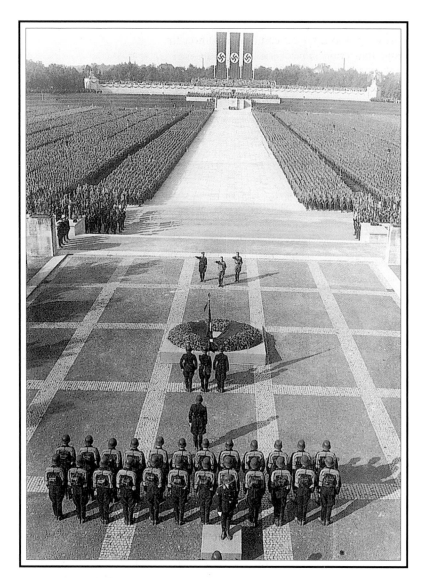

ABOVE: Hitler, Himmler and Lutze give the Nazi salute at a mass rally at Nuremberg, 1934. By this time, Röhm was dead and the SA emasculated, leaving Himmler and his SS the power behind the throne in Nazi Germany.

nists, but Jews quickly followed, then gypsies, homosexuals, trade unionists, habitual criminals and dissenters of all kinds. The demand for space into which to cram all these people soon led to the creation of further camps at Buchenwald and Sachsenhausen, then Belsen, Mauthausen and Theresienstadt.

The SS-Verfügungstruppe

In 1934, Theodor Eicke began a reorganisation of the Totenkopfverbände, which was eventually to lead to the creation of the third Waffen-SS fighting division: the *Totenkopf* (the camp guards were all SS members). Another armed SS formation would later form the cadre of two more premier fighting divisions. On 16 March 1935, Hitler announced the reintroduction of conscription and, thumbing his nose at the Treaty of Versailles, an increase in the size of the Army to 36 divisions. On the same day he announced that the existing Political Purpose Squads were to be amalgamated into a new formation called the SS-Verfügungstruppe (Special Disposal Troop), which was to form the basis of a full-scale SS fighting division. To begin with, although the situation would soon change, the *Leibstandarte* was also considered a part of this new unit. To diminish Army fears of this new rival organisation, a year later it was placed on the police budget, along with the Totenkopfverbände.

A few months afterwards, on 1 October 1936, Hitler established the SS-VT Inspectorate and appointed Paul Hausser as its commandant. Hausser, one of the most influential men in the moulding of the Waffen-SS, and later to become one of Germany's most distinguished field commanders, had retired from the General Staff of the Reichswehr in 1932. He quickly became an influential name in the Stahlhelm organisation and a standartenführer in the SA, following the merging of the two organisations, before transferring to the SS to take charge of its first officer cadet training school in Brunswick. Now promoted to SS-Brigadeführer, it was his ultimate responsibility to lick the Verfügungstruppe into fighting shape.

At this time the strength of the armed SS comprised the 2600 men of the *Leibstandarte*, the 5040 men in the two SS-VT Standarten *Deutschland* and *Germania* (whose ranks would be further swelled by the addition of *Der Führer* after the annexation of Austria in 1938), the 3500 men in the Totenkopfverbände battalions, and 759 staff in the training schools in Brunswick

But the armed SS was still small, which did not satisfy Himmler. Apart from the *Leibstandarte* and Eicke's concentration camp guards, plus a number of 'Political Purpose Squads' in key cities, its total strength was barely that of an entire infantry regiment. This situation was soon to change, however, even though the main growth in the Waffen-SS would not take place until after 1940.

But the armed units were only a component of the SS, which was now a power to be reckoned with in Nazi Germany, as the enemies of the Reich began to fill the concentration camps. The first ones were the hutted compounds which were built in the aftermath of the Reichstag fire, to be quickly followed by more permanent installations, such as the one at Dachau. Originally they were called 're-education centres', a title that was soon abandoned because they were in truth 'concentration camps', in which the leaders of the Third Reich could incarcerate all their enemies. To begin with most inmates were commu-

and newly established Bad Tölz. However, Totenkopf personnel were not classed as being part of the SS-VT because the Army refused to recognise membership in their ranks as being equivalent to military service.

From these humble beginnings, the armed SS would eventually grow to a strength of nearly a million men. However, even at its height it never exceeded around 10 per cent of the Wehrmacht's own strength, and thus was never the threat that the discredited SA might have been. Nevertheless, Hitler still had to prove to the Army that the SS would not challenge its right to be the state's sole armed protector.

The role of the armed SS

Hitler's own thinking behind the creation of the SS-Verfügungstruppe is revealed in a conversation he had with Himmler in 1934: 'In our Reich of the future, the SS and police will possess the necessary authority in their relations with other citizens only if they have a soldierly character. Through their past experience of glorious military events and their present education by the NSDAP, the German people have acquired such a warrior mentality that a fat, jovial, sock-knitting police such as we had during the Weimar era can no longer exert authority. For this reason it will be necessary for our SS and police, in their own closed units, to prove themselves at the front in the same way as the Army and to make blood sacrifices to the same degree as any other branch of the armed forces.'

In public, however, Hitler was less frank about the intended role of the armed SS. Officially, its 'original and most important duty' was 'to serve as the protector of the Führer'. In 1935, he amplified this by saying that 'in time of war the SS-VT will be incorporated into the Army'. Himmler was not happy with this, and in 1936 stated that the role of the SS was to 'guarantee the security of Germany from the interior, just as the Wehrmacht guarantees the safety of the honour, the greatness and the peace of the Reich from the exterior'. Since these two statements were clearly contradictory, Hitler was forced in 1938 to clarify the situation, writing that in time of 'national emergency' the SS-VT would be used for two purposes: 'By the Commander-in-Chief of the Army within the framework of the Army. It will then be subject exclusively to military law and instructions; politically, however, it will remain a branch of the NSDAP'; adding, 'at home, in accordance with my instructions, it will be under the orders of the Reichsführer-SS'.

The armed SS was by this time rapidly growing into a far different organisation to any that could have been realistically conceived when it was first formed. This was largely due to the work of Paul Hausser and his training schools. It is appropriate at this point, therefore, to look at those factors which influenced men to join the Waffen-SS in the first place, rather than the Army; and those factors that made them such tough and often fanatical opponents in the field, earning themselves sobriquets such as 'fighters not soldiers' (applied to the 12th SS Panzer Division *Hitlerjugend*) or 'soldiers of destruction' (given to the 3rd SS Panzer Division *Totenkopf*).

SS recruits

There were many reasons why a man might choose to join the armed SS rather than another branch of the armed forces. To give one example, the commando leader Otto Skorzeny originally wanted to join the Air Force, but his height rendered him ineligible for air crew duties. More often, though, the reasons were ambition and a desire to belong to an elite. After the reintroduction of conscription, the Army's standards fell because it had to make up the specified 36 divisions with the material available, rather than being able to pick and choose, as under the restrictions of the Treaty of Versailles. Realising this, and seeing the high standards the armed SS demanded of its recruits, the Army imposed rigid constraints upon the number of men eligible for national service whom it would allow to join the SS. This situation was only partially ameliorated when Hitler put the SS on the police budget, giving the Army more money to play with; it also exempted members of other SS branches from conscription, making them available

BELOW: A group of officers and NCOs of the **Leibstandarte Adolf Hitler** *photographed wearing a mixture of earth-brown and black service uniforms. The* **Adolf Hitler** *cuffband of the SS-Untersturmführer is clearly visible. Many of those executed during the Night of the Long Knives were shot at the* **Leibstandarte's** *Bad Lichterfelde barracks in the capital Berlin.*

to volunteer for the fighting formations. However, it was an unhappy situation that was never totally resolved to the satisfaction of either side.

There were two principal differences between volunteers for the armed SS and the Army. Although SS physical requirements were higher (see below), its educational ones were lower: nearly half of all Waffen-SS recruits had received only minimal schooling, and officer candidates in particular were accepted with far lower academic qualifications than their counterparts in the Army. This tended to make them far more amenable to the tough discipline and ideological indoctrination (this was not necessarily true in other branches of the SS, which attracted a high proportion of very capable administrators and lawyers, as well as members of the aristocracy).

Standards of entry

The second difference, as noted earlier, is that the majority of volunteers for the Waffen-SS came from rural areas, whereas the bulk of the Army's ranks were composed of city dwellers. This may seem unimportant, but rural living conditions in Germany during the first half of the twentieth century were far more primitive than they are now. Thus, it soon became apparent, especially in Russia, that the majority of men in the Waffen-SS divisions were not only more comfortable living in the field and off the land, but were also more adept at fieldcraft. As one of the principal requirements of a soldier is to be able to simply endure in order to continue fighting, this was not an insignificant asset.

Armed SS recruits in the early days, before wartime conditions forced a relaxation of standards to prevent the SS division from being starved of recruits, had to satisfy stringent physical and moral conditions. 'Sepp' Dietrich, commander of the *Leibstandarte* until 1944, wanted mature men rather than acned schoolboys, so he only recruited from those aged between 23 and 35, with the added requirements that they had to be at least five feet eleven inches tall and in excellent physical condition. No man was accepted if he had a criminal record, and he obviously had to be able to prove his 'Aryan' ancestry. In fact, to begin with – before he was forced to lower his standards in order to replace casualties – Dietrich would not accept a man into the *Leibstandarte* if he had a single tooth filled! He was determined that his regiment would be the toughest, fittest and most highly disciplined unit in the Führer's ser-

vice, and correspondence with now ageing survivors reveals that they still firmly believe they were. Indeed, right to the end the *Leibstandarte* attracted the cream of German volunteers for the Waffen-SS.

Membership of the Allgemeine-SS (the general body of the SS) was a different matter. Between his accession to power in 1933 and the Blood Purge in 1934, huge numbers of men had flocked to join the ranks of the SS, as well as the SA and NS-DAP. These 'March Violets', as they were known, were not of the same calibre as the pre-1933 membership, so Himmler instituted a ruthless weeding-out process during 1934-35, throwing out thousands on the grounds of alcoholism, criminality, homosexuality or dubious racial background.

In the armed SS, initial enlistment was four years for other ranks, 12 for NCOs and 25 for officers, while candidates were only allowed to apply for officer training after serving at least two years in the ranks (unless they had previous experience in the Army, as in the case of Paul Hausser, for example). Despite these lengthy commitments, and despite the tough physical, moral and racial requirements, there was no shortage of volunteers. However, there was a lack of combat-experience field officers in the beginning, and this was to prove a contributory factor in the high losses the Waffen-SS suffered during the invasion of the West in 1940.

Military training

Initial training was carried out in depots outside each regiment's home town. Thus, Dachau for *Totenkopf*, Munich for *Deutschland* and *Hamburg* for Germania. Officer candidates then went on to either Bad Tölz or Brunswick, where light and airy barracks and classrooms had been purpose built. In his efforts to train his SS men, Hausser had the help of two very experienced officers: Felix Steiner and Cassius Freiherr von Montigny.

Steiner had been an officer in a Stosstruppe (assault troop) during World War I, and he wanted to imbue the armed SS with a similar style and elan. These assault troops, direct forerunners of today's special forces, consisted of small groups of heavily armed volunteers. They were true light infantry, just as the grenadiers of the Waffen-SS were to become. They carried only weapons, ammunition, water bottles and field dressings, and were not weighed down with heavy pack loads. This, Steiner decided, would be the style of the SS: it would be composed of frontline fighters.

'Of a hundred men we can use on the average ten or fifteen, no more. We ask for the political record of his parents, brothers and sisters, the record of his ancestry as far back as 1750, and naturally the physical examination and his record from the Hitler Youth.'

– Himmler, *Organization and Obligations of the SS and the Police,* 1937

Montigny, a World War I U-boat captain who had subsequently joined the Totenkopfverbände, had similarly strong ideas on discipline. Between them, he and Steiner set out to create a force of men who would be tough, ruthless and, equally important, highly disciplined. To a large degree they succeeded, although it was largely a lack of the last-named quality, together with a total recklessness and callous disregard for human life, which was to lead to several atrocities.

The training programme evolved for the *Deutschland* and *Germania* Regiments was broadly followed by the *Leibstandarte Adolf Hitler,* although, because of its ceremonial and guard duties, the *Leibstandarte* had to endure a great deal more 'spit and polish', leading to its men being nicknamed 'asphalt soldiers'. Similarly, the same programme was more or less followed when Theodor Eicke began the transformation of part of the Totenkopfverbände into the *Totenkopf* Division.

The daily routine

The normal day's routine began at 0600 hours with the recruits dressed in PE kit being put through an hour's callisthenics before breakfast. Afterwards, the men would change into fatigues or service dress, depending on the day's programme. Of all the aspects of training, weapons usage received the greatest emphasis. First the men had to learn how to strip, clean and reassemble their rifles. This took place in the classroom, the instructor using a large wall chart, which showed the weapons in exploded view, to explain the function of each part. Then the men had to practice on their own rifles, repeating the disassembly and reassembly processes until they could do them blindfold. They were shown how to clear blockages and effect simple field repairs. Then it was out on to the firing butts for target practice at steadily increasing ranges. Those who proved 'gun shy', or who simply had no aptitude despite patient encouragement, were eased out into clerical and other tasks, because the SS needed signallers, clerks, drivers and cooks as much as any other military formation.

Once the men were familiar with their weapons they would begin to learn infantry assault techniques, charging at sandbags with bayonets fixed. The instructors put great emphasis on aggression, constantly stressing speed and ferocity in the attack, both as a means of winning quickly and to minimise casualties. To this end the men were taught the techniques of unarmed

combat by qualified unarmed combat instructors and, later, when they were sufficiently skilled to practice on each other without causing injury, they would fight mock battles using rifles and bayonets.

To further the aggressive spirit, boxing featured as a major part of the curriculum, helping the trainees to get over the instinctive fear of being hurt and teaching them that the best way to avoid just that was getting their own blows in first. In fact, sport of all types played a major role in the Waffen-SS training programme, much more so than in the Army. All forms of field and track events were encouraged, not just for relaxation but as part of the training itself, as a means of enhancing physical fitness and reflexes. And of course there were endless route marches and cross-country runs, both with and without full kit, to develop stamina and endurance.

Ideological indoctrination

After the morning's work was finished the trainees were given a hearty lunch, then settled down to a 'make and mend' session, during which barracks were scoured, boots cleaned, uniforms repaired and pressed and any other chores attended to. Then it was out into the open again for further exercise. In the evening the trainees could read, listen to the radio, write letters and play cards or chess (the latter being encouraged to develop both logical thinking and mental flexibility). Those recruits lucky enough to have secured a pass could go into town, after first passing a rigorous inspection by the duty officer of the guard.

So far, apart from those already noted, there were few differences between the

ABOVE: The man who shot Ernst Röhm in his cell at Stadelheim prison: Theodor Eicke. Appointed commandant of Dachau concentration camp by Himmler, Eicke set about transforming the guards into what he described as 'an outstanding body of men showing a splendid corps spirit...[whose] ideals were loyalty, bravery and duty-fulfilment.' Any thoughts of compassion towards the inmates were quickly squashed. Eicke left the guards in no doubt as to their task: 'You stand as matchless soldiers even in peacetime day and night against the enemy, against the enemy behind the wire!'

BELOW: Victor Lutze, the SA leader in Hanover, who assumed the command of the SA after the Night of the Long Knives. He relayed to Hitler Röhm's plans to turn the SA into a National Socialist army, and he accompanied Hitler to Munich to arrest Röhm. After the purge Lutze assumed the command of the SA, though by this stage it was an organisation in decline. Lutze himself quickly became a minor figure in the Nazi hierarchy, and he was killed in a car crash in May 1943.

training of an SS man and his Army counterpart. What they had to endure additionally were formal lectures, given at least three times a week, covering the policies of the NSDAP, and intense indoctrination in SS philosophy, particularly the theories of racial superiority, which destined them to rule over the *untermensch*, the so-called 'subhuman' Slavs and Jews (gypsies, freemasons and communists were also classed as *untermensch*). In a typical address to the troops, Himmler said at the beginning of Operation 'Barbarossa' (the codename for the invasion of Russia in June 1941): 'When you, my men, fight over there in the east, you are carrying out the same struggle, against the same subhumanity, the same inferior races, that at one time appeared under the name of Huns, another time – a thousand years ago – at the time of King Heinrich and Otto I, under the name of Magyars, another time under the name of Tartars, and still another time under the name of Genghis Khan and the Mongols. Today they appear as Russians under the political banner of

Bolshevism.' Ironically, thousands of these 'subhumans', particularly from the Baltic states and the Ukraine, would shortly join the ranks of the SS.

The SS creed

What the ideological lectures aimed at producing were men who firmly believed in their own destiny as missionaries of the new Aryan order, which would eventually rule the world. They were thoroughly indoctrinated in Nazi philosophy so they would know what they were fighting for. While many believed, or came to believe in, in this creed, others were certainly more cynical and believed that they were fighting to make their country strong again. That said, these factors, coupled with their personal oath of allegiance to Hitler, goes a long way towards accounting for the almost suicidal determination and courage of the Waffen-SS soldiers and their disdain of death. Few were taken in by Himmler's crackpot pseudo-medieval mythology. However, strangely, being the recipient of a Totenkopfring was an award coveted almost as much as a Knights Cross. The silver Totenkopfring had a skull and crossbones on the front and runic symbols around the band, which were supposed to reinforce the wearer's 'psychic' Germanic virtues. It was not a military decoration, but a personal reward for service from Himmler himself, and the ring was supposed to go to the grave with its wearer.

Austrian intrigues

At the end of World War I, Austria's fortunes, or misfortunes, closely paralleled those of its German neighbour. The driving force of the Austro-Hungarian Empire had been humbled, with much of its territories lost and its home front in turmoil. Both countries were governed by shaky regimes and on both sides there was a notable willingness to consider the advantages of a union, or *Anschluss*. The Allies, however, having just spent over four years of fighting to subdue the Central Powers, were in no mood to sanction any such union, and the idea was dropped.

The capital, Vienna, was known as a hotbed of political intrigue and, like Berlin, contained a considerable proportion of communist sympathisers. So much so that it was commonly known as 'Red Vienna'.

The rise of the left in Austria was viewed with considerable alarm by the Christian Democratic government, whose own leanings were distinctly conservative. In order to prevent leftist influence growing, the government began moves to limit the power of the socialists, and the government, civil service and Army were purged of unreliable elements. In response, the leftists formed their own paramilitary force, the Schutzbund.

As tension in Austria increased, a myriad of right-wing nationalist groups arose, intent on halting the rise of the left. By the late 1920s, many of them began to look to Germany and Hitler for support, and the Austrian Nazi Party grew steadily (the Depression had the same effect in Austria as it had in Germany: weakening the government and encouraging the rise of extremist groups on both sides).

The Austrian Nazis

At the time of Hitler's accession to power in Germany in 1933, the Austrians, on the face of it, had a strong government in place. Their chancellor was Engelbert Dolfuss, a conservative supported by a tough Justice Minister, Kurt Elder von Schuschnigg, and the Chief of the Heimwehr, von Starkenberg, who was vice chancellor. Dolfuss was determined not to allow political extremists of either persuasion to overthrow his government, and in March 1933 he banned the Austrian Nazi Party. In this he had the full support of Italy, though Mussolini insisted he should move against the leftists also.

In February 1934, a socialist uprising was vigorously suppressed by the police and elements of the regular Army. However, although on the face of it Dolfuss had acted swiftly and decisively to restore order, he had also served the purposes of the Nazis by eliminating their socialist enemies. Now the right could become even more strident in Austria.

The Austrian Nazis, however, were by no means as strong or as well organised as their German counterparts, and they had to accept there was little chance of a seizure of power. Instead, intrigue and conspiracy were to be the main weapons used against Dolfuss and his government.

The Austrian Nazis hatched a plot, armed and assisted by the SS, to assassinate Dolfuss and his entire cabinet during an assault on the Chancellory. Aided and abetted by Nazi sympathisers in the Austrian police and Army, the assault was to be carried out by a group of some 150 armed SS men disguised as policemen. The plot was fully approved of by Hitler.

The attack was to take place on 24 July 1934 during a cabinet conference. One of the conspirators, however, a police offi-

cer, lost his nerve and leaked details of the plot. The authorities declined to act upon unsubstantiated allegations, and by the time the reality of the threat was established it was almost too late. Dolfuss was warned in time to send his cabinet members to safety, but he himself elected to remain in the Chancellory, and he was still present when the assassins arrived. At the last moment he attempted to escape, but was intercepted by a squad of SS men under the command of Otto Planetta, who fired on Dolfuss with his pistol, mortally wounding him. (the Vienna Allgemeine-SS Regiment, SS-Fuss-Standarte 11, was later named after Otto Planetta in honour of his 'achievements'). Dolfuss was laid out on a couch by his assailants but was refused aid or comfort, and died from his wounds a few hours later, as his assassins abused him for refusing to accept Hitler as his Führer.

It was intended that the assassination would be the signal for a Nazi uprising and seizure of power. As in Germany, however, the rank and file of the Nazi stormtroopers were mistrustful of the elitist SS. As the assassins had failed in their plan to elimi-

ABOVE: SS-Gruppenführer Paul Hausser. Born in 1880, he had retired from the Reichswehr in 1932. On 1 October 1936, the Inspectorate of Verfügungstruppen was established to supervise the administration and military training of the field units of the SS, and Hausser was appointed to head it. Proving himself more than able to fulfil his duties, he went on to command I SS Panzer Corps in 1943 and Army Group B in the West in August 1944. He was wounded while leading a relief attack to keep the gap open out of the Falaise Pocket. He was affectionately known as 'Papa' to his men.

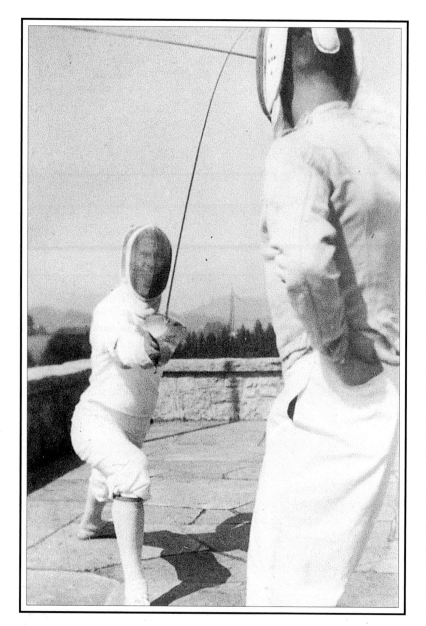

ABOVE: Sporting activities at Bad Tölz. Physical fitness played a large part in Waffen-SS training, which produced soldiers who had an aggressive fighting spirit. Waffen-SS officer candidates in particular were characterised by toughness and loyalty. They led from the front and, whatever their men may have thought of them, they were always obeyed. This resulted in a reckless bravery in battle which often carried all before it, but at a price: Waffen-SS units generally suffered high casualties.

nate the entire cabinet, the stormtroopers were reluctant to come to their aid. Indeed, the cabinet ministers who had escaped had gone straight to the Defence Ministry and raised an armed force, which then returned and surrounded the Chancellory. The assassins surrendered when it became obvious their plot had failed. The government then moved swiftly, rounding up the conspirators and jailing thousands of Nazis.

Mussolini was furious at Hitler's intrigues and moved some 50,000 Italian troops to the border with Austria, insisting that they would be used against the Germans if they attempted to invade. Schuschnigg was sworn in as the new chancellor and for a time it seemed the crisis was over.

Schuschnigg realised, however, that Hitler would not give up his designs on Austria so easily, and as Germany's relations with Italy grew more cordial he

realised he could not count on Mussolini's assistance in the future. Schuschnigg was forced to engage in dialogue with the Germans, who had appointed the conservative Franz von Papen as ambassador to Austria, reckoning he might be more likely to strike up a rapport with the Austrians than a fervently Nazi politician.

Schuschnigg did, in fact, reach an agreement with von Papen, by which Germany would recognise Austria's sovereignty and accept that any conflict between the Austrian government and the Austrian Nazis was an internal Austrian affair in which Germany would not meddle. Austria, on the other hand, would agree not to enter into any anti-German alliances and would proclaim an amnesty for her Nazi political prisoners.

Schuschnigg, for his part, kept his side of the bargain, and some 17,000 Austrian Nazis were released from captivity, and almost immediately returned to their subversive activities.

Hitler, of course, had no intention of honouring the agreement and by November 1937 was openly expressing to his aides his intent to annex Austria into the Reich. Mussolini's acquiescence was gained by Hitler's promise to give him control of the German-speaking South Tyrol.

Schuschnigg at the Berghof

As Schuschnigg prepared for what was to be a fateful meeting with Hitler at the Berghof in February 1938, he prepared a list of concessions he was prepared to make to Hitler and naively involved lawyer Arthur Seyss-Inquart in his deliberations. Seyss-Inquart was one of the few pro-German Austrians whom Schuschnigg trusted. In the event his trust was to prove misplaced, as Seyss-Inquart immediately betrayed his confidences to Germany. Hitler's bargaining position was thereby strengthened by his foreknowledge of what Schuschnigg was prepared to concede.

As might have been expected, Hitler opened the discussions with a stream of invective against the Austrians. Threats and insults abounded before he 'invited' Schuschnigg to cooperate with his plans for Austria. Schuschnigg refused and the meeting broke for lunch. Afterwards, the Austrian chancellor was presented with a list of Hitler's demands, which included Seyss-Inquart's reward – his appointment as Minister of the Interior. Schuschnigg refused to concede without consulting President Miklas. Hitler, after further outbursts, agreed to give Schuschnigg just three days to agree to his terms.

On his return to Austria, Schuschnigg had little option but to agree to Hitler's demands and Seyss-Inquart was duly appointed Minister of the Interior. The latter immediately began conspiring with Hitler and Himmler to undermine Schuschnigg, and the Austrian Nazis began to cause even more trouble and unrest. Needless to say, Hitler refused to honour his promise to reaffirm Germany's commitment to Austrian sovereignty.

On 24 February, Schuschnigg appeared before the Austrian parliament and said that Austria would never surrender its independence. He announced that a plebiscite would be held to give the people the chance to decide their own fate. Hitler was furious at this, and on 10 March ordered that preparations be made for the invasion of Austria. On 11 March, the border between the two countries was closed.

The *Anschluss*

Alarmed by these developments, Schuschnigg attempted further negotiations with Hitler only to be met with fresh demands, which included his resignation and replacement by Seyss-Inquart. Reluctantly Schuschnigg agreed, but President Miklas refused to swear in Seyss-Inquart as chancellor. Rumours swept the country that German troops had already crossed the border, and this panicked Schuschnigg into announcing over the radio that the Austrian Army would offer no armed resistance to the Germans. The rumours were false, but on hearing of Schuschnigg's broadcast Hitler ordered the invasion to proceed knowing that his troops would meet no resistance. The German 8th Army flowed over the border unopposed.

Hitler's initial intent was to install a puppet government under the leadership of Seyss-Inquart. However, on realising that the Austrians seemed to be in favour of the events, decided to go for full annexation of Austria as a province of the Reich. In a new plebiscite held soon after the *Anschluss*, some 95 per cent of the voters were in favour of Hitler and the union with Germany. Austria's fate was sealed.

With *Anschluss* came the inevitable repression of all whose of suspect loyalty. Mass arrests began as the SS and Gestapo went to work. Within weeks over 160 former government officials had been sent to Dachau. The Austrians, however, were soon to have their own concentration camp, at Mauthausen, where over 30,000 people perished.

The invasion of Austria, however, was not only an important step in the development of the security and police organs of the SS, but also gave valuable experience to the units of the fledgling SS-Verfügungstruppe, ultimately to become the Waffen-SS. The *Leibstandarte*, along with the *Deutschland* and *Germania* Regiments, formed part of the invasion force. Almost immediately after the annexation, a new SS-Verfügungstruppe regiment entitled *Der Führer* was raised in Vienna.

German desires on Czechoslovakia

Czechoslovakia had been created at the end of World War I, principally from territories of the former Austro-Hungarian Empire. It had also gained the German-speaking Sudetenland, to the north of Bohemia. In fact, there had been a considerable number of ethnic Germans concentrated in Bohemia and Moravia for over seven hundred years. Not surprisingly, this very nationalistic section of the population followed the rise of Hitler and his National Socialists with great interest. The Czechs were very wary of this potentially disloyal group, and were determined not to allow

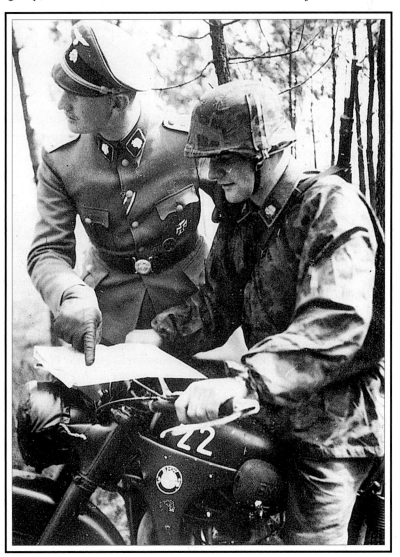

BELOW: Recruits of the **Totenkopf** *Division in training. The division's commander, Theodor Eicke, instilled into his men a contempt for death and the need for speed and aggression in the attack. This tied in with the ideology of the Waffen-SS as a whole. Hitler stated his SS troops to be 'inspired by a fierce will, troops with an unbeatable turn-out – the sense of superiority personified.' Such attributes were invaluable to a commander in battle, but they also resulted in Waffen-SS soldiers killing without compunction and placing a low value on all human life.*

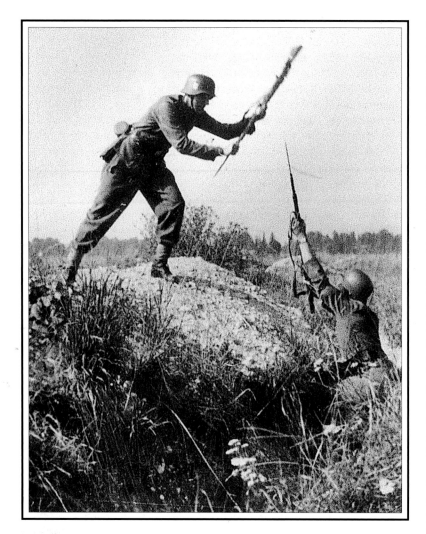

ABOVE: Waffen-SS recruits simulating trench assaults. In every SS barracks there hung a sign, upon which was a quote from Nietzsche which read: 'Praise be that which toughens!'

the German nationalists in their country to endanger the stability of the nation. From 1935, however, the Germans began to openly support and financially subsidise the Sudetendeutsch Partei under Konrad Henlein, an ultra right-wing supporter of Nazism. Well aware of the potential threat this posed to his country, the Czech President, Eduard Benes, busied himself organising treaties with France, Russia, Romania and Yugoslavia in an attempt to procure a measure of security.

As soon as the *Anschluss* with Austria had been successfully concluded, Hitler pressured Henlein to antagonise the Czechs as much as possible in the hope of provoking action against the Sudeten Germans, which Hitler could then use as an excuse to come to their aid. At the same time, Hitler began a propaganda war against the Czechs, accusing them of atrocities against the Sudeten German population. Some of these accusations were based on actual incidents, but many had been blown up out of all proportion. Henlein's outrageous demands to the Czechs included almost complete autonomy for the Sudetenland and compensation for alleged atrocities. At

the same time, Hitler ordered his Armed Forces High Command to prepare plans for the ultimate invasion of Czechoslovakia. The military were somewhat aghast at this, as the Czechs had a strong army and would undoubtedly defend their land with vigour.

Britain and France were intent on appeasing Hitler, and encouraged Benes to make concessions to the Germans. Despite this, the Czechs mobilised over 170,000 reservists and reinforced their border areas. British and French pressure eventually prevailed, however, and on 5 September 1938 Benes acceded to Henlein's demands.

Another easy German victory

This, of course, was the last thing that Hitler really wanted. His orders were for Henlein to provoke the Czechs into action, not reach agreement with them. Henlein reacted by provoking a confrontation between Sudeten German nationalists and Czech police on 7 September, which Hitler used as an excuse to break off negotiations. Benes was forced into declaring martial law and sent troops into the Sudetenland to restore order.

On 12 September, Hitler gave a speech to a Nuremberg rally in which he ranted on at length about the alleged atrocities perpetrated by the Czechs on the Sudeten Germans. This inflammatory speech was heard on a radio broadcast by the Sudeten population, and resulted in violent anti-Czech riots in Sudeten cities.

As the Germans began preparation for military intervention, Britain and France rushed to appease Hitler in their desperation to avoid a war in Europe. The British Prime Minister, Neville Chamberlain, flew to Munich on 15 September and heard Hitler categorically insist he was prepared to go to war to solve the Sudeten problem. Within three days the British and French governments, without consulting the Czechs, had agreed that the Sudetenland should be ceded to Germany, leaving Czechoslovakia without much of its industrial capacity, and neutralising much of its border defences with Germany.

Left with little choice, as the British and French governments declared themselves unwilling to take any further interest in Czechoslovakia's fate if Benes refused to agree, the president agreed to surrender control of the Sudetenland to Germany.

The Poles also moved to demand the Teschen district and the Hungarians the provinces of Ruthenia and Slovenia. Hitler, however, now wanted not only political and economic control of the Sudetenland, but insisted that all Czech forces be withdrawn from the area and replaced by German occupation troops. The Czechs rejected this demand and once again Europe seemed on the brink of war, as the Czechs mobilised their reserves to face the 30 German divisions facing them. The French massed troops along the Maginot Line and the Royal Navy was put on alert.

The Americans and British pleaded with Mussolini to intercede with Hitler, who was perhaps now beginning to believe that the British and French might well go to war with him, and he agreed to back down. Chamberlain, together with Mussolini and Daladier, were invited to a conference in Munich on 29 December. The Czechs were not invited as delegates, but were forced into the undignified position of attending as observers with the British, and being confined to their Hotel rooms by the Gestapo. The conference in effect did little more than ratify Hitler's demands.

The SS in Czechoslovakia

The Czech Army was more than willing to face up to Hitler's Wehrmacht, but Benes refused to take his country into a war he felt they could not win without the support of Britain and France. On 1 October 1938, German troops entered the Sudetenland. Once again, among the units used were the elements of the SS-Verfügungstruppe, including the *Leibstandarte* and the Regiments *Deutschland*, *Germania* and *Der Führer*. In fact, the *Deutschland* Regiment had also, rather ironically, provided the honour guards for the visiting heads of state during the Munich peace talks.

The period of peace gained by the Munich agreement was, however, to be very brief. As soon as the Sudetenland had been occupied, Hitler set about destabilising the Benes government. Benes soon resigned, to be replaced by the weak and inexperienced Emil Hacha. On 14 March 1939, Hitler claimed that the Czech nation was in such turmoil and chaos that the German Army might feel compelled to occupy the country to restore order.

Hacha was warned that if the occupation was unopposed the Czechs would be treated benevolently, but if any opposition was encountered it would be swiftly crushed and the Czechs treated as a subjugated enemy. Hacha was no match for Hitler's threats and caved in. According to the document signed by Hacha, he willingly placed the fate of his country and people into the hands of Adolf Hitler.

As soon as the Germans had occupied the entire country, the SS and its security elements lost no time in making their presence felt. Although Czechoslovakia, now known officially as the Protectorate of Bohemia and Moravia (Bohmen-Mahren) had as its titular head the moderate Constantin von Neurath as its Reichsprotektor, the real power lay with the SS in the person of SS-Gruppenführer Karl Hermann Frank, an unscrupulous and brutal thug. Soon, Heydrich's SD and Gestapo would be fully occupied rounding up those elements of the Czech populace considered undesirable by the Nazis, with the Jews at the top of Heydrich's list of targets.

Crystal Night

By 1938, any respite from persecution gained by the Jewish community because of the Olympic Games and the Nazis fear of adverse international reaction had long since receded. The regime's measures against the Jews were becoming more and more extreme, and one resulted in the expulsion of 8000 Jews of Polish ancestry in mid-1938. Many of these Jews had settled in Germany and had lived there for over 25 years, but were uprooted with little or no warning and deported with no more than the clothes they stood up in. All their property and savings were forfeited to the state. This caused an outcry in the foreign press, but Hitler no longer cared for the opinions of his detractors abroad.

The unfortunate deportees were shoved into railway carriages and unceremoniously dumped a couple of kilometers (1.5 miles) from the Polish border. From here, they were forced to march the remaining distance under a constant hail of physical and verbal abuse from their SS guards.

BELOW: A wargaming exercise at Bad Tölz. As well as practical lessons, all Waffen-SS recruits were given ideological indoctrination in the tenets of National Socialism. In this way they would carry out their orders without hesitation. A Nazi Party document put it succinctly: 'Obedience must be unconditional. It corresponds to the conviction that National Socialist ideology must reign supreme...Every SS man is therefore prepared to carry out blindly every order issued by the Führer or given by his superior, regardless of the sacrifice involved.'

ABOVE: German troops march into Austria during the **Anschluss**, *March 1938. Himmler was closely involved with the takeover of Austria, as he controlled the underground Austrian SS, which was commanded by the notorious Ernst Kaltenbrunner. The seizing of the country resulted in 'enemies of the state' being imprisoned in concentration camps, and at least 76,000 Austrians were sent to Dachau, including Chancellor Schuschnigg.*

Even when they had reached Polish soil their lot did not improve dramatically. The physical abuse may have ended, but little comfort was provided for them in the way of food and accommodation, some families being forced to shelter in cattle pens or stables still filthy with animal dung.

Once such deportee was Zindel Grynszpan, who had lived in Hanover for many years and had raised a son there. The son was, at that time, studying in Paris, and he soon received a letter from his father detailing the misfortunes and brutal treatment the deportees had suffered. The son was enraged at his father's plight and determined to revenge himself against the Nazis. On 7 November 1938, armed with a pistol, he marched into the German Embassy in Paris and shot the first official to come within range. Ironically, his victim was Ernst vom Rath, an Embassy official who was being monitored by the Gestapo for his anti-Nazi leanings. Rath was seriously wounded and rushed into hospital.

This provided Himmler and Heydrich with a perfect excuse to implement an 'action' against Germany's Jews. They had been planning such a move for some time; now was their chance.

On 9 November, a secret wire was sent by Heinrch Müller, Gestapo chief, to his Gestapo offices. It stated they were to liaise with the Ordnungspolizei to ensure only Jewish properties suffered. Later, Heydrich himself wired all Gestapo and SD offices, ordering them to coordinate actions with Nazi political leaders. SA and SS men were tasked with the destruction of Jewish businesses, homes and, most of all, synagogues. The action was to be portrayed as a spontaneous outburst of rage from the German people against the perfidious Jews. In fact, it was highly orchestrated to the extent that official guidelines were laid down as to what exactly could be destroyed, to control the extent of the damage and ensure that non-Jewish property was not touched.

For instance, a Jewish-owned property, detached from its neighbours and standing on its own ground, could be attacked and totally destroyed without fear of retribution, but a Jewish shop next door to a German-owned business could be attacked and damaged, but care had to be taken not to cause any harm to the adjacent German property. Thus, arson in these cases was prohibited as potentially dangerous to

German property. Looting of Jewish property was also prohibited. The intent was to portray the action as the work of an outraged German people intent on punishing the Jews for the murder of vom Rath. Looting would allow the foreign press to portray the mob as a thieving rabble (which many were!). Therefore, looting would thus be punished, as would attacks on foreign nationals, even if Jewish.

With Himmler and Heydrich having their excuse, the full terror of the Nazi fury was turned against Germany's Jewish community. Mobs of SA and SS men, closely monitored by the Gestapo to ensure the 'guidelines' were followed, wreaked havoc. Synagogues, being among the prime targets, were gleefully desecrated. Shops, offices, houses and even cemeteries were violated over a 24-hour period, as Hitler denounced the death of vom Rath as the result of a Jewish plot.

Over 30,000 Jews were rounded up and put in concentration camps. Although most were released some three months later, over 1000 had died in total due to the merciless beatings they had sustained in the camps (91 were killed on the night of 9/10 November). Some 7500 Jewish businesses were destroyed and over 260 synagogues damaged or destroyed. The streets of the Jewish quarters were awash with sparkling shards of broken glass from the shattered windows, giving this atrocity its nickname Kristallnacht – Crystal Night.

The Nazis, however, had made one major miscalculation in their plans to wreak havoc on the Jewish business community: most of the Jewish properties were insured with German companies, who would now have to foot the bill for the damage. The massive claims looked set to ruin many German insurance companies.

According to Nazi reasoning, however, the destruction wrought on Kristallnacht was entirely the fault of the Jews themselves. As the Jews were responsible for all this, they must foot the bill. Hermann Göring came up with a scheme by which a fine of one billion Reichsmarks would be levied upon the Jews. This would be raised by all those with savings in excess of RM 5000 losing 20 per cent of their property. This decision was enshrined in a government decree of 12 November.

So, the Nazi regime had succeeded in terrorising and brutalising the Jewish population of the Reich, destroying a huge proportion of Germany's synagogues and Jewish businesses, murdering over 1000 Jews and incarcerating some 30,000 in concentration camps, and had handed the bill for these excesses to the Jews themselves.

Crystal Night was to be a turning point in the Nazi treatment of the Jews. Only three days after the decree of 11 November, further anti-Jewish measures were promulgated, including the banning of Jewish children from being educated in German schools. Soon the Nazis would make sure that there was no place for Jews in German society. The Gestapo and the security arm of the SS, Heydrich's Sicherheitsdienst, would make sure of that.

BELOW LEFT: Wrecked Jewish shops after Crystal Night. A secret SD report after the event summed up the aims of the exercise, as laid down by Heydrich: 'The action manifested itself in general in the destruction or burning down of synagogues and the demolition of almost all Jewish businesses, which were thereby forced to sell up. In part the homes of Jews were affected in the action...In resisting a number of Jews were killed or wounded.' In fact, 91 Jews were killed on the night, 20,000 arrested, 815 shops and 171 homes destroyed, and 191 synagogues burnt. To pay for the damage, Germany's Jews were collectively fined one billion marks and Jewish businesses and property were confiscated. The aforementioned report concluded by stating that 'Jewry – so far as German nationals and stateless persons are concerned – has finally been excluded from all areas of the German community so that only emigration remains to the Jews to safeguard their existence.' For Nazi Germany, Crystal Night was a major step on the road that would lead to the gas chambers of the Final Solution.

FORGED IN BATTLE

In September 1939, the military units of Himmler's SS empire were untried in battle. However, the campaigns in Poland and the West were to show the Wehrmacht and the world that the Waffen-SS, whose motto was 'loyalty is my honour', was staffed by dedicated officers and first-rate soldiers.

The German attack on Poland on 1 September 1939 brought the fledgling military formations of Hitler's SS-Verfügungstruppe the opportunity to show their detractors just what they were capable of. In the event, despite generally acquitting themselves well, they still failed to win the respect of most of the Army's senior commanders, probably unfairly, and were considered by their Army counterparts to have been too brash and reckless, suffering disproportionately high casualties as a result. The SS, in turn, was critical of the Army, insisting its units had been misused, and had been given the most difficult and dangerous tasks. The truth probably lies somewhere in between.

Individual SS units did not find the Poles to be the pushover many had expected, but the losses suffered by the SS were largely due to aggressive and daring tactics instilled into its recruits during training, rather than to inexperience or poor leadership, as some of its Army detractors had suggested.

At the outbreak of war, the principal armed units of the SS-Verfügungstruppe consisted of the following: *Leibstandarte SS Adolf Hitler*, the premier SS formation at this point. It consisted of a fully motorised battalion-sized unit led by SS-Gruppenführer Josef 'Sepp' Dietrich.

SS troops watch a flight of German dive-bombers overfly their position during the campaign in France, May 1940. These men are probably from the **SS-Verfügungsdivision.**

ABOVE: German troops dismantle a Polish border post on 1 September 1939. For the SS, and the German Army as a whole, the campaign in Poland was a staggering success. However, the Poles did put up a spirited resistance, and the aggressively led SS units suffered high casualties as a result. The Army quickly seized on this as evidence that the SS, particularly its officer corps, was inadequately trained. Himmler and his commanders, however, believed the SS in Poland had been deliberately misused by the Army, and argued that only independent SS-led divisions would truly demonstrate the military potential of SS soldiers. Himmler did eventually get his divisions, but throughout they remained under the control of the Army High Command.

OPPOSITE: A German 37mm Pak 35/36 anti-tank gun engages Polish armour on the outskirts of Warsaw in September 1939.

SS-Standarte *Deutschland*: a motorised infantry regiment based in Munich and commanded by SS-Standartenführer Felix Steiner, who was one of the most able soldiers of the SS and eventually reached the rank of SS-Obergruppenführer.

SS-Standarte *Germania*: a Hamburg-based motorised infantry regiment which was commanded by SS-Standartenführer Carl-Maria Demelhuber.

SS-Standarte *Der Führer*: raised in Vienna shortly after the *Anschluss*, it was composed principally of Austrian volunteers and was commanded by SS-Oberführer Georg Keppler.

SS-Nachrichtensturmbann: originally garrisoned in Berlin, the signals battalion of the SS-Verfügungstruppe was established in March 1935. By the spring of 1939 it was a highly efficient and well-trained unit under the command of SS-Sturmbannführer Weiss.

SS-Artillerie Regiment: established at Munsterlager in the summer of 1939, the regiment was worked up very rapidly with the assistance of the Army. Within only eight weeks it was pronounced combat ready. The commanding general of VIII Corps, General Busch, said of it at its final review: 'Either you have achieved a miracle or we have been going about establishing and training our new artillery units in the wrong way. The SS-Artillery Regiment is completely combat ready.' The regiment itself was commanded by SS-Obersturmbannführer Peter Hansen.

SS-Aufklärungsabteilung: the reconnaissance battalion of the SS-Verfügungstruppe consisted of two motorcycle companies, an anti-tank platoon, an armoured car platoon and a signals platoon, and was led by SS-Sturmbannführer Brandt.

SS-Pionieresturmbann: established in Dresden in 1935, the SS pioneer battalion was equipped with the most up-to-date kit, such as bridging gear, and was commanded by SS-Sturmbannführer Blumberg.

It had been decided, much to the annoyance of SS commanders, that for the Polish campaign SS units would not operate as a single cohesive force, but would rather be dispersed among the various Army formations. The inspector general of the SS-Verfügungstruppe, SS-Gruppenführer Paul Hausser, for example, served on the staff of Panzer Division *Kempf*.

For the Polish campaign the SS regiment *Deutschland*, the newly formed artillery regiment, the reconnaissance battalion and the signals battalion, plus an Army tank regiment, were part of a fully motorised division under the command of Major-General Werner Kempf. This unit was in turn part of I Corps in General Fedor von Bock's Army Group North.

SS-Standarte *Germania* was initially part of the reserves of General Wilhelm List's 14th Army in East Prussia. The SS-Standarte *Der Führer* saw no part in the Polish campaign, being held in reserve in Germany. The *Leibstandarte*, together with elements of the SS-Pionieresturmbann, served as part of the 10th Army under General Walther von Reichenau. Being a fully equipped motorised unit, it was especially valuable to von Reichenau during the advance, and was used mainly for reconnaissance duties and defending the flanks of the slower Army units. Only one Totenkopf unit, the *SS-Heimwehr Danzig*, a so-called home defence force, took part in the seizing of that city, but played no major role in the campaign itself.

The SS victorious in Poland

When war broke out on 1 September 1939, German units were in excellent positions. From the northeast, General Georg von Kuchler's 3rd Army in East Prussia aimed to push south and approach Warsaw from its eastern side, then link up with General von Kluge's 4th Army, which was to launch its attack from Poland's northwestern frontier. On the southwest frontier the 14th Army, under General List, planned to drive towards the Vistula to cut off any Polish retreat. From the west, General von Reichenau's 10th Army would drive east in a two-pronged movement to cut off the bulk of Polish forces west of Warsaw. The 10th Army would have its flanks protected by the 8th Army under General Johannes Blaskowitz.

ABOVE: A column of German panzers advance through wooded terrain during the campaign in Poland. The use of white crosses on the hulls was soon discontinued – they made good aim marks for anti-tank gunners!

RIGHT: An Unter-scharführer of the Deutschland Regiment. Commanded by SS-Standartenführer Felix Steiner, the regiment was aggressively led in Poland. In one incident, for example, it stormed enemy fortifications northwest of Warsaw in half a day. Note the '1' on this man's collar patch, signifying his membership of the Deutschland Regiment.

As Kempf's division launched its attack from Niedenburg in East Prussia towards the Polish defence lines at Mlava, SS-Standarte *Deutschland* was tasked with breaching the enemy's defences. Led by SS-Standartenführer Steiner, the regiment made a determined frontal assault supported by panzers. However, the SS men had rather underestimated the extent of the Polish anti-tank defences, and the Germans soon got bogged down, becoming sitting targets for enemy heavy artillery. In addition, promised Luftwaffe dive-bomber support failed to materialise. Nevertheless, the SS soldiers, unsupported, pushed on, and battled to within 100m (110yd) of the Polish bunkers before being ordered to withdraw.

On the following day the SS troops were rushed to Chorzele, where the Germans had broken through the Polish lines, and joined in the rapid advance to Rozan on the River Narew, before running into stiff opposition and counter-attacks from Polish cavalry. However, devoid of air support and outnumbered, the Poles could only delay the inevitable,

and the SS was soon advancing again, crossing the River Bug and thereafter being ordered to intercept Polish units withdrawing towards Warsaw. The latter, though poorly equipped, did not lack fighting spirit, and much fierce combat took place before they were crushed and Warsaw itself encircled.

Battlegroups from *Deutschland* then took part in the attack on the major Polish fortifications at Modlin and Zacrozym, northwest of Warsaw. Steiner led his men into the attack and took Zacrozym within 90 minutes, and later that afternoon the fortifications also fell. Meanwhile, in the central sector, the *Leibstandarte* saw considerable fighting in its reconnaissance role and defending the flanks of the 17th Infantry Division, as it drove to the area west of Warsaw. It was then transferred to the 4th Panzer Division to take part in the advance towards Lodz, before finally reaching the western outskirts of the Polish capital.

As the 4th Army closed in from the north and the 10th Army struck from the centre, a large number of Polish troops

The Polish campaign
September 1939

Königsberg
LITHUANIA
BALTIC
Polish corridor
Danzig
EAST PRUSSIA
KEY
→ German forces
POLAND
Bydgoszcz
Torun
Vistula
Modlin
Poznan
Sochaczev
Warsaw
Brest-Litovsk
Warta
Bzura
Breslau
Lodz
Pertrikau
Lublin
Bug
Oder
GERMANY
SILESIA
Katowice
Kraków
Lvóv
Carpathian mountains
SLOVAKIA

Germany invaded Poland on 1 September 1939. Nine armoured divisions – including the 4th Panzer Division – swept through Poland in just 18 days, putting the armoured vehicles, and the tactics that became *blitzkrieg*, to the test for the first time.

were trapped around Posen. Rather than attempting to withdraw eastwards to beat the pincer movement, the Poles attacked south and ran into elements of the German 8th Army, which was protecting 10th Army's northern flanks. Though temporarily thrown off-balance, the Germans soon recovered and successfully encircled the Poles. The *Leibstandarte* itself was then withdrawn westwards and attached to the forces taking part in the encirclement of Polish forces on the River Bzura.

SS-Standarte *Germania*, unlike its counterparts *Deutschland* and *Leibstandarte*, was not used as a cohesive unit. It initially took part in the push through the industrial areas of Upper Silesia before having its strength depleted by the removal of its armoured reconnaissance platoon, which was attached to the 5th Panzer Division, then, four days later, losing a reinforced motorcycle unit to each Corps. The remnants of the regiment were then attached to XXII Army Corps. On its arrival, it was tasked with securing the flanks of the 2nd Panzer Division and the 4th Light Division.

On 13 September, the 15th Company, under the command of SS-Hauptsturmführer Johannes Muhlenkamp, sur-

BELOW: German troops parade in Warsaw, October 1939.
The campaign had been a vindication of Blitzkrieg tactics. Hitler was impressed by the SS's performance, and gave his permission for the formation of three SS divisions. The call went out for recruits (see posters opposite), and many so-called Volksdeutsche answered it with enthusiasm.

prised a retreating Polish battalion and took over 500 prisoners. However, it was then attacked by a larger Polish force trying to reach Warsaw and was forced to withdraw, having been badly mauled. Four days later, the regiment was attached to XVII Corps as a flank protection force, a role it undertook for the rest of the campaign. After the surrender of Poland, all the sub-units were reunited and the regiment moved to Beraun near Prague.

Overall the SS had played only a minor role in the Polish campaign, though the *Leibstandarte* in particular had demonstrated the effectiveness of fully motorised infantry units, as it was rushed from one sector of the front to another. Later in the war, whole SS divisions would be used in the same way on the Eastern Front in so-called 'fire brigades', hurrying from one sector to another. In addition, individual SS units had displayed the high valour that was to become common during the campaign in Russia.

The high command of the Army, however, was unimpressed by the performance of the SS, preferring to stress the negative aspects of its performance, such as the high losses suffered by SS units. The Army, as mentioned earlier, attempted to

*Symbols of an elite:
ceremonial SS dagger,
SS collar patches, the
Knights Cross award,
the **Leibstandarte***'s
cuffband and its
standard.*

put this down to poor leadership at junior officer level, allied to recklessness in the attack. Himmler was incensed at this, and immediately came to the SS's defence, citing what he insisted was the Army's tendency to always give the most difficult and dangerous tasks to the SS, and complaining that the distribution of SS units among Army formations had been detrimental to his men.

Additionally, as an ominous foretaste of things to come, there were a few instances of SS troops killing civilians, specifically Jews. Himmler refused to allow the military courts to prosecute those involved, insisting that only an SS court was competent to try an SS man. Needless to say, the sentences passed were exceptionally light. In return, however, the Army was, for a short time at least, able to insist that no Gestapo, SD or Security Police prosecution of Wehrmacht personnel would be permitted – only military courts were deemed competent to try Army members.

It should not be assumed, however, that these incidents were part of an official policy in SS units at this time. They were isolated atrocities that occurred as

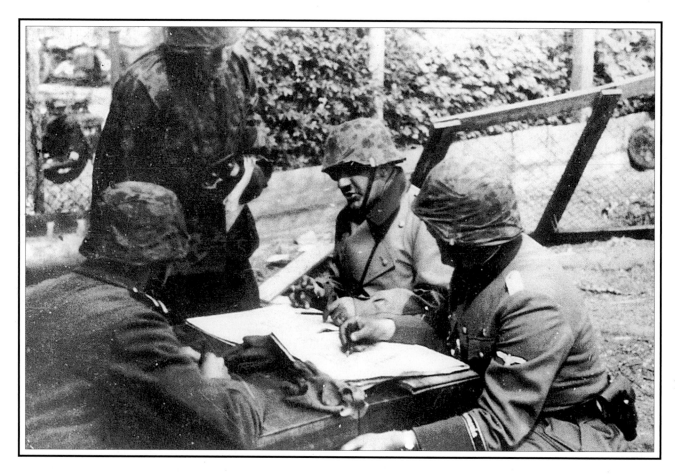

ABOVE: Soldiers of the SS-Verfügungsdivision on the eve of the campaign in the West. These men are from the Germania Regiment, as denoted by the cuffband of the man on the right. Note also the national eagle worn on the left arm, a simple way of differentiating between Wehrmacht and SS military personnel. The man standing is wearing the SS camouflage tunic, which was initially ridiculed by the Army.

a consequence of the strong political and racial indoctrination given to individual SS soldiers (some Wehrmacht personnel also committed atrocities).

The expansion of the Waffen-SS

Hitler was well aware of the ill will that existed between the Army and SS, and as usual sought to play one side off against the other, agreeing with Himmler's request that in future SS units should be used cohesively, but also acquiescing in the Army's demand that it should retain overall command of SS units in the field. The Führer also agreed to the establishment of three new SS divisions, a decision that infuriated the Army, which believed its recruits would be diverted into the SS. Himmler, however, circumvented the normal recruitment channels by a number of ways, including recruiting ethnic Germans from the occupied territories. As these men were not eligible for conscription into the Wehrmacht, the Army could not interfere. Thus, for the forthcoming campaign in the West the SS would be a much better organised and larger fighting force.

The expanded SS-Verfügungstruppe, which from March 1940 became officially known as the Waffen-SS, consisted of the reinforced *Leibstandarte*, now at regimental strength, the newly formed *SS-*

Verfügungsdivision, the *Totenkopf* Division and the *SS-Polizei* Division. The *SS-Verfügungsdivision* had been formed at the close of the Polish campaign by amalgamating the three SS-Verfügungstruppe Standarten: *Deutschland*, *Germania* and *Der Führer*, along with support units such as the artillery, signals and the pioneers. The *Totenkopf* Division was formed in October 1939 from members of the SS-Totenkopfverbände who had been based at the original concentration camps at Dachau, Sachsenhausen, Buchenwald and Mauthausen. Its commander, SS-Gruppenführer Theodor Eicke, was a brutal thug who despised the Army and was even contemptuous of other SS units. Despite his many failings, Eicke was an accomplished organiser who was idolised by his men. He soon whipped them into shape, giving them a degree of military skill which made a favourable impression upon General von Weichs when he inspected the division on the eve of the campaign in the West. The *Polizei* Division was recruited from members of the Ordnungspolizei. Compared to the other Waffen-SS units it was second-rate, not being fully motorised and equipped with old and captured hardware.

Despite being substantially reorganised and enlarged, however, the Waffen-SS was still only a tiny proportion of the German forces massed for the attack in the West, having only three divisions and the regimental-sized *Leibstandarte*, compared to the Army's 136 divisions.

For the campaign in the West, the *Leibstandarte* and the *SS-Verfügungsdivision*'s *Der Führer* Regiment, attached to the 28th Army, were tasked with the seizure of road and rail bridges on the Dutch border. The *Totenkopf*, much to Eicke's disgust, was initially held in reserve, and the *Polizei* Division was also in reserve behind the upper Rhine front of Army Group C. The remainder of the *SS-Verfügungsdivision* formed part of the second wave of the 28th Army's forces for the attack on Holland.

Both the *Leibstandarte* and *SS-Verfügungsdivision* had gained battle experience in Poland, and were thus grudgingly accepted by the Army as suitable for frontline tasks. However, both the *Totenkopf* and the *Polizei* Divisions were untried in battle and their background, as former concentration camp guards and policemen, did little to promote any confidence in them among the Army's hierarchy.

The plans for 'Fall Gelb'

The German plan employed three army groups: A, B and C. Part of Army Group B was tasked with occupying Holland, giving the Germans a base from which to launch their attack southwards into France and Belgium, and thus luring the bulk of Allied forces northwards, where they could be engaged on the Germans' terms. The *Leibstandarte* and *SS-Verfügungsdivision* were part of this force. The remainder of Army Group B, plus Army Group A, was to push through southern Belgium and Luxembourg into northern France. The *Totenkopf* formed part of the reserves available to Army Group A. The *Polizei* Division was assigned to Army Group C, which was positioned opposite France's Maginot Line and took no active role in the first 45 days of the campaign. Once Holland and Belgium had been overrun, Army Groups A and B would unite and push on into central France.

The *Leibstandarte* was the first SS unit into battle. On 9 May 1940, at 0530 hours, it crossed the Dutch border and, moving with great speed, advanced 100km (70 miles) by midday, capturing Zarolle and the nearby bridges over the Yssel. Two of the bridges had been blown by the Dutch Army, but the *Leibstandarte* forced a crossing and captured Hoven to the south. SS-Obersturmführer Hugo Krass became

the first SS officer to win the Iron Cross First Class in the Western campaign during these actions. The *Leibstandarte* then moved south to join the 9th Panzer Division and the *SS-Verfügungsdivision* on the drive towards Rotterdam.

On 10 May 1940, the *Der Führer* Regiment crossed the Yssel near Arnhem, and on the following morning the 9th Panzer Division and the bulk of the *SS-Verfügungsdivision* crossed the Maas, meeting only light opposition. The French immediately sent troops north to counter this threat, their plan being to send forces to Breda and then clear the Germans from the Moerdyk bridges. However, the French were intercepted by the 9th Panzer Division and the *SS-Verfügungsdivision*. One French column ran straight into the German panzers and their motorised SS infantry support, while a second was caught by Ju 87 Stuka dive-bombers. The French fell back to Breda in disarray.

On 12 May, the Luftwaffe was ordered to bomb Rotterdam in an effort to hasten the capitulation of Holland and therefore release German troops for the attack on France. Because of a breakdown in communications, the aircraft bombed the city unaware that a surrender had already been negotiated. Immediately following the raid, the *Leibstandarte* moved into Rotterdam, again in support of the 9th Panzer Division. A number of Dutch soldiers were standing idly around awaiting the result of surrender talks being conducted between their officers and Generals Student and von Cholitz. As the *Leibstandarte* soldiers roared past they spotted the Dutch soldiers and, unaware of the talks, opened fire. A stray bullet hit

ABOVE: A Pak 35/36 of the **SS-Verfügungsdivision** *engages Dutch targets in May 1940. Though SS units as a whole approached the campaign in the West with their usual enthusiasm, they were in for a few nasty surprises, not least the fact that their Pak 35/36s could not knock out the heavily armoured British and French tanks.*

BELOW RIGHT: The ruins of Rotterdam after it had been bombed by the Luftwaffe. Following the raid, the Leibstandarte was one of the first German units to enter the city. The Dutch, stunned by this display of air power and their country overrun by enemy forces, surrendered on 15 May.

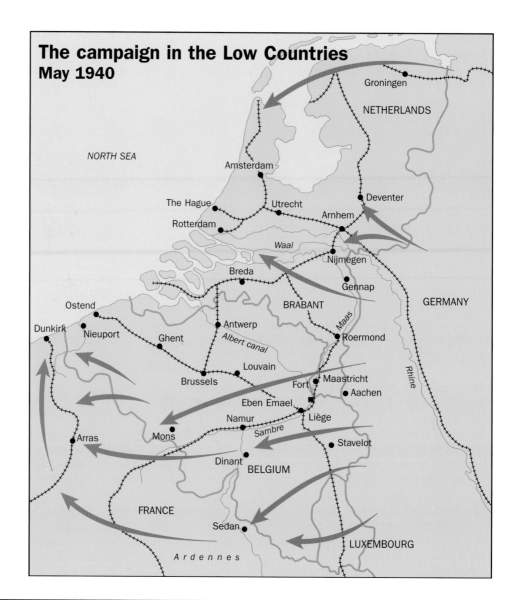

The campaign in the Low Countries
May 1940

Student in the head, seriously wounding him. The fast-moving *Leibstandarte* pushed its way through the city and headed for Delft, sweeping aside opposition and taking nearly 4000 prisoners. The next day it reached The Hague, just in time for the Dutch surrender. Meanwhile, SS-Gruppenführer Paul Hausser led the *SS-Verfügungsdivision* and some Army units against the French remnants in Zeeland, quickly forcing his way through to the coast as the French desperately evacuated their troops by sea.

Allied counterattack at Cambrai

With Holland defeated and the Belgian defences overrun, the French and British were drawn northwards in an attempt to stem the attack by Army Group B. Meanwhile, Army Group A drove west into France and, on 16 May, the *Totenkopf* Division was released from the reserves and sent into battle in support of General Hoth's XV Panzer Corps. Eicke's men struggled to reach the front over roads congested with military traffic and refugees. Eventually reaching the front, the SS men fought a number of battles against French armour and colonial troops from Morocco trying to hold back the German advance. As the Germans attempted to consolidate their hold on the area around Cambrai, the flanks of the *Totenkopf* and the 7th Panzer Division were hammered by Allied armour on 21 May, with over 130 French and British tanks taking part. The SS troops received a shock when they discovered their small 37mm anti-tank guns had little effect against the heavily armoured Allied tanks, and Eicke's men were forced to use their heavy artillery, firing over open sights. In this way the Allies were held at bay until the arrival of Ju 87s turned the tide, though not before a number of *Totenkopf* soldiers had fled in panic.

On 22 May, French forces trapped in the east attempted to break out of the German trap. The *Leibstandarte* at this point was moving south from Holland and was rapidly rushed into position to fend off a number of French attacks. Within two days the Allied forces in Flanders had been confined into a roughly triangular area, the southern part of which was a series of canals, which were used as defence lines. By now the *Totenkopf*, *Leibstandarte* and *SS-Verfügungsdivision* were all poised along this southern line, ready to cross at a moment's notice.

Patrols from the *SS-Verfügungsdivision* established that some French units had

already pulled out of the line before the British troops detailed to relieve them had arrived. Taking advantage of this, the SS soldiers established a bridgehead over the canal and some of their comrades were already across when Hitler's famous 'halt order' was given on the afternoon of 24 May. The *Leibstandarte*, which had not yet crossed the line, had come under heavy artillery fire from the enemy and so its commander, 'Sepp' Dietrich, decided to solve the problem by ignoring Hitler's orders and led his men over the canal. In total, the SS managed to breach the Allied defences in four places. For the next two days the SS units suffered a number of attacks from British formations intent on holding the line, while the bulk of Allied troops withdrew towards Dunkirk. Some of these attacks were fierce and succeeded in driving the SS back and recapturing lost ground, albeit temporarily.

On the night of 26 May, the Führer's halt order was rescinded. The *Germania* and *Der Führer* Regiments of the *SS-*

ABOVE: Luftwaffe general Kurt Student. Instrumental in founding Germany's parachute forces, he was negotiating the surrender of Dutch troops in Rotterdam in May 1940 when elements of the **Leibstandarte,** *unaware of what was going on, opened fire on idling Dutch soldiers. Student himself was wounded by an SS bullet, though he recovered and went on to mastermind the airborne assault on Crete in May 1941.*

ABOVE: Soldiers of the newly formed **Totenkopf** *Division about to cross a river in France, during the drive to the English Channel. The division quickly established its fighting reputation in this campaign, which Field Marshal von Manstein later stated to be 'great dash in the assault and steadfast in defence'.*

Verfügungsdivision attacked through the deep woodlands of the de-Nieppe forest and encountered heavy resistance, suffering a considerable number of casualties, especially among their officers. The remaining infantry regiment, *Deutschland*, was temporarily attached to the 3rd Panzer Division and took part in the attack on British units on the Lys Canal near Merville. The SS infantry forced a bridgehead over the canal, but then found themselves being counterattacked by a detachment of British tanks. Having no heavy weapons, the SS men had to defend themselves with small arms. Only the timely arrival of troops from the *Totenkopf*'s anti-tank company saved the day However, the British tanks, safely beyond the range of the *Totenkopf* gunners, continued to shell the Germans, delaying the crossing of the canal and allowing the bulk of the British forces to withdraw.

Meanwhile, the bulk of the *Totenkopf* Division had crossed the Lys at Bethune. Once again fierce British opposition meant the Germans were only able to advance at the cost of heavy casualties. At Le Paradis some 100 men of the Royal Norfolk Regiment successfully held off a number of *Totenkopf* assaults by 4 Kompanie of Infanterie Regiment 2, inflicting severe casualties before they were forced to surrender. The SS had lost 17 killed and 52 wounded, and, more importantly, their arrogant pride had been badly dented. As a result, the British prisoners were machine gunned on the orders of SS-Obersturmführer Fritz Knöchlein, the company commander, who was hanged by the British after the war for the atrocity.

This incident caused considerable disquiet within Waffen-SS units, and it is said that some of Knöchlein's fellow officers, enraged at his behaviour, challenged him to a duel, while others threatened to resign from the SS in protest. Some of the reservists who were discharged after the French campaign are said to have requested that should they be recalled for future Waffen-SS service, that they be posted to another unit, not the *Totenkopf*. Himmler, however, succeeded in covering up for Knöchlein, who was never punished. He eventually reached the rank of SS-Obersturmbannführer and went on to be decorated with the Knights Cross of the Iron Cross for gallantry.

On 28 May, while the *Leibstandarte* was advancing towards Dunkirk, its commander, 'Sepp' Dietrich, came under fire when his staff car unwittingly drove to within 50m (52yd) of the British positions near Wormhoudt. Dietrich and his driver flung themselves from their vehicle as it burst into flames, and took shelter in a roadside ditch. As burning petrol from the vehicle threatened to engulf them, they were forced to cover themselves in wet mud to shield themselves from the intense heat. They remained there for five hours.

The atrocity at Wormhoudt

Meanwhile, the *Leibstandarte*, infuriated by the apparent loss of its commander, attacked the British defenders in a fury. Some 80 prisoners taken by a company from the 2nd Battalion were herded into a barn and hand grenades thrown in. As they tried to escape, they were mercilessly cut down. Some 65 were killed, but 15 survived to point the finger of blame at SS-Hauptsturmführer Wilhelm Mohnke.

Shortly afterwards, the *Leibstandarte* was pulled back for rest and refit in preparation for the next phase of the campaign: the drive south to smash the remnants of the French Army. On 5 June, a total of 140 German divisions struck southwards, outnumbering French forces two to one. The *Leibstandarte* and *SS-Verfügungsdivision* formed part of Panzergruppe *Kleist* in the advance on Paris. To Eicke's chagrin, the *Totenkopf* Division was once again held in reserve. By the following day, the *SS-Verfügungsdivision* had already crossed the Somme. At first opposition was light, but on 7 June the division's spearhead units became pinned down by French artillery around the River Aire. The division eventually forced bridgeheads over the river, but French resistance con-

ABOVE: An MG34 machine gun team of the Polizei Division in France, late May 1940. The division had a hard time of it during the Western campaign, overcoming French units only after heavy hand-to-hand fighting.

LEFT: Totenkopf soldiers go onto the attack against Allied units near Dunkirk. Though the division performed well in France, it had a nasty surprise at Cambrai, when a French and British armoured counterattack resulted in some of Eicke's men fleeing for their lives, especially when their 37mm anti-tank shells bounced off the hulls of the Allied tanks.

tinued to stiffen and Kleist's command lost around 30 per cent of its armour.

The shaken panzer group was withdrawn from this sector and moved farther east, where German forces had already smashed through the French defences as far as the Aisne. By 9 June, the *SS-Verfügungsdivision* had been pulled back over the Somme. The *Leibstandarte*, however, was given no respite and drove southwards in pursuit of the retreating French, crossing the Marne on 12 June.

The *Totenkopf* was now released from the reserve and eagerly joined the advance.

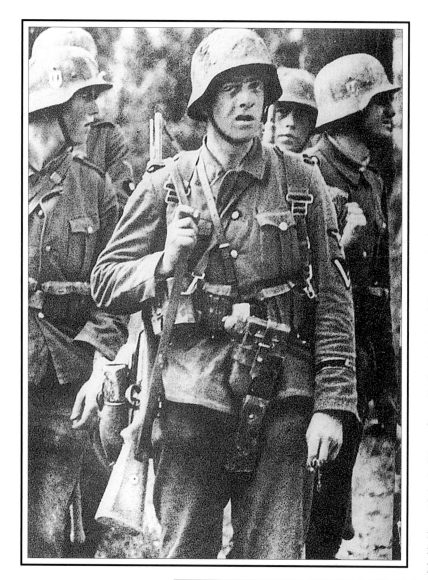

Panzergruppe *Kleist*, now including the *Leibstandarte*, *Totenkopf* and *SS-Verfügungsdivision*, headed towards Dijon, intent on preventing the French forces in Alsace from retreating southwest. Huge numbers of French prisoners started to fall into SS hands. On 16-17 June, French units attempting to escape encirclement tried to break through the *SS-Verfügungsdivision*'s lines. Their efforts were futile, however, and over 30,000 French prisoners were taken by Hausser's men.

The *Leibstandarte* also enjoyed considerable success at this time, capturing the airfield at Clermont-Ferrand, along with 200 aircraft, 4000 prisoners and masses of military materiel. The *Totenkopf* also took a large number of prisoners – 6000 at Tarare alone. The slower *Polizei* Division had less success: near Voncq it saw bitter fighting against determined French opposition, and in the Argonne forest it only overcame the French rearguard elements after bitter hand-to-hand combat.

By the time the cease-fire came into effect on 22 June, the *Totenkopf* and *SS-Verfügungsdivision* were in Bordeaux preparing for occupation duties, the *Polizei* Division was in reserve, and the *Leibstandarte* was preparing for its part in the planned grand victory parade in Paris.

Once again the performance of the SS in battle engendered mixed opinions. For its part, the SS itself was satisfied with its performance in the face of a determined

TWO VIEWS OF THE LEIBSTANDARTE *IN* FRANCE, MAY-JUNE *1940.*

ABOVE: A weary NCO leads his platoon south after the evacuation of French and British troops from Dunkirk. Note his holster for the wooden stock of the Mauser C96 handgun.

RIGHT: At the end of a long day's march, the men settle down to a bout of weapons maintenance. As the premier Waffen-SS unit, the Leibstandarte *had some of the most highly trained and motivated men in the German armed forces.*

ABOVE: To the victor the spoils. 'Sepp' Dietrich, who himself had been awarded the Knights Cross of the Iron Cross for his leadership of the Leibstandarte in the West, bestows honours on his men. The fall of France had seen the SS go up in the Army's estimation, and Himmler was delighted at the performance of his men.

LEFT: Preparing for a campaign that never materialised. Soldiers of the SS-Verfügungs-division haul a 105mm howitzer aboard a landing craft for Operation 'Sea Lion', the codename for the invasion of Britain.

RIGHT: Following the conquest of western Europe, the call went out for suitably racially qualified young men to join the ranks of the Waffen-SS. The call was successful: eventually over 125,000 west Europeans joined up, the vast majority of them volunteers. This recruiting poster urges Norwegians to enlist.

'It is not surprising that units of the Waffen-SS and the branches that had thus been employed in extermination actions and in the execution of civilians are also to be found violating the laws of warfare when carrying on ordinary combat operations.'
– Nuremberg Trials, prosecution statement

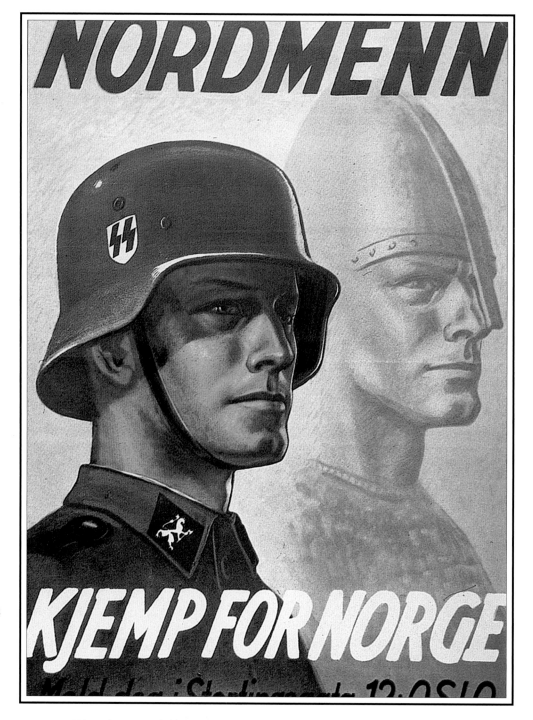

enemy. Himmler was delighted at the achievements of his troops, and no less so was the Führer himself. In fact, Hitler approved the award of the Knights Cross of the Iron Cross, Germany's highest possible award for gallantry and distinguished service at that time, to six soldiers of the Waffen-SS. 'Sepp' Dietrich received the award for his successful command of the *Leibstandarte* during the campaign on 5 July 1940, and SS-Oberführer Georg Keppler was also so decorated on 15 August 1940 for his command of the SS-Regiment *Der Führer*. On the same date, SS-Oberführer Felix Steiner received his Knights Cross for his leadership of the SS-

Regiment *Deutschland*. On 4 September 1940, SS-Sturmbannführer Fritz Witt joined the ranks of the Ritterkreuzträger in recognition of his command of I Battalion of the SS-Regiment *Deutschland* during the Western campaign. Not only senior commanders received awards: on 4 September, SS-Obersturmführer Fritz Vogt received the Knights Cross for his leadership of the 2nd Company of the SS-Aufklärungsabteilung, and on the same day SS-Hauptscharführer Ludwig Kepplinger, a platoon commander in the 11th Company of the SS-Regiment *Der Führer*, was also awarded the Knights Cross. In all these cases the soldiers involved went on to have extremely distinguished military careers, and many were further rewarded for subsequent acts of bravery and distinguished leadership of their men.

The Army, though it was now beginning to grudgingly admit that some Waffen-SS troops fought very well, still had considerable misgivings. SS soldiers were, after all, considered to be political soldiers, and the lack of self-control which led to such atrocities as Le Paradis and Wormhoudt did nothing to improve the reputation of the SS with its Army counterparts. In addition, whereas the *Leibstandarte* and the *SS-Verfügungsdivision* were led by officers who had combat experience as a result of the Polish campaign, and who could temper their natural aggressive and reckless daring with a little caution, the *Totenkopf* and *Polizei* Divisions had no such experience and suffered high casualties as a result.

Despite the Army's overt and covert moves to block the expansion of the Waffen-SS, however, Himmler's troops had managed to ensure that at least the *Leibstandarte* and *SS-Verfügungsdivision* were well equipped. Eicke, too, by begging, stealing and borrowing, managed to equip his *Totenkopf* Division to a reasonable standard. Only the *Polizei* Division could be regarded as being second-rate.

Now that Hitler had been satisfied that his Waffen-SS troops could perform well on the battlefield there was no turning back. He would ensure that the SS would receive equipment as good as, sometimes better than, its Army counterparts. Hitler's

campaigns in the East would eventually see the formation of 38 Waffen-SS divisions, still small in relation to the Army, but whose influence on the course of the war cannot be overestimated.

But already the SS soldiers were displaying their dark side. Whereas the incident at Wormhoudt was the responsibility of just one company, the same cannot be said of Eicke's division. Schooled in the brutality of the concentration camps, the atrocity at Le Paradis was by no means unique, and the numerous cases of *Totenkopf* soldiers shooting 'racially inferior' French colonial prisoners was a portent of things to come.

For the fledgling Waffen-SS as a whole, however, it was a time to celebrate its victories, both over the enemy and over its detractors in the German military. For Himmler's troops, a period of expansion and conquest was about to begin, which would see the military formations of the SS in action in the Balkans and fighting at the gates of Moscow and Leningrad.

Though the Waffen-SS tried to recruit west Europeans as part of a crusade against Bolshevism, and posters stressed this in Holland (above) and Denmark (above left), research has shown that this was not the reason non-Germans from western Europe donned Waffen-SS uniform. Rather, they were motivated by such factors as boredom, better food, a desire to avoid the dreaded compulsory labour service, a lust for adventure and the glamour of wearing an SS uniform.

THE SS TURNS EAST

The spring and summer of 1941 witnessed a string of victories for the SS, as its units stormed through the Balkans and then into the Soviet Union. These successes were misleading, however. The war in the East was to be long – and ultimately disastrous.

After the fall of France in 1940, SS-Obergruppenführer Gottlob Berger continued his policy of recruitment of suitable Germanic stock from the occupied territories, a source of manpower the Army had no jurisdiction over. Up until this point Berger had had to rely principally on *Reichsdeutsche* German recruitment, and he had blatantly exceeded the quotas of manpower allocated to him. The Army had become more and more disturbed by the claim of the Waffen-SS on its manpower resources, as both organisations had to be fed from the same pool of recruits. To exacerbate the situation further, Hermann Göring's Luftwaffe was also demanding a larger share of the manpower cake. As a result, Army recruitment authorities began to refuse to release men to Waffen-SS units.

Despite the many obstacles in his way, Berger was remarkably successful in his recruiting campaign. By the summer of 1940, for example, all Waffen-SS units were at full strength, including the replacement units. By the end of July, Reichsführer Himmler had even demobilised some of his reservists.

In August 1940, the *Leibstandarte* was enlarged from regimental to brigade status. Hitler, meanwhile, had reassured the Army that he had no intention of allowing

Das Reich *soldiers take part in the encirclement of Minsk, June 1941. For the SS, the invasion of Russia was the start of the longed-for crusade against Bolshevism.*

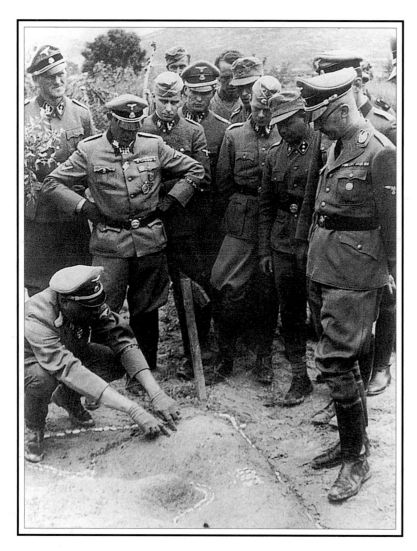

ABOVE: Himmler (right) and 'Sepp' Dietrich (hands on hips) with officers of the 1st Battalion, Leibstandarte Division, after the division had captured the Klidi Pass, Greece, in April 1941. Up until the attack on the pass, the Leibstandarte had suffered only five casualties in the Greek campaign. At Klidi that all changed. Faced by determined Australians and New Zealanders, it took two days of hand-to-hand fighting before the pass was captured. Nevertheless, its seizure meant the Germans had possession of the gateway to Greece.

the SS unrestricted expansion. He envisaged the SS to be a state police force after the successful conclusion of the war, its sacrifices and achievements on the field of battle were merely ways to gain moral authority for its post-war tasks. The Waffen-SS was to remain at a maximum of 10 per cent of the peacetime strength of the Army. This being 64 divisions, the Waffen-SS had a ceiling of six divisions. Hitler had therefore sanctioned the raising of a new Waffen-SS division which, as a sop to the Army's complaints over the demands made by the Waffen-SS on manpower, was to be staffed principally by Germanic volunteers.

In December 1940, the new division was formed around a nucleus provided by the transfer of the SS-Regiment *Germania* from the *SS-Verfügungsdivision*. To it was added the Germanic volunteer units *Nordland* and *Westland* and SS-Artillerie Regiment 5. The new division was to be entitled *Germania*, but due to the confusion caused by naming it after an existing regiment, it was quickly changed to *Wiking*. The reorganised *SS-Verfügungs-*

division was also renamed, becoming the *Das Reich* Division. In addition, around this time a number of personnel from the various Totenkopf regiments were formed into a new kampfgruppe – *Nord* – for service in the far north, though under Army command. Himmler also still retained a number of Waffen-SS units at his own personal disposal, including SS-Infantry Brigades 1 and 2, SS-Cavalry Regiments 1 and 2, and SS-Infantry Regiment 5.

At this time the *Leibstandarte, Das Reich, Totenkopf* and *Polizei* Divisions were training in France, supposedly for the intended invasion of Great Britain. However, Hitler soon lost his enthusiasm for this undertaking; his mind turned instead to the conquest of Russia. But first, there was to be a Balkan adventure.

The SS in the Balkans

In October 1940, much to Hitler's fury, the Italians invaded Greece. Mussolini was jealous of Hitler's military successes and sought to achieve some glory for himself by taking on the Greeks in what he thought would be an easy campaign. The Greeks were no pushovers, however, and the Italians soon found themselves floundering woefully. Hitler was disgusted at the Italians' blundering attempts to subdue the plucky Greeks. However, as he needed the Balkans secured to protect his flanks for the forthcoming attack on the Soviet Union, he was forced to provide military aid to the Italians.

On the diplomatic front, the Germans had negotiated a pact with the Yugoslavs which would leave the Greeks isolated in the Balkans. However, as Prime Minister Cvetkovic and Foreign Minister Cincar-Markovic returned from signing the pact in Vienna on 26 March 1941, they found themselves overthrown by a military coup. Incensed by this, Hitler ordered that the plans for the invasion of Greece be expanded to include Yugoslavia.

At the beginning of February 1941, the *Leibstandarte* had been moved from France and journeyed to Bulgaria, joining General List's 12th Army. Together with the 9th Panzer Division, the *Leibstandarte* was attached to General Stumme's XL Panzer Corps. The attack was launched on 6 April 1941, with the corps being split into two prongs. The northerly prong, containing the 9th Panzer Division and the *Leibstandarte*, was tasked with seizing the Kriva Pass and pushing on to take Skopije, some 100km (70 miles) inside Yugoslavia. After only one day, both objectives had been taken. The second prong, consisting of the 73rd Infantry Division, took the town of Prilep and then sent out patrols to link up with the Italians to the west. These rapid advances threatened Greek forces in Albania, but the Greeks, refusing to give ground to the Italians, were reluctant to withdraw any part of their 1st Army to meet the German threat.

The next German objective was to force the Monastir Gap and thrust deep into Greece itself. On 11 April, the *Leibstandarte* pressed on through the town of Vevi and began probing the defences of the Klidi Pass. At dawn on 12 April, an artillery barrage pinned down the defending Australian and New Zealand troops while German pioneers cleared a path through the minefields. As the tanks of the 9th Panzer Division rolled forward, the infantrymen of the *Leibstandarte* took on the defenders in bitter hand-to-hand fighting. The Germans lost some 37 men killed and nearly 100 wounded or missing, but they took one of the key defensive positions in northern Greece.

The capture of the Klissura Pass

The rapid German advance now continued towards the Klissura Pass, which was strongly held by Greek infantry. The narrow mountain roads and tracks proved difficult for the Germans, who were held up by numerous roadblocks and attacks by Greek troops. Assault groups tried to infiltrate the Greek positions by coming through the hills behind them, but the SS soldiers became dispersed as darkness fell. The attack was delayed until the following morning when, supported by fire from a battery of the Germans' dreaded 88mm guns, the SS infantrymen rushed the defenders. At one point SS-Sturmbann-führer Kurt Meyer and the men of his Aufklärungsabteilung became pinned down by intense Greek small-arms fire. Even the tough SS troopers were somewhat subdued by the intensity of the enemy fire, and the attack was in danger of becoming bogged down. Meyer, though, overcame the reluctance of his men to leave the cover of their positions by pulling the pin from a hand grenade and rolling it behind them. Thus motivated, the SS men clearly decided that the Greek fire was the lesser of the two evils and they rushed forward, capturing the enemy positions. By the afternoon the pass had been secured and a considerable number of prisoners taken.

On 15 April, the heights around Kastoria were taken after an assault by *Leibstandarte* troops in torrential rain, the town itself falling during the afternoon of the same day. The *Leibstandarte* then moved swiftly southwest and secured the Messover Pass, isolating the Greek armies west of the Pindus mountains.

The *Leibstandarte* victorious

The Greeks now realised that their situation was hopeless and sued for peace. Dietrich himself accepted the surrender of 16 Greek divisions from General Tsolakoglou, treating the beaten Greeks with the honours due to a gallant foe. The Italians, however, were infuriated that the Greeks had surrendered to the Germans and not to them, and Mussolini made his displeasure known to Hitler, who in turn berated Dietrich for his actions. The Führer, however, was secretly delighted at the elan shown by the brigade bearing his name.

With the Greeks beaten, only the British and Commonwealth troops remained to be dealt with, and the *Leibstandarte* set off in pursuit of them as they rapidly withdrew. The division excelled itself, crossing over 350km (180 miles) of almost impassable terrain in a vain attempt to cut off the British before they could evacuate at Corinth. However, they arrived too late.

To continue the chase, Meyer requisitioned local fishing boats to ferry his troops across the Gulf of Patras to Nafpaktos. By 27 April, the *Leibstandarte* was advancing down the west coast of the Peloponese to reach Pirgus, where it captured elements of the Royal Tank Regiment. Meanwhile, troops from the

BELOW: Soldiers of the Das Reich Division photographed during the campaign in Yugoslavia. The man on the left is a motorcycle despatch rider, while the two on the right are SS-Untersturmführers. Though the division fought in Yugoslavia with the Waffen-SS's usual elan, there were bad feelings between many Army and Waffen-SS personnel. In one incident, for example, a Das Reich column of vehicles attempting to negotiate muddy Yugoslav roads was overtaken by an Army column. However, the commanding SS officer stopped the Army column from passing by threatening to order his men to open fire if it did so. These incidents between Army and SS personnel were to result in a formal complaint from the Army's Commander-in-Chief, Field Marshal von Brauchitsch, to Himmler.

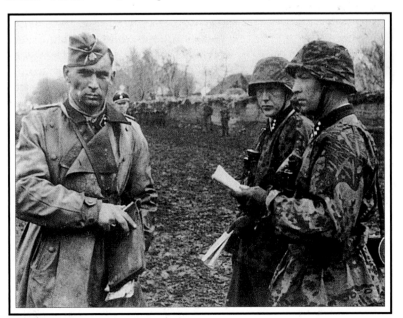

RIGHT: *The man who captured Belgrade single-handedly. On 13 April 1941, SS-Hauptsturmführer Fritz Klingenberg, a company commander in the* **Das Reich** *Division's reconnaissance battalion, captured the city with 10 men. For his daring exploit, Hitler awarded him the Knights Cross. Four days later the Yugoslavs capitulated to the Germans. This picture shows Klingenberg a few months later in Russia. He is wearing his Knights Cross for the capture of Belgrade, a feat that particularly annoyed the Army because the SS beat its elite* **Grossdeutschland Regiment** *to the Yugoslav capital. Klingenberg later went on to command the 17th SS Panzergrenadier Division* **Götz von Berlichingen,** *before being killed in action in April 1945.*

Aufklärungsabteilung under SS-Hauptsturmführer Hugo Krass advanced along the coast, eventually making contact with German paratroopers who had been dropped at the Corinth Canal. This link-up brought to an end the *Leibstandarte's* part in the campaign. The brigade then took part in a major victory parade in Athens before being transported to barracks in Czechoslovakia to prepare for the attack on the Soviet Union.

The Greek campaign was a triumph for the *Leibstandarte*, whose troops had acted with great skill, elan and daring and no small measure of personal gallantry. It was also notable for the chivalrous way in which it had treated its foes. British survivors of the campaign have testified to their good treatment by their Waffen-SS captors. SS-Hauptsturmführer Gerd Pleiss, commander of 1 Kompanie of the *Leibstandarte*, and SS-Sturmbannführer Kurt Meyer of the Aufklärungsabteilung were both decorated with the Knights Cross for their gallantry during the seizure of the Klidi and Klissura Passes.

While the *Leibstandarte* was enhancing its reputation during the Greek campaign, the *Das Reich* Division had entered Yugoslavia along with XLI Panzer Corps, commanded by General George-Hans Reinhardt. *Das Reich* was among the forces tasked with striking directly towards Belgrade, the Germans having assumed that Yugoslav resistance would quickly crumble once the capital had been taken. The division's line of advance, however, was over very marshy terrain, and it had great difficulty in making any progress.

The motorcycle reconnaissance unit, however, under SS-Hauptsturmführer Fritz Klingenberg, found that its light vehicles could make good headway by travelling along railway tracks and embankments, and it took off at speed towards Belgrade while the remainder of the division laboured in the mud.

The delays resulted in *Das Reich* being ordered to halt at the banks of the Danube, its objectives having been cancelled. Klingenberg and his men reached the river just outside Belgrade, well ahead of any other German units. He decided to take a small volunteer group of 10 men and, commandeering a small boat, crossed over to the opposite bank and entered the city. His group fortuitously met up with some staff members of the German Embassy, who asked that he take the building and its staff under his protection. Klingenberg, however, had become aware of how lightly defended the city was at that moment, and so he decided to try a monstrous bluff. Using the Embassy telephone, he summoned the mayor of the city and warned him that he was merely the advance group of a huge German assault force, and that if the city was not surrendered to him immediately he would use his radio to order a massive air raid. The frightened mayor agreed, not knowing that Klingenberg had no communication with the main German forces and that the men around him was his entire force.

Preparations for 'Barbarossa'

By the time Army units from the 11th Panzer Division arrived, they found, much to their chagrin and the delight of the Waffen-SS, that a mere handful of SS troopers had already secured the surrender of the city. For his audacity, Klingenberg was awarded the Knights Cross. A few days later the Yugoslav Army surrendered and the Balkan campaign was over.

Over the next few weeks all the Waffen-SS divisions were concentrated in the east, ready for their part in the opening moves of Operation 'Barbarossa'. On the eve of the attack, German forces were divided into three main army groups: Army Group North under Field Marshal von Leeb, which included the *Totenkopf* and *Polizei* Divisions; Army Group Centre under Field Marshal von Bock, which included the *Das Reich* Division; and Army Group South under Field Marshal von Rundstedt, which included the *Leibstandarte* and *Wiking* Divisions. In addition, Kampfgruppe *Nord* was assigned

SS-Division Reich
The Race to Belgrade April 1941

In the months immediately following the outbreak of World War II, the Balkan region of Europe remained at peace. The countries in the area had been intimidated by the German occupation of Czechoslovakia, and by the signing of the German-Soviet pact in 1939. However, when Greece repelled an Italian invasion in 1940, the situation began to change. On 27 March 1941 a coup d'état overthrew the Yugoslav government, bringing into power a regime less sympathetic to the Germans. Adolf Hitler, alarmed by the appearance of a Greek-Yugoslav bloc, planned an immediate invasion. The assault included the men of SS-Division 'Reich', who moved up to the Yugoslav border from their positions around the town of Denta in Romania. As part of the XLI Corps, the division was given the objective of capturing Belgrade, the Yugoslav capital.

Key

→ Advance of SS-Division *Reich*

→ Advance of *Grossdeutschland* Regiment

Operation Marita

GERMANY • ROMANIA • BULGARIA • Zagreb • Belgrade • Sarajevo • YUGOSLAVIA • ITALY • Dubrovnik • ALBANIA

Key

→ German attacks

→ Italian attacks

Veliki Gaj · Jermenovici · Vrsac · Margita · Viasecki Canal · Seleus · Kamlovac · YUGOSLAVIA · ① · Alibunar · Tamis · Pancevo · Dunav · ② · Belgrade

First into Belgrade

12 April The leading elements of SS-Division Reich resume their advance and reach the River Tamis.
13 April Hauptsturmführer Fritz Klingenberg leads ten men across the Danube into Belgrade, and receives the city's surrender.

The Road to Alibunar

11 April 0905 SS-Division Reich advances into Yugoslavia from Romania, part of the general German-Italian-Hungarian invasion.
2130 Despite adverse weather conditions, the division's motorcycle battalion reaches Alibunar first, ahead of the German Army's Grossdeustschland Regiment.

---

to the Finnish front under the command of General von Falkenhorst.

The *Totenkopf* Division was not used in the initial strike by General Erich Hoepner's 4th Panzer Group on 22 June 1941. The group advanced in a two-pronged movement. The left prong consisted of General Max Reinhardt's XXXI Panzer Corps: the 1st and 6th Infantry Divisions and the 36th (motorised) Infantry Division. The right prong consisted of the 8th Panzer Division, 3rd (motorised) Division and 290th Infantry Division, all in General von Manstein's LVI Panzer Corps. The *Totenkopf* and the 269th Infantry Division were initially held in reserve, the intent being to allocate

them to whichever panzer corps achieved the most rapid rate of advance.

In the event, the *Totenkopf* was committed on the night of 24 June, with instructions to cover von Manstein's right flank. Manstein's panzer group had advanced at an incredible pace, having reached Wilkomiercz, some 160km (100 miles) from its start point, within two days of the beginning of the attack. The *Totenkopf* reached Dvinsk on 30 June, having spent six days mopping up the battered remnants of the Soviet units caught in the initial assault. Its line of advance took it through Latvia, where, on 2 July, it ran into the Red Army's 42nd Rifle Division. The *Totenkopf*'s lead battalion,

BELOW: The driver's view from a PzKpfw III during the first few days of Operation 'Barbarossa', the German invasion of the Soviet Union. The first line of Soviet resistance has been brushed aside and the panzers are free to roam over the steppes. Overhead the Luftwaffe has complete mastery of the skies, and the Red Army is reeling. The **Blitzkrieg** *would take the German Army, and the Waffen-SS, to the gates of Moscow itself.*

under the command of SS-Oberführer Max Simon, was halted with the loss of 10 men killed and 100 wounded. The enemy gave the *Totenkopf* no time to recover from the initial shock, the Germans being forced to give ground under Russian pressure. Only with the help of a concentrated attack by Luftwaffe Stuka dive-bombers was the town eventually taken. Further heavy fighting ensued before the *Totenkopf* captured the town of Opochka on 11 July. The division's advance slowed as Russian opposition intensified, and its losses were high: 82 officers and 1620 NCOs and men being killed or wounded, almost 10 per cent of its strength.

From mid-July to late August, the *Totenkopf* was engaged in fierce combat against Soviet troops in the heavily wooded and marshy terrain around Leningrad. In late September, the Red Army launched a series of counterattacks south of Lake Ilmen which the *Totenkopf* helped to repulse, but by the end of the month its

losses had reached a staggering total of over 6500. As the year drew to a close, the *Totenkopf* dug in between Lakes Ilmen and Seliger, anxiously awaiting the anticipated Soviet winter offensive.

In the central sector of the front, *Das Reich* was grouped with the Army's 10th Panzer Division and the elite *Grossdeutschland* Regiment in XLVI Panzer Corps under the command of General Freiherr von Vietinghoff. This corps formed the reserve of the 2nd Panzer Group under one of Germany's greatest military commanders: General Heinz Guderian. The panzer group had crossed the River Bug either side of the Brest-Litovsk fortifications, and within a week, in conjunction with General Hoth's 3rd

Panzer Group, had advanced some 400km (250 miles) into Belorussia along a 200km-wide (125 mile) front. On 27 June, in one of the great encirclements of the war, the city of Minsk and its 500,000 defenders was cut off by Guderian and Hoth.

XLVI Panzer Corps was brought into action on 26 June to protect the left flank of the 2nd Panzer Group, and took part in the successful encirclement of the Bialystock Pocket. By 2 July, *Das Reich* had reached the Beresino and the Aufklärungsabteilung succeeded in forming a bridgehead on the opposite bank. Guderian then ordered a general advance towards the Dnieper, with *Das Reich* again providing flanking cover. After the successful crossing, the 10th Panzer Division and *Das Reich*, with *Grossdeutschland* covering the flank, advanced on Gorki, which was eventually reached on 14 July, though only after heavy fighting and considerable losses. By the following day, *Das Reich*, again accompanied by the 10th Panzer Division, advanced past the south of Smolensk and reached the River Yelnya, which they then held for several days in the face of determined enemy attacks.

Das Reich in the Ukraine

In late July the 10th Panzer Division was withdrawn, its place being taken by the 268th Infantry Division. Hitler now made his ill-fated decision to divert the main thrust of the attack from Moscow to the south. Guderian's 2nd Panzer Group was ordered to head south towards Comel, though *Das Reich* remained in its positions in defence of the left flank of the Yelnya salient. Relentless Soviet counterattacks of up to 11 divisions in strength saw *Das Reich* stretched to near breaking point, and on 8 August it was pulled out of the line for a badly needed period of rest in the area to the northeast of Smolensk.

By the beginning of September the southern push was experiencing problems, and so *Das Reich* had to be thrown into action once again. Guderian personally visited the division and gave SS-Obergruppenführer Hausser the order to prepare to attack Sosnitza on 4 September. The Russian weather, however, was now starting to affect operations, and the heavy rains turned the roads into quagmires. Nevertheless, despite these problems *Das Reich* reached its objective and took Sosnitza after only one day's fighting.

During the following weeks *Das Reich* slogged over terrible terrain and against stubborn Soviet resistance, the enemy launching counterattacks with air and armour support as the Red Army desperately sought to prevent the German encirclement and capture of Kiev. On 26 September, however, the battle came to an end with the surrender of some 665,000 Soviet troops and huge numbers of tanks and other military equipment.

Operation 'Typhoon'

Four days later, Operation 'Typhoon', the assault on Moscow, began. *Das Reich* formed part of Guderian's spearhead, together with three Army panzer divisions, a motorised division and *Grossdeutschland*. *Das Reich* successfully completed its task of cutting the main Smolensk-Moscow highway, and then captured the strategic town of Gshatsk after fierce fighting in the surrounding woods. When the infantry of the division's *Deutschland* Regiment entered the town they found the bodies of many civilians whom the NKVD had brutally executed before fleeing.

The Russians did not give up easily, however, and fighting in the area around Gshatsk continued for several days as the Red Army tried to build up forces in preparation for an attempt to retake the town. But the Russian efforts were broken up by determined attacks by the division's *Der Führer* Regiment.

Das Reich continued its advance against Moscow against ever-increasing opposition. By mid-October, the weather had deteriorated drastically and the division was battling through snow storms. As it advanced further, its soldiers were nearing total exhaustion, while Russian resistance was increasing in intensity. Near the main Moscow highway, some 100km (60 miles) west of the city, lay the battlefield of Borodino, where Napoleon had come to grief some 129 years earlier. Stalin had decreed that the German invaders should meet the same fate, and so some of his most combat-hardened troops were sent into battle to hold back the Germans: the 32nd Siberian Rifle Division from near Vladivostock, supported by a number of infantry brigades and two brigades of armour equipped with the new T-34 tank.

The Russians fell upon the SS troopers with a fury, and in the savage fighting that ensued no quarter was asked or given. The German anti-tank gunners found their weapons were almost useless against the T-34's armour, and they had to resort to using satchel charges of explosive, which had to be physically placed on the tank or its tracks. On 15 October 1941, Borodino

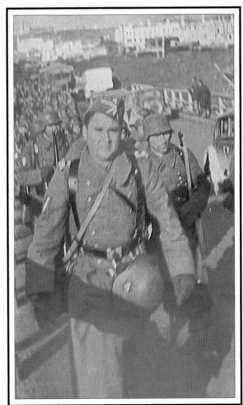

ABOVE: A **Totenkopf** *sniper takes aim with his Kar 98 bolt-action rifle during the opening phase of 'Barbarossa'. The 18,754-strong division was attached to Army Group North for the attack on the Soviet Union in June 1941, and it saw heavy fighting. By the middle of July it had lost 1702 officers and men killed or wounded.*

LEFT: The drive east. Himmler left his Waffen-SS commanders in no doubts as to their prime task in Russia, stating: 'We have only one task, to stand and to pitilessly lead this race-battle.'

ABOVE: *German troops clear a Russian town in July 1941. The Germans achieved incredible feats of arms during the first weeks of the Russian campaign. For example, the envelopment of Minsk at the end of July resulted in the capture of 280,000 prisoners. The Germans seemed unstoppable, and in the ideological vanguard was the Waffen-SS, imbued with an almost religious zeal for its campaign against the* untermensch.

RIGHT: *The strain begins to show. German motorcyclists take a rest during the advance on Moscow.*

eventually fell to the *Der Führer* Regiment. *Das Reich* was then tasked with capturing the vital road junction at Mozhaisk, which was achieved on 18 October, though only after bitter fighting.

As the division's advance continued, the *Deutschland* Regiment ran into two battalions of Mongolian infantry near the village of Otyakova. Well equipped and not in the least discouraged by the freezing temperatures, the Mongolians attacked the Waffen-SS infantrymen in an almost incredible bravery. Ignoring their dreadful losses as they were cut down by German machine guns, they attacked time and time again, only to be finally beaten off. The SS troopers held, but at a cost; indeed, by this stage of the campaign *Das Reich* had nearly 7000 of its soldiers posted as killed, wounded or missing in action (it had a strength of 19,000 men at the start of Operation 'Barbarossa').

The Germans falter before Moscow

The cold weather did have one advantage: the mud had frozen over, making movement by foot somewhat easier. That being said, the division's advance was almost at an end, halting just 20km (11 miles) west of the outskirts of Moscow. The German advance as a whole had far outstretched its supply lines, and ammunition began to run out. German soldiers lodged on the edges of the Soviet capital were now little more than a shadow of their former selves. Still dressed in their summer campaign clothing, many were literally freezing to death. They were exhausted, filthy and starving, but their esprit de corps was still intact. Many believed that the fall of Moscow was imminent. However, Marshal Zhukov had gathered 18 fresh, full-strength divisions and was about to launch a massive counteroffensive against the Wehrmacht before the gates of Moscow.

Army Group South, under von Rundstedt, was responsible for the invasion forces on the southern sector of the front. The northern part of its forces consisted of the 6th and 17th Armies, together with Kleist's 1st Panzer Group, and was tasked with advancing east along the southern edge of the Pripet Marshes and into the vast plains of the Ukraine, with the city of Smolensk being the main objective. In the south the 11th Army was to operate in conjunction with two Romanian armies.

The *Leibstandarte* was allocated to XIV Corps of the 1st Panzer Group in the area around Lublin, Poland, and was not committed to battle until 27 June when, along with *Wiking*, it formed the panzer group's reserve. On 1 July 1941, the *Leibstandarte* crossed the Vistula and was soon at the former Soviet frontier. Shortly thereafter it was in action against Soviet armoured units attempting to sever the main highway at Dubno and Olyka. These battles lasted for several days and saw the *Leibstandarte* capturing Moszkov, before receiving orders to hold the Rovno-Luck line to fend off Soviet attacks.

Kleist's panzers were advancing with such rapidity that the supporting infantry could barely keep pace, and in some extreme cases were left up to 80km (50 miles) behind the fast-moving tanks. This left the German flanks precariously exposed, a situation which the Soviets did their best to exploit. Such a situation developed with the 11th Panzer Division, when its rate of advance left the supporting infantry well behind. Here again, though, the advantages of fully motorised units such as the *Leibstandarte* were apparent, as it was rushed in to fill the gap between the fast-moving armour and the hard-pressed infantry, who often had to make long forced marches on foot.

The *Leibstandarte* takes Rostov

The *Leibstandarte* smashed through the Soviet defences at Miropol and continued its rapid advance towards Zhitomir. Just north of the highway at Romanovka, the spearhead units of the division ran straight into strong enemy forces in the dense surrounding woodlands. Despite being greatly outnumbered, they held the Soviets at bay until the bulk of the division arrived. Meyer's Aufklärungsabteilung then rushed on to capture the vital road junction at Kudnov on 8 July. At the same time, however, a desperate Soviet counteroffensive along the entire southwestern front was just beginning. Massed Russian attacks often led to vicious hand-to-hand fighting, some German units losing more casualties in just two days of fighting than they had lost in all their previous campaigns.

The momentum of the German attack was too great to be halted, however, and after huge losses the Soviet assaults abated. The *Leibstandarte* went on to the offensive again, capturing Shepovka in a night assault before turning northwest towards Zhitomir, which fell soon afterwards. At this point Hitler interfered with von Rundstedt's plans to capture Kiev, and directed the 6th Army southeast towards Uman. The intent was to cut off the Soviet forces engaged against the 11th

and 17th Armies. Once again the *Leibstandarte* was tasked with covering the flanks of the main assault force as it struck southeast, and it came under severe pressure as a number of divisions from the Soviet 5th Army tried to smash their way through the German flanks. The *Leibstandarte* was instrumental in helping to rescue the beleaguered 16th Panzer Division when the latter came under attack from a combined force of three Soviet armoured divisions. When von Rundstedt's forces finally took Uman in late July, some 100,000 Red Army soldiers from the Soviet 6th and 12th Armies had been taken prisoner.

Two views of the **Das Reich** *Division in Russia. A motorcycle team prepares to move on following the destruction of a Russian village (below), and a column of weary but cheerful foot sloggers pass through wooded terrain on their way east (bottom). The division was part of Field Marshal Fedor von Bock's Army Group Centre.*

The *Leibstandarte*'s advance continued, the division taking Bubry on 9 August and then seizing the road junction at Sasselje. The SS armoured reconnaissance and field artillery units then beat off a number of savage Soviet counterattacks. From

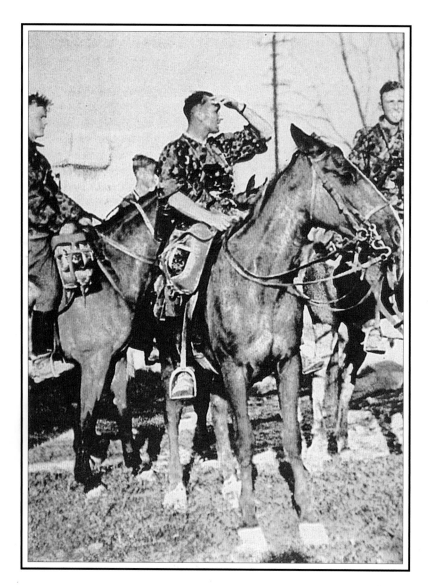

ABOVE: The invasion of Russia resulted in a rapid growth in the number of SS field divisions. One of these was the 8th SS Cavalry Division Florian Geyer, which saw service in Russia and was destroyed fighting in the defence of Budapest in February 1945.

on the city in dreadful weather conditions, with heavy snow fall and plummeting temperatures. Early in the assault, a daring attack across the main railway bridge over the Don led by SS-Hauptsturmführer Heinrich Springer succeeded in capturing the bridge intact. With a small force from 3 Kompanie and some pioneers, Springer held the bridge against determined Russian attacks to recapture it. With this vital crossing in their hands, the Germans seized the city on 20 November. For his actions Springer was decorated with the Knights Cross.

German supply lines, however, were now dangerously over-stretched and under enemy pressure. As many as 15 Soviet divisions were attempting to cut off the German spearheads. As ammunition began to run low, the *Leibstandarte* was forced to abandon Rostov and consolidate its positions on a shortened front, as an exceptionally severe winter began to curtail military operations.

In the same sector of the front as the *Leibstandarte*, SS-Brigadeführer Felix Steiner and his *Wiking* Division began their campaign on 29 June, advancing through Lemberg and on to Tarnopol and Zhitomir. As well as German cadre personnel, *Wiking* boasted volunteers from Denmark, Holland, Belgium, Norway and Finland. Reaching Byela Tserkovusin by the end of July, it then took part in the encirclement of Soviet forces at Uman on 3 August. Thereafter the division pushed eastwards towards the Dnieper, overcoming determined enemy resistance at Dniepropetrovsk at the end of the month. *Wiking* then advanced towards Stalino and Rostov, bypassing the actions in the Crimea and ending the year dug in to await the anticipated Soviet winter offensive after the withdrawal from Rostov.

Sasselje the *Leibstandarte* turned south, its new objective being the large industrial city of Cherson. Three days of intense house-to-house fighting were required before the defenders were finally driven out on 20 August. The division was then granted a spell of well-earned rest, when it was briefly sent into the reserve.

In early September 1941, the *Leibstandarte* rejoined the advance towards the Black Sea, meeting heavy enemy resistance as the Red Army's battered divisions pulled back towards the Crimean Peninsula. Dietrich's men then swung east, heading towards Rostov on the Don, capturing Romanovka, Berdyansk and Mariupol in the face of bitter fighting. Taganrog fell on 17 October and Stalino three days later, but by then the weather was deteriorating and the *Leibstandarte's* vehicles were finding the going very difficult. Progress slowed, and Rostov was not reached until mid-November.

On 17 November the *Leibstandarte*, as part of III Panzer Corps, began its assault

The Demyansk Pocket

On the northern sector of the front, the Red Army offensive began on the night of 7 January 1942. The 1st, 11th and 34th Shock Armies smashed through the German lines in the area between Lake Ilmen and Lake Seliga. At the same time, a further assault penetrated through the German positions to the south of Lake Seliga. The whole of the German 16th Army was in danger of being encircled.

The *Totenkopf* Division detached two infantry battalions, its reconnaissance battalion, the pioneer battalion and part of the artillery regiment, which were all rushed to Staraya Russa on 9 January

1942, with instructions to hold the vital road and rail junction at all costs. Two further battalions were sent to Demyansk a few days later to bolster the vulnerable German southern flank.

Within days the situation had deteriorated to crisis point. Fearing the encirclement of his forces, Field Marshal von Leeb requested Hitler's permission to make a tactical withdrawal behind the River Lovat. Unsurprisingly, Hitler refused, insisting that the 16th Army stand firm. The Führer thereupon accepted von Leeb's proffered resignation and replaced him with General von Küchler. The situation continued to worsen, however, and both II and X Army Corps were squeezed into a pocket at Demyansk. By 20 January, all land communications with the remainder of the 16th Army had been lost, and the encirclement of the beleaguered Germans was almost complete. The Luftwaffe was forced to undertake the resupply of the entrapped forces by air, and barely sufficient levels of supply were only just maintained.

The SS holds – but at a price

Totenkopf units at Staraya Russa were instrumental in blunting the attacks of the Soviet 11th Army and forcing it to turn to the south, frustrating its attempts to break through to the 16th Army's rear. However, on 8 February 1942 the Soviet 1st Shock Army and 11th Army closed the last remaining gap, trapping the *Totenkopf* Division and five other Army divisions.

The main German force now set about building defensive positions to the west of the Lovat, from where they could launch an attack aimed at freeing the trapped units. In the pocket, meanwhile, the Germans held on, and none more so than the *Totenkopf*. Split into battlegroups of regimental strength, *Totenkopf* units were used in the most hard-pressed areas of the pocket. On 27 April, having been encircled for some 73 days, the siege was lifted and the mauled *Totenkopf* Division escaped from the Demyansk Pocket. However, it remained at the front in a defensive role until October, when it was finally relieved. By that time it was a shadow of its former self, having suffered devastating losses. The remnants were moved first to Sennelager in Germany and then France for rest and refitting. From the original number of 17,000 men at the start of 'Barbarossa', some 12,600 had been either killed or wounded, half of them in the Demyansk Pocket.

LEFT: SS-Hauptsturmführer Heinrich Springer of the Leibstandarte Division, who won the Knights Cross for his capture of a bridge over the River Don in November 1941. By this date the division had travelled 1600km (1000 miles) in just over four months. However, though it captured Rostov, its overstretched supply lines and Soviet resistance meant the city had to be relinquished. For Springer and his comrades, a long, hard winter on the steppes was ahead.

During these winter battles from January to March 1942, 11 officers and men of the *Totenkopf* Division were decorated with the Knights Cross of the Iron Cross for their gallantry. No other Waffen-SS division achieved such a high number of awards in such a brief period.

Marshal Zhukov's counteroffensive in front of Moscow had been launched at the beginning of December 1941, and by the end of the month virtually all of the gains made by the Germans during Operation 'Typhoon' had been lost. On the defensive from January to March 1942, the *Das Reich* Division had suffered some 4000 casualties. In March, therefore, it was decided to withdraw it to France for rest and refitting. However, as Army Group Centre could not afford to lose the whole division, two mixed battalions from the *Deutschland* and *Der Führer* Regiments, under the command of SS-Obersturmbannführer Werner Ostendorff, remained in the east as a battlegroup until they too were released from the front in mid-June.

On 1 June 1942, a new regiment joined the division. Entitled SS-Infanterie Regiment *Langemarck*, its II Battalion and staff came mainly from 4 SS-Infanterie Standarte, with its I Battalion being formed around the division's Kradschutzenbataillon. In November 1942, while still in France, the new regiment took part in the attempt to prevent the scuttling of the French fleet at Toulon (27 November). During the same period, *Das Reich* was upgraded to the status of a panzer-grenadier division, remaining in France

RIGHT: The beginning of Operation 'Typhoon', the German attempt to take Moscow in October 1941. An NCO of the **Der Führer** *Regiment,* **Das Reich** *Division. The division spearheaded the drive on the Soviet capital, and got to within 20km (32 miles) of the city's outskirts. Note the improvised snow camouflage smock and helmet cover, both made from sheets.*

BELOW: As the ground hardened when temperatures fell, the panzers were able to advance towards Moscow, but they had inadequate supplies and the men had no winter clothing.

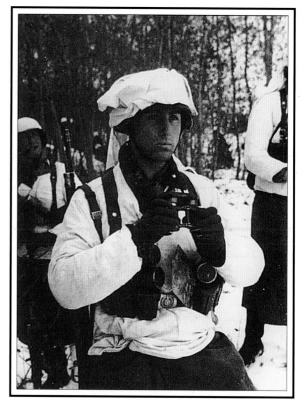

until January 1943, when it was recalled to the Eastern Front.

In the south of Russia, the Red Army had attempted to break through German lines in a major offensive in January 1942. The *Leibstandarte*, as part of III Panzer Corps, participated in the halting of a Soviet incursion into the German positions near Dniepropetrovsk. German attempts to launch a summer offensive were pre-empted by a Soviet attack in mid-May, but within a week the Germans had sealed off the Soviet salient near Kharkov.

The *Leibstandarte* then moved to Stalino for an intended refit, but German intelligence had warnings of a possible Allied landing attempt in the West and so the division was rushed to France, where it stayed for the remainder of the year.

What, then, had Himmler's Waffen-SS achieved in the Russian Campaign during 1941-42? The principal Waffen-SS divisions – *Leibstandarte, Das Reich, Totenkopf* and *Wiking* – had certainly proved themselves on the field of battle. In the

attack they had shown themselves to be daring, aggressive and fearless almost to the point of foolhardiness. They had absorbed their training well, eschewing outdated tactics and quickly assimilating the most modern of military concepts. Of all the components of the German war machine, the Waffen-SS was probably the most suited to fast, modern land warfare.

The training to which Waffen-SS soldiers were subjected was far removed from that given to the typical Wehrmacht recruit. In the Waffen-SS virtually all class barriers were removed: all officers had to serve a period in the ranks and the title 'sir' was rarely used when speaking to a superior officer, the military rank only being the preferred method of address. The bonds of comradeship between Waffen-SS officers and men were thus much stronger than those in other armies. In addition, Waffen-SS soldiers who took part in the early stage of the Russian campaign were not only superbly fit, well trained and equipped, but were also ardent supporters of National Socialism, seeing the Soviets as their natural enemies. With supreme confidence in their beliefs, their leadership, Nazism and, most importantly, themselves, these Waffen-SS troops were a truly formidable force.

Himmler made many speeches exhorting his troops to consider the enemy as Bolshevik subhumans, but whatever their political beliefs at the start of Operation

'Barbarossa', the soldiers of the Waffen-SS were quick to develop a healthy respect for the determination and tenacity of the individual Soviet soldier.

The reputation of the Waffen-SS

When two such fanatical ideologies clashed, it was inevitable that combat of such ferocity would lead to excesses being committed (see Chapter 11). Both sides were guilty of atrocities, though history has rightly emphasised the Russians as the victims of Nazi aggression. However, Red Army units, especially NKVD units, were guilty of committing atrocities of such barbarity that their behaviour was reminiscent of the Middle Ages. The soldiers of the Waffen-SS had no compunction in retaliating in kind, and war in the East became marked by innumerable atrocity reports. When the *Leibstandarte* took Taganrog, for example, it found the bodies of some of its men who had been captured and literally hacked to death with spades and axes by the local GPU (security police). Dietrich ordered that the *Leibstandarte* take no prisoners for three days, and so over 4000 Red Army soldiers who were captured were executed on the spot.

Waffen-SS losses were extremely high. By mid-November 1942, for example, it had lost over 8400 men killed in action and in excess of 27,115 wounded and 935 missing in action. However, its combat achievements silenced many of its detractors once and for all. Though there were still many in the Army who found the SS and its methods distasteful, few now questioned its military prowess and gallantry in action. Senior Wehrmacht commanders, who had once treated the Waffen-SS with disdain or contempt, were now glad to have troops of such a high calibre operating alongside them. General Eberhard von Mackensen, for example, wrote personally to Himmler in a totally unsolicited letter regarding the *Leibstandarte* and its status in his eyes: 'a genuine elite unit I am proud and happy to have under my command and, furthermore, one that I sincerely and hopefully wish to retain.' General Wöhler, commander of the 8th Army, also spoke of the Waffen-SS in glowing terms, praising its 'unshakeable fortitude'.

The mainstream Waffen-SS units had proved themselves beyond Himmler's wildest dreams, not only in the attack but also in their fanatical determination and stubborn, fanatical gallantry, even when greatly outnumbered and when other units had given up.

However, if these elite Waffen-SS units had earned reputations which would see them go down as some of history's toughest soldiers, there were other SS units whose fighting records were less than impressive, and others whose actions were

ABOVE: An SS-Rottenführer of the Totenkopf Division in the Demyansk Pocket, February 1942. On his left collar he wears rank insignia, while his right collar bears the death's head patch. He is armed with an MG34 machine gun with a drum magazine, stick grenades and a handgun.

LEFT: A Totenkopf patrol quickly goes to ground in the Demyansk Pocket as a Russian flare bursts over them.

Army Group North – the drive to Leningrad, June – Sept 1941

FINLAND

Lake Ladoga

Kronstadt • Leningrad

28 Aug

Helsinki

GULF OF FINLAND

Volkhov

20 Aug

Narva •

Luga

14 July

Chudovo •

Tallin •

Lake Peipus

Novgorod •

BALTIC SEA

E S T O N I A

Illmen

Parnu •

Tartu •

Soltsy •

• Staraya Russa

Pskov •

4 July

Ostrov •

• Kholm

Riga •

L A T V I A

S O V I E T

Dvina

• Opochka

• Liepaja

30 June

Rezekne •

U N I O N

L I T H U A N I A

26 June

• Nevel

Memel •

26 June

Ger 18th Army

Key

German forces

Soviet forces

Soviet pocket

Ger 4th Pz Group

Kaunas •

Ger 16th Army

• Wilno

Soviet front line, 1 Sept 1941

EAST PRUSSIA

Neiman

altogether more sinister. In the far north, for example, the newly formed SS-Kampfgruppe *Nord* had been involved, along with Army troops and some Finnish units, in an attack on a Soviet strongpoint at Salla. The first two attacks by the SS soldiers were beaten back, and when they launched a third assault it too was defeated. Then the Soviets launched a counterattack which resulted in the SS fleeing in a wild panic. Some 73 members of the kampfgruppe were killed, 230 wounded and nearly 150 missing in action. Luckily for the kampfgruppe, the Army and Finnish units either side of it were made of sterner stuff and drove back the Soviet attack. The Army was disgusted by the cowardly behaviour of the SS, and shortly afterwards the kampfgruppe was withdrawn from the front for retraining and reorganisation as a mountain troop unit. It was upgraded to divisional status and renamed the 6th SS Gebirgs Division *Nord*. It eventually returned to the same sector of the front, where the dank forests

and mosquito-infested swamps did little to improve the unit's low morale.

The *Polizei* Division, serving with Army Group North, also failed to win itself any real glory, though it did perform adequately. It took part in most of the actions around Leningrad, though it was never accepted as a 'true' Waffen-SS division, only having the prefix SS- added to its divisional title in 1942. Up till then its personnel wore police-pattern collar patches and police escutcheons on their helmets in place of the SS runes. Although the division was upgraded to the status of a panzergrenadier division in June 1943, it never reached the level of combat proficiency of its fellow units. In fact, it earned a somewhat unpleasant reputation for brutality in its actions against the partisans.

In addition to these units, there were of course the notorious Einsatzgruppen (action squads), which streamed into the Soviet Union hard on the heels of the combat units. Brutalities against the civil population began almost immediately, lightning advances, stunning victories – albeit at the cost of the lives of so many of their comrades – and the hardships and suffering of the hellish Russian winter. In future years the hardships would grow, while the victories would become fewer and fewer. However, for the moment morale was high as Hitler bestowed his country's highest honours on the officers and men of his Waffen-SS.

The first Knights Cross of the campaign went to SS-Gruppenführer Paul Hausser in recognition of his distinguished service as commander of the *Das Reich* Division. Hausser believed, as did most of his SS counterparts, in leading from the front, a factor which cost the lives of so many senior Waffen-SS officers, and Hausser himself lost an eye during the battle for Yelnya in October 1941. The eye-patch he subsequently wore became something of a trademark of this able general.

The second Knights Cross off the campaign was a posthumous award to SS-

LEFT: A Ukrainian peasant woman offers refreshment to a soldier of the Wiking *Division. This image of friendliness between SS soldiers and Ukrainian civilians has to be treated with caution. It was difficult for soldiers imbued with the tenets of National Socialism to regard the eastern Europeans as anything more than subhuman.*

BELOW: Hermann Fegelein, commander of the Florian Geyer *Division. Despite being Eva Braun's brother-in-law, he was shot in April 1945 for attempting to flee Berlin.*

with the unfortunate Jewish community being the prime victims, though many other innocent members of the indigenous populations were to suffer at the hands of these murder squads.

It has often been written that it was the activities of the SS that turned the Russian population in the occupied regions against the Germans. This is a somewhat inaccurate theory, as many Waffen-SS combat units were welcomed as liberators on their arrival in some areas, as the locals celebrated the expulsion of their communist overlords. Much photographic evidence exists showing the festive reception which greeted the young Waffen-SS soldiers, especially in areas such as the Ukraine, as they were greeted with gifts of flowers, food and drink. These soldiers, too, would have reason to curse the activities of the Einsatzkommandos, (see Chapter 5) who turned so many friendly locals into hate-filled enemies.

The fact that many of the Einsatzgruppen personnel wore uniforms which seemed to be the same as the young Waffen-SS infantrymen did not help matters either. Russian civilians could not be expected to notice that the SS men of the Einsatzkommandos did not wear honour titles on their sleeves, unlike the soldiers of the elite Waffen-SS combat units.

For the young soldiers of the elite Waffen-SS, however, the 1941-42 campaign would be remembered as one of

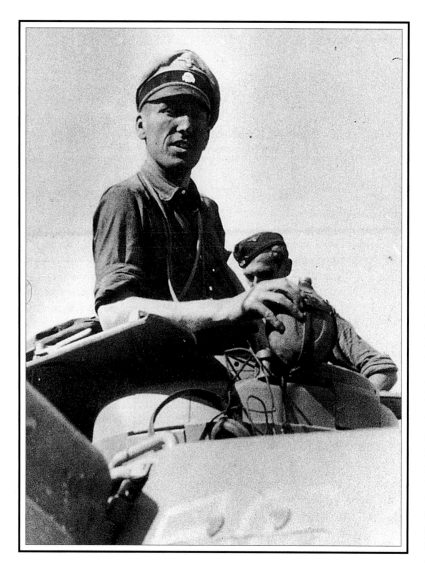

ABOVE: A tank commander of the Wiking Division. This unit fought consistently well in Russia. It was initially part of Field Marshal von Rundstedt's Army Group South, and was heavily involved in the Caucasus and Ukraine in 1942.

Unterscharführer Erich Rossner from SS-Panzerjäger Abteilung 2, who personally knocked out 13 Soviet tanks before being fatally wounded. He died on 30 July 1941, and was posthumously awarded the Knights Cross on 25 August. The fanatical determination of the typical Waffen-SS soldier is probably best illustrated by the case of SS-Sturmmann Fritz Christen of the *Totenkopf* Division. An anti-tank gunner, Christen and his unit had come under attack from a concentrated force of enemy tanks and infantry. One by one the *Totenkopf* guns were knocked out and their crews killed, until only Christen was left. Facing the enemy attack entirely alone, he fought on, loading, aiming and firing by himself. He knocked out over a dozen enemy tanks and around 100 Soviet infantrymen before reinforcements finally arrived. Christen was deservedly awarded the Knights Cross on 24 September 1941.

All in all, between June 1941 and the end of December 1942, a total of three Knights Crosses had been awarded to *Leibstandarte* personnel, eight to *Das*

Reich, nine to the *Polizei* Division, eight to *Wiking* and two to members of the SS cavalry brigade. Of the total figure of 48, some 42 were of officer rank, although many were very junior grade officers.

While both Hitler and Himmler were delighted at the combat performance of the Waffen-SS divisions on the Eastern Front, the horrific cost in casualties, plus the tenacity of the Soviet defence, made it clear that it was going to be a long, hard campaign. The German successes had indeed been spectacular, but the Russian bear was by no means dead or even mortally wounded. German losses had been massive and now the invasion force was exhausted. Clearly, reinforcements in great numbers would be required if the campaign was to be brought to a successful conclusion. As a result, in the forthcoming year Hitler would allow a massive expansion in the ranks of the Waffen-SS.

New Waffen-SS divisions

During 1942, the huge numbers of Soviet troops cut off in the great pincer movements of the German armies caused the invaders considerable problems. By no means all of the entrapped Red Army troops surrendered to the Germans. Many took to the great forests, from where they carried out guerrilla attacks on Axis supply routes. The situation became so acute that considerable numbers of German soldiers, badly needed at the front, were required to police and protect these rear areas. These duties were unpopular and unwelcome for the Wehrmacht, and so increasing numbers of police regiments were allocated to Russia in an attempt to release combat troops for the front. As Himmler held the appointment of Chief of German Police as well as Reichsführer-SS, these police troops also came under the auspices of the SS. It has subsequently been established that these police personnel were responsible not only for ant-partisan and security actions, but were also involved in the rounding up and murder of much of the Jewish population in the occupied areas. They were assisted in both types of actions by willing accomplices, in the form of volunteer auxiliary police units raised from the non-Jewish members of the indigenous populations.

As far as the Waffen-SS was concerned, two new divisions were formed during 1942. The first was the 7th SS Freiwilligen Gebirgs Division *Prinz Eugen*, raised in northern Serbia in the spring of 1942. For the remainder of the year it was

LEFT: *Soldiers of the artillery regiment of the* **Wiking** *Division photgraphed in the summer of 1942. The division was upgraded to panzergrenadier status in November 1942 and became a panzer division in October 1943. It was ably led by SS-Gruppenführer Felix Steiner, who later went on to command III SS Panzer Corps.*

BELOW: *A frozen soldier of the* **Polizei** *Division in Lapland during the winter of 1941-42. Attached to Army Group North for 'Barbarossa', the division's poor training and inadequate equipment meant its overall level of performance was low.*

involved principally in organising and training and saw no combat action.

The second new division was the 8th SS Cavalry Division *Florian Geyer*. In 1941, an SS cavalry brigade had been formed from two of the pre-war SS-Totenkopf Reiterregiments. This brigade was used primarily for anti-partisan duties and was commanded by SS-Standartenführer Hermann Fegelein, and it quickly gained an unsavoury reputation for its dealings with the partisans. It was expanded and upgraded to divisional status in the autumn of 1942. Command of the division passed to SS-Gruppenführer Wilhelm Bittrich, an extremely able soldier, from 1942 to 1943, before returning to Fegelein, who eventually reached the rank of SS-Gruppenführer. Promoted well above the level of his abilities, he was married to the sister of Eva Braun, Hitler's mistress. However, this did not save him when the Führer ordered his execution after discovering his attempt to flee Berlin in the closing days of the war dressed in civilian clothes and with a suitcase of valuables.

In early 1942, however, the Waffen-SS could bask in the glory of its tremendous combat achievements. The reputation it had established for itself would result in its men being in greater and greater demand on all fronts as the war continued.

HOME SERVICE

Himmler's SS administered a vast empire within the borders of the Third Reich, which had under its control the Gestapo, the uniformed police, the notorious Einsatzgruppen and the various economic enterprises that worked thousands of concentration camp inmates to death. The tentacles of this empire spread into many spheres of the domestic front.

In wartime Germany, under the direct control of the Reichsführer-SS, were a number of hauptamter (main offices) which controlled the various functions of the SS. Those which impinged upon life in wartime Germany and the occupied territories in a major way will be looked at in some detail below. However, there were other hauptamter which certainly had their principal effect on the home front rather than on the battlefield or outside the Reich, though the average citizen may never have been aware of their existence.

The Hauptamt SS-Gericht

The legal department of the SS was based in Munich, the birthplace of National Socialism. It was principally responsible for administering and enforcing the SS disciplinary code and controlled the SS und Polizei Gerichte, both in German cities and in the occupied territories.

The Hauptamt SS-Gericht was controlled by SS-Obergruppenführer Franz Breithaupt and carried out, in addition to its other duties, investigations into alleged disciplinary offences, and prepared and prosecuted cases brought against those who had been charged with violating the SS code of honour. This hauptamt also controlled the SS and police prisons.

A group of Gestapo officers pose for the camera. At its height in 1943, the Gestapo had 45,000 men, 60,000 agents and up to 100,000 informers enforcing Nazi rule.

ABOVE: Himmler (centre) and Heydrich (second from left) inspect an SS honour guard in Prague in October 1941. Heydrich had been appointed Protector of Bohemia and Moravia in September in place of Freiherr Neurath. At first his administration began in terror, but then he astutely introduced the 'carrot and stick' approach to the Czechs. Additional ration cards and clothing were introduced as a reward for increased production, and the population responded positively. The British government and Czech government in exile decided to assassinate Heydrich, believing that it would result in a period of unrestrained violence against the Czech people that would destroy the fragile cooperation that was emerging in Czechoslovakia. The assassination squad struck on 27 May 1942, and Heydrich died on 4 June from his wounds. The reprisals that followed were brutal, and ensured the lasting hostility of the Czechs.

Although its remit included actions against offenders from the Allgemeine-SS in wartime Germany, and a small number of concentration camp personnel were prosecuted for corruption (usually the theft of valuables taken from inmates upon their arrival at the camps), its impact on the ordinary citizen would have been fairly negligible.

The SS-Hauptamt

As its name suggests, this department was originally the principal main office of the entire SS. However, as the organisation rapidly expanded it was considered to be over-worked, so various new hauptämter were created to take over a number of its functions. It eventually lost nearly 70 per cent of its official functions, and thus its overall power and influence was considerably reduced when war broke out.

Under SS-Obergruppenführer Gottlob Berger, however, it was responsible for the care and maintenance of all personal files for NCOs and lower ranks of the SS, and, more importantly, for the recruitment of personnel for the Waffen-SS from 1941 onwards. Berger was involved in all sorts of Machiavellian plots to poach manpower from the Army, and was instrumental in organising recruitment for the foreign volunteer units (see Chapter 6).

SS-Führungshauptamt

Under the overall command of SS-Obergruppenführer Hans Jüttner from 1942, this was the Operations Headquarters of the SS. It boasted a massive 45,000 staff by the end of the war, and was responsible for the operational control of both the Waffen-SS and Allgemeine-SS. Its functions with regard to the former included organisation, supply, training, deployment and mobilisation.

Persönliche Stab Reichsführer-SS

Located in Berlin, the personal staff of the Reichsführer-SS was responsible for all matters which did not come under the remit of the other SS-Hauptämter. Its main impact on the domestic front was its responsibility for the Lebensborn organisation. This had been formed in 1936 to promote the bearing of good Aryan children by mothers of sound racial stock, whether married or not. In November 1939, just after the outbreak of war, an order promulgated by Himmler stated: 'Every war involves the shedding of the best blood. Numerous victories mean a loss of vigour and blood. The death of the best is not the worst fate. What is worse is the absence of children who have not been procreated by the living during the war and cannot be procreated afterwards. Quite apart from civil law and normal custom, it must now be the duty of all German women and girls of good blood to become mothers of children of SS soldiers serving at the front, not frivolously, but in all moral seriousness.' In addition, the future of these children would be assured: 'Official guardians will take over the wardship, in the name of the Reichsführer-SS, of all illegitimate children of good blood whose fathers have fallen in battle...The head of the Rasse- und Siedlungs Hauptamt and his staff will observe discretion in the maintaining of documentation relating to the parentage of these children...SS men must see clearly that, in complying with this order, they will perform an act of great importance. Mockery, disdain and non-comprehension will not affect us, for the future is ours.'

Thus, official assistance was promised to unmarried mothers and illegitimate children, so long as they were of good blood, and Himmler went to great lengths to protect the blood line. In August 1942, he ordered that when an SS family had only one remaining son, and he was of an age to be serving in the military, he would be removed from the front and sent home to ensure the continuance of the family line. This practice was adhered to until quite late in the war.

Himmler's fanaticism concerning good Germanic bloodstock did not restrict itself to the Reich. As German armies swarmed over the conquered lands of Europe, suitably 'Nordic' children orphaned by the war were rounded up and sent to Germany, and, ultimately, what amounted to virtual kidnapping of suitable children occurred. This even applied to some Polish children who, as Slavs, would appear to be unsuitable for Himmler's plans. However, they were all taken to Germany and fostered out to suitable SS-approved families.

In the Reichsführer's plans these children, once grown, would eventually be returned to their homelands, suitably Germanised, to form a stock of loyal Nordic subjects in all the conquered lands and thus keep the 'lower' races under control.

Rasse-und Siedlungs Hauptamt (RuSHA)

By 1940, this main office had lost some of its original functions but still retained four main duties: Race, Family, Resettlement and Organisation and Administration.

Each SS-Oberabschnitt (territorial division) in wartime Germany had an officer of the RuSHA, and every town an SS Family Welfare Officer. Despite wartime demands on the SS and its administration, RuSHA personnel continued to check racial details of any prospective member of the SS. Whereas meticulous checks were made prior to the outbreak of war in 1939, the rapid expansion of the SS thereafter rendered such in-depth research impossible in many cases. Only officers and their prospective spouses, therefore, had their background and family lineage fully investigated. For noncommissioned ranks, a signed declaration that their lineage was free from non-Aryan blood was deemed sufficient, with fuller enquiries to be made after the war. Germanic volunteers were likewise accepted on the basis of a signed declaration.

The other major function performed by this department was the resettling of Germans into the conquered eastern territories, where the indigenous populations were often simply evicted from their lands and farms and replaced with German families.

Hauptamt Dienststelle Heissmeyer

The most important effect of this Main Office on home life in wartime Germany was in the field of education. It controlled the Nationalpolitische Erziehungsanstalten (NPEA), the Nazi Political Education Institutions. These were formed in 1933 to allow the best of Germany's educational talent to be cultivated into a suitable pool of aspirants for the highest positions in the SS and NSDAP. Himmler eventually gained control of the NPEA insidiously, first offering to supply clothing and equipment, then scholarships and funding. In

1936, his efforts were rewarded when SS-Obergruppenführer August Heissmeyer was appointed as Inspector General of the NPEA. Himmler then pushed for all NPEA staff to be enrolled in the SS.

By 1940, the SS had taken full control of the schools, introducing SS-style uniforms and ranks for their staff, the SS prefix to the rank being replaced by NPEA, thus an SS-Oberführer became an NPEA-Oberführer, and so on. NPEA schools were also opened outside of Germany's borders to cope with suitable recruits from the *Volksdeutsche* communities.

The fact remains, however, that despite the importance placed in the NPEA by Himmler, only a tiny proportion of Germany's youth ever passed through these schools, and thus its influence on German life was minimal.

Reichs Sicherheitshauptamt

The Reich Central Security Department, under the command of SS-Obergruppenführer Reinhard Heydrich, probably had more impact upon life in the Third Reich than any other SS organisation.

There were seven main sections within the RSHA itself, including Ideological Research under SS-Obersturmführer Dittel, which dealt with investigation of those seen as 'ideologically dangerous' to the National Socialist creed, including communists, Jews, pacifists, freemasons and others, Administration under SS-Standartenführer Spacil, and a Training and Personnel Selection under SS-Oberführer Ehrlinger. In addition to these, the most important offices were the Geheime Staatspolizei (Gestapo) under SS-Gruppenführer Heinrich Müller, the Kriminal Polizei (Kripo) under SS-Gruppenführer Arthur Nebe, the Ausland (External) SD under SS-Brigadeführer

BELOW: The rubble that was the village of Lidice, following its destruction by the Germans. The village was chosen to be an example to the world of Nazi vengeance. It had only been tenuously linked (two families who lived there had sons serving with the Czech forces in Britain) with the assassination of Heydrich. However, the Führer wanted revenge. His orders went out to the Gestapo chiefs in Prague and Kladno: all adult male inhabitants to be shot, all females to be sent to a concentration camp, the children to be either 'Germanised' or to undergo 'other forms of education', and the village to be flattened. The Gestapo later reported that 199 men were executed and 195 women arrested and sent to Ravensbruck. Of the 95 children, nine were considered fit for 'Germanisation' and were delivered to SS families; the rest simply vanished (only 16 were traced after the war). The village was then systematically destroyed (even the graveyard was disinterred).

Walter Schellenberg, and the Inland (Internal) SD under SS-Brigadeführer Doctor Otto Ohlendorf. Of the above, those that impinged most upon the lives of the citizens in wartime Germany were the Inland SD, the Kripo and the Gestapo.

Hitler had, from the earliest days of its existence, granted the Gestapo, under its founder Hermann Göring, extremely wide powers. He decreed that interference from other security organs into matters which were considered to be within the remit of the Gestapo would not be tolerated.

A considerable number of Gestapo officials during the early part of its history were former career policemen from the Kriminal Polizei (broadly equivalent to the plain clothes Criminal Investigation Department of the British police), many of whom were not members of the NSDAP or the SS. A large number of these officers could boast years of solid police experience, if not academic qualifications.

Gestapo and SD rivalry

In contrast to these Gestapo officials, the typical SD officer came from an educated middle-class background, was articulate, and a loyal NSDAP and SS member. The SD had responsibility for counter-intelligence and the rooting out of enemies of the state, but had no executive powers of arrest and often felt a degree of resentment towards its Gestapo counterpart. The Gestapo had no restrictions as to its powers of arrest, and it often trespassed into areas which were properly the responsibility of the SD. Relations between the two, therefore, were often far from cordial.

The Gestapo, having been formed in the main from former Kripo personnel, had a ready-made 'field force' of informers in place, which was rapidly expanded. For example, each large apartment building would have its own resident Gestapo informer, who would keep a suspicious eye on his fellow tenants, ever ready to inform on the slightest indiscretion. Government employees in particular were actively encouraged to spy and inform on their colleagues, and the slightest problem would be exaggerated out of all proportion and used as an excuse to dispense with the services of any employee not considered suitably loyal to the regime. Even children were encouraged to spy on, and denounce, their own parents for any suspected disloyalty.

By the outbreak of war in 1939, the Gestapo had expanded to a strength of around 20,000 functionaries, while the SD remained at a mere 3000. The latter had

around 50,000 informers on its payroll, but by 1943 the Gestapo had 100,000 informers. The lack of goodwill between the two security organs was exacerbated by the Gestapo's seeming ability to get whatever funding it required to function, whereas the SD had to beg its paymasters for funds. The Gestapo's personnel also had better pension rights than the SD.

Things began to change when the police agencies of the Third Reich were reorganised and Heydrich was given command of the SD, Gestapo and Kripo under the umbrella of the RSHA, while SS-Obergruppenführer Kurt Daluege took command of the remaining police duties under the banner of the Ordnungspolizei.

Heydrich quickly installed his own men: former Kripo Officer Heinrich Müller to head the Gestapo, and Walter Schellenberg to command the SD. As a Kripo officer in Bavaria, Müller had connived with the Nazis to cover up the death of Hitler's niece, Geli Raubal.

When war broke out in 1939, the paranoia of the Nazi state went into overdrive. Not only had the SD and Gestapo to counter the potentially disaffected elements in Germany, such as the Church, whose sermons were carefully monitored for covert criticism of the regime, but masses of foreign diplomats, businessmen, members of the press and other foreign nationals also had to be carefully watched.

Early Gestapo successes

The beginning of the war saw the security services scoring major propaganda coups. In November 1939, a communist watch repairer named Georg Elser had planted a bomb in the Bürgerbraukeller in Munich. Concealed behind wood panelling, it was intended to explode and kill Hitler as he addressed a meeting of trusted Party comrades. Unfortunately for Elser, Hitler left the building before the scheduled time and, though the bomb exploded, Hitler had already gone. The Gestapo's network of agents soon discovered who had been responsible and a nationwide manhunt began. Elser was captured as he attempted to cross the border into Switzerland. The attempt on Hitler's life was presented to the German people as a plot by the British and its failure as proof that destiny was on Hitler's side. Elser was held in so-called 'protective custody' but never brought to trial. He was executed at Sachsenhausen concentration camp in April 1945.

In 1940, a further intelligence coup was carried out by the SD. Under the pre-

'By the end of 1934, the SA had been fairly well eliminated and the SS, the members of which wore elegant black suits and were therefore called elite guards, became almost identical as functionaries with the Gestapo.'
– Raymond H. Geist, United States Consul in Berlin, 1930s

text of being members of an anti-Nazi resistance group, SD agents made contact with the British, apparently seeking to negotiate peace terms once Hitler had been overthrown. British agents Captain Best and Major Stevens were lured to a meeting place at Venlo on the Dutch side of the Dutch/German border, whereupon SD agents led by Alfred Naujocks crossed the border, stormed the meeting place and abducted the British agents.

Once again the German people were presented with evidence of a British plot to ferment unrest and overthrow Hitler. In addition, Hitler was presented with so-called Dutch complicity in the scheme, which he then used to help excuse his attack on Holland.

Hitler's enemies in Germany were somewhat cowed by these successes of the security services. In any case, during the first two or three years of war, when victories seemed to come thick and fast and shortages had not yet become acute, there was no real groundswell of dissatisfaction among the populace, and opposition to Hitler had little opportunity to flourish.

As the war progressed, however, and shortages at home began to affect the civilian population more drastically, dissatisfaction and resentment grew. The security services were well aware of the drop in morale, but there was little they could do to combat this, other than watch carefully for signs of defeatism and disaffection. In any case, strange as it may seem, very little of this ill feeling was directed at Hitler personally – most of the population still had faith in their Führer.

Reinhard Heydrich

As head of an apparently successful RSHA, Heydrich's standing with Hitler was extremely high. In the East, the so-called 'Protectorate of Bohemia-Moravia', actually part of Czechoslovakia, was administered by Reichsprotektor Constantin von Neurath, a diplomat of the old school whom Hitler considered too soft on the subjugated Czechs. His deputy, SS-Gruppenführer Karl Frank, coveted the post for himself and used every possible opportunity to undermine von Neurath's status. However, when Hitler did remove von Neurath it was Heydrich who was appointed acting Reichsprotektor.

Heydrich was delighted with this important new post, though he did not give up his command of the RSHA. Much to everyone's surprise, Heydrich's attitude towards the Czechs was entirely uncharac-

teristic of the man. Rather than brutal repression, Heydrich chose a 'carrot and stick' approach. The carrot was the provision of a good level of rations and fair treatment of the Czechs, so long as they were industrious and well behaved. The stick was the harshest possible sentencing on anyone aiding the Czech resistance or sabotaging the war effort (he also dealt extremely harshly with any Germans found guilty of actions against the interests of the Reich). Thus, to many Czechs he seemed a fair, if very firm, administrator, and acts of resistance decreased. The Czech government in exile was alarmed at this situation. Allied interests and propaganda would be best served if the Czech population could be shown to hold only hatred and contempt for a brutal Nazi oppressor. The British and the Czech gov-

BELOW: Admiral Wilhelm Franz Canaris, the head of German military intelligence, the Abwehr. A complex character, Canaris eventually became disillusioned with National Socialism. As such, he was well placed to give protection to those who were actively opposing Hitler. Implicated in the July 1944 Bomb Plot (although no one knows his exact role), he was arrested and eventually hanged at Flossenbürg concentration camp.

ernment in exile resolved to assassinate Heydrich, knowing that the inevitable retribution handed down to the Czechs would turn them all irrevocably against the Germans. A team of exiled Czech soldiers were parachuted into Czechoslovakia by the British in May 1942. On the 27th of that month, as Heydrich drove to his office in his open topped staff car, he was attacked by the parachutists. In the gunfight which ensued, a grenade was thrown which exploded in the car beside Heydrich and he was seriously injured, dying in hospital from a secondary infection on 4 June. Hitler reacted entirely predictably. Thousand of Czechs were arrested and the village of Lidice, falsely associated with the assassins, was ordered to be destroyed.

Units of the Sicherheitspolizei levelled the village and murdered most of its inhabitants. Only a tiny handful escaped. The assassins were betrayed and their hiding place in the Karel Boromejsky Church in Prague surrounded. After a brief battle, the Czech parachutists, realising that escape was impossible, committed suicide.

Heydrich was given a state funeral, and a Waffen-SS regiment was named in his honour. Lidice was razed to the ground and its name removed from the map. Heydrich's position as head of the RSHA was taken by the Austrian Doctor of Law, Ernst Kaltenbrunner, an SS-Obergruppenführer and General of Police.

Back in Germany, criticism of the regime was becoming more outspoken. For some time the Bishop of Munster had been an opponent of Nazism, and his highly critical sermons left no one in any doubt of his viewpoint. Remarkably, however, he remained unmolested, perhaps due

to his high position. Professor Huber of the Department of Philosophy at the University of Munich, a dedicated anti-Nazi, had taken up the Bishop's critical stance and had written a leaflet based on his sermons and had it duplicated and secretly distributed around the university. These leaflets reached a number of like-minded students, and an active resistance movement was established. Under the pseudonym 'White Rose', the group restricted itself to passive resistance, which consisted of distributing anti-Nazi leaflets.

News of this growing unrest reached the gauleiter, Paul Geisler, who decided to make a personal speech to the students.

He berated them for their low morale and lack of loyalty to Hitler, threatening male students with compulsory military service and suggesting that female students should be used to bear children for the Reich, leeringly hinting that he himself would be prepared to assist in this. The students had had enough and attacked Geisler and his guards. Street riots broke out and slogans, such as 'Down with Hitler', began to appear painted on walls.

The authorities had no hard evidence against individual students, but they kept a close watch on the university. Eventually, a Gestapo informer who was working as a janitor at the university spotted two students, brother and sister Hans and Sophie Scholl, scattering leaflets from a balcony and immediately denounced them. They were at once arrested and brought to trial before the notorious Nazi Judge, Roland Freisler. The Scholls, together with another student, Christoph Probst, were pronounced guilty and sentenced to death by decapitation. The sentences were carried out without delay. Shortly afterwards, the other members of the 'White Rose', including Professor Huber, were arrested and executed.

Despite such setbacks, resistance continued to grow and the SD and Gestapo were forced to remain on constant watch for further signs of discontent and opposition.

The July 1944 Bomb Plot

By the end of 1943, the RSHA was aware of a strong anti-Hitler element in the Wehrmacht, but seemed unable to unearth positive evidence against many individuals. Those suspects they had identified were left unmolested, presumably in the hope that close scrutiny of their movements and contacts would lead the SD and Gestapo to their ringleaders. The security forces had to move carefully because the SS courts had no jurisdiction against Wehrmacht personnel, and, as military courts were unlikely to use Gestapo methods of interrogation against soldiers suspected of disloyalty, confessions were unlikely. The SD and Gestapo bided their time.

As military defeat in the war became more and more certain, the loyalty of senior Wehrmacht officers was put under strain. A number of them had for some time favoured action against the regime, specifically to remove the Führer himself, but in the past could not depend upon public support while Hitler's adventures continued to bring victory. By mid-1944, they reasoned, time was ripe for action.

An Army training exercise, codenamed 'Valkyrie', had been designed, in which the Army occupied Berlin to defend the city against a theoretical uprising by Germany's mass of slave labourers, escaped prisoners and the like. If Hitler could be removed, the plotters were confident that their forces, under the guise of carrying out this exercise, could successfully occupy Berlin and depose the Nazi government. The commander of the Abwehr (military intelligence), Admiral Wilhelm Canaris, knew, and tacitly approved, of the plot. An enthusiastic National Socialist, he disapproved of the excesses of the regime. Although Canaris had lived near to, and often socialised with, Heydrich, the latter had coveted Canaris' position, and the two security branches, the RSHA and Abwehr, had a mutual distrust of each other.

The main conspirators

The plotters' main problem was to breach Hitler's tight personal security. A plan was hatched in which an Army staff officer would plant a bomb in Hitler's Rastenburg headquarters and kill the Führer. A volunteer was found in the person of Colonel Klaus Schenk, Graf von Stauffenberg, an aristocratic war hero who had lost an eye, an arm and two fingers of the remaining hand in action in North Africa, yet had refused to be invalided out of the service. He was perceived as a totally loyal and dedicated soldier, and thus unlikely to attract suspicion.

Senior members of the General Staff in Berlin, including General Hans Oster, General Ludwig Beck and General Friedrich Olbricht, agreed to the plan and were supported by other senior field commanders in occupied Europe, who were to move against the SS and security elements in their areas. General Fromm in Berlin knew of the plot and promised support, but in fact was too frightened to commit himself fully.

Some of Germany's most senior soldiers were involved in the plot, including two field marshals, von Witzleben and von Kluge, and a number of senior generals. Field Marshal Rommel knew of the plot but took no active part in it (he had been seriously injured on 17 July when his car had been strafed by Allied aircraft). However, his mere foreknowledge of it was later sufficient to seal his fate.

On 20 July 1944, Stauffenberg duly arrived at Rastenburg to attend a military briefing that Hitler was to address. He planted a bomb concealed in his briefcase under the conference table and left, ostensibly to take an important phone call. Unfortunately, one of the other officers present tripped on the briefcase and moved it behind one of the stout oak pedestals of the table. The bomb exploded as planned, and Stauffenberg, hearing the detonation, assumed Hitler was dead and made his hurried departure. He was unaware that the pedestal had shielded Hitler from the blast. Although badly shaken, the Führer was relatively uninjured.

It was, however, the ineptitude of the plotters in Berlin which destroyed any hope of wresting control of Germany from the Nazis. On receiving the signal from Stauffenberg that Hitler was dead, they neglected to seize all means of communication, including the radio stations. The Berlin Guard Regiment, mobilised under

BELOW: Hitler shows Mussolini the damage following the attempt on his life. Himmler believed that failure was proof that Hitler had God on his side: 'By preserving the Führer Providence has given us a sign. The Führer lives, invulnerable – Providence has spared him to us so that we may bring the war to a triumphant conclusion under his leadership.' The subsequent purge was an orgy of brutality, with suspects being tortured and executed.

'Valkyrie', and believing a revolt had started, moved to secure a number of government buildings, including the office of Propaganda Minister Josef Göbbels. Due to the failure of the plotters to sever communications, Göbbels was able to make direct telephone contact with Hitler himself. When Oberst Remer of *Wache Regiment Berlin*, part of the elite *Grossdeutschland* Division, arrived to secure the building, Göbbels was able to put him on the telephone link direct to Hitler, who promoted him on the spot and ordered him to quell the rebellion.

General Fromm, seeing the plot beginning to waver, acted to save his own skin and ordered the arrest and immediate execution of the other plotters after a drumhead court martial. Olbricht, Stauffenberg and others were executed by firing squad. Fromm hoped thereby to eliminate those who might testify to his own knowledge of the plot. Himmler suspected Fromm's motives, however, and despatched a group of officers from the RSHA to prevent any further executions.

Elsewhere, the plotters had more success. In Paris, 1200 SS and Gestapo staff were rounded up and put in the Fresnes military prison. However, the conspirators blundered here, too, and overlooked a vital teleprinter link to Berlin, and the RSHA was soon aware of the fate of its Paris personnel.

On hearing that Hitler had survived, Kluge immediately switched sides and denounced his fellow conspirators. This did him no good because Himmler was aware of his complicity. Hard evidence, though, may have been difficult to obtain, and Hitler did not wish the scenario of Germany putting one of its most senior soldiers on trial for treason. Himmler despatched SS-Brigadeführer Jurgen Stroop to deal with the problem, and the latter dutifully murdered von Kluge, arranging the death to look like suicide.

Meanwhile, the threat of military force persuaded General von Stulpnagel in Paris to release the imprisoned SS and Gestapo staff. Amazingly, Stulpnagel then sat drinking champagne with the head of the Paris Gestapo as if nothing had occurred, both wishing the whole event could be swept under the carpet, Stulpnagel because of his complicity in the plot and the Gestapo chief out of embarrassment for not having detected the treasonable plotting going on around him in Paris.

Nazi reprisals after the Bomb Plot

Himmler prepared to unleash a wave of terror on suspects such as had never been seen before, rooting out once and for all any elements not totally loyal to Hitler. In the roundup which followed, 16 generals and two field marshals fell from grace. A wave of arrests swept through Germany, and anyone who even knew any of the suspects became a suspect themselves. Even the most tenuous link was sufficient for the SD and Gestapo to assume guilt. A series of show trials were held, presided over by Judge Roland Freisler. These could only have one possible outcome: vilification, abuse, guilty verdict and death. But it was not the honourable death of a soldier before a firing squad; rather, the victims were hanged at Plotsensee prison from meathooks by thin hempen ropes to ensure a slow and agonising strangulation, which was filmed for Hitler's gratification.

A special commission was formed, with 400 Gestapo investigators attempting

to flush out any remaining conspirators. A dragnet was thrown over the Reich. Of course the RSHA used this as an excuse to settle many old scores, and denunciations were common, as those implicated sought to conceal their guilt by denouncing and thus eliminating fellow conspirators.

SD chief Walter Schellenberg now took his chance to move against Admiral Canaris and the Abwehr. Evidence had emerged of the Admiral's knowledge of the plot. He was arrested and held, initially at least, under a fairly civilised house arrest. This soon changed, however, to incarceration in the cells of the dreaded Gestapo headquarters in the Prinz Albrechtstrasse. Although Canaris was not subjected to excessive physical abuse, he was put through considerable psychological torture before being thrown into Flossenbürg concentration camp, where he was executed on Himmler's orders a few days before the camp was liberated at the end of the war.

Many old scores were settled during this period. One of the Abwehr's legal experts, Hans von Dohnanyi, had helped to expose the Gestapo plot to discredit General Blomberg in 1938. The Gestapo was now to have its revenge, as evidence was unearthed showing Dohnanyi's close links with some of the conspirators. He was arrested and subjected to the usual brutal Gestapo interrogation. Knowing he could not withstand this treatment for long, he arranged for his wife to smuggle some diphtheria bacilli into prison during a visit the Gestapo had permitted, hoping that the severe illness which ensued would prevent further interrogations. In fact, the Gestapo responded by throwing him into Sachsenhausen concentration camp, where he was interred until April 1945. As the war drew to a close, he was given a brief show trial which reached the inevitable guilty verdict and he was hanged. He was so ill at this time that he was hanged while propped up, still in his stretcher.

By late 1944, the Gestapo and SD wielded virtually unrestricted power in Germany as Hitler's paranoia raged unchecked. Sections of the civil population lived in fear that the slightest hint of defeatism in an unguarded conversation might bring the dreaded knock on the door in the middle of the night, and subsequent arrest by the Gestapo.

The Einsatzgruppen

Certainly the most sinister of all of the Nazi security organs were the notorious Einsatzgruppen of the RSHA. Few other

---

'...the SS man is prepared to carry out blindly every order that comes from the Führer or is given by one of his superiors even if it demands the greatest sacrifice of himself.'

– Organization Book of the NSDAP, 1943

units in history could rival the reputation and record of the Einsatzgruppen for committing the most terrible atrocities.

The Einsatzgruppen owed their origin to a specially formed group of Sicherheitspolizei and Gestapo agents, who had worked in close conjunction with the Austrian police to arrest anti-Nazi elements in Austria following its annexation by Germany in 1938. The process was then further developed during the invasion of Czechoslovakia in March 1939, when two special Einsatzstabe were formed to carry out similar actions.

The Einsatzgruppen in Poland

When Hitler invaded Poland in September 1939, a special Einsatzgruppe was attached to each of the five German armies of the invasion force, with a sixth based in Posen. Einsatzgruppe I was attached to the 14th Army, Einsatzgruppe II to the 10th Army, Einsatzgruppe III to the 8th Army, Einsatzgruppe IV to the 4th Army and Einsatzgruppe V to the 3rd Army. Einsatzgruppe VI was based in Posen. Each Einsatzgruppe was subdivided into Einsatzkommandos of 100 men.

Throughout the battle zone and in the area immediately behind the frontline, the Einsatzkommandos came under Army control. In rear areas, however, the Army had no power to interfere with the activities of the Einsatzkommandos. As far as the military were aware, the task of the Einsatzkommandos was to suppress any anti-German elements in the rear areas, to arrest undesirables and to prevent sabotage. In reality, the task Himmler had allocated to these units was the complete extermination of the Polish intelligentsia.

Himmler felt that once Poland's best brains and most able leaders had been annihilated, the Polish people would become a subservient slave race under Nazi domination. In areas controlled by the Army the Einsatzkommandos were forced to exercise some discretion, but in the rear areas they were under no such restrictions and openly carried out their policy of mass murder. Once the Einsatzgruppen had eliminated their initial victims, their full fury was turned on Poland's Jews, with horrific results.

Once victory over Poland had been achieved, the occupied territories were split into military districts under Army control, and senior Army commanders greatly resented the behaviour of Himmler's murder squads. The worst offender had been Einsatzgruppe *z.b.v. von Woyrsch*, com-

manded by the brutal SS-Obergruppenführer Udo von Woyrsch, who had already struck terror into the Jewish population of upper Silesia. By late September 1939, the Army had become so incensed at the brutal behaviour of Woyrsch's men that the commander of Army Group South, General von Rundstedt, demanded that the anti-Jewish measures be immediately halted, insisting that the Army would no longer tolerate their presence. Hitler retorted by abolishing military rule and installing a number of gauleiters to bring direct Nazi rule to occupied Poland. Gauleiter Forster was appointed in West Prussia, Gauleiter Greiser in Poznan (renamed the Wathegau), Gauleiter Wagner in the newly amalgamated Silesia and Upper Silesia, and Hans Frank was appointed to rule the remainder of Poland, now entitled the Generalgouvernement.

Under control of the gauleiters, the occupied areas were once again at the mercy of the Einsatzgruppen, now formed into static Gestapo Leiststellen (regional HQs) and SD Abschnitte (regional HQs), responsible in each district to the local Security Police and SD Commander, who in return was responsible to the Security Police and SD Commander, who answered directly to the RSHA. A directly parallel command structure was also organised for units of the Ordnungspolizei. All SS and police functions were placed under the control of a Höhere SS-und Polizeiführer, senior SS and police commander (HSSPF).

The Army, however, had not yet admitted defeat in its struggle against the Einsatzgruppen in Poland. General von Rundstedt had resigned in disgust and was replaced by General Johannes Blaskowitz, who was made of sterner stuff. The rapid expansion of Himmler's extermination

ABOVE: Concentration camp slave labour. Himmler and his acolytes in the SS, particularly Oswald Pohl, the head of the SS Economic and Administrative Department, soon realised that the thousands of people in the camps could be used in factories to aid the war effort, instead of being a 'drain' on the state's resources (Himmler widened the list of 'anti-socials', such as tramps, beggars and pimps, who could be arrested to provide more workers for the SS's economic ventures). In this way the SS became an immensely rich organisation, not least because of the vast amounts of gold and jewellery seized from prisoners. For the SS's economic schemes, Pohl advocated that prisoners should not be beaten but should be offered better food and clothes as an incentive to work harder. However, the prisoners were still slaves who had no rights and could be mercilessly beaten by the camp guards for the most minor offence.

BELOW: Thousands of slave labourers were literally worked to death by the SS. For most concentration camp prisoners the day began between 0400 and 0500 hours in the summer and between 0600 and 0700 hours in the winter. After a breakfast of gruel and the roll call, the working parties were marched out of the main gate, each prisoner removing his cap in deference to the slogan over it. They were then worked at a frenetic pace until the late afternoon, when they might be allowed another bowl of gruel. The working day finished at 2000 hours in the summer and 1700 hours in the winter. For those who had not died of exhaustion, the agony continued. The evening roll call was a particularly brutal event, during which inmates could stand for hours in freezing conditions as the camp guards added up their tallies. The surviving inmates were then allowed to eat their evening 'meal' – a small piece of bread, perhaps some margarine and a spoon of cheese curd. Such was the life of the workers of Himmler's SS empire.

programme finally forced Blaskowitz to act. He collated a number of reports of these atrocities committed by the Einsatzgruppen and sent them to Hitler, making the Army's repugnance clear. Hitler was enraged at what he regarded as the interference by Blaskowitz in non-military matters. Blaskowitz was undeterred, however, and continued to submit even more critical reports. By February 1940, things had reached the stage where Blaskowitz was openly expressing in his reports the attitude of abhorrence and even hatred prevailing in the military towards the actions of the Einsatzgruppen, stating that every soldier was 'disgusted and repelled' by these crimes. It is said that even at Hitler's headquarters, Army officers were refusing to shake hands with SS leaders.

The invasion of the Soviet Union

Gauleiter Frank then intervened with Hitler and personally requested the removal of Blaskowitz. Hitler was happy to comply, and the troublesome Blaskowitz and his staff were removed from the occupied territories, ostensibly to prepare for the forthcoming campaign in the West. Himmler's murder squads were once again free to roam the occupied areas, bringing death and destruction as they drove the indigenous Polish and Jewish populations from their homes and replaced them with racially acceptable *Volksdeutsche* settlers.

Although the actions of the Einsatzgruppen in Poland had been monstrous, worse was to come after Hitler unleashed his military might in the east once again, this time against his erstwhile Soviet allies in mid-1941. Four Einsatzgruppen were initially committed: Einsatzgruppe A to work in the area covered by Army Group North, Einsatzgruppe B in the area covered by Army Group Centre, and Einsatzgruppen C and D to the area covered by Army Group South. As the war

progressed, a further four were formed: E, G, H and Einsatzgruppe *Kroatien*.

As the German armies advanced into Russia, the Einsatzgruppen followed behind with orders to exterminate any of the unfortunate categories on their lists, which included political commissars, NKVD Agents, anti-Nazi ethnic Germans, partisans and anyone giving them aid, Jews, insurgents and 'undesirable elements', the latter category being a catch-all which virtually permitted the Einsatzgruppen to execute anyone they saw fit. In many cases the Einsatzgruppen were able to call on anti-semitic elements in the local population to help them in the persecution and murder of Jews. In areas which fell to the Germans, a static Security Police and Order Police command structure was set up similar to that in Poland.

It had been decided prior to the invasion of the Soviet Union that the Einsatzgruppen would only come under Army jurisdiction in terms of movement, accommodation and supply of rations. In all other respects the Army could only forbid Einsatzgruppen actions if they actually interfered with military operations. In other words, the Einsatzgruppen were to have a virtual free hand yet again.

Heydrich's instructions

The chief of the RSHA, SS-Obergruppenführer Heydrich, sent his men into action with the exhortation: 'Communist functionaries and activists, Jews, Gypsies, Saboteurs and Agents must be regarded as persons who, by their very existence, endanger the security of the troops and are therefore to be executed without further ado.' So close behind frontline combat units were some of these Einsatzkommandos, that they often entered captured enemy towns and villages at the same time as German military units, and set about their grisly work almost immediately.

At first many Jews, still woefully unaware of the true nature of Nazi policy towards them, saw the invading Germans as liberators who had driven off the hated communists. The Einsatzkommandos were quick to disabuse them of this illusion, and rapidly adapted to using deceit as well as brute force in their determination to destroy the Jews. For example, Einsatzgruppe C, on entering Minsk, posted notices instructing the Jewish community to report for resettlement to a new location. Some 30,000 unsuspecting civilians turned up and were promptly taken away and executed.

By the first winter of the war in the Soviet Union, almost half a million Jews had been murdered by the Einsatzgruppen. Einsatzgruppe A alone had murdered almost a quarter of a million, B some 45,500, C 95,000 and D 92,000. Behind the Einsatzkommandos came police and auxiliary volunteers from the occupied territories to deal with any stragglers the Einsatzkommandos had missed, and a grisly race ensued to see who could report the highest 'score' of executions.

Army and Waffen-SS combat units, who had in many cases been feted by the local populace as liberators, were soon dismayed to find that these once friendly locals often became willing helpers of the partisans, their friendly feelings turned to hatred by the abominable behaviour of the Einsatzkommandos.

So abhorrent was the behaviour of these men that the murderers themselves began to suffer nervous breakdowns, as their minds rebelled at the enormity of their crimes. Several committed suicide, and many could only operate when their senses had been dulled by drink. Himmler's response was merely to exhort his men to be hard and to steel themselves to fulfil their heavy task.

The war against the partisans

Einsatzgruppen also became involved in the war against the partisans, Himmler being pleased to be able to disguise the real nature of these troops behind the excuse that they were carrying out essential work to secure the rear areas against partisan attacks. However, matters became so bad that even the gauleiter began to complain of their excesses. No Jew was spared by the Einsatzkommandos, even those who had skills which were essential to Germany's war effort. As a result, the economies of the occupied areas were affected. At one point even the known anti-semitic gauleiter of Belorussia, Wilhelm Kube, rebelled at the prospect of German Jews being deported from the Reich into his area for execution. Kube apparently had no qualms about the mass murder of Russian Jews, but the prospect of German Jews, some of whom had served in the German Army in World War I and had been decorated, being murdered in his territory was too much for him, and he took these German Jews under his personal protection. Kube was not alone in this, and several other gauleiter began to intervene to save 'their' Jews. Kube even leaked information about intended SD

raids on Jewish areas to allow the intended victims to escape.

Unfortunately for the Jews, and much to Himmler's delight, Kube was killed by a bomb planted by his Russian housemaid, who was an agent of the partisans. By then, however, the activities of the mobile Einsatzgruppen were beginning to run down as the principal implementation of the so-called 'final solution of the Jewish question' was transferred from them to the static death factories that were the concentration camps.

Einsatzgruppen uniforms

It is interesting to note that although the personnel of Himmler's death squads were entitled Einsatzgruppen der Sicherheitspolizei und des SD, it is estimated that as little as three per cent of the personnel were actually SD men. In order to distinguish the men of the Einsatzkommandos from other military and police units, they were ordered to wear the field-grey service dress of the SD. In fact, some 35 per cent were SS, 20 per cent Polizei, 10 per cent Gestapo and five per cent Kripo. There was even a small number of Army personnel, presumably serving in an administrative function. It must be said, however, that close examination of the few photographs which survive showing the Einsatzkommandos at work, show men wearing what appears to be Army insignia participating in the executions. Thus, Army personnel may also have been deeply implicated in the murders.

Among the range of other functions which came under the auspices of Heydrich's RSHA was the provision of Gestapo personnel, during the early months of the war at least, to supplement the border control units of the Zollgrenzdienst (Customs Service). These Gestapo personnel wore field-grey dress and were distinguished by a cuffband bearing the title *Grenz Polizei*. They were presumably used to help secure Germany's eastern borders, but had been disbanded by late 1941.

Another of Heydrich's smaller units was the Stab RFSS Kriminal Kommando. This select unit, under the control of the Sicherheitspolizei, provided personal bodyguards for senior Nazi personalities, including Hitler himself. Hitler's bodyguard unit, the *Leibstandarte SS Adolf Hitler*, had become a frontline unit, and so the day-to-day security of Hitler and his staff fell to the RSHA, although a number of the bodyguard personnel were on

'The moment one Jew had been killed, the marksman would walk across the bodies of the executed Jews to the next Jew, who had meanwhile lain down, and shoot him.... The children were kept with their mothers and shot with them.'
– Witness testimony to the Babi Yar massacre, Ukraine, 1941

attachment from the *Leibstandarte*. Hitler's personal safety was the responsibility of SS-Brigadeführer Hans Rattenhuber, who remained in the bunker with Hitler until the latter's death, after which men of Rattenhuber's Kommando were responsible for the attempted incineration of Hitler's corpse.

Hitler's security when travelling to various headquarters locations, when making public appearances, and on any occasion when it was felt that a potential risk to his safety might occur, was the responsibility of the *Führer-Begleitkommando*, whose numbers also included some members of the *Leibstandarte* on attachment.

Although Hitler retained a retinue of loyal SS guards until the end of his life, the day-to-day responsibility for guarding his headquarters and escorting his movements eventually passed to the *Führer-Begleitbrigade*, an elite Army unit, which, like the *Leibstandarte*, grew to become a full-blown frontline combat division.

The Gestapo

The Geheime Staatspolizei (Gestapo) was one of the most infamous police organisations in the 1930s and 1940s. The leather-overcoated figure beloved of post-war satire and television comedy shows was far from being a humorous figure in Germany or the occupied countries during the period of the Third Reich.

As originally formed, the Gestapo represented the Secret State Police of Prussia only. Formed by Hermann Göring and based in Berlin, the Gestapo passed through a phase of being a severe thorn in the flesh of the SS. Under one of its early commanders, Arthur Nebe, Gestapo agents had arrested SS men who had exceeded their authority on a number of occasions. The Gestapo was eventually brought to heel under the command of the man whose name has become synonymous with that of the Gestapo itself, SS-Gruppenführer Heinrich Müller, popularly known as 'Gestapo Müller', who became an enthusiastic pursuer of the perceived enemies of the Third Reich.

The task of the Gestapo was to track down subversive elements, and it had little or nothing to do with the fight against 'ordinary' crime, this being the province of the Kripo and Orpo.

After a brief period when the two main security organs of the state were in conflict with one another, the Gestapo came to work very closely with the SD. The SD would be principally involved in

gathering information on subversives, while the Gestapo was responsible for the actual arrests. Low-level Gestapo officers could use powers of preventative arrest of up to seven days, while the Geheime Staatspolizei Amt (Gestapa) could order the detention of its victims in the concentration camps indefinitely.

As with most security organs, its functionaries ranged from academics who preferred to use their often considerable powers of guile and persuasion, along with psychological techniques, to obtain information and confessions, to the brutal thugs who were more than happy to use almost medieval torture methods. Some of the more prominent members of German society who fell into the clutches of the Gestapo were fortunate enough to be interrogated by the former, while many other victims were left to the thugs.

The Gestapo was also widely represented in the occupied zones, France alone having a major Gestapo HQ, in Paris, and 17 other regional offices, which were involved in tracking down personnel of the Resistance and members of the Jewish community. A Gestapo representative was also posted to each concentration camp.

The Kriminal Polizei

The Kriminal Polizei (Kripo) was made up of Germany's professional career detectives. They wore civilian clothes and were primarily involved in the investigation of serious crimes, such as murder, rape and arson. They were not an overtly political force like the Gestapo, but there were inevitably cases where investigations by either force would overlap. There was also a good deal of movement between the two, with Kripo officers serving on secondment to the Gestapo, on transfer, or merely assisting with Gestapo investigations.

Obviously, during wartime the potential for serious crime increases, with blackout conditions and bomb damage providing the criminal element in society with cover for its activities. In particular, of course, in any wartime economy theft, to supply the inevitable black market, increases dramatically. The Kripo was therefore kept busy during the wartime years, but these policemen had no great impact on the lives of the average law-abiding German citizen, certainly no more than they had had in peacetime. It is probable, however, in the paranoid atmosphere of wartime Germany, any plain clothes policeman was likely to arouse fear, as they would almost certainly be assumed to

'Göring considered neither the Munich philistines nor Göbbels sufficiently aristocratic for him and therefore avoided all social relations with them; whereas Himmler, filled with the elitist missionary zeal of the SS felt far superior to all the others.'
– Albert Speer, *Inside the Third Reich*, 1970

be Gestapo, and treated with the same fear and loathing that the latter organisation engendered.

Wirtschafts-und Verwaltungshauptamt

This branch, the SS Economics and Administrative Department (WVHA), was formed in March 1942 under the command of SS-Obergruppenführer Oswald Pohl. It eventually developed five main sections:

Amt A – Finance, Law and Administration, under SS-Brigadeführer Fanslau.
Amt B – Supply, Administration and Equipment, under SS-Gruppenführer Lorner.
Amt C – Works and Buildings, under SS-Gruppenführer Kammler.
Amt D – Concentration Camps, under SS-Gruppenführer Glucks.
Amt W – Economics

The WVHA was responsible for the control of the above five aspects of the Allgemeine-SS. In effect, however, by the time war broke out the Allgemeine-SS was already fading in significance next to the meteoric growth of the SS-Verfügungstruppe and then Waffen-SS. The administration of the Waffen-SS divisions alone was a huge undertaking. In addition, all the SS-Totenkopfverbände, including the concentration camps, were administered by the WVHA, though the SS-Totenkopfverbände were effectively made part of the Waffen-SS from as early as 1941 to simplify administration and supply matters. In early 1944, when the Administrative Command of the Ordnungspolizei was put out of action by Allied bombing, the WVHA took over responsibility for its administration also.

The financing of the Waffen-SS as a whole was complicated by the fact that it was considered to be an organ of the state, and was thus funded by the Reichs Finance Ministry, which exercised control over its budget. The Allgemeine-SS, however, was deemed an organ of the NSDAP and was administered by Party Treasurer Franz Xaver Schwarz, who was much more liberal with its funding.

Thus, the unlikely situation arose whereby the Waffen-SS divisions engaged fighting at the front, had their budgets strictly controlled, while the Allgemeine-SS, whose significance to the war effort was much less, experienced no real financial restrictions.

The WVHA ran its own SS-Verwaltungsschule to train its own administrative staff, and it was responsible for maintaining its own supply system in conjunction with the SS-Führungshauptamt (operational HQ of the whole SS). The FHA was responsible for the procurement of arms and ammunition, and the WVHA for rations, uniforms and personal equipment.

Even before the outbreak of war, the SS had begun to dabble in economic ventures. These had initially been on a relatively small scale such, as the Allach porcelain factory or the Apolenaris mineral water plant. However, as the armies of the Third Reich began their conquest of Europe, Himmler found himself with not only a wide range of economic enterprises ripe for plunder, but an almost limitless supply of slave labour from the subjugated populations of the occupied countries.

The interest of the SS was by no means limited to ventures concerned with

BELOW: Members of a police regiment in Russia. Formed mostly for anti-partisan duties and the murder of Jews and political prisoners, they were composed of men over 45 years of age, youths of pre-draft age and wounded war veterans no longer fit for frontline duties. Himmler also created a number of auxiliary police troops from 'savage peoples' – Latvians, Lithuanians, Estonians and Poles – for rounding up Jews in the occupied territories. The men below, unusually, are wearing combat decorations.

the manufacturing of goods important to the war effort. Concerns as varied as farming, forestry and fish farms all fell under the control of the SS in Himmler's lust for power. This does not mean, however, that the average German citizen was necessarily aware of the growing influence of the SS on economic life. In fact, the SS often went to great pains to conceal its ownership of certain businesses, in view of the Party hierarchy's unease at the ever-expanding power and influence of the SS, as Himmler's economics office continued its plunder of the occupied areas.

In Germany itself, SS control of manufacturing concerns expanded rapidly. By 1945, over 500 different businesses were

BELOW RIGHT: A recruiting poster for the 12th SS Panzer Division Hitlerjugend. Hitler, and the SS, were keen to inculcate Germany's youth with the ideas of National Socialism. If the performance of the division was anything to go by, they succeeded. The Führer had no reservations about Germany's youth, declaring to Himmler: 'the youngsters who come from the Hitler Youth are fanatical fighters...These young German lads, some only sixteen years old, fight more fanatically than their older comrades.'

controlled by the SS, including the majority of the German soft drinks industry. At least one of today's most popular soft drinks was a thriving concern in Germany during the period of the Third Reich!

The Allach porcelain factory

The acquisition of the porcelain factory at Allach, near Munich, is one of the most interesting examples of the forays made by the SS into the world of commerce and the arts. This factory was first established as a small private concern in 1935. Himmler's staff, knowing his infatuation with Aryan mysticism and his intention of enforcing his own particular brand of Germanic culture on the nation, saw the acquisition of a porcelain factory as an astute move. Rightly so, as Germany was world famous for the quality of its fine porcelain. The factories at Meissen and Dresden had classic reputations for the quality of their work. With its own factory, the SS could produce works in keeping with its own particular concept of what constituted Germanic art. Perhaps surprisingly, in view of the somewhat garish nature of some Nazi 'art', the work produced by the Allach factory was indeed of the finest quality. Delicately executed, beautifully detailed and magnificently glazed, Allach porcelain can stand comparison with some of the world's best.

Himmler's personal staff, the Stab-RFSS, contained a section dealing with artistic and architectural matters. Headed by SS-Obersturmbannführer Professor Diebitsch, himself an artist of some repute, it was this section which, in 1936, acquired the Allach factory.

Dachau inmates at the factory

Almost immediately, the SS scoured Germany for artists of the highest calibre to work at Allach. Few would be foolish enough to refuse the 'invitation' to work for the Reichsführer-SS, and soon master craftsmen such as Professor Theodor Karner and Professor Fichter of the State Porcelain Works at Dresden were producing work for the Allach concern. SS-Obersturmbannführer Professor Diebitsch also became involved, producing work himself and acting as factory manager.

The factory, as well as producing the finest of porcelain artwork, also produced more mundane, basic products, such as ceramic crockery. As production increased, the Allach concern soon outgrew its small factory location. It was therefore decided to move production to a new temporary

facility at Dachau, near to the concentration camp. In fact, some of the inmates were used as labour at the new plant. Nothing seems to have been recorded of the conditions under which they worked, but although undoubtedly harsh, they would presumably have been better than those in the camp itself.

While production continued at Dachau, the original plant was enlarged and improved, and in 1940 ceramic production returned to Allach, with fine porcelain manufacture remaining at Dachau. It was, in fact, intended that all production plants be greatly extended, with special showrooms being opened in Berlin and other major cities. The war, however, put paid to such grandiose plans.

Both Hitler and Himmler took a great personal interest in the Allach plant, a large percentage of the output of the porcelain factory being reserved for the Stab-RFSS. These were in the main used by the Reichsführer-SS as personal presentation pieces for leading dignitaries and for rewarding deserving SS officers and men. For example, SS-Sturmbannführer Willi Kment was presented with the rare and superbly executed 'Swordsman' for his efficiency in carrying out his duties as an officer on Himmler's personal staff.

Although the majority of Allach pieces were white-glazed, a proportion were painted, being intended for public consumption. Painted pieces were exquisitely executed but somehow seem to lack the simple beauty of the white pieces.

Of all the paraphernalia of Hitler's Third Reich still in existence, SS Allach porcelain is among the most sought after, and original undamaged examples now fetch extremely high prices. Although some Allach pieces, such as the mounted SS officer or SS standard bearer figures, are obviously of Nazi origin, the majority of production has no such political imagery. Figures in national dress, such as traditional Bavarian farmers, were produced alongside superb historical figures like the mounted figure of Frederick the Great, and delicate wildlife pieces ranging from 'Scottie' Dogs to 'Bambi'-type young deer. These figures are identifiable as coming from the Allach factory by the unique Allach trademark on their base, with the interlinked SS Sig-runes being the only clue to the sinister past of this magnificent German porcelain.

Slave labour deaths

Himmler was aware of the value of the inmate labour of the concentration camps to his economics empire, and he instructed the sifting out of those inmates whose skills might prove useful to the WVHA, and even ordered that they be given slightly better treatment and rations. How much effect was given to his orders is debatable, as around 500,000 slave labourers are estimated to have died from ill-treatment.

In the concentration camps Himmler had access to a vast range of skills and a large army of slave labour. In some cases the entire cycle, from raw material, through manufacture, distribution and ultimate consumption, was under the control of the SS in some way or other. This

did not go unnoticed, though, and many senior Party functionaries sought to inhibit such expansion. However, when the government introduced restrictions on who might be permitted to own a particular concern in order to prevent an SS takeover, Pohl simply set up a holding company as a cover, and many firms whose owners appeared to be ordinary German businessmen or industrialists were actually owned by those who held SS rank.

When war broke out in September 1939, there were four main economic concerns controlled by the SS: Deutsche Erd & Steinwerke GmbH, which owned some 14 stone works and quarries; Deutsche Ausrüstungswerke, which owned all plant and machinery within the concentration camp; Deutsche Versuchsanstalt für Ernährung und Verpflegung, which studied food and nutritional research, one of Himmler's personal obsessions; and the Gesellschaft für Textil und Lederverwertung, which used inmate labour to rework worn uniforms and equipment for reissue to the military.

The wartime structure of the WVHA was controlled by many who were neither Nazis nor even particularly interested in the tenets of National Socialism, or Himmler's racial theories. Such a man was Dr Hans Hohberg, who was in charge of Amtsgruppe W but was not a member of either the Nazi Party or the SS. He was purely and simply a capitalist exploiter who was happy to use the opportunities offered to him by his SS employment to further his own ends.

Within his Amtsgruppe W were the following sub-divisions:

Amt I – Excavations and Quarries

Deutsche Erd und Steinwerke GmbH, under SS-Obersturm bannführer Mummenthey. This branch covered the following production:

Amt I(i) – Brickworks. The concentration camps situated at Buchenwald, Neuengamme, Sachsenhausen and Stutthof all produced bricks.

Amt I (ii) – Quarries. Granite was quarried at the camps at Gross-Rosen, Mauthausen and Natzweiler, which later also controlled an oil shale distillery. Stone was quarried at Rotau and Linz.

Amt I (iii) – Porcelain and Pottery. The best known of these factories was the famous Allach concern, though there were others in the protectorate of Bohemia-Moravia.

'Most of you must know what it means when one hundred corpses are lying side by side, or five hundred, or one thousand. To have stuck it out and at the same time – apart from exceptions caused by human weakness – to have remained decent fellows, that is what has made us hard.'
– Himmler, speech to SS officers, Poznan, 1943

> 'One basic principle must be the absolute rule for the SS men. We must be honest, decent, loyal, and comradely to members of our own blood and to nobody else. What happens to a Russian, to a Czech, does not interest me in the slightest.'
> – Himmler, speech to SS officers, Poznan, 1943

Amt II – Building Materials

Baustoffswerke und Zementfabriken, under SS-Obersturmbannführer Bobermin.

Amt II (i) – Building Materials: at Posen, Bielitz and Zichenau.

Amt II (ii) – Cement. The concentration camp at Auschwitz was the greatest provider of labour for the manufacture of cement at the Golleschau factory.

Amt II (iii) – East. A considerable number of Soviet businesses were absorbed in their entirety by the SS after the invasion of the Soviet Union and were controlled by this office.

Amt III – The Food Industry

Amt III (i) – Mineral Waters. The Sudetenquell, Mattoni and Apollinaris mineral water firms, together with a bottling plant, Rheinglassfabrik, were among the firms controlled by the SS.

Amt III (ii) – Meat. Auschwitz, Dachau and Sachsenhausen concentration camps carried out meat processing operations.

Amt III (iv) – Bread. Auschwitz, Dachau, Herzogenbosch, Lublin, Plasnow and Sachsenhausen camps operated busy bakeries.

Amt IV – German Equipment

Amt IV (i) – Military. The SS had two main functions in the manufacture of military equipment. First, it owned its own factories manufacturing small arms, repairing weapons and equipment and processing scrap. Most of these concerns were based at camps like Auschwitz, Neuengamme, Dachau and Sachsenhausen. In addition, the SS provided inmate labour on a contract basis to assist in the manufacture of components for firms such as Messerschmitt, Heinkel and Junkers.

Amt IV (ii) – Carpentry. Vast quantities of wooden furniture for both military and, to some extent, civilian use were produced at most camps.

Amt IV (iii) – Clothing. A number of Bekleidungswerke were established at camps producing uniforms for both the police and SS. Some insignia was also produced. The central SS clothing and insignia depot was at Dachau. A smaller amount of woven equipment, such as webbing, belts and straps, was also produced on contract for the Wehrmacht.

Amt V – Land, Forestry and Fisheries

Amt V (i) – Food and Nutrition. As well as his racial theories, Himmler was known to have had a great interest in 'alternative medicine', such as herbal remedies. At a number of concentration camps, therefore, he ordered herbs and spices to be grown in special garden areas. This office was also involved in breeding animals for laboratory tests.

Amt V (ii) – Forestry. This office controlled the administration of forests on land owned by the SS.

Amt V (iii) – Fisheries. The SS also owned a minor fish-processing operation under the guise of a private limited company.

Amt VI – Textil und Lederverwertung

This branch dealt with the reworking of uniforms, leather belts, straps and boots by inmate labour at the Dachau and Ravensbruck camps.

Amt VII – Bücher und Bilder

Amt VII (i) – This office ran a publishing house entitled Nordland-Verlag, which produced books and magazines dealing in the main with Germanic culture and history.

Amt VII (ii) – An SS-run art restoration company operating under the title of Bauer und Cie which carried out work for a number of European art collections, and also helped to acquire art works used to decorate Himmler's castle at Wewelsburg.

Amt VIII Kulturbauten

Amt VIII (i) – This section was responsible for the maintenance of historical monuments and buildings, and was also responsible for the Damascus Blade facility set up under master craftsman Paul Müller at Dachau.

Amt VIII (ii) – Himmler's infatuation with King Heinrich I (Henry the Fowler) was reflected in the special section founded to control the King Heinrich Memorial Trust.

Himmler was fascinated by Germanic mythology: virtually all SS insignia was based on ancient German symbols. The Reichsführer's castle at Wewelsburg was a shrine to Nordic mythology, and even included an Arthurian-style round table at which his trusted 'Knights' were to sit.

Not surprisingly, swords and daggers were important aspects of this symbolism. Indeed, the SS was among the first organisations to receive its own dagger when, in 1933, a stylish weapon with a wide, spear-point blade bearing the SS motto *Meine Ehre Heisst Treue* and a black scabbard and handle was introduced. This design was based on the so-called Holbein Dagger, which had an almost identical shape and proportions. The Holbein Dagger, an artwork of great age, was so named because of the rendering of Holbein's painting 'The Dance of Death' on its scabbard, the artist being the court painter to King Henry VIII of England. In 1936, the dagger was followed by a special SS sword based on the model carried by the police. This attractive straight-bladed sword featured a large set of SS runes on its black wooden grip.

Edged weapons manufacture was highly important to the German economy, and the explosion in output of blade manufacture helped in a considerable way to lift the German cutlery industry out of recession. The presentation of edged weapons (swords, dagger, bayonets, etc.) with inscribed blades had long been a way of expressing gratitude or appreciation, and the Nazi leadership, Himmler in particular, continued with this tradition. Before long, special presentation versions of the SS dagger and sword were being produced. Initially these consisted of merely an additional etching to the reverse face of the blade, celebrating a special event, or in some cases a personal dedication, such as those given by Himmler himself, which bore the legend *In herzlichen Kameradschaft H Himmler*. Soon, however, beautifully hand-crafted Damascus blades with gilded inscriptions were also produced.

Damascus blades

Damascus blades had been very popular since the eighteenth century. Extremely beautiful, they were also very expensive and labour-intensive to manufacture. Costing as much as 25 to 30 times the price of a standard blade, few could afford them. Damascus blades were truly a labour of love, and by the 1930s had become a dying art since modern methods of artificially reproducing the Damascus effect by acid etching had been introduced, which reduced costs. Probably only half a dozen swordsmiths in all Germany were capable of producing true Damascus blades. All were superb craftsmen, but first among equals was Paul Müller.

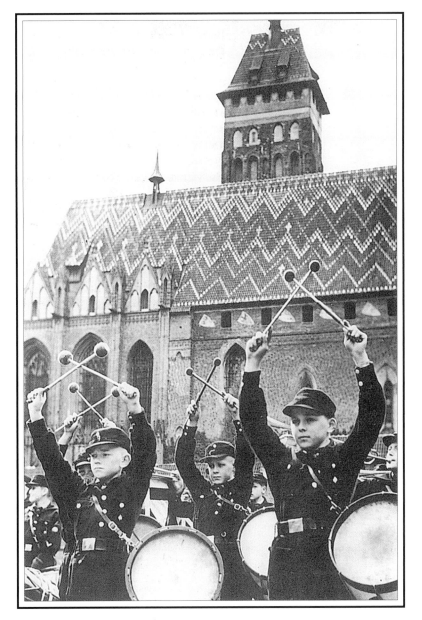

Himmler was determined that this great skill should not be allowed to die out, and so Müller was contracted to set up a Damascus blade school at Dachau on highly favourable terms. From 1939 onwards, with a team of 10 apprentices, he began to produce special presentation swords and daggers to be used as gifts from the Reichsführer-SS to particular dignitaries or deserving soldiers of the SS.

In the Damascus process, several hundred thin layers of steel of differing grades were beaten together and, when the white-hot blade was immersed in oil, a beautiful pattern would appear on the blade. It was an extremely time-consuming process requiring the highest level of skills, not unlike the great Japanese craftsmen who produced the world-famous Katana swords for the Samurai warriors.

The serving officers of the *Leibstandarte SS Adolf Hitler* commissioned a

ABOVE: The Nazis indoctrinated German youths from a very early age. For young boys between the ages of 10 and 14 the Party established the Jungvolk, and for girls the same age the Jungmädel. A boy entering the Jungvolk had to undergo an initiation test, which involved reciting the Horst Wessel song, running 50 metres in 12 seconds and learning weapons drill. The next step was the Hitler Youth, which was compulsory for boys aged between 15 and 18.

special presentation sword for their commander, Josef 'Sepp' Dietrich, with its Damascus blade bearing all of their names. Hitler presented special commemorative swords to his SS officers who were part of the honour guard to welcome the Duke of Windsor to his mountain retreat at Berchtsegaden in 1936. The blades bore the legend *Obersaltzberg 1936*, testimony to the high regard Hitler had for the Duke, 'The man with whom I could have made my treaty of friendship with England', as he later remarked.

Müller and his small team were kept busy fulfilling orders. However, wartime demands on manpower saw his group of apprentices being called up for military service one by one, until only Müller himself remained, and for the last two years of the war he worked virtually alone. He survived the war and continued to make Damascus blades until a few months before his death in 1971. Before he died, he in turn passed on his skills to master craftsman Robert Kürten.

The organisation of slave labour

As already mentioned, in many cases the businesses controlled by the SS were held in the names of private individuals or various holding companies to disguise the fact of their SS ownership. For all intents and purposes, therefore, in the eyes of the public, the government, and often even the workforce, these were private companies unconnected with the SS. However, in many cases these firms represented little more than a new avenue to financial profit and empire-building by the SS.

When Amtsgruppe W (Industrial Directorate) of the WVHA is considered along with Amtsgruppe D (the concentration camps), the full extent of the SS economic empire becomes apparent.

The huge pool of manpower held in the 25 or so 'official' concentration camps and numerous other labour camps was so brutalised and cowed into submission that only a very small guard element was required to run each camp, in comparison to the huge numbers of inmates. Habitual criminals incarcerated in these camps, who were often as brutal as the guards themselves, were utilised as 'trustees', and they ruled the other prisoners with an iron fist.

The average concentration camp inmate with sufficient useful skills to allow his survival of the initial 'selection' process, through which each new arrival at the camps passed, was required to work each day regardless of the weather, often

in the most appalling conditions. In view of the disease-ridden environment in which they were kept, the totally inadequate rations, and the brutality with which they were treated, it is not surprising that the mortality rate was extremely high. This was of little concern to Oswald Pohl, however, as the supply of replacements seemed virtually inexhaustible (after the war Pohl was sentenced to death in 1947, though four years were spent in appeals and debate before he was hanged at Landsberg prison in 1951).

Amtsgruppe C

Kammler's Amtsgruppe C also used some 175,000 camp inmates as slave labour on his construction projects. In many cases these workers were utilising raw materials excavated by their fellow inmates in the camp quarries at little or no cost to the SS, but at a huge cost in human lives. Kammler was not a career SS officer, but a former civil servant who had been persuaded by Himmler to accept SS rank and take over this particular part of its economics branch. Kammler saw in this move almost unlimited prospects for advancing his own power and influence. His only loyalty was to his personal ambition, and he undertook an extensive construction programme building factories, underground workshops, and even became involved in the V2 rocket programme. Kammler, an SS-Gruppenführer by 1944, cared little how many lives were sacrificed on the altar of his ambition. By the end of the war he had progressed from being a minor civil servant to a senior SS officer responsible to Hitler personally, all at the cost of countless lives of slave labourers supplied willingly by Amtsgruppe D.

Hauptamt Ordnungspolizei

The history and fortunes of the uniformed police, usually referred to as the Order Police, or Ordnungspolizei (Orpo), was inextricably linked with that of the SS once Himmler had successfully intrigued his way into being nominated to the post of Head of the German Police – Chef der deutschen Polizei.

The vast bulk of the German police were professional, career policemen who had been just as likely to arrest Nazi miscreants as those opposed to Hitler. Indeed, the police had given Himmler a few headaches before he took over the reins of power in 1936. Himmler had appointed the former Berlin SS chief Kurt Daluege to command the Orpo as a separate SS-

'The battalion commander gave orders not to take Russians under a thousand men prisoners. When it happened once that they had a batch under seven hundred he volunteered for the job because he got cigarettes and schnapps for it. The Russians were led to a sand-pit, shot at with machine guns and covered with earth.'
– Information about SS unit on Eastern Front, British report, 1945

Hauptamt, and Daluege made every effort to eject any politically unreliable elements from the police.

Once Daluege had purged the police of any personnel unsympathetic to the Nazi cause, he discovered that in doing so he had thereby lost a vast pool of professional police expertise which left the police greatly emasculated. The Hauptamt Orpo was obliged to sanction the re-employment of many of those it had dismissed, but only after they had undergone a period of 're-education'. There is no doubt, however, that a fair percentage of the police remained ambivalent in their attitude towards the Nazis.

Daluege further sought to politicise the police by urging members of the Allgemeine-SS to seek a career in the Ordnungspolizei. This certainly had the effect of bringing in a considerable inflow of younger, more politically indoctrinated personnel. Older, experienced policemen often found themselves working alongside young, brash Nazi fanatics who were encouraged to keep their eyes open for any signs of political unreliability in their older colleagues, and the inevitable mutual mistrust resulted.

As more and more younger Nazi sympathisers joined the police, its fanatical adherence to the Nazi cause grew. When war broke out, however, a large number of these younger policemen found themselves called up for military service. Thus, police duties on the home front once again reverted, in the main, to the older career policemen, many of whom were the very types Himmler wished to lose.

The police regiments
Between 1940 and 1942, some 30 or so polizei regiments were created. These regiments, formed along military lines, were split into 500-strong battalions and equipped with light infantry weapons. They were used primarily in anti-partisan duties in the occupied territories, although polizei units did collide on occasion with frontline enemy combat units. One example of this was the battle for Cholm in Russia, in which polizei troops were among the German forces surrounded by vastly superior Soviet forces. A special award, the Cholm Shield, was instituted on 1 July 1942 to recognise the steadfast defence of the area by Army and polizei units between January and May 1942.

Some, but not all, of the soldiers in these polizei regiments were SS or Party members who were fanatically loyal to

Himmler as titular head of the SS and police. They were occasionally used to assist the Einsatzgruppen in rounding up members of the Jewish populations of the occupied areas for deportation, and earned an unsavoury reputation for brutality.

By 1943, Daluege's Hauptamt Ordnungspolizei controlled not only the uniformed police, but also other subsidiary forces such as the Railway Police, Fire Brigades, Postal Protection Police and Technical Emergency Units. In addition, the SS gained control of all indigenous police forces in the occupied zones.

In February 1943, the polizei units were re-titled SS-Polizei Regiments to differentiate between German police units and those foreign auxiliary formations raised from among the local populace in areas occupied by the Germans.

Many of these communities were fervently anti-communist and were eager to come forward and offer their services to the Germans to defend their areas against Soviet partisan bands, which roamed behind the German lines. The numbers who came forward were quite astounding. From among the *Volksdeutsche* elements in Poland, some 12 polizei regiments were formed; in Estonia, 26 regiments. Latvia and Lithuania between them raised 64 battalions totalling around 28,000 men, and in the Ukraine an astonishing 70,000 volunteers came forward, sufficient to form 71 battalions. In the Balkans the Croats produced some 15,000 volunteers, the Serbs some 10,000, and even Albania was

ABOVE: Fritz Witt (left), the man who commanded the Hitlerjugend division in Normandy in 1944. The division, and the Hitler Youth units that defended Berlin in 1945, fought with a bravery bordering on the insane. They were the flower of the Nazi Party, believing themselves superior. This is not really surprising, given the indoctrination they had received. An example of this was provided by Himmler in 1936, when he addressed a meeting of the Hitler Youth thus: 'The German people, especially German youth, have learned once again to value people racially – they have turned away once again from the Christian theory, from the Christian teaching which ruled Germany for more than a thousand years and caused the racial decay of the German Volk, and almost caused its racial death.'

'My program for educating youth is hard. Weakness must be hammered away. In my castles of the Teutonic Order a youth will grow up before which the world will tremble. I want a brutal, domineering, fearless, cruel youth.'

– Hitler, speech, 1943

able to produce sufficient volunteers to form two police battalions.

The behaviour of some of these auxiliary police units against their own countrymen equalled, and in some cases exceeded, the worst excesses of the Einsatzgruppen. For example, when the German Army moved through Poland, the *Volksdeutsche* population formed its own self-defence militia (selbstschutz) – claims of pre-war Polish atrocities against the ethnic German population were by no means all Nazi propaganda, many had actually happened. The Army initially undertook the training and equipping of these units, but Hitler ordered their reorganisation under the control of the Hauptamt Orpo. Many of these *Volksdeutsche* were fanatical Nazis who were eager to settle old scores with the Poles who had mistreated them. These units were often only too willing to help the Einsatzkommandos in their grisly tasks. So bad was their behaviour that at least one gauleiter requested their disbandment once a civil administration had been formed.

Similar events occurred when the Germans invaded the Soviet Union. The Army set up auxiliary volunteer units, only to have them poached by the Einsatzgruppen in the rear. In November 1941, Himmler ordered that all auxiliary units be formed into police units named schutzmannschaften. The reorganisation was somewhat patchy, however: some units remained with the Ordnungspolizei while others came under direct SS control. The performance of these units was variable. They were certainly effective at instilling fear into the civil populace, but their performance was less impressive against tough Soviet partisan units.

The Hitler Youth

Although compulsory service in the Hitler Jugend (HJ) had been introduced some six months before the outbreak of war for all male 17 year olds, it was not until September 1941 that membership of the Nazi youth organisations became obligatory for both sexes, from 10 years of age upwards. The SS took a great interest in the HJ, seeing it as an opportunity to groom the best of German youth for eventual membership of the SS.

The Hitler Youth had in fact introduced its own elite formation, the HJ Streifendienst, or Hitler Youth Patrol Service, which was responsible for policing HJ meetings and rallies in the same way the SS did for the NSDAP. These youths

were even issued with a unit cuffband very similar in style to those worn in the SS; indeed, by late 1938 the training and equipping of this unit was in the hands of the SS. These boys were heavily indoctrinated in the right-wing, anti-semitic, elitist tenets of National Socialism, and many of them may well have had eventual membership of the SS in mind.

Both the Army and Waffen-SS were involved in the preparatory military training of the HJ, which included three-week training courses in special camps established throughout Germany. On the completion of the course, SS recruiting agents often tried to persuade the boys to volunteer for the Waffen-SS, thus circumventing their almost certain induction into the Army on reaching the age of military service.

The *Hitlerjugend* Division

The SS was also involved with the HJ Landdienst, which trained selected youths to provide voluntary farming help in the eastern provinces, and ultimately to train as so-called Wehrbauern, very much fitting in with Himmler's dream of the occupied territories in the East being controlled and defended by Nordic peasant warriors. Suitable volunteers from the occupied 'Germanic' lands were also welcomed.

As the war progressed and military losses necessitated the lowering of the age for military service, more and more youths found themselves going directly from the HJ into the military. In 1943, the enticement of these youths into the SS reached its peak when Himmler and the Reichsjugendführer Artur Axmann determined between them to take full advantage of Hitler's agreement that volunteers as young as 17 years old, three years under the usual conscription age, could be accepted into the armed forces. It was decided that an entire Waffen-SS division should be formed from Hitler Jugend volunteers, and a camp was established at Beverloo in Belgium for this purpose.

Only the best candidates with a sufficient degree of National Socialist fervour and unswerving loyalty to Hitler were to be accepted. This was, from the earliest days, intended to be a truly elite unit, a fact accentuated by the transfer of a cadre from the *Leibstandarte SS Adolf Hitler* to form the core of the division. Some 1000 of the *Leibstandarte*'s best men were transferred to the new unit, ultimately to be entitled the 12th SS Panzer Division *Hitlerjugend*. A smaller number of experienced personnel from other SS divisions were also transferred to the new formation, as were a few Army officers, one of whom was Major Gerhard Hein, an Oakleaves winner with the Army's Jäger Regiment 209. Hein also held the position of HJ-Oberbannführer and commander of the HJ Wehrertüchtigungslagern, or military training camps.

The division saw service in the Normandy battles, earning a fearsome reputation for fanaticism and reckless bravery. By the time the division escaped through the Falaise Gap in August 1944, only 600 of its original strength remained. It was rebuilt and saw action in the Ardennes Offensive, in Hungary and in Austria. The young grenadiers of the *Hitlerjugend* Division displayed a suicidal contempt of danger, but it was to no avail – the almost total air superiority and overwhelming land strength of the Allies rendered their best efforts ineffectual.

The ideology of the Hitler Youth

In the closing stages of the war, the loss of almost every able-bodied man to the front left only the very young and the very old to serve in Germany's 'Home Guard', or Volkssturm, units. On the crumbling Eastern Front, HJ boys in their droves lost their lives in futile last-ditch attempts to halt the inexorable advance of the Red Army before the gates of Berlin. As with their only slightly older compatriots in the *Hitlerjugend* Division, the individual youths in the ad hoc Volkssturm units of the last few days of the war often performed feats of great gallantry (one of Hitler's last acts was to personally congratulate Hitler Youths fighting in the defence of the Reich's capital).

While vast numbers of the membership of the Hitler Jugend saw the organisation as little more than the equivalent of the Boy Scouts under a different name, and were aware of no great efforts to indoctrinate them (even some former battle-hardened Waffen-SS veterans fall into this category), there is no doubt many did fall under the influence of the worst of Nazi dogma, and became fanatical acolytes of Adolf Hitler.

In view of the short combat life of this division, it is certainly true that few lived long enough to become the cynical, worldly-wise pragmatists that many of their comrades in other Waffen-SS divisions had become. Such was their level of fanatical loyalty to the Führer and Fatherland, however, that they were willing to lay down their lives without hesitation, filled with pride at being soldiers of the Waffen-SS.

The Totenkopfverbände

By the outbreak of war in 1939, the Totenkopfverbände consisted of five regiments; Totenkopf Standarte I, *Oberbayern*, based at the original concentration camp at Dachau; Totenkopf Standarte II, *Brandenburg*, at Buchenwald; Totenkopf Standarte III, *Thuringen*, at Sachsenhausen; Totenkopf Standarte IV, *Ostmark*, at Mauthausen; and the newly formed Totenkopf Standarte V, *Dietrich Eckhardt*. These units were controlled by the SS-Totenkopfverbände Führungstab and were supported by medical, signals and transport elements.

In October 1939, the formation of the *Totenkopf* Division, with Theodor Eicke, the infamous former Inspector of Concentration Camps and SS Guard Units, as its commander, began at Dachau concentration camp, which had been temporarily cleared of its inmates for this purpose. From the first four Totenkopf regiments, plus a considerable number of police rein-

forcements, the *Totenkopf* Division and a number of Totenkopf infantry and cavalry units were formed.

Thereafter, the concentration camp guard elements were comprised of elderly reservists, unfit for frontline service, and young Totenkopf soldiers who had not yet reached the age of liability for conscription. These personnel were formed into Totenkopf Wachsturmbanne.

Normally, the concentration camp chain of command would commence with the kommandant, who usually held a field rank from SS-Sturmbannführer to SS-Standartenführer, and had responsibility for the efficient running of the camp. Day-

BELOW: The Hitler Youth was founded in 1926 as a branch of the Sturmabteilung, and by the end of 1934 had grown into a movement 3,500,000 strong.

'On 11 September 1944, in the presence of SS Sturmbannführer Dr. Ding, Dr. Widmann, and the undersigned, experiments with aconite nitrate bullets were carried out on five persons.... The calibre of the bullets used was 7.65 millimetres, and they were filled with poison in crystal form.'
– Report from the office of the Reich Surgeon of SS and Police, 1944

to-day responsibility, however, was usually delegated to his adjutant.

Next in line came the commander of the so-called 'Protective Custody Compound', the schutzhaftlagerführer, who would often share his office with the resident representative of the Gestapo. A senior NCO, often with the rank of SS-Hauptscharführer, would hold the post of rapportführer and be responsible for the regular thrice-daily roll calls. Thereafter, each block in the camp would be the responsibility of a more junior NCO, or blockführer. Within each block a trusted inmate was usually appointed as a supervisor, or kapo. These men tended to be from the criminal element in society, rather than political prisoners, Jews or other prisoners. In addition, many of the clerical or administrative positions in the camp would be held by prisoners with the requisite skills. The guards, under the command of their duty officer, were usually accommodated outside the camp itself.

The organisation of the camps

In April 1941, due to a major reorganisation to establish clearly which SS units came under the definition of Waffen-SS, the entire concentration camp guard system found itself included. The guards were issued with standard field-grey Waffen-SS uniforms, rank insignia and carried standard Waffen-SS paybooks. As part of the Waffen-SS, the camps came under the control of the SS-Führungshauptamt.

This situation continued until 1942, when the vast inflow of new inmates from the conquered territories in the East stretched both the accommodation and administration system to their limits.

As the camps were by now regularly supplying virtual slave labour for a number of SS-run and private industries, the administration of the camps was transferred to the WVHA as its Amtsgruppe D, subdivided into four principal sections: (i) Central Office, (ii) Inmate Labour, (iii) Medical and Hygiene, and (iv) Administration. Although the camps were now under the control of the WVHA, the responsibility for guarding the camps remained with the Wachsturmbanne.

The head of the WVHA, SS-Obergruppenführer Pohl, began to feel dismay at the conditions and high mortality rate in the camps. This was not through any humanitarian feelings on his part. He saw the inmates as a valuable labour force and knew that more effort could be extorted from them if they were kept under better conditions and fed better rations. His protests had little effect, however. The RSHA saw the camps as a method of disposing of the enemies of the Reich and little more. It had no interest whatsoever in the well-being of the inmates, especially the Jews. Quite the opposite, in fact. Heydrich went to great lengths to obstruct Pohl in his attempts to extend the 'working life' of the inmates, especially the Jews.

Expansion of the camps

The number of concentration camps expanded rapidly between 1941 and 1944, until there were well over 20 official camps, plus over 150 forced labour camps. The first concentration camp, Dachau, had opened in March 1933, the last, at Mittelbau in October 1944.

From the earliest days of the concentration camp system, the treatment meted out to the inmates had been harsh in the extreme. In fact, the first kommandant at Dachau, SS-Oberführer Hilmar Wäckerle, had been charged as an accessory to the murder of several inmates, the attendant adverse publicity infuriating Himmler.

Although the level of violence and brutality common under Wäckerle did moderate a little under Eicke, the improvement was marginal. It was claimed that punishment was only given when an inmate was found guilty of some offence, but in fact some of the offences were often imaginary and the punishments meted out were out of all proportion to the 'crime'. In the early days, however, some inmates did have at least a faint hope of eventual release. Some were given their freedom when, for instance, they were considered suitably 're-educated', or on some special occasion, such as Hitler's birthday, when an amnesty might be declared for minor offenders. Before being released, however, inmates had to sign a declaration that they had been well treated and undertake not to discuss conditions within the camps.

Most of the original inmates of the concentration camps had been political enemies of the National Socialists, such as communists, socialists, pacifists and others. As time progressed, however, the majority of those committed to the camps were the victims of Hitler's racial persecution: Jews, Gypsies, Slavs and other unfortunates considered 'undesirable'.

As the Gestapo's Amt IVB4, under its 'Jewish Expert' Adolf Eichmann, scoured Europe for Jews to be deported for 're-settlement' in the East, the Einsatzkommandos roamed the conquered territories of eastern Europe attempting to outdo each other in their 'scores' of Jews liquidated, proudly reporting back to their master, Reinhard Heydrich, as each new area was declared 'Jew-Free'.

So vast were the numbers now involved that even the dedicated efforts of Heydrich's murder squads could not cope with the number of victims, despite the horrifying ingenuity of some of their methods. A number of new camps were established in Poland which were little more than death factories. At the so-called Vernichtungslagern at Belzec, Sobibor, Majdanek and Treblinka, for example, there was little real effort made to establish any sort of SS-controlled industrial processes, as the inmates were not intended to live long enough to produce any sort of goods.

At camps like Auschwitz, extermination facilities operated alongside industrial plants. Once the last ounce of strength had been squeezed out of inmates, they were eliminated, along with the sick and old. It is estimated that 80 per cent of those who entered Auschwitz perished there.

Camp guards and military service

As the younger Totenkopf guards reached the age of military service, they were called up for the Wehrmacht or volunteered for the Waffen-SS. They were then replaced by reservists, or those no longer fit for frontline service, and thus there was a continual rotation of personnel through the camps. In May 1944, Himmler ordered the transfer of some 10,000 reservists into the concentration camp guard units. Even Luftwaffe and Kriegsmarine personnel found themselves transformed into camp guards, as their respective branches of the German armed forces dwindled in military importance.

Often, fewer than 25 per cent of the camp guards at these establishments were actually German, the remainder comprising, in the main, auxiliary volunteers from the occupied territories, the Ukraine in particular. These auxiliaries were often as brutal as the SS guards, and many of the worst atrocities reported by survivors of the camps concern the actions of Ukrainian auxiliaries, who were noted for their virulent anti-semitism. In 1943, SS-Gruppenführer Odilo Globocnik gained Himmler's approval to raise a concentration camp guard unit from Russian volunteers. These men were trained at Trawniki, near Lublin, and gained a well-earned reputation for the most barbaric behaviour.

As well as being utilised as slave labour in the concentration camp industries, or being hired out to private concerns, those fit to work were also used in highly dangerous bomb disposal work, the clearing of bomb-damaged buildings and the repair of bomb-damaged railway tracks. The camps at Sachsenhausen, Neuengamme, Buchenwald and Auschwitz are known to have had such so-called Baubrigade at their locations.

Mention should also be made of the women overseers recruited to guard the female inmates in the concentration camps. Recruitment of these women began as early as 1937. They were trained at the women's camp at Ravensbruck and many gained reputations for brutality every bit as bad as some of the male guards.

ABOVE: His death's head badge clearly visible, an SS-Unterscharführer of a Totenkopf regiment, undoubtedly a former concentration camp guard, poses for the camera. The commandant of Auschwitz, Rudolf Höss, stated that Theodor Eicke, the head of the concentration camp guards, instilled into the guards 'a hate, an antipathy, against the prisoners which is inconceivable to those outside.'

HITLER'S FOREIGN LEGIONS

As the Third Reich overran much of Europe, the Waffen-SS formed numerous volunteer units from suitably 'Nordic' countries. At first recruitment was selective, but as the demands of war increased the SS was forced to create military formations from races that were decidedly non-Aryan.

During the early years of the SS, a constant struggle existed between the SS on the one hand, hungry for expansion, and the SA on the other, worried over the rising power and influence of Himmler's elite (see Chapter 1). As a result, the SA used every means at its disposal to hinder the expansion of its rival.

When war broke out in 1939 the SA was no longer a problem, but the SS now had a new opponent, one with much more power and influence than the SA. Himmler now faced competition from what was until then the sole legitimate bearer of arms in the defence of the nation: the Wehrmacht. Although the Wehrmacht, in terms of numbers, was vastly superior to the SS, the Oberkommando der Wehrmacht (High Command of the Armed Forces) greatly resented the expansion of the SS as a military force. It insisted that the number of recruits allowed into the SS be severely restricted. During peacetime the Wehrmacht accepted that SS men could consider their service in the SS as being in lieu of the usual two years of military service. However, in wartime it wanted priority when it came to recruits – the SS would come second. Hitler initially accepted the Wehrmacht's point of view, and the SS was restricted to a small percentage of the Army's peacetime strength. Of the total number of

*Dutch SS soldiers: members of the **Nederland** Division. The grimness in their faces is understandable: they are about to embark for the Eastern Front.*

ABOVE: Soldiers of the Nederland divison being inspected by SS-Gruppenführer Hans Albin Rauter, head of police and SS operations in the Netherlands. Gottlob Berger, in charge of SS foreign volunteer recruitment, admitted to Rauter that many of the Dutch volunteers had no moral integrity and some were even criminals. However he argued that many criminals could become very good soldiers, if properly led. He was proven right, the division fighting extremely well in the Soviet Union in 1942–43, before forming the core of the 4th SS Freiwilligen Panzer-grenadier Brigade in May 1943.

recruits taken into the Wehrmacht, for example, the Army claimed two thirds, with the remainder being split between the Navy and Air Force – the SS received its men from the Army's share.

In December 1939, a special SS recruiting office was set up in Berlin under the leadership of SS-Obergruppenführer Gottlob Berger, entitled Ergänzungsamt der Waffen-SS (Waffen-SS Recruiting Office). While it was accepted that recruitment of German nationals within the borders of Germany itself, the *Reichsdeutsche*, was heavily restricted, no such restraints were placed on the recruitment of ethnic Germans living outside Germany's borders, the so-called *Volksdeutsche*. These included such groups as the Sudeten Germans in Czechoslovakia, for example. Nor, indeed, was there any restriction on the recruitment of volunteers from those European countries where the population was accepted as being suitably 'Germanic' in its origins. Thus, as early as May 1940 there was already a small number of foreign volunteers, mostly Swiss, serving in the Waffen-SS.

As the campaign in the West proceeded, more of the so-called 'Germanic' nations fell under German dominance: Denmark, Holland, Norway and Flanders, all of which were to prove fertile recruiting grounds for Berger.

Hitler still hesitated to upset his Army generals by allowing a major expansion of the military SS, but he did give his permission for the establishment of a division of Germanic volunteers. In this way the elite *Wiking* Division was born, based around the Dutch/Flemish *Westland* Regiment and the Danish/Norwegian *Nordland* Regiment, and bolstered by the addition of the *Germania* Regiment, which had been drawn from the *SS-Verfügungsdivision*.

As an enticement, suitably Germanic recruits were offered German citizenship at the end of their terms of service if they volunteered. Himmler himself was very keen on the recruitment of Germanic volunteers, and is on record as saying: 'We must attract all the Nordic blood in the world to us, and so deprive our enemies of it, so that never again will Nordic or Germanic blood fight against us.'

In 1941, aware of the demands that the forthcoming attack on the Soviet Union would make on manpower, Himmler pushed recruiting harder, although he refused to lower the standards required of potential recruits. It was, after all, assumed that the campaign in the East would be a short one and the enemy quickly defeated. This over-optimistic view led to some ludicrous situations. In Belgium, for example, the Flemish population was considered Germanic and thus eligible to serve in the Waffen-SS, but the Walloons (who would prove themselves to be excellent Waffen-SS soldiers) were not considered to be of sufficiently Germanic blood and were thus rejected and passed to the Army. The luxury of such selectivity was not to last for long.

The first foreign SS recruits

In many of the occupied countries, indigenous fascist or neo-Nazi political organisations already existed. The DNSAP in Denmark, the VNV in Belgium, the NS in Norway and the NSB in Holland all leaned heavily towards the tenets of National Socialism. Most, however, were fervently nationalist in their own right and their members were not necessarily pro-German. Few were willing to join the Waffen-SS proper, and even fewer yearned for the 'prize' of German citizenship. The bulk of volunteers at this stage, therefore, were recruited on the basis of a two-year contract for service with the SS. They were not to be considered as SS members per se, merely attached to the organisation. Under international law they were required to wear German uniform, and were usually identified by an arm shield in their own national colours, together with a cuffband bearing their unit's name. Once the attack on the Soviet Union had got under way in June 1941, recruiting did pick up as volunteers answered the call to join Hitler's much publicised 'Crusade against Bolshevism' (aided by the fact that it did look as though the Red Army would crumble quickly).

Unfortunately for these idealistic recruits, they were in for a rude awakening when they reported for training at the various barracks in Germany. Few were accustomed to the rigid discipline, spartan conditions and hard training of the Waffen-SS. The tough SS training NCOs had little sympathy for the hurt feelings of their charges, and the usual training NCO bluster and bullying of recruits was liberally sprinkled with abuse concerning their nationality, which the recruits took to heart. The complaints about the treatment of the recruits by their German officers and NCOs even reached Himmler's ears. As a keen advocate of the recruitment of Germanic volunteers, he was enraged that his good work was being undone by the thoughtlessness of the training staff, and he saw to it that the culprits were dealt with. An increase in the number of suitable volunteer officers and NCOs alleviated the situation, and the more sympathetic handling of the recruits by both officers and NCOs of their own nationalities led to a marked improvement in morale.

BELOW: Recruits of the Freiwilligen Legion Niederlande on parade. Clearly visible, below the sleeve eagle, is the special arm shield in the Dutch colours of red, white and blue, and the cuffband bearing the unit title. Volunteers usually wore national arm shields on the left arm, though there are photographs showing them on the right arm.

BELOW: A young Flemish soldier of the Freiwilligen Legion Flandern. Note the 'Trifos', the three-legged swastika design on the collar patch. The unit served with distinction on the Eastern Front in 1941–43, though they were initially treated with contempt by their German SS instructors.

The volunteer legions raised in the Germanic countries fought consistently well when they eventually reached the Eastern Front, and gained a commendable reputation for combat reliability. Unfortunately, however, these reputations, indeed the reputations of most of all the better Waffen-SS units, were usually only earned at the cost of heavy losses. When their two-year contracts ended in 1943, therefore, few were willing to re-enlist for a further period of service, or to join the Waffen-SS proper. Thus, most of the legions were disbanded in 1943, with the remnants of their personnel being absorbed into newly formed volunteer divisions of the Waffen-SS proper.

As the war progressed and wartime losses produced greater and greater demands on Germany's manpower resources, Himmler was forced to lower his racial standards and allow the entry of non-Germanic volunteers. The aforementioned Belgian Walloon volunteers, for example, initially fought as a volunteer legion in the Army. By 1943, however, the Walloons were considered acceptable for the Waffen-SS. Eventually the situation became so serious that Himmler abandoned any attempt at racial selection for the Waffen-SS, and the once 'pure' Nordic stock of his military legions became diluted by the acceptance into the ranks of Slavic volunteers, Moslems, Indians and other Asiatics, as Himmler constantly struggled to make up for battlefield losses and further expand his SS empire. The quality of these later SS units was worlds away from the original *Reichsdeutsche* formations or the early Germanic volunteer units, and although some did gain good reputations under combat conditions, others were only good for committing atrocities and had to be disbanded.

Foreign volunteer insignia

Ultimately, all foreign volunteers came under the direct control of the Reichsführer-SS himself, whether or not they actually wore SS uniforms and insignia, and by the war's end almost anyone who was fit to carry a weapon was considered suitable material. To the end, however, the SS did seek to distinguish between the 'real' SS men and foreign volunteers. Only those accepted as true SS men were entitled to use the SS prefix to their rank. An SS-Sturmbannführer in a *Reichsdeutsche* unit, for example, would have as his direct equivalent in a volunteer unit a Waffen-Sturmbannführer, or perhaps a Legions-Sturmbannführer, emphasising that the latter were not genuine SS men, only attached to the SS on a temporary basis. Great store was set by the wearing of the SS runes by 'real' SS men, and many alternative collar patches were introduced for wear by the various volunteer units.

Many of the foreign volunteer units of the Waffen-SS only reached regimental strength, despite being designated a legion or division, and they therefore lacked the full support elements of a true combat division. They were, therefore, often attached to a German division for administrative and support purposes. The main foreign units that fought in the Waffen-SS in World War II are listed below.

Freiwilligen Legion *Niederlande*

Holland's largest National Socialist movement was the Nationaal Socialistische Beweging (NSB) of Anton Mussert, a long-time admirer of Adolf Hitler. Its activities were actively encouraged by the Germans, who saw the Dutch as a particularly valuable stock of good Nordic blood. An SS recruiting office was established in The Hague soon after the German occupation, and, initially at least, acceptable recruits were channelled into the *Westland* Regiment of the *Wiking* Division. In July 1941, however, a Dutch volunteer legion was formed under the command of the Chief of the Dutch General Staff, General Seyffardt. Having such a prominent and respected member of the Dutch military as head of the legion gave it a prestige which greatly assisted recruitment, though his command was largely nominal. In fact, so large was the number of recruits coming forward that it was thought that a full division might be formed. However, the Germans rejected a number of Dutch officers and NCOs as having no combat experience and replaced them with German personnel. The friction this caused and the subsequent cavalier treatment of the recruits by German training staff caused great problems for the legion, leading to some disgusted volunteers resigning.

The Freiwilligen Legion *Niederlande* reached the Eastern Front in January 1942 and was allocated to the northern sector in the Volkhov region, north of Lake Ilmen. After many weeks of intense fighting the Dutch volunteers mounted a counterattack against the Red Army in their sector, but by March had been beaten back to their start lines with heavy losses. Only 20 per cent of its strength remained intact, but its fighting spirit earned the Dutch a special commendation from the Oberkommando der Wehrmacht.

In the spring of 1942, the unit was reformed and once again committed to the northern sector of the Eastern Front near Leningrad as part of Army Group North, only to suffer severe losses yet again. Morale was also hit by the assassination of General Seyffardt by Dutch resistance fighters in Holland.

In the spring of 1943, as the two-year contract of its first intake of volunteers came to a close, few were willing to sign on for a further period of service. It is unlikely that any now believed in German

ABOVE: Soldiers of the Freiwilligen Legion Flandern are inspected by SS-Sturmbannführer Conrad Schellong, their commander. In Russia the legion was to suffer crippling losses in March 1942 and early 1943. The unit was withdrawn to Poland in May 1943 and was disbanded, its survivors having little enthusiasm to re-enlist.

promises of a quick victory in the East. As insufficient numbers were prepared to sign on again, the Freiwilligen Legion *Niederlande* was disbanded in May 1943.

Members of the legion wore a special collar patch with the so-called 'Wolf's Hook' insignia in place of the SS runes, and wore a special arm shield in the national colours of red, white and blue over a cuffband bearing the unit title.

During its brief existence, Freiwilligen Legion *Niederlande* earned a praiseworthy reputation as a dependable combat unit. Among its most noted members was the young Legions-Sturmmann Gerardes Mooyman. Only 20 years of age, Mooyman served as an anti-tank gunner with the Panzerjäger Kompanie. During a heavy Soviet tank attack, Mooyman knocked out 13 enemy T-34 tanks, continuing to operate the weapon alone after his fellow gun crew members had been killed or disabled. For this, Mooyman became the first European volunteer to win the Knights Cross of the Iron Cross, and he was ultimately commissioned as an SS-Untersturmführer.

Freiwilligen Legion *Flandern*

The Flemish area of Belgium had several nationalist parties, the most important of which was the Vlaamsch Nationaal Verbond (VNV). The VNV had advocated the break-up of Belgium, with the Germanic Flemings forming a new 'Greater Netherlands' with the Dutch. When the country was occupied by the Germans in May 1940, all other smaller nationalist groups were ordered to merge with the VNV. The Germans had a very favourable attitude towards the Flemish nationalists, and even agreed to the setting up of a Flemish Allgemeine-SS. As they were of Germanic race, the Flemings were considered ideal material for recruitment into the Waffen-SS. In 1941, therefore, the Freiwilligen Legion *Flandern* was formed.

The core of the unit was a group of some 400 or so Flemings who had already volunteered for military service in the SS-Freiwilligen Regiment *Nordwest*. The first commander of the Flemish volunteers was SS-Sturmbannführer Lippert. Former soldiers of the Belgian Army, and officers and NCOs in particular, were greatly coveted by the Germans, and were promised rank and status equal to that they had previously held in the Belgian Army if they agreed to sign on for the duration. As with their Dutch counterparts, however, the recruits found that not all was as had

been promised, and Himmler's personal intervention was once again required to rectify matters.

In the autumn of 1941, Freiwilligen Legion *Flandern* was committed to the northern sector of the Eastern Front near Leningrad, and in the early part of 1942 it was instrumental in repulsing strong Soviet attacks near Novgorod, being cited for its gallant conduct. In March 1942, the Flemings went briefly on to the offensive, but suffered crippling losses and were eventually driven back. They spent the remainder of 1942 in the Volkhov sector, until the unit was moved back to the Leningrad area at the start of 1943. It went into the reserve in February 1943.

After a short period of rest and refitting, Freiwilligen Legion *Flandern* went back into action around Krasny-Bor. The fighting in this area was extremely fierce. In one week alone, for example, the unit lost over 1000 men, and ended up with a strength of only some 60 soldiers. The survivors were withdrawn from the front to Debica in Poland in May 1943. Like their Dutch compatriots, most of the survivors were loathe to sign on for another tour of duty once their two-year contracts came to an end. The legion was therefore disbanded, though some members did go on to join the newly formed SS Freiwilligen-Sturmbrigade *Langemarck*. The Flemish volunteers had suffered the same grievous losses as the Dutch, but had likewise gained a formidable fighting reputation as first-class soldiers.

Unit members wore a special collar patch showing the 'Trifos', the three-legged swastika, though the SS runes also seem to have been widely worn. Above the cuffband bearing the unit title was worn a shield-shaped insignia in yellow thread with a black rampant lion thereon.

Freikorps *Danmark*

Denmark had been invaded by the Germans in April 1940 in a virtually bloodless coup. Hitler was keen to promote the image of Denmark as the 'model protectorate', and the population was left relatively unmolested, with their monarchy and parliament intact. So long as the Danes were prepared to behave as the Germans requested, interference in Danish matters was kept to a minimum. In general, therefore, Danish resistance to the Germans took the form, initially at least, of fairly passive non-cooperation and consisted mainly of trying to ignore the invaders as much as possible.

OPPOSITE: A highly successful Belgian recruit in the service of the Waffen-SS. The soldier on the left is SS-Sturmmann Remy Schrÿnen, who single-handedly knocked out seven Russian tanks, despite being wounded at the time. He is seen here accompanied by SS-Untersturmführer Koslovsky on the occasion of his receiving the Knights Cross for his gallantry. Schÿnen was in the 27th SS Freiwilligen-Panzergrenadier Division Langemarck.

RIGHT: *The commanding officer of* Freikorps **Danmark**, *SS-Sturmbannführer Christian Frederich von Schalburg, who was described by his German superiors as a 'reliable National Socialist'. Note the national arm shield and cuffband.*

'Every SS man must be deeply imbued with the sense and essence of the National Socialist movement. He will be ideologically and physically trained so that he can be employed individually or in groups in the decisive battle for the National Socialist ideology.'
– *Organization Book of the NSDAP, 1943*

The Danes did have their own indigenous Nazi movement, the Danmarks National Socialistiske Arbejder Parti (DNSAP), which had been formed as early as 1930. Few Danes, however, were persuaded to enlist in the Waffen-SS (even fewer when the Danes learned of the abuse their men had received at the hands of SS instructors), and by the autumn of 1941 only some 2-300 volunteers were serving, mostly in the *Nordland* Regiment of the *Wiking* Division.

Following negotiations, however, and due mostly to the Danes' status as a protectorate as opposed to an occupied country, special terms were agreed to induce more volunteers to come forward. Any ex-

Danish Army personnel who volunteered to join the Waffen-SS, for example, would be permitted to keep their original seniority dates from the Danish Army, and would also retain their pension rights. With this tacit approval of the Danish government recruiting levels improved, and by September 1941 some 1000 or so Danish volunteers had come forward.

In May 1942, the Danish volunteer unit, entitled Freikorps *Danmark*, was despatched to the front to support the *Totenkopf* Division, which was involved in fierce defensive actions around Demyansk. The commanding officer of Freikorps *Danmark*, SS-Sturmbannführer Christian Frederich von Schalburg, a former youth leader of the DNSAP, was killed in action during these battles. In June 1942, the Red Army retook the town of Vassiliev-schtshina and Freikorps *Danmark* was ordered to drive them out again, which it did despite furious Soviet attacks supported by aircraft and tanks. The unit was cited for gallantry for its conduct, but once again a Germanic volunteer unit had only received such praise after suffering horrendous losses. By August 1942, only 22 per cent of the unit strength remained.

The freikorps returned to Denmark for four weeks rest and recuperation. The home-coming parade held in its honour was far from successful, however. Instead of lining the streets to welcome the returning heroes, the hostile crowd jeered at the freikorps veterans.

In December 1942, Freikorps *Danmark* returned to the front in the Velikje Luki region, where it suffered heavy attacks from a division of the notorious NKVD internal security troops and was driven from its positions. Although it retook them on the following day, heavy losses were suffered. Then, in January 1943, German forces withdrew from the area, which was reoccupied by the Soviets. Freikorps *Danmark* moved northwards and destroyed the Soviet positions at Taidy. In March 1943, it was withdrawn to Gräfenwohr in Germany, where it was disbanded in May of that year.

The Danish volunteers were unique in wearing a version of their national flag on their collar patch, though the SS runes also appear to have been worn. A shield, also bearing the Danish colours of a white cross on a red field, was worn above the cuffband bearing the unit title.

Freiwilligen Legion *Norwegen*
As early as May 1933, a nationalist party entitled Nasjonal Sammling (NS) had been founded in Norway and was led by former Defence Minister Vidkun Quisling (who also held the title of honorary Commander of the Order of the British Empire). The latter was a great admirer of Adolf Hitler, and when Norway fell to Germany in June 1940 he installed himself as head of state. Hitler was having none of it, however, and appointed his own representative, Reichs-kommissar Josef Terboven, to rule occupied Norway, although the Führer did eventually grant Quisling the status of Minister President in 1942.

Almost immediately after Norway fell, the SS opened a recruiting office in Oslo and enlistment of suitable Norwegian vol-

unteers, many of whom were members of Quisling's NS, began. Those volunteers who were accepted were posted to the *Nordland* Regiment. Recruitment figures were hardly startling, though, with only some 300 coming forward in the first year. Quisling was rather suspicious of German intentions, and he urged his own supporters to join so he would have a degree of influence among the SS volunteers.

In August 1941, a new volunteer unit, the Freiwilligen Legion *Norwegen*, was formed, though the fact that it was to be controlled by the SS was at first hidden from prospective volunteers. The original volunteers who served with the *Nordland*

BELOW: A Sturmmann of Freikorps **Danmark.** *Note the machine-woven cuffband bearing the unit title.*

RIGHT: An Unterscharführer of the Freiwilligen Legion Norwegen. Alongside their Flemish, Dutch and Danish colleagues, this unit was thrown into the battle for the northern sector of the Eastern Front, where they were almost completely wiped out.

'If the Waffen-SS had not existed, Europe would have been overrun entirely by the Soviets by 1944. They would have reached Paris long before the Americans. [...] Without SS resistance the Soviets would have been in Normandy before General Dwight D. Eisenhower.'
– Leon Degrelle, Commander 28th Waffen-SS Division *Wallonien*

Regiment were initially intended for police duties in occupied Norway, but those who came forward for the new unit did so on the understanding that they would be fighting the communists in Russia. The Norwegians were highly sympathetic towards their neighbours the Finns, who had already suffered from a Soviet invasion, and it appears that many thought the new force would be a Norwegian national unit that would support the Finns against Soviet ambitions in Scandinavia.

Two battalions were initially formed – *Viken* and *Viking* – and by March 1942 some 1200 men were trained and ready for combat duties. The first commander of the Norwegian volunteers was Jorgen Bakke,

but a degree of friction between him and the Germans led to his replacement by Legions-Sturmbannführer Arthur Quist, who was to command the unit until its eventual disbandment.

The Norwegians, like their Flemish, Dutch and Danish counterparts, were committed to action in the northern sector of the Eastern Front, near Leningrad. Rather than taking part in major battles, Freiwilligen Legion *Norwegen* was worn down by continuous patrol and skirmishing actions until May 1942, by which time it had been virtually annihilated. Recruitment in Norway had slackened, and the legion was only slowly brought back up to strength. In late 1942, the remnants were attached to the 1st SS Infantry Brigade, alongside their Danish compatriots in Freikorps *Danmark*. At the end of the year it was moved north once again and fought around Konstantinovka and Krasny Bor with the 2nd SS Infantry Brigade. By early 1943, however, it was badly depleted and in March was withdrawn from the front altogether and sent back to Norway.

In May 1943, Quisling called upon the Norwegian volunteers to enlist in the newly formed *Norge* Regiment as its 1st Battalion, a call that resulted in 600 men coming forward. The remainder of the Freiwilligen Legion *Norwegen* was demobilised, and in May 1943 it was formally disbanded.

In addition to the above, a volunteer Norwegian ski battalion was formed. However, it numbered only some 200 men and fought alongside the 6th SS Gebirgs Division *Nord* in the far north of the Eastern Front. It was disbanded at the same time as the legion – in 1943.

Soldiers of the Freiwilligen Legion *Norwegen* wore a special collar patch bearing a rampant lion carrying an axe. An arm shield bearing the colours of the Norwegian flag was also worn above the cuffband containing the unit title.

Finnische Freiwilligen-Bataillon der Waffen-SS

Formed in June 1941 as the SS Freiwilligen-Bataillon *Nordost*, this small unit of Finnish volunteers was renamed in September of that year and was eventually attached to the elite *Wiking* Division as a component of the *Nordland* Regiment, but in mid-1943 it was disbanded and its personnel returned to duty with the Finnish Army. No special collar patch or cuffband was produced for these troops, but an arm shield depicting a rampant lion holding a straight-bladed sword, standing over a scimitar-type sword, was produced in both yellow threads on a blue base, and white threads on a black base.

The Indian Legion

Initially formed as Indisches Infanterie Regiment 950 of the German Army in April 1943, this unit was formed from Indian prisoners of war captured while serving with the British in North Africa. The unit was taken over by the SS in November 1944, but it is doubtful if it ever saw any action and its usefulness was purely in terms of propaganda. No special Waffen-SS insignia was issued, though a collar patch bearing a stylised Tiger's head was manufactured. Members of this unit

BELOW: Volunteers of the Freiwilligen Legion Norwegen in May 1942. Though the national legions were built up quickly and they performed well in combat, the 'Germanic' foreigners had many grievances against their German superiors. For example, many foreign volunteers were not released from service at the end of their enlistments, and as a result some Danes and Norwegians deserted while on leave. Worse, the Germans believed all the foreign volunteers were ardent National Socialists who would tolerate any treatment out of idealism. They were wrong, and the mistreatment of foreigners at the training depots by SS instructors resulted in much disillusionment.

ABOVE: John Amery (left), the leader of the British Free Corps, is arrested in Milan. The idea of a British SS unit came about in 1943, following the Waffen-SS's success in recruiting former enemy soldiers from POW camps. In an effort to aid recruitment, Himmler granted British Free Corps personnel the right to wear English uniforms with German insignia. However, the response was very poor, and by the spring of 1944 only 50 Britons were at the unit's camp at Hildesheim. The corps never saw combat and its use to the Germans seems to have been purely for propaganda purposes. Amery, the son of one of Churchill's ministers, was hanged by the British after the war for treason.

continued to wear their Army sleeve shield showing a leaping tiger over the Indian national colours of orange, white and green, with the title *Freies Indien* above.

British Free Corps

This unit, which was little more than propaganda value to the Germans, was formed in the spring of 1944 and at most is thought to have numbered around 60 men, who were recruited from British prisoners of war. A sorry bunch, this group caused the Germans many problems because of their indiscipline. It is perhaps not surprising in view of the calibre of men who volunteered. Only a few individual members saw action in the closing days of the war, attached to the 11th SS Freiwilligen-Panzergrenadier Division *Nordland* during the battle for Berlin, some being killed in action there. The survivors who were captured mostly received minor punishments; some were only fined. The exception was John Amery, the ringleader, who was hanged for treason.

Despite it numerical insignificance, the unit had great propaganda potential for the Germans, and a full range of special insignia was manufactured, issued and worn by these men: a collar patch showing three lions couchant, a Union Jack arm shield, and a cuffband bearing the unit title.

Some of the members of this unit are still alive, but are, understandably, generally unwilling to discuss their service with the SS, suffering from acute 'loss of memory' regarding this period of their lives.

5th SS Panzer Division *Wiking*

Initially established in May 1940 as SS Division (motorisierte) *Germania*, the title was altered only days later to SS Division (mot) *Wiking*, being formed around a core of *Reichsdeutsche* personnel from the *Germania* Regiment, who had been transferred wholesale from the *SS-Verfügungs-division*. To this core was added the two existing Germanic volunteer regiments *Nordland* and *Westland*. The first truly international division of the Waffen-SS, it numbered Germans, Dutch, Danes, Norwegians and Flemings among its personnel, together with a smattering of *Volksdeutsche* from the Balkans.

The division first went into action in the southern sector of the Eastern Front, as far as possible from their countrymen fighting in the volunteer legions around Leningrad. It took part in the drive through the Caucasus and quickly earned itself a reputation for efficiency and dependability under fire. In late 1942, it was reformed as a panzergrenadier division and played an important role in the ill-fated German armoured offensive at Kursk in July 1943.

Although it suffered heavy losses, it achieved an excellent reputation, even earning the grudging respect of the Soviets in several battle reports for its pugnacious fighting spirit (Soviet commanders were always concerned to learn that their troops were facing the soldiers of the *Wiking* Division). In October 1943 the division was reformed yet again, and emerged as a fully fledged panzer division. The significance of this should not be underestimated. Considering the disdain shown for many of the foreign volunteer units by their German masters, the fact that a predominantly 'foreign' division should be accorded panzer division status and equipped with the latest tanks was a tribute to the regard in which it was held.

The 'Wikingers' were fast attaining an elite status to equal the best of the original Waffen-SS divisions. In February 1944, Wiking took part in the furious fighting around Cherkassy and suffered heavy losses, though its morale and esprit de corps remained high. Withdrawn into Poland, it took part in the defensive battles around Warsaw in the autumn of 1944 before moving south to assist in the attempt to relieve Budapest. When this failed the division was withdrawn into Austria, where it fought in the final battles to defend Vienna in 1945.

The qualities of the *Wiking* Division as a combat unit are ably testified to by the number of Knights Crosses of the Iron Cross awarded to its soldiers. A total of 54 such gallantry awards were made, a figure surpassed only by the 73 of the *Das Reich* Division.

The division was first commanded by SS-Obergruppenführer Felix Steiner, one of the finest and most highly decorated soldiers of the Waffen-SS, who went on to command III Panzer Corps and the 11th Panzer Army. Steiner was followed by SS-Obergruppenführer Herbert Otto Gille, who was awarded the Swords, Oakleaves and Diamonds to the Knights Cross for both his own, and the division's, achievements in battle. The final commander was SS-Standartenführer Johannes Mühlenkamp, who had already been awarded the Knights Cross as commander of the division's panzer regiment, and was subsequently awarded the Oakleaves in recognition of his distinguished leadership of the division as a whole.

To the end the men of the division fought like tigers. In defeat they retained

their pride in having given service above and beyond the call of duty, and to this day the phenomenal esprit de corps engendered within this elite division lives on through a thriving veterans organisation. The *Wiking* Division was without a doubt the finest of all the SS volunteer formations, and indeed one of the best units in the entire German armed forces.

Although a special collar patch showing the prow of a Viking longship was produced for wear in the division, no evidence has yet emerged to show that it was ever worn, and the men of *Wiking* generally wore the standard SS runes. In addition, those who had first served with the volunteer legions continued to wear their national arm shields. Members of the *Nordland*, *Westland* and *Germania* Regiments wore cuffbands showing the names of their regiments, while soldiers not attached to a named regiment wore the *Wiking* cuffband.

It has been suggested that a special version of the *Wiking* cuffband with the lettering in finely executed gothic script, rather than the latin script normally used, was specially made for Herbert Otto Gille. While Gille did indeed wear such a cuffband, it was by no means unique, being identified in photographs as having been worn by junior NCOs and other ranks of the division.

6th SS Gebirgs Division *Nord*

Raised in Austria in late 1940, this unit was first given the title SS Kampfgruppe *Nord* in February 1941. It comprised mainly volunteers from Hungary, Romania and a few Norwegians (principally the SS Ski Battalion) built around a German cadre. Despite its poor training, the kampfgruppe was sent to the far northern front in June 1941, striking through Finland into Russia in an attempt to take the port of Murmansk in support of German Army units. In September 1941, it was upgraded to divisional status.

The initial performance of the division was anything but inspiring. However, it must be admitted that the conditions in which it fought were atrocious. The dank, dark forests and predominantly swampy ground were a haven for mosquitoes. Morale was low and the incidence of illness high. Nevertheless, the division was constantly engaged in this region until 1944. As the Red Army drove westwards, the division was pulled back into Norway to Oslo, from where it was evacuated by sea to Denmark.

'Bosnians! Join the ranks of the Waffen SS. Defend your beautiful homeland, your wives, and children.'
– Text of a Waffen-SS recruitment poster, 1944

ABOVE: Two members of the 5th SS Panzer Division Wiking. *The man beaming proudly on the right is SS-Hauptsturmführer Oeck of the division's Panzerjäger Abteilung (tank destroyer detachment). He is photographed after a successful tank-busting engagement. There is no doubt that the* Wiking *Division was one of the finest fighting formations in the entire Waffen-SS. The division had Germans, Danes, Dutch Flemings, Walloons, Norwegians and Finns in its ranks. First committed to action in mid-1941 as part of Operation 'Barbarossa', it maintained a very high fighting reputation until its surrender to the Americans in Czechoslovakia in May 1945. Interestingly, a number of its men managed to evade capture and enlist in the French Foreign Legion, and subsequently served in Indo-China.*

By December 1944, it was positioned in the Saar region of Germany fighting the Western Allies. The unit performed better here than it had done in Russia, but was gradually pushed back until it was cut off on the west bank of the Rhine by the advancing Allies in March 1945. It put up a spirited fight before being forced to surrender. In total, seven soldiers from the Division were decorated with the Knights Cross of the Iron Cross, all of which were won from mid-1944 onwards, attesting to the improved quality of the division as time progressed.

The Division *Nord* was initially commanded for a short period by SS-Obergruppenführer Georg Keppler (who also commanded the *Das Reich* Division), who passed on command to SS-Obergruppenführer Mattias Kleinheisterkamp, a former commander of the *Das Reich* Division and a highly decorated and able soldier. Its final commander was SS-Obergruppenführer Friedrich Wilhelm Krüger, who was decorated with the Knights Cross for his command of the division in October 1944.

Most of the soldiers of the division wore the SS runes collar patch, though some soldiers of SS Gebirgsjäger Regiment 11, which had evolved from SS Totenkopf Standarte 6, continued to wear the death's head collar patch. Although the division was granted the title *Nord*, no special cuffband was introduced, though some personnel took to wearing the cuffband of the Allgemeine-SS's SS-Oberabschnitt *Nord* unofficially. Within the division, personnel from SS Gebirgsjäger Regiment 11 wore the cuffband *Reinhard Heydrich*, those from SS Gebirgsjäger Regiment 12 the cuffband *Michael Gaissmair*, those from the Norwegian Ski Battalion the cuffband *Norge*, and a few the cuffband of the Norwegian volunteer legion *Frw Legion Norwegen*.

7th SS Freiwilligen-Gebirgs Division *Prinz Eugen*

Recruited predominantly from the *Volksdeutsche* community in Croatia and the Banat, this unit was founded in March 1942 as the SS Freiwilligen Gebirgs Division, receiving its honour title *Prinz Eugen* a month later. By October 1942 its title had reached its final form, being accorded seventh place in the order of battle of Waffen-SS divisions.

The division, however, was a volunteer unit in name only. Almost from the beginning volunteer recruitment was backed up by widespread coercion and conscription. A number of Serbs, Romanians and Hungarians also found their way into the division. Some members of the Croat Einsatz Staffel, broadly equivalent to the German SS, were also persuaded to enlist.

Although the manpower required to raise the unit to divisional status was found through various means, equipment was to be more problematic. As it was intended to utilise *Prinz Eugen* for internal security and anti-partisan duties, the Germans were unwilling to give it large quantities of first-rate arms and equipment, and in the event a large supply of obsolete and obsolescent material found its way into the divisional arsenal. This included French, Belgian, Yugoslav, Czech and Italian weapons. Even so, the *Prinz Eugen* Division was comparatively well manned and certainly fully, if variably, equipped, even to the extent of boasting a panzer detachment equipped with captured French tanks.

Prinz Eugen was commanded by SS-Obergruppenführer Artur Phleps, a former general of the Romanian Army. Its first major action was at the battle of the Neretva in early 1943, where the German forces attempted to encircle and destroy Tito's partisan forces once and for all. Although the action certainly saw the partisans suffering heavy losses, Tito and a good part of his force escaped the encirclement to regroup and reform, and they continued to represent a major thorn in the flesh of the German forces for the remainder of the war. As a consequence, the *Prinz Eugen* Division spent much of its time engaged in anti-partisan duties. In October 1944, it was moved into the area around Belgrade to cover the withdrawal of German forces through Yugoslavia. It suffered heavy losses due to almost continuous action during this period, and morale was also affected by the loss of Phleps, who was captured by an advance unit of the Red Army and shot. He was posthumously awarded the Oakleaves to his Knights Cross on 24 November. The division ended the war in the Balkans, the bulk of the survivors going into Soviet captivity, from which few returned.

It is difficult to assess the fighting qualities of the *Prinz Eugen* Division as it spent most of its combat career in anti-partisan actions rather than facing front-line enemy combat units. When it did come up against units of the Red Army in the latter stages of the war, it was virtually annihilated. It is probably fair to say that while it was certainly not one of the best Waffen-SS divisions, it was far from being the worst, though it did commit many atrocities during its anti-partisan actions.

After the death of Phleps, command of the division passed to SS-Brigadeführer Carl von Oberkamp and then to SS-Brigadeführer Otto Kumm, an accomplished former regimental commander of the *Das Reich* Division, who earned the Swords to his Knights Cross for his command of the *Prinz Eugen* Division. Kumm passed command to SS-Brigadeführer August Schmidthuber when he left to take command of the elite *Leibstandarte SS Adolf Hitler* in the closing stages of the war. A total of six soldiers from the division were decorated with the Knights Cross of the Iron Cross.

Members of the division wore a cuffband with the divisional title *Prinz Eugen* in latin script, and a collar patch bearing the so-called 'Odalrune'.

11th SS Freiwilligen-Panzergrenadier Division *Nordland*

Established in February 1943, this was an attempt by the Germans to set up an international SS division manned and commanded by foreign volunteers. Although the elite *Wiking* Division had a considerable number of foreign troops in its ranks, the senior NCOs and officers were predominantly German. In *Nordland*, the Germans hoped to utilise a far greater proportion of foreign volunteer senior ranks. Considerable use was made of the remnants of the disbanded Germanic legions in staffing the division, and it certainly carried the widest range of nationalities to be found in any single Waffen-SS

division. By the end of the war, Danes, Dutch, Norwegians, Estonians, Finns, French, Swedish, Swiss and even British volunteers had either served in the division itself or had been attached to it.

By the autumn of 1943 the division was training in Croatia, and in January 1944 was judged to be ready for combat. It was attached to Army Group North on the Eastern Front in an unsuccessful attempt to prevent the Red Army from breaking the siege of Leningrad. It also took part in the Battle of Narva (early 1944), where it suffered heavy casualties (so many volunteer units saw action at Narva that it became known as the 'Battle of the European SS').

In September 1944, over a period of just four days, the division undertook a forced march from Narva to Riga, where its arrival prevented the encirclement of the German 18th Army by Soviet forces. As the Red Army's advance continued, *Nordland* slowly withdrew into the Courland Pocket, fighting doggedly all the way, from where it was evacuated to Germany in early 1945. It saw heavy fighting around Danzig, Stettin and Stargard, before becoming part of the force defending Berlin. The division was finally destroyed in the battle for the city in April/May 1945.

Nordland was a full-strength, well-equipped unit which included a powerful armoured element: SS Panzer Abteilung 11 *Hermann von Salza*. Overall, it acquitted itself well in action and was one of the better non-German SS divisions. This is reflected in the total of 30 Knights Crosses awarded to its members, ranking it fifth in the table of Waffen-SS units in terms of Knights Cross awards.

BELOW: PzKpfw IIIs of the **Wiking** *Division in the Soviet Union. The success in wielding the many nationalities present in the division into an effective fighting force was due in no small part to the considerable talents of SS-Obergruppenführer Felix Steiner. His views on leadership were widely different to some of the other SS commanders, Theodor Eicke in particular. For example, Steiner wrote to his officers: 'The more reasonably, thoughtfully and sympathetically a unit is led, the stronger is its cohesion and the greater its combat value. Especially because of our Nordic volunteers, a humane leadership seems to me to be of decisive importance.'*

RIGHT: Two soldiers of the 7th SS Freiwilligen Gebirgs Division Prinz Eugen. The idea for the division came from Gottlob Berger, who wanted to create an SS division from the ethnic Germans living in Yugoslavia. However, the initial call for volunteers in Serbia and Croatia was not answered with enthusiasm, and so coercion and conscription were employed. Equipped with a variety of captured and obsolete weapons, the division spent much of its career engaged in anti-partisan actions in Yugoslavia. As such, its activities included burning villages, massacring civilians and torturing captured partisans. It saw combat against the Red Army in late 1944 and suffered accordingly, taking heavy casualties and losing many men through desertion. It fought on until May 1945, when it surrendered to Yugoslav forces in Slovenia. A number of its personnel were subsequently executed for their participation in atrocities.

The division was initially commanded by SS-Obergruppenführer Fritz von Scholz, holder of the Swords and Oakleaves, who was killed in action on 28 July 1944 near Narva. Command then passed to SS-Brigadeführer Joachim Ziegler, who fell in Berlin on 2 May 1945.

Soldiers of the division wore a special collar patch showing a so-called curved swastika. The members of SS Panzer Grenadier Regiment 23 wore the title *Norge*, members of SS Panzer Grenadier Regiment 24 the title *Danmark*, and mem-bers of SS Panzer Abteilung 11 the title *Hermann von Salza*. All other members of the division wore the title *Nordland*. Generally speaking, soldiers of the division also wore their own particular national arm shield.

13th Waffen-Gebirgs Division der SS *Handschar* (kroatische Nr 1)

Himmler ordered the raising of a new unit of Bosnian Moslem volunteers in February 1943, to be used for anti-partisan duties within Yugoslavia, and from this order sprang the kroatische SS Freiwilligen Division. The Croat dictator Ante Pavelic was highly suspicious of Himmler's moves, suspecting the Reichsführer-SS of some sort of Machiavellian plot to turn Moslem against Christian and destabilise the state. Himmler simply ignored his protests, however, and recruiting went ahead regardless. The quality of recruits, though, left much to be desired. In September 1943, the division moved to France for training and trouble started almost immediately. The German officers and NCOs in charge of training were often contemptuous of their Moslem charges. Bearing in mind that many of these Germans were early SS recruits imbued with Himmler's ideas of Germanic racial purity, it must have been galling indeed for them to be placed in command of a hotchpotch of poor-quality Moslem recruits, who wore their semi-comic fez headgear and came complete with their retinue of imams to administer their daily devotions towards Mecca.

Tensions ran high, and the usual foul-mouthed epithets used by training NCOs were taken to heart by the Moslem volunteers, who promptly mutinied and murdered several of the German cadre staff. Himmler was furious at the heavy-handed treatment of his Moslem volunteers by the training cadre, but with German personnel having been murdered he had little option but to quell the mutiny with all necessary force. The mutiny was put down and the ringleaders executed without delay. The division, however, the only one in the SS ever to mutiny, was not disbanded.

Viewed with great suspicion by the Germans, it was despatched back to Yugoslavia to combat partisan activity. It then proceeded to earn itself an unenviable reputation for savagery. Many atrocities were committed by its members, primarily against members of the Serb community.

By the end of 1944, German forces were on the retreat in the Balkans. The Moslem element of the division, being considered to be useless for frontline combat situations, was finally disbanded. The German and *Volksdeutsche* elements, however, were formed into a kampfgruppe and fought on in the withdrawal through Hungary and Austria, before finally surrendering to the Soviets.

It is interesting to note that although five Knights Crosses were awarded to soldiers in the *Handschar* Division, to SS-Brigadeführer Desiderius Hampel, SS-Obersturmbannführer Karl Liecke, SS-Obersturmbannführer Hans Hanke, SS-Sturmbannführer Albert Stenwedel and SS-Sturmbannführer Helmut Kinz, all were to German cadre personnel and were all awarded in May 1945, after the Moslem element had been disbanded.

Despite its dire disciplinary record and poor performance, the division had been granted the name *Handschar* by Himmler in May 1944, and a special collar patch showing a hand holding a short scimitar-like sword, or handschar, over a swastika had also been authorised, indicative perhaps of Himmler's genuine desire for his experiment with Moslem personnel to be successful. Despite the division being allocated a name, no cuffband was ever authorised. The arm shield worn by personnel in this division was in the red and white chequered colours of Croatia.

14th Waffen-Grenadier Division der SS (ukrainische Nr 1)

The western part of the Ukraine had at one stage been a part of the sprawling Austro-Hungarian Empire, and though the August 1939 Russo-German Pact had agreed that this area was well within the Soviet sphere of influence, its population was far from being ardent supporters of Stalin's brand of communism. The years of iron-hard Soviet control had so affected the peoples of the western Ukraine that when the Germans launched their attack on the Soviet Union in the summer of 1941, they were invariably welcomed as

LEFT: Otto Kumm, seen here wearing the uniform of an SS-Obersturmbannführer. Kumm was the third commander of the Prinz Eugen Division, the first two being Artur Phleps and Carl von Oberkamp. Kumm is best remembered for his exploits with the Das Reich Division in Russia. In February 1942, Kumm was commander of the Der Führer Regiment of the division, which was battered by savage Soviet assaults in the area of Rzhev. When the attacks had stopped, Kumm took his regiment to divisional headquarters. There he met Field Marshal Model, commander of the 9th Army, who told him: 'I know what your regiment has been through, Kumm, but I still can't do without it. How strong is it now?' Kumm pointed to the window. 'My regiment is on parade outside.' In the cold stood 35 men, the remains of a unit that had gone into combat 2000 strong. Kumm was awarded the Knights Cross for his gallantry in February 1942, the Oakleaves on 6 April 1943 and the Swords on 4 April 1945. His career ended as the last commander of the Leibstandarte Division.

liberators by the Ukrainians (though this would abate somewhat when the Einsatzgruppen began their activities).

In August 1941, the western Ukraine, which Himmler insisted on calling Galicia, was pronounced part of the Generalgouvernement, the Nazi-administered area comprising most of Poland. The military commander of the area was SS-Brigadeführer Wächter, who was sympathetic to the peoples under his control. The area thus remained comparatively peaceful, the populace content to have thrown off their Soviet oppressors.

In March 1943, Wächter sought, and was given, permission to raise a 'Galician' police regiment. As manpower shortages due to combat losses grew more acute, Himmler suggested that the proposed regiment be increased to a division. Such was the level of anti-Soviet feeling in the area that up to 70,000 volunteers came forward. This was sufficient to man the projected division, with enough manpower remaining to form a further five police regiments. Some 350 volunteer officers and 2000 NCOs were sent to Germany to be trained up to what the Germans considered a sufficiently high standard to meet combat requirements.

The western Ukraine is predominantly Catholic and so Himmler, a Catholic himself, even granted the concession of allowing the Ukrainian units to have their own chaplains. This was common enough in the German Army, but almost unheard of in the SS, where soldiers were permitted to record their religion as 'a believer in God', but where membership of an established religion was not encouraged.

In mid-June 1944, the division saw its first action when it was thrown into the line near Brody in an attempt to halt the Soviet summer offensive. With no opportunity to build up its combat experience gradually, the division was virtually annihilated. Of some 14,000 troops who went into action, only 3000 survived. Many of those lost were in fact cut off behind Soviet lines, where they roamed for several years after the war's end as partisan units harrying the Soviets, such was their hatred for the communists.

Fortunately for the Germans, the vast number of volunteers coming forward allowed them to quickly reform the division to make up its losses. In the autumn of 1944, one regiment from the division was sent to Czechoslovakia to help suppress the Slovak uprising. In January 1945, the whole division was sent into

Yugoslavia to assist in the battle against Tito's partisans, but in the event saw relatively little action. Two months later, too late to have any useful effect, the division passed under the control, on paper at least, of the Ukrainian National Army under Pavlo Shandruck. Shandruck was a former general staff officer of the Polish Army, and the division was intended to form part of his force.

The bulk of the division was able to withdraw westwards in the closing days of the war and surrender to Anglo-American forces. Allied confusion over the status of personnel labelled as Galicians led to many being able to avoid forced repatriation to the Soviet Union. Despite their having served in the Waffen-SS, Polish General Anders took the pragmatic view that their past could be forgiven in consideration of their potential future usefulness as dedicated anti-communists, and he supported their claim to be Polish rather than Russian. Few other Waffen-SS volunteer units were so fortunate.

Despite its combat record, only one member of the division, its German commander, SS-Brigadeführer Fritz Freitag, was awarded the Knights Cross of the Iron Cross. Soldiers of the division wore a special sleeve shield in blue bearing a yellow rampant lion and three crowns. A special collar patch, also showing a rampant lion, was produced and worn.

15th Waffen-Grenadier Division der SS (lettische Nr 1)

After the Soviets had been successfully driven out of Latvia in 1941, the Germans set up a number of Latvian police regiments under German command to guard essential supply lines from possible attack by Soviet partisans. In early 1943, some of these police units, together with a number of German officers and NCOs, were attached to Army Group North on the Eastern Front to gain combat experience.

When it was announced that a Latvian Legion was to be formed to fight against the Soviets, a total of 32,000 volunteers came forward. On 9 March 1943, former Latvian Minister of War, General Rudolf Bangerskis, was appointed to command the unit, being accorded the rank of SS-Gruppenführer.

In November 1943, the Latvian volunteers first saw action at Novo Sokolniki in defensive actions against the Soviet winter offensive. The Latvians were resolute fighters in the defence, and they successfully held off the enemy attacks, though only

'Thanks to its policy of recruiting, the SS will be a nursery of rulers. One hundred years from now, we will control this entire empire without having to rack our brains to look for the proper men.... That's why I'm so glad we are secure in Norway and all over the place.'
– Hitler to Himmler, 1942

at the cost of heavy losses. As one Soviet attack was repulsed another followed, and the division became continuously involved in a series of desperate defensive actions, but to no avail – by July 1944 the enemy was on Latvian soil. Despite its losses, the division continued to fight well, earning the respect of its German comrades. The division was pulled out in time to avoid encirclement and found itself in West Prussia. Riga, the Latvian capital, fell to the Soviets on 13 October 1944. The division was then swept gradually westwards by the inexorable advance of the Red Army, and eventually surrendered to British forces in April 1945.

Five of the division's soldiers, SS-Brigadeführer Nikolaus Heilmann (a German), Waffen-Standartenführer Karlis Aperats (a Latvian), SS-Oberführer Adolf Ax (born in Flanders), SS-Sturmbannführer Erich Wulff (a German) and Waffen-Unterscharführer Karlis Sensbergs (a Latvian), were awarded the Knights Cross of the Iron Cross.

Standard SS runic collar patches were widely worn within the division, even though it was non-German. A further special patch showing a swastika was worn for a period, before the final pattern – showing three stars within a surround of the sun's rays – was issued. No cuffband was ever authorised. An arm shield in the Latvian colours of red with a white diagonal stripe was worn, both with and without the title *Latvija* at the top.

18th SS Freiwilligen-Panzergrenadier Division *Horst Wessel*

Hungary was not, initially at least, considered to be an occupied country, but an independent sovereign state allied to Germany. There was a sizeable number of *Volksdeutsche* within Hungary who, despite their German ancestry, were considered Hungarian citizens, and as such were subject to conscription into the Hungarian armed forces. As might be expected, Himmler's covetous eyes fell upon the Hungarian *Volksdeutsche* as a potential source of recruits for the Waffen-SS.

After much cajoling, persuading and the use of thinly veiled threats, Himmler prevailed upon the Hungarian government to allow the Waffen-SS to recruit from the *Volksdeutsche* population. However, the Hungarians did insist on certain conditions: that the recruitment must be of genuine volunteers, no coercion was to be permitted, that any volunteers under the

age of 18 must have parental consent, and any who did volunteer for service with the Germans must renounce their Hungarian citizenship. By mid-summer 1942, almost 18,000 volunteers had been accepted for service and most were allocated to the 7th SS Freiwilligen Gebirgs Division *Prinz Eugen* and the 8th SS Kavallerie Division *Florian Geyer*.

By 1943, manpower shortages were becoming acute and Himmler had been forced to increase the upper age limit for volunteers. This raised a further 30,000-40,000 volunteers, most of whom found their way into the 11th SS Freiwilligen-Panzergrenadier Division *Nordland* and some into the 16th SS Panzergrenadier Division *Reichsführer-SS*.

By 1944, Hungary's independence was a mere sham and Himmler's authority was sufficient to allow him to demand that Hungarian *Volksdeutsche* be given no option other than to complete their military service within the Waffen-SS. These moves coincided with Hitler's growing

ABOVE: SS-Sturmbannführer Christian von Schalburg (left) shakes hands with SS-Unterscharführer Soren Kam of the 11th SS Freiwilligen-Panzergrenadier Division Nordland. The division was formed from the remnants of the national legions, transfers from the Wiking Division and new recruits from the 'Germanic' lands under Nazi control. Note the cuffband on Soren Kam's left arm.

ABOVE: A Waffen-SS recruiting appeal that had a large degree of success – an appeal to Italians to join the Italian Legion of the SS. Around 15,000 Italian fascists eventually answered the call to arms.

'Volunteer' (Freiwilligen) was of course a mockery, since there was very little volunteering being done at this late stage in the war, most recruits having very little option. It was built up during the winter of 1943/44, and in July 1944 a kampfgruppe from the division was sent to the Ukraine to help bolster the crumbling front there, rejoining the division in December. Thereafter, the division served in the retreat through Poland and Slovakia and ended the war east of Prague, before being taken into Russian captivity.

The sight of an SS unit wearing a cuffband bearing the name of one of the great hero figures of the SA, and wearing a collar patch bearing the SA runic device in place of the SS runes, must have been anathema to Himmler. The division, however, was a fully manned and well-equipped combat formation which, though it did not reach the level of efficiency and reliability as some, certainly did not disgrace itself in combat, a fact demonstrated by the award of seven Knights Crosses to its members.

The commanders of the *Horst Wessel* Division were SS-Brigadeführer August Wilhelm Trabandt, who had joined as commander of SS Infanterie Brigade (mot.) 1, SS-Oberführer Georg Bochmann, a highly decorated panzer officer from the *Totenkopf* Division, and, finally, SS-Standartenführer Heinrich Petersen, a *Prinz Eugen* veteran who commanded the division during the final weeks of the war, and who committed suicide rather than go into Soviet captivity.

insistence that a new division be formed to bear the honour title of the party's great martyr, Horst Wessel. This irked Himmler because of the poor relations between the SS and SA. Nevertheless, Hitler insisted (the Army and Air Force already had units into which former members of the SA were specifically recruited). Both the Army and Air Force had units bearing the honour title *Feldherrnhalle*, into which SA members were recruited, and the Air Force had a bomber squadron bearing the honour title *Horst Wessel*.

Himmler decided to comply with Hitler's instructions by conscripting ethnic Germans into this new division, justifying the use of the 'honour' title *Horst Wessel* by the fact that these men were, after all, of German bloodstock.

The division itself was formed in 1943 around a cadre of personnel from SS Infanterie Brigade (mot.) 1. Its title

19th Waffen-Grenadier Division der SS (lettische Nr 2)

This second Latvian volunteer division was formed in March 1944 to take advantage of the excellent response to the recruiting campaign of the Waffen-SS in the Baltic states. Its parent unit was the 2 lettische Freiwilligen Brigade, which had been in action on the Eastern Front since late 1943. The division reached a strength of some 10,500 men and, like its companion Latvian division, was committed to the fierce defensive battles during the retreat from the Leningrad front and into the Courland Pocket.

One of the division's finest soldiers, Waffen-Oberführer Voldemars Veiss, commander of SS Freiwilligen Grenadier-regiment 42, was the first Latvian to win the Knights Cross of the Iron Cross for gallantry in action. Indeed, the 19th Waffen-Grenadier Division could boast an impressive total of 11 Knights Cross winners, giving a combined total, with the 15th Waffen-Grenadier Division, of 16 Knights Crosses – testimony to the ferocious fighting qualities of the Latvian soldiers in defence of their homeland.

The division was slowly pushed back by the Red Army into the Courland Pocket, where it was encircled when the war ended. Most of its personnel were murdered by the Soviets on the pretext that, their homeland having been forcibly annexed by the Soviet Union prior to the outbreak of war, they were thus Soviet citizens and guilty of treason for having supported the Germans.

Divisional troops wore the swastika collar patch used for a short period by the 15th Division, in conjunction with the Latvian arm shield.

20th Waffen-Grenadier Division der SS (estnische Nr 1)

After their country was forcibly annexed by the Soviet Union, many Estonian soldiers took to the woods and waged a partisan war against their Soviet oppressors. Naturally enough, these men saw the Germans as liberators in 1941, and the Germans in turn were quick to exploit the presence of a number of trained soldiers who were fervently anti-communist. A number of self-defence units were raised, but such was the Estonian response that sufficient numbers came forward to raise three full-strength Army battalions, a number of police battalions and six border guard regiments.

The head of the Nazi administration, Generalkommissar Litzmann, called for the raising of an Estonian Legion to fight alongside the Germans on the Eastern Front in 1942. The response was very encouraging, as the Germans had astutely made their appeal on the first anniversary of the liberation of Tallin, the Estonian capital, by German forces. Enough recruits (mainly former conscripted Estonian Army personnel) came forward to form three battalions for the newly formed estnische SS Freiwilligen Grenadier Regiment 1, and a single battalion from the regiment saw action on attachment to the elite *Wiking* Division.

By May 1943, the remainder of the regiment was expanded to brigade status, becoming estnische SS-Freiwilligen Brigade 3. The brigade consisted of SS Freiwilligen Grenadier Regiments 45 and 46. During 1944, Himmler decided to create a new Estonian division by amalgamating the

brigade with elements from the existing Estonian volunteer battalions in the German Army and some police battalions. One of these Army units, estnische Bataillon 658, was commanded by an Estonian officer, Major Alfons Rebane, who had already proved his worth as a soldier by winning the Knights Cross of the Iron Cross in February 1944.

In April 1944, the battalion that had been attached to the *Wiking* Division returned, to join the new division as SS Fusilier Bataillon 20. The divisional commander was SS-Brigadeführer Franz Augsberger, an Austrian, who took his new division into action at the Battle of Narva in mid-1944. Despite its spirited performance, the division was pushed back through its homeland and into the Courland Pocket, where the bulk of it was successfully evacuated to Germany. The division was returned to the Eastern Front in December to oppose the Soviet drive

BELOW: A poster aimed at recruiting British prisoners of war for the SS. The call for volunteers mainly fell on deaf ears, and British members of the SS were few in number.

into Silesia, and thence into Czecho-slovakia. Franz Augsberger was killed in action on 17 March 1945 during the division's breakout from a Soviet encirclement at Falkenberg. He was replaced as divisional commander by SS-Oberführer Berthold Maack.

In May 1945, part of the division was captured by the Soviets. Most of those unfortunate enough to fall into the hands of the Red Army were put to death. Some of their more fortunate comrades succeeded in fighting their way westwards and surrendered to Anglo-American forces.

A special collar patch, in two versions, was produced for the members of this division. The first pattern depicted an armoured arm bearing an upheld sword, with the letter 'E' in the crook of the arm. This was temporarily replaced by one showing simply the letter 'E' with a sword superimposed on it. This proved unpopular, however, and the first type, which had been only unofficially made, was reintroduced as the official pattern. Two versions of Estonian arm shield were also produced. One bore the Estonian colours of blue, black and white as horizontal bars, the other as diagonal bars, and both bore three lions couchant superimposed, facing left, upon the bars. No cuffband was ever authorised for this unit. A total of six members of the division were awarded the Knights Cross of the Iron Cross.

21st Waffen-Gebirgs Division der SS *Skanderbeg*

Albania had been conquered by the Italians in March 1939, prior to the outbreak of war, and remained under Italian control until the latter's surrender to the Allies in 1943. At this point the Germans took over, but, initially at least, treated the Albanians with moderation. Himmler saw in the Albanian Moslems a potential source of manpower for the war against the partisans, most of whom were predominantly Serb, and sought to use the traditional enmity of these two groups for his own ends.

In April 1944, Himmler established a new Albanian volunteer division named after the great Albanian Moslem hero Iskander Beg, who was responsible for driving the Turkish invaders from Albania in the fifteenth century. The division also drew a good number of recruits from the former Yugoslav area of Kossovo, which had been annexed by Italian-controlled Albania in 1941. The quality of recruits was poor, however, and only some 6000 or

so were eventually judged to be suitable to receive training. Numbers were padded out by drafts of personnel from other Waffen-SS units. The officer and NCO cadre, for example, was predominantly German or *Volksdeutsche*.

By August 1944, the division had been formed and was judged as ready for action as it would ever be. It was considered only fit for policing actions, though, and even then its performance was dire. The bulk of the Moslem personnel seemed only interested in settling accounts with their Serb enemies, which resulted in a number of atrocities. Over 3500 desertions were recorded in just two months. Himmler then drafted in nearly 4000 naval personnel who, because of the lack of ships, were surplus to the Navy's requirements. This had little effect on the division's fighting abilities, however, and Himmler ordered its disbandment in early 1945. The German cadre element was formed into a kampfgruppe, which in turn was amalgamated into the *Prinz Eugen* Division for the remainder of the war.

Despite its poor record, a full range of special insignia was introduced for members of the division. A collar patch portraying a helmet with a goat's head device on the crown was made, but saw little use. A cuffband was made and widely worn, showing the title *Skanderbeg* and an Albanian arm shield showing the black Albanian double-headed eagle on a red field. It is also said that many of the division's Moslem personnel wore a traditional skull cap-type headgear, in field-grey, rather than the standard SS field cap.

22nd SS Freiwilligen-Kavallerie Division *Maria Theresia*

As the status of Hungary in relation to Nazi Germany changed from that of an independent ally, then puppet regime, to finally being an occupied country, so the pace of Himmler's recruiting drives accelerated. He planned to form four Hungarian SS divisions in total, of which two would be *Volksdeutsche* and the remainder ethnic Hungarian.

In the autumn of 1944 a new division, entitled SS Division *Ungarn*, was formed. Its personnel, however, were a confused mix of both *Volksdeutsche* and Hungarians, with the resultant language problems. Himmler therefore ordered the Magyar-speaking contingent removed and formed into a separate kampfgruppe named after its commander, Waffen-Obersturmbannführer Karoly Ney, which

'For the fulfilment of these missions a homogeneous, firmly welded fighting force has been created, bound by ideological oaths, whose fighters are selected out of the best Aryan humanity.'
– Organization Book of the NSDAP, 1943

Two views of the men of the 13th Waffen-Gebirgs Division der SS Handschar: relaxing over a meal (LEFT) and on parade (BELOW LEFT). Recruited from members of the Islamic faith, Himmler thought the idea of enlisting Bosnian Moslems, who had a traditional hatred of the Christian Serbs (the latter comprised the bulk of Tito's partisans), an excellent one. The division was granted many privileges, such as special rations and permission for the men to observe their religious rites. These religious privileges were supposedly at odds with the anti-religious ideology of the SS, but Himmler stated to Göbbels that he had 'nothing against Islam because it educates the men in this division for me and promises them heaven if they fight and are killed in action; a very practical and attractive religion for soldiers!' The reality was slightly different. The division fought a number of actions against the partisans, and committed many atrocities in the process, but in the face of the Red Army its men deserted en masse. It was eventually disbanded as a division in October 1944.

führer Anton Ameiser, commander of SS Kavallerie Regiment 22, SS-Oberscharführer Paul Reissmann, killed in action on 8 November 1944 and awarded the Knights Cross posthumously, and SS-Obersturmführer Werner Dallman, also killed in action and awarded his Knights Cross posthumously.

Kampfgruppe *Ney*, with a strength of some 5000 men, escaped the fate of the division and carried out a fighting withdrawal westwards before surrendering to US Army units at Salzburg, Austria. The division was commanded by SS-Brigadeführer August Zehender, who was killed in action when the division was decimated in the defence of Budapest.

Despite being awarded the title *Maria Theresia*, the division was never authorised a cuffband. It was, however, supplied with a special collar patch showing a cornflower.

23rd Waffen-Gebirgs Division der SS *Kama* (kroatische Nr 2)

Activated in January 1944, this division was intended to consist of Bosnian Moslems, plus a cadre of German and *Volksdeutsche* personnel, with a contingent of Croat Moslem officers and NCOs on detachment from the 13th Waffen-Gebirgs Division *Handschar*.

By October 1944, while it was still in the process of its formation, disciplinary problems had become so acute that Himmler ordered its immediate disbandment, no doubt influenced by the recent embarrassment he had experienced over the mutiny

would remain connected to the division. By September 1944, SS Division *Ungarn* had been renamed and given the honour title *Maria Theresia*.

Unfortunately, the division was committed to action before it was fully prepared. As part of IX SS Corps it took part in the Battle of Budapest (November 1944-February 1945) and was all but annihilated. Despite fighting well, it was overwhelmed by the sheer weight of the Soviet assault. Three of the division's men, however, won the Knights Cross of the Iron Cross in its short life: SS-Obersturmbann-

TOP: Latvians in action against the Red Army, late 1944.

BOTTOM: Latvians dive for cover on the Eastern Front, late 1944. Latvian dislike of the Soviet Union was strong, and approximately 32,000 Latvians volunteered for the Waffen-SS in 1943. Two divisions were eventually formed, the 15th and 19th Waffen-Grenadier Divisions.

Anton Mussert, the Dutch Nazi leader, however, was affronted by the idea of a merger of his Dutch volunteers with other nationalities, and he sent his protest to Hitler. The Führer agreed, and instructed Himmler to exclude the Dutch volunteers from the projected division.

As there were insufficient Dutch volunteers to form a division on their own, a brigade-sized unit of two regiments was set up as SS Freiwilligen Panzergrenadier Brigade *Nederland*. The two regiments bore the honour titles *General Seyyfardt* and *De Ruiter*. The brigade's first action was against partisans in Croatia, before moving into the area in which its predecessor legion had served – the Leningrad front. Committed to the Battle of Narva in 1944, the brigade was almost completely wiped out.

In December 1944, in a largely paper reorganisation, the brigade was given divisional status as the 23rd SS Freiwilligen Panzergrenadier Division and re-committed to the front as part of the 3rd SS Panzer Army. By early 1945, *Nederland* had withdrawn into the Courland Pocket and was evacuated by sea to Stettin, only to be thrown back into action on the rapidly crumbling Eastern Front in Pomerania. It was remorselessly driven westwards, and eventually surrendered to the Americans at Fürstenwalde. Despite its short combat career, the fighting qualities of these troops should not be underestimated. Some 20 Dutch volunteers in the Waffen-SS received the Knights Cross of the Iron Cross for gallantry in action.

The official collar insignia for the division portrayed the so-called 'wolf's hook' emblem in both horizontal and vertical forms. An arm shield in the Dutch colours of orange, white and blue was worn just above the cuffband. Cuffbands were produced for both the *General Seyyfardt* and *De Ruiter* Regiments, as well as a divisional cuffband *Nederland*.

of the *Handschar* Division in France. The division's illustrated sunburst motif collar patch was never issued.

23rd SS Freiwilligen Panzergrenadier Division
Nederland

During the early part of 1943, the Freiwilligen Legion *Niederlande* was withdrawn from frontline service after being badly mauled in the fighting around Leningrad, and was sent back to Holland for rest and refitting. Himmler, meanwhile, was intent on amalgamating his four Germanic volunteer units into one powerful division, to be called *Nordland*.

24th SS Gebirgs Division
Karstjäger

In the summer of 1942, a mountain troop company was formed to deal with the growing partisan problem in northern Italy. In November of that year, it was decided to expand the unit to a battalion. By the summer of 1943, the battalion had been worked up and was dispatched to northern Italy just after the overthrow of Benito Mussolini.

Its first mission was to capture and disarm the Italian Army garrison at

Tarvisio, which it did successfully, before going on to carry out actions against communist partisans in the Trieste, Udine and Gorizia regions. Gratified with its success, Himmler authorised its upgrading to a division in July 1944 (in the event, its total strength never exceed 7000 men). Most of its recruits came from the south Tirol, Istria and Slovenia, along with a smaller number from Croatia, Serbia and even the Ukraine. From its base in Udine, it spent the bulk of its life in action against communist partisan bands. Ironically, one of its first senior officers was a SS-Obersturmbannführer Karl Marcks, and one of his fellow officers in the division bore the name of Engels!

As the war drew to a close, the division found itself in action against enemy frontline combat units for the first time – it acquitted itself well. Finally, its remnants were formed into a kampfgruppe with the remains of other Waffen-SS units and under the command of SS-Brigadeführer Heinz Harmel, a veteran of Arnhem, and acted as a rearguard to protect other German units withdrawing from Yugoslavia. It did not surrender until 9 May 1945, one day *after* the official end of the war in Europe.

25th Waffen-Grenadier Division der SS *Hunyadi*

First formed in mid-1944, this supposedly totally ethnic Hungarian unit was still being worked up to operational status when it and Hungary were overrun by the Red Army. Despite not having reached operational status, special insignia in the form of a collar patch bearing a large letter 'H' had been manufactured and issued.

26th Waffen-Grenadier Division der SS *Hungaria*

Formed in Germany in September 1944 around a nucleus of existing units, including the 49th SS Panzergrenadier Brigade and Panzer Brigade *Gross*, it also picked up a small number of Hungarians and Romanian soldiers fleeing from the advancing Red Army. It was still not fully organised when Hungary fell, being rapidly swamped by the enemy and never reaching operational status.

27th SS Freiwilligen-Panzergrenadier Division *Langemarck*

In May 1943, Freiwilligen Legion *Flandern* was withdrawn from the front, having suffered a severe mauling near Leningrad.

Pulled back to Bohemia for rest and refitting, it was joined by a fresh group of recruits from Belgium. However, many of the first intake of volunteers were nearing the end of their two-year contract and, unsurprisingly, did not wish to re-enlist. The legion was therefore disbanded.

The total of those who were willing to re-enlist, plus the new group of recruits, was insufficient to build a new legion, however. A Finnish battalion was added to bolster numbers, and the assembled force added to a cadre from the SS Infanterie Regiment *Langemarck*, which had been withdrawn from the *Das Reich* Division. The new body was named SS Freiwilligen Sturmbrigade *Langemarck*. Commanded by SS-Obersturmbannführer Conrad Schellong, a Knights Cross holder, it was dispatched to the southern sector of the Eastern Front in December 1943. By the summer of the next year it was in the north and took part in the attritional Battle of Narva.

In September 1944, the brigade was expanded to a division, though its strength at this time probably did not exceed 3000 men. It was all but wiped out during heavy fighting in December 1944, and its remnants pushed back through Poland and Pomerania. Some of its veterans survived to take part in the defence of Berlin.

During its short history, this Flemish unit earned a good reputation for combat reliability. One of its junior NCOs, SS-Sturmmann Remy Schrÿnen, was decorated with the Knights Cross of the Iron Cross on 21 September 1944 for extreme gallantry in the face of the enemy. As an anti-tank gunner, he had continued to man his weapon alone after the other crew members had all been killed, and he himself had been ordered to withdraw. He refused to leave his post, and single-handedly knocked out three 'Stalin' tanks and four T-34s before being severely wounded. After the war, this brave soldier was rewarded with a sentence of 10 years imprisonment for having served with the Germans. Not surprisingly, on his release he left Belgium and now lives in Germany.

Although many members of the division wore the standard SS runes collar patch, the three-legged swastika, or 'Trifos', collar patch was also worn, as was the Flemish arm shield showing a black rampant lion on a yellow field. A *Langemarck* cuffband already existed for that regiment within the *Das Reich* Division, and it continued to be worn by members of this division.

'This faith in higher ideals inspired four hundred thousand German SS, three hundred thousand Volksdeutsche or Germanic SS and three hundred thousand other European SS. Volunteers all, one million builders of Europe.'
– Leon Degrelle, Commander 28th Waffen-SS Division *Wallonien*

28th SS Freiwilligen-Panzergrenadier Division *Wallonien*

As mentioned above, after Belgium was occupied in 1940 the Flemish half of the population was considered Germanic and thus eligible for service in the Waffen-SS, while the Walloons were considered fit only for service in the Wehrmacht.

In Belgium there existed a right-wing, predominantly Catholic, nationalist political organisation – the Rexists – under the charismatic leadership of Léon Degrelle. Degrelle and his followers naturally supported the German attack on the 'godless' Soviets in 1941, and when the Germans called for volunteers for their 'Crusade against Bolshevism', they received a willing and eager response from the Rexists. Over 1000 Walloons came forward to volunteer almost immediately, among them Degrelle himself. Pleased at having such an important political figure, and mindful of his position as the leader of the Rexists, the Germans offered him a commission in their Walloon volunteer force. Modestly, Degrelle refused the offer, insisting that as he had no military training he would prefer to first gain experience in the ranks.

In August 1941 the volunteers left for Poland, where they were to undergo military training. The unit joined the order of battle of the German Army as 373 Infanterie Bataillon, and was initially used in anti-partisan duties until February 1942 to allow the troops to build up their military skills before being sent to the front. During this period Degrelle justified the confidence the Germans had shown him by winning the Iron Cross both Second and First Classes, and eventually being commissioned a lieutenant in May 1942.

The Walloon volunteers then moved to the front and saw heavy combat action on the Don and in the Caucasus, suffering severe casualties. In order to provide battle casualty replacements, and to allow for the expansion of the battalion, the lower age limit for recruits was dropped and the upper limit raised. By May 1943, its strength stood at around 1600 men.

Now Himmler cast his covetous eyes on the Walloons. Having proved themselves in battle, he now considered them suitable material for the Waffen-SS. In June 1943, therefore, they were taken into the SS as the SS Sturmbrigade *Wallonien* and attached to the *Wiking* Division in the southern sector of the front in late 1943.

January 1944 saw the Walloon brigade embroiled in the battle for the Cherkassy Pocket, where almost 60,000 German troops were in danger of being cut off and wiped out. The breakout, though successful, was costly in terms of losses and *Wallonien* emerged with only 632 men, though with its reputation considerably enhanced. On 20 February 1944, Degrelle, now holding the rank of SS-Hauptsturmführer and commanding the brigade, was decorated with the Knights Cross of the Iron Cross for his gallantry in action. Hitler took great personal interest in the progress of the brigade, and Degrelle became one of his personal favourites.

The brigade was withdrawn from the front to regroup, but had to be rushed back into action soon afterwards because the situation on the Eastern Front had deteriorated rapidly. In July 1944, the remnants of Sturmbrigade *Wallonien* were involved in the Battle of Narva, again incurring heavy losses.

Withdrawn from the front again for rest and regrouping, the brigade was upgraded to a division in the autumn of 1944. At this time Degrelle was again personally decorated by Hitler: with the Oakleaves to his Knights Cross along with the prestigious Close Combat Clasp in Gold, which was awarded for 75 days of hand-to-hand fighting.

A division on paper only, it never reached full strength. It returned to the Eastern Front in January 1945 and was thrown into the line at Stettin. After a few weeks hard fighting its strength was down to a mere 700 men, as it was gradually pushed farther and farther west. In the closing days of the war what was left of the division withdrew into Denmark, from where Degrelle managed to escape to Norway and then by plane to Spain, where he lives to this day.

In addition to Degrelle himself, two other Walloons received the Knights Cross: SS-Untersturmführer Leon Gillis and SS-Untersturmführer Jaques Leroy. The latter lost his right arm and right eye in the battle at Cherkassy, but he refused to be invalided out of the unit. In April 1945, he took charge of 1 Kompanie of SS Freiwilligen Panzergrenadier Regiment 69. During three days and nights of hand-to-hand combat the 40-man unit lost 32 of its strength, but Leroy manifested such fine qualities of courage and leadership that, on 20 April, he was recommended for an immediate award of the Knights Cross. Although the award was approved, it is not known if the decoration itself was physically given to him.

Soldiers of the division generally wore the standard SS runes collar patch, together with a cuffband *Wallonien* (German spelling) and an arm shield in the national colours of black, yellow and red vertical stripes, with the title *Wallonie* above.

29th Waffen-Grenadier Division der SS (russische Nr 1)

This notorious unit had its origins in early 1942 in the town of Lokat in central Russia. Red Army units had been driven from the area, but large numbers of them lurked in the nearby forests, from where they carried out partisan attacks on German supply lines. The town's mayor sought, and was granted, permission from the Germans to raise a self-defence force of around 500 men to defend the area against these attacks. The unit was a great success and partisan activity in the area decreased dramatically. The volunteers were fervent anti-communists and pursued their enemy with great vigour. The mayor was eventually killed during combat with the partisans and so a replacement had to be sought. One candidate for the post was considered particularly suitable by the Germans: Bronislav Kaminski, an educat-ed man with a career in chemical engineer-ing who spoke fluent German and had spent a period of imprisonment in a Soviet labour camp, which had engendered in him a fanatical hatred for all communists. He was given command of the self-defence force and proved himself a skilled organis-er and administrator, if over ambitious and arrogant. He served his German mas-ters well, however, and pursued the parti-sans mercilessly. So pleased were the Germans that they permitted an expansion of his self-defence force, until by the autumn of 1943 it resembled more a pri-vate army, having 10,000 men and even a number of captured tanks.

The unit saw continuous action against the partisans in the forests near Bryansk, where Kaminski himself earned the Iron Cross Second and First Classes. By 1944, the force had assumed the rather grand title of Russian Liberation Peoples Army, its Russian initials RONA appearing as POHA in cyrillic script. The unit had its own arm shield, which bore these letters on a dark-green base over a red-edged white shield, which enclosed a black Maltese cross.

The unit eventually came to Himmler's attention for its 'successes' (widespread

BELOW: Dutch SS recruits swear the oath of allegiance. Following the disbandment of the Dutch legion, recruits from Holland were formed into a Waffen-SS panzergrenadier brigade, and then the 23rd SS Freiwilligen Panzergrenadier Division Nederland. They performed consistently well in battle.

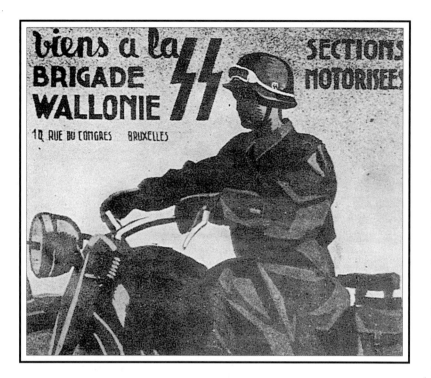

ABOVE: A publicity postcard for the motorised section of the Sturmbrigade Wallonie *(Walloon spelling). Initially recruits in the Wehrmacht, the Walloons were taken into the Waffen-SS after they had proved themselves to be excellent soldiers.*

atrocities) against the partisans, and it ultimately came under Waffen-SS control. It was taken into the SS as the Sturmbrigade *RONA*, and Kaminski was granted the rank of Waffen-Brigadeführer. Its final designation was the 29th Waffen-Grenadier Division, though it never actually reached divisional strength.

It was undergoing training in Hungary in August 1944 when the Warsaw uprising broke out. One of the *RONA*'s regiments was detached and sent to assist in the suppression of the rebellion. The scenes that followed were more reminiscent of medieval barbarity than twentieth-century warfare, as the *RONA* troops murdered, looted, raped and pillaged their way through Warsaw in an orgy of savagery. Other German units which attempted to prevent these outrages found themselves threatened by Kaminski's men. As their rampage continued, the SS commander in charge of the Warsaw action, SS-Obergruppenführer Erich von dem Bach-Zelewski, was inundated with complaints about their behaviour. *RONA* troops were by now totally out of control and the SS was forced to act.

Kaminski was arrested and brought to trial. He was charged, not with the tens of thousands of murders committed by his troops, but with looting. Found guilty after a brief trial he was quickly executed. In order to avoid a mutiny by the division, a fake partisan ambush was staged in which Kaminski was reported to have been killed. The *RONA* then deteriorated into a lawless rabble, its morale destroyed by the loss of its venerated leader. The

sorry remnants found their way into the Russian Army of Liberation of General Andrei Vlassov, or into the 30th Waffen-Grenadier Division der SS.

29th Waffen-Grenadier Division der SS (italienische Nr 1)

When the Italian government surrendered to the Allies in 1943, there remained an ample number of pro-fascist Italian troops willing to continue the struggle on the side of Germany, and so a volunteer legion of some 3000 soldiers, led principally by German officers and NCOs, was raised in October 1943. By the end of that year, sizeable numbers of Italian troops in the unliberated north, shamed by their country's surrender, joined and increased its strength to around 15,000 men.

These volunteers were formed into an SS sturmbrigade and spent a period of time training in the south of Germany, before being returned to Italy as the *Legion Italia* under the command of SS-Brigadeführer Peter Hansen. Initially used in antipartisan operations, in February 1944 the unit was reorganised and renamed as a volunteer brigade with the intention of employing it eventually in frontline combat duties. With this in mind, much of the brigade was sent back to Germany for more intensive training.

Interestingly, although this unit was comprised of staunch fascists who until recently had been allies of the Germans, Himmler was reluctant to grant the unit full SS status, and so the Italian troops utilised insignia embroidered on a red, rather than the traditional SS black, base. The collar patch bore the Italian fasces emblem in place of the runes (though runic collar patches on a red base also exist), and the traditional SS-style arm eagle worn by these troops held a fasces, not a swastika, in its talons.

In April 1944, the Italian troops found themselves in action against the Allied landings at Anzio and performed so well that they were cited for their gallantry. However, the price had been high: over half the unit's strength had been lost in the battle. Himmler was so impressed that he proclaimed: 'Because of the demonstration of courage and devotion to duty displayed by the volunteers of the Italian SS, they are designated as units of the Waffen-SS, with all of the rights and duties which that implies.' In fact, however, only these portions of the brigade that had fought at Anzio, the so-called *Vendetta* Battalion and SS Fusilier Bataillon 29, were so honoured. These soldiers were now permitted to wear the correct black-backed SS insignia and the runic collar tabs.

In April 1945, the brigade was given official divisional status, though it never reached division strength. It saw further action against the communist partisans in the rear and US Army combat units at the front in the closing days of the war, and performed consistently well.

Part of the division surrendered to the Americans near Gorgonzola on 30 April. The remainder saw continued action against the partisans in the Lake Como area until the last days of the war, when, after running out of ammunition, it unwisely surrendered to the partisans. The survivors were massacred to a man. One Italian Waffen-SS officer, recovering from serious wounds, was even dragged from a hospital bed and shot.

30th Waffen-Grenadier Division der SS (weissruthenische Nr 1)

The Belorussian area of the Soviet Union, being its most westerly region, was one of the first areas to be occupied by the Germans and the last to be retaken by the Soviets. The Belorussians were far from committed communists, and the German troops who occupied the area in 1941 were generally well received by the population and were considered as liberators. In return, the Belorussians were treated less harshly by the Germans than were the occupants of many other areas. In October 1941, the Nazi kommissar for the area, Wilhelm Kube, sanctioned the raising of a volunteer self-defence unit to counter any potential threat from Soviet partisans.

As the harsh realities of occupation by the Germans became clear, the attitude of the Belorussians changed from that of open support to one of considering the Germans as the lesser of two evils. Despite this change in attitude, there was still an ample supply of volunteers prepared to come forward and offer their services to defend their homeland against the Soviets.

In the summer of 1944 these volunteers were moved to Germany for training, where they were formed into the 30th Waffen-Grenadier Division der SS. As a number of its personnel already had experience of police-style actions against the partisans in the self-defence units, it was considered by the Germans that the unit would be best used by continuing in this role, and in September 1944 it was sent, not to defend its homeland, but to France to combat the French Resistance, the *Maquis*. Its performance was lamentable and a large number of desertions ensued, which resulted in it being downgraded to brigade statue. It saw some action in the defence of the Rhine against the Allies, but was easily pushed back.

In early 1945, its German cadre personnel were withdrawn and most were seconded to the newly formed 38th SS Panzergrenadier Division *Nibelungen*, while the Belorussian troops were passed over to Vlassov's Russian Army of Liberation. They were captured by the Red Army in May 1945 and executed out of hand as traitors.

German cadre personnel in the division wore the standard SS runes collar tab, while the Russian personnel are believed to have worn a plain blank patch.

31st SS Freiwilligen Grenadier Division

This short-lived division was raised in the autumn of 1944 from a mixture of German and *Volksdeutsche* personnel from the so-called protectorate of Bohemia-Moravia (part of Czechoslovakia). It was rushed to the crumbling Eastern Front before it had been properly formed or fully trained, and was quickly annihilated in May 1945. Many of its cadre personnel had come from the disbanded *Kama* Division. Unconfirmed reports state that the division had the honour title *Böhmen-Mähren*. No special insignia was ever introduced for this unit.

BELOW: The leader of the Walloons: Léon Degrelle, seen here holding the rank of SS-Sturmbannführer. Note the Army-style Edelweiss badge worn on his field cap. Strangely, it is worn with the stem pointing to the rear rather than the front of the cap. Degrelle, the founder of the fascist Rexist Party, was heavily influenced by the extreme French nationalist Charles Maurras, Italian fascism and the German Nazi Party. Ironically, he only joined the Waffen-SS to stop Himmler's plans to incorporate Flemish-speaking Belgium into the Reich. Nevertheless, he proved to be an outstanding leader of men, winning the Knights Cross and Oakleaves for his gallantry. He eventually reached the rank of SS-Oberführer, and managed to escape his nation's retribution after the war had finished by fleeing to Norway and then to Spain.

ABOVE: Léon Degrelle and other survivors of the Cherkassy Pocket, when 1368 were killed and wounded out of a total of 2000 men from SS Sturmbrigade Wallonien. The courage of the Walloons convinced the Germans of their worth, and Degrelle, their highly-decorated commander, was given permission to form the 28th Freiwilligen-Panzergrenadier Division Wallonien.

33rd Waffen-Grenadier Division der SS *Charlemagne*

The forerunner of this division was the *Légion des Volontaires Français*, a French volunteer force raised in 1941 under the control of the German Army. It was initially designated as the Army's Infanterie Regiment 638, first seeing action on the Eastern Front as part of the 7th Infantry Division during the drive on Moscow during the winter of 1941/42. It suffered heavy losses and so, from spring 1942 to autumn 1943, was out of frontline service and utilised principally in anti-partisan operations in the rear areas. At this point in its career it was fragmented and used in individual battalion-sized units. It was regrouped again in January 1944, but still continued with its anti-partisan duties.

In June 1944, the legion returned to the central sector of the Eastern Front to take part in successful defensive actions against the Red Army. So impressive was the performance of these French troops that the Red Army thought it was facing two French divisions, while in fact the French strength had been reduced to

around half a battalion. The French soldiers had proved their combat worth.

In September 1944, the French volunteers were inducted into the Waffen-SS. SS recruiting in France had begun in earnest in 1943 from a recruiting office based in Paris. In August of that year, the first 800 volunteers were sent to Alsace for training as the *französiche* SS Freiwilligen Sturmbrigade. In November 1943, some 30 or so French officers were sent to the SS-Junkerschule at Bad Tölz in Bavaria, and around 100 NCOs to various Unterführerschulen to upgrade their training to Waffen-SS standards.

Meanwhile, a number of French volunteers had seen service on the Eastern Front while attached temporarily to the 18th SS Freiwilligen-Panzergrenadier Division *Horst Wessel*. After seeing fierce combat against the Red Army, they were withdrawn from the line to regroup and refit. At this point, because of the Frenchmen's combat record, it was decided to merge them with the remnants of the legion and an intake of French militiamen to form a new Waffen-SS division.

This most unusual of Waffen-SS divisions also included a number of personnel from the French colonies, including French Indo-China, and even a lone Japanese. It is also claimed that a few French Jews managed to escape detection in the ranks of the *Charlemagne* Division.

The division was formed during the winter of 1944/45, and early in the new year was committed to the front in Pomerania. Constant ferocious combat against the numerically vastly superior Red Army saw the division badly battered and split into three fragments. One battalion-sized unit retreated into the Baltic and was evacuated by sea to Denmark, eventually finding its way to Neustrelitz, near Berlin. A second group was totally decimated by furious Soviet artillery barrages, and a third attempted a fighting withdrawal westwards but was virtually wiped out, its personnel being either killed or captured by the Russians.

Those remnants at Neustrelitz were assembled by the divisional commander, SS-Brigadeführer Gustav Krukenberg, who released from their oath of allegiance any who no longer wished to serve. Some 500 men, however, volunteered to go with their commander to the defence of Berlin. Around 700 remained at Neustrelitz.

The 500 volunteers who went into action during the battle for Berlin fought exceptionally well, despite knowing by then that all was lost. Their gallantry was recognised by the award of three Knights Crosses to divisional personnel. One went to SS-Obersturmführer Wilhelm Weber, one of the German cadre personnel, and two to individual French soldiers: Waffen-Unterscharführer Eugene Vaulot and Waffen-Oberscharführer Francois Apollot. All three awards were made for personal gallantry in single-handedly knocking out a number of Soviet tanks. Both Vaulot and Apollot were killed just three days later; Weber survived the war.

Those members of the *Charlemagne* Division who had elected not to go on fighting made their way back to voluntary captivity in the West. Doubtless they anticipated that they would be more fairly treated by the Western Allies than by the Russians. Those who surrendered to their compatriots in the Free French forces, however, were to be shockingly disabused of this illusion.

It is reported that when confronted by Free French soldiers who asked why they would wish to wear German uniform, the French SS soldiers queried the US uniforms worn by the Free Frenchmen. Infuriated at this retort, the French commander had the Waffen-SS men shot on the spot, without any due process of law. As far as the Free French were concerned, they were guilty of the worst crime in the military calendar: 'traitorous collaboration with the enemy'. Needless to say, the murderers of the French SS volunteers went unpunished. Ironically, French SS men who had taken part in the atrocity at Oradour in 1944 were much more leniently treated. Regarded as unwilling conscripts and thus 'victims', they were, after a properly constituted trial, acquitted. The reason behind this surprising verdict would appear to be a political one. These SS men were from the province of Alsace, which had changed hands between France and Germany on a number of occasions. It was felt that a guilty verdict against those involved in the Oradour outrage might create unrest in Alsace.

Thus, the situation arose whereby French Waffen-SS men who had taken part in the executions of a considerable number of French citizens were allowed to go unpunished, while members of the *Charlemagne* Division, who had fought the Red Army or communist partisan groups in the East, were put to death after having surrendered.

34th Waffen-Grenadier Division der SS *Landstorm Nederland*

In March 1943, a Dutch territorial home guard unit was established, known as the *Landwacht Nederland*. The men were, however, conscripts and not true volunteers. In October 1943, control of the unit passed to the SS and its name was changed from

BELOW: A celebratory dinner held to honour the return of the SS Sturmbrigade Wallonien from the Cherkassy Pocket. There was a special celebration in the Belgium capital on 1 April 1944, with 'Sepp' Dietrich himself being the senior German officer present.

Landwacht to *Landstorm*. It was originally intended purely for internal security duties, but at least some elements saw action at Arnhem in September 1944.

The *Landstorm Nederland* Division was inducted into the Waffen-SS proper in November 1944, and was stiffened by additions from the SS recruiting staff in the Netherlands and members of the Dutch Nazi NSB youth movement, the approximate Dutch equivalent of the Hitler Youth, plus other formerly non-combatant elements of the *Landstorm*.

By March 1945, it was considered that sufficient numbers had been gathered to form a new Waffen-SS division. However, due to its extremely short combat life of only a few weeks, it played no significant role in the closing stages of the war in Europe, fighting in only minor defensive skirmishes before German forces surrendered in May 1945.

Despite its late war origin, a full range of insignia was produced for this unit. A collar patch showing a flaming grenade was worn, though examples of the 'wolf's hook' patch were also used. A machine-woven cuffband bearing the title *Landstorm Nederland* was worn also, as was a sleeve shield with the Dutch colours of orange, white and blue in either horizontal or diagonal stripes.

37th SS Freiwilligen-Kavallerie Division *Lützow*

Hurriedly assembled in February 1945 as the situation on the Eastern Front deteriorated rapidly, the division was built around a cadre of personnel from the remnants of the 8th and 22nd SS Cavalry Divisions. Theoretically the division included two full regiments, but in effect the entire division never reached the strength of even a single regiment. It existed for just over three months only, and was then swamped in the Red Army's advance.

Spanish Volunteers

Spain had for some time fielded a full division of volunteer troops on the Eastern Front as part of the German Army. As the war turned against the Germans, pressure from the Western Allies eventually persuaded the Spanish dictator Franco to order the recall of his famed 'Blue' Division in 1943. A large number of its dedicated anti-communist members, however, refused to return to Spain. From these volunteers the Waffen-SS formed a small legion comprising just two companies: SS Freiwilligen Kompanie (span.) 101 and SS Freiwilligen Kompanie (span.) 102.

Both units were committed to battle and saw action during the fighting around Krasny Bor. Some also participated in the

Battle of Berlin and were captured by the Red Army. Those unfortunate enough to fall into the hands of the Soviets were held prisoner until 1954, by which time around 30 per cent of their number had perished.

Swedish Volunteers

A small number of Swedes, probably between 100 and 130 in all, served in the Waffen-SS, although there was no specific Swedish volunteer unit. Apparently, however, a number of them were concentrated in 3 Kompanie, SS Aufklärungs Abteilung 11, a part of the multi-national *Nordland* Division. So much so, in fact, that the unit became known as the 'Swedenzug'.

It is also known that at least 20 Swedish officers passed out from the SS-Junkerschule at Bad Tölz in Bavaria. A few others served in the elite *Wiking* Division, and a scattering of individuals saw service in other Waffen-SS divisions. At least five Swedish officers served in the SS Kriegsberichter *Kurt Eggers* unit as war correspondents.

There were no Knights Cross winners among the Swedish volunteers, but it is known that a number won the Iron Cross Second or First Class, that one was awarded the Honour Roll Clasp of the German Army, and that a Swedish oberscharführer serving in the 10th SS Panzer Division *Frundsberg* was decorated with the German Cross in Gold.

The Cossacks

As a fiercely nationalistic and independent race, many of the various Cossack nations were eager to serve with the Germans in their war against the hated Soviet communist regime. By 1944, a number of independent Cossack cavalry units were already serving in the German Army, as well as a powerful Cossack division commanded by a dedicated German cavalry officer, General Helmuth von Pannwitz. In November 1944, the Waffen-SS took over control of all Cossack units and stated its intention to form an entire corps – the XV Cossack Cavalry Corps – comprising two full divisions of Cossacks.

In the event, it appears that the SS control of the Cossack volunteers was a purely administrative matter. No Waffen-SS officers were attached to any Cossack unit, no SS insignia was issued and all members retained their German Army paybooks. For all practical purposes, the Cossack formations remained under the control of the Army rather than Waffen-SS, and as such are thus outside the compass of this study.

'In our treatment of the foreign ethnic groups in the east, we must attempt to recognize and foster as many individual groups as possible, i.e. apart from Poles and Jews, the Ukrainians, White Ruthenians, Gorales, Lemkes and Kashubians. If there are any more ethnic splinter groups to be found, then these too.'
– Himmler, 'Thoughts on the Treatment of the Alien Population in the East', 15 May 1940

LEFT: Rumanian soldiers in the service of the Waffen-SS on the Eastern Front take a rare opportunity to rest, despite the harsh conditions. The vehicle in the background is a Sturmhaubitze, a variant of the StuG III armed with a 105mm gun.

HOLDING THE LINE

On the Eastern Front, the Soviet offensives of late 1942 and early 1943 threw the Germans onto the defensive. But then I SS Panzer Corps retook Kharkov, and the Führer became convinced his·SS legions were unbeatable. But the Waffen-SS was struggling to contain the Red Army, and the Battles of Kursk and Narva would see his elite divisions bled white.

As the premier formations of the Waffen-SS, the *Leibstandarte Adolf Hitler, Das Reich* and *Totenkopf* Divisions, were undergoing retraining and reorganisation in France in the second half of 1942, the German armies in Russia were coming under intense pressure from the Red Army.

The German offensive in the south had ground to a halt in September at Stalingrad, and in October the renewed German push on Leningrad was equally unsuccessful. By November 1942, the Red Army was counterattacking at Stalingrad, and on the 23rd of that month the German 6th Army had been surrounded. The end of November also saw the Red Army going over to the offensive in the central sector of the front. By the end of the year the situation was worsening, as the Italian 8th Army collapsed on the Don front and Hitler had to order the withdrawal of Army Group A from the Caucusus to prevent its destruction.

On 9 January 1943, the newly formed I SS Panzer Corps, consisting of the *Leibstandarte, Das Reich* and *Totenkopf* Divisions, was rushed to the Eastern Front from France. The *Leibstandarte* and *Das Reich,* under the command of SS-Obergruppenführer Paul Hausser, were immediately sent into positions around Kharkov.

Tiger tanks of the **Das Reich** *Division advance during the Battle of Kursk, July 1943. Despite the tenacity of SS and Army units, for Germany 'Zitadelle' was a failure.*

BELOW: Fritz Witt (right) photographed in March 1943 as a commander of a regimental battlegroup of the **Leibstandarte Division.** *He holds the rank of SS-Standartenführer, but, as with many SS soldiers on the Eastern Front, he has abandoned military etiquette and opted for comfort and warmth, commandeering a loose sheepskin jacket. Note also the non-regulation headgear of the man he is addressing! Witt, the decorated veteran of the war in the Soviet Union who participated in the capture of Kharkov, went on to forge the 12th SS Panzer Division* **Hitlerjugend** *into a crack fighting unit, and was killed in action leading it during the campaign in Normandy in June 1944.*

The *Leibstandarte* was ordered to hold a defensive bridgehead at Chegevayev that stretched for over 100km (70 miles) along the banks of the River Donetz. *Das Reich*, meanwhile, held the area to the east of the river. The *Leibstandarte* Division was weakened somewhat by the removal of Fritz Witt's Panzergrenadier Regiment *LSSAH*, which was ordered to defensive positions at Kupyansk on the River Oskol. In early February, the outermost positions held by the *Leibstandarte* were overrun by the enemy, but the main defensive positions held firm, repulsing massed Soviet attacks with heavy losses on both sides.

Das Reich was slowly pushed back to the Donetz, putting up a spirited fight as it withdrew. Unfortunately, few of the other units in the sector were as tenacious in the defence as the Waffen-SS troops, who found themselves cut off by the Red Army's advance. A wide gap of some 65km (40 miles) appeared between the *Leibstandarte* and its neighbouring unit, the Army's 320th Infantry Division. The Army unit took a pounding from the Soviets and was soon cut off behind enemy lines. A kampfgruppe under the command of SS-Sturmbannführer Joachim Peiper was formed and tasked with penetrating some 40km (25 miles) behind enemy lines, contacting the 320th Infantry

Division, and guiding it back to the German lines. This was no small undertaking, but was one which Peiper accomplished with great success and remarkably little loss of life. For his achievement, Peiper was awarded the Knights Cross of the Iron Cross. It was the first of many daredevil exploits which would be carried out by this remarkable soldier.

A larger kampfgruppe, under the command of SS-Obergruppenführer 'Sepp' Dietrich and consisting of the Aufklärungsabteilung of the *Leibstandarte*, the *Der Führer* Regiment from *Das Reich*, the panzer regiment of the *Leibstandarte,* and the panzergrenadier regiment *LSSAH* was tasked with cutting across the salient formed by the Soviet advance and establishing contact with the bulk of the trapped German units.

Dietrich's force lanced into the Soviet salient in temperatures as low as minus 20 degrees, piercing 45km (30 miles) into enemy territory and cutting off the Soviet VII Guards Cavalry Corps. The fighting continued for several days, as objectives were taken, lost, retaken and lost yet again. Finally, Hausser, fearing that his forces were in great danger of being cut off, requested permission to make a tactical withdrawal and reorganise his units. He was probably somewhat less than totally surprised when Hitler refused. Hausser, however, had no intention of allowing his troops to be encircled and withdrew anyway. On 16 February, the Red Army captured Kharkov. By now, however, it was the Red Army's turn to feel exhausted. Its supply lines were stretched to their limits, its men exhausted and its units weakened by dreadful losses.

Field Marshal von Manstein was aware of the Soviets' precarious position and decided that an immediate counterattack could be successful. Timing was of the essence. A successful attack now would stun the enemy, leaving him with no time to mount a response before the spring thaw turned the front into an impassable sea of mud. This would then give the Germans themselves time to prepare for their own spring offensive.

Manstein decided on a massive pincer attack, in which Hausser's I SS Panzer Corps, which now included the *Totenkopf* Division, would be the northern spearhead. The attack began on 19 February and met with almost immediate success. In just one week the Soviet 6th Army had been annihilated, losing over 23,000 killed, with over 600 tanks and 1000 guns captured. Most of its manpower, however, did escape across the frozen Donetz.

I SS Panzer Corps takes Kharkov

Fearing a counterattack by 3rd Guards Tank Army to the south, the *Leibstandarte* launched an attack on the heights commanding the vital Berevka-Yefomevka highway, before turning towards Valuiki in the east, with the *Totenkopf* covering its flanks. In fierce fighting lasting some three days, the Soviet 15th Guards Army was encircled. By 6 March, Valuiki had fallen with huge Soviet losses. Three days later, *Leibstandarte*'s lead units had reached Polevaya and forced the enemy back over the Donetz there. As the rampaging Waffen-SS units pursued the fleeing Russians, the *Totenkopf* Division lost its commander when Theodor Eicke's light observation aircraft was shot down by enemy gunfire, killing all on board.

Hausser now deployed his I SS Panzer Corps for the capture of Kharkov. Attacking from the north and west, the Waffen-SS slammed into the city's defences and battled the Russian garrison in five days of intense house-to-house fighting, before Kharkov was finally taken. However, it was only gained at a considerable cost in lives, the corps having lost some 11,500 killed and wounded.

What counted to the Germans, however, was that it was a great victory. Following the disastrous surrender at Stalingrad on 31 January and the Soviet's success in preventing the capture of Leningrad, it was a much needed boost to morale. Hitler, at least, still believed that ultimate victory on the Eastern Front was still very much possible.

Although Hitler had been enraged by Hausser's withdrawal from Kharkov, disobeying his express orders to stand firm, the Waffen-SS had once again shown itself in his eyes to be among the finest troops he had. Contemptuous of what he saw as the lack of fighting spirit shown by the Italian 8th Army when it was crushed by the Russians in the south, Hitler insisted that his I SS Panzer Corps was worth at least 20 Italian divisions!

His prized Waffen-SS had performed as well as the best troops the Army could field; indeed, better than most, and he had no hesitation in agreeing to the formation of two further SS corps. The revamped I SS Panzer Corps would consist of the *Leibstandarte* plus the new *Hitlerjugend* Division; II SS Panzer Corps would consist of *Das Reich* and *Totenkopf*; and III SS Panzer Corps of *Wiking* and the new *Nordland* Division.

However, by early March 1943 the *Hitlerjugend* Division was still very much in its early stages of formation. The *Nordland* Division was formed in spring 1943 by detaching the *Nordland* Regiment from the *Wiking* Division and adding the new regiments *Norge* (principally manned

ABOVE: SS soldiers fighting in the suburbs of Kharkov, March 1943. The bipod-mounted machine gun is an MG42, one of the finest small arms of the war. The decision by Paul Hausser, commander of I SS Panzer Corps, to abandon the city to the Red Army the month before, despite the Führer's orders not to do so, enraged Hitler (as soon as he heard the city was lost he flew to the headquarters of the commander of Army Group South, Field Marshal Manstein, at Zaporozhye and demanded an immediate assault on the city). When he retook Kharkov, however, Hausser was partly redeemed, though Hitler delayed four months before including him among the Kharkov medal winners. The fighting for the city was savage, and the Soviets actually outnumbered the SS in terms of equipment and men.

ABOVE: Street fighting in Kharkov. The Red Army capture of the city in February 1943 had prompted Stalin to state: 'The mass expulsion of the enemy from the Soviet Union has begun.' He was rather premature, for as soon as the Germans had relinquished the city they launched a counterattack, hitting Soviet forces between the Donetz and the Dnieper. By the time the battle came to an end on 2 March, the 1st and 4th Panzer Armies had forced the Red Army to retreat, the latter losing 23,000 dead and 9000 men captured. In Kharkov itself, the Soviet 1st and 2nd Guards Tank Corps, plus four infantry divisions, put up a spirited resistance. For example, on 11 March elements of the Deutschland Battlegroup of the Das Reich Division was initially repulsed from the outskirts of the city in the face of Soviet fire.

by members of the disbanded Norwegian volunteer legion) and *Danmark* (likewise principally containing former members of the Danish volunteer corps). Smaller numbers of volunteers from other nations also served in this unit, including some Britons, and *Nordland* eventually acquired its own panzer battalion – *Hermann von Salza*. Also in the process of being formed around this time were two new elite *Reichsdeutsche* divisions: the 9th SS Panzer Division *Hohenstaufen* and the 10th SS Panzer Division *Frundsberg*. These units, however, would spend most of the year working up and training, and would see no combat until 1944.

In March 1943, in a further attempt to overcome the problems being caused by partisan activity in the occupied eastern territories, the Croat volunteer *Handschar* Division was formed. Its dire combat record is recorded in Chapter 6, and little more will be said of it here, as it played no significant part in the principal campaigns of 1943-44. It is significant, however, that by this stage of the war any pretence at retaining the elite status of the SS, at least in racial terms, had been abandoned. New volunteer formations were raised from what would, on the face of it, appear to be totally unsuitable material for the military branch of Hitler's praetorian guard.

By the end of 1943, the above units were joined by the 14th SS Waffen-Grenadier Division, the 15th SS Waffen-Grenadier Division, the 16th SS Panzergrenadier Division *Reichsführer-SS*, and the 17th SS Panzergrenadier Division *Götz*

von Berlichingen. The Waffen-SS had expanded considerably since the invasion of the Soviet Union, but over the next 12 months the rate of expansion would increase dramatically in an attempt to bolster the flagging German war machine.

With Kharkov itself recaptured, the Germans set about consolidating their positions and recovering from the deprivations of the winter. A period of relative calm ensued over the 12 weeks after Kharkov was retaken. Between the city and Orel in the north, however, a huge Soviet-controlled salient, centred around Kursk, bulged deep into German-held territory. This salient had the effect of extending the frontline by some 400km (250 miles), requiring large numbers of German troops for its defence. Across its base, however, the salient measured only some 120km (70 miles). If it could be eradicated it would shorten the front and release a great number of German troops, who could be used to counter the expected Allied invasion of southern Europe.

Preparations for Kursk

In addition, after the debacle at Stalingrad the Germans needed to regain the initiative in the East, both politically and militarily. Hitler hoped to persuade Turkey to join the war on his side, and a major military success would help, as well as reassuring his eastern European allies. There was another consideration: a successful offensive would result in the capture of large numbers of Russians, who could then be used as forced labour for the war effort. And it would also blunt the Soviet capacity for further offensive operations on the Eastern Front for some time to come.

By mid-March, Hitler had decided in principal to launch a two-pronged attack on the salient. Army Group Centre, under Field Marshal von Kluge, would attack from the northern perimeter of the salient, while Army Group South, commanded by Field Marshal von Manstein, would attack from the south. Unfortunately for the Germans, it was obvious that an offensive would be launched against the salient: the vast movements of men and material prior to the operation would hardly have gone unnoticed by the Russians. The Soviet High Command, STAVKA, decided that rather than launch its own pre-emptive strike against the Germans, it would draw the enemy into a deliberate defensive battle designed to bleed the attacking armies white, then launch its own massive counterattack as a *coup de grâce*.

The Soviets put in motion their plans. Vast quantities of mines were laid, which were placed to funnel the German attacks into areas where the Soviet anti-tank and artillery defences would be provided with a perfect killing ground. Every available member of the local civil populace was put to work digging anti-tank ditches and strongpoints.

The Soviet forces were commanded by Marshal Georgi Zhukov, who split his force into three. In the northern half of the salient General Rokossovsky commanded seven armies, one of which was a tank army. In the southern half, General Vatutin commanded six armies, including one tank army and two guard tank armies. In reserve, ready to deliver the fatal blow once the Germans had been drained of their strength, was General Koniev with six fresh armies. These forces represented a colossal total of some 1,300,000 men, 3300 tanks, 20,000 pieces of artillery and 2600 aircraft.

To attack these Soviet forces, the Germans fielded around 900,000 men, 2700 tanks, 10,000 artillery pieces and 2000 aircraft. The two armies were fairly evenly matched, especially when the quality of men and equipment is taken into consideration, but the Soviets did have the advantage of foreknowledge of the German plan, and were in well-prepared defensive positions.

For this great offensive, codenamed Operation 'Zitadelle', which both sides realised would probably be the war's turning point, the Germans had assembled their largest concentration of armour. The Wehrmacht had used some 3300 tanks for the invasion of the Soviet Union in 1941. Now, for the destruction of a salient just 120km (70 miles) wide, 2700 tanks and self-propelled guns were being deployed.

Such was the significance placed on the 'Zitadelle' offensive that several new and untried weapons were rushed into service on the German side. A number of the formidable PzKpfw VI 'Tiger' tanks, which had already earned a fearsome reputation, were committed to the battle, as was the new PzKpfw V 'Panther'. The latter was armed with a high-velocity 75mm gun and was to become the war's finest tank. However, at this stage it was still suffering from teething problems. Also new was the heavy tank destroyer 'Elefant', which mounted the superb 88mm gun, and the Brumbär self-propelled gun, which was armed with a 150mm howitzer on a modified PzKpfw IV chassis.

In the southern sector, von Manstein fielded two major forces: Group *Kempf*, comprising XI Corps, XLII Corps and III Panzer Corps, and the 4th Panzer Army, which comprised XLVIII Panzer Corps, LII Corps and SS-Obergruppenführer Paul Hausser's II SS Panzer Corps. The latter

BELOW: The **Totenkopf** *Division rolls into Kharkov. The morale of the division had been dealt a blow when its commander, Theodor Eicke, was shot down and killed during an aerial reconnaissance on 24 February. The aircraft crashed behind enemy lines, but a party of volunteers managed to retrieve his body. The* **Totenkopf** *Division had been decimated in the Demyansk Pocket, and Eicke had worked hard to bring it back up to combat readiness. As the division's actions in early 1943 demonstrated, he had succeeded. Despite his death, the* **Totenkopf** *Division continued to fight the way Eicke had taught it. As he himself said: 'Hardness saves blood. In fact hardness saves more. It saves bitterness, it saves shame, it saves worry, it saves sorrow.'*

ABOVE: Soldiers of the Leibstandarte Division take a breather during the fighting for Kharkov in March 1943. The division had entered the city on 11 March, its flanks covered by the Das Reich Division on the left and the Totenkopf Division on the right. The performance of the Leibstandarte, and particularly the leadership of 'Sepp' Dietrich, during the Kharkov battles impressed Hitler greatly. The Führer believed Dietrich to be a 'great strategist'. But even great strategists take casualties, and when the fighting for Kharkov was over I SS Panzer Corps had lost a total of 11,500 dead, wounded or missing.

comprised the *Leibstandarte*, commanded by SS-Brigadeführer Theodor 'Teddi' Wisch, *Das Reich*, under SS-Gruppenführer Walter Kruger, and *Totenkopf*, under SS-Brigadeführer Hermann Priess. All three SS panzergrenadier divisions included a heavy company equipped with 15 Tiger tanks in their panzer regiments.

Hoth's 4th Panzer Army was tasked with smashing through the Soviet defence lines along the Voronezh Front, before wheeling northeast to take Prokhorovka, from where it was assumed any Soviet counterattack would come. Once Soviet forces in this area were destroyed, the 4th Panzer Army would turn northwest towards Kursk and link up with Model's 9th Army advancing from the north.

The three SS divisions were deployed along parallel lines of advance, each division having an armoured wedge, at the tip of which was the Tiger company. On 5 July, II SS Panzer Corps launched its attack, breaking through the first line of Soviet defences reasonably easily, before hitting the extensive minefields and anti-tank defences. Nevertheless, by the end of the first day the Waffen-SS divisions had been able to penetrate some 18km (15

miles) into Soviet-held territory, the massive power of the Panzerkeil (armoured wedge) being well supported by air strikes from Luftwaffe ground-attack aircraft.

Not for the first time on the Eastern Front, the Waffen-SS divisions were making faster progress than their flanking Army units, and by dawn on 6 July were already preparing to assault the Soviet second line of defences. However, the second day of the battle was to prove more difficult, and the *Leibstandarte* engaged in fierce tank battles with the 1st Guards Armoured Brigade. At long ranges the Russian tank guns were incapable of penetrating the thick armoured plating of the German panzers, especially the Tigers, and the Soviets took a severe beating.

Soon, a considerable gap had been opened up in the sector of the Russian line covered by the 6th Guards Army. Hausser immediately took advantage of this and led his SS divisions through it. The rapidity of the SS's advance, however, was beginning to leave the flanking Army units behind, and the *Totenkopf* was forced to cover the flanks of the SS corps, diverting essential armour from the spearheads in the process.

The Soviets now began to move some of their reserve units to the Prokhorovka area, ready to challenge the German advance. On the third day of the offensive, *Leibstandarte* and *Das Reich* pressed on towards the north, where concentrations of Soviet armour were reported near Teterevino. A furious battle developed against strong Soviet defensive positions, but once again the strength of the Tigers in the armoured spearheads won the day,

tearing a gap in the defences and allowing SS assault troops to capture the village and the entire staff of a Soviet brigade. A considerable number of Russian prisoners were beginning to flow in, and the entire front of the 6th Guards Army was starting to look precarious.

By 10 July, *Totenkopf* had moved from covering the left flank of the SS corps and had joined the *Leibstandarte* and *Das Reich* for the attack on Prokhorovka. By

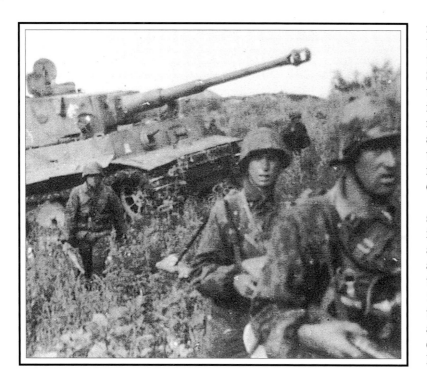

ABOVE: A Tiger tank and infantry of the **Das Reich** *Division advance during the Battle of Kursk. The division had moved into its start positions to the south of the Belgorod-Tomarovka railway line on 3 July, and began its offensive in the early hours of 5 July. Right from the start the fighting was heavy, and in one sector the men of the* **Deutschland** *Regiment became involved in hand-to-hand fighting with entrenching tools while attempting to clear an anti-tank ditch. The conditions on the ground were poor on the first day: the constant rain had turned the ground to mud in many places, which had held up the advance of the tanks and self-propelled guns. This meant the SS infantry often had to struggle on unsupported in the face of Soviet counterattacks, air strikes and artillery barrages The omens for the rest of the offensive were not good.*

late afternoon, Waffen-SS troops had crossed the River Psel and captured Krasny Oktabyr, and were in a favourable position to wheel round to the rear of the Soviet forces building up at Prokhorovka. Hausser's SS corps could field nearly 600 tanks for the assault on a front only 10km (6 miles) wide. Fearing that the German attack would hit them before they were up to full strength, the Soviets launched a pre-emptive strike. Vatutin threw the entire 5th Guards Tank Army into the battle, a force of some 850 tanks and self-propelled guns.

On 12 July 1943, one of the greatest tank battles in history occurred at the village of Prokhorovka. It was an engagement that had profound consequences, for it halted the German advance in the battle, and spelled the end of 'Zitadelle'.

Clash at Prokhorovka

The Soviets were aware of the superior armament of many of the German tanks, to say nothing of the massive armour of the Tigers, and knew that their only hope was to close the distance between them and the Germans to give their guns any chance of penetrating the enemy armour. The Russians hurled themselves at the German panzers at top speed, and soon the battlefield was a swarming mass of tanks squeezed into an area of only a few square kilometres. Over 1500 tanks blasted away at each other at virtually point-blank range in a battle that raged for eight hours. The sun was behind the Soviets as they attacked, blinding the German gun-

ners. Many Tigers and Panthers were blown apart as the T-34s blasted their thinner side armour at close ranges. Some Soviet tank crews made suicide attacks on the Germans by ramming their tanks at full speed into the heavier panzers, the resultant explosions blowing both vehicles apart. By the end of the day, some 700 tanks lay burned out and gutted on the field of battle. Needless to say, few of the crews survived the action.

The sky was soon black with the thick smoke of battle, and the *Totenkopf* was forced onto the defensive as it came under attack by the 31st Guards Tank Corps and the 33rd Guards Rifle Corps. The battle-hardened tankers and grenadiers of the *Totenkopf* held their ground, however, and the Soviet attack was beaten off, but only at a horrendous cost in both men and equipment. By this time the division had lost half its strength.

The offensive falters

A critical stage in the offensive had been reached, whereby it seemed that whichever side could bring up reinforcements first would win the day. On the German side, III Panzer Corps was making every effort to reach Prokhorovka against determined Soviet attempts to delay it. By 12 July, it had broken through the Russian defences, but too late – Rotmistrov's 5th Guards Tank Army had beaten the Germans to it.

Considering that they had attacked an enemy whose forces were numerically superior to their own, had foreknowledge of the attack, and were in well-prepared defensive positions, the achievements of Hausser's II SS Corps were considerable. The crack Waffen-SS panzer regiments had carried out their tasks with their customary elan and total contempt for danger, and several young Waffen-SS panzer officers gained legendary reputations. The most famous, perhaps, was SS-Unter-sturmführer Michael Wittman, who ran up a personal score of 30 enemy tanks during the Kursk offensive, and went on to become the highest scoring tank ace in history, before being killed in action in Normandy in June 1944.

It was now clear, however, that the objectives of 'Zitadelle' could not be met. The attack in the north had made little headway, principally because the Soviets had wrongly anticipated that this was the direction from which the main German push would come from, and had fortified their positions accordingly. Although good progress had been made in the south, it had been achieved only at an unacceptable cost in both casualties and armour. On 13 July, Hitler called off the offensive. He was extremely concerned about the situation in the Mediterranean, where the Allies threatened Germany's southern flank. In addition, a massive Soviet build-up was evident in the Donetz area. Manstein tried to persuade the Führer that success could still be achieved, but when a fresh Soviet assault towards Orel threatened to cut off Model's 9th Army, he was forced to finally accept that the operation had failed.

'Zitadelle' was Germany's last major offensive in the East and it had been a costly one. Army Group South had lost some 20,700 men killed and wounded, while Army Group Centre suffered 10,000 casualties in just two days. Hausser's command, which had boasted some 700 tanks at the start of the offensive, emerged with only 280 still intact. The Red Army lost over 2100 tanks and 33,000 of their men taken prisoner. The number of Soviet dead is not known, but it must have been high.

The *Leibstandarte* gained a brief period of respite after the cessation of 'Zitadelle', but a fresh Soviet attack on the Bryansk-Orel railway line saw the division thrown back into the fighting along the River Mius defence lines. Its stay was brief, however, because on 3 August it was withdrawn from the Eastern Front altogether and sent to Italy to reinforce German forces there, following the collapse of Mussolini's government.

Now fully on the defensive, German forces in the southern sector of the Eastern Front were sent reeling as Soviet forces smashed through the Mius defences and advanced rapidly towards Stalino and Taganrog, along the northern coast of the Sea of Azov. Field Marshal von Kleist and his Army Group A, on Manstein's southern flank, were in danger of being cut off. Manstein therefore shifted his reserves to assist Kleist, weakening his own forces so much that he was unable to resist the momentum of Vatutin's attack on the Voronezh Front. Kluge's Army

BELOW: Himmler with the man who commanded II SS Panzer Corps at the Battle of Kursk: Paul Hausser.

BELOW: SS troopers display a swastika flag to ensure they are not strafed by German aircraft during the Battle of Kursk. Of the SS divisions, the Totenkopf *made the greatest advance on the first day, reaching the Belgorod-Kursk railway line. However, resistance had been fierce and the Germans were facing formidable defences: six belts of defences, consisting of anti-tank, machine gun and mortar positions, plus tens of thousands of mines. The only thing in the Germans' favour was that the Soviets had expected the main assault to come from the north, and had deployed the bulk of their forces there. However, Zhukov had made sure he had a strong reserve.*

Group Centre was also gradually pushed back towards Smolensk, its own problems too serious to allow it to assist Manstein. To the north, Model's 2nd Panzer Army was threatened with encirclement and was forced to withdraw across the neck of the Orel salient.

By mid-August, a 55km-wide (34 miles) gap had opened up in the German lines west of Kursk, and Soviet forces began to pour through it, threatening to take Kharkov once again. *Wiking, Das Reich* and *Totenkopf* were all thrown into the battle to prevent the loss of the city. Although weakened by the 'Zitadelle' disaster, *Das Reich* had received all of *Leibstandarte*'s armour before the latter had been transferred to Italy, and it was still a formidable fighting force. In a reversal of the German capture of Kharkov in March, it was now the Red Army's turn to launch a massive pincer attack, with the 53rd Army driving in from the north and the 57th Army from the south – the 5th Guards Tank Army was to apply the *coup de grâce*. The Russian attack was not quite as effective as the previous German one, though. The Soviets ran into strong defences, and on just one day of fighting Waffen-SS anti-tank gunners knocked out

over 180 Russian tanks. However, they could only delay the Red Army, and Manstein, fearing encirclement, ordered the city abandoned on 22 August.

A fighting withdrawal

Over the next few weeks the *Wiking, Das Reich* and *Totenkopf* Divisions scored some outstanding successes in localised combats with armoured units of the Red Army. On 12 September, for example, *Das Reich* destroyed 78 enemy tanks in one engagement. However, the Russians seemed to have little problem in replacing such great losses, whereas the hard-pressed Waffen-SS units found it increasingly difficult to maintain their own strength.

Hitler agreed to von Manstein's Army Group South withdrawing to the line of Melitopol and the River Dnieper, thus retaining the western Ukraine in German hands. The withdrawal, undertaken in the face of Soviet pressure, was completed by 30 September. By that time a total of 68 German divisions – 1,250,000 men and over 2000 tanks of Army Group South – was tasked with holding the river line at all costs. Opposing them, however, the Red Army fielded a force almost twice as strong and in better shape.

In late August Soviet forces began to advance, and the Waffen-SS took part in a spirited withdrawal towards the Dnieper. Yelnya fell to the Red Army after two days of bitter fighting, but the Russians were made to fight for every metre of ground and had to pause within a week to regroup. Then the red onslaught continued, capturing Bryansk, Smolensk and Roslavl in quick succession. By 2 October the Germans had been driven back almost 240km (150 miles).

In November 1943, the *Leibstandarte* was released from service in Italy and was sent back to the Eastern Front. It was allocated to XLVIII Panzer Corps of the 4th Panzer Army, situated to the south of Kiev, in the Ukraine. Despite the best efforts of the *Das Reich* Division, which was operating near Kiev, the city fell to the enemy on 7 November. The *Leibstandarte* did have some localised successes against Red Army units in the Kiev sector, but the respite was short-lived.

Between mid-November and the end of the year, both the *Leibstandarte* and *Das Reich* took part in a number of counterattacks as part of XLVIII Panzer Corps, but the weakness of the German forces was all

too apparent. At Korosten, for example, the *Leibstandarte*, together with the 1st and 7th Panzer Divisions, attempted to encircle a number of Red Army units. This was achieved, but the Germans were spread so thin that they couldn't maintain their positions, and soon the Germans were themselves fighting desperately to avoid encirclement. At Brusilov, XXIV Panzer Corps, to which *Das Reich* had been allocated, was overwhelmed in bitter hand-to-hand fighting. The remnants of the division, together with the *Leibstandarte*, conducted a fighting retreat towards Zhitomir. The *Leibstandarte* was then moved to Berdichev, where it linked up with the 1st Panzer Division and succeeded in halting the Soviet attack in that sector, albeit for a short time.

The remaining division of II SS Panzer Corps, the *Totenkopf* Division, had assumed the role of a fire brigade, continuously rushing from one threatened sector of the front to another. In November and early December, it served with Hube's 1st Panzer Army, which was attempting to hold Krivoi Rog and the defensive positions on the Dnieper. On 12 December, it was moved to LVII Corps and, together

ABOVE: Waffen-SS soldiers hitch a lift during 'Zitadelle'. On 6 July the Germans had made some gains, in the north reaching the high ground north of Kashara, and in the south breaching the Soviet line in two places. The Army's elite Grossdeutschland Division did particularly well, and II SS Panzer Corps itself had penetrated 32km (20 miles) towards the village of Prokhorovka. However, German losses in terms of men, aircraft, tanks and self-propelled guns had been high, and a very worrying development was that many of the new Panther tanks had broken down or burst into flames before reaching the battle zone.

ABOVE: Waffen-SS infantry at Kursk.

*BELOW: The **Das Reich** Division advances towards Prokhorovka. By 7 July all units of the division were engaged in combat with Red Army units.*

with the 11th and 13th Panzer Divisions, launched a counterattack which halted the Soviet advance in that sector.

On Christmas Eve 1943, the Russian forces in the southern sector of the front renewed their push westwards from their positions around Kiev. Zhitomir was quickly recaptured, and only a determined effort by Manstein's forces slowed the enemy advance, though not before some

German units had already been pushed back by as much as 160km (100 miles). At this point the Soviets attempted to smash German forces around Kirovgrad. They captured the town on 8 January 1944, but found German resistance stronger than expected. Some 11 German divisions were involved, including *Wiking* and the SS Sturmbrigade *Wallonie*, the Belgian Walloon volunteer unit recently transferred from Army to Waffen-SS control. These strong German units posed a serious threat to Koniev's northern flank and Vatutin's southern flank. This German-held salient would have to be eliminated to ensure the success of the Soviet offensive. Koniev renewed his attack on 25 January, and by the 29th 60,000 Germans had been encircled near Cherkassy. An unseasonal rise in temperature caused a sudden thaw which turned the terrain into a boggy morass, making movement all but impossible. The airfield within the pocket, which the Luftwaffe was using to resupply the beleaguered divisions, was rendered unusable. Constant pressure from the Russians saw the salient shrink rapidly, until it measured 65 square kilometres (40 square miles) by 9 February.

True to form, Hitler refused to countenance any talk of a breakout by the

Operation Zitadelle
July 1943

Key

➤ German offensive, 4–12 July
(Operation Zitadelle)

➤ Soviet counter-offensive, 12 July

—— Front line, 4 July

– – – Front line, 6 July

········· Front line, 12 July

trapped units, insisting that only an offensive by Manstein's forces to relieve them be considered. The Soviets, however, had thrown a ring of 35 divisions around the salient, and any escape attempt by the trapped forces looked unlikely to succeed. Eventually the Führer was persuaded to allow the encircled units to attempt a breakout. The only armoured unit in the pocket, the 5th SS Panzer Division *Wiking*, commanded by SS-Obergruppenführer Herbert Otto Gille, would cover the flanks, while SS Sturmbrigade *Wallonie* formed the rearguard.

Escape from the Cherkassy Pocket

On the night of 16 February, the breakout began. Movement over the waterlogged terrain was difficult, and once the Soviets became aware of what was happening a murderous barrage of artillery and rocket fire was laid down on the retreating Germans. The wounded had to be left behind, as did most of the artillery and other heavy equipment. SS Sturmbrigade *Wallonie* suffered dreadful losses covering the rearguard, with 70 per cent of its strength left dead on the battlefield. As the remnants of the brigade drew near to the German lines, they were in danger of being swamped by the mass of pursuing

Soviets. In a typical example of the type of self-sacrifice to which the Waffen-SS units would become accustomed, *Wiking*'s few remaining panzers turned back and held off the enemy for just long enough to allow the last of the brigade to reach the German lines, before being overrun.

Some 32,000 Germans escaped with their lives, and despite the fact that a great deal of equipment had been left behind, a major disaster had been averted. If the pocket had been totally destroyed, Manstein's Army Group South would have been dealt a fatal blow.

For the distinguished performance of their troops, both Gille and SS-Hauptsturmführer Léon Degrelle, commander of the Walloons, were summoned to Hitler's headquarters in Prussia and decorated. Gille received the Oakleaves and Swords, and Degrelle the Knights Cross.

The *Das Reich* Division, now totally exhausted, was withdrawn from the front and sent to France for rest and refitting in February 1944. A battlegroup from the division, under the command of SS-Oberführer Heinz Lammerding, remained on the Eastern Front.

During March 1944, Army Group South was forced to make a gradual withdrawal to the Dniester river, on the border with Romania. On 11 March 1944, elements of the *Totenkopf* were airlifted to Balta to form the core of a new defence line. Events were moving too fast, however, and both the 6th and 8th Armies were too weak to prevent the Red Army from crossing the Dniester on a wide front before the new defences were ready, the Russians pushing deep into Romanian territory. The *Totenkopf* Division, attached to XLVIII Panzer Corps, battled its way west to avoid encirclement. The exhausted SS men fought off the Soviet spearheads for three weeks, as the withdrawal continued through Balta and Romania and across the River Sireth to Targul Frumos and into the Carpathian mountains.

Armies at Proskurov. Before the breach could be sealed, the entire 1st Panzer Army found itself surrounded in a pocket at Kamenets-Podolsk. Among the units trapped were the *Leibstandarte* and Lammerding's *Das Reich* kampfgruppe.

At this point Hitler agreed to allow the reconstituted II SS Panzer Corps, which consisted of the elite 9th SS Panzer Division *Hohenstaufen* and the 10th SS Panzer Division *Frundsberg*, to be rushed to the Eastern Front. These two divisions, though untried in battle, were elite units of the highest standard. They were manned primarily by *Reichsdeutsche* Germans and equipped and trained to a high level. Also of significance was the fact that the units were built around cadre personnel from

The Soviet offensive eventually ran out of steam, and the month of May was relatively peaceful. On 9 June, the division was pulled out of the line for some much needed rest and refitting, receiving sorely needed tanks and armoured vehicles, as well as around 6000 replacement troops. Many of these were *Totenkopf* veterans returning to duty after recovering from wounds, but around three-quarters were raw recruits hastily transferred from the recently formed 16th SS Panzergrenadier Division *Reichsführer-SS*.

In March 1944, as Army Group South struggled to reorganise its left flank, it was struck by a new Soviet offensive which shattered it completely, tearing a massive gap between the 1st and 4th Panzer

tried and tested units, such as *Das Reich* and the *Leibstandarte*, and had been fortunate enough to be allowed a full year of training. Both units were to display combat performances equal to that of the best Waffen-SS divisions. *Hohenstaufen* was commanded by SS-Brigadeführer Willi Bittrich and *Frundsberg* by SS-Brigadeführer Karl von Treuenfeld.

Meanwhile, as much fuel and ammunition as possible was being airlifted into the Kamenets-Podolsk Pocket in order to avoid Manstein's forces having to abandon much of their heavy equipment and armour when the time came to break out. On 27 March, under cover of blizzard conditions, the withdrawal began. *Hohenstaufen* and *Frundsberg*, as part of the 4th

Panzer Army, took part in the counterattack launched to take the pressure off the retreating 1st Panzer Army as it fought its way west. Contact was made on 7 April, and over the next nine days the bulk of Manstein's forces made it back safely into German-held territory. Unlike the breakout from Cherkassy, this escape was achieved without serious losses; indeed, it is estimated that several hundred Soviet armoured vehicles were destroyed during the German withdrawal.

In April, the *Leibstandarte* was withdrawn from the East and moved to France for rest and refitting, and around the same time the remnants of Lammerding's kampfgruppe rejoined the *Das Reich* Division in France. *Hohenstaufen* and *Frundsberg* were held in reserve in Poland, but when the Allies landed in Normandy in June they were both rushed back to the Western Front. The *Wiking* Division, badly battered in the escape from the Cherkassy Pocket, was withdrawn from the front for rest and refitting, leaving a kampfgruppe behind.

Retreat from Leningrad

In northern Russia, 1944 had begun badly for the Germans. The Red Army, having lifted the siege of Leningrad, had gone on to the offensive and gradually drove the German armies westwards towards Estonia and Latvia. It was in this sector of the front that most of the west and east European SS volunteer units were concentrated. The main Waffen-SS force in this area was III (germanisches) SS Panzer Corps, commanded by SS-Gruppenführer Felix Steiner, and containing the 11th SS Freiwilligen Division *Nordland* and SS Freiwilligen Brigade *Nederland*. Within these two units alone were to be found volunteers from Norway, Denmark, Holland, France, Finland, Sweden and Switzerland. In addition, allocated to the same sector of the front were the 15th and 19th Waffen Grenadier Divisions from Latvia, the 20th Waffen Grenadier Division from Estonia, as well as the Flemish *Langemarck* Brigade and the Walloon Sturmbrigade *Wallonie*.

By the end of January, the Red Army had reached the German defence lines at Narva. These ran from the city of Narva itself, south along the banks of the River Narva, to the shores of Lake Peipus and down to Polotsk, northwest of Vitebsk. A concentrated effort by the Red Army along the entire line was expected; it came on 2 February. Any hopes that the

German defences would easily crumble were soon dashed. Narva had been a strategically important city for hundreds of years, and was the gateway to Estonia. Defensive positions had been established along the west bank of the River Narva, and for the next few months Steiner's men and other SS units stood firm against anything the enemy could throw at them. So prominent were the foreign volunteer units of the Waffen-SS in this sector that the defence of Narva was to become known as the 'Battle of the European SS'.

The Battle of Narva

The Germans had established a fairly large and strongly defended bridgehead covering a substantial area of territory on the eastern approaches to Narva, directly opposite the city itself. Here, soldiers from Division *Nordland* and Brigade *Nederland* dug in and awaited the inevitable assault. German forces in the Narva area were a mixture of Army, Waffen-SS, Air Force, Navy and police troops. Opposing them were the Soviet 8th and 47th Armies and the 2nd Shock Army.

At the beginning of February, the Red Army began its attempts to soften up the German defences with heavy shelling, and some Russian units forced a crossing of the river between Hungerburg and Narva and established a small bridgehead. The Waffen-SS grenadiers, however, were able to throw the enemy back, and on 3 February a further attempt by the Soviets to establish a bridgehead was defeated by *Nordland*'s own 11th Panzer Battalion *Hermann von Salza*. Eventually, the enemy did succeed in establishing a small bridgehead at Ssivertski, to the northwest of the city, but an attempt to break out of the bridgehead into the German rear areas was quickly halted by an SS battlegroup. This thorn in the side of the defenders was finally destroyed in a concerted assault by elements from *Nordland* and *Nederland*.

The Soviets forced yet another bridgehead on the west bank at Vopsküla, which was supported by heavy artillery. However, it too was destroyed, by the 19th Waffen-Grenadier Division, following bitter hand-to-hand fighting. Estonian volunteer Waffen-Unterscharführer Haralt Nugiseks was decorated for extreme gallantry during this action. He had exposed himself to enemy fire on three occasions to urge on his assault troop, on each occasion being hit by enemy fire, yet he continued to lead his men in close-quarter combat with the enemy, driving them out of

'In the months that have gone by since we met in June 1942 many of our comrades were killed, giving their lives for Germany and the Führer. In the first rank – and I ask you to rise in his honour and in honour of all our dead SS men, soldiers, men, and women – in the first rank our old comrade and friend from our ranks, SS Lieutenant General Eicke.'
– Himmler, speech to SS officers, Poznan, 1943

The Ukrainian and Belorussian fronts
Dec 1943 – April 1944

Army Group Centre

Brest-Litovsk

Lublin

POLAND

Army Group
North Ukraine

2nd Belorussian
Front

Chernigov

Desna

1st Ukrainian Front

Kiev

Army Group
South

Korsun-
Shevchenkovskiy

Moshny

Dniepr

Cherkassy
Gorodishche

Vinnitsa

Lysyanka

2nd Ukrainian Front

Dnepropetrovsk

Kamenets Podolsky

Kirovgrad

3rd Ukrainian Front

HUNGARY

Chernovtsy

Krivoy Rog

Dniest

Key

Army Group A

4th Ukrainian
Front

Jassy

Kishinev

Army Group
South Ukraine

Odessa

SEA OF AZOV

BLACK SEA

CRIMEA

Danube

On 24 December 1943, the Red Army launched a new offensive by the 1st Ukrainian Front, followed during January by attacks on the fronts further south. The German 1st Panzer Army was trapped in a pocket near Korsun-Shevechkovskiy. Supplied from the air, the isolated German divisions fought fiercely, and finally on 16 February began a breakout.

Key
- → Soviet forces
- → German forces
- ⟳ German pockets
- ···· Front line, 23 December 1943
- — · — Front line, 24 January 1944
- ——— Front line, 4 March
- — — — Front line, 21 March
- ——— Front line, April
- — — Russo-Polish border, 1939
- ···· Russo-German border, 1940

RIGHT: Waffen-SS troops engage Red Army units during the fighting in southern Russia after Kursk. Both the Totenkopf *and* Das Reich *Divisions were involved in trying to stem the Soviet advance, with limited success. By 6 November 1943, the Red Army had liberated Kiev, and by the end of December most of the important bridgeheads over the Dnieper were in Soviet hands. For the Third Reich, the floodgates in the East were creaking.*

INSET: 'Sepp' Dietrich, whose Liebstandarte *Division was rushed to Italy following the Battle of Kursk.*

their positions. He was awarded the Knights Cross of the Iron Cross on 2 May 1945 for his achievements. Five days later he was captured and spent many years in captivity in a Siberian prison camp.

Frustrated by their lack of success, the Soviets decided to attempt an amphibious assault on the coast to the west of Narva, bypassing the defenders and striking deep into the German rear. German units, it was reasoned, would be lured away from the Narva defences to deal with this threat, and a renewed Soviet assault would succeed in breaking through.

The seaborne assault force was ferried in a motley collection of fishing boats and steamers, but did manage to land undetected and overrun the defenders in the immediate area of the beach near Merekula. The defenders were soon alerted, however, and although the Soviet force managed to push forwards into the town, they got no further. German reinforcements were called up in the shape of Waffen-SS grenadiers and Stuka ground-attack aircraft, and the invasion force was swiftly crushed with heavy losses.

To the south, near Krivasso, the Red Army established a strong bridgehead from which to launch its attack into German-held territory. This sector was manned by Army troops, including the elite *Feldherrnhalle* Division. By 24 February, the Soviets looked likely to break out and sweep up the rear of III (germanisches) SS Panzer Corps. Troops from *Nordland* were quickly moved to the

scene and initially made good progress in their counterattack, before becoming bogged down. Then the Soviets counterattacked, and the fighting quickly degenerated into ferocious hand-to-hand combat. Only the arrival of some Army Tiger tanks enabled the Waffen-SS troops to withdraw safely. Fierce fighting continued throughout March and April, with the Soviets making little headway against the tenacious German defenders.

When the Waffen-SS troops recaptured Sirgula in March, they discovered the corpses of many Estonian civilians who had been used as forced labour to carry ammunition for the Red Army. The Russians had slaughtered the civilians before fleeing. Several Danish volunteers had also been captured and shot by the Russians at Hrastovica.

The Soviets intensify their attacks

In early March, Soviet artillery and aerial bombardment of the Narva area increased dramatically. On 7 March, massed Russian air attacks went on for 12 hours, then the artillery opened up. However, the civilian population of Narva had been evacuated, and the Waffen-SS defenders merely dug deeper into the rubble of the city. The main Soviet attack following the softening up was against the area held by the Dutch volunteer *General Seyffardt* Regiment. The Dutch soldiers repulsed every Soviet attack, and even launched their own counterattack. The regimental commander, SS-Obersturmbannführer

ABOVE: A **Wiking** *panzergrenadier at Cherkassy. He wears a fur-lined 1942 SS winter combat anorak and winter trousers, and is armed with an MP40 submachine gun.*

ABOVE LEFT: A photograph that amply conveys the conditions faced by the men of the **Wiking** *Division in the Cherkassy Pocket.*

TOONT U EEN WAARACHTIG NEDERLANDER

Til vakt ved Nordens grense mot øst'!

SS-SKIJEGERBATALJON NORGE

OP - TEGEN HET BOLSJEWISME
MELDT U AAN BIJ DE
WAFFEN SS
STADHOUDERSLAAN 132 DEN HAAG

ABOVE: Waffen-SS recruiting posters aimed at Norwegian (above) and Dutch (above right) recruits, two of the nationalities that fought at Narva in the early months of 1944. There were many Norwegians in the 11th SS Freiwilligen-Panzergrenadier Division Nordland, which took part in the battle, and Dutch participation was represented by the SS Freiwilligen Brigade Nederland.

Wolfgang Joerchel, was decorated with the Knights Cross of the Iron Cross on 21 April 1944 in recognition of the achievements of his regiment.

The main thrust of the Soviet attack then moved against the positions at Lilienbach, held by another Dutch volunteer regiment – *De Ruiter*. After bitter fighting the enemy broke through the Waffen-SS positions, but were driven back by reinforcements from the *Nordland*'s *Danmark* and *Norge* Regiments

Despite the spirited, and often successful, defensive actions by the Dutch SS troops at Lilienbach, it became clear that this part of the bridgehead on the east bank of the Narva could not be held much longer. Waffen-SS losses in terms of manpower and equipment had been too high, and the Soviet strength was increasing. By June 1944, however, the Red Army had still not taken Narva, though the German bridgehead on the east bank, opposite the city, had been greatly reduced. The Germans, aware of the disasters befalling their comrades in the central and southern sectors of the front in Russia, realised that their position at Narva was becoming more precarious with each day, and so it was decided to pull back to a new defen-

sive position further west, to the so-called Tannenberg Line.

On 24 July 1944, the northern prong of a massive pincer attack forced the 20th Waffen-Grenadier Division der SS back over the River Narva. The Estonian volunteers were forced to retreat westwards, fighting every inch of the way in defence of their homeland. Having experienced Soviet occupation once before, they had no wish to repeat it, and they fought tenaciously. On 24 July, the Waffen-SS units still on the east bank of the Narva slipped quickly over the river and into the city, destroying the bridges as they did so. By the close of the next day, the city itself had been evacuated. During the retreat to the Tannenberg positions, though, the Dutch unit General *Seyffardt* was cut off and annihilated by the Soviets.

On 26 July, the Russian assault at Tannenberg began. Subtle tactics were eschewed in favour of a massed assault on the greatly outnumbered Germans and the European volunteers. The fighting seesawed back and forth, first one side having the advantage then the other. Despite its many successes, the Waffen-SS suffered great losses, while the enemy poured ever increasing numbers of fresh troops over the Narva and into the battle. The SS, for all its tenacity, was being bled white: virtually all its armour was gone, and its artillery was the only remaining heavy weaponry. The Russian attacks slackened somewhat in August, as the Red Army gathered its strength for one final all-out assault on the beleaguered Waffen-SS. The battered European volunteers could only await the mortal blow with apprehension.

By this time the European volunteers knew that the Soviet offensive was tearing holes in the front. For example, on 22 June, the Red Army had launched its summer offensive across the entire front. Codenamed 'Bagration', it was deliberately timed to start on the third anniversary of the German invasion of Russia. The Red Army had built up a massive force of some six million men, compared to the Wehrmacht's two million. Army Group Centre, which was destined to take the main brunt of the offensive, could field around three-quarters of a million men, under 1000 tanks and 10,000 artillery pieces. Opposing it, however, were over two million Red Army soldiers, 4000 tanks and nearly 29,000 guns.

LEFT: Sylvester Stadler, seen here as an SS-Sturmbannführer in the **Das Reich** *Division. He later went on to command the 9th SS Panzer Division* **Hohenstaufen.** *The latter, together with the 10th SS Panzer Division* **Frundsberg,** *were formed at the beginning of 1943 from conscripted native Germans. Despite the fact that conscription had to be resorted to, both divisions turned out to be excellent fighting formations. By the second half of 1943, both were entering the final phase of their training. Both were first sent into action on the Eastern Front in April 1944, at Tarnopol, to stem the Soviet offensive and rescue the* **Leibstandarte** *and other units from the Kamenets-Poldosk Pocket. The recruits to the* **Hohenstaufen** *Division may have been conscripts, but the indoctrination they received at the training depots was the same as that given to volunteers in the SS. The men were not allowed to forget they were Hitler's warriors. Educational material distributed to the division's soldiers stated that the lessons of history 'showed the necessity for an unflinching force at the disposal of the leadership of the Reich in any situation, even when this implies maintenance of order at home by the use of all methods.'*

THE SS: HITLER'S INSTRUMENT OF TERROR

BELOW: A PzKpfw IV of the **Leibstandarte** *in the Kamenets-Podolsk Pocket. The division had been recalled to the Easter Front from Italy in November 1943, but was swept west in the wake of the massive offensives launched by the Red Army. By April 1944, these offensives had lasted for four months and had destroyed the entire southern wing of the German armies. For this task the Red Army had employed four million troops, 4000 tanks and artillery pieces and 4000 aircraft.*

At this point in the war the average Red Army conscript was no longer the half-trained, poorly equipped peasant who had faced the might of the Wehrmacht in the summer of 1941. By 1944, the Red Army's frontline combat units were composed, in the main, of experienced veterans who had excellent equipment. The latest T-34 tank, for example, with its uprated 85mm main gun, and the new Josef Stalin heavy tank, armed with a 122mm gun, were a match for any panzer. In air power, too, the Soviet Air Force was technically equal to the Luftwaffe, having excellent fighters and ground-attack aircraft, plus overall superiority in numbers.

Although 1943 and the first half of 1944 had been a period of disasters for the armies of the Third Reich on the Eastern Front, Hitler had reason to be greatly pleased with the performance of his elite Waffen-SS divisions. Time and time again SS units had stood firm against almost impossible odds, while Wehrmacht troops retreated. Even the most fanatical Waffen-SS troops must have realised that military

success in the east was now impossible, yet they continued to make sacrifice after sacrifice, often holding the line to allow other units to escape.

Few other units in the Wehrmacht could engender such confidence from their Führer as did those of the Waffen-SS. However, though proud of their achievements and their deserved elite status, Hitler's confidence in them was a double-edged sword. With increasing regularity, Waffen-SS divisions were rushed to threatened areas of the front and expected to save the day. That they did so is testament to the fact that they were elite troops. However, they were not supermen, and there would come a time when not even the Waffen-SS could stave off defeat.

Although the Waffen-SS at this point in the war represented only around five per cent of the fighting strength of the Wehrmacht, it is significant that some 20 per cent of the Waffen-SS units were panzer divisions of the highest standard. In fact, just over 25 per cent of all panzer divisions were Waffen-SS, and around 30

ons antwoord:
Het geweer
ter hand!

Griekland
Nijpland
Engeland!

Vlamingen
alle in de ⚡⚡ Langemarck!

per cent of all panzergrenadier divisions. Yet, despite this fact, apart from the 12 Waffen-SS divisions that could truly be called elite, the remainder were indifferent, often, as in the case of those formed late in the war, of divisional strength in name only and sometimes poorly equipped. In view of these figures, the military significance of the Waffen-SS's achievements on the Eastern Front is indisputable.

Despite the Waffen-SS's efforts, the Red Army in the summer of 1944 had only been delayed, not halted. And its next offensive would drive the Germans back into the Reich itself. But, in June, Hitler had pressing matters in western Europe to deal with, as the Allies poured ashore after D-Day. Once again the Führer looked to his Waffen-SS divisions to save the military situation.

ABOVE: A recruiting poster for the 27th SS Freiwilligen-Panzergrenadier Division **Langemarck,** *a unit that suffered heavy losses during the Battle of Narva. For the Waffen-SS, 1944 was a catalogue of defeats and withdrawals. Though many units had performed superbly in battle, there seemed to be nothing that could stem the Soviet tide. Hitler had stated: 'if one fought bitterly for every foot of ground and made the enemy pay dearly for every step he advanced, even the Soviet armies' offensive power must some day be exhausted.' He was wrong – the Waffen-SS was being exhausted.*

BATTLES IN THE WEST

Mid-1944 was a bad time for the Third Reich. The Soviets launched a major offensive in the East and there was an attempt on the Führer's life. In the West the Allies landed in Normandy, and the Waffen-SS was thrown into battle in a desperate attempt to stop them securing the bridgehead.

By August 1943, the German armies in North Africa had been thoroughly defeated, and those units that had evaded capture in Tunisia had been further driven out of Sicily and onto the Italian mainland. The subsequent Allied invasion of the mainland at Salerno (September 1943) saw Axis forces in Italy driven slowly northwards. The Germans, however, fought a highly successful fighting withdrawal with moderately low losses, and the Allies faced a long and costly campaign to drive them out of Italy.

The British and Americans therefore decided to land a seaborne invasion force south of Rome at Anzio. The subsequent drive inland would cut Highways 6 and 7, which were the main German supply routes for the western end of the Gustav Line, where the Allied advance was stuck in front of Monte Cassino. The Germans, threatened from the rear, would withdraw from the line and allow Allied troops to reach Anzio. It was at Anzio that Waffen-SS units took the field for the first time against Anglo-American forces.

In the summer of 1943, a new SS panzergrenadier division bearing the honour title *Reichsführer-SS* was formed. It was built around a cadre of personnel from SS-Sturmbrigade *Reichsführer-SS*, which in turn had

Tiger tanks of the Leibstandarte Division move through the French countryside on their way to Normandy in June 1944. By August the division had lost all its tanks.

BELOW: Panther tanks, reportedly of the **Leibstandarte,** *in north Italy in 1943. The division had been sent there after Kursk, Hitler giving as his reason: 'Down there, I can only accomplish something with elite formations that are politically close to Fascism.' Nevertheless, the division's stay in Italy was not a happy one, and it became involved in a number of atrocities against civilians before returning to Russia.*

OPPOSITE TOP: StuG III self-propelled guns of the 16th SS Panzergrenadier Division Reichsführer-SS *move through an Italian town in early 1944. The division fought well at Anzio and was engaged in anti-partisan activities in northern Italy.*

OPPOSITE BELOW: SS tank ace SS-Obersturmführer Michael Wittmann.

been formed from soldiers of Himmler's personal escort unit. The commander of the new division was a former regimental commander in Theodor Eicke's *Totenkopf* Division: SS-Brigadeführer Max Simon. It had been formed in Corsica, but was transferred to the Italian mainland in October 1943 when the Allies took the islands of Sardinia and Corsica. When the Allies landed at Anzio, the division was still being worked up and so elements had to be quickly rushed to the front. These elements are believed to have been several companies from SS-Panzergrenadier Regiments 35 and 36, plus the assault gun unit SS-Panzerjäger Abteilung 16. They remained in combat in the Anzio/Nettuno bridgehead until 9 March 1944.

The *Reichsführer-SS* in Italy

Meanwhile, Hitler had become concerned with the possibility of his erstwhile Hungarian allies abandoning the Axis cause and going over to the Soviets. To pre-empt this he launched Operation 'Margarethe', and most of the remaining elements of the division were transferred to Hungary to take part in the seizure of power from Admiral Horthy's regime.

The continued Allied advance through Italy soon saw these units returned, however, and the division was reunited in time to take on the British 8th Army, which drove it relentlessly back past Siena and Pisa to Carrara. Engaged in heavy defensive fighting for the remainder of 1944, it became embroiled in anti-partisan actions

and its reputation was severely dented by the killing of a large number of civilians at Padule di Fuceccio and Sant'Anna di Stazzema. In addition, the division was involved in the massacre of civilians at Marzabotto in September, though German sources have claimed that the civilians were not executed but were the victims of crossfire between German troops and heavily armed partisans.

Command of the division passed to SS-Oberführer Otto Baum in October 1944, another former *Totenkopf* regimental commander, and by January 1945 *Reichsführer-SS* was in position in the far northeast of Italy. Hitler then decided to add it to his forces being assembled for the counterattack in the Lake Balaton area.

The only other major Waffen-SS unit to serve in Italy was the elite *Leibstandarte SS Adolf Hitler* Division, which had been transferred from the Eastern Front in July 1943, leaving its heavy equipment and armour in Russia. It took part in the disarming of Italian Army units after the overthrow of Mussolini's regime in September 1943, and was also used in anti-partisan actions before returning to the Eastern Front in the autumn.

In addition to the German SS units, there were of course a number of Italian volunteers, loyal to the fascist regime, who served in Waffen-SS formations. The Italian SS Legion, for example, fought alongside units of the *Reichsführer-SS* Division at the Anzio/Nettuno bridgehead, performing so well that it was mentioned in the official Wehrmacht war reports. The major part of the combat life of the legion, later to become the 29th Waffen-Grenadier Division der SS (italienische Nr 1), was spent in action against the predominantly communist partisans in the Po Valley area. This fighting was extremely bitter. Italian volunteers also made up a significant part of the 24th SS Gebirgs Division *Karstjäger*, a mountain warfare formation which spent most of its life in action against partisan bands in the far north of Italy, and particularly along the Adriatic coast.

Although the Waffen-SS did not play a major role in the Italian campaign, the security elements of the SS left their mark on the Italian people. The SD representative in Rome, SS-Obersturmbannführer Herbert Kappler, had some 335 civilian hostages shot in reprisal for the killing by partisans of 32 members of a police unit in Rome on 23 March 1944. In a particularly callous and brutal operation, the hostages were driven out of Rome to the ancient Ardeatine Caves and executed by pistol shots to the back of the head. The caves were then dynamited to seal them up. Kappler was arrested after the war and sentenced to life imprisonment.

By the beginning of June 1944, Hitler was no longer in any doubt that an Allied

invasion attempt on the French coast was imminent. What he could not be sure of, however, was the location, and he was therefore unable to concentrate his forces in any one area. When the Allied invasion forces hit the beaches of Normandy on 6 June, the Führer refused to believe that this was the real invasion attempt, insisting that it was a feint intended to draw German forces away from where he felt the real invasion would be made: the Pas de Calais. Consequently, by the time he was persuaded that it was not a feint, a fatal delay in striking back had already been suffered.

On the morning of 6 June, the *Leibstandarte* was located near Bruges, Belgium, and was not called into action immediately, being part of the Armed Forces High Command's strategic reserve, which could not be committed to battle without Hitler's express permission. It subsequently left its location to head for the battlefield 11 days after the D-Day landings had commenced, and was finally committed to combat around Caen. The *Leibstandarte*'s sister unit, the *Hitlerjugend* Division, was already in the area around Dreux, between Paris and Caen, and was the first Waffen-SS unit to go into action in Normandy. Another first-class Waffen-SS unit, the 17th SS Panzergrenadier

Division *Götz von Berlichingen*, had been formed in November 1943 and was working up in the area around Tours/Angers. It was brought into the line within a week of the initial landings.

Actions around Caen

The *Das Reich* Division was initially stationed in the south of France near Toulouse, in expectation of a possible Allied strike against the underbelly of occupied France. It was ordered north to the invasion front soon after D-Day, and its march northwards was marked by intervention against *Maquis* units along the way, including a number of executions in Tulle and the atrocity at Oradour sur Glane (see Chapter 11). The division had reached the Normandy area by 10 July, and was moved into the line near Périers.

The Allied forces initially maintained pressure at the eastern end of their bridgehead. One of the main objectives of the British 21st Army Group, under the command of General Bernard Montgomery, was the city of Caen. The first attempt to take the city was by direct assault on 6 and 7 June, supported by British and Canadian aircraft. The *Hitlerjugend* Division moved into positions around Caen on 7 June and immediately set about forming an assault force to intercept the advancing British forces. Under the command of SS-Standartenführer Kurt 'Panzer' Meyer, a kampfgruppe, comprising three battalions of infantry and a con-

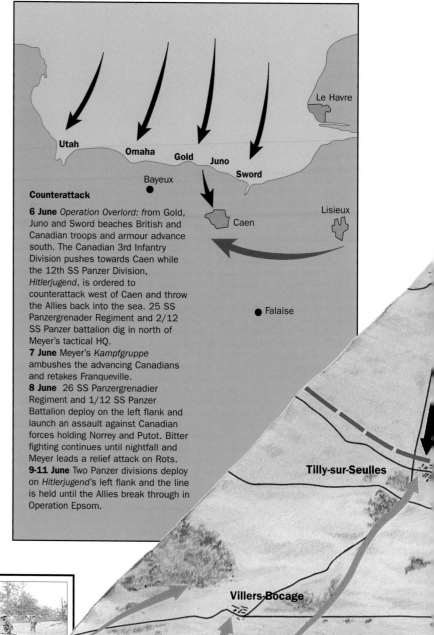

Counterattack

6 June *Operation Overlord:* from Gold, Juno and Sword beaches British and Canadian troops and armour advance south. The Canadian 3rd Infantry Division pushes towards Caen while the 12th SS Panzer Division, *Hitlerjugend*, is ordered to counterattack west of Caen and throw the Allies back into the sea. 25 SS Panzergrenader Regiment and 2/12 SS Panzer battalion dig in north of Meyer's tactical HQ.
7 June Meyer's *Kampfgruppe* ambushes the advancing Canadians and retakes Franqueville.
8 June 26 SS Panzergrenadier Regiment and 1/12 SS Panzer Battalion deploy on the left flank and launch an assault against Canadian forces holding Norrey and Putot. Bitter fighting continues until nightfall and Meyer leads a relief attack on Rots.
9-11 June Two Panzer divisions deploy on *Hitlerjugend*'s left flank and the line is held until the Allies break through in Operation Epsom.

siderable number of PzKpfw IV tanks from the division's panzer regiment, in conjunction with the Army's 21st Panzer Division, went on to the attack and the British advance was soon halted, with over 30 Allied tanks being destroyed for the loss of just two panzers. The Allied advance was only temporarily brought to a halt, however, and the Germans were

ABOVE: British troops await a German attack in Normandy, June 1944. Allied air superiority was a decisive factor in the Germans' defeat in France.

Battle for Caen
Normandy, 1944

Key

Panzer Lehr Division

2nd Panzer Division

12th SS Panzer Division 'Hitlerjugend'

Hitlerjugend Tactical Headquarters

Hitlerjugend Divisional Headquarters

Hitlerjugend Artillery emplacements

Allied forces

Front line up to Operation Epsom

Bayeux

British 50th Infantry Division

Putot-en-Bessin

Bretteville-l'Orgueilleuse

Canadian 3rd Infantry Division

Franqueville

le Mesnil-Patry

Rots

Buron

St Manvieu-Norrey

Carpiquet

Cheux

Authie

St Contest

Epron

Airfield

Verson

Caen

Gavrus

Hill 122

**26 SS Panzergrenadier Regiment
2/12 SS Panzer Battalion
8 June**

River Orne

**25 SS Panzergrenadier Regiment
1/12 SS Panzer Battalion
6 June**

From Caen to Falaise

26 June Operation Epsom, the Allied attempt to encircle Caen from the west, begins with an assault on Cheux and St Manvieu. Hitlerjugend bears the brunt of the attack and is pushed steadily south.

27 June Hitlerjugend launches a desperate counterattack on Cheux but fails to retake it and is pushed back to the slopes of Hill 112.

28-30 June After three days of bloody fighting, Hitlerjugend and other Panzer divisions force an Allied withdrawal from Hill 112. The Allies remain in position south of the Odon and continue their attacks on Hill 112 well into July.

3 July On the right flank, Hitlerjugend continues to hold the line north of Caen through Buron.

4 July Operation Charnwood begins with a Canadian assault on Carpiquet. By evening the north of Carpiquet airfield is in Allied hands.

4-9 July Hitlerjugend is pushed back from Buron and suffers heavy casualties as it contests the Allied advance into Caen.

11 July Hitlerjugend withdraws to Potigny to regroup.

18-20 July As the Allies attempt to break through German lines from the northeast during Operation Goodwood, Hitlerjugend returns to the fight south of Caen.

7-20 August Operation Totalise: in a fighting withdrawal down the road to Falaise, the remnants of Hitlerjugend hold off the Allied advance and keep the north of the Falaise Gap open for two days.

20 August Meyer withdraws across the River Dives with the surviving elements of the division.

CHARNWOOD

Putot-en-Bessin

Buron

Epron

EPSOM

Authie

Caen

St Manvieu-Norrey

Carpiquet

Cheux

Verson

GOODWOOD

Hill 112

River Odon

River Orne

TOTALISE

to Falaise

Potigny

not strong enough to force the British infantry and armour to retreat.

By 9 June, Major-General Fritz Bayerlein and his Panzer *Lehr* Division were also in position around Caen after a nightmare 150km (90 mile) trek to reach the front, all the time under constant attack by Allied fighter-bombers, which cost the division over 200 vehicles of all types. But it meant that Caen and the vital Carpiquet airfield were now defended by three powerful panzer divisions.

Montgomery now decided to make use of two of his most experienced units: the 51st (Highland) Division and the 7th Armoured Division, both veterans of the 8th Army in North Africa. The Scots were tasked with bypassing the 6th Airborne Division's positions east of the Orne river, while the 7th Armoured Division advanced against Caen from the northeast. In vicious fighting lasting three days, however, the British made little or no progress in the face of tenacious resistance from the Germans, and the attack eventually petered out.

On 10 June, the 7th Armoured Division attempted to force its way past the British 50th Division just to the west of Caen, but likewise made little progress. A gap in the German defences between Caumont and Villers-Bocage had been spotted by the British, and the 7th Armoured Division immediately attempted to exploit this, British armour entering Villers-Bocage on the morning of 13 June. Unfortunately for them, at the same time SS-Obersturmführer Michael Wittmann,

commander of 2 Kompanie, schwere (heavy) SS-Panzer Abteilung 101, was also entering the village with a force of four Tiger tanks and one PzKpfw IV. Wittmann himself encountered four British Cromwell tanks on entering the village, and in a brief firefight knocked out three while the fourth tried to outflank him. However, it too fell victim to his deadly 88mm gun. Wittmann then rejoined the other Tigers and proceeded to attack an entire British armoured column from the 22nd Armoured Brigade. Driving along the side of the column, Wittmann knocked out a further 23 British tanks at point-blank range, as well as a similar number of half-tracks and lighter armoured vehicles. The shells of the British tanks merely bounced off the Tigers' massive armour plating, even at such close range.

By the time the four Tigers and the PzKpfw IV returned through the village, however, British tanks and a 6-pounder anti-tank gun were waiting for them, and all five were knocked out by shots through their thinner side armour at close range. The panzer crews escaped. Nevertheless, Wittmann's action had saved the flanks of the Panzer *Lehr* Division, and for his achievements he was deservedly decorated with the Swords and Oakleaves to his Knights Cross.

By 14 June, the gap in the German lines had been sealed. Within a few days of the invasion, Oberkommando der Wehrmacht (OKW) realised that this was indeed the real thing and that it was in danger of losing control of the battlefield to the enemy unless reinforcements could be brought to the front as soon as possible. To that end, the 9th SS Panzer Division *Hohenstaufen* and the 10th SS Panzer Division *Frundsberg* were immediately ordered from Poland to Normandy, but they did not arrive until almost the end of the month.

Meanwhile, SS-Brigadeführer Werner Ostendorff's 17th SS Panzergrenadier Division *Götz von Berlichingen* was facing American troops south of Carentan, along with Fallschirmjäger Regiment 6. The town had been taken by American troops, who had broken out from the Omaha and Utah beaches. On 14 June, *Götz von Berlichingen*, not yet at full strength and short of its heavy weapons, and the fallschirmjäger, now little more than ground troops, unsuccessfully attempted to oust the enemy, suffering heavy casualties in the process. The division remained in this sector for the remainder of June and most of July, struggling valiantly to hold back the Americans.

Defeating Operation 'Epsom'

On reaching Normandy on 25 June, both *Hohenstaufen* and *Frundsberg* were fed into the line between Caen and Villers-Bocage. Their arrival was timely, coinciding as it did with Montgomery's Operation 'Epsom' (his attempt to take Caen). The British VIII Corps attacked along a 6km (4 mile) front between Carpiquet and Rauray. Once again Montgomery used some of his finest and most experienced troops, including the 15th (Scottish) Division, 11th Armoured Division and 43rd Wessex Division. The attack opened with massive artillery and naval bombardments, but what initially seemed to be good progress deteriorated quickly into a vicious battle for every metre of ground as the German defenders fought tenaciously to blunt the Allied advance. The Germans counterattacked on 27 June, but their assault was stopped in its tracks by the 11th Armoured Division, which then followed through to cross the Odon river on the following day and take the crucial Hill 112 on 29 June.

In reply, SS-Obergruppenführer Paul Hausser launched a major counterattack using both *Hohenstaufen* and *Frundsberg*, but the Waffen-SS soldiers were beaten back. Fortunately for the Germans, however, the Allies had expected an even heavier attack and had withdrawn the 11th Armoured Division back across the Odon, so Hill 112 was soon back in German hands once again.

Meanwhile, American forces had resisted all attempts to dislodge them and had broken out of their bridgehead area to capture the essential port of Cherbourg. However, the German demolition engineers had been so efficient at destroying the port facilities when they retreated that barely 10 per cent of the anticipated level of supplies could be brought into the port by the Allies. The Americans now prepared for a major drive to the south towards Coutances, St. Lô and Caumont.

In Caen, the grenadiers of the *Hitlerjugend* Division held on desperately despite severe artillery, aerial and naval bombardment. The SS troops were gradually forced to give way, however, and the British eventually reached the Orne river, which ran through the centre of Caen, but only at a heavy cost in casualties – the remainder of the city was still in the hands of the

OPPOSITE TOP: US troops engaged in bitter fighting in the **Bocage,** *June 1944.*

OPPOSITE BELOW: A grenadier of the 12th SS Panzer Division **Hitlerjugend** *in the Normandy campaign. Note his Italian camouflage uniform, a consequence of uniform shortages in Germany.*

BELOW: A Tiger tank of schwere SS-Panzer Abteilung 101 moves through a French town on the way to the Normandy front.

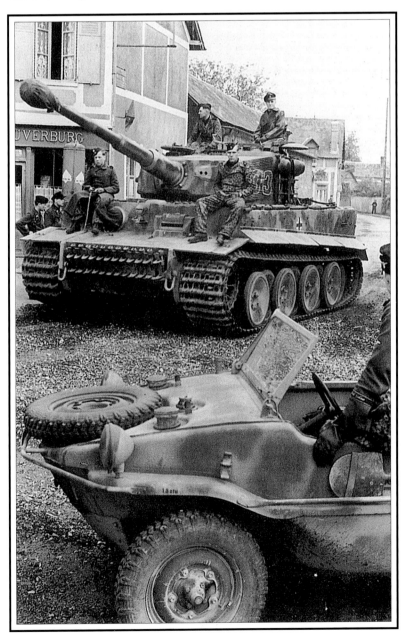

Hitlerjugend Division. Then the *Leibstandarte* reached the front and took over the *Hitlerjugend*'s positions at Caen, allowing the 12th SS Panzer Division to go into reserve north of Falaise.

On 18 July, the British launched Operation 'Goodwood', in which a massive armoured assault force planned to advance along a corridor blasted through the German lines by a massed Allied bombing attack. Once again, however, a promising initial rate of advance soon foundered, as the Germans quickly recovered from the three-hour bombardment, and tank and anti-tank fire soon began to exact its toll on Allied armour. Although the *Leibstandarte* was forced to relinquish most of Caen, the Allies lost over 400 tanks and the main German defence line was still relatively intact.

'Barkmann Corner'

On its arrival in Normandy, the 2nd SS Panzer Division *Das Reich* had joined *Götz von Berlichingen* in facing the Americans as they attempted to drive inland. During the early stages of the division's involvement in the Normandy battles, one of its most proficient tank killers was to considerably enhance his already high standing in the division. SS-Oberscharführer Ernst Barkmann had already proved himself to be one of the finest tank commanders in SS Panzer Regiment 2 during his service on the Eastern Front. On 8th July, he scored his first kill in the West when a US M4 Sherman tank fell victim to his Panther's 75mm high-velocity gun. On 13 July, three more M4s were added to his score, but it was on 27 July that Barkmann earned his place as one of Nazi Germany's top panzer aces at an isolated crossroads on the St. Lô-Coutances road, which subsequently became known as 'Barkmann Corner'. His Panther tank parked in the shade of a large oak tree, Barkmann watched as a large American armoured column of some 14 or so M4s approached his position. Once they were well within range he opened fire, and the first two lead Shermans were soon ablaze. Behind them came a petrol tanker truck, and the panzer ace lost no time in taking out this choice target. As the wreckage of the Shermans and the tanker truck blazed furiously, two more Shermans attempted to edge past the blockage. The first was quickly despatched, though the second managed to get off a couple of shots. They were no match for the Panther's thick armour, however, and this Sherman was

also soon ablaze, as Barkmann's gunner picked off his targets.

The Panther then came under attack from Allied fighter-bombers, and had a track blown off and the ventilation system damaged. Under the cover of the air strike two more Shermans approached, only to find that Barkmann's tank had not suffered any serious damage and was still more than capable of fending off their challenge. The two Shermans were soon reduced to burning hulks. Barkmann managed to destroy one more Sherman before deciding discretion was the better part of valour and ordering his driver to reverse their way back out of danger. This in itself was no mean feat in a badly damaged Panther tank.

Nine out of the 14 Shermans which had attacked this lone Panther were destroyed. In addition, despite fighter-bomber attacks and his tank being severely damaged, Barkmann managed to get his vehicle and crew back safely to German lines. He was decorated with the Knights Cross of the Iron Cross on 27 August for his achievements.

Allied pressure pushes back the SS

Earlier, on 25 July, the Americans had launched Operation 'Cobra', preceded by the customary massive aerial bombardment, in which many of their own troops were killed by 'friendly' fire. The stubborn defence put up by *Götz von Berlichingen* resulted in it becoming dangerously exposed, and so it was forced to withdraw. The Germans were suffering terribly from the attentions of rocket-firing Allied fighter-bombers – 'Jagdbomber' or 'Jabos' to the Germans. The effect of these rocket attacks was especially deadly against German tanks attempting to negotiate the narrow, hedge-lined country roads of this *bocage* country. Most German movements had to be made under the cover of darkness, a factor which led to many accidents, including the death of the *Leibstandarte*'s Knights Cross winner, SS-Obersturmführer Georg Karck, when his jeep ran into an unlit ammunition truck.

On 26 July, the US 1st Infantry Division and 3rd Armored Division, attacking in the direction of Marigny, met strong resistance from the badly battered *Das Reich* and the Army's 353rd Infantry Division, and after two full days of bitter fighting were still 2km (1.5 miles) away from the town. Their plan of pushing on through to Coutances now had little hope of succeeding.

'We came to Munich with Patton. There was a firefight between Americans and SS troops in a square.... The Americans were taking a tremendous beating. But they were battle-hardened, had lost a lot of guys, and were not to be trifled with. The SS troops surrendered.'
– Photographer Walter Rosenblum in Studs Terkel, *The Good War* (1985)

The Americans had more success on their left flank, with the 22nd Infantry Division meeting little more than sporadic resistance from the Germans in that sector, and over the next two days they exploited this lack of concerted resistance to the full as US forces rolled back the Germans. Still fighting around Marigny, *Das Reich* was forced to rapidly reform its defences to guard against the danger this posed to its flanks. Despite its best efforts, however, the momentum of the American attack was impossible to resist and Coutances fell on 28 July.

On 29 July, a combined force from *Das Reich* and *Götz von Berlichingen* smashed through the US 67th Armored Regiment and the 41st Armored Infantry near St. Denis le Gast, but the attack ran out of steam in the face of overwhelming Allied numerical superiority, and to avoid encirclement the Waffen-SS units were forced back towards Avranches, which fell to the tanks of the US 4th Armored Division on 30 July.

On the same day, the British VIII Corps launched Operation 'Bluecoat', an assault in the direction of Vire on the boundary between American and British forces. Although the 11th Armoured Division quickly seized the high ground around Le Bény Bocage, the drive to capture Vire was not followed through swiftly enough and the Germans were able to reinforce their positions. A chance to roll up the entire German 7th Army had been missed, and Vire was subsequently able to hold out for a further seven days.

The American battle plan now revolved around driving on beyond Mortain and Avranches to swing up to the Caumont-Fourgères line, before sweeping south via Le Mans and Alençon. With Avranches secured, the German units in the Contentin peninsula were in great danger of being cut off. In an effort to split the American forces in two, Hitler ordered an offensive towards Avranches. Taking part were the 2nd Panzer Division, 116th *Windhund* Panzer Division and elements of the *Leibstandarte* and *Das Reich* Divisions. The attack was launched on the night of 6 August, and *Das Reich* soon took Mortain and the high ground around St. Hilaire.

ABOVE: King Tiger tanks of the Waffen-SS in woods in northern France. Note the British prisoners being used for menial duties. The Luftwaffe's almost total absence from the air during the Normandy battles meant Allied aircraft could roam at will. Therefore, German armour was forced to use camouflage as much as possible and conduct movement at night. Only wooded terrain such as that here offered a degree of protection to the tanks of the SS divisions. However, Allied rocket-armed ground-attack aircraft still inflicted heavy losses on German vehicles throughout the campaign.

BELOW RIGHT: An SdKfz 234/2 Puma armoured car of the Hitlerjugend Division photographed in Normandy in July 1944. The division fought superbly throughout the Normandy campaign, its performance a testimony to the training it had received, its leaders and the calibre of its individual recruits. However, its fighting qualities were to no avail in the face of the Allies' so-called 'materialschlacht', their overwhelming strength in tanks, aircraft, motorised infantry and artillery. To the young and old Waffen-SS troopers alike, this was a new and demoralising experience. The Hitlerjugend had initially been positioned to the west of Caen, and it was here that the young recruits had their first taste of combat. Against the Canadian 3rd Division they performed well. But a subsequent counter-attack by its Panther tanks stalled in the face of intense Allied air attacks. The division fought superbly, some would say fanatically, but by 9 July it had lost an estimated 60 per cent of its original manpower strength, and only had a third of its 150 tanks left. Its original complement had been 21,300 men, but by the end of August the Hitlerjugend Division mustered only 300 men and 10 tanks, and its commander, Fritz Witt, had also been killed. What was left of the division was pulled out of the line and sent to Germany.

The 2nd Panzer Division also made good progress, almost reaching Juvigny before being slowed down by determined American resistance. Unfortunately, the 116th Panzer Division became bogged down almost at the start, and the whole offensive soon began to falter.

Meanwhile, II Canadian Corps had begun an assault along the Caen-Falaise road as part of Operation 'Totalize', even as the Germans launched their own attack towards Avranches. As the American XV Corps rapidly moved towards Argentan, the Canadians in the north endeavoured to link up with it. The Germans were again facing the danger of encirclement. Hitler therefore approved a withdrawal from the Mortain area on 11 August, with the *Leibstandarte* and 116th Panzer Division assembling their battered remnants around Carrouges for a counterattack on the approaching Americans. Elements of the 116th Panzer Divisions did temporarily halt the US advance near Mortrée, but it was a brief respite. The *Leibstandarte* and 2nd Panzer Division arrived in Argentan on 13 August, but almost immediately had to cancel any thoughts of a counterattack because the situation was deteriorating rapidly. *Frundsberg*, meanwhile, was battling to hold back the Americans around Domfront. It soon became clear that only an immediate retreat through the Falaise-Argentan gap would save the German forces in Normandy.

Withdrawal towards the River Orne began on 16 August, and initial progress was swift. However, by 17 August the 4th Canadian and 1st Polish Armoured Divisions were pushing south determinedly, while units of General Patton's US 3rd Army drove north, with the *Hitlerjugend* Division desperately battling to hold open the gap. *Das Reich* and *Hohenstaufen*, which had both passed through the gap earlier, turned about and launched counterattacks against the Allies in a desperate attempt to gain time for their comrades trapped in the pocket. German armour still within the pocket, caught in an ever-shrinking perimeter, became a prime target for Allied fighter-bombers, resulting in horrendous German losses.

The end of the Normandy battles

British and American units finally met at Chambois on the night of 19 August and the gap was closed. The line, though continuous, was not particularly strongly held at all points, and some German units did manage to break through, one of them being *Götz von Berlichingen*, which passed through the Canadian-held section of the line north of Mont Ormel. By the afternoon of 21 August 1944, the battle for the Falaise Pocket was over.

The first part of the campaign for western Europe had been a costly one for the Waffen-SS, with many of its finest units being decimated. Although the average Waffen-SS soldier had proved yet again that he was capable of the highest level of gallantry and self-sacrifice, against such massive material superiority, especially in the air, he could now only delay the enemy, not defeat him. In addition, the undoubted gallantry of the young Waffen-SS grenadiers was once again besmirched by the atrocities committed by a number of soldiers and officers from the *Hitlerjugend* Division.

A report issued by Army Group B on 22 August 1944 listed the following strengths for the eight surviving panzer divisions which took part in the battle for Normandy: the *Leibstandarte* had only weak infantry elements remaining – all of its tanks were lost and its artillery was totally destroyed; *Das Reich* had only some 450 men and 15 tanks remaining; *Hohenstaufen* fared only slightly better, with 460 men and around 25 tanks surviving; *Frundsberg* had no tanks or artillery left and only four battalions of infantry; and the *Hitlerjugend* had only 300 men, 10 tanks and no artillery. The Army had fared little better: the 2nd Panzer Division had no tanks or artillery and only one battalion of infantry; the 21st Panzer Division had 10 tanks and four battalions of Infantry; and the 116th Panzer Division *Windhund* had one battalion of infantry, 12 tanks and two battalions of artillery. The Panzer *Lehr* Division had ceased to exist as a cohesive unit, and the 9th Panzer Division was wiped out at Mortain.

The remnants of the *Leibstandarte* were withdrawn to Aachen for rest and rebuilding. Likewise, *Das Reich* was withdrawn into Germany to the Schnee Eifel area. The *Hitlerjugend* pulled back to the area east of the Maas to lick its considerable wounds, and *Götz von Berlichingen* was relocated to Metz. When a site was sought for the two sister panzer divisions *Hohenstaufen* and *Frundsberg* to rest and refit after the Normandy battles, a quiet spot in Holland was selected. Well behind German lines, it was considered that the two units would be left relatively undisturbed at Arnhem.

After the comprehensive defeat of the German forces in Normandy, Field Marshal Montgomery (he had been promoted on 1 September) pressed for permission to push on through Holland, while General Patton argued that an attack through the Siegfried Line defences via Lorraine was the best route into the Reich. After much argument, Montgomery eventually persuaded Eisenhower to approve a combined ground and airborne assault through Holland entitled 'Market Garden'. This plan called for the capture of the bridges at Eindhoven and Nijmegen by US airborne forces, while the British would capture the furthest bridge at Arnhem. Meanwhile, the British XXX

ABOVE: Two members of the **Hitlerjugend** *Division examine the hull of a disabled Sherman tank. Despite its horrendous losses in northern France and its failure to throw the Allies back into the sea, the division managed to hold open the northern end of the corridor out of the Falaise Pocket to allow trapped German units to escape.*

*ABOVE: SS-Obersturmbannführer Werner Ostendorff. Born in August 1903, he served in the **Das Reich Division** before assuming command of the 17th SS Panzergrenadier Division **Götz von Berlichingen**. The division was created in France in late autumn 1943 and saw action in Normandy, particularly around Carentan and Avranches. Ostendorff was wounded in March 1945 and died two months later, by which time he had been awarded the Oakleaves to his Knights Cross.*

*ABOVE RIGHT: SS-Unterscharführer Georg Karck, circa 1933. Karck served with the **Leibstandarte Division** with great distinction, before being killed in action in Normandy in a motoring accident.*

Corps, under Lieutenant-General Brian Horrocks, would push through from its starting point in Belgium and link up with the airborne assault troops along its line of advance.

The audacious assault was launched on 17 September, and as the vast Allied airborne armada began to deposit its human payload into the Dutch skies, reports quickly reached the commander of Army Group B, Field Marshal Walter Model, who immediately placed his forces, including II SS Panzer Corps under SS-Obergruppenführer Willi Bittrich, on the alert. This 'Panzer Corps' consisted of the battered remnants of the once mighty 9th and 10th SS Panzer Divisions, both of which had been decimated in the battle for Normandy. Nevertheless, they contained first-class troops, and their presence would come as a shock to the British 1st Airborne Division which landed at Arnhem.

While the American paras of the 82nd and 101st Airborne Divisions quickly consolidated their positions, taking the bridge and town of Eindhoven and reaching Nijmegen on schedule, they began to falter against unexpectedly strong German resistance. At Arnhem things were even worse. Because of unfavourable terrain, the troops had been landed as far as 13km (8 miles) from the city itself, and were soon

to find themselves in a hornets' nest of tough Waffen-SS panzer troops. Bittrich immediately despatched Kampfgruppe *Hohenstaufen* to halt the British airborne troops at Arnhem, while Kampfgruppe *Frundsberg* was sent to Nijmegen to help block the advance of XXX Corps. These two kampfgruppen were by no means the only contribution made by the Waffen-SS to the battle at Arnhem, however. Smaller, *ad hoc* kampfgruppen from the staff of the SS-Unterführerschule at Wolfheze, some 400 troops from the 16th SS-Stammbataillon, and a number of Dutch SS police also took part.

By the end of 17 September, the 2nd Parachute Battalion, under Lieutenant-Colonel John Frost, had forced its way on to the northern end of the Arnhem bridge and had taken the surrounding houses. Overnight, a few troops from the 1st Parachute Brigade arrived to bring Frost's forces up to a strength of around 600 men. The British were by no means strong enough to take the whole bridge, however, as its southern end was held by Waffen-SS panzergrenadiers.

Curiously, the Germans had local, if temporary, air superiority over the battlefield. As a consequence, Allied aerial resupply aircraft ran into difficulties. Losses were considerable, and the small amount of supplies reaching the battle zone often fell into the enemy's hands, so fluid was the situation on the ground. John Frost's troops found themselves squeezed between the Waffen-SS armoured reconnaissance troops to the south of the bridge and, advancing quickly on them from the north, Kampfgruppe *Hohenstaufen* led by SS-Obersturmbannführer Walter Harzer. Just to the west of the city, between Arnhem and Oosterbeek, was SS-Kampfgruppe *Spindler*, and farther west still SS-Kampfgruppe *Krafft*.

The fighting at Arnhem

The Germans soon discovered, however, that the British airborne troops who had appeared in their midst would be no easy prey for the tough SS panzer troops. As the battle quickly degenerated into house-to-house and hand-to-hand fighting, it became clear that Frost's men had a firm grip on the northern end of the bridge and would not be easily dislodged by mere infantry attacks.

Next to appear on the scene was SS-Panzeraufklärungsabteilung 9, under the command of SS-Hauptsturmführer Victor-Eberhard Grabner, who had recently been decorated with the Knights Cross for gallantry in the Normandy battles. Grabner led his recce troops in a head-on assault across the bridge. The attack was a total disaster, with Grabner being killed and over 20 of the unit's vehicles left burning and shattered on the bridge. Greater force would obviously be needed to throw the British from their positions, and in fact reinforcements for the Germans in the form of artillery and armour were already beginning to reach Arnhem.

On the morning of 19 September, an attempt by the bulk of 1 Para Brigade to force its way to the bridge was routed by German units, including SS-Kampfgruppe *Spindler*. To the west of the city, Polish glider-borne troops landed in between the battling 4th Airborne Brigade and SS-Kampfgruppe *Krafft* and were cut to pieces. At the bridge, Frost's strength was down to a mere 250 men, but he was still able to repulse all German attempts to dislodge him. All the while, Lieutenant-General Horrocks' XXX Corps was struggling to force its way through to Arnhem in the face of stiff German resistance and heavy aerial bombing attacks.

At midday on 21 September, SS-Kampfgruppe *Knaust* (actually commanded by a highly experienced Army panzer officer, Oberst Hans-Peter Knaust) finally

forced its way over the bridge at Arnhem, ending Frost's gallant stand. Knaust had no time to celebrate his victory, however, as he was immediately sent south to block those Allied troops who had finally forced their way over the Nijmegen bridge. Now only some 17km (11 miles) separated the XXX Corps from the remnants of the British force around Arnhem, which was being squeezed into a pocket at Oosterbeek. This was close enough for XXX Corps to provide artillery support for the beleaguered airborne troops, commanded by Major-General Robert Urquhart.

On 21 September, Major-General Stanislaw Sosabowski landed at Driel with the 1st Polish Parachute Brigade, to find himself faced with a German force which had by now decidedly gained the upper hand. Facing him was a rapidly assembled blocking force under SS-Obersturmbannführer Harzer, comprising a mixture of Naval, Luftwaffe, Army and Coastal Defence troops, as well as Dutch SS.

Both sides were by now exhausted, but it was the Germans who received the first significant reinforcements in the shape of schwere Panzer Abteilung 506, which had

*BELOW LEFT: One of the **Das Reich** Division's tanks aces: SS-Oberscharführer Ernst Barkmann. With his lone Panther tank he destroyed 13 American Sherman tanks in Normandy between 8-28 July 1944, and deservedly won the Knights Cross for his achievements. He fought in the German Ardennes Offensive of December 1944, and had an amazing escape near Manhay when his lone Panther encountered a large number of tanks of the US 2nd Armored Division. At one period in the battle his Panther collided with a Sherman and the two vehicles were locked together, the Panther's engine then cutting out. His driver managed to get the engine started, and the Panther pulled itself away from the American tank and then retreated. It was followed by another Sherman, which was destroyed by Barkmann with a single shot. He then headed off the road and drove through snowy woods to reach his battalion. Barkmann survived the war and lives in Germany.*

a full complement of the awesome PzKpfw VIB King Tiger tanks, against which the light weapons of the British Paras were all but useless. Two companies of Tigers were despatched to Kampfgruppe *Frundsberg* to help hold back the advance of XXX Corps, while the third was turned against the embattled survivors in the Oosterbeek area. The remnants of the British assault force were ordered to withdraw on the night of 25/26 September. The battered survivors withdrew over the Lower Rhine at Oosterbeek and retreated south. The wounded had to be left behind with volunteer medical staff and, fully aware of the often unsavoury reputation of the Waffen-SS (both sides had in fact shot prisoners during the Arnhem battle), must have awaited their captivity with some trepidation. In the event, however, those taken prisoner were treated with considerable care by their Waffen-SS captors. Almost 17,000 casualties had been suffered by the Allies during Operation 'Market Garden'. German casualties were reckoned to have been somewhere between 4000 and 8000.

Although the Germans, weakened and exhausted after the Normandy battles, had inflicted a major defeat on the Allies, the benefits to Army Group B were limited and of extremely short duration. Within 10 days, for example, Bittrich's II SS Panzer Corps had given up its attempts to repulse the advance of XXX Corps and the bridge at Arnhem had been closed to German traffic by Allied bombing raids.

The Ardennes Offensive

Since September 1944, though, Hitler's attention was already elsewhere, as he gathered his troops for what was to be his final attempt to regain the military initiative in the West: the ill-fated Ardennes Offensive. Codenamed 'Wacht am Rhein', it was intended as a three-pronged assault towards Antwerp. Its main strike component, the 6th Panzer Army under the command of SS-Oberstgruppenführer 'Sepp' Dietrich, was to attack through the Ardennes forests, force a crossing of the River Meuse between Liège and Huy, and then drive on towards Antwerp.

General Hasso von Manteuffel, commander of the 5th Panzer Army, was to sweep northwest along Dietrich's southern flank, cross the Meuse between Namur and Dinant and push for Brussels, while the 7th Army, under General Erich Brandenberger, was to drive for the Meuse on the southern flank. Vital to the plan was the capture, intact, of the bridges over the

Meuse, after which the drive towards Antwerp would be supported by the 15th Army, under General Student, in Holland, trapping the American 1st and 9th Armies, British 2nd Army and Canadian 1st Army.

The panzer element of Dietrich's 6th Panzer Army consisted of I SS Panzer Corps, whose principal components were the 1st SS Panzer Division *Leibstandarte* and the 12th SS Panzer Division *Hitlerjugend*. In reserve was II SS Panzer Corps, comprising the 2nd SS Panzer Division *Das Reich* and the 9th SS Panzer Division *Hohenstaufen*. The infantry element was made up of the 12th, 272nd, 277th and 326th Volksgrenadier Divisions and the 3rd Fallschirm Division.

Kampfgruppe *Peiper*

The importance of capturing the bridges over the Meuse intact as early as possible led to the creation of a special force – Panzerbrigade 150, commanded by SS-Sturmbannführer Otto Skorzeny. English-speaking volunteers, some dressed as military police, were kitted out in American uniforms and issued with American weapons and vehicles. They were sent into action ahead of the main strike force to mingle with the retreating Americans and spread confusion along the way, misdirecting the fleeing Americans and sowing the seeds of panic.

The spearhead of the 6th Panzer Army was to be formed by I SS Panzer Corps, which was tasked with punching through the American lines between Hollerath and Krewinkel and driving through to the Liège-Huy sector, with the *Hitlerjugend* on the right flank and the *Leibstandarte* on the left. The route was confined to narrow, twisting roads due to the terrain being unsuitable for cross-country movement, and the number one priority was to gain control of the road network. The Germans were well aware of the difficulties even a small number of determined defenders could cause in such country, and so the lead in the attack of I SS Panzer Corps was given to a particularly powerful assault group. It was led by an officer who had proved himself in combat on numerous occasions: SS-Obersturmbannführer Joachim Peiper.

Although Hitler had achieved virtual miracles assembling such a huge assault force at this late stage of the war, the quality of the average German soldier taking part in the Ardennes Offensive could not compare with those who had routed the Allies in France in 1940 and steamrolled into the Soviet Union in 1941. Now, the typical German soldier was dressed in a poor-quality, shoddy uniform, was ill-equipped and lacking in adequate training. Even the better-quality units, such as the Waffen-SS divisions, had their share of troops drafted from the Luftwaffe and Kriegsmarine, men who were not trained for tank and infantry warfare.

On the morning of 16 December 1944, a massive artillery barrage heralded the opening of Hitler's last gamble in western Europe. The 12th Volksgrenadier Division punched through the weak American defences around Losheim and made a breach in the enemy's line, which Kampfgruppe *Peiper* was quick to exploit. Two companies of PzKpfw IV tanks led, followed by two companies of the excellent PzKpfw V Panther and accompanying infantry-carrying half-tracks. Artillery and combat pioneers followed, with the awesome King Tiger tanks of schwere SS-Panzer Abteilung 501 bringing up the rear.

Progress along the congested roads was slow, though, with Kampfgruppe *Peipe*r becoming entangled with slower-moving units, such as the 12th Volksgrenadier Division and fallschirmjäger elements. By late evening, the kampfgruppe was approaching Losheim, where the 3rd Fallschirm Division had forced a breach in

the enemy lines to the south of the village, and Peiper immediately rushed his force through the gap and sped on towards Lanzerath and linked up with Fallschirmjäger Regiment 9. He pressed on through the night, and just before dawn on 17 December the Germans found themselves amidst retreating American units moving through Honsfeld. The soldiers were taken completely by surprise by the appearance of an SS kampfgruppe in their midst, and surrendered after offering token resistance.

By now running low on fuel, Peiper diverted towards Büllingen and captured an American fuel dump there, which allowed his force to replenish its fuel stocks, before pressing on to capture Schoppen, Ondenval and Thirimont by the middle of the day. The kampfgruppe's line of advance now led it towards Ligneuville, where it met some resistance from American armour before taking the town. Peiper remained in the town to confer with the commander of the *Leibstandarte*, SS-Oberführer Wilhelm Mohnke, while the kampfgruppe continued on towards Trois Ponts and Beaumont (it was on the 17th that the Malmédy massacre occurred – see Chapter 11).

Without its leader, however, the kampfgruppe acted with uncharacteristic caution when it met resistance at Stavelot,

ABOVE: The aftermath of Arnhem. A StuG III of the 9th SS Panzer Division Hohenstaufen *and captured British Paras. SS soldiers from both* Hohenstaufen *and* Frundsberg *were involved in the battle, and their treatment of the prisoners afterwards was exemplary. Lieutenant-Colonel John Frost, one of the British officers who took part and was captured, describes the SS thus: 'We had all heard of them shooting their prisoners or herding them into burning buildings, but these men were kind, chivalrous and even comforting.' After Arnhem,* Hohenstaufen *was pulled back to Germany to prepare to take part in the Ardennes Offensive. It then took part in the abortive attempt to retake Budapest.*

BELOW RIGHT: 16 December 1944 – the start of the German Ardennes Offensive. In the vanguard of the attack were the men of the 6th SS Panzer Army, commanded by SS-Oberstgruppenführer 'Sepp' Dietrich. The plan was simple and daring: German forces would drive through the Ardennes, cross the Meuse and then advance to capture the port of Antwerp, the main Allied supply port. Though many of his generals, such as von Rundstedt, believed the war in the West was already lost, Hitler thought otherwise. He had given his views to his commanders in August 1944: 'If necessary we will fight on the Rhine. It makes absolutely no difference. Regardless of the circumstances we will continue the long struggle until, as Frederick the Great said, one of our damned enemies becomes too tired to fight any more and until we secure a peace that will endure the existence of the German nation for the next 50 or 100 years.' For the offensive the SS was assigned the main role: to drive along the northern flank of the assault, which was the shortest route to Antwerp. The morale of the SS was high. A young lieutenant of the Hitlerjugend Division wrote to his sister: 'Some believe in living but life is not everything! It is enough to know that we attack and will throw the enemy from our homeland. It is a holy task.'

its lead vehicles having come under fire from American troops. The Germans drew back for the night and prepared to attack again in the morning.

By daybreak, Peiper had returned to his unit and the town was stormed after a heavy artillery barrage. The bridge at Stavelot was captured intact, and by mid-morning the kampfgruppe was leaving the town behind and pressing on towards Trois Ponts, which gained its name from the three bridges over the River Amblève and the Salm at this location. The Americans, however, succeeded in blowing the bridge over the Amblève, and subse-

quent attempts to ford the river were unsuccessful. Peiper was forced to turn north, and an alternative bridge was found at Cheneux, near Stoumont.

Despite being delayed by fighter-bomber attacks, Peiper had now only two bridges between him and his primary objective: Huy. One of these bridges, however, the one at Neuf Moulin, was blown as Peiper's troops approached. Two alternative bridges were found nearby, but both were too small to support Peiper's heavy vehicles, and the kampfgruppe had no heavy bridging equipment. Leaving some troops behind to guard the bridge at

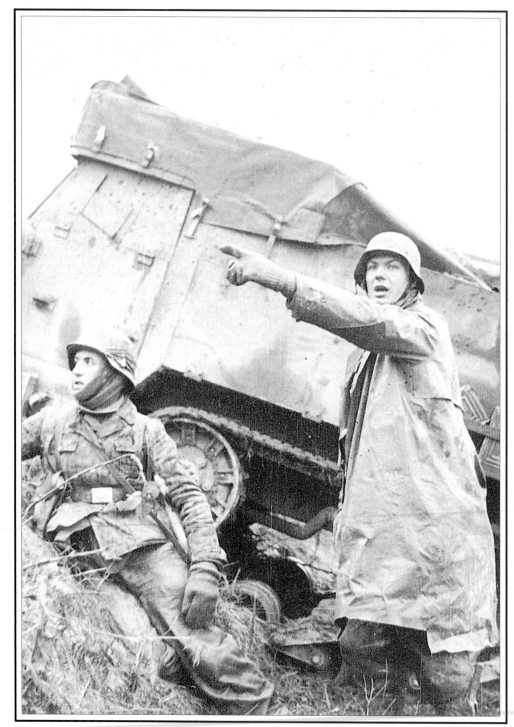

Cheneux, Kampfgruppe *Peiper* withdrew into woods near Stoumont for the night.

At Stavelot meanwhile, American infantry, supported by armour, had all but retaken the town, and Peiper's force was in danger of being cut off. The *Leibstandarte* was ordered to support the kampfgruppe, and Stavelot was the focus of an unsuccessful counterattack to drive the Americans out.

On 19 December, Peiper reached Stoumont, where a two-hour pitched battle with the American defenders ensued before the Germans took the town. Peiper's tanks pursued the retreating enemy for a few kilometres out of the town, before hitting an American roadblock and losing several tanks.

Unfortunately for the Germans, the Allies were by now recovering from the initial shock of the attack and resistance was stiffening somewhat. On 21 December, Peiper decided to concentrate his forces around La Gleize and try to hold the bridge at Cheneux. In the town of Cheneux itself, savage hand-to-hand fighting raged for several hours, costing the Americans over 200 dead before the Germans were driven out.

The offensive stalls

On 22 December, the Americans began probing the German defences around La Gleize. Peiper was now out of fuel and low on ammunition, and an air drop by the Luftwaffe saw most of the supplies fall into American hands. Peiper was given permission to break out to the east on 23 December. After destroying his vehicles, Peiper and his remaining 1000 men set out for the German lines on 24 December, leaving only a small rearguard to hold off the American pursuers. The remnants of Kampfgruppe *Peiper* crossed the Salm and linked up with the *Leibstandarte* just before dawn on Christmas Day.

Elsewhere, the 12th SS Panzer Division *Hitlerjugend* had had little good fortune in its attack on American positions on the Elsenborn ridge, and after three days of heavy fighting was still struggling to take the villages of Rocherath and Krinkelt. It was then diverted to the *Leibstandarte*'s southern flank to assist in the push against the US 7th Armored Division near Poteau on 19 December. The *Hitlerjugend* Division, having little success in its current operation, was re-routed south to clear the Büllingen-Malmédy road. Heavy losses were incurred, particularly in the fighting for Büfenbach, and the division was with-

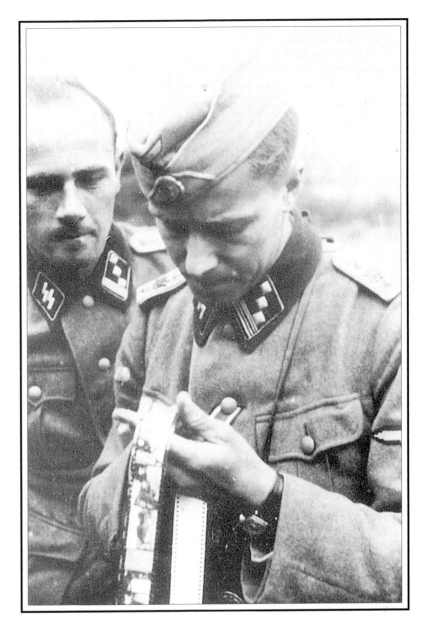

ABOVE: Joachim Peiper, commander of Kampfgruppe Peiper, a battlegroup of the Leibstandarte Division, which was the spearhead unit of the Ardennes Offensive. Seen here earlier in the war with the rank of SS-Hauptsturmführer, he fought in the Ardennes as an SS-Obersturmbannführer. For his part in the Malmédy massacre he was sentenced to hang by the Allies. He requested to be shot instead, which was granted. However, the sentence was eventually commuted.

drawn on 23 December to regroup in the Moderscheid/Born area.

Das Reich had been waiting in its assembly area near Jünkerath for orders to follow *Hohenstaufen* into action when it was attached temporarily to Manteuffel's 5th Panzer Army, and fought in the St. Vith salient on 22 December. *Das Reich* captured the vital crossroads at Baraque de Fraiture on 23 December, and a night attack on the 24th took Manhay, but further progress was prevented by increasingly determined American actions. By 27 December Manhay had been lost again.

Hitlerjugend, *Das Reich* and *Hohenstaufen* were all involved in an attack in the Manhay sector on 27 December, but failed to penetrate the American lines. One aspect of the Manhay action which did prove successful for the Germans was the attack by SS-Panzerregiment 2 on US armour in that sector. Once again, panzer

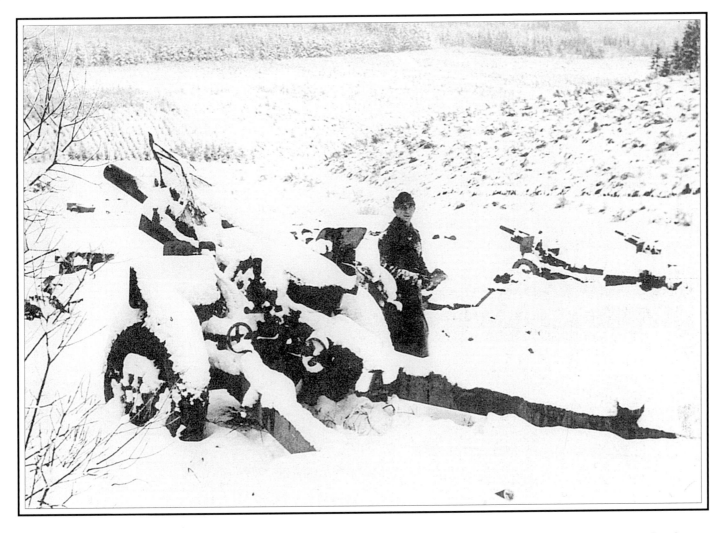

ace SS-Oberscharführer Ernst Barkmann proved his worth, taking out several M4 Shermans. His comrade, SS-Hauptscharführer Franz Frauscher, also inflicted considerable damage on the Americans, destroying or capturing nine Shermans. Frauscher was awarded the Knights Cross on 31 December for his achievements.

The whole offensive was now bogged down, as Allied numerical superiority and air power, combined with German supply problems, began to take their toll. All hopes of reaching Antwerp were forgotten as Hitler came up with a new plan designed to draw Allied power away from the Ardennes sector and give some relief to the stalled assault forces. This new offensive, Operation 'Nordwind', was launched on 1 January 1945. It was aimed at the weak American forces in the province of Alsace. Among the Waffen-SS units taking part were the 17th SS Panzergrenadier Division *Götz von Berlichingen* and the 6th SS Gebirgs Division *Nord*, recently evacuated from the far north of the Eastern Front. Although initial successes were achieved and several hundred American prisoners

taken, the attack foundered within a few days. A fresh assault by *Frundsberg*, aimed at Strasbourg, also quickly ground to a halt, and no further German gains in Alsace were made.

In the Ardennes, the *Hitlerjugend*, *Leibstandarte* and *Hohenstaufen* Divisions were all heavily involved in the attempt to take Bastogne before it could be relieved by Patton's 3rd Army, but by 24 January the situation in Hungary had deteriorated so seriously that all four Waffen-SS divisions initially committed to the Ardennes Offensive were withdrawn and transferred to the crumbling Eastern Front.

By 10 February 1945, the last German units were back over the River Rhine. The Wehrmacht's last, carefully gathered reserves had been squandered in the Ardennes, and the remaining Waffen-SS units on the Western Front could do little more than fight a dogged, but hopeless, rearguard action, as the Americans, Canadians, French and British pushed deep into the Reich itself. On the Eastern Front, meanwhile, the Führer gathered his forces for what was to be the death ride of the Waffen-SS panzer divisions.

OPPOSITE: A Panther tank rumbles forward in the Ardennes, late December 1944. Despite the strength of the 6th SS Panzer Army, it is ironic that the bulk of its units never got into combat. Because of the weather conditions and the wooded terrain, there were many bottlenecks that resulted in tanks being held up in massive jams. As a consequence, only the lead elements of the panzer columns clashed with the enemy. In fact, the deepest penetration of the Allied line was made not by the SS but by the Army's 2nd Panzer Division.

ABOVE: Captured US 105mm howitzers lay abandoned in the snow.

DEATH RIDE

With the failure of the Ardennes Offensive, all hopes of victory in the West had gone. In the East, meanwhile, the Red Army was sweeping all before it. The Third Reich was crumbling, but the soldiers of the Waffen-SS fought on, conducting a fighting withdrawal to Berlin. There the SS died doing what it had been created for – defending its Führer.

From August 1944, as the apparently unstoppable Red Army drove through Romania and Bulgaria, Hitler's east European allies, having little choice as the Soviets approached their borders, left the Axis cause and sided with the Soviets. No doubt this was done partly in the hope of receiving more lenient treatment for their countries after the defeat of Germany. However, if this was their hope it was a vain one, as the subsequent iron control in their nations by Stalin would show.

As Army Groups E and F, under Field Marshal von Weichs, were forced back through Yugoslavia, the ethnic volunteer SS divisions *Prinz Eugen*, *Skanderbeg* and *Kama* found themselves not only facing Tito's increasingly strong partisan forces, but frontline troops of the Red Army as well. *Skanderbeg* and *Kama* were annihilated during these battles, while *Prinz Eugen* was decimated fighting Red Army units south of Vukovar in January 1945, its remnants thereafter withdrawing into Austria.

In Hungary, the capital Budapest came under the protection of General Otto Wöhler's Army Group South. Units committed to the defence of the city included the 8th SS Kavallerie Division *Florian Geyer*, 22nd SS Freiwilligen-Kavallerie Division *Maria Theresia* and 18th SS Freiwilligen-Panzergrenadier Division *Horst Wessel*,

Troops of the Red Army hoist the banner of the Soviet Union over the charred ruins of Berlin, the culmination of a campaign that had begun four years before.

although elements of the latter were to be detached to assist the German defences in Galicia and to help suppress the Slovak uprising (August-October 1944).

In October 1944, it became clear to the Germans that the Hungarian head of state, Admiral Horthy, was about to join the Romanians and Bulgarians in negotiating terms with the Soviets, and so, in a coup d'etat led by Hitler's commando extraordinaire, SS-Obersturmbannführer Otto Skorzeny, Horthy was overthrown and a puppet government loyal to the Nazis installed. The situation was temporarily stabilised. At the beginning of the month, however, the Red Army had crossed the Hungarian border and raced for the Danube, reaching the river to the south of Budapest and establishing a bridgehead on the west bank, from where it could launch future operations.

Attempts to relieve Budapest
To the southwest of the city lay Lake Balaton (the *Platensee* to the Germans), between which and the area around Budapest the Germans had established strong defensive positions. By 20 December 1944, the Soviets had advanced across the Danube and reached the southern shore of Lake Balaton. The main German defences, however, proved a difficult nut for the Red Army to crack (by this stage of the war in the East, the Germans were making use of natural defences, such as rivers, and 'fortress cities'). The Soviets had also outstretched their supply lines. Nevertheless, the respite for the Germans was brief. Marshal Tolbukhin diverted the main thrust of his attack past the eastern edges of Budapest, and with the 6th Guards Tank Army attacking from the northeast and the 46th Army from the south, the city was eventually encircled in a massive pincer action. Fighting raged for some time, the Soviets unable to rout the Germans and the latter unable to throw back the attackers.

On 26 December, IV SS Panzer Corps, comprising the 3rd SS Panzer Division *Totenkopf* and the 5th SS Panzer Division *Wiking*, were transferred from the Warsaw area in an attempt to relieve Budapest. Two attempts to raise the siege of the city were beaten back by the Soviets, before they in turn launched a counterattack which forced IV SS Panzer Corps on to the defensive. The beleaguered garrison struggled on until 11 February 1945, when some 30,000 of the remaining troops inside the city attempted a breakout to the west.

In the nightmare battles that ensued, the fleeing Germans were cut to pieces. *Florian Geyer* and *Maria Theresia* were annihilated, and only some 700 soldiers eventually reached the safety of German lines. Budapest surrendered on 12 February.

Plans for 'Spring Awakening'
The few survivors of the two SS cavalry divisions were to form the nucleus of a new unit: the 37th SS Freiwilligen-Kavallerie Division *Lützow*. However, it never reached the strength of a single regiment, and existed for only three months before being swallowed up in the Soviet advance.

The surrender of Budapest released a large number of Soviet troops for a fresh offensive on the German Army. As a consequence, the German-held oilfields at Nagykanizsa, Hungary, were in danger of being overrun by enemy forces, which were now only 80km (50 miles) away. Hitler was horrified at the thought of losing this precious source of oil, and decided that only a new offensive could throw the Soviets back over the Danube and save the overall situation in Hungary.

Hitler's plan involved assaults by Army Groups South and Southeast. Army Group South, under General Wöhler, would comprise the 6th SS Panzer Army, 8th Army, 6th Army and the Hungarian 3rd Army, and would strike south from the Margarethe defence lines, while Army Group Southeast's 2nd Army would attack from the west of the Soviet lines. This pincer movement, it was hoped, would crush Tolbukhin's 3rd Ukrainian Front, comprising the 4th Guards Army, 26th Army, 57th Army and 1st Bulgarian Army. Meanwhile, IV SS Panzer Corps would remain in the Margarethe positions around Lake Balaton.

Commanded by SS-Oberstgruppenführer 'Sepp' Dietrich, the 6th SS Panzer Army consisted of the 1st SS Panzer Division *Leibstandarte*, 2nd SS Panzer Division *Das Reich*, 9th SS Panzer Division *Hohenstaufen* and the 12th SS Panzer Division *Hitlerjugend*. All newly arrived from the abortive Ardennes Offensive, none of these units were anything like the mighty formations they once were, but they could still cause serious problems for the Soviets. The *Leibstandarte*, commanded by SS-Brigadeführer Otto Kumm, and the *Hitlerjugend*, commanded by SS-Oberführer Hugo Kraas, were grouped together as I SS Panzer Corps, while *Das Reich*, temporarily commanded by SS-Standartenführer

'Dietrich [Sepp Dietrich, commander 6th Waffen-SS Panzer Division] openly criticized actions taken by the Führer. He complained that the Führer does not give his military staff enough self-determination and that this tendency is so deep-seated that the Führer even controls the deployment of individual companies.'
– Göbbels diary entry for 2 March 1945

Rudolf Lehmann, and *Hohenstaufen*, led by SS-Oberführer Sylvester Stadler, formed II SS Panzer Corps.

Hitler's fanatical insistence on total secrecy for the operation, codenamed *Frühlingserwachen* ('Spring Awakening'), certainly fooled the enemy, but it was taken to ludicrous extremes. For example, none of the SS commanders were allowed to reconnoitre the areas in which their units would operate in case the enemy began to suspect an operation was about to be mounted. All identifying insignia were removed, unit names were changed, and even individual soldiers were ordered to remove identifying insignia in an effort to fool the enemy.

The area around Lake Balaton is predominantly marshy, but under normal circumstances the severe frosts during the early part of the year renders the ground hard enough to bear the weight of heavy vehicles. Unfortunately, in the spring of 1945 the thaw came much earlier than expected and the terrain was turned into a glutinous sea of mud, into which 'Sepp' Dietrich's panzers sank – all the way up to their turrets in some extreme cases.

The opening of the offensive

As a preliminary to the main attack, I SS Panzer Corps had smashed the Soviet bridgehead around Estergom with little difficulty. Once the Soviets became aware of a large body of elite Waffen-SS troops in the region, however, they quickly realised that a major offensive was indeed imminent and began to strengthen their defences accordingly, thickening up their minefields and preparing anti-tanks defences in depth. This prelude to the main attack, though successful in its own right, had merely forewarned the Red Army of what was to come.

When the day of Operation *Frühlingserwachen* dawned (6 March), heavy snow had made conditions even worse. In addition, to increase the element of surprise, which to all intents and purposes had been lost anyway, soldiers moving to the front were dropped off by their transport vehicles some 18km (12 miles) back from the launch point of their attack; they had to cover the remaining distance on foot so the Soviets would not detect any troop movements. Unfortunately, this meant the Waffen-SS grenadiers were soaked, freezing and exhausted by the time they reached their start points. In fact, few were in position at the appointed time when the artillery barrage intended to soft-

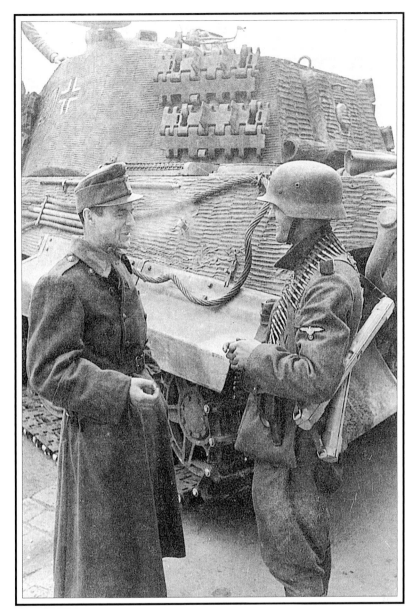

en up the Soviet positions began at 0430 hours. By the time some units started their attack, the barrage had long since ended and the enemy, thus alerted, was waiting.

I SS Panzer Corps was best placed for the attack, the men having reached their positions in time, but II SS Panzer Corps was still floundering in the mud, its heavy vehicles finding the going almost impossible. Not surprisingly, the German attack began to suffer heavy losses almost from the start. Despite this, though, the Waffen-SS troops threw themselves into battle with their customary elan and determination, driving the enemy back, in the case of I SS Panzer Corps, for distances of up to 40km (25 miles). II SS Panzer Corps however, could only manage penetrations of around 8km (5 miles) at best.

The Soviets had the luxury of being able to make good their losses relatively quickly, while the Germans, though they

ABOVE: A Hungarian soldier and machine gunner of the **Totenkopf Divison** *share a joke next to a* **King Tiger** *tank in Budapest, in early December 1944. In reality there was not much to smile about – by the end of the month the Red Army had encircled the city and Hungary itself had declared war on Germany. Note the tubes containing spare barrels slung across the SS trooper's back. The* **Totenkopf Division** *was involved in the abortive attempt to relieve the city in January 1945.*

ABOVE: A Waffen-SS machine gun opens up with tracer fire against Red Army positions in Hungary, January 1945. After Budapest had been surrounded, Hitler ordered the Wiking and Totenkopf Divisions, grouped together in IV SS Panzer Corps, to raise the siege. They began their efforts at the beginning of January, and for two weeks the Waffen-SS struggled in vain against intense Soviet opposition. Eventually they were forced to give up. Reichsführer-SS Himmler had stated that the Waffen-SS 'has never under any circumstances caused disappointment and it will not – even under the most severe hardships to come – disappoint in the future.' However, the men in the individual divisions knew that such statements were empty words in early 1945.

did receive some reinforcements, obtained personnel who were often very poor quality, such as former Luftwaffe and Kriegsmarine members. These men were frequently poorly trained and equipped, and had no motivation to sacrifice their lives at this late stage in the war. The offensive slowed up, and German aerial reconnaissance began to see evidence of a massive Soviet build-up, obviously intended for a counterattack.

The Soviet offensive began on 16 March along the entire sector west of Budapest. The Russian sledgehammer blow stopped the German offensive in its tracks. Dietrich desperately reshuffled his forces to reinforce the areas most endangered, but when he did so the Soviets soon swamped the areas from which the reinforcements had been taken. The 6th SS Panzer Army was in great danger of being completely cut off, as IV SS Panzer Corps struggled to maintain the German base line. *Das Reich* desperately battled to hold open a corridor of escape for its comrades, but the defection of the Hungarian Army left the flanks of II SS Panzer Corps wide open to the enemy. *Frühlingserwachen* was completely routed, and the Germans had no option but to order a full retreat or lose the best remaining divisions they still possessed on the Eastern Front. By 25 March, the Russians had torn a 100km (60 mile) gap in the German defences.

As well as the four elite panzer divisions of the 6th SS Panzer Army and the two panzer divisions of IV SS Panzer Corps, the 16th SS Panzergrenadier Division *Reichsführer-SS* was also committed to battle around Lake Balaton. The *Horst Wessel* Division had been fortunate enough to escape the encirclement of Budapest and retreat into Slovakia. Within 10 days of the offensive being launched, however, it had been totally wiped out.

Hitler was infuriated at this 'betrayal' by his elite Waffen-SS divisions when they failed to hold their positions. General Heinz Guderian was ordered to the front from Hitler's headquarters to demand the removal of the cuffbands worn by these SS divisions as punishment for their offence. Guderian refused, insisting that only the Reichsführer-SS himself was competent to so punish units of the Waffen-SS. Himmler did not have the courage to face his commanders with such an order in person, and so transmitted it in writing.

Dietrich, incensed by this insult to the gallantry and self-sacrifice shown by his soldiers, called a meeting of his divisional commanders, in which he informed them of Hitler's orders and then promptly ordered them to disobey. Not one cuffband, which the soldiers of these elite units wore with such pride, was to be removed. Apocryphal stories abound of chamber pots full of decorations and cuffbands being sent back to Hitler to return the insult with interest. Whatever the truth of the matter, Hitler had certainly lost the last few vestiges of respect which many of these Waffen-SS soldiers still held for him. From now on, many of the hard-bitten soldiers of the Waffen-SS would remain primarily loyal to the Waffen-SS itself, to their own divisions and regiments, and to their own commanders. But they would continue to fight for the Führer.

After smashing the German offensive around Lake Balaton, the Soviet advance continued to the west of Budapest in a two-pronged movement towards Pápa and Gyór. By 2 April, the Red Army had reached the Neusiedler Lake, on the border between Hungary and Austria, and two days later the last German soldiers had been driven out of Hungary. The Soviet 46th Army was then transported by boat along the Danube to attack Vienna from the north, while the 4th Guards Army drove towards the city from the southeast. Of the Waffen-SS divisions which had fought in Hungary, most had withdrawn into Austria to defend Vienna.

Hohenstaufen had been bady cut up in Hungary and so its remnants were formed into small kampfgruppen, which fought a rearguard action during the withdrawal towards Vienna. The *Totenkopf*, too, fought in defence of the Austrian capital, while the *Hitlerjugend* withdrew into strong defensive positions in the mountainous area around Wienerwald, to the southwest of the city, but was forced out of its positions by the unrelenting Soviet pressure after only a few days.

Das Reich put up a stubborn defence to the south of Vienna, before withdrawing into the city itself and becoming involved in bitter fighting around the Florisdorf bridge on 13/14 April. Despite its efforts, it was gradually driven out of the city by intense Soviet pressure. Elements continued to fight in the area to the west of Vienna, but the bulk of the division's remnants were sent to the region east of Dresden to help attempt to hold back Soviet units swarming into the Reich itself. *Reichsführer-SS* withdrew into Untersteiermark in the south of Austria, but became fragmented. Everywhere the Germans were on the retreat.

In the closing days of the war in eastern Europe, most Waffen-SS soldiers realised that the war was irrevocably lost. They had one thought uppermost in their minds: surrendering to Anglo-American forces rather than the Soviets. Few of them harboured any illusions as to the

BELOW: Soviet infantry advance towards German positions in Hungary in February 1945. Budapest fell to the Red Army on 13 February, which resulted in some 188,000 men of the German/Hungarian force being knocked out of the war. The Wehrmacht could not afford such losses, and everywhere in the East its resources were stretched to the limit. The Red Army's offensives in Hungary had resulted in German forces being withdrawn from Army Group A in the north. Thus when the Soviet offensive began in Poland on 12 January, the Germans were ill-equipped to mount an effective defence. As a result, the Red Army advanced 480km (300 miles) in two weeks.

*ABOVE: Warsaw burns as the Germans suppress the August uprising. To crush the revolt, Himmler assembled a motley band of SS soldiers: the **Dirlewanger Brigade**, the **Kaminsky Brigade**, regular police units, and elements of the 22nd SS Freiwilligen-Kavallerie Division **Maria Theresia** (there were also Army units involved). The uprising was finally extinguished on 2 October 1944, some two months after it had erupted. The fighting spirit of the Poles had been superb, but short of small arms, artillery and ammunition, as well as the hoped-for Red Army support, they could not hold out for long. Some 15,000 of the Polish Home Army died, together with an estimated 200,000 civilians, many of them butchered by Himmler's SS soldiers.*

kind of treatment they would receive as prisoners of the Russians. Both sides had committed many atrocities against the other's prisoners, and few Waffen-SS men expected to survive Soviet captivity. With these thoughts in mind, the SS formations tried to take appropriate action.

Elements of *Reichsführer-SS* surrendered south of the River Drau, while others withdrew towards Klagenfurt and surrendered there to the Western Allies. The *Hitlerjugend* trekked some 96km (60 miles) westwards to surrender to the Americans at Linz on 8 May. *Hohenstaufen*'s pitiful remnants surrendered to the Americans at Seyr in Austria, as did the *Leibstandarte*. The *Totenkopf* had withdrawn to the northwest of Vienna and surrendered to the Americans on 9 May. Any relief its members felt at being taken prisoner by the Americans was short-lived, however, as they were promptly handed over to the Soviets, who had a score to settle with this particular division. Very few *Totenkopf* soldiers survived Soviet captivity.

Although by the end of April the bulk of *Das Reich*'s remnants were in the area to the east of Dresden, one of its units had further business to attend to in the southern sector. At the end of April, SS-Obersturmbannführer Otto Weidinger, commander of the *Der Führer* Regiment, was ordered to Prague to report to the senior SS commander there. Although

things seemed peaceful on the surface, a Czech revolt was anticipated as the Red Army drew closer. Weidinger was briefed on his task of covering the evacuation of the German population in Prague should events deteriorate, and was ordered to concentrate his unit to the west of the city.

By the time Weidinger returned to his unit to organise its move eastward, a Czech uprising had indeed begun. Despite the large number of Germans in Prague, the majority were totally demoralised now that utter defeat was only days away, and Czechs had become openly defiant. They had not, however, anticipated the appearance of a powerful SS kampfgruppe in their midst. These SS men may have realised the end was near, but their intense unit pride ensured they would do their duty to the bitter end.

The evacuation of Prague

As Weidinger's kampfgruppe neared Prague, more and more roadblocks were encountered, and then news was received that it was cut off from its parent unit. It was placed under the direct command of Field Marshal Ferdinand Schörner, a fanatical Nazi who ordered them to crush the Czech revolt.

On 6 May, *Der Führer* entered Prague to find its way barred by an enormous roadblock, too large to be destroyed with explosives. It had to be dismantled piece by piece, with the soldiers working into the night under the headlights of their vehicles, all the time under constant harassment from snipers. By the next morning the route was clear and Weidinger, a seasoned combat veteran and holder of the Knights Cross of the Iron Cross with Swords and Oakleaves, was in no mood to be trifled with. Setting off again, *Der Führer* encountered another roadblock on the approaches to a bridge and came under small arms fire. A Czech officer appeared and offered a negotiated truce if the Germans would withdraw. Weidinger refused outright, but he did agree to a temporary ceasefire. However, it soon became obvious that the Czechs were stalling for time, and so a furious Weidinger ordered his troops to attack across the bridge. A second Czech officer appeared, and Weidinger made it quite clear that he would use all the force at his disposal to continue on his way, and if the Czechs attempted to interfere with him they would pay dearly. An armistice was agreed, allowing the *Der Führer* Regiment to enter the city.

A number of stragglers attached themselves to this highly disciplined unit as Weidinger prepared for the evacuation. It soon became obvious that the Germans had nowhere near enough transport, and so every available vehicle was requisitioned. Matters were made worse when it was discovered that a troop train full of German wounded had been abandoned in a railway siding. Weidinger was determined that these men would not be left to the mercy of the Soviets, but should be evacuated, along with a number of female signals auxiliaries who had appeared. By the time Weidinger's evacuation convoy was ready to depart it numbered over 1000 vehicles. His plan now consisted simply of making his way west towards Pilsen as soon as possible to surrender to the Americans, and he ignored attempts by senior SS officers in the city to divert him from this aim.

On its journey the convoy ran into another roadblock, where it was demanded that all its weapons be surrendered. Weidinger acceded to this demand but had the weapons spiked before being handed over. The convoy was then allowed to proceed and eventually surrendered to American troops at Rokiczany. Thus, the last official action by Waffen-SS units in this sector was not in their characteristic role of aggressive shock troops, but in the rescue of thousands of civilians and wounded from an uncertain fate at the hands of the Soviets. In fact, persecution and murder of ethnic Germans in Czechoslovakia after its liberation by the Red Army was widespread as countless 'scores' were settled.

The fall of Vienna (13 April 1945) had netted the Soviets over 125,000 prisoners. However, rather than pursue the retreating Germans, Stalin halted major operations in Austria and concentrated on the final push on Berlin, fearing the Western Allies would wrest this great prize from under the very nose of the Red Army.

In the north, by the spring of 1944, STAVKA had decided that Byelorussia was to be the next major priority for the Red Army. Although the Germans had

BELOW: A Tiger tank of the **Wiking** *Division situated just outside Warsaw in late 1944. The division saw heavy fighting against the Red Army on the Vistula Front up to December 1944, when it was transferred to Hungary. Though it fought very well up to its surrender in May 1945, neither it nor the Waffen-SS as a whole were capable of stopping the Soviets in the East. Nevertheless, their Reichsführer-SS was insistent that 'bitter as it is, they must do their duty now more than ever, and only if the west is guarded now will the German forces in the east...become active again.'*

ABOVE: Red Army soldiers on the attack. For the final drive on Berlin, through Poland, the Soviets assembled a massive force of some 2,200,000 men, 33,500 artillery pieces and mortars, 7000 tanks and assault guns and 5000 aircraft. Against such numbers the Germans could only muster 980,000 men, 1800 tanks and assault guns and 800 aircraft. The quality of many German troops, Waffen-SS included, was variable at this stage of the war. Yet still Hitler believed that his SS legions could pull off a miracle and save the day.

suffered a number of crippling defeats, they still held considerable amounts of Soviet territory and fielded a large number of troops in the central sector, not too far removed from Moscow itself. Stalin intended the next offensive to remove this potential threat once and for all, and the plan was ambitious in its scope. It was intended that the Red Army would drive from its starting point, east of Lake Peipus along a line running through Gorki in the centre, skirting the Pripet Marshes, and on to Odessa on the shores of the Black Sea, and push the Germans back some 650km (400 miles) to the very gates of Warsaw. For this it mustered 19 armies and two tank armies, in all 1,500,000 men, over 30,000 artillery pieces, over 5000 tanks and 50,000 aircraft. In opposition, the Germans could only field 1,200,000 men, 9500 guns and 900 tanks, with some 1300 or so aircraft in support.

On the night of 22 June 1944, the main assault began and several Soviet Armies

crashed through the lines of Army Group Centre. Within just seven days, the entire length of a 320km (200 mile) front stretching from Ostrov on the Lithuanian border and Kovel on the edge of the Pripet Marshes had been completely overrun. In the weeks that followed, some 350,000 German troops, representing the equivalent of 28 divisions, were eliminated as the Red Army raced for the borders of Poland and East Prussia.

On 25 June 1944, the 3rd SS Panzer Division *Totenkopf* was immediately ordered north from Romania to help fend off the Soviet attack west of Minsk. The roads, however, were chaotic and the *Totenkopf* did not reach its assigned destination until 7 July. By then the Red Army was advancing rapidly towards Grodno, endangering the southern flank of the 4th Army and the northern flank of the battered remnants of the 2nd Army. The *Totenkopf* held the line at Grodno for 11 days against overwhelming odds, before being ordered to withdraw towards the southeast to join the mass of German troops retreating slowly towards Warsaw. It was joined by the Luftwaffe's elite *Hermann Göring* Division at Siedlce, east of Warsaw, and both units held open an escape corridor for the 2nd Army as it retreated towards the Vistula.

With the Red Army rapidly approaching the Polish capital, the Polish Home Army resistance movement under the leadership of Major-General Bor-Komorowski rose up in open revolt against the German occupiers on 1 August, confident of receiving support from the approaching Red Army. The Germans were stunned at the initial strength of the uprising, and initially lost almost two thirds of the city to the Poles. With the Red Army so near and the Germans apparently in full retreat, the Poles were justified in feeling considerable optimism.

The crushing of the Warsaw revolt

What the Poles did not realise, however, was that the Red Army's advance was rapidly running out of steam. Having advanced almost 750km (450 miles) and outrun its supply lines, it was now exhausted. It reached the very suburbs of the city, but the Germans were aware of the tired state of the Soviet troops and their resistance stiffened. In addition, Stalin saw the opportunity to allow the Germans to rid him of some troublesome Poles, whose sense of patriotism would be unlikely to see them quietly submit to Soviet subjugation after the war's end. Far better for him to sit back and watch, his armies resting and regaining their strength as Poles and Germans fought to the death on the streets of Warsaw.

Once the Germans had eliminated Polish resistance, they in turn would be forced to retreat, and his troops could take the Polish capital free of obstruction from the pro-Western Home Army. Although the Western Allies did attempt to drop supplies to the Poles, by the time it was organised the Germans had regained control of most of the city, and the bulk of the supplies dropped fell into German hands. In addition, Stalin refused the Western Allies the use of Soviet air bases from which to launch supply missions.

Meanwhile, in Warsaw, SS-Obergruppenführer Erich von dem Bach-Zelewski, commander of anti-partisan forces, was determined to crush the Polish revolt with every means at his disposal. Unfortunately for the Poles, this included two of the most notorious military formations in history: the 29th Waffen-Grenadier Division der SS (russische Nr 1) and the 36th Waffen-Grenadier Division der SS.

Both units, though nominally of divisional status, were in fact only of brigade strength. The 29th Waffen-Grenadier Division was commanded by Bronislav Kaminski and consisted of anti-communist Russians who had previously been engaged in suppressing Soviet partisan activity. The 36th Waffen-Grenadier Division was recruited from the lowest criminal elements who could be dredged from the prisons and concentration camps of the Third Reich. Under the command of SS-Oberführer Oskar Dirlewanger, who had himself been imprisoned by the Nazis for a string of crimes, including sexual offences against a young girl, this unit and Kaminski's men had no compunction in conducting themselves with the utmost barbarity. The catalogue of atrocities committed by these men revolted those German frontline combat troops involved in the fighting for Warsaw, and complaints from senior German military officers flooded in. The troops of both Waffen divisions even threatened any German Army troops who tried to interfere with their debauchery, as they indulged themselves in an orgy of looting, rape, torture and murder.

IV SS Corps stalls the Red Army

Eventually Himmler was forced to act. Kaminski was now too much of an embarrassment to the SS and was murdered, his death explained to his men as being the result of an attack by Soviet partisans. Dirlewanger was more fortunate in having influential friends in high places and he survived the war. He got his just desserts, however, when he was spotted by some former concentration camp inmates and beaten to death.

In Warsaw, Bor-Komorowski was eventually forced to surrender on 2 October when his supplies of food and ammunition ran out. He was offered honourable surrender terms by Bach-Zelewski, who had been impressed by the gallantry of the Polish Home Army and offered to treat the surrendering Poles as prisoners of war. To the surprise of many of the Poles, the surrender terms were honoured.

The Soviet offensive had been renewed on 14 August, with an attempt to surround the Polish capital with attacks over the Vistula to the north and west of the city. However, IV SS Panzer Corps, with a

'On 23 April 1943 the Reichsführer-SS issued an order via the Higher SS and Police Leader in Cracow, to assault the ghetto more vigorously.... I therefore decided to undertake the total destruction of the ghetto block by block.'
– Report from SS-Brigadeführer Jürgen Stroop to Himmler, 1943

RIGHT: A 75mm Pak 40 of the 8th SS Kavallerie Division Florian Geyer outside Budapest. The division was destroyed trying to flee the city. Hitler chose Hungary as the site for the last German offensive of the war, codenamed 'Spring Awakening'. He had said: 'I want the best sort of attack to get a big fast gain. The Russians have to be thrown out of the oilfields along Lake Balaton and back across the Danube.'

BELOW: A Wiking *grenadier in Hungary.*

powerful force comprising the *Totenkopf* and *Wiking* Divisions, was ready and waiting. For a full week the Russians battered against the German positions without success, and were eventually forced to withdraw to regroup. On 25 August, a massive new offensive was launched, principally against the *Totenkopf*'s positions, and gradually the Germans were forced to fall back towards Warsaw. The *Totenkopf* Division did attempt a counterattack against the Soviets on 11 September, however, which drove back enemy units. The Soviet steamroller was temporarily halted.

Despite these successes, the *Totenkopf* faced the same problem with regard to being unable to rapidly make good its losses, whereas the Soviets were back up to strength and ready to launch yet another attack against the city by 10 October. This time the weakened Germans were forced back to the northwest of the city, but managed to stabilise their positions quickly and halt the Soviets once again.

By the end of October 1944, Romania and Bulgaria had capitulated and gone over to the Soviets, while in the north, Finland had sued for peace terms. The Red Army's 1st Baltic Front had retaken Memel in Lithuania on 10 October, while Yeremenko's 2nd Baltic Front had captured Riga, the Latvian capital. The Soviet offensives had resulted in two entire German armies being cut off in Courland, comprising some 33 divisions of desperately needed troops. Rather than tie up a considerable number of troops in trying to eliminate these units, STAVKA decided on an air and sea blockade of the pocket. However, the Kriegsmarine was still more than a match for the Red Navy at this time and was able to evacuate the equivalent of 12 divisions by sea.

Among the units able to escape by sea were the remaining Dutch SS volunteers from the *Nederland* Brigade. The ship evacuating them was attacked and sunk, but some of the Dutch SS men did survive and formed the nucleus of the 23rd SS Freiwilligen Panzergrenadier Division *Nederland*. The unit went back into action at Stargard in Pommerania and also saw action at Stettin, before being forced back towards Berlin.

In January 1945, the Red Army's first priority was to drive the Germans out of Poland. Marshal Zhukov and his 1st Byelorussian Front was to aim for Poznan, while Marshal Koniev would direct his assault towards Breslau to the south. Each massive force comprised over one million men, with over 30,000 guns and 7000 tanks between them. Opposing them was Army Group Centre with only 400,000 men and just over 1000 tanks. The Germans, however, still had some 580,000 troops in East Prussia which could cause the Soviets considerable problems.

The Red Army clears Poland

On 12 January, Koniev's attack began after a massive artillery barrage lasting one and three quarter hours. Two days later Zhukov's forces joined in the assault, his forces aiding the Soviet-formed 1st Polish Army in taking Warsaw. During the second half of January the Red Army seized Silesia, one of Germany's most important industrial regions, rich in coal deposits, and by early February had reached the River Oder. Those German strongpoints which had withstood the Soviet onslaught, such as Breslau, were merely bypassed. Many German cities overrun by the Red Army at this time were subjected to an orgy of rape and pillage, rivalling the behaviour of the *Dirlewanger* and *Kaminski* Brigades in terms of barbarity, though it generally seems to have been the case that these excesses were in the main carried out by second-rate, not frontline, units.

By the spring of 1945, most of the so-called 'classic' Waffen-SS divisions were carrying out a fighting withdrawal through Hungary and into Austria, while in the central and northern sectors of the Eastern Front those SS units still in action were principally east and west European volunteer units. The level of determination shown by these volunteers in their attempts to hold the Soviet advance was quite exceptional, if not entirely surprising.

These units raised from eastern European states no longer had any homelands to return to, as their nations had been 'liberated' by the Soviets and were now in Stalin's iron grip. To surrender to the Russians would mean almost certain death, thus many felt they had no option but to fight on. Those who did survive generally did so either because they had been able to fight their way to the West and surrender to the Anglo-Americans, or because they returned to their native soil and continued to fight a guerrilla war against the Soviets for several years after the war's end. Those who surrendered to the Soviets, or were handed over to them after giving themselves up to the Western Allies, were usually shot out of hand.

Those volunteers from the western European nations were in a similar predicament, their own homelands by now having been in most cases overrun by the Allies, and with new governments unlikely to welcome them with open arms. Rather than face an uncertain future in their own countries, many chose to fight on to the death. It should also be remembered that many of these men were fighting with a sense of genuine, if misguided, idealism, and were determined to fight to their last breath to defend Europe from what they perceived as the 'evils of Bolshevism'.

Most of the Waffen-SS foreign volunteers did indeed get killed on the battle-

BELOW: Bulgarian troops as allies of Germany. Bulgaria had officially withdrawn from the war in August 1944, but Stalin, mindful that he wanted eastern Europe to be Soviet controlled after the defeat of Germany, declared war on Bulgaria on 5 September 1944. Three days later the Red Army entered the country and occupied it; there was no resistance. While Romania and Bulgaria fell easily to the Soviets, the conquest of Hungary was a bloody affair and took nearly five months.

The Eastern Front
January – May 1945

BALTIC SEA

Pommersche Bay

Gulf of Danzig

Tilsit

Königsberg

LITH-UANIA

Danzig

Elbing

Marienburg

EAST PRUSSIA

Rostock

Stettin

Narew

Berlin

Frankfurt

Warta

Poznan

Vistula

Modlin

Warsaw

POLAND

Magdeburg

Oder

Glogau

Lodz

Elbe

Liegnitz

Breslau

Sandomierz

Dresden

Key

← Soviet attacks

——— Front line 11 January

– – – Front line 2 February

–·–·– Front line 16 April

··—··— Front line 25 April

········ Front line 8 May

Prague

Cracow

CZECHOSLOVAKIA

In the early hours of 12 January 1945, Soviet forces on the River Vistula launched one of the greatest offensives of World War II. Outnumbered four to one all along the front, the Germans reeled under the ferocity of the attack. By the end of March the Red Army was on the banks of the Oder, and by 24 April, after heavy fighting, they had surrounded Berlin itself.

RIGHT: Weary Waffen-SS soldiers retreat in the face of the Red Army. 'Spring Awakening' had petered out in mid-March 1945, by which time the 6th SS Panzer Army had only 185 vehicles left in service. By this time supplies had virtually dried up. The **Totenkopf** *Division, for example, was almost bereft of fuel, ammunition and spares. By early April what was left of the 6th SS Panzer Army, minus its heavy equipment, had withdrawn across the Austrian border.*

fields of eastern Europe. The *Wiking* Division, with its predominantly west European volunteers, was decimated in the fighting for the approaches to Vienna. *Nordland* was destroyed in the Battle of Berlin; the 14th Waffen-Grenadier Division der SS from the Ukraine surrendered to the Soviets in Czechoslovakia, and the bulk of its surviving personnel were promptly executed. Part of the 15th Waffen-Grenadier Division der SS from Latvia took part in the defence of Berlin, and following the war's end its survivors suffered the same fate as their Ukrainian counterparts. *Horst Wessel*, with its Hungarian volunteers, surrendered to the Soviets near Prague. The Estonian volunteers from the 20th Waffen-Grenadier Division der SS also surrendered near Prague, many of its personnel being executed on the spot.

The *Maria Theresia* Division, predominantly Hungarian, was destroyed in the fighting for Budapest. The Red Army also overran the predominantly Hungarian volunteer 25th and 26th Waffen-Grenadier Divisions while they were still working up. *Nederland*, nominally a division though little more than regimental strength, was wiped out in the fall of Berlin, and the battered remnants of the Belgian *Langemarck* and *Wallonien* Divisions were also wiped out during the fighting for the Reich's capital city, as were the remaining volunteers of the French *Charlemagne* Division. The Russian volunteers of the 30th Waffen-Grenadier Division were transferred to General Andrei Vlassov's Free Russian Army and fell into Soviet hands, where they met certain death.

The nature of the contribution of the foreign volunteers from both west and east Europe to the defensive battles on the Eastern Front in 1945 can be gauged by the number of Knights Crosses awarded to Waffen-SS soldiers during this period. Considering Himmler's dreams of the SS as a purely Germanic racial elite, those

decorated with this highly coveted award for gallantry and distinguished service included a substantial number of soldiers with distinctly non-Germanic names.

In January 1945, the following east European volunteers joined the ranks of Knights Cross winners: Waffen-Hauptsturmführer Robert Ancans (Latvian), Waffen-Hauptscharführer Zanis Ansons (Latvian), Waffen-Hauptsturmführer Miervaldos Adamsons (Russian), Waffen-Obersturmführer Nikolajs Galdins (Latvian), and SS-Hauptscharführer Gustav Wendrensky (Slovak). In February and March respectively, two Danes, SS-Obersturmführer Soren Kam and SS-Hauptsturmführer Johannes Helmers, also received the Knights Cross, and in April SS-Obersturmführer Jacques Leroy, a Belgian, and Waffen-Unterscharführer Eugene Vaulot, Waffen-Oberscharführer Francois Apollot and Waffen-Hauptsturmführer Henri Fenet, French volunteers from the *Charlemagne* Division, all received the Ritterkreuz.

In the closing weeks of the war, five Latvians – Waffen-Unterscharführer

ABOVE: SS panzers in eastern Germany in 1945. From the divisional markings on the front tank, these vehicles would appear to belong to the 23rd SS Panzergrenadier Division **Nederland,** *which was virtually wiped out in Pomerania.*

Karlis Sensberg, Waffen-Unterscharführer Alfreds Rieksins, Waffen-Untersturmführer Andreys Freimans, Waffen-Obersturmführer Roberts Gaigals and Waffen-Sturmbannführer Voldemars Reinholds – were among the last soldiers to be awarded the Knights Cross. All of these words were proof, if any were needed, that from among the ranks of the foreign volunteers of the Waffen-SS, even as the Reich crumbled about them, came some of the bravest soldiers to have served in the German armed forces in World War II.

As the battered German armies on the Eastern front retreated deep into the Reich, the Waffen-SS divisions were once again to play a major role as rearguard units. *Frundsberg*, serving in Pomerania as part of SS-Obergruppenführer Felix Steiner's 11th Panzer Army in early 1945, took part in an attack on Zhukov's 1st Byelorussian Front as it advanced on Berlin. On 16 February, *Frundsberg*, *Nordland*, *Nederland* and *Wallonien* attacked in a southwesterly direction, smashing into Zhukov's northern flank. The weakened German divisions, however,

did not have the strength to seriously deflect the massive Soviet assault and were driven back within a couple of days.

On 1 April, Stalin met with his senior commanders to establish their plans for the final drive on Berlin. In the north was Rokossovsky with the 2nd Byelorussian Front, in the centre Zhukov with the 1st Byelorussian Front, and in the south Koniev with the 1st Ukrainian Front. The demarcation lines between the areas allocated to each front were to be relaxed some 65km (40 miles) from Berlin, and from then on it was to be a race to see which commander could reach the Reich's capital first. Stalin, like Hitler, often made good use of the rivalry between his senior commanders, and few were such determined rivals as Koniev and Zhukov. By encouraging this he could be sure that no opportunity would be lost by either in their attempts to reach Berlin.

Zhukov had established a bridgehead over the Oder at Küstrin (which had been taken on 28 March), from where he would launch his attack. Wishing to achieve maximum impact, he decided to open his

ABOVE: A knocked-out SdKfz 251 of the **Wiking** *Division. By the end of March 1945, the front in the East was collapsing, and with it the German armies ordered to hold it. The* **Wiking** *Division had been decimated during Hitler's last offensive, and had taken heavy losses trying to hold the Hungarian town of Stühlweissenburg. It had received an order to hold the town at all costs, but to do so would have meant certain destruction, and so the division was withdrawn to avert its annihilation.*

OPPOSITE: A brief period of rest to service the vehicles before the next Soviet onslaught.

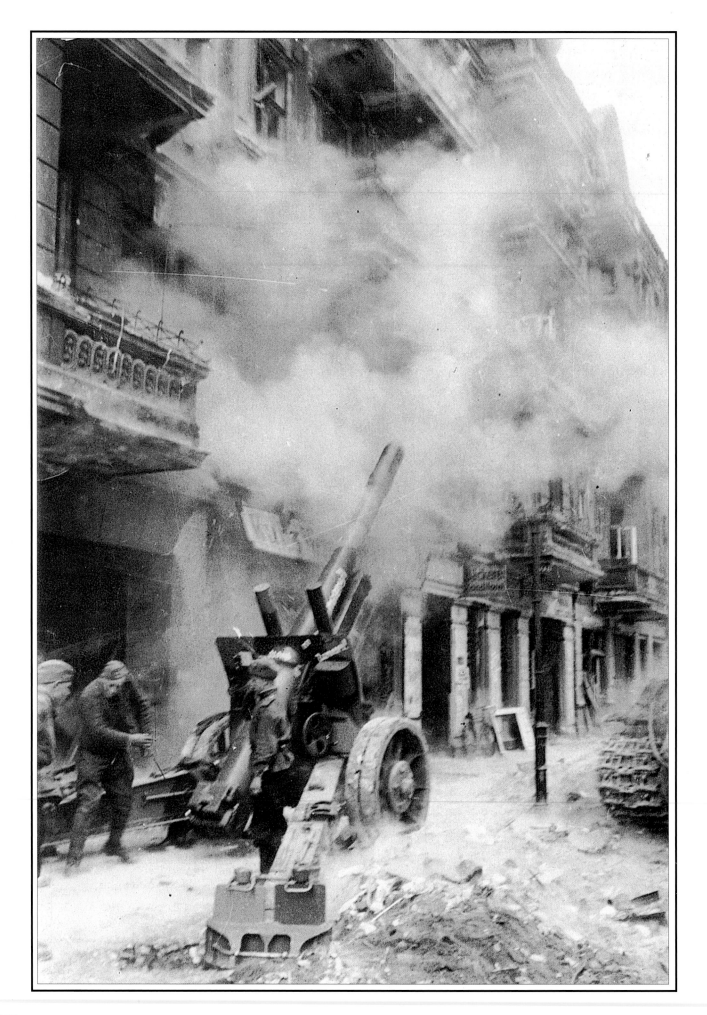

attack with an artillery barrage of unparalleled ferocity, employing over 8000 artillery pieces in a 30-minute barrage. This would be followed by an immediate and massive assault. Zhukov had nearly 150 searchlights brought up to the launch point, intending to bounce their powerful beams off the low cloud cover and blind the German defenders. Koniev, on the other hand, was taking no chances, and intended a prolonged barrage of some 145 minutes duration, followed by an attack under the cover of darkness.

The first probing attacks began on 14 April, and, two days later, the main assault began. The German defenders, however, were aware of Zhukov's plan and withdrew from their positions before the artillery barrage began. Once it had ended they quickly returned to their positions and were ready and waiting for the Soviet assault troops. The searchlights, intended to blind the Germans, merely illuminated the attacking Soviets, making them ideal targets. Despite Zhukov's threats, his troops could not throw the Germans out of their strongly defended positions on the Seelow Heights, opposite his bridgehead. Instead of the immediate victory he had expected, three full days of the most bitter fighting were required before the Germans could be slowly forced back. By 19 April, though, the German defences had been overrun and the Seelow Heights captured, and Rokossovsky's push from the north launched.

The drive on Berlin
Koniev ordered his 3rd and 4th Guards Tank Armies to break into the city on 20 April, but by the 23rd Stalin had declared that it was to be Zhukov's troops who would make the main assault. He then redrew the boundaries within which the units were to operate in Berlin to give Zhukov's armies the honour of capturing the area, including the Führer bunker and the Reichstag.

On 21 April, Hitler had ordered an attack to relieve the city. General Theodor Busse, defending the Oder Line with his 9th Army to the southeast of Berlin, was to turn about and march to the relief of the city. To the west, General Walther Wenck, holding back the Americans at the Elbe, was to do the same, and Steiner's 11th Panzer Army was to launch an all-out attack from the north to relieve Berlin. Quite how Hitler expected this to be achieved was not explained. If Busse and Wenck had abandoned their positions to

march to the relief of the city, their pitifully few troops would have been instantly overwhelmed. As for Steiner, his 'panzer army' existed on paper only, as his best troops had already been sacrificed or sent into the city. For example, *Nordland* had been sent into Berlin, *Nederland* was sent south to contain a Soviet attack, and the Walloons were cut to pieces trying to hold a bridgehead at Altdamm.

The battle for the Reichstag
By 25 April Berlin was completely surrounded, and the next day around half a million Red Army troops swarmed into the city itself. The battle for the city was a desperate one: savage hand-to-hand fighting in many places with knives, rifle butts and bayonets, and the Waffen-SS took part in the last, apocalyptic fight for the Third Reich. Ironically, most of those wearing SS uniforms were non-German volunteers. Apart from the host of Hitler Youth and Volkssturm personnel and two understrength Army divisions of LVII Corps, the only other regular German troops in Berlin were the men of the *Nordland* and *Charlemagne* Divisions, a battalion of Latvians from the 15th Waffen-Grenadier Division der SS and 600 men of Himmler's Escort Battalion.

On 28 April, the Soviets broke through the inner city defences and stormed towards the Reichstag. As usual, the SS fought with great tenacity. The battered building had been turned into a fortress, with heavy machine guns and artillery emplaced behind makeshift gun ports. The first Soviet assault went in on 30 April, supported by artillery and Katyusha rocket launchers. Three battalions of infantry charged forward in the face of heavy fire and managed to breach the defences. Inside the building the fighting degenerated into hand-to-hand combat. The SS had turned the cellar into a fortress, and it took two days of heavy fighting before they were defeated. Some 2500 of the Reichstag's defenders were killed, with another 2600 taken prisoner. By that time Hitler was dead and the battle for Berlin was over. At 1500 hours on 2 May, Lieutenant-General Weidling surrendered the city to the Russians. Although their Führer was dead and Germany's capital in Soviet hands, there were still groups of Waffen-SS troops fighting in various pockets of the shrinking Reich. They continued to fight until all the formal surrender negotiations had been completed. In fact, as mentioned above, some former Waffen-

OPPOSITE: Soviet artillery on the outskirts of Berlin pounds German positions a few kilometres away. Hitler had stated: 'If the war is lost, the German nation will also perish. There is no need to take into consideration the basic requirements of the people. Those who will remain after the battle are those who are inferior; for the good will have fallen.' He was determined that the Reich should be engulfed in an all-consuming whirlwind of destruction, and into this nightmare was sucked the Waffen-SS. On 24 April, the Red Army forged a ring of steel around Berlin, and the final assault on the capital of the Reich began two days later.

ABOVE: Part of the 4000-strong force of tanks the Soviets used to crush German resistance in Berlin. Despite its overwhelming superiority in tanks, artillery and aircraft, the Red Army had a hard time of it in Berlin. Fanatical Hitler Youth, non-German Waffen-SS soldiers, Army personnel and aged Volkssturm battled with grim ferocity. During these final days of the Third Reich, SS soldiers of Himmler's Escort Battalion roamed Berlin looking for deserters and shirkers and hanging them when they found them.

OPPOSITE: 3 May 1945 – Berlin falls.

SS men fought on for years in eastern Europe, as the men serving in the Baltic and Ukrainian Waffen-SS knew that they faced certain death if they surrendered.

For the majority of Waffen-SS soldiers, however, their duty had been fulfilled and in their own eyes at least they could lay down their arms and surrender in the knowledge that no military formation in existence could have achieved more. Many Waffen-SS troops marched into captivity with their pride and esprit de corps still intact. Both Western and Eastern Allies in their drives across Europe had, however, encountered a far more sinister side to the SS when they liberated the few surviving inmates of the death camps. Even these battle-hardened soldiers could hardly believe the almost indescribable horrors they encountered. The camp guards wore the same uniforms and insignia as the soldiers of the Waffen-SS, and this influenced the treatment received by Waffen-SS combat soldiers who were subsequently taken prisoner.

As the Third Reich entered its death throes, Hitler had become increasingly

contemptuous of those whom he considered had 'failed' him. At first it was the Wehrmacht which had borne the brunt of his contempt. Even the Waffen-SS had its limits, however, and when his elite troops also became unequal to the monumental tasks set for them, being usually overwhelmingly outnumbered, low on ammunition and food, and freezing without adequate winter clothing, their Führer had no sympathy for them. He heaped insult and scorn upon them, even his own bodyguard unit. Their own supreme SS commander, Reichsführer-SS Heinrich Himmler, was a moral coward who made no attempt to stand up for his men in the face of Hitler's wrath. His own total incompetence as a military leader had been amply demonstrated by his abject failure as commander of Army Group Vistula.

Former Waffen-SS men, scornful of their Allgemeine-SS counterparts and the concentration camp guards, who rarely, if ever, put their lives at risk, took immense pride in their military achievements. No one would be able to deny their military skill and gallantry.

WEAPONS AND EQUIPMENT

At first indifferently armed and equipped, the Waffen-SS developed into a fighting force that was supplied with some of the finest hardware the German armaments industry could produce. The elite SS panzer divisions, especially, were equipped with Germany's best tanks and military vehicles.

The title of this chapter is perhaps somewhat misleading, in that there were few, if any, weapons specifically designed and produced solely for use by the SS, the exception being a few ceremonial edged weapons. The bulk of the hardware used by the Waffen-SS was identical to that used by the Wehrmacht, though there were certainly a number of weapons, particularly small arms of foreign origin, which saw considerable use with the Waffen-SS due to the Army's reluctance to supply sufficient quantities of German-produced armaments to Himmler's elite. This chapter, therefore, will cover the principal types of weaponry used by the Waffen-SS: everything from small arms to heavy tanks.

One of the most famous German military firearms of all time is the Pistole 08, referred to by the Germans as the P08 but known throughout the world as the Luger, after its designer, Georg Luger. This highly regarded and versatile weapon was produced with barrel lengths of four, six and eight inches, and could accept a wooden shoulder stock and even a drum magazine to replace the standard eight-round box magazine contained within the grip. It fired a 9mm parabellum cartridge with a muzzle velocity of around 350mps (1500fps), and had an effective combat range, like most of its counterparts, of

The Totenkopf *Division in action in France, May 1940. The artillery piece is the 37mm Pak 35/36 anti-tank gun, which was used in Poland and in the West in 1940.*

Kar 98K

manual safety — sear — firing pin — bolt — chambered round
firing pin nut —
stock —
lug —
integral 5-round magazine
rear sight assembly
trigger
trigger guard — follower and spring

RIGHT: A soldier of the **Leibstandarte** *armed with a Walther P38 handgun, a weapon that had a double-action trigger mechanism and was produced throughout the war. Production of the weapon was resumed by Walther in 1957, when it was issued to the Bundeswehr.*

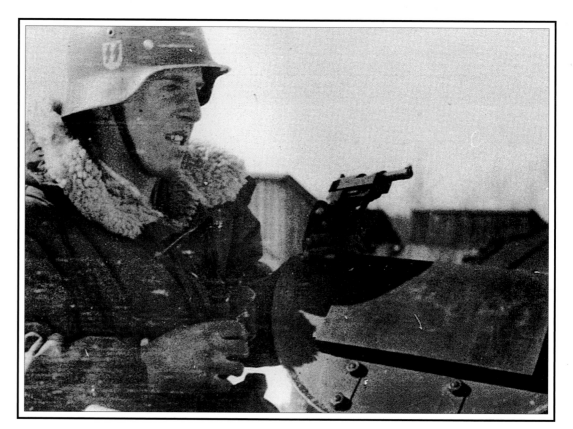

around 30m (32yd). The P08 was a high-quality weapon, though somewhat over-engineered and thus not always fully up to rigorous frontline combat use. It was prone to jamming with anything other than high-quality ammunition, and occasionally went off by accident if dropped. Despite being largely superseded by the beginning of World War II, it remained in production until 1942 and was a very popular weapon, many of them remaining in service throughout the war.

The replacement for the P08 handgun was the Pistole 38, or P38, manufactured by Walther. This was a more rugged handgun, and at 0.96kg (2.1lb) heavier than the P08. It also had an eight-round box magazine and fired its 9mm parabellum ammunition with a muzzle velocity comparable to that of the P08. It was a sturdy and

fore sight assembly — barrel nut — chambe rou
barrel
barrel cap
barrel jacket — resting bar — firing pin

Calibre 7.92mm
Length 110.7cm
Weight (unloaded) 3.9kg
Magazine 5-round integral box
Muzzle velocity 755mps

highly popular weapon, and was much easier to field strip and maintain than the P08. The Waffen-SS used considerable quantities of this excellent weapon, and it was such a success that it was reintroduced into service in the West German Army in 1957 as the P1. Many are still in use today with the German Army.

Probably the most unusual of the handguns used by the Waffen-SS during World War II was the Mauser C96, commonly known as the 'broomhandle' due to

LEFT: **Das Reich personnel firing their Kar 98 bolt-action rifles during Operation 'Barbarossa' in 1941. The Kar 98 was a robust, reliable weapon that was produced in Germany up until 1945. By this time, however, many Waffen-SS soldiers were using submachine guns as their personal weapons.**

MP40 SMG

Calibre 9mm
Length (stock extended) 83.3cm
Weight (loaded) 4.7kg
Magazine 32-round box
Rate of fire (cyclic) 500rpm
Muzzle velocity 381mps
Maximum effective range 200m

FG42

rear sight assembly

firing pin

bolt

barrel extension

buffer spring

operating rod

fore grip

stock

grip

trigger

piston

trigger sear

cocking handle

its distinctive round, wooden handle. This large, heavy handgun had its magazine sited in front of the trigger guard, and was loaded with a stripper clip in the same way as most rifle magazines were loaded. It was available in 7.65mm and 9mm calibres, and some versions produced were capable of automatic fire. One particularly interesting aspect of its design was the wooden holster, which doubled as a shoulder stock. With the stock attached, the C96 could achieve a good degree of accuracy in the hands of a marksman. Somewhat bulky and cumbersome, it was nevertheless popular. Several photographs of soldiers from the SS-Verfügungstruppe in France in 1940 show them carrying C96s.

The above handguns were all highly popular and effective weapons, and were used primarily by NCOs and lower ranks. Officers preferred more compact weapons, which were also favoured by the crews of tanks and other armoured fighting vehicles, where the small space made their size advantageous. The three most widely used in this category were the Walther PP and PPK and the Mauser HSc.

The Walther PP, or Polizei Pistole, was produced in both 7.65mm and 9mm calibres. It was very compact in size and shape and featured a 99mm (3.9in) barrel and eight-round magazine in the grip. It developed a muzzle velocity of around 289mps (950fps) and had an effective combat range of around 30m (32yd). Its small size and the ease with which it could be concealed on the person made it a favourite with police and security personnel. These same attributes applied equally to the slightly smaller Walther PPK, though its barrel length was 86mm (3.4in) and its magazine carried only seven rounds. Apart from being slightly smaller, however, it was visually very similar to the PP.

The Mauser HSc came in 7.65mm calibre, featured an 85mm (3.375in) barrel and an eight-round magazine in the grip. A more modern- and stylish-looking handgun than the Walther models, it was a favourite with many officers. All three of these handguns were extremely easy to field strip.

As well as German-made handguns, a number of captured foreign types were used by the Waffen-SS. Among the most

MG34 GPMG

recoil booster

muzzle catch

barrel casing

barrel

fore sight

mounting for anti-aircraft sight

flash hider

bipod (folded position)

port   barrel   bayonet

fore sight assembly

gas nder

bipod (folded)

Calibre 7.92mm
Length 94cm
Weight 4.5kg
Magazine 20-round box
Rate of fire (cyclic) 750rpm
Muzzle velocity 762mps

popular was the superb Browning High Power, a 9mm automatic handgun carrying a 13-round magazine in the grip. It was manufactured by Fabrique Nationale of Belgium, and the Germans continued production after occupying the country in 1940. Many were used by the Waffen-SS, though substantial numbers were sabotaged by Belgian workers before they left the factory. The Czech CZ38 and the Polish Radom were both 9mm automatics similar in appearance to the Browning, as was the Soviet Tokarev, a 7.65mm eight-

round automatic which became a popular souvenir for German troops serving on the Eastern Front.

Where rifles were concerned, the earliest SS units tended to be equipped with the Gewehr 98 (G98), a bolt-action, five-round rifle with a barrel length of 740mm (29in). It weighed 3.8kg (8.8lb), had a muzzle velocity of 870mps (2850fps) and an effective range of about 550m (600yd).

ABOVE: The Waffen-SS often made use of captured weapons, especially on the Eastern Front. The NCO on the right is armed with a Soviet PPSh submachine gun. Crude but extremely effective, over five million were produced by the Soviets during the war.

ABOVE LEFT: Waffen-SS grenadiers armed with MP40 submachine guns at the Battle of Kursk, July 1943. This weapon was the first submachine gun to be produced without any wood in its stock or furniture, and the first to be manufactured for use with fast-moving mechanised units.

rear sight assembly
feed cover hinge
bolt
feed cover
feed mechanism
firing pin
feed cover hatch
stock
buffer spring (compressed)

stock catch

firing pin spring
amber
trigger guard
interruptor
trigger
grip
sear

50-round drum magazine

Calibre 7.92mm
Length 122cm
Weight 12.1kg
Feed belt, 50-round drum or 75-round saddle drum
System of operation short recoil
Rate of fire (cyclic) 800-900rpm
Muzzle velocity 756mps

207

Like most pre-war German weapons, it was a high-quality design.

By the outbreak of war, the G98 had been largely superseded by the shorter Mauser Karabiner 98 (Kar 98). Slightly lighter at 3.66kg (8lb), this carbine version of the Mauser rifle had a shortened barrel and a muzzle velocity of 745mps (2445fps). Its effective range was comparable to the G98. Originally developed from a cavalry weapon, the shoulder strap slotted through a hole in the side of the butt, allowing the weapon to be carried comfortably across the back of mounted personnel. Like the G98, early examples were beautifully crafted, but later wartime pieces had cheap laminated wooden stocks and metal parts with an inferior finish. Both the G98 and Kar 98 were made under licence in various European countries.

German assault rifles

German attempts at producing a semi-automatic rifle to rival the American M1 Garand resulted in the Gewehr 41, or Gew 41, which featured a 10-round magazine and used the same 7.92mm ammunition as the G98 and Kar 98. An improved version, the Gew 43, was introduced, but these weapons never came close to replacing the Kar 98 as the standard German rifle of World War II.

Undoubtedly the most important German development in the rifle field were the assault rifles, the MKb42 and MP43. In 7.92mm calibre and featuring 30-round box magazines, they had a cyclic rate of fire of 600rpm and 500rpm respectively. They were superb weapons, and one glance at their shape clearly shows their influence on the development of the post-war Soviet Kalashnikov family of assault weapons. Both weapons were used primarily on the Eastern Front.

Submachine guns

As far as submachine guns (SMGs), or machine pistols as they were known to the Germans, are concerned, the weapon which certainly became one of the best known of all World War II SMGs is the MP38/40, erroneously referred to as the 'Schmeisser'. How it got this name is uncertain, as Hugo Schmeisser had nothing to do with its design or manufacture. The MP38 was a 9mm calibre submachine gun with a 32-round box magazine feeding from underneath the weapon. It weighed 3.97kg (8.75lb) and had a cyclic rate of fire of around 500rpm. Although a few early models did have a wooden stock, the

'The front was a few streets away. At the street corner diagonally opposite our house Walloon Waffen SS had taken up position; wild, desperate men who had nothing to lose and who fought to their last round of ammunition.'
– Juergen Thurwald, *Flight in the Winter* (1951)

vast majority featured a collapsible metal stock. The MP40 was an improved version of the MP38, which utilised cheaper manufacturing methods. For example, many of its machined parts were replaced by stamped metal items. Visually, however, it was almost identical to the MP38.

Ironically, it was the Army's reluctance to supply the Waffen-SS with a sufficient number of MP38s which resulted in SS troops being equipped with earlier German models and foreign weapons, which were often better quality than the MP38/40. Such a weapon was the Bergmann MP28. This extremely well-made weapon, also in 9mm calibre, featured a full wooden stock and a perforated sleeve around the barrel. It also had the magazine feeding horizontally from the left, a boon to the soldier as it allowed easier firing from a less exposed prone position. The later MP34/35 was almost identical, but had the magazine feeding horizontally from the right. Both were used by the SS in considerable numbers. In fact, the MP35 was the standard submachine gun of the Waffen-SS, and a total of 40,000 were produced during the war.

Foreign SMGs in Waffen-SS use

Another submachine gun popular with Waffen-SS soldiers was the Italian 9mm Beretta MAB 38A, numbers of which fell into German hands after Italy's surrender to the Allies in September 1943. It was similar to the MP28 in featuring a full wooden stock and perforated sleeve around the barrel.

Of all the captured enemy weapons used by Waffen-SS troops, the most popular by far was the Soviet 7.62mm PPSh submachine gun. It featured a wooden stock, perforated sleeve around the barrel and a distinctive 71-round drum magazine. Huge numbers of these fell into German hands on the Eastern Front, and they were extremely popular with the troops. With its cyclic rate of fire of 900rpm, it was a highly effective weapon and, like much Soviet equipment, very robust (it could operate without lubricating oil). Other foreign weapons used by the Waffen-SS included the the Czech ZK 383 and the excellent Finnish Suomi M/31.

Fewer different types were used where medium and heavy machine guns were concerned. The principal type in use on the outbreak of war in 1939 was the superb MG34. This versatile, belt-fed 7.92mm machine gun weighed just over 12kg (26.5lb) and fired at a rate of

900rpm, with a muzzle velocity of 726mps (2500fps). Generally fitted with a bipod, it could also be mounted on a heavy tripod for the sustained fire role, and an anti-aircraft mount was also available. Like most weapons dating from pre-war days, it was exceptionally well made, albeit rather expensive to produce.

The MG42 machine gun

As the war progressed, the Germans needed a machine gun that could be easily produced in large numbers and withstand the rigours of combat better than the MG34. The result was the MG42. Similar to the MG34, it was made of stamped metal parts and was designed to be easy to maintain in the field. Weight and muzzle velocity were similar to the MG34, but the rate of fire was increased to 1200rpm. This made it a devastating weapon, though it could be extremely wasteful of ammunition if carelessly used.

Also used by Waffen-SS units was the Czech ZB 30. This weapon saw service with the *Polizei* Division, the *Prinz Eugen* Division and several others. It was an excellent light machine gun, and a variant was adopted by the British as the Bren Gun. It featured a 30-round box magazine feeding from the top of the weapon, and its rate of fire was 500rpm. Captured Soviet Degtyaryov 7.62mm light machine guns, with their distinctive top-mounted magazines, were also occasionally used by Waffen-SS units.

As well as these basic infantry weapons, the Waffen-SS soldier was supplied with a fairly typical range of mortars and light anti-tank weapons. Mortars were produced in three basic sizes: the light 50mm mortar, the leGrW36, which could throw a 0.9kg (1.98lb) projectile up to a range of 520m (569yd); the 80mm sGrW34 medium mortar, which could throw a 3.5kg (7.72lb) projectile up to a range of 2400m (2625yd); and the schw GrW42 in 120mm calibre, which could throw a hefty 15.9kg (35lb) projectile up to a distance of 5500m (6000yd).

Anti-tank weapons

Although 7.92mm Panzerbüchse anti-tank rifles were used by the Waffen-SS, they were rather ineffective against most Allied armour unless the user could achieve some very lucky shots. Far more useful was the single-shot Panzerfaust, which fired a 3kg (6.6lb) hollow-charge projectile and was then simply discarded. With a range of around 30m (32yd), it could knock out just about any known Allied tank, providing the user could get within range. It was particularly effective against tanks if used in urban areas, where tank-hunting teams had the advantage of good cover. Less commonly used was the Panzerschreck (RpzB 54), a virtual copy of the American Bazooka and capable of penetrating up to 160mm (6.3in) of armour with its 3.25kg (7.16lb) rocket.

Artillery used by the Waffen-SS was in effect identical to that supplied to the Army, and can be divided into three broad categories: light, medium and heavy. The lighter artillery piece, at 75mm calibre, was the leFk 18, which fired a 5.83kg (12.85lb) shell up to a range of 9425m (10,310yd). Medium pieces included the 105mm calibre leFH (leichte Feld Haubitze) 18, a light howitzer firing a 14.81kg (32.6lb) shell up to a range of 12,325m (13,478yd). A typical heavy weapon was the lumbering sFH (schwere Feld Haubitze) 18, which could throw a hefty 43.5kg (95.5lb)

BELOW: The 80mm sGrW 34 mortar, a weapon that had good accuracy and rate of fire, and which was used from 1939 until the end of the war. Having a straightforward design and being well made, it was robust and could be broken down easily into man-portable loads. Throughout the war German mortar crews were expert at getting their weapons in and out of action quickly, which often gave them the edge in many encounters. An advantage of the sGrw 34 was that it could fire a wide range of captured ammunition.

150mm shell to a distance of up to 13,325m (14,570yd).

The principal types of anti-tank artillery used by Waffen-SS units were the 37mm Pak (Panzer Abwehr Kanone) 35/36, which could only penetrate 38mm (1.48in) of armour, the slightly more effective 50mm Pak 38, which could fire a 2.06kg (4.5lb) shell up to a range of 2650m (2900yd) and penetrate 101mm (3.98in) of armour, and the excellent 75mm Pak 40, which could penetrate up to 98mm (3.86in) of armour up to a range of 2000m (2190yd).

The 88mm guns

The most famous, or infamous, however, were the superb 88mm guns. They were actually anti-aircraft weapons which had been found to be equally effective against armour: the Flak 18, Flak 36 and Flak 37. An improved 88mm gun, designed specifically for the anti-tank role, was the Pak 43, which fired a 10.16kg (22.4lb) shell up to a range of 15,150m (16,570yd) and was capable of penetrating up to 184mm (7.244in) of armour. This weapon was at its most effective up to a range of 2000m (2190yd), but at least one case is known of a Pak 43 knocking out a Soviet tank at a range of almost 4000m (4380yd).

Before the first of the Waffen-SS panzer regiments were formed, most SS units listed armoured reconnaissance units in their orders of battle. The most important types of armoured cars used by these units fell into two categories: the four-wheeled light armoured cars and the eight-wheeled heavy vehicles (a few six-wheeled armoured cars were also used by the Waffen-SS, though they only saw service in the very early part of the war).

Armoured cars

The four-wheeled variety, known as the SdKfz (Sonder Kraftfahrzeug) 222, weighed in at 4.8 tonnes, had a top speed of just under 80km/hr (50mph) and a cross-country range of 180km (110 miles). It usually carried a crew of three and was armed with a 20mm cannon and 7.92mm machine gun, both mounted in a small, open-topped turret. The SdKfz 222 served well in France during 1940, though in Russia, because the amount of fuel carried in its internal fuel tanks restricted its operational range, it was replaced by the SdKfz 250/9 half-track.

The eight-wheeled, heavy armoured car, known as the SdKfz 231 (8-Rad), weighed just over eight tonnes, had a top speed of 85km/hr (52mph) and a cross-

OPPOSITE: The radical MG34 machine gun. Radical because it introduced the concept of the multi-purpose machine gun, and also the use of a belt feed in a light gun. Ammunition was usually carried in 50-round belts of 7.92mm calibre, which could be linked together to form 250-round belts, or the 75-round saddle drum (shown here) could be used. The MG34 was strong, though it did have a tendency to jam in dust, dirt and snow.

BELOW: Das Reich Division infantry at Kursk in 1943. The soldier at the front is carrying an MG42 machine gun, a weapon that had a high rate of fire of 1200 rounds per minute – devastating firepower.

ABOVE: A 75mm Pak 40 in action with Belgian volunteers in the Waffen-SS. This highly effective anti-tank gun was in production until the end of the war, and, as can be seen by the 22 stripes on the barrel denoting kills, in the hands of an expert crew was lethal on the battlefield.

RIGHT: Lithuanian volunteers in the Waffen-SS train with an 8.8cm Raketen-panzerbüchse (RPzB) 54 anti-tank weapon. Nicknamed Panzerschrek (tank terror), the RPzB 54 was a light and portable weapon and was a great success for the Germans on all fronts in World War II.

country range of 150km (95 miles). It had a crew of four and a typical armament of a 20mm cannon and 7.92mm machine gun in a small, enclosed turret.

SdKfz half-tracks

Each of these basic types was followed by a series of variants with differing armament and equipment, each new model taking the next number in sequence, ie following the SdKfz 231 was the 232, 233 and so on. The 234 version featured some interesting variants of its own, including the 234/2 Puma, which had a two-man turret mounting a 50mm cannon, and the 234/4, which mounted the excellent 75mm Pak 40 anti-tank gun in an open-topped fighting compartment.

One of the vehicles most widely used within the Waffen-SS was the half-track armoured personnel carrier. Two basic types were in widespread use: the SdKfz 250, which weighed five tonnes, had a crew of two and was capable of carrying four infantrymen, and the larger SdKfz 251, which weighed just over seven tonnes, had a crew of two and could carry up to 10 infantrymen. Both were only lightly armoured and their only armament were two 7.92mm machine guns.

The SdKfz vehicles, especially the SdKfz 251, were made in a bewildering range of variants, including flame-thrower vehicles, bridging vehicles, ambulances, mortar carriers, radio vehicles and many more. There were in fact 22 official variants of the SdKfz, and over 16,000 of all types were built in total. The vehicle was so successful that its manufacture was continued post-war in Czechoslovakia.

The panzers

By the time the first of the Waffen-SS panzer regiments was formed in 1942, the lightweight and very lightly armed and armoured PzKpfw (Panzerkampwagen) I was no longer a significant part of Germany's armoured formations. Only a

BELOW: Originally an anti-aircraft gun, the 88m Flak 18 became one of the most formidable anti-tank guns of World War II. It was used to devastating effect in Poland, the West in 1940 and in the North African desert, where the open spaces meant that the 88's long range could be employed to the full. It was fortunate indeed for the Germans that they had the gun for the invasion of the Soviet Union in 1941, for it was the only anti-tank gun currently in German service at the time that could knock out the T-34.

ABOVE: A Das Reich Division SdKfz 222 light armoured car in Russia in the summer of 1941.

BELOW: An SdKfz 231 during the campaign in France, May 1940.

few soldiered on, mostly in training units or second-rate formations.

The PzKpfw II was also obsolescent by this time, but during the early part of their development each battalion in an SS panzer regiment would be equipped with a company of PzKpfw IIFs. This particular version weighed around 10 tonnes and was powered by a 6090cc petrol engine, which gave it a maximum speed of around 55km/hr (34mph). It had a crew of three and was armed with a 20mm cannon and single co-axial 7.92mm machine gun. Its armour was thin, however, and it was no match for the heavier-armed and armoured Soviet tanks, such as the T-34 and KV-1. It was, nevertheless, highly effective against lighter armoured vehicles, such as half-tracks and so-called 'soft skinned' vehicles, ie trucks. Like most German tanks of the period, it had rather narrow tracks, which put it at a disadvantage in snow or muddy terrain. When it finally went out of frontline service, however, its chassis proved useful as the basis for a number of self-propelled artillery and anti-tank designs.

The PzKpfw III

A much more effective tank was the PzKpfw III, which in its 'J' version was the mainstay of the early Waffen-SS panzer regiments. Weighing in at 22 tonnes, this tank was powered by an 11,867cc petrol engine, allowing it to match the top speed of the PzKpfw IIF. This tank required a crew of five: driver, radio operator/machine gunner, gunner, loader and commander. It had a useful cross-country range of around 87km (56 miles) and was armed with a 50mm cannon and two 7.92mm machine guns, one co-axial in the turret and one in the hull. Its main weapon, though far superior to that of the PzKpfw II, was still at a distinct disadvantage when it came up against the T-34, whose armour could easily withstand the effects of the German shells, except at very close range. Even then, the Germans often had to try to disable the enemy tank by blowing off its tracks or hitting the thinner rear armour.

The schurzen

In order to improve the PzKpfw III's own defensive capabilities, thin steel skirts (schurzen) were hung from brackets along the hull sides and turret sides and rear, intended to detonate enemy shells before they struck the body of the tank itself. While of some use against lighter anti-tank weapons, the benefits of these skirts were often more psychological than actual when dealing with the excellent 76.2mm main armament of the T-34.

Like the PzKpfw II, the IIIJ had rather narrow tracks, and so to improve its cross-country performance in snow and on soft boggy terrain, track extensions were fitted to the outer edge to help spread the ground loading.

The PzKpfw IV

The tank that was to become the mainstay of the Waffen-SS panzer regiments was the PzKpfw IV. It remained in production throughout the entire war, being constantly improved and upgraded. Of the various versions produced, the most effective were the IVF2 and the IVG. Only slightly heavier than the PzKpfw III, it weighed 25 tonnes and featured an engine of the same size as the PzKpfw III, giving it a comparable top speed. It too was manned by a crew of five, but in addition to its two 7.92mm machine guns it boasted an effective long-barrelled 75mm gun (the original short-barrelled version was found to be ineffective against Soviet tanks). A third machine gun could also be fitted on a special external mount on the commander's cupola. With a cross-country range of 175km (110 miles) and a main gun which could just about hold its own against that of the better Soviet tanks, this tank went a long way to restoring the confidence of

BELOW: SdKfz 251 half-tracks of the **Leibstandarte** *Division in Kharkov, March 1943. This ubiquitous vehicle was used widely by Waffen-SS divisions throughout the war, and in different versions, such as an anti-aircraft variant, rocket launcher, engineer vehicle and personnel carrier.*

BELOW: A PzKpfw III of the Das Reich *Division in Kharkov. Note the divisional marking on the front of the vehicle.*

Germany's panzer crews in their vehicles. Like its predecessors, however, it was fitted with relatively thin bolted-on armour – its sides being especially vulnerable – and so the use of schurzen on the PzKpfw IV was widespread. The PzKpfw IV gave sterling service to the Waffen-SS panzer regiments on all fronts on which they served, and its versatile chassis was also the basis for a number of highly successful self-propelled guns and other specialised vehicles.

It was with the arrival of the PzKpfw V Panther in 1943, however, that the

Germans at last had a tank which could not only match the best Soviet tanks, but could also outclass just about every other tank in service with any army at that time. At 45 tonnes, this tank was able to achieve a top speed of 46km/hr (29mph) thanks to its powerful 23,880cc engine. Thicker, sloped armour provided excellent protection for the five-man crew, and meant that the Panther was a difficult beast for the enemy to kill. In addition, its interleaved road wheels and wide tracks gave it good cross-country performance in all terrains.

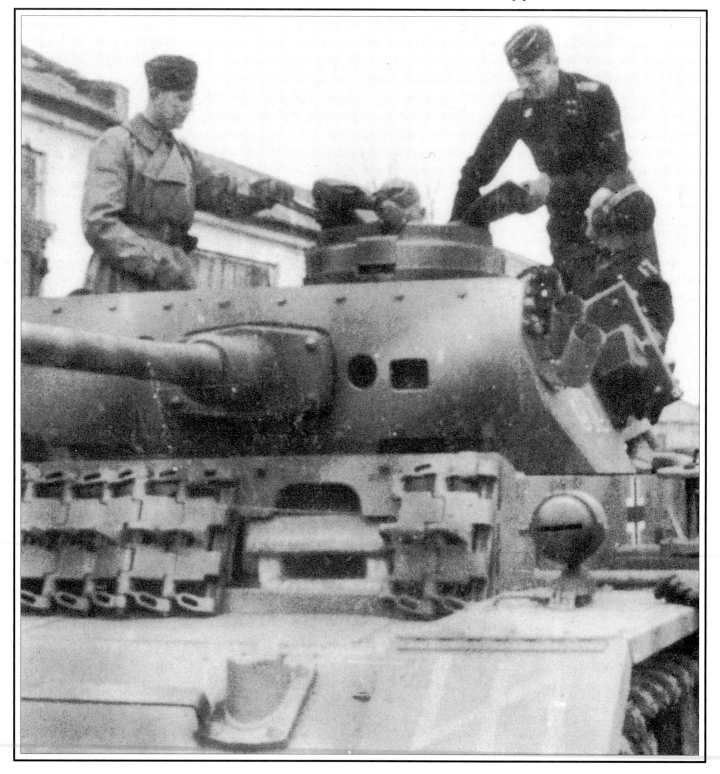

The main armament of the Panther was a high-velocity 75mm gun, which could penetrate the armour of all Soviet vehicles at that time, long before the latter could get close enough to bring their own guns into action. It also carried a 7.92mm machine gun in the bow, one co-axially in the turret and a third could be mounted on the commander's cupola if required.

Unfortunately, this superb tank was rushed into service too quickly, before its designers had the opportunity to iron out several teething problems, and its initial impact at the Battle of Kursk in July 1943 was disappointing. Nevertheless, it went on to become one of the finest medium tanks of World War II, and many of Germany's top panzer aces achieved their finest victories in this vehicle. Soldiers like SS-Oberscharführer Ernst Barkmann, who in an exposed spot with his sole Panther knocked out nine American M4 Shermans before withdrawing, were quick to prove the outstanding qualities of this tank. Other Waffen-SS panzer aces, such as SS-Hauptscharführer Franz Frauscher (nine

M4 Shermans destroyed and many more captured in a single day's combat) and SS-Obersturmführer Horst Gresiak, were to become some of the most successful tank commanders in the Waffen-SS thanks to their skilled employment of this magnificent weapon.

The Tiger

Of all Germany's tanks, however, none had as much psychological impact on the enemy as the dreaded PzKpfw VI Tiger. At 55 tonnes, this fearsome weapon mounted the excellent 88mm gun. With an engine of the same size as that installed in the lighter Panther, though, the Tiger could only manage a top speed of 38km/hr (24mph). But the Tiger carried massive armour protection, which made its frontal aspect almost impenetrable, and to have any hope of killing a Tiger an enemy tank had to come perilously close and attempt to hit its comparatively thinner side or rear armour.

The 88mm main armament was supported by the usual hull- and turret-

BELOW: The crew of a Das Reich PzKpfw IV pose for the camera during the Battle of Kursk. This tank was used throughout the war by the German armies and was the mainstay of the panzer formations. The original short-barrelled 75mm gun was found to be inadequate against Soviet tanks, and so, from 1943, a long-barrelled 75mm cannon was fitted. With this improvement the PzKpfw IV could hold its own against most enemy tanks. Though the chassis remained unchanged throughout its life, more armour was added to later models to combat enemy anti-tank weapons.

BELOW: The best tank of the war: the Panther. Introduced into action prematurely at the Battle of Kursk, where many broke down before they got into combat, it was a splendid fighting machine. Its 75mm gun could deal with any Allied tank, and its thick, well-sloped armour could deflect all but the heaviest armour-piercing rounds. As well as the 75mm main gun, the Panther was armed with a 7.92mm machine gun mounted co-axially with the main gun, another machine gun in the hull front, and one more on the turret.

mounted 7.92mm machine guns, and was capable of penetrating the armour of any Allied tank of the period, and doing so at a range beyond Allied tank guns.

Although slow and somewhat cumbersome, the massive Tiger was an awesome weapon in the hands of a skilled crew and commander, especially in defensive situations, where it could be sited in specially selected locations to give it an advantageous field of fire.

Michael Wittmann – tank ace

It is no surprise that the most successful tank commander in history, the famed Michael Wittmann, served in a Tiger battalion. The appearance of a mere handful of Tigers had been known to turn the tide of more than one battle, even against overwhelming odds. Probably the best known example of the Tiger's power and potential was at Villers-Bocage, during the Normandy battles, when SS-Obersturm-

führer Michael Wittmann met a tank and vehicle column of the British 7th Armoured Division and immediately attacked. Driving along the enemy column at close range, the enemy shells merely bounced off his Tiger's massive armour, while Wittman's own shells hit home with deadly effect. Around 27 British tanks and over 20 half-tracks and other vehicles were destroyed by this single Tiger.

Wittman's final score was to reach 138 enemy tanks destroyed and 132 guns, all in the course of a two-year period. This record has never been equalled, and it is extremely unlikely that it ever will. Michael Wittmann, and the Tiger tank, have deservedly earned their place in the annals of warfare.

The last German tank to go into operational service was the PzKpfw VI Königstiger, usually referred to as the King or Royal Tiger. In fact, it owed few of its design characteristics to the Tiger I,

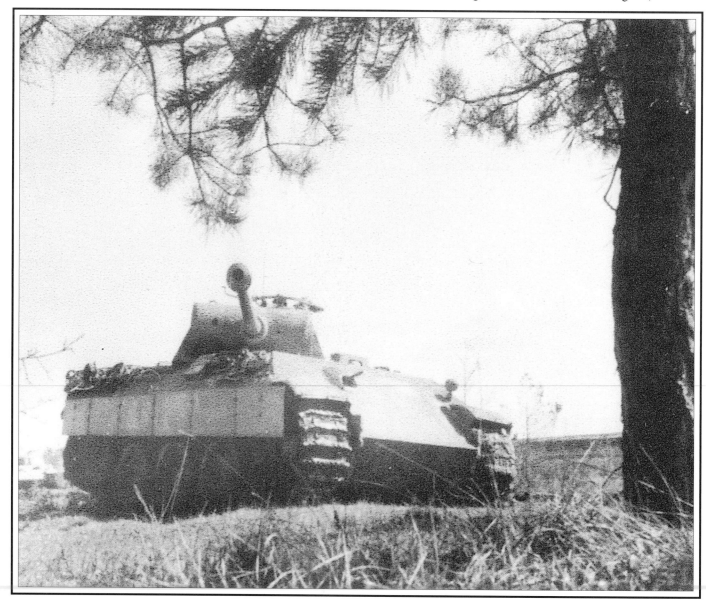

its sloped front and side armour bearing a much stronger resemblance to the Panther. The King Tiger weighed some 69 tonnes, and its 23,880cc engine gave it a creditable top speed for such a heavy vehicle: 38km/hr (24mph). Its main armament was an 88mm gun specially designed as a tank weapon, unlike the 88mm gun from the Tiger I, which was adapted from the existing anti-aircraft weapon.

The Tiger II

Its extremely wide tracks gave it good cross-country performance despite its excessive weight, and once again the combination of massive armour protection and a superb high-velocity main gun, which could out-range almost anything in the enemy arsenals, made the King Tiger a difficult and dangerous beast to kill. Few, if any, were ever knocked out by shots penetrating their frontal armour. As well as the main armament, the King Tiger carried a 7.92mm hull machine gun and a co-axial 7.92mm machine gun in the turret. A third was often mounted on the commander's cupola as an anti-aircraft weapon.

The King Tiger carried a crew of five and was allocated to the heavy tank battalions of the Waffen-SS panzer divisions: schwere Panzer Abteilungen 501, 502, and 503, whose use was usually decided at corps, not divisional, level.

French tanks in German use

In addition to German-manufactured tanks, a number of captured enemy weapons were utilised by SS formations. These ranged from the heavily armoured but obsolescent French Renault and Souma types, to the superb Soviet T-34s. The French types were commonly used by second-rate units employed mostly in anti-partisan duties, such as the 7th SS Freiwilligen Gebirgs Division *Prinz Eugen*, where their inability to perform well against enemy tanks was of less significance.

T-34s in SS service

A considerable number of T-34s fell into German hands on the Eastern Front, and many were either captured intact or in such a condition that their repair was feasible. So many, in fact, were to become available, that in the panzer regiment of the 2nd SS Panzer Division *Das Reich* a T-34 abteilung was formed. These captured tanks were marked with extremely large German crosses on the turret sides to ensure that friendly German troops were

in no doubt as to which side they belonged. Nevertheless, it took great courage to serve in this abteilung, where there was always the possibility that in the heat of battle one might end up being shot at by one's own side, as indeed some German T-34s were. One such T-34 crewman was SS-Hauptscharführer Emil Seibold, a panzer ace who ended the war with a score of 69 Soviet tanks destroyed. Seibold was decorated with the Knights Cross of the Iron Cross on 6 May 1945.

Self-propelled guns

Almost as important to the Waffen-SS as its panzers were the self-propelled guns and tank destroyers – the Sturmgeschütz and Panzerjäger. These vehicles consisted almost invariably of the chassis of a tried and tested tank design fitted with a fixed superstructure, either enclosed or open-topped, and a main armament that had a limited traverse. The entire vehicle had to be pointed towards the enemy, and final adjustments made by what limited traverse was available. Some of these vehicles used the chassis of tanks which were no longer suitable for frontline service, while others were manufactured alongside the corresponding tank. The benefits of these vehicles included their generally very low silhouettes, making them a difficult target, and the fact that they were cheaper to manufacture and maintain than the equivalent tank, while often being equally effective.

The StuG III

The most widely used and certainly most successful of these self-propelled guns was the Sturmgeschütz, or StuG III, which was based on the chassis of the PzKpfw III. A number of variants were produced, of which the most successful was probably the StuG IIIG. With a crew of four, it weighed 23 tonnes and had the same 11,867cc engine as the PzKpfw III. Armament consisted of a 75mm gun, but a version carrying the 105mm howitzer was also produced, making it a very potent weapon indeed. Over 8000 StuG IIIs were built and used, mainly by artillery battalions, though many Waffen-SS panzergrenadier divisions were issued with Stug IIIs in place of tanks.

When production of the StuG III was halted by the bombing of the Alkett factory which manufactured the vehicle, production was switched to Krupp for a short period. Krupp utilised an almost identical design of superstructure, but based its vehicle on the chassis of the PzKpfw IV.

'It could not take much longer now, whatever the Walloon and the French Waffen SS or the fanatic Hitler Youth with their 2 cm anti-aircraft guns could do. The end was coming and all we had to do was survive this final stage.'
– Juergen Thurwald, *Flight in the Winter* (1951)

ABOVE: The tank with which Michael Wittmann, of the Leibstandarte Division, became Germany's leading tank ace in World War II: the Tiger. With its thick armour and dreaded 88mm main gun, the PzKpfw VI Tiger was an outstanding tank design. This photograph shows a Tiger of the Das Reich Division at the Battle of Kursk in July 1943. The Tiger was in production from August 1942 to August 1944, with a total of 1350 being built.

This StuG IV was slightly heavier than Alkett's vehicle and a little slower, with a top speed of some 40km/hr (24.8mph).

Also based on the PzKpfw IV chassis was the excellent Jagdpanzer IV. This vehicle was designed specifically as a tank destroyer, and it mounted the same excellent 75mm gun as used on the later PzKpfw IV models. A second version was also produced, which mounted the high-velocity 75mm gun from the Panther tank. Around 1800 of both types were produced by the Vomag firm.

Several of the SS panzer divisions also made use of the Nashorn tank destroyer. This vehicle was based on a hybrid PzKpfw III/IV chassis, with an open-topped fighting compartment mounting an 88mm gun. A similar vehicle, known as the Hummel, was produced mounting a 150mm howitzer. Both, however, were

produced in relatively small numbers compared with the StuG III.

The versatile PzKpfw IV chassis was also used as the carriage for the quadruple 20mm flak 'vierling' cannon, either in an open-platform configuration with collapsible side panels, known as the Möbelwagen (Furniture Van), or with the armament in an armoured revolving turret, known as the Wirbelwind (Whirlwind). As well as being used primarily in the anti-aircraft role, these weapons were also devastating when used against enemy infantry. In fact, this weapon was also to be found mounted on the SdKfz 7, a half-tracked prime mover, which was also used in the anti-aircraft/ground role.

The earlier German tanks, such as the PzKpfw II, and the captured Czech tank, the PzKpfw 38(t), had their chassis used for assault guns and tank destroyers.

PzKpfw II chassis were used for the Marder (Marten) II, and the Czech chassis for the Marder III. Both of these vehicles were made in versions which were armed with the German 75mm gun, or in versions mounting captured Soviet 76mm guns. Even the elderly PzKpfw I was utilised to provide the chassis for the sIG 33, giving its 150mm howitzer a useful degree of mobility. The PzKpfw II chassis was also used to provide the carriage for the 105mm howitzer, in a vehicle known as the Wespe (Wasp).

The Hetzer

One of the most successful of these mobile gun carriages, however, was the tank destroyer variant based on the chassis of the Czech PzKpfw 38(t). Known as the Hetzer (Baiter), this vehicle was small and light (14.5 tonnes), but featured good, well-sloped armour protection and packed a mighty punch with its 75mm high-velocity gun. Though cramped, the vehicle was extremely popular with its crews. So suc-

cessful was the design, that production continued in both Czechoslovakia and Switzerland after the war, and several are still in existence today.

Mention should also be made of what were undoubtedly the most powerful of the Panzerjäger, the Jagdpanther and Jagdtiger. The Jagdpanther was a 46 tonne tank destroyer based on the Panther chassis, but with a fixed superstructure mounting the same 88mm gun carried by the King Tiger. It featured excellent, well-sloped armour and was an awesome weapon. To add to its protection, it was coated with a substance called Zimmerit, a plaster-like coating that made the attachment of magnetic charges against the hull more difficult. Despite flaking off after a while, it did work against smaller charges. Though the space inside the hull was rather cramped for the five-man crew (the Jagdpanther carried 60 rounds of ammunition for the main gun inside the tank), there was room to work. In addition, the vehicle's engine had more than

BELOW: Tiger crews stand to attention on their tanks during a ceremony for the award of Knights Crosses to members of the **Das Reich** *Division after the Battle of Kursk. Though the Tiger was an excellent design, it did have a number of problems, such as the overlapping wheel suspension, which became clogged with mud and stones. On the Eastern Front the mud often froze overnight, immobilising the tank by the morning. Note the 20mm Flakvierling 38 anti-aircraft combination on the SdKfz half-track in the background.*

adequate power and the vehicle drove very well. It was first used in action during the Normandy battles after D-Day, and it took a fearful toll of Allied tanks out of all proportion to the number of Jagdpanthers involved. The Allies were fortunate that only 400 were produced.

The Jagdtiger was based on the chassis of the King Tiger and featured a massive slab-sided superstructure carrying a deadly 128mm anti-tank cannon, which was capable of piercing the armour of any known tank of its day. Only 74 were built, and allocated to schwere Panzerjäger Abteilungen.

Although no such weapon was built around the chassis of the Tiger I, the

Porsche prototype of the Tiger, which was never put into production, had its chassis design used for a huge tank destroyer known variously as the Elefant or Ferdinand (after Dr Ferdinand Porsche). Again featuring a huge, box-shaped superstructure with only slightly sloped sides, it was armed with an 88mm gun. Early models lacked a hull machine gun for self-defence and easily fell prey to Soviet infantry. Only around 90 were built, and after its disastrous debut on the Eastern Front the remaining vehicles were transferred to Italy.

OPPOSITE: The early version of the StuG III, which had a short-barrelled 75mm gun.

BELOW: As the StuG III's short-barrelled gun was found to be ineffective against many targets at short ranges, it was replaced by a long-barrelled version. This is a StuG III at the Battle of Kursk.

JUST SOLDIERS?

The SS was the standard bearer of Nazism. As such, it was responsible for implementing the racial policies of the Third Reich, policies that sanctioned the extermination of hundreds of thousands of people. The concentration camp guards and Einsatzgruppen were directly involved in mass murder, and the Waffen-SS also assisted in Himmler's racial policies.

To the question 'were the SS soldiers just like any others?', there is no simple answer. To attempt to be as objective as possible, it is necessary to consider the SS not as a single entity but as four broad groupings. First, there were those who served on either the home front or to the rear of the combat zones, such as the SD and Gestapo. Second, the *Totenkopf* Division, part of the Waffen-SS but inextricably linked with the concentration camp guard units. Third, the foreign volunteers who served Germany in the ranks of the SS, and fourth, the so-called 'classic' Waffen-SS divisions, most of which were *Reichsdeutsche* in origin.

In addition to considering the qualities, or lack of them, of the men who served in these units, it is also worthwhile considering the backgrounds from which these men came, together with the attributes of their counterparts in the Wehrmacht and in the Allied armies. But why were Germans in the 1930s so easily led down the path of nationalism and extreme anti-semitism?

Maltreatment of the Jews was by no means a particularly German phenomenon. Anti-semitism had been rife in Europe for centuries. Even in the twentieth century, blatant anti-semitism smouldered just under the surface, waiting to be ignited. In virtually every country occupied

An SS execution of partisans in Russia. In the East, the SS's Reich Central and Security Department (RSHA) conducted a reign of terror against the civilian population.

ABOVE: Einsatzgruppen personnel search for partisans behind the lines in Russia, 1943. Each Einsatzgruppe had its own headquarters personnel, which were drawn from the Gestapo, Kripo and the SD. Their tasks were outlined in a memo sent from Heydrich to the Chiefs of the Sipo and SD dated 2 July 1941: 'the immediate goal is the security-police pacification of the newly occupied areas...To be executed are all functionaries of the Comintern (as are the Communist professional politicians in general); the senior, middle-ranking and radical low-ranking functionaries of the Party, the Central Committees, the District and Area Committees; other radical elements (saboteurs, propagandists, snipers, assassins, agitators, etc.); Jews in Party and state posts.' Himmler himself visited Minsk, the headquarters of Einsatzgruppe B, in August 1941 and witnessed an execution.

by the forces of Hitler's Third Reich, the Germans were able to find members of the indigenous population, sometimes in great numbers, who were willing and eager to assist in the persecution of the Jews. Indeed, some of the worst atrocities committed during this dark period in history were carried out by foreigners serving with the Germans.

To return to the Germans themselves, however, anti-semitism had existed long before the National Socialists had appeared on the scene. It was, though, a fairly passive form of prejudice and no more extreme than the levels of anti-semitism found in other European countries. When Hitler came to power, though, he twisted a number of verifiable statistics to help convert the populace, or at least a portion of it, to his extremist views.

The legacy of World War I

Almost every German family had suffered grievous losses, both in World War I, losing husbands, sons or brothers in battle, and in the subsequent Great Depression, when millions had their lives ruined by unemployment and rampant inflation, some being reduced to abject poverty almost overnight. In these circumstances the victims are almost always happy to be presented with a scapegoat on which to blame their troubles; the Jews were to be Germany's scapegoats.

Within a few years of the end of the war, the 'stab in the back' theory had taken a firm hold in Germany. Many of those countless thousands of German families who had seen their loved ones sacrificed in a war which had gained the coun-

try nothing were eager to blame the politicians who had agreed the surrender terms. Chancellor Ebert, head of the government that had signed the Treaty of Versailles, was Jewish. As post-war Germany degenerated into utter chaos, one of the greatest dangers, as perceived by the average citizen, was that Germany would suffer a Bolshevik revolution like the one in Russia. One of the leading figures in the communist movement in Germany had been Rosa Luxemburg, a Jewess. Thus, by historical coincidence the anti-semites in Germany were presented with two scapegoats upon whom they could blame many of Germany's problems and back their theories of a Jewish-Bolshevik menace.

Laying the foundation of hatred

In the economic and social spheres, statistics show that during the chaotic post-World War I period in Germany, some 17 per cent of the country's bankers were Jewish, 10 per cent of doctors were Jews, 25 per cent of the retail trade and an astounding 79 per cent of department stores were in Jewish ownership. These figures, of course, do nothing to show that many of Germany's Jews were also suffering from the ravages of unemployment and spiralling inflation. However, taken out of context, as they were by Nazi propagandists, these statistics were powerful weapons in Hitler's attempts to show that the Jews had not only been partly responsible for Germany's problems, but were among those suffering least from her dire economic position. According to the Nazi propagandists, while the German population suffered the Jews grew rich and prospered. The fact that many Jewish businesses, in an attempt to help ease the problems of their Gentile customers, extended their credit was often used against them in an attempt to portray them as cynical usurers. To young Germans growing up during this period, it was easy to believe that the Jews were indeed at the root of Germany's misfortunes.

Of course, once Hitler came to power in 1933 the anti-Jewish propaganda increased, as the Nazis worked hard to indoctrinate the nation's youth from the earliest possible age. Teachers unsympathetic to the National Socialist line were quickly replaced with those who could be depended upon to spread the word of Nazi theorists without question.

Many future grenadiers of the Waffen-SS grew up in this atmosphere of prejudice and mistrust, even hatred, of the Jews, so that by the time they had passed through the Hitler Youth and joined the Waffen-SS, many had been imbued with a considerable level of anti-semitism. This, together with the further political and racial indoctrination many received, particularly concentration camp guards or Einsatzgruppen personnel, inflated this minor level of racial prejudice into an all-consuming hatred, which resulted in total indifference to the sufferings and deaths of millions.

The Gestapo

On the home front, most members of the Gestapo came from a background in the Kriminal Polizei and were career policemen, in the early days at least, though many were also committed Nazis and may also have been members of the SS. The two did not automatically go together, as many senior SS officers were not even members of the Party. The treatment of their victims by the Gestapo has been well documented in numerous scholarly works, and seems very much to have depended on individual interrogators. Some, considering themselves intellectual, would attempt to obtain information from their prisoners by the use of wit and guile, as well as psychological methods, such as disorientation techniques and drugs. In this they were little different to the secret service organisations of any other nations. Some, however, were sadistic thugs who appeared to enjoy extorting information and confessions from their victims by the use of almost medieval methods of torture. However, this was not unique to the Gestapo, as those who had been unfortunate enough to fall into the hands of Stalin's notorious NKVD, or numerous other secret police forces, would no doubt confirm. Thus, had the Gestapo been involved in merely police work it may well have gone down in history as a particularly harsh and sinister organisation, but in many ways not very different from other security organs in other parts of the world.

However, the Gestapo was deeply involved in the persecution and extermination of the Jewish population in Germany and the occupied zones. While the concentration camps were run by staff from the notorious Totenkopf-Wachsturmbanne, each camp also had a resident Gestapo official attached. Of the Gestapo's numerous branches, none was more terrifying than Amt IVB4, commanded by Heydrich's so-called 'Jewish Expert' Adolf Eichmann. Despite his lowly rank – by the end of the war he had only reached SS-

Obersturmbannführer – Eichmann held considerable influence in the Reich Central Security Department (RSHA), and pursued and persecuted the Jews of Europe with an almost religious fervour. At the notorious Wannsee Conference in 1942, when the 'final solution of the Jewish question' was decided, Eichmann proudly reported to the assembled audience the total numbers of Jews liquidated in each of the occupied lands. Heydrich, Eichmann and other RSHA officials may not have pulled a trigger themselves, but they undoubtedly died with the blood of millions on their hands.

The SD

There was such a degree of overlap between the SD and Gestapo that it is often difficult to establish, from photographic evidence, to which organisation a particular individual belonged. For example, Eichmann was an official of the Gestapo but wore an SD uniform. Gestapo officials serving in Germany mostly wore civilian dress, but those serving in the occupied lands usually wore SD

BELOW: 'I walked round the mound and found myself confronted by a tremendous grave...The people went down some steps which were cut in the clay wall of the pit and clambered over the heads of those who were laying there to the place which the SS man directed them. They lay down in front of the dead and wounded. Some caressed the living and spoke to them in a low voice. Then I heard a series of shots. I looked into the pit and saw that in some cases their bodies still twitched, in others that their heads lay motionless on top of the other bodies before them.' (An Army witness to an SS execution.)

'Again and again during these confidential conversations I was asked; is it necessary that we do this? Is it necessary that hundreds of thousands of women and children be destroyed? ... There was no doubt in the mind of any of us that Hitler's order had to be obeyed regardless, and that it was the duty of the SS to carry it out. Nevertheless we were all tormented by secret doubts.'
– Rudolf Höss, Auschwitz commandant, statement in 1951

uniform. Most of the personnel serving in the Einsatzgruppen, whether SD members or not, wore full SD service dress. Those who were actually SD men wore a small, black, diamond-shaped insignia on the lower left sleeve which contained the embroidered letters 'SD'. Those who had served in the Gestapo wore similar badges, but ones that had silver cord edging.

As described in Chapter 5, the original members of the SD tended to be academics with law degrees who were primarily involved in intelligence gathering, threat analysis and counter-espionage. They had no powers of arrest, unlike their Gestapo counterparts. However, their commander, SS-Obergruppenführer Heydrich, had undeniable complicity in mass murder. The involvement of the Einsatzgruppen in the deaths of hundreds of thousands of civilians in eastern Europe while wearing SD uniform means that the SD as a whole must be considered deeply involved in one of the most heinous crimes in history.

Eastern European anti-semitism

The Einsatzgruppen and other security personnel who served in uniform in the occupied areas may well have considered themselves as soldiers, but in no way can they be regarded as 'just like any others'. Even those who performed purely clerical or administrative functions must have been aware that many of the orders they were processing related to monstrous and unforgivable crimes abhorrent to any civilised nation.

Eastern Europe, like many areas in the world, has had a long history of intolerance and persecution of the Jews. Unfortunately for the Jews in more modern times, a number of the leading figures in the rise of communism were Jewish, a fact used to great effect by their opponents to expound the theories of a Jewish-Bolshevik conspiracy. For Jews in the western provinces of the Soviet Union, their greatest hatred was reserved for their erstwhile communist masters and not, on the whole, for the German armies which, in mid-1941, were often welcomed as liberators from communist oppression.

However, there would be no freedom from oppression for the Jews in these areas, nor indeed for vast numbers of the non-Jewish indigenous populations, for it was in the East that Himmler and his SS would fully implement National Socialism's racial policies. The Jews were to be killed outright. For the Slav peoples of the East, Nazi rule meant subjugation as slaves of the 'master race'. According to Nazi dogma, Germany needed *lebensraum* (living space) for its people, and the *untermensch* (subhuman) peoples of the East would provide it. For its part, the SS had a Race and Resettlement Department to plan for and carry out the settlement of German and suitably 'Nordic' people on forcibly vacated lands.

Atrocities in Poland

The first mass atrocities were in Poland after its fall to the Germans in September 1939. The Polish intelligentsia and Poland's Jews were the targets. The task, Himmler described in a later speech, was at first hard, but it was necessary for the survival of future generations of Germans: 'An execution must always be the hardest thing for our men. And despite it, they must never become weak, but they must do it with tightly clenched lips. In the beginning that was necessary.'

As part of Himmler's empire, the Waffen-SS was constantly reminded of the need for it to fulfil its racial obligations, however unpalatable it might be. In the autumn of 1940, Himmler addressed the officers of the *Leibstandarte* about events in Poland: 'where, in a temperature forty degrees below zero, we had to drag away thousands, tens of thousands, hundreds of thousands – where we had to have the hardness – you should listen to this, but forget it at once – to shoot thousands of leading Poles, where we had to have the hardness, otherwise it would have rebounded on us later. In many cases it is easier to go into battle with a company of infantry than it is to suppress an obstructive population of low culture or to carry out executions or drag people away.'

The Einsatzgruppen in Russia

The invasion of the Soviet Union in June 1941 heralded a period of unprecedented savagery towards the civilian populations of the conquered lands, as the SS sought once and for all to deal with what was described to them as the Jewish-Bolshevik subhuman enemy. Einsatzgruppen killings started almost immediately, with execution centres being set up at Minsk and Lvov. Jews, and anyone else who was on Heydrich's death list, were usually rounded up and marched off to nearby woods. They were made to undress, hand over their valuables and were then marched in single file to long graves, where they were lined up and shot. For the men of Himmler's SS, indoctrinated to despise Jews and 'lower races' and taught to be 'hard', there was no remorse. An SS NCO who participated in Einsatzgruppen activities stated: 'What can they be thinking? I believe each still has the hope of not being shot. I don't feel the slightest pity. That is how it is and has got to be.'

Einsatzgruppen personnel

The extermination units were mostly officered by Gestapo, SD and Kripo personnel, though the rank and file appear to have been drawn from the Waffen-SS and the Ordnungspolizei. The executions themselves were grisly affairs. An Army witness to a shooting at Dubno in October 1942 reported that: 'We heard shots from the vicinity of the pit. Those Jews who were still alive had been ordered to throw the corpses into the pit, then they themselves had to lie down in the pit to be shot in the neck.' Not all were shot. An Einsatzgruppe report compiled soon after the invasion of Russia stated: 'Only the children were not shot. They were caught by the legs, their heads hit against stones, and they were thereupon buried alive.'

Einsatzgruppen commanders

The leaders of the Einsatzgruppen took pride in their work. SS-Obergruppenführer Friedrich Jeckeln, the SS leader in Riga, boasted that he had invented the 'sardine packaging' method of killing, whereby the victims were lined up at the edge of long graves (see above). Jeckeln later stated that it had 'the merit of saving space.' Otto Ohlendorf, chief of Einsatzgruppe D, favoured gas vans for the killing of Jews: 'Other group leaders demanded that the victims lie down flat on the ground to be shot through the nape of the neck. I did not approve of these methods because both for the victim, and for those who carried out the executions, it was, psychologically, an immense burden to bear.'

From the beginning, Waffen-SS soldiers appear to have been members of the Einsatzgruppe, with varying degrees of enthusiasm. Georg Keppler, one of the commanders of the *Das Reich* Division, stated attachment to an Einsatzgruppe could be a result of a misdemeanour: 'They are late or fall asleep on duty. They are court-martialled but are told they can escape punishment by volunteering for Special Commandos...Well, these commandos are murder commandos. When the young men realise what they are being asked to do and refuse to take part in mass murder, they are told the orders are

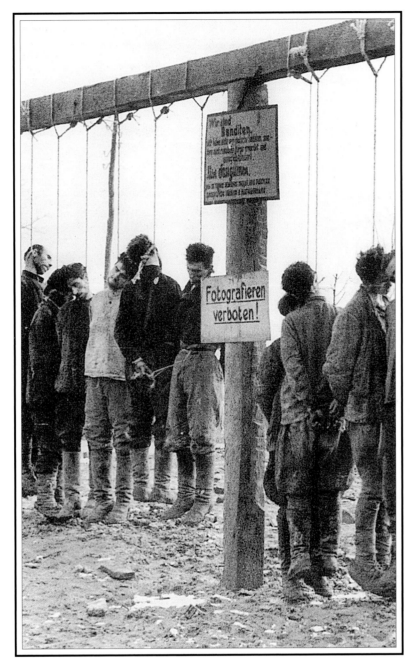

given them as a form of punishment. Either they can obey and take that punishment or they can disobey and be shot... By such methods decent young men are frequently turned into criminals.'

By early 1943, by the reckoning of the SS's own statisticians, the Einsatzgruppen had murdered 633,330 Jews in the Soviet Union (100,000 more are estimated to have been killed in the period 1944-45). To the eternal shame of the people involved, they were often assisted in their tasks by members of the indigenous populations.

Vast numbers of the indigenous populations came forward to serve in the German crusade against the Bolsheviks, as well as to show their determination to ensure that the liberation of their homelands was permanent. Unfortunately, their

ABOVE: Execution of partisans in Russia, January 1943. At the beginning of the war, Theodor Eicke, later the commander of the infamous **Totenkopf Division,** *left his concentration guards in no confusion as to the SS's role in the coming conflict: 'Every enemy of the state, every war-saboteur is to be liquidated. The Führer desires from the SS that they protect the homeland from all hostiles.'*

ABOVE: A Jewish mother and her children make their way to the gas chambers at Auschwitz concentration camp. Throughout the war there was a continual exchange of personnel between the field divisions of the Waffen-SS and the concentration camps. For example, Rudolf Höss, the commandant of Auschwitz between May 1940 and December 1943, later testified that during his term of office 2500 members of his staff were posted to Waffen-SS units, with a similar number replacing them from SS units. This transfer of personnel included both enlisted men and officers. In particular, officers who proved they were unfit for a field command were often assigned a concentration camp command. This interchange of personnel nullifies the claim that the Waffen-SS had no connection with the camps and did not know of the genocide policy.

hatred of the communists, twisted by Nazi propaganda into a great crusade against the supposed Jewish-Bolshevik menace, combined with their own latent anti-semitism, which was present in many eastern European regions, where the religion was either Catholic or Russian Orthodox. For those with strong religious beliefs, it was easy to believe the propagandists' portrayal of the enemy as being godless communists and Jewish 'Christ Killers'. This was the excuse which many would use to try to excuse or rationalise their barbaric treatment of their Jewish compatriots.

Ukrainian auxiliaries

Some of the eastern volunteers who fought in frontline combat units of the Waffen-SS and Wehrmacht did so with great gallantry and distinction, and would be justified in feeling proud of their military record. Unfortunately, the record of many of those who fought in the SS-controlled auxiliary police units was distinguished not by gallantry but by atrocity. Many of the Ukrainian auxiliaries, for example, earned themselves a dreadful reputation for brutality against civilians, often working in conjunction with the Einsatzkommandos in rounding up and murdering Jewish civilians. Most of the German units who served with these auxiliary units had nothing but contempt for them. Indeed, after using them to assist in anti-Jewish atrocities, the Einsatzkommandos often also murdered the auxiliaries, to avoid any witnesses to the event surviving.

If the Einsatzkommandos were happy to use the services of the auxiliary police

units to carry out some of their 'dirty work', the concentration camp guard units were even more willing to enlist such aid in the dirtiest work of all: guarding the camps. From special training camps, such as the one at Trawniki near Lublin, came some of the most brutal criminals in history, whose behaviour towards the inmates matched the worst excesses of their German counterparts.

Concentration camp guards

At Auschwitz, Belzec, Sobibor, Majdanek and others, the reports made by survivors almost invariably identify the auxiliaries as their most cruel tormentors. These auxiliaries were identifiable by the special identity card they were issued with at Trawniki, and by the fact that they were rarely issued with field-grey Waffen-SS uniforms. Instead, they were issued with obsolete pre-war, black Allgemeine-SS service dress, altered by the addition of light-green or light-blue facings to the collar and cuffs.

These men could not under any circumstances be described as soldiers, and would have been fortunate to survive even a few minutes had they encountered frontline enemy combat troops. To the camp inmates, however, they were all-powerful. Though not SS men proper, auxiliaries such as these were employed by the SD and the Wachsturmbanne, the latter being, administratively at least, an official part of the Waffen-SS, which thus must take its share of responsibility for their criminality.

Theodor Eicke

The SS-Totenkopfverbände were originally known as the SS-Wachverbände – units which guarded the first concentration camps at Dachau, Sachsenburg, Oranienburg and elsewhere. At the first concentration camp at Dachau, the guards were commanded by the unsavoury and sadistic SS-Oberstumführer Hilmar Wäckerle, under whose command Dachau became a cesspit of corruption. Himmler was forced to dismiss Wäckerle after the police charged him, and other members of the camp staff, with complicity in the murder of camp inmates. Himmler was furious at the bad publicity this caused and replaced him with SS-Oberführer Theodor Eicke.

Eicke set about tightening up discipline and improving morale. The circumstances of the inmates, however, scarcely improved, as the camp continued to be used by SS-Oberabschnitt Süd (the SS territorial division in which Dachau was situated) to off-load its more undesirable elements.

Eicke complained to Himmler, who responded by declaring Eicke's command independent of the SS-Oberabschnitt.

Eicke now had what amounted to his own empire free from outside interference. He made every attempt to harden his men to the circumstances of the inmates and the conditions in the camps. They were trained to hate their charges, and any feelings of sympathy for the inmates was treated as a sign of weakness. Eicke's men were also expected to renounce their membership of any church or religious organisation to which they belonged. From now on their loyalty was to be strictly to the SS-Totenkopfverbände and Eicke himself.

Service in the SS-Totenkopfverbände, unlike that in the SS-Verfügungstruppe, was not considered acceptable as an alternative to military service, and Eicke's men

were required to fulfil their two-year obligatory service in the Wehrmacht before returning to duty in the camps.

On the outbreak of war, members of the SS-Totenkopfverbände of an age which rendered them liable for military service were called up, leaving those too old or unfit for frontline duty, and those who were still below the age limit for conscription (20 years of age at this stage of the war). As the war brought more and more conquered territories under German control, new camps sprang up throughout the occupied lands, as large numbers of so-called 'enemies of the Reich' found themselves rounded up by the security services. As the best of Germany's manhood was called up for service in the frontline combat units, the concentration camp guard units had to settle for the 'left

BELOW LEFT: The 'lucky ones'. Survivors of Buchenwald concentration camp, where some 6000 inmates died each day from starvation, torture, beatings and sickness. Buchenwald was not an extermination camp, but supplied labour to local manufacturing plants. Nevertheless, it was a place of brutal punishments, as testified to by one of the survivors, Dr Dupont: 'The SS were present at these hangings in full-dress uniform, wearing their decorations. The prisoners were forced to be present under threat of the most cruel beatings. When they hanged the poor wretches, the prisoners had to give the Hitler salute. Worse still, one prisoner was chosen to pull away the stool on which the victim stood. He could not evade the order as the consequences to himself would have been too great.' Such was the regime under which the camp inmates lived and died. Some of the experiments carried out on prisoners in the camp were horrific. Russian prisoners, for example, were burned with phosphorus to test drugs for use in the treatment of Germans burned by Allied incendiary bombs. The sufferings of these men were indescribable, as their flesh was burned to the bone. When captured and shown pictures of the scenes of horror at Buchenwald, Himmler is reported as saying: 'Am I responsible for the excesses of my subordinates?'

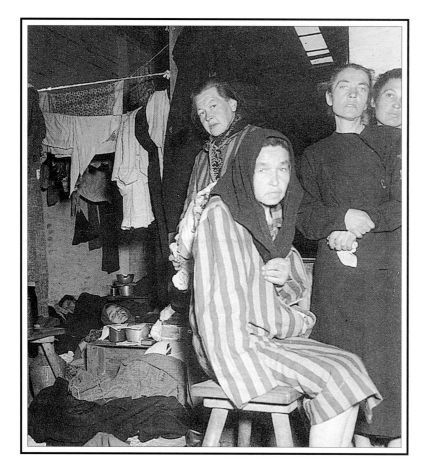

ABOVE: 'The Jews are the eternal enemies of the German people and must be exterminated. All Jews we can reach now, during the war, are to be exterminated without exception. If we do not succeed in destroying the biological basis of Jewry, some day the Jews will annihilate the German Volk.' Himmler to Rudolf Höss, commandant of Auschwitz, June 1941.

overs'. In many cases these were indeed the dregs of Germany's manpower.

Eicke had moved on to command the *Totenkopf* Division at the front, but his departure did not in any way alleviate the brutal conditions in the camps. Although it was not uncommon for personnel to be posted for service in the camps whether they liked the idea or not (undoubtedly some certainly did not), there can be no doubt that many seemed to take great pleasure in their cosy rear-area postings, with almost unlimited opportunities for corruption and mistreatment of the inmates. Corruption, for example, especially theft of valuables taken from the inmates at their arrival at the camps, was almost endemic in the camp system. Those caught were severely punished, but the problem was never solved.

Many guards must have grown rich from inmates who, having managed to conceal some precious keepsake on entering the camp, were forced by their circumstances to barter their remaining possessions for a few scraps of rotten meat or mouldy bread. The sadistic behaviour of the concentration camp guards, who also included women who were just as bad as their male colleagues, is sufficiently well documented in countless post-war studies. However, one example of their work will

give the reader some idea of what type of people they were.

The following is a description by an SS officer at Belzec concentration camp: 'Even in death one knows the families. They squeeze each other's hands, clenched in death, so that there is difficulty tearing them apart in order to evacuate the chamber for the next consignment. The cadavers, damp with sweat and urine, legs spattered with excrement and blood, are hurled outside. Children's corpses fly through the air. There is no time, the whips of the Ukrainians drive on the work-Kommando. Two dozen dentists open the jaws with hooks and look for gold. Gold left without gold right. Other dentists break the gold teeth and crowns from the jaws with pliers and hammers.'

None of the excuses they offered for their behaviour after the war could exonerate the inhuman conditions in which the prisoners were held, or the starvation level of the rations, nor the tortures, beatings and mass executions of millions carried out in the camps. The usual excuse that the guard was just an ordinary soldier doing his duty is totally unacceptable. Under German military law, for example, any soldier was entitled to refuse to obey an illegal order. The theory that had they done so they would have been executed has been disproved, as some who did refuse such orders were transferred to other duties, nothing more.

It should also be noted that a number of Naval and Air Force personnel were transferred to the concentration camp guard units during the latter stages of the war. Thus, former Wehrmacht personnel, and not just SS and foreign auxiliaries, must also bear their share of responsibility for the inhuman conditions in the camps.

Waffen-SS camp personnel

Many of the personnel in the concentration camps had seen service in frontline units before being posted to the camps. The infamous Doctor Joseph Mengele, for example, served as a medical officer in a Waffen-SS unit at the front before being posted to Auschwitz. From 1942, when the concentration camp guard units were absorbed into the Waffen-SS for administrative purposes, the guards carried the standard Waffen-SS paybooks and wore standard field-grey Waffen-SS uniforms. Thus, unfortunately for the reputation of the Waffen-SS, the camp guards could indeed claim to be soldiers in this respect, but under no circumstances could they claim that they were just like any others. Even the soldiers of the notorious *Totenkopf* Division eventually sought to distance themselves from those of the Wachsturmbanne, both during and after the war. So much so, in fact, that Himmler introduced a special collar patch bearing a double swastika to replace the Totenkopf collar patch worn by the Wachsturmbanne. This never replaced the original patch to any great extent, however.

The most horrifying aspect of the behaviour of the concentration camp guards, and indeed many of the Gestapo and SD personnel of the Einsatzkommandos, was not so much their sadism, but their total indifference to the hellish conditions around them and their victims' fate – they simply did not care.

Those members of the Totenkopfverbände who were of the appropriate age and fitness, together with personnel from the Allgemeine-SS and those who had been designated as police reinforcements, were gathered together in 1939 to be formed into the *Totenkopf* Division and the numerous Totenkopf infantry and cavalry regiments. After the conclusion of the Polish campaign, these Totenkopf regiments were, in the main, used as garrison troops in the occupied areas or for security duties, earning themselves an unsavoury reputation in the process. Meanwhile, Eicke prepared his *Totenkopf* Division for its first major combat action: the Western Campaign of 1940.

Massacre at Le Paradis

On 10 May the German attack began, and within just 17 days the *Totenkopf* Division had become involved in an atrocity at the small village of Le Paradis in France. Elements of the division had captured a number of British soldiers from the Royal Norfolk Regiment after hand-to-hand combat, and had executed them by machine-gun fire after they had been disarmed. The Army was furious when it discovered what had transpired and General Hoepner, commander of XVI Panzer Corps, demanded action against the perpetrators. Even Himmler was irate that his Waffen-SS was the subject of such bad publicity, its reputation sullied within just a few days of the opening of the campaign. Eventually the matter was hushed up, much to the Army's indignation. The officer responsible, however, SS-Obersturmführer Fritz Knochlein, survived the war and was subsequently tried and hanged by the British. On a number of occasions the *Totenkopf* Division came up against French colonial troops – Moroccans and Algerians – and took no prisoners from among these 'racial inferiors'.

After the conclusion of the campaign in the West, the Totenkopf regiments, which had been under the command of the Inspector of SS-Totenkopf Standarten, were transferred to the Waffen-SS proper. From these various units were formed nine Totenkopf infantry regiments, two SS cavalry regiments and an assault unit (SS Kampfgruppe *Nord*), with the remaining five infantry and two cavalry regiments being assigned to 'special duties' in the rear areas. All these units were thereafter used behind the lines for security duties on the Eastern Front, and earned a reputation for brutality, often working in conjunction with the Einsatzgruppen.

The *Totenkopf* Division in Russia

In Russia the *Totenkopf* Division continued its ruthless attitude to its enemies. SS-Oberführer Max Simon, commander of the SS-Totenkopf Infanterie Regiment 1,

BELOW: 'During work the SS men and women who stood guard over us would beat us with cudgels and set their dogs on us. Many of our friends had their legs torn by the dogs. I even saw a woman torn to pieces under my very eyes when Tauber, a member of the SS, encouraged his dog to attack her and grinned at the sight.' The testimony of Madame Vaillant-Couturier, an Auschwitz survivor.

'...the Tribunal has heard evidence of the conspirators' criminal program for aggressive war, for concentration camps, for the extermination of the Jews, for enslavement of foreign labour and illegal use of prisoners of war, for deportation and Germanization of inhabitants of conquered territories. Through all this evidence the name of the SS ran like a thread.'

– Prosecution statement, Nuremberg Trial

exhorted his troops to be even more brutal, declaring that the Russians were 'bandits who must be slaughtered without pity.' It is said that partisans captured by *Totenkopf* troops were often executed by shots aimed deliberately at the stomach to ensure a slower, more agonising death. Whether this is true or not, it certainly illustrates the sinister reputation these men were rapidly earning. The skills these hardened *Totenkopf* troops had learned in Eicke's concentration camps were much in demand in Russia. At one stage, an entire battalion from Einsatzgruppe A was transferred to the division as battle casualty replacements. It is also interesting to note that of the principal atrocities which were committed by Waffen-SS troops during World War II, almost all were by units under the command of officers who had previously served in Eicke's *Totenkopf* Division. It would be wrong to suggest that every single soldier of the *Totenkopf* Division was some sort of mass murderer. However, for soldiers imbued with the ideology of National Socialism, and hardened by the leadership of Theodor Eicke, it was impossible to show mercy towards the foe.

Despite the more positive reputation the division was to earn for its tenacity in battle, and the gallantry of many of its individual soldiers, it was ultimately to be fatally compromised by the regular interchange of its personnel with those from the concentration camps. *Totenkopf* soldiers who were no longer able to serve at the front through illness or injury often found themselves posted to the camps, and many of the younger camp personnel on reaching the age of conscription found themselves in the *Totenkopf* Division.

Soldiers of destruction

The *Totenkopf* Division contained many contrasts. Its men would engender a reputation for fighting bravely in the most appalling situations, so that even some of Germany's finest soldiers would compliment its qualities. Field Marshal von Manstein said of it: 'I had it under my command on frequent occasions later on, and I think it was probably the best Waffen-SS division I ever came across.' Yet these were the same soldiers schooled in hatred and brutality by Eicke, with claims that the enemy was a 'Jewish-Bolshevik subhuman, intent on annihilating the Reich unless prevented. Such prevention was to be achieved without mercy or pity; commissars were to be slaughtered along with other prisoners.'

Such training was to produce, from the ranks of the *Totenkopf* Division, criminals like the aforementioned SS-Obergruppenführer Friedrich Jeckeln, who became Höhere SS-und Polizei Führer for southern Russia and commander of Einsatzgruppe C, which was responsible for the murder of tens of thousands of Jews in the Riga Ghetto. Jeckeln not only commanded these troops, but admitted in his post-war interrogation to having taken part in the actual slaughter himself, to 'set an example' to his men.

The men of the *Totenkopf* Division may well be able to claim that they fought as well as any other units of the Wehrmacht or Waffen-SS, and even better than some, but here, for most of them, the similarity ends. Too many of the *Totenkopf*'s soldiers were brutalised fanatics for them to be able to claim that they were soldiers like any others.

The Waffen-SS

To turn to the Waffen-SS proper, two categories will be considered. First, the foreign volunteer units, a number of which were of east European origin. Second, the so-called 'classic' Waffen-SS divisions, which consisted in the main of German or *Reichsdeutsche* personnel.

Many former members of Waffen-SS tried to maintain after the war that it had committed no more atrocities than any other military formation. Kurt 'Panzer' Meyer, writing in 1957, stated that SS troops 'committed no crimes except the massacre at Oradour [see below], and that was the action of a single man. He was scheduled to go before a court-martial, but he died a hero's death before he could be tried.' Meyer also condemned the theory of collective guilt, further stating that SS soldiers 'did nothing more than fight for their country.' Heinz Guderian, writing in the forward of Paul Hausser's history of the Waffen-SS, stated: 'After the collapse [surrender of Germany] this formation faced exceptionally heavy and unjust charges. Since so many untrue and unjust things have been said and written about them, I welcome most cordially the initiative of their pre-war teacher and one of the most outstanding wartime commanders, who has taken up his pen to give evidence of the truth.' However, the truth was that the Waffen-SS did commit atrocities throughout the war, both at the front and behind the lines.

In the early days of the Waffen-SS, Himmler would only accept foreign volunteers from racially acceptable 'Germanic' populations, but as the war progressed he rapidly abandoned any real attempts at racial selection when recruiting foreign volunteers. The later foreign units were really more a reflection of Himmler's lust for personal power and glory, and often used up invaluable time and resources to produce units of little or no military value.

The Moslem units raised in the Balkans, for example, were particularly troublesome in this respect. Himmler attempted to exploit ancient religious

The *Handschar* Division, as recorded in Chapter 6, had earned the mistrust of its masters by its mutiny and the murder of German personnel while still training in France. Himmler, however, had no hesitation in turning these troops loose on the population of Yugoslavia. If anything, the atrocities committed by them had a negative effect. They were of such low calibre that their military effectiveness was almost zero, yet the crimes they committed only served to harden the attitudes of the partisans, resulting in the war degenerating into

BELOW: A Russian village burns after being attacked by an SS unit. Whether an Einsatzgruppe or Waffen-SS detachment, such actions were all too typical in what Himmler descibed as 'an ideological battle and a struggle of races.'

enmities in this area to his advantage. Where partisans from a predominantly Christian Serb background were causing the German occupation forces great concern, Himmler intended to field against them units of Croat Moslem volunteers, in the full knowledge that the traditional hatred which these two communities held for each other would almost certainly lead to excesses. Once Moslem units such as the *Handschar* and *Skanderbeg* Divisions were turned loose in a particular area where partisan activity was rife, reports of atrocities soon emerged.

one of gross brutality, with atrocities being committed regularly by both sides.

In addition to the Moslem volunteers from the Balkans, considerable numbers of Russians and Balts also volunteered for service with the Waffen-SS. Of these, the Balts were to form by far the most effective units from a military point of view, and the Estonian and Latvian volunteers in particular often displayed great gallantry and determination in battle, especially when defending their homelands, and even afterwards. Several of them were very highly decorated, and the Baltic SS

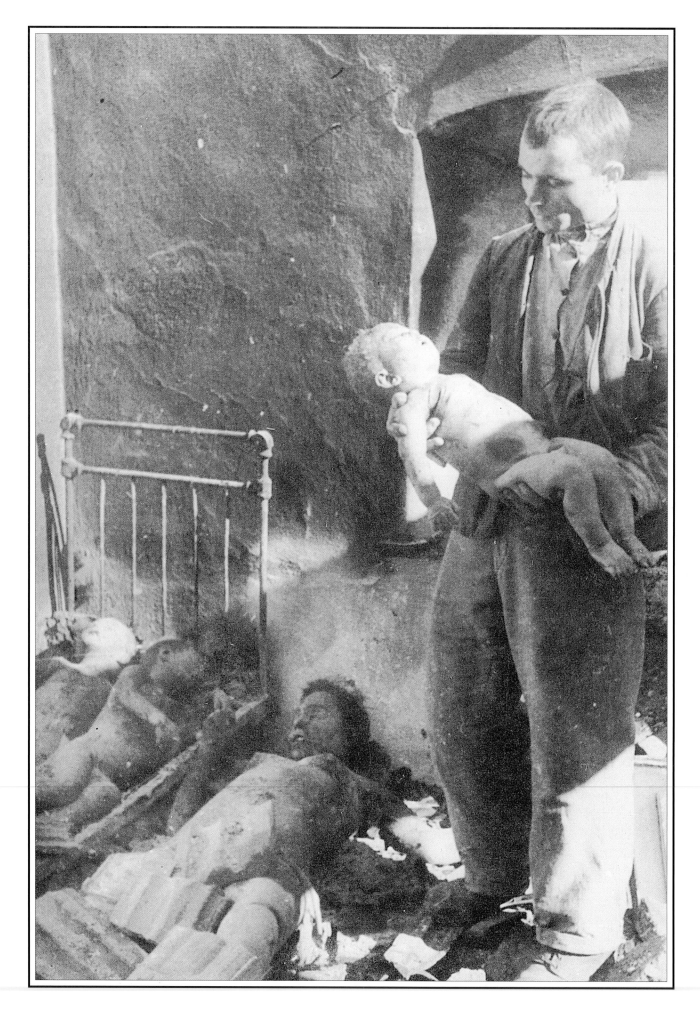

units generally earnt the respect of their German comrades.

Unfortunately, this was not always the case with the Russian and Ukrainian recruits. Although great numbers came forward to volunteer, often in sufficient numbers to fully man a division, with enough remaining to form several police units for rear area security duties, the calibre of the recruits was not particularly high. Most came forward because of their hatred of the communists, though there were many who were also mere opportunists who sought to exploit the situation to their own advantage and gain extra rations and pay, or to be in a position of advantage over their personal enemies. Those who did have genuine idealistic reasons for joining were often sadly disillusioned in their given duties, a case in point being the 30th Waffen-Grenadier Division der SS, whose soldiers joined to fight the Soviets yet found themselves posted to France to combat the *Maquis*. Little wonder, then, that the morale and efficiency of this unit was not of the highest level.

In any case, by the time Himmler had overcome his basic racial prejudice against the Slavs and allowed them to serve in the Waffen-SS, the tide of war had turned against Germany. Suffering defeat after defeat, they were inexorably pushed westwards through their homeland and out of Russia altogether. This hardly helped increase the morale and enthusiasm of these Russian volunteers.

If, in general, the Baltic SS units were of good quality, the bulk of the Russian units variable at best, and the Balkan Moslem units all but useless, there is one particular volunteer unit which gained a reputation second to none for extreme brutality: the 29th Waffen-Grenadier Division der SS, under Bronislav Kaminski. Of all of the units which gained unsavoury reputations for excesses against the civilian populace, Kaminski's troops were undoubtedly the worst. Although they did possess a degree of military skill, as their successes against the partisans in the forests of central Russia showed, when they were released against the Polish Home Army defenders of Warsaw in the 1944 uprising they acted with a degree of savagery which shocked even the battle-hardened Germans. The catalogue of atrocities for which Kaminski's men were responsible was truly horrendous.

Thus, with a few exceptions, such as the Baltic SS divisions, most of the east European volunteers units were at best of indifferent quality as combat units, and at worst little more than savages, responsible for some of the war's worst atrocities.

East European divisions

Himmler refused to accept these divisions as true Waffen-SS men, and the nomenclature used in the official designations of the units bears this out. For example, the official title of the *Handschar* Division was the 13th Waffen-Gebirgs Division der SS, or Armed Mountain Division of the SS, and not SS Gebirgs Division. This differentiated these volunteers as being in the service of the SS but not actually SS. Regulations even forbade the use of the SS runes as a collar patch for these units, and this spawned a bewildering array of special collar patches for their use. However, the regulations were often ignored and SS runes patches were worn.

Despite this slight difference, these units did wear standard Waffen-SS uniforms, and all carried the standard SS paybook, though sometimes in dual latin and cyrillic script. One can hardly expect the populations blighted by the appearance of these troops, or post-war investigators of alleged war crimes, to concern themselves with such subtleties in differentiating between these volunteers and 'real' Waffen-SS men. Certainly, in the immediate post-war period, when sympathy towards the Germans was rare, these units were considered simply as SS troops, with no consideration deemed necessary for the fine distinctions between these rather Byzantine volunteer units and the so-called 'classic' Waffen-SS divisions. The eastern volunteer units must therefore bear a fair degree of responsibility for the perception that the Waffen-SS was a particularly brutal or ruthless organisation.

The 'classic' Waffen-SS divisions

The Western volunteers, from Denmark, Holland, Belgium, Norway and France, were in the main of fairly high quality and emerged from the war with very positive reputations for dependability and combat efficiency. Allegations of atrocities against these soldiers are also conspicuous by their rarity. All in all, these units may be said to have enhanced the reputation of the Waffen-SS, rather than sullied it.

But what about the so-called 'classic' Waffen-SS divisions? This term has often been used to identify those divisions formed using a fair degree of selectivity, and producing units whose manpower consisted overwhelmingly, if not totally, of

OPPOSITE: 'On the other side stands a population of 180 million, a mixture of races, whose very names are unpronounceable, and whose physique is such that one can shoot them down without pity and compassion. These animals, that torture and ill-treat every prisoner from our side, every wounded man that they come across and do not treat them the way decent soldiers would, you will see for yourself. These people have been welded by the Jews into one religion, one ideology that is called Bolshevism, with the task: now we have Russia, half of Asia, a part of Europe, now we will overwhelm Germany and the whole world.' Thus spoke Himmler to soldiers of the Waffen-SS in July 1941. The result of such exhortations was the picture opposite: Russian civilians killed 'without pity and compassion'. In the Soviet Union the Waffen-SS built up a grim record of atrocities against the civilian population. For example, in the summer of 1941 the SS Cavalry Brigade, later the **Florian Geyer** *Division, undertook a 'pacification operation' in the Pripet Marshes, during the course of which some 259 Russian soldiers were killed and 6504 civilians executed. In September 1941, members of the* **Das Reich** *Division assisted in the massacre of 920 Jews near Minsk. Many civilians were also reportedly killed by the Waffen-SS in Kharkov.*

German nationals or *Reichsdeutsche,* who fulfilled the stringent entry qualifications laid down for full membership of the SS. These divisions were, for the most part, well equipped, usually carried an honour title worn on a cuffband, and had an exceptionally high level of esprit de corps. It is usually suggested that those divisions with an order of battle number less than 20 fell into this category. It is certainly true that few of the divisions with a higher number gained anything like the prestige and reputation for combat efficiency of these earlier units, and it is also true that the majority of these later divisions contained a preponderance of east European volunteers, the standard of whom, with a few exceptions, was poor.

Qualities of an elite

However, not all of the early divisions were of an equally high standard. The 4th SS *Polizei* Division, for example, was equipped to a lower standard than its counterparts, as was the 7th SS Gebirgs Division *Prinz Eugen*, both being used primarily for anti-partisan duties and being allocated a degree of obsolete and captured equipment.

Those Waffen-SS divisions which *were* considered to be the true elite did indeed come from the first half of the SS order of battle. Divisions such as the *Leibstandarte, Das Reich, Wiking, Hohenstaufen, Frundsberg, Hitlerjugend* and *Götz von Berlichingen* all earned enviable reputations for military prowess, sometimes reckless disdain of danger, and phenomenal esprit de corps, their morale remaining high and their spirits unbroken even in the direst of circumstances. These are the divisions which can reasonably claim to be purely combat soldiers like any others. However, even some of these prestigious divisions had allegations of having committed atrocities laid against them.

Hitler's bodyguard

Undoubtedly the most famous of the Waffen-SS divisions was the elite *Leibstandarte SS Adolf Hitler*, Hitler's bodyguard unit, which grew to become one of Germany's most powerful armoured formations. The men of the *Leibstandarte* were an elite within an elite. Restrictions on recruitment were rigidly enforced, with only the very best being accepted. Only the fittest, tallest, most racially pure and politically loyal applicants would be permitted to enlist in this unit. It is said that a single filling in a tooth would be suffi-

cient for a recruit to be rejected. The men of the *Leibstandarte* were immensely proud of their status and of carrying the name of their Führer on their sleeve. Unlike in the Army, where officers usually tended to come from a different social class than the men, the men of the *Leibstandarte* were all considered social equals. The rigid class system of the Army was anathema to the Waffen-SS, where all men were comrades.

Officers were required to perform their duties for a period as rankers before they could go forward for officer training and be commissioned. Junior ranks referred to their superiors by their SS ranks, and officers were not afforded the prefix 'Herr-' as in the Wehrmacht. Soldiers were not permitted to use padlocks on their lockers as this suggested mistrust of their comrades, upon whom, some day, their lives might well depend. Military training was carried out using the very latest tactics, and officers and men went through it together. All of these factors served to mould the *Leibstandarte* Division into a first class fighting formation – well equipped, well trained, supremely confident and with morale second to none. Rapport between officers and other ranks was much closer in the Waffen-SS, which is not surprising in view of the fact that even senior commanders of the Waffen-SS were often relatively young men.

Atrocity in Poland

Almost from the start of hostilities in September 1939, Waffen-SS soldiers gained a reputation for reckless gallantry when compared to their Army colleagues. This, though, is hardly surprising in view of the training they had received. The Army, however, viewed this lack of caution with considerable mistrust, citing the high casualty rates of SS units in its battle reports. SS units, on the other hand, complained that the Army would often give them the more difficult tasks rather than risk its own troops. Whatever the truth of the matter, the Waffen-SS quickly gained a reputation for achieving its allocated goals with some elan, but often only at a high cost in lives.

It was in Poland that the first recorded Waffen-SS atrocity occurred on 19 September 1939. An SS soldier called Ernst, of the SS-Artillery Regiment, and an Army policeman herded 50 Jews into a synagogue and shot them. The SS soldier was then court-martialled, the prosecutor demanding the death penalty. However, a senior judge in Germany quashed the

'The pit was nearly two-thirds full. I estimated that it already contained about a thousand people. I looked for the man who did the shooting. He was an SS man, who sat at the edge of the narrow end of the pit, his feet dangling into the pit. He had a tommy-gun on his knees and was smoking a cigarette.'
– German eyewitness to Einsatzgruppen executions of Jews from Dubno, Ukraine

death sentence, saying that the SS soldier 'was in a state of irritation as a result of the many atrocities committed by the Poles against ethnic Germans. As an SS man he was also particularly sensitive to the sight of Jews and the hostile attitude of Jewry to Germans; and thus acted quite unpremeditatedly in a spirit of youthful enthusiasm' (note the reference to the anti-Jewish indoctrination of the SS).

The *Leibstandarte* Division was expanded and reinforced for the attack in the West in 1940, and took part in the drive through Holland and into France, pushing towards the Channel coast at Dunkirk. On 27 May 1940, a number of British soldiers who had been captured by the Waffen-SS were herded into a barn near the village of Wormhoudt and killed by grenade and small arms fire. The perpetrators maintained that one of the prisoners had concealed a revolver, which he used to fire at them, thus provoking the shooting. However, this seems unlikely. No conclusive evidence to support this version of the events of that day have ever been produced, and the killings must

remain a blot on the reputation of the *Leibstandarte*, though it should be noted that this does seem to have been an isolated incident involving only a single company of this large force, and no other similar incidents were reported involving the division. In contrast, when the *Leibstandarte* subsequently met up with British forces again during the German invasion of Greece in 1941, some of those British troops captured went to great pains to record their chivalrous treatment by their Waffen-SS captors.

The *Leibstandarte* in the East

By the summer of 1941, when the *Leibstandarte* stood poised on the eastern borders of the Reich, ready to strike into the Soviet Union as a part of Hitler's invasion force assembled for Operation 'Barbarossa', it had gained a fine reputation for gallantry and elan, and, apart from the incident at Wormhoudt, could be justifiably proud of its achievements.

War in the East, however, introduced the young Waffen-SS grenadiers to a far more brutal and unrelentingly savage form

ABOVE: An example of the 'New Order' in Yugoslavia. The 7th SS Freiwilligen-Gebirgs Division **Prinz Eugen** *was engaged in anti-partisan duties in the country between 1942 and 1944, and committed many atrocities. Photographs taken by men of the division, and later captured by the Russians, show the unit carrying out many massacres and burnings of villages.*

ABOVE: The crushing of the uprising by the Jews of the Warsaw ghetto in April/May 1943, in which units of the Waffen-SS were involved. The operation was directed by SS-Brigadeführer Jurgen Stroop (executed in 1951 in Warsaw), who, by his own estimates, had taken or killed 37,359 Jews by the end of April. Asked after the war if he had regretted his actions, Stroop replied: 'Whoever wanted to be a real man in those days, that is to say a strong man, had to act as I did.'

of warfare. The SS had been taught to regard the Russians as despised and hated communist enemies, anathema to all that National Socialism stood for. The Soviets, on the other hand, saw the Germans as hated fascist invaders. This mutual aversion expressed itself on the field of battle in fierce hand-to-hand fighting, with no quarter being asked or given. What may be acceptable in the heat of battle, however, is an entirely different matter outside combat, and the *Leibstandarte* was accused of the cold-blooded murder of a large number of Soviet prisoners of war in October 1941 during the battle for Taganrog. The *Leibstandarte*'s commander, 'Sepp' Dietrich, did give an order that for a period of several days no enemy prisoners were to be taken, in reprisal for Soviet atrocities against his own men.

Russia - war without mercy

The war on the Eastern Front was a particularly savage and ruthless affair. The Soviets were fighting for their very existence, and even some of their own people were volunteering to fight for the Germans against them. No mercy was shown to the hated invaders or those who aided them.

German veterans who fought on the Eastern Front will often express disdain of the opinions expressed by those who did not personally experience the horrors of serving in Russia. Savagery and brutality were common, and reports of atrocities committed against surrendered Germans were just as widespread as the allegations made against the Germans themselves by the Soviets. The Germans even had their own War Crimes Bureau investigating atrocities carried out against its soldiers – the Wehrmacht-Untersuchungsstelle.

The atrocity at Oradour

In the West, however, the conduct of warfare rarely degenerated to the level of savagery common in the East, and in general the rules of warfare were more or less adhered to. There were, nevertheless, a number of incidents which did serve to blacken the reputations of even the 'classic' Waffen-SS divisions, and it is perhaps worthwhile examining two of the most notorious cases.

The first major incident of the campaign in the West occurred in the summer of 1944 in France, as the *Das Reich* Division prepared to head northwards to the Normandy battlefields. On its march the division was tasked with the suppression of partisan activity in the region around Limoges. In particular, the town of Tulle was under virtual siege by communist partisan bands and the German garrison troops, III Battaillon of Sicherungsregiment 95, were cut off. These troops were not frontline combat troops. Part of the *Der Führer* Regiment was detached from the division to relieve the town, and it easily drove off the partisans, who were no match for the Waffen-SS soldiers. On entering the town, the Germans discovered the bodies of some 40 of the garrison troops who had surrendered and then been murdered and mutilated.

At the same time as these events in Tulle, two of the division's officers, SS-Obersturmführer Gerlach and SS-Sturmbannführer Kampfe, were abducted by partisans while travelling unescorted. Kampfe was shot and his body not discovered until after the war; Gerlach himself escaped. On his return Gerlach reported to his regimental commander, SS-Standartenführer Stadler, relating that at one point his captors had taken him to a village he identified as Oradour-sur-Glane. SS-Sturmbannführer Diekmann was dispatched with a company of troops to investigate.

On his arrival at Oradour he sealed the village, rounded up all the inhabitants and exacted his revenge. In the violence that followed, 642 people of all ages and sexes, including 207 children, were either shot or herded into buildings and burned to death. When Diekmann reported back to his unit, Stadler was furious at his conduct and immediately called on the divisional commander, SS-Brigadeführer Lammerding, to institute court martial proceedings. In the event, Diekmann was killed in action shortly afterwards and so the proceedings were dropped.

LEFT: Men of the notorious **Dirlewanger** *Brigade during the Warsaw uprising of August 1944. Commanded by Oskar Dirlewanger, the unit was composed of poachers, criminals, cashiered officers, court-martialled servicemen and SS soldiers on punishment. It cut a swathe of violence through the city during the course of the quelling of the revolt, killing, looting and raping anyone who came into contact with it. Even hospitals were attacked, their staff and patients, including nurses and nuns, were robbed and raped. For his disgraceful actions in Warsaw, Dirlewanger was awarded the* **Knights Cross.**

It is said that Diekmann, on his way to Oradour, discovered a German medical unit that had been attacked by partisans. The wounded had been murdered and the medics tied up in their vehicle, which was then set alight, the medics being burned alive. If this was true, it would certainly go some way to explaining, though in no way condoning, his outrageous conduct at Oradour. Finding the murdered medics, coming hard on the heels of the loss of the two officers and the killing of the German troops in Tulle, may well have been the last straw for Diekmann, sending him into the fury which resulted in the deaths of so many innocents.

The Malmédy massacre

The other major incident which occurred during the Western Campaign in 1944 was the massacre of a number of American POWs at Malmédy. There is no real controversy over what happened. A number of American prisoners had been assembled at the Baugnez crossroads, near Malmédy, as spearhead units of I SS Panzer Corps streamed past. They were guarded by two Mk IV tanks and their crews. German sources claim that only some 20 POWs were involved, Belgian witnesses say around 35, and the Americans claim over 120. Whatever the numbers involved, a crewman in tank number 731, a Romanian *Volksdeutsche* named Georg Fleps, fired his automatic pistol into the mass of pris-

oners. As they scattered the other Germans opened fire and most of the prisoners were killed. This was clearly a crime for which the perpetrators would have to be brought to justice. The controversy arose over the way in which the investigations were handled. The Americans sought to show that this massacre was the result of a German policy decision not to take prisoners. The order was said to have emanated from SS-Oberstgruppenführer Josef 'Sepp' Dietrich.

After the war some 500 Waffen-SS soldiers from I SS Panzer Corps, including Dietrich, SS-Gruppenführer Hermann Priess, commander of the *Leibstandarte*, and SS-Obersturmbannführer Joachim Peiper, commander of the spearhead unit, Kampfgruppe *Peiper*, were imprisoned. The senior officers were charged with transmitting an illegal order: that prisoners were to be executed. No written evidence was ever found to substantiate these charges (though the US 328th Regiment of the 26th Infantry Division did have a written order that 'no SS troops...will be taken prisoner but will be shot on sight'), but the Americans were able to come up with witness testimony that such orders were given, as many junior SS soldiers testified against their officers. As a result, a total of 42 death sentences were passed down by the court, as well as 28 life sentences.

It was later discovered, however, that the testimony obtained from those soldiers who incriminated their officers was obtained by illegal means. US Army investigators had used both physical and psychological torture to extort false confessions; their methods were more suited to the Gestapo than the US Army. So badly tainted were the proceedings that rumours of what had occurred leaked out in the USA, causing an outcry. A special commission was founded to investigate the trial proceedings, which were found to be so flawed that all the death sentences had to be commuted. As a result 'Sepp' Dietrich was released in 1955 and Joachim Peiper in 1956.

The Waffen-SS at Arnhem

Less reported was the chivalrous treatment accorded British paratroopers captured at Arnhem by Waffen-SS troops led by SS-Obergruppenführer Willi Bittrich. Both sides had fought hard and well, often in ferocious hand-to-hand fighting, yet the Waffen-SS had developed a great respect for the tough British Paras. When they were eventually forced to surrender, the British were impressed at the humane manner in which they were treated, especially the wounded, their appreciation being expressed after the war in personal messages to the German commanders.

So, even at this late stage in the war, and despite many of them having suffered

the brutalising effect of service on the Eastern Front, Waffen-SS troops could still be found who were willing to fight with a considerable degree of chivalry against an enemy they respected.

The SS legacy

As Germany's war machine slowly disintegrated, it was invariably the elite Waffen-SS units that were rushed in to fill the gaps in the Reich's crumbling defences. The almost continuous combat and fierce actions resulted in high casualty rates, yet the esprit de corps of most of the elite Waffen-SS units remained undiminished. By this time many of these Waffen-SS soldiers had become hardened cynics, with no real feelings of loyalty to their political masters or their Reichsführer; their loyalty instead being directed towards their comrades and their unit. In this sense these Waffen-SS grenadiers had become very much like the Freikorps soldiers of the 1920s. Himmler's blundering attempts at military leadership – Hitler made him commander of Army Group Vistula – had shown him totally incompetent to lead an army in the field, and had earned him the contempt of many of his battle-hardened Waffen-SS troops.

Whatever the merits or otherwise of the Waffen-SS divisions as fighting formations, there is no doubt that a greater proportion of war crimes were alleged to have been committed by them than by any other branch of Germany's armed forces. Clearly, in the case of some of the so called 'classic' divisions at least, the bulk of any excesses which they have been charged with were carried out in the heat of battle by only a small element, and often in response to similar excesses being carried out by the enemy. Even Simon Wiesenthal, the celebrated investigator of Nazi was crimes, who has spent over 40 years researching atrocities committed by the Nazis during World War II, has stated his opinion that, during the early years of the war at least, a man serving in the Waffen-SS had neither more nor less to answer for than any other German soldier.

The judgement of Nuremberg

Clearly, for much of the SS there can be no redeeming factors. The International Military Tribunal at Nuremberg stated that the SS 'was utilised for purposes which were criminal under the Charter [of the International Military Tribunal], involving the persecution and extermination of the Jews, brutalities and killings in concentration camps, excesses in the administration of occupied territories. the administration of the slave-labour programme and the mistreatment and murder of prisoners of war.' It also went on to record that the Waffen-SS 'was in theory and practice as much an integral part of the SS organisation as any other branch of the SS', and it was 'directly involved in the killing of prisoners of war and the atrocities in occupied countries. It supplied personnel for the Einsatzgruppen, and had command over the concentration camp guards after its absorption of the Totenkopf SS.' As such, it thus had complicity in the extermination of six million Jews, hundreds of thousands of slave labourers and the murder of untold numbers of civilians in eastern Europe.

No one could possibly seek to condone or justify the actions of the Einsatzgruppen, the Gestapo, the Totenkopfverbände and others. In addition, it is inconceivable that history will ever consider that it has been unjust in its treatment of some of the Waffen-SS units, such as the notorious Moslem volunteers or the Ukrainian auxiliaries who served in the police units or as concentration camp guards. Those units must go down as monstrous aberrations. Their claim to be soldiers like any others must be rejected absolutely.

Those soldiers from the elite units of the *Reichsdeutsche* Waffen-SS and some of the Germanic volunteers, however, can probably be justified in claiming the right to be considered soldiers like any others, even if this consideration is not accorded to the Waffen-SS as a whole. These troops were not involved in genocide or crimes against humanity on a divisional basis, but were nevertheless soldiers who were imbued with the tenets of National Socialism and all its harebrained racial theories. This often translated itself into minor and major atrocities.

Perhaps, in the fullness of time, when all of the official documents relating to World War II have been opened, and the full facts are known about the actions of both sides, history may look upon some units of the Waffen-SS less harshly. This will never be the case for the bulk of Himmler's legions. however. which will surely forever remain damned.

BELOW: Hermann Priess, commander of the Leibstandarte, *who was sentenced to death for his part in the Malmédy massacre. This was later commuted, and Preiss was released from prison in 1954.*

SS Biographies

From Heinrich Himmler to Wernher von Braun, this is a selection of biographies of some of the infamous individuals who belonged to the SS, ranging from the soldiers who fought in the front line to the bureaucrats responsible for the various SS organizations operating throughout the Third Reich.

KEY:
E.A. – Executed by Allies   A – Accidental death
K.I.A. – Killed in action   E.R. – Executed by the Reich
M.I.A. – Missing in action   M – Murdered
D – Died of natural causes   E – Escaped
S – Suicide

A

D'ALQUEN, Gunter
RANK: SS-Standartenführer
BORN: 24 October 1910
DIED: 15 May 1998 (D)
PARTY NUMBER: 66689
SS NUMBER: 8452
AWARDS: Golden Party Badge;1939 Iron Cross Second Class; War Merit Cross Second Class with Swords; SS Honour Ring; SS Honour Sword.

D'Alquen was editor of the SS newspaper, *Das Schwarze Korps*, founded by Heydrich (q.v.) in 1934. Under his protection, it was one of the only papers free from the heavy handed censorship of Göbbels' propaganda ministry. D'Alquen also wrote an official pamphlet for Himmler, *Die SS*, based on Himmler's magisterial address to the higher leadership of the SS on 2 July 1936, at a ceremony for the thousandth anniversary of Henry the Fowler's death. In his capacity as war correspondent of the *Wehrmacht* propaganda section, d'Alquen visited Le Paradis in Normandy the day after the infamous massacre of prisoners in 1944. He saw the bodies and was told the implausible story that dumm-dumm bullets had been used by the Second Royal Norfolks. Soon after the 20 July Bomb Plot, Himmler commissioned him to orchestrate a recruiting campaign for Russian deserters. Towards the end of the war he became head of the *Wehrmacht* propaganda section, in succession to General Wedel, a particular enemy of Göbbels, who declared that Wedel had increased the propaganda section to the size of a division. D'Alquen also assisted Prützmann (q.v.) in the creation of the Werewolf organisation. He was fined by a Berlin de-Nazification court in July 1955 DM60 000.

AMANN, Max
RANK: Reichsleiter, SS-Obergruppenführer
BORN: 24 November 1891
DIED: 31 March 1957 (D)
PARTY NUMBER: 3
SS NUMBER: 53143
AWARDS:1914 Iron Cross Second Class; Golden Party Badge; Coburg Badge, 14 October 1932; Blood Order; Pioneer of Labour Decoration, 1 May 1941; SS Honour Ring; SS Honour Sword.

Amann, an uncouth but shrewd man, was born in Munich. During World War I he served in a Bavarian infantry regiment, where he was Hitler's sergeant. He joined the SA (*Sturmabteilung*, the Brownshirts), and was one of the original party members. From 1925, he was in the SA Central Office, and his business training led him to become party treasurer and to undertake the running of its paper, the *Völkische Beobachter*. When Hitler wrote a book called *Four and a Half Years of Struggle Against Lies,*

Stupidity and Cowardice, it was Amann who conceived a shorter, more memorable title: *Mein Kampf*. Amann took over responsibility for the book, arranging publication, organising the royalties, which were Hitler's main source of income, and supervising the dozens of editions which were published during Hitler's lifetime.

With *gleichschaltung* of the press (with the coming to power of the Nazis in January 1933, all newspapers were required to conform to the party line or else risk punishment), Amann became president of the Reich association of newspaper publishers and president of the Reich press chamber. He also bought the Hugenbergs' press empire for the party in 1943. His toughness and greed made him a millionaire, but at the war's end he was tried by a de-Nazification court and stripped of his property; he died in Munich in poverty.

B

BACH-ZELEWSKI, Erich von dem
RANK: SS-Obergruppenführer und General der Waffen-SS und Polizei
BORN: 1 March 1899
DIED: 8 March 1972 (D)
PARTY NUMBER: 489101
SS NUMBER: 9831
AWARDS: 1914 Iron Cross Second Class; 1914 Iron Cross First Class; Cross of Honour 1914-1918 Combatants; 1914 Wound Badge Black Class; War Merit Cross Second Class with Swords; War Merit Cross First Class with Swords; Knight's Cross of the Iron Cross, 30 September 1944; German Cross in Gold, 23 February 1943; 1939 Iron Cross Second Class Bar, 31 August 1941;1939 Iron Cross First Class Bar, 20 May 1942; Golden Party Badge; Danzig Cross First Class; SS Honour Ring; SS Honour Sword.

Born in Lauenburg, Pomerania, into a Junker family, Bach-Zelewski became a professional soldier serving at the front in World War I. After the war, he joined in succession the police service, the NSDAP in 1930 and the SS in 1931. When Hitler came to power, he was promoted quickly and for a time commanded the SS-District Southeast in Breslau-Silesia. Between 1932 and 1934 he was a Reichstag deputy. From 1941-42 he was senior SS and Police Leader in the Central Army Group area in Russia, where he was head of all anti-partisan units, and directly responsible to Himmler (q.v.). Despite his zeal, he became ill in 1942 due to the horrors being committed in the East, being admitted to the SS hospital in Hohenlychen suffering from a nervous breakdown. He suffered hallucinations connected with the shooting of Jews.

The change in control did not change the involvement of the Army or the Luftwaffe in these operations. Bach-Zelewski controlled the task of combatting guerrillas or partisans behind the lines on the Eastern Front and in the mountain reaches of the Balkans, and gave the SS control of the *Wehrmacht* and non-German soldiers fighting as volunteers in the *Wehrmacht*.

Bach-Zelewski was in command of all German units employed in curbing the Warsaw Uprising during August to October 1944. During the brutal suppression, the Soviet forces in the region made no attempt to aid the Poles, but stood firm on the eastern banks of the Vistula to await the predictable outcome. As with the earlier revolts, Himmler wished to see this as a battle honour for the SS, so the Warsaw Shield was instituted on 10 December 1944 to be awarded 'as a battle badge to members of the Armed Forces and non-military personnel who between 1 August and 2 October 1944 were honourably engaged in the fighting in Warsaw.' However, Bach-Zelewski was unable to award a single medal as the factory producing them was bombed out. The panzer leader General Guderian said of the putting down of the revolt: 'What I learnt was so appalling that I felt myself bound to inform Hitler about it that same evening and to demand the removal of the two brigades from the Eastern Front.'

In order to prevent his extradition to Poland after the war, Bach-Zelewski became a prosecution witness during the Nuremberg Trials. He was sentenced by the Allies in 1951 to 10 years' special labour, which in effect meant house arrest. In 1958, he was re-arrested and charged with murders committed in 1941-42. As more evidence about his wartime activities emerged, he was again retried and sentenced in 1961 to life for murders which had occurred in Breslau-Silesia during the period 1942-44 when it was under his command. He died in Munich-Harlaching in 1972.

BACKE, Herbert

RANK: SS-Obergruppenführer
BORN: 1 May 1896
DIED: 6 April 1947 (S)
PARTY NUMBER: 22766
SS NUMBER: 87882
AWARDS: Golden Party Badge; War Merit Cross Second Class without Swords; War Merit Cross First Class without Swords; SS Honour Ring; SS Honour Sword.

Born in Batum in the Caucasus, Backe was educated at the Russian Tifliser Gymnasium and Göttingen University. He was imprisoned by the Russians for most of World War I. An agricultural specialist, he served as State Secretary in the Ministry of Food from 1933 until 1942, when he assumed the position of Food Minister, a post he held until the end of the war. One of the ministers named in Hitler's last testament, he was imprisoned in Nuremberg after the war and hanged himself on 6 April 1947.

BARBIE, Klaus

RANK: SS-Obersturmführer
BORN: 25 October 1913
DIED: 23 September 1991 (D)
PARTY NUMBER: —
SS NUMBER: —
AWARDS: 1939 Iron Cross Second Class.

The infamous 'Butcher of Lyons', Barbie was born in Triers, the son of a village school master. He joined the SS and was assigned to the SD, beginning a long career in espionage that survived the Third Reich.

On 2 May 1941, Barbie was posted to the Bureau of Jewish Affairs in the Hague as an intelligence officer. His next appointment was the Amsterdam Gestapo headquarters in Euterpestraat. Barbie's orders were to concentrate on the Zionists, Jewish financiers, Marxists and, especially, Freemasons, whom the Nazis regarded as a special threat. Eichmann (q.v.) was impatient, intelligence gathering was a slow, laborious business and he wanted the RSHA section IVB4 to be providing the cargoes for the deportation trains. By May 1942 the first had arrived in Holland, but Barbie had moved to France by then and took up his appointment in Lyons in November 1942.

Barbie's first commander was SS-Sturmbannführer Rolf Müller, who took an immediate dislike to him and distanced himself from Barbie, leaving him uncontrolled in Lyons, well away from his supremo, SS-Standartenführer Helmut Knochen (q.v.) of Amtix at Sipo-SD headquarters in Paris. Barbie's brief from Knochen was crudely simplistic: penetrate and smash the Resistance in Lyons. Barbie chose as his headquarters the Hotel Terminus, a luxurious four-star establishment. Those who had dealings with him encountered a person with a split personality. He affected a pose of informality, sometimes refusing to use an offi-

cial protected car so he could meander through the streets, meeting fellow pedestrians as acquaintances. Barbie had a love of good food, and the waitress who served him found him generous, but this side to him could be replaced by uncontrollable rages and sadism.

Two incidents stand out in Barbie's unspeakable career. On 2 June 1943, information gleaned from an unknown source led him to the local doctor, Dugougon, who was using his house for a meeting of prominent Resistance members. The most influential was a Monsieur Martel, whose cover was that he was a patient needing treatment for rheumatism. When the Gestapo broke in they savagely arrested all inside, but had particular interest in 'Jean Martel', or Jean Moulin, the organiser and coordinator of the various Resistance cells in the area. Moulin, one of the great heroes of the French Resistance, endured a long, slow death at the hands of Barbie, who knew all the refinements of torture. An eyewitness recounted: 'he was unconscious, his eyes dug in as though they had been punched through his head. A mute rattle came out of his swollen lips.'

Desperately ill with a fractured skull and suspected brain damage, he was transported to Paris where he spent several days in a coma at the residence of SS-Standartenführer Boemelberg. Early in July, the barely conscious Moulin was transported to Germany, and died en route. His death certificate verified he died at Metz of heart failure on 8 July 1943.

Barbie's reign of terror knew no bounds, and he was responsible for the deportation of 842 people to concentration camps, of whom at least 373 were known to have perished. Of that total, 52 were children, with 44 of them being sent to the gas chambers from the children's home at Iziev. A special haven for Jewish children from all over France, Iziev was betrayed by informers, and the home was raided by Barbie and his forces in April 1944.

After the war some of the strangest, and as yet unexplained, events occurred. John Loftus, former prosecutor with the US Office of Special Investigations, stated that both America and Britain recruited ex-SS men to infiltrate communist cells in Eastern Europe. In 1945, MI6, the British intelligence-gathering organisation, secretly flew SS-Brigadeführer Walter Schellenberg (q.v.) to London, where he provided a list of all his most important agents. Barbie's contact with MI6 was through SS-Untersturmführer Hans Markus, one of Schellenberg's key men. At first Barbie was used as a 'runner', distributing supplies and money to new agents. Later, with numerous contacts he set up his own intelligence operation and the network grew. The supreme irony was that while MI6 had no qualms about using Barbie, MI5 and British military intelligence were trying to track him down for war crimes. Barbie knew he was living dangerously and went to a doctor in Hamburg to have his SS blood group tattoo removed. Shortly afterwards he was arrested in the city by British soldiers and beaten up. He and two other SS men were locked in the coal cellar of a house for three days, but were allowed to escape. Conveniently, they found an iron bar to force open the door. There was only one guard on duty and he was playing a flute when they fled. Barbie was so shaken by the beating he vowed he would never work for the British again, so he switched his allegiance to the Americans from 1947 to 1950.

Asked to penetrate the German Communist Party and detect Soviet agents, Barbie was given his own office in Augsburg and 100 informers. The Americans described him afterwards as 'invaluable'. He used his new position with the Americans to help ex-SS men escape from Germany. Years later he boasted how easy it had been to fool the Allies. Towards the end of 1950, the Americans found Barbie too 'hot' to keep.

The French knew he was in the American zone and demanded that he should be made to pay for his atrocities, so Barbie slipped out of Augsburg in June 1951 in a US Army truck. American agents gave him false papers and a new identity, Klaus Altman. He eventually turned up in Bolivia and remained safe for over 30 years, until 5 February 1983, when he was handed over to the French.

Klaus Barbie was tried for his war crimes in 1987. He put up no defence and for much of the proceedings insisted on withdrawing from the dock altogether. The survivors who testified said, 'he loved to play God,' and recalled the Gestapo chief's devotion to cruelty and inflicting pain. Barbie's family spoke of an apparently devoted husband and a father who had been inconsolable after the death of a son. He was found guilty and sentenced to life imprisonment, dying in prison in 1991.

BAUR, Hans

RANK: SS-Brigadeführer
BORN: 19 June 1897
DIED: 17 February 1993 (D)
PARTY NUMBER: 48113
SS NUMBER: 171865
AWARDS: Combined Pilot and Observer Badge in Gold with Diamonds; SS Honour Ring; SS Honour Sword.

Baur was a pilot in World War I and afterwards joined Lufthansa. He made many international flights and showed great expertise in the commercial flying world, earning a reputation that brought him to Hitler's notice. Baur joined his personal staff and Hitler seldom flew with any other pilot, admiring not only his aeronautical skills but also enjoying his company.

Baur was in the bunker at the end of the war and implored Hitler to let him fly him to Japan or Argentina, assuring him that they could still escape. Hitler's response was unequivocal: 'one must have the courage to face the consequences. I am ending it all here. I know that by tomorrow millions of people will curse me.' In recognition of his long and faithful service Hitler shook his hand and gave him his treasured portrait of Frederick the Great. Baur attempted to break out of Berlin and was captured by the Soviets, losing a leg. Imprisoned by the Allies after the war, he was released in 1955, when he confirmed Hitler's suicide.

BECHER, Kurt

RANK: SS-Obersturmbannführer
BORN: 12 September 1909
DIED: 5 August 1995 (D)
PARTY NUMBER: 4486195
SS NUMBER: 234478
AWARDS: German Cross in Gold; 1939 Iron Cross Second Class; 1939 Iron Cross First Class; War Merit Cross Second Class with Swords.

A former grain salesman from Hamburg, Becher was a skilled negotiator and head of an SS Remount Purchasing Commission from 1942. Fegelein (q.v.) noticed his skill in acquiring the Baron Oppenheim racing stud for the SS. Becher served in Budapest in the SS personnel office, and was introduced to Himmler's (q.v.) intimate circle of advisers, probably by Schellenberg (q.v.) after the 'occupation' of Budapest, when Becher once more handled a negotiation for the SS, acquiring the Jewish Mannfred Weiss steel combine.

In 1944-45 Himmler dreamt up an alternative method of disposing of the Jews: he proposed selling them to the Western Allies. Becher was required to go to Istanbul to offer the lives of 700,000 Jews in exchange for 10,000 lorries to be delivered by the Allies to the port of Salonika. Accompanied by Brand, Becher departed for Istanbul and tried to make contact with the British Embassy in Ankara and the Jewish Agency in Palestine. British military intelligence arrested him on the Turkish-Syrian border and interned him in Cairo. He was permitted to see the Jewish Agency representative, Moshe Sharell, who forwarded proposals to London, but they fell on stoney ground. Once made public, however, the proposals caused Himmler acute embarrassment in Germany.

Becher also visited Switzerland in his efforts to obtain foreign currency for Jewish lives. This was partly successful, and two trains left Belsen in 1944 and another in February 1945.

BECKER, Helmuth

RANK: SS-Brigadeführer und Generalmajor der Waffen-SS
BORN: 12 August 1902
DIED: 28 February 1952 (E.A.)
PARTY NUMBER: 1592593
SS NUMBER: 113174
AWARDS: 1939 Iron Cross Second Class, 24 May 1940; 1939 Iron Cross First Class, 22 June 1940; Knight's Cross 7 September 1943; Oakleaves, 21 September 1944; German Cross in Gold, 26 September 1942; 1939 Wound Badge Black Class; 1939 Wound Badge Silver Class; SS Honour Sword.

Becker was born in Alt-Ruppin, Brandenburg, and saw service in the Reichswehr before joining the SS-*Totenkopf Standarte Oberbayern*. He soon assumed command of its first battalion and saw service in Poland and France before being transferred to Russia. During the battle of Demjansk he commanded a battle group with considerable success. He replaced Hermann Priess (q.v.) and, taking over I SS Panzer Corps, he commanded the remnants of the 3rd SS Panzer Division *Totenkopf*, where he and his men were involved in bloody battles. He was awarded the Knight's Cross of the Iron Cross in recognition of these activities and four years later was the 595th recipient of the Oakleaves.

Becker's excesses in Russia, before and during his stint as commander of the *Totenkopf* Division, were bad enough to embarrass even the SS. In July 1944, Himmler (q.v.) launched an investigation into allegations of his sexual and military misconduct. Evidence showed that Becker organised and led an orgy in his regimental office canteen in France at Christmas 1942. While drunk, Becker allegedly broke furniture, smashed windows and rode a horse to death in the canteen before fornicating with revellers. He kept prostitutes in his forward command post in the Ukraine in the spring of 1943 and then, to celebrate Hitler's birthday in April 1943, a drunken Becker ordered a 10-minute salvo salute from all the heavy guns in his regiment, wasting precious ammunition and forcing the men in adjacent units to take cover. He publicly raped Russian women and was insensibly drunk while in frontline command. Himmler was unable or unwilling to punish Becker, or even prevent him from obtaining command of the *Totenkopf* Division. Becker's combat successes, the attrition of capable SS field commanders, plus Hitler's personal admiration, all combined to keep him in authority until the end of the war. After the war Becker was sentenced by the Russians to 25 years' hard labour. While commanding a reconstruction brigade, he was reported for allowing an unexploded grenade to be cemented into a wall. He was tried by a military court, found guilty and shot on 28 February 1952.

BEHRENDS, Dr Hermann

RANK: SS-Gruppenführer
BORN: 11 May 1907
DIED: 1946 (E.A.)
PARTY NUMBER: 981960
SS NUMBER: 35815
AWARDS: 1939 Iron Cross Second Class; War Merit Cross Second Class with Swords; War Merit Cross First Class with Swords; 1939 Wound Badge Black Class; SS Honour Ring; SS Honour Sword

Behrends was the first leader of the Berlin SD, when it was officially only a party office with no foreign intelligence or military section. He was probably responsible for preparing the death lists for the purge of the SA in 1934. On 17 January 1937 Himmler (q.v.) addressed an army officers' group, stating that 'detailed problems of execution do not concern the SD, but only ideological problems'. In contradiction to this, Behrends controlled the Tuchachewski forgeries (Tuchachewski was a Russian opponent of Stalin; the letters purported to show his group in contact with the *Wehrmacht*). At the end of 1936, Heydrich (q.v.) had invented an ingenious scheme that resulted in the notorious Moscow Generals' Trials, and the execution of the generals Tuchachewski, Uberewitch, Eideman and Putna on 12 June 1937. Heydrich thought he had destroyed the Russian high command.

Behrends went on to direct the racial German office in Yugoslavia. The worst excesses were committed by him in Slovenia. He was tried in 1945 and hanged in Belgrade in 1946.

BERGER, Gottlob

RANK: SS-Obergruppenführer
BORN: 16 July 1896
DIED: 5 January 1975 (D)
PARTY NUMBER: 426875
SS NUMBER: 275991
AWARDS: 1914 Iron Cross Second Class; 1914 Iron Cross First Class; Cross of Honour 1914-1918 Combatants; 1914 Wound Badge Silver Class; War Merit Cross Second Class with Swords; War Merit Cross First Class with Swords; Knight's Cross of the War Merit Cross with Swords, 15 November 1944; German Cross in Silver, 1 July 1943; 1939 Iron Cross First Class Bar; Golden Party Badge; SS Honour Ring; SS Honour Sword.

Born in Gerstetten, Württemberg, the son of a sawmill owner, Berger served as an officer in World War I and was seriously wounded. After the war he joined the Freikorps; he was a teacher in Gerstetten and also held the post of director of the Regional Gymnastic Institute in Stuttgart. Berger wormed his way into Himmler's (q.v.) confidence and became his chief adviser, as well as an adviser to Alfred Rosenberg, the anti-Semitic writer. He was an early member of the SA, but after the murder of Röhm gave his loyalty to the SS. He became head of the SS Sports Office on 1 August 1938; once in charge the SS main office began a reorganisation. From 1 April 1940 he was head of the main recruiting office for the Waffen-SS, and it was he who exploited the availability of non-ethnic Germans for recruitment into the Waffen-SS, particularly as the other branches of the military had no call on their service. He was also responsible for the welfare of German and non-German members of the Waffen-SS, and was Himmler's liaison representative to Rosenberg's ministry.

For a short time Berger held the post of commanding general in Slovakia, where he 'imposed the peace of the graveyard' during the Slovak uprising. He was relieved part-way through the uprising by General Höfle, and from 20 July 1944 was responsible for all POW affairs. He was tried at Nuremberg for the wartime murder of Jews and was sentenced to 25 years' imprisonment in 1949. He was released in 1951 and died in Gerstetten in 1975.

BEST, Dr Werner

RANK: SS-Obergruppenführer
BORN: 10 July 1903
DIED: 5 July 1976 (D)
PARTY NUMBER: 341338
SS NUMBER: 23377
AWARDS: Golden Party Badge; War Merit Cross Second Class with Swords; War Merit Cross First Class with Swords; SS Honour Ring; SS Honour Sword.

A law student from the Rhineland, Best was imprisoned during the French occupation of the Ruhr after World War I for his outspoken

nationalist views. He became a legal adviser to the NSDAP and was the drafter of the Boxheim Papers, a plan for a Nazi putsch, which was disclosed in 1931 and caused no little embarrassment to them. In 1933 he became police commissioner for Hesse and in July of that year state governor. He strengthened his career by becoming deputy to Heydrich (q.v.), and as first legal adviser to the SD and Gestapo he laid the foundations of their strength. He was a disciple of Ernst Jüttner and an ardent admirer of Hitler. RSHA was divided into seven departments and Best controlled the personnel department, Amt I, from 1939 to 1940. At the start of the war, however, Best found himself opposed to the new tendencies in National Socialism, and from 1940 to 1942 he led the SD in France. He was then made Plenipotentiary to Denmark, arriving in Copenhagen on 5 November 1940 to take up his duties. His rule was lenient by Nazi standards, and he seems to have tried to soften the effect of the 'Final Solution' in Denmark. There is evidence that he leaked a warning to the Danish resistance, which enabled them to effect the escape of almost all of Denmark's Jews to Sweden. On 30 December 1943, Best was summoned to Hitler's headquarters, where the Führer reiterated that the most effective deterrent to 'terror' was the use of greater 'terror'. Best tried to counter this argument, but Hitler was adamant that for every victim of resistance, five Danish hostages must die. Best returned to Copenhagen, determined to thwart this directive as far as possible. His enlightened attitude was not, however, shared by the military governor von Hanneken or the SD, and 1944 was to prove one of the bloodiest in Danish history.

In 1946, Best was found guilty of murder by a Danish court and condemned to death, commuted to life imprisonment. Released from Copenhagen prison on 29 August 1951 he returned to Germany, where in 1958 he was found guilty of mass murder and imprisoned. He was released in 1972 due to ill health.

BITTRICH, Willi

RANK: SS-Obergruppenführer und General der Waffen-SS
BORN: 26 February 1894
DIED: 19 April 1979 (D)
PARTY NUMBER: 829700
SS NUMBER: 39177
AWARDS: 1914 Iron Cross Second Class; 1914 Iron Cross First Class; Cross of Honour 1914-1918 Combatants; 1914 Wound Badge Black Class; 1939 Iron Cross Second Class Bar, 25 September 1939; 1939 Iron Cross First Class Bar, 7 June 1940; Knight's Cross, 14 December 1941; Oakleaves, 23 August 1944; Oakleaves with Swords, 6 May 1945; SS Honour Ring; SS Honour Sword.

A dedicated professional soldier, Bittrich was born in Wenigerode in the Harz mountains. During World War I he served as an army officer and then qualified as a pilot. He volunteered to serve with the *Grenzschütz Ost* and subsequently joined the *Reichswehr*; he continued his flying in Russia under an agreement with the Soviets, which circumnavigated the aviation ban in the Treaty of Versailles. He joined the SS-*Verfügungstruppe* in 1934 and the *Leibstandarte* in 1939.

During the Polish and French campaigns he commanded the regiment *Deutschland*, and was awarded the Knight's Cross for actions on the Russian Front. His divisional commands included the *Das Reich* and *Hohenstaufen* Divisions. In his role as commander of II SS Panzer Corps he was awarded the Oakleaves, becoming the 563rd recipient. Bittrich's greatest victory came while commanding this corps at Arnhem in 1944, the last German battlefield victory. His name is etched on the memory of every British paratrooper who landed there, for it was his troops who destroyed the airborne division. While still in command of the corps, he was awarded the Swords, becoming the 153rd recipient. After the war he was tried by the French for war crimes and acquitted in 1954. He died in Wolfratzhausen, Bavaria, in 1979.

BORMANN, Martin
RANK: Reichsleiter and SS-Obergruppenführer
BORN: 17 June 1900
DIED: unknown
PARTY NUMBER: 60508
SS NUMBER: 555
AWARDS: Blood Order, 17 February 1939; Frontbann Badge; SS Honour Ring; SS Honour Sword.

Born in Halberstadt in Lower Saxony, Bormann was one of Hitler's closest confidantes. Called up as a gunner towards the end of World War I, he did not see action. After the war he was unemployed and then worked as a steward on an estate. He joined the Rossbach Freikorps and later the Frontbann, the paramilitary force organised by Röhm after the banning of the SA in 1923.

He and Höss were jailed for the murder of Walter Kado, a teacher they claimed was an informant in the French-occupied Ruhr. He was released in 1925 and he joined the NSDAP working first as head of the press service in Gau Thüringen, then rising to become Gauleiter in 1928, before transferring to the staff of the supreme SA leadership towards the end of that year.

Bormann's fund-raising abilities became legendary; he was made party treasurer and was Hitler's intermediary as overseer of the 'Adolf Hitler Fund'. Donations and extortions were deposited and used for multifarious enterprises. He ensured that the scandal surrounding the mysterious death of Hitler's niece, Geli Raubel, was hushed up by using the fund to pay off the police inspector, Heinrich Müller (q.v.).

In September 1929 Bormann married Gerda Buch who was, if possible, even more fanatical in her beliefs than her husband. Bormann hated everything about Walter Buch, her father, coveting only his Blood Order, the award worn by veterans of the 1923 Putsch. On 30 May 1938 Bormann considerably expanded the conditions for the award of the Blood Order, much to the dismay of the *Alter Kämpfers* (veterans). New conditions for recipients included: the imposition of a death sentence which was later commuted to life imprisonment; to have served at least a one-year jail sentence for political crimes; or to have been severely wounded. Thus, not eligible for his involvement in the putsch, Bormann was able to confer the award on himself under either clause one or two and his ambition was fulfilled.

Hitler trusted him to conduct his financial affairs, and Bormann was responsible for rebuilding the Berghof. He may also have encouraged or helped Hess's (q.v.) flight to Scotland in 1941. Hess's office was renamed Parteikanzlei and Bormann was promoted to head it and to act as chief of staff to the Führer's deputy. He also became a member of the Council of Ministers for the Defence of the Reich.

Bormann possessed a ruthless and crafty mind, and during the war he became an almost invisible courtier who wielded enormous power. After his appointment as Hitler's Secretary on 12 April 1943 he controlled access to Hitler, preventing even the most senior leaders from seeing the Führer. He witnessed Hitler's will and marriage, and attempted to have Göring executed. He transmitted Dönitz's succession as Führer and ordered the mass breakout from the bunker. His fate is unknown, there was one theory that he died at the Lehrta bridge. An American investigator, McCabe, concluded that he could have committed suicide, been killed in Berlin, been a Russian or British agent, or

escaped to Argentina. He was tried in absentia at Nuremberg, found guilty and sentenced to death.

BOUHLER, Philipp
RANK: SS-Obergruppenführer
BORN: 2 September 1899
DIED: 10 May 1945 (S)
PARTY NUMBER: 12
SS NUMBER: 54932
AWARDS: Golden Party Badge; Blood Order No 29; Culture Badge; SS Honour Ring; SS Honour Sword.

After being severely wounded in World War I, Munich-born Bouhler became involved in publishing. In 1921 he became an early member of the NSDAP, which subsequently entitled him to be known as an Alter Kämpfer and worked on the *Völkischer Beobachter*, being its business manager from 1925 to 1934. In 1933 he was promoted to Reichsleiter and followed Himmler (q.v.) as Police President of Munich in 1934. Later in the year, he was appointed head of Hitler's private Chancellery, a most important move, effectively making him part of Hitler's secretariat. Holding a number of posts associated with the publishing industry, Bouhler also became chairman of the Censorship Committee, which nominated books to be approved or damned according to Nazi policy.

Hitler entrusted Bouhler and Dr Karl Brandt (q.v.) with responsibility for the programme of euthanasia in 1939. However, public concern about the programme forced Hitler to abort it. Bormann's (q.v.) ambitions contributed to the absorption of the private Chancellery by the party Chancellery, and by 1944 Bouhler was sidelined. He and his wife committed suicide at Zell am See when the Americans tried to arrest him in 1945.

BRANDT, Prof Dr Karl
RANK: SS-Gruppenführer
BORN: 8 January 1904
DIED: 2 June 1948 (E.A.)
PARTY NUMBER: 1009617
SS NUMBER: 260353
AWARDS: SS Honour Ring; SS Honour Sword.

Having been asked to treat SA-Obergruppenführer Wilhelm Brüchner, who had been injured in a car crash in 1933, Brandt made such as impression on his patient, who was Hitler's chief personal adjutant, that he quickly became part of Hitler's inner circle as a result. In September 1939 Brandt and Bouhler (q.v.) were given command of the Third Reich's official programme of euthanasia. On its cessation, Brandt was appointed Reich Commissioner for Sanitation and Health in 1942 and became one of Hitler's doctors.

Hitler's personal physician was Theodor Morell, who had taken a post as ship's doctor after graduation from medical school, then began a practice as a specialist in skin and venereal diseases in Berlin. Heinrich Hoffman, Hitler's court photographer, developed a dangerous infection in 1936 and Morell cured it with sulphanilamide, a new wonder drug he had imported from Hungary. Morell was engaged by Hitler on this recommendation. Brandt competed with Morell for Hitler's favours, advising him against the use of countless drugs which Morell was administering by injection. Hitler refused all criticism of Morell, and Brandt was dismissed in October 1944, being replaced by Ludwig Stumpfegger.

During his tenure in office Brandt was continually criticised by the Bishop of Münster, Clemens von Galen, one of the bravest opponents of the Third Reich in Germany. It was the bishop who had first raised doubts about the euthanasia programme, and his sermons on the matter had led to its suspension. Later, Brandt reported to Himmler that the bishop was raising doubts about the evacuation of mental patients from institutions in areas subject to air raids. Himmler himself had wanted to arrest the bishop in 1941, but had not for fear of the trouble this might cause in Westphalia. In this he would have been supported by both Hitler and Heydrich (q.v.), who despised what they called the 'black crows' of the Christian churches. Hitler himself saw Nazism itself as a religious faith, but the whole religious debate bored him.

However, he was impressed by the machinery of the faiths, Roman Catholicism in particular. Needless to say, those religious groups which fell foul of Nazism, such as the Jehovah's Witnesses, who refused to do military service, were ruthlessly suppressed.

Two weeks before his suicide Hitler became aware that Brandt had secreted his family in a position of safety where they could surrender to the Americans rather than fall into Soviet hands. Hitlerian rage resulted in Brandt being summarily tried for treason, found guilty and condemned to death, although Himmler (q.v.) and Speer succeeded in staying the execution by calling for new witnesses. Although he dodged the sentence imposed by Hitler's court, Brandt was tried by a US court for having approved medical experiments by SS doctors at concentration camps. His defence was that 'any personal code of ethics must give way to the total character of the war'. He was found guilty and condemned to death. He offered his body for experimental purposes similar to those he had sanctioned, but this was declined. He remonstrated that his execution was political revenge, and his farewell address from the scaffold was curtailed as the black hood was placed over his head.

BRAUN, Prof Dr Wernher von

RANK: SS-Sturmbannführer
BORN: 23 March 1912
DIED: 16 June 1977 (D)
PARTY NUMBER: 5738692
SS NUMBER: 185068
AWARDS: War Merit Cross Second Class with Swords; War Merit Cross First Class with Swords; Knight's Cross of the War Merit Cross with Swords, 28 October 1944.

Wernher von Braun (right in picture) was the Third Reich's most celebrated rocket scientist. He was born in Wirsitz, Westpreussen, which is now part of Poland. He belonged to the Verein für Raketen as an 18-year-old student and, by the end of the 1920s, to a group of technicians researching rocket propulsion, as an assistant to Nebel and Riedel. From 1 October 1932 he was an employee of the army's weapons department at the testing grounds in Kümmersdorf. As technician in charge, he was prominent in the founding of the Army Technological Research Institute from 1936, and took part in creating the 'wonder weapons'.

While Director of Rocket Research at Pennemünde, he created the Flüssigkeitsgrossrakete 'A4', better known as the V-2 rocket. In July 1943, at the instigation of Armaments Minister Albert Speer, a colour film showing the successful start flight of a V-2 missile was shown to Hitler himself, who until then had been against the project. After the presentation Hitler said to von Braun, 'I thank you. In the face of this missile one can only say that Europe and the world, from this point onwards, are too small for a war. With these weapons a war would be unbearable for mankind.'

For his contributions von Braun received the title of Professor on 21 July 1943. Between January 1944 and April 1945 around 6000 V-2s were built, with some 2315 being launched against Antwerp, London, and other British targets.

Von Braun surrendered to the Americans on 2 May 1945, together with his entire staff and a goods train full of technical documents, and he was taken to the USA. There he entered the service of the US Missile Department and accepted American citizenship in 1955. The basis for this was a decree from President Truman about the employment of captured German scientists in the USA: 'They receive special treatment because of their technical or scientific expertise. A personality from the Nazi regime who holds a high position or has been awarded honours will not receive exceptional treatment on that basis alone.'

When a reporter asked von Braun his reasons for changing citizenship, he answered: 'My country has lost two world wars. Next time, I would like to be on the winning side.' As the leader of a development team, which worked with technicians of the HVP under the control of the US Army, he succeeded in launching the first American satellite, Explorer. At the beginning of 1970, von Braun was appointed Deputy Director of NASA and Leader of Planning. He died in 1977.

BUCH, Walter

RANK: SS-Obergruppenführer
BORN: 24 October 1883
DIED: 15 September 1949 (S)
PARTY NUMBER: 7733
SS NUMBER: 81353
AWARDS: Golden Party Badge; Coburg Badge, 14 October 1932; Blood Order; NSDAP Long Service Medal 25 Years; NSDAP Long Service Medal 15 Years; NSDAP Long Service Medal 10 Years; SS Honour Ring; SS Honour Sword.

The son of a prominent judge, Buch was born in Bruchsal, Baden. He saw service in the army in World War I, rising to the rank of major, a title he used throughout his career. After the war he was a member of several ex-servicemen's organisations. In 1922 he joined the SA, becoming the commander of the Nuremberg force in 1923 and fighting in the 1923 Putsch. He was made president of the USCHLA, the NSDAP disciplinary tribunal. He was to become 'lord high executioner' of the party, a vengeful man from whom nobody was immune. In this capacity he accompanied Hitler on the arrest of Röhm at Weissensee, and he took charge of the liquidations at Stadelheim prison. Eyewitnesses recounted his enjoyment as he watched his victims die, some of them old comrades whom he butchered with his own hands. As president of the tribunal he judged all cases in accordance with Hitler's views. Buch's article in German Justice on 21 October 1938, stating: 'the Jew is not a human being. He is an appearance of putrescence. Just as the fission-fungus cannot permeate wood until it is rotten, so the Jew was able to creep into the German people, to bring a disaster only after the German nation had begun to rot from within', provoked anti-Semitic riots on 9 November 1938. Buch decreed that Nazis who raped Jewish women were to be expelled from the NSDAP and surrendered to the courts, whereas murderers were given minor punishments. Party members who killed Jews were merely carrying out orders.

Hated, despised and ignored by his son-in-law Martin Bormann, he was nevertheless made Reichsleiter, but his power was short-lived, as most of his functions were taken over by the SD and he became an irrelevance. After the war he was arrested, tried and given five year's hard labour. Whilst in captivity he committed suicide, slashing his wrists and drowning in Ammer Lake in Bavaria.

C

CLAUBERG, Karl

RANK: SS-Oberführer
BORN: 1898
DIED: 9 August 1957 (M or S)
PARTY NUMBER: —
SS NUMBER: —
AWARDS: Golden Party Badge (Honour Award)

Clauberg was the oldest son of a rural craftsman who later established a weapons business. He joined the army in 1916, seeing action in France and being taken prisoner by the British. After the war he became a gynaecologist and later a professor whose early researches on female hormones during the 1920s and early 1930s led to the discovery of the chemicals progynon and prolutons for the treatment of infertility. He joined the NSDAP in 1933 and, after being introduced to Himmler (q.v.) in 1940, began to concentrate his researches on methods of mass sterilisation. He was a member of the SD and Himmler employed him in experiments of mass sterilisation on Jewish women from July 1942, first at Ravensbrück and then Auschwitz. This led to the infamous 'Auschwitz sterilisation experiments'. In the latter part of 1944, Clauberg was engaged in a new project on sterility and reproduction as chief of a new institution known as the 'City of Mothers'.

Captured by the Russians on 8 June 1945, Clauberg was imprisoned for three years in the Soviet Union before being tried for war crimes. He was sentenced to 25 years' imprisonment, but was repatriated with others in October 1955, totally unrepentant. Charges were brought against him in November 1955 by the Kiel Court, but suddenly and mysteriously he died in his cell on 9 August 1957. It was generally believed that he was about to name names at the top of the Nazi medical hierarchy, and as a result colleagues helped bring about his demise.

CONTI, Dr Leonardo

RANK: SS-Obergruppenführer
BORN: 24 August 1900
DIED: 6 October 1945 (S)
PARTY NUMBER: 72225
SS NUMBER: 3982
AWARDS: Golden Party Badge; War Merit Cross Second Class without Swords; War Merit Cross First Class without Swords; SS Honour Ring; SS Honour Sword.

Conti was born in Lugano, Switzerland, and after taking his medical degree he moved to Berlin where he joined the Nazi Party, becoming in 1923 the first SA physician in Berlin. Hitler appointed him to be Reich Health Leader and State Secretary for Health in 1939. He instituted the euthanasia programme for killing Germans of unsound mind and mental defects with the avowed intention of cleansing the Nordic race. Conti committed suicide while awaiting trial in Nuremberg Prison. The Berlin de-Nazification Tribunal fined his estate DM3000 four years after his death.

COOPER, Thomas Hellor

RANK: SS-Unterscharführer
BORN: 29 August 1919—
PARTY NUMBER: —
SS NUMBER: —
AWARDS: 1939 Wound Badge Silver Class.

The only Englishman to receive a German combat award during World War II, Cooper was the son of a British soldier/photographer and a German mother. After World War I his parents returned to Britain, where Thomas was born. Unable to join the police because of his mother's nationality, an embittered Cooper joined the BUF (British Union of

Fascists) and subsequently looked to Germany for work. In 1939 he sought the help of the German academic exchange organisation in London and was eventually sent to Stuttgart.

He was offered a teaching job at a school in the Taunus Mountains and he started on 20 August. With the outbreak of war he was dismissed as an enemy alien, but secured a post as a private tutor. It was suggested that he might join the German Army, and eventually he was presented to Gottlob Berger (q.v.), who enrolled him in the SS. On 1 February 1940 he reported to the *Leibstandarte* for basic training. He found life difficult and had run-ins with members of the unit. He was moved to a new unit, SS-*Totenkopf*, based at Radolfzell and repeated his basic training. In July 1940 Cooper was transferred to the 8th company of the 5th *Totenkopf* Infantry Regiment where he received temporary NCO rank and acted as an instructor, remaining with the regiment until 1941, with the rank of Rottenführer.

Cooper finally saw action in February 1943. In the face of a heavy barrage and onslaught by infantry and tanks, Cooper collected his unit together and withdrew. Having travelled only 500m (1640ft), he fell, his legs severely wounded by shrapnel. However, he qualified for a wound badge, becoming the only Englishman to win a German combat decoration. He was subsequently placed in charge of the British Freikorps. In 1945 he was tried at the Old Bailey for high treason, found guilty and condemned to death. This was commuted to life imprisonment.

D

DALUEGE, Kurt

RANK: SS-Oberstgruppenführer und Generaloberst der Polizei Chef der Ordnungspolizei
BORN: 15 September 1897
DIED: 20 October 1946 (E.A.)
PARTY NUMBER: 31981
SS NUMBER: 1119
AWARDS: 1914 Iron Cross Second Class; Cross of Honour 1914-1918 Combatants; 1914 Wound Badge Silver Class; Gau Berlin Badge, Gold Class; Frontbann Badge; German Cross in Silver, 10 September 1942; Knight's Cross of the War Merit Cross with Swords, 1 September 1943 (6 September 1943); SS Honour Ring; SS Honour Sword.

Born in Kreuzberg-Oberschlesien, Daluege was wounded several times during World War I. Professionally Daluege was an engineer, having studied at the Berliner Technischer Hochschule and passing the state exams for the Engineering Diploma in 1923. He worked as a site manager with different canal and tram constructions, later changing to be a technical assistant in the Prussian Ministry of Agriculture. From 1927 until 1933 Daluege worked at the Berlin Refuse Collection Department as an engineer. Politically, he was involved in the growing success in different right-wing radical groups from the end of World War I, in particular the National Socialists, where he rose to the level of leader. He entered the Freikorps Rossbach in 1922, as well as the NSDAP after the banning of the *Grossdeutschen Arbeiterpartei* in 1923. After the legalisation of the NSDAP and *Sturmabteilung* (SA) in 1925, he was promoted to deputy gauleiter and leader of the first SA unit in Berlin. During the re-banning of the SA, he was the founder and leader of the Frontbanns-Nord. At the end of 1928 Daluege left the Berlin SA and joined the SS. On 25 July 1930, he was promoted to SS-Oberführer, then to SS-Gruppenführer on 1 July 1932, remaining leader of the SS-Gruppe Ost until August. From 24 April 1933 until its dissolution, he belonged to the Prussian Landtag as a specialist of the NSDAP coalition party for police matters, and was a representative from 12 November 1933. In June 1933, he was elected to the Prussian Staatsrat.

On 30 January 1933, the day the National Socialists assumed power, Daluege began his appointment as Kommissar by special appointment in the Prussian Home Office through Hermann Göring, and was promoted to the chief of all police informers. On 11 May, he took over the leadership of the police in Prussia, simultaneously being appointed as Ministerialdirektor.

On 15 September 1933, he was promoted to Generalleutnant of the Prussian Landespolizei. Two months later he took on the leadership of the police department in the Reich Home Office. Daluege was promoted to SS-Obergruppenführer in the same month. In June 1936, he was appointed to the position of Chef der *Ordnungspolizei* in the newly created *Hauptamt Ordnungspolizei* (the civil police, known as Orpo), and on 17 June he was promoted to the rank of General der *Ordnungspolizei*. On 20 April 1942, he was promoted to Generaloberst der *Ordnungspolizei* and SS-Oberstgruppenführer, the only police officer with this rank.

Heydrich (q.v.) loathed Daluege and scathingly nicknamed him 'Dummi-Dummi', so it is ironic that his successor as Deputy Reichsprotektor of Bohemia and Moravia was none other than Daluege, who took over on 30 May 1942. He remained until 14 October 1943, and ordered the massive reprisals, murders and imprisonments that followed the assassination. From the summer of 1943 he was continually ill.

After the war Daluege was charged by the Czechs as a war criminal, found guilty and condemned to death. Due to his ill health he was only semi-conscious when he was hanged in Prague on 24 October 1946.

DARGES, Fritz

RANK: SS-Obersturmbannführer
BORN: 8 February 1913
DIED: unknown
PARTY NUMBER: —
SS NUMBER: —
AWARDS: 1939 Iron Cross Second Class, 15 July 1940; 1939 Iron Cross First Class, 19 August 1942; Knight's Cross of the Iron Cross, 5 April 1942.

Born in Dülseberg near Salzwedel, Altmark, Darges was Martin Bormann's (q.v.) SS adjutant from 1936 to 1939, and from October 1940 was an SS aide with periods of frontline duty until he was wounded. He was Hitler's personal adjutant from 1 March 1943 until 18 July 1944. During one conference, a house fly kept returning to a point on the map Hitler was concentrating upon, producing an angry Hitlerian outburst with attempts to shoo it away. Darges was grinning as Hitler looked his way. Immediately taking him aside, he had him transferred to the Eastern Front. Here, as the commander of the 5th Panzer Regiment, 5th SS Panzer Division *Wiking*, he was awarded the Knight's Cross of the Iron Cross.

DEGRELLE, Léon

RANK: SS-Standartenführer der Reserve
BORN: 15 June 1906
DIED: 31 March 1994
PARTY NUMBER: —
SS NUMBER: —
AWARDS: 1939 Iron Cross Second Class, 2-13 March 1942; 1939 Iron Cross First Class, 18-21 May 1942; Knight's Cross of the Iron Cross, 20 February 1944; Oakleaves, 27 August 1944; Close Combat Clasp Gold Class, 14 September 1944; Infantry Assault Badge Silver Class, 30 August 1942; Belgium Badge of Honour of 'Rex' Gold Class.

Léon Degrelle was born in Bouillon, Belgium, and became the most famous foreign volunteer in the Waffen-SS. He entered Belgian politics in May 1935 calling his movement 'Rexisme', for he disliked the term

'political party'. In the general election of May 1936 the Rexists won a sensational victory, gaining 21 seats in the lower house and 8 in the senate. Degrelle was offered a cabinet post by the King of the Belgians, which he later declined. He wanted much more than just a ministerial portfolio for himself and some minor positions for his party.

The ascendance of Degrelle's movement was meteoric; so, equally, was its decline: the Rexists lost most of their gains in the April 1939 general election, holding on to only four seats with Degrelle suffering defeat at the hands of the then prime minister, Paul van Zeeland, in a straight fight for a Brussels seat. Degrelle looked set for political oblivion until the occupation of his country in May 1940 catapulted him once more onto the political stage. The Rexist party was the main collaborationist faction in Wallonie under the occupation, but was never entrusted with political power, although some members held minor posts in the civic administration.

Degrelle spent most of the war on the Russian Front with a legion of Walloon Volunteers, and in May 1943 Himmler (q.v.) decided that they had proved themselves worthy of admission into the Waffen-SS. This did not imply any question of merging them with the existing Flemish Waffen-SS. On 1 June 1943 the Walloon legion became the SS-Sturmbrigade *Wallonie* and joined the *Wiking* Division in the southern Ukraine in November.

In January 1944, 56,000 German troops were trapped in the action at Cherkassy, where their effort to fight their way out lasted for several weeks and was enormously costly. On 14 February, over 200 members of the Walloon assault brigade were killed, including the commander, Lucien Lipert, and Degrelle was promoted to replace him. When the Germans finally broke out, the *Wiking* Division was down to 4000 men, and only 632 of the original 2000 Walloons came through unscathed. The survivors were sent to Wildflecken in Franconia to regroup but, in fact, received little respite. A desperate situation had developed in Estonia and the Walloon assault brigade was rushed in to take part alongside their Flemish compatriots in the Battle of the European SS at Narva in July 1944. Degrelle won the Knight's Cross of the Iron Cross, and had the Oakleaves conferred upon him by Hitler personally, becoming the 355th recipient. Hitler held Degrelle in high esteem, saying: 'If I had a son, I would wish him to be like you'.

In January 1945, the newly created panzergrenadier division was ordered to the front with two other badly under-strength volunteer divisions, the Flemings and the French, which made up the grandly titled, SS Army Corps West. They joined battle with the Russians in the region of Stettin and within a matter of weeks were reduced to a strength of little more than 700 men. By mid-April, what was left had been almost completely destroyed on the west bank of the River Oder. Some remnants of this shattered division were evacuated by sea to Denmark. Degrelle escaped to Norway, and flew on to Spain in Speer's plane. After the war he was tried in absentia by the Belgians and sentenced to death. He lived in Spain until his death. When Degrelle died, the Belgian Government took active measures to prevent Belgians who had fought beside him attending the funeral.

DIEBITSCH, Prof Karl

RANK: SS-Oberführer
BORN: 3 January 1899
DIED: unknown
PARTY NUMBER: 4690956
SS NUMBER: 141990
AWARDS: SS Honour Ring; SS Honour Sword.

Professor Diebitsch was the head of the *Hauptamt Persönlicher Stab Reichsführer-SS*, Chefamt Munich. It was his job to deal with 'all artistic and architectural questions' which interested the Reichsführer-SS.

Diebitsch's creations included the police and SS sword, as well as the much sought-after 1936 chained dagger. He was also responsible for the 'touch mark', commonly referred to as the 'SS proof mark' which was the logo denoting his work. It has also been observed on some of the ceramic works decorating the walls of the SS-Junkerschule in Bad Tölz. He was also responsible for the design of SS uniforms, coats of arms for senior SS leaders and insignia, such as the long-service medals.

The famous Allach SS porcelain factory came under his control in 1939, when he was named director and he used a similar touch mark as its logo on the base of all its creations. The SS acquired the small porcelain factory in Allach in 1937, and it was one of its first economic enterprises. The factory had been established as a small private concern in 1935 – Himmler viewed its acquisition as a major triumph. It was moved to the SS complex at Dachau where it produced high quality porcelain and official SS gifts, such as the pseudo-Germanic Yuletide candle holder.

Diebitsch summed up his sense of artistic and architectural excellence when he stated: 'we know that all we may produce will be critically examined by those who come after us and we do not want these later generations to give a poor verdict on our work.' His perception of stylistic lines and runic forms intricately laced together has left a legacy of some of the finest collectables of the Third Reich period.

DIELS, Rudolf

RANK: SS-Oberführer
BORN: 16 December 1900
DIED: 18 November 1957 (D)
PARTY NUMBER: 3955308
SS NUMBER: 187116
AWARDS: Cross of Honour 1914-1918 Combatants; SS Honour Ring; SS Honour Sword.

The first chief of the organisation that became the Gestapo, Diels was a survivor who somehow outwitted his former agents after the 20 July Bomb Plot. He was born in Berghaus in Taunus, the son of a prominent landowner. He studied medicine and law at the Universities of Giessen and Marburg, but his preoccupations, however, were seen to be anything but academic. His interests encompassed fighting duels, being a prodigious drinker, and, rumour had it, a glass chewer.

Diels joined the Prussian Ministry of the Interior in 1930, becoming a high-ranking police official. In 1932 he became a party member and subsequently married Göring's cousin. Diels persuaded Göring, a good friend, that a secret police force was necessary to monitor the activities of the communists, and on 26 April 1933 the *Geheime Staats Polizeiamt* (GESTAPA) was established, (later renamed *Geheime Staats Polizei*, or Gestapo), as a new department of the Prussian State Police, affiliated to the Ministry of the Interior, and headed by Diels.

The Nazi Party was engaged in widespread illegal practices, of which Diels became aware. The Gestapo became the target for Himmler (q.v.), who was rising to power and was desperate to control it, bringing Diels in conflict with him. On the eve of the arsonist's attack on the Reichstag, 27 February 1933, Diels reported to Hitler that it was the work of a single demented pyromaniac and that the culprit, Marinus van der Lubbe, was in custody. Hitler, however, blamed the communists and bleated out in fury: 'This is a cunning plot! Every communist official must be shot. All communist deputies must be hanged this very night.' As a result, Diels was ousted from his position in the Gestapo, but with Göring's help still managed to hold a number of government posts, including Assistant Police Commissioner of Berlin and Administrative President of Köln. During the 1940s, he refused to participate in anti-Jewish measures. He eventually became reconciled with Himmler, however, and was allowed to wear an honourary Standartenführer's uniform.

After the 20 July Bomb Plot, Diels was seized by the Gestapo and thrown into prison. After the war he went back to the role which he played best: that of the loyal civil servant, in Lower Saxony. He accidentally shot and killed himself while on a hunting expedition on 18 November 1957.

DIETRICH, Josef 'Sepp'

RANK: SS-Oberstgruppenführer, Panzer-Generaloberst der Waffen SS, zuletzt Oberbefehlshaber der Panzer Armee
BORN: 28 May 1892
DIED: 21 April 1966 (D)
PARTY NUMBER: 89015
SS NUMBER: 1177
AWARDS: Golden Party Badge; 1914 Iron Cross Second Class; 1914 Iron Cross First Class; Cross of Honour 1914-1918 Combatants; First World War Commemorative Tank Battle Badge; 1939 Iron Cross Second Class Bar, 25 September 1939; 1939 Iron Cross First Class Bar, 27 October 1939; Knight's Cross of the Iron Cross, 4 July 1940; Oakleaves, 31 December 1941; Oakleaves with Swords, 16 March 1943; Diamonds, 6 August 1944; Combined Pilot and Observer Badge in Gold with Diamonds 1943; Blood Order No 10; SS Honour Ring; SS Honour Sword.

A Bavarian, Dietrich enlisted at 19 in the 4th Field Artillery Regiment. During World War I he served first with the artillery, then the infantry and, finally, with the newly introduced tank units. At the war's end he was demobbed with the rank of sergeant. He had a number of jobs, including a runner and hat maker.

Dietrich joined the Bund Oberland and was present at the 1923 Putsch. In June 1932 he became head of Hitler's bodyguard. He was noted as being a stern but fair commander, and his overriding ambition was to train and maintain the best political and combat personnel possible. His *Leibstandarte* saw service in the Polish campaign in 1939, suffering heavy casualties due to lack of experience and military training. They were transferred to the Western Front and saw action in the Low Countries and France in 1940. Dietrich was awarded the Knight's Cross of the Iron Cross for actions in this campaign. The *Leibstandarte* was later employed in Yugoslavia, and then conducted a brief but costly campaign in Greece and pressed on into the Soviet Balkans, where he was awarded the Oakleaves, becoming the 41st recipient. The *Leibstandarte* fought on the Russian Front, often with heavy casualties, and for these activities he was awarded the Swords. His unit was transferred to France in 1944 where he was to achieve his greatest level of recognition.

While commanding I SS Panzer Corps his units were engaged in a bitterly contested two-month battle in the Caen region. In recognition of the bravery of his troops Hitler awarded him the Diamonds, making him the 16th recipient. He assumed command of the 6th SS Panzer Army and his units fought during the Ardennes Offensive. It is still remembered for incidents such as the Malmédy Massacre, when some of Dietrich's troops shot US prisoners of war. As the war closed, his units again turned eastwards, this time with the hope of halting the tide of the 3rd US Army through Austria. Eventually Dietrich's forces surrendered to the Americans.

After the war, 'Sepp' Dietrich was imprisoned in Landsberg and tried for the Malmédy Massacre. He was given a 25-year sentence on 16 May 1946. Released in 1956, he was re-arrested for complicity in the murder of Ernst Röhm. He served a further 18 months, was released and died in Ludwigsburg in April 1966.

DIETRICH, Dr Otto

RANK: SS-Obergruppenführer
BORN: 31 August 1897
DIED: 22 November 1952 (D)
PARTY NUMBER: 126727
SS NUMBER: 101349
AWARDS: 1914 Iron Cross Second Class; 1914 Iron Cross First Class; Cross of Honour 1914-1918 Combatants; Golden Party Badge; SS Honour Ring; SS Honour Sword.

Otto Dietrich graduated as a doctor after serving in World War I, turning to news work as Munich representative for several large newspapers, which brought him into contact with the NSDAP. He was appointed press chief of the NSDAP in 1931, and from 1937 was Göbbel's state secretary in the Ministry of Propaganda.

Time and again, he showed extraordinary talent for fabrication and dissimulation. He devised the 'editor's law', which made each editor responsible for any anti-Nazi articles in their papers. After the Röhm purge he eloquently described Hitler's shock at the moral degeneracy of the old comrades he had liquidated. When Hess (q.v.) flew to Scotland, Dietrich reported his death in an accident over enemy territory. In October 1941, Dietrich boasted that 'Soviet Russia is done with and the British dream of war on two fronts is dead.'

This pronouncement ultimately proved fallacious, and cast a shadow over Nazi propaganda. Hitler dismissed him from his position of President of the Reich Press Chamber in March 1945. He was tried at Nuremberg by a military tribunal in 1949, being sentenced to seven year's imprisonment. He was released from Landsberg Prison in December 1949 and died in Düsseldorf in 1952.

DING, Dr Erwin

RANK: SS-Sturmbannführer
BORN: 19 September 1912
DIED: 1945 (S)
PARTY NUMBER: 1318211
SS NUMBER: 280163
AWARDS: 1939 Iron Cross Second Class; SS Honour Ring; SS Honour Sword.

Before the war Ding had served as a surgeon in the SS-*Totenkopf* Verband and as camp physician in Buchenwald concentration camp. In October 1939 he was transferred to the *Totenkopf* Division as adjutant to the chief surgeon of the division and remained with the unit until August 1940. He joined the staff of the Hygiene Institute of the Waffen-SS and was assigned the job of organising and conducting the infamous typhus experiments carried out on prisoners at Buchenwald in 1942 and 1943. As a result of his experiments with injections of typhus bacilli, Ding was responsible for the deaths of nearly 600 inmates at the Buchenwald camp. After being arrested and charged by the American military authorities in 1945, he committed suicide before being brought to trial.

DIRLEWANGER, Dr Oskar

RANK: SS-Oberführer
BORN: 26 September 1895
DIED: 7 June 1945 (M)
PARTY NUMBER: 1098716
SS NUMBER: 357267
AWARDS: 1914 Iron Cross Second Class; 1914 Iron Cross First Class; Knight's Cross 30 September 1944; 1939 Iron Cross Second Class Bar, 24 May 1942; 1939 Iron Cross First Class Bar, 16 September 1942; German Cross in Gold, 5 December 1943; Knight's Cross of

the Iron Cross, 30 September 1944; Close Combat Clasp Bronze Class; Slovakia – War Victory Cross Order First Class with Swords.

Dirlewanger, a totally unsavoury character, was born in Würzburg, Franconia. He was a former member of a Freikorps unit and later joined the French Foreign Legion. Gaoled for sex crimes in 1935, on his release he volunteered for the Condor Legion in the Spanish Civil War. He approached the head of the SS recruitment office, Gottlob Berger (q.v.), and suggested that a special unit be set up to recruit convicted criminals incarcerated in concentration and penal camps, thus enabling felons to atone for their crimes. This unit, which was to be a Sonderkommando, was responsible for operations against the partisans in Eastern Europe from 1942. Its reputation became notorious, peopled as the division was by murderers, rapists and other criminals. The brigade was most notorious for its actions in Warsaw during the Polish Uprising. Dirlewanger apparently entertained the officers of his mess with the death struggles of Jewish girls to whom he had given strychnine injections. At the end of the war all the members of his brigade were executed by the Russians. Dirlewanger's fate is unclear. He was either killed by former brigade members or concentration camp inmates in 1945 at Altshausen. He is buried in the local cemetery.

DYCK, Anton van

RANK: SS-Untersturmführer
PARTY NUMBER: —
SS NUMBER: —
AWARDS: 1939 Iron Cross Second Class; War Merit Cross Second Class with Swords, 4 April 1942.

Van Dyck was born in Belgium, the son of a fervent Flemish nationalist. The Flemish equivalent of the German Allgemeine-SS was established in Antwerp in September 1940. Anton van Dyck was adjutant to Jef van der Wiele, leader of the Flemish SS, and served with the 1st Freiwilligen Legion Flandern. He was also adjutant to Jef François. He was leader of the Germanic SS in Flanders from 9 November 1943 to 15 September 1944. He was the first Fleming to be awarded the Iron Cross when he was only 20 years old. On 23 December 1943, he married Ingeborg Scharl in an SS wedding service that took place in the Hall of Pacification in Ghent. It is also reported that a further ceremony was held on the 20 May 1944 in Munich. One of his last missions was on 14 February 1945 to Bad Saran, looking for men to join the Langemark Regiment.

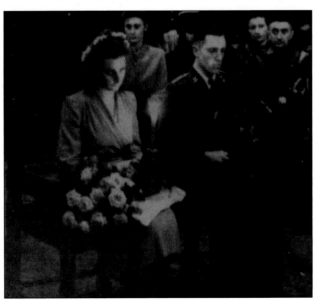

E

EBERSTEIN, (Friedrich) Karl von

RANK: SS-Obergruppenführer
BORN: 14 January 1894
DIED: 10 February 1979 (D)
PARTY NUMBER: 15067
SS NUMBER: 1386
AWARDS: Golden Party Badge; 1914 Iron Cross Second Class; 1914 Iron Cross First Class; Cross of Honour 1914-1918 Combatants; War Merit Cross Second Class with Swords; War Merit Cross First Class with Swords; SS Honour Ring; SS Honour Sword.

Von Eberstein was an early member of the SS, joining in 1928. Lina von Osten enlisted his help to bring Heydrich (q.v.) to Himmler's (q.v.) notice, which he did on 14 June 1931. In 1934, he was the commander of the SS Higher Section for Dresden. At the time of the Röhm Purge, it appeared that Himmler was fermenting discord between the army and the SA in order to incite the two factions into rebelling against one another. To this end, he ordered Eberstein to muster his men in an army barracks and to keep contact with the military area command, thus strengthening Himmler's position against the SA. This worked to Himmler's advantage, in that the SS came through the 'Night of the Long Knives' as the dominant force and their loyalty endeared them to Hitler. The purge effectively emasculated the SA, and it appears that at least 1000 people lost their lives as a result of the action. The SA was commanded by Victor Lutze after Röhm's death, but he quickly became a minor Nazi Party figure. Eberstein himself became Higher SS and Police leader for Munich, and the spokesman for the SS at Nuremberg.

EICHMANN, Adolf

RANK: SS-Obersturmbannführer
BORN: 19 March 1906
DIED: 31 May 1962 (E.A.)
PARTY NUMBER: 899895
SS NUMBER: 45326
AWARDS: War Merit Cross Second Class with Swords; SS Honour Ring.

Fanatically anti-Semitic, Eichmann was born in Solingen and educated in Linz, Austria. He became a travelling salesman and member of the Austrian Nazi party soon after leaving school. As a party activist he was forced to move to Germany in 1932. Here he wrote for Der Stürmer, an anti-Semitic newspaper, and afterwards joined the SD as a Jewish affairs expert. He visited Palestine in 1937 to meet Arab leaders, but the British mandate police deported him. Initially, he favoured the Zionists as a means of encouraging Jews to leave Europe, but this became totally impractical as immigration quotas for Palestine were vastly over-subscribed.

Eichmann was Head of Gestapo Section IV BG in 1941, the department of Jewish affairs. At the Wannsee Conference on 12 January 1942, which introduced the 'Final Solution', the programme to eliminate all Jews, Eichmann pedantically took down the agenda. He obtained the final decree, signed by Bormann (q.v.), which deprived Jews of all rights of appeal, on 1 July 1943. Eichmann organised the transportation to the camps and had gas chambers installed, as the most efficient method of killing. He viewed the extermination of the Jewish race as his chief ambition in life. In the spring and summer of 1944, for example, he took an avid part in the transportation of Hungarian Jews to Auschwitz, 400,000 of them dying there.

There were rumours that Eichmann had Jewish relations, even a Jewish mistress when he lived in Vienna. His whereabouts at the end of the war and his escape from an American internment camp to South America, using a Vatican passport under the name of 'Ricardo Klement',

are confused. His reported involvement with American and British intelligence is unsubstantiated, but highly probable. He settled in Buenos Aires in 1950 and it was here that he was discovered and kidnapped by Israeli agents in 1960. He stood trial in Israel, where his confession under intense interrogation was characteristically full and factual – ever the good bureaucrat – running to some 3500 pages. He was found guilty of crimes against humanity and hanged at Ramle on 31 May 1962.

EICKE, Theodor

RANK: SS-Obergruppenführer und General der Waffen-SS
BORN: 17 October 1892
DIED: 26 February 1943 (K.I.A.)
PARTY NUMBER: 114901
SS NUMBER: 2921
AWARDS: 1914 Iron Cross Second Class; Cross of Honour 1914-1918 Combatants; 1939 Iron Cross Second Class Bar, 26 May 1940; 1939 Iron Cross First Class, 31 May 1940; Knight's Cross, 26 December 1941; Oakleaves, 20 April 1942; SS Honour Ring; SS Honour Sword.

One of the most infamous Waffen-SS divisional commanders, Eicke was born in Huedingen, Alsace-Lorraine. He was an army paymaster in World War I, subsequently joining the Freikorps and fighting the Polish incursions on Germany's eastern borders. Employed by I. G. Farben as an industrial counter-espionage agent in 1923, he joined the police in 1927, but was dismissed the following year for his outspoken comments about the French occupying forces and the Weimar Republic. He joined the NSDAP as an SA man, transferring to the SS and rising to command an SS regiment in Rhein-Palatinate. He was sentenced to two years imprisonment in March 1932 for his part in bombing political opponents, but fled to Italy, returning the following year when Hitler assumed power.

Eicke was a key figure in the liquidation of Röhm and his supporters, shooting Röhm at midday on 1 July 1934 in his cell at Stadelheim prison after Röhm had refused to shoot himself. In the summer of that year, and as a direct result of the Röhm Putsch, most of the unofficial camps were closed. The remaining SA camps were removed from the jurisdiction of the civil authorities and taken over by the SS. The first full-time SS concentration camp unit was recruited from members of the Allgemeine-SS and was entirely under the overall command of the SS district south, who made it a depository for its unwanted personnel. The conditions that the guards lived under were little better than the inmates. In June 1933, Eicke took command. He improved conditions, lifted the morale and discipline of his men and formulated service regulations for both guards and prisoners which remained virtually unchanged until the end of the war. In recognition Himmler, in 1934, appointed him Inspector of Concentration Camps and Head of the SS Totenkopf Verbände, the unit created specifically to guard the increasing numbers of concentration camp inmates.

By the end of 1938 Eicke's men had all received some basic military training. When World War II broke out, he formed a division from the Totenkopf units, undergoing further military training at Obermünsigen Württemberg during the winter of 1939. It saw action in northern France during the 1940 campaign, but Eicke was unhappy that it was not properly deployed by army command. The Totenkopf Division fought in Russia, distinguishing itself and its leader at Demjansk. Fighting in the pocket was severe and losses were heavy on both sides.

The Totenkopf lost 7000 men between December 1941 and mid-March 1942. What was worse, the division was held at the front until October 1942, continually trying to defeat the Russian attacks thrown against it. This it managed to do, but in the process being decimated. In one action, for example, the division lost over 1000 men in a matter of hours in the face of a furious Red Army assault. By the time of its withdrawal the *Totenkopf* numbered 6400 men.

On 26 February 1943, Eicke was on an inspection flight in a Fiesler Stork when he was shot down, crashing behind enemy lines. He was idolised by his men, who recovered his body with the loss of several lives. He was given a Viking-style burial at a divisional cemetery near Orelka, Russia.

ERBPRINZ ZU WALDECK UND PYRMONT, Josias
RANK: SS-Obergruppenführer
BORN: 13 May 1896
DIED: December 1967 (D)
PARTY NUMBER: 160025
SS NUMBER: 2139
AWARDS: Golden Party Badge; 1914 Iron Cross Second Class; 1914 Iron Cross First Class; Cross of Honour 1914-18 Combatants; 1914 Wound Badge Black Class; 1939 Iron Cross Second Class Bar; 1939 Iron Cross First Class Bar; SS Honour Ring; SS Honour Sword.

Himmler's (q.v.) first 'blue-blooded' recruit joined the SS in 1928 and witnessed the executions of Röhm's supporters in Munich. Unlike Hitler, Himmler was not anti-royalist and made his attacks on the nobility begrudgingly; thus the prince remained in office as SS Police Leader in Kassel-Mainfranken until May 1945.

With jurisdiction over Buchenwald concentration camp, Waldeck was arrested at the end of the war, and on 11 April 1947 the trials of the Buchenwald staff opened at Dachau. Waldeck was one of the main defendants and the only member of a German princely house to be tried for war crimes. He was held responsible for the appalling conditions that had prevailed there, was found guilty and sentenced to life imprisonment – some would say a lenient sentence. Released in December 1960, he died seven years later in Schaumburg.

F

FEGELEIN, Hermann Otto
RANK: SS-Gruppenführer und Generalleutnant der Waffen-SS
BORN: 30 October 1906
DIED: 29 April 1945 (E.R.)
PARTY NUMBER: 1200158
SS NUMBER: 66680
AWARDS: 1939 Iron Cross Second Class, 15 December 1940; 1939 Iron Cross First Class, 28 June 1941; Knight's Cross of the Iron Cross, 2 March 1942; Oakleaves, 25 December 1942; Oakleaves with Swords, 30 July 1944; 1939 Wound Badge Black Class; 1939 Wound Badge Silver Class; '20 July 1944' Wound Badge Silver Class; German Cross in Gold, 1 November 1943; Close Combat Bar in Silver, 5 December 1943; War Merit Cross Second Class Bronze with Swords; Medal for the Winter Campaign in Russia 1941-1942, 1 April 1942; German Horseman's Badge Gold; SS Honour Ring; SS Honour Sword.

A career soldier, Fegelein enlisted in the 17th Cavalry Regiment in 1925. He served briefly in the Freikorps Rossbach and also with the Bavarian State Police. On 1 March 1933, he joined the cavalry branch of the SS. He rode in professional competitions and represented Germany as a member of the equestrian team at the 1936 Olympics. On 12 January 1939, Hermann Fegelein, with other members of the SS show-jumping team, Temme-Waldemar, were interviewed in front of German cameras with their horse Firster. Fegelein became an adjutant attached to the SS District South and eventually commanded the SS cavalry school at Munich. He formed the first Waffen-SS cavalry units from reinforced SS-*Totenkopf* Verbände in Warsaw.

Apart from serving in the Polish campaign in 1939, all Fegelein's service was on the Russian Front, where he was involved in actions against Red Army units and partisans. When Germany attacked the Soviet Union in June 1941, thousands of Russian soldiers managed to evade capture and fled into the swamps and dense forests. Operating from

these refuges they began to threaten German supply lines and soon represented a formidable challenge to the German war effort. Army Group Centre formed special units to fight the partisans, consisting of the SS Cavalry Brigade, the 1st and 2nd SS Infantry Brigades, and some smaller army and police units. After several months of fierce and bloody fighting, during which both sides sustained heavy losses, the supply lines were made safe. Field Marshal Model awarded Fegelein and his unit a citation for actions in support of Army Group Centre, and Fegelein himself received the Knight's Cross of the Iron Cross. Wounded three times during these actions, Fegelein's most famous injury occurred during the attempted assassination of Hitler on 20 July 1944, when he was serving as Himmler's (q.v.) personal adjutant to Hitler. Fegelein had married Eva Braun's sister, Margarete, on 3 June 1944, just one month earlier. Afterwards he returned to the Russian Front in command of the 8th SS Kavallerie Division *Florian Geyer*, then returned to serve once again as SS-adjutant at Hitler's headquarters.

At the end of the war he was in the Berlin bunker with Hitler and his immediate entourage. On 27 April 1945, Fegelein vanished from the bunker; once aware of his absence, Hitler ordered a search. The Gestapo arrested him at his home in Berlin under suspicious circumstances: he was in civilian dress and had on his person a large amount of Swiss francs and jewellery. He was returned to the bunker and here Hitler, who had begun to doubt Himmler's loyalty, turned his vengeance upon Fegelein, who ardently protested his innocence. Eva pleaded for her brother-in-law's life, pointing out that her sister was pregnant. Hitler acquiesced to her request and spared him, after rebuking him for his lack of courage. A few hours later the BBC reported that Himmler had offered to surrender the German Army unconditionally to the Allies. Hitler became uncontrollable, had Fegelein court-martialled, found guilty, and condemned to death for his perceived part in Himmler's disloyalty. However, Fegelein's disloyalty was most likely to his wife, for there were rumours that he intended to run off with a beautiful Hungarian girl. To exacerbate the situation further, some of the jewellery found upon him was believed to be Eva's, so she remained silent as Fegelein was escorted by an SS squad into the Chancellery garden where they executed him on 28 April 1945.

FELDMEIJER, Johannes Hendrik
RANK: SS-Standartenführer
BORN: 30 November 1910
DIED: 22 February 1945 (K.I.A.)
PARTY NUMBER: —
SS NUMBER: 440001
AWARDS: 1939 Iron Cross Second Class; 1939 Wound Badge Black Class; SS Honour Ring.

A Dutchman, Feldmeijer joined the NSB in 1932 and became director of NSB propaganda by 1936. The NSB (*Nationaal-Socialistische Beweging*) was founded on 14 December 1931 by civil engineer Anton Mussert, although clearly inspired by German example. It tried to stress its Dutch patriotism. In August 1939 Feldmeijer formed the 'Mussert Guard', the embryonic Dutch SS. In May 1940, together with other NSB leaders, he was arrested and imprisoned in France, but was freed after its fall. Feldmeijer was one of Mussert's principal lieutenants, and it was at his instigation that the Dutch formed their own SS.

The *Nederländische-SS* was formed on 11 September 1940 as the contemporary of the German Allgemeine-SS. It adopted the same black uniform and the same system of ranks, although Feldmeijer held the unique rank of Voorman which had no SS equivalent. In March 1943 this was changed to Standartenführer, however. No facilities existed for training, and initially the recruits were obliged to go to Germany for instruction. In May 1941 a training school was opened at Auegoor near Arnhem. On 1 November 1942, the title was changed to the more general term 'Germanic SS in Holland', thus loosening the ties between it and the NSB. It was now a part of a larger non-German Teutonic SS movement, which embraced all the so-called Nordic countries.

Feldmeijer worked with Rauter (q.v.) to undermine the position of the Dutch Nazi leader, Mussert, but as Feldmeijer was neither forceful nor shrewd, Mussert survived relatively unscathed. Feldmeijer introduced the German SS concept of 'sponsoring members', i.e. civilians who paid a subscription of not less than 1 Florin per month, earning them the right to wear a badge of SS runes. By 1944 there were some 4000 sponsoring members.

Feldmeijer transferred to the Waffen-SS and saw service in the Balkans and Russia. He was killed in action on 22 February 1945.

FRANK, Karl Hermann

RANK: SS-Obergruppenführer
BORN: 24 January 1898
DIED: 22 May 1946 (E.A.)
PARTY NUMBER: 6600002
SS NUMBER: 310466
AWARDS: Golden Party Badge; War Merit Cross Second Class with Swords; War Merit Cross First Class with Swords; SS Honour Ring; SS Honour Sword.

Frank was a fanatical Sudeten-German Freikorps leader, as well as deputy leader of the Sudeten-German Party and adjutant to Henlein (q.v.). A close associate of Himmler (q.v.) during the Munich crisis of 1938, Frank was made head of the Czech police force after the German takeover as a reward for his loyalty, although this force was really a puppet of the SD. He became Higher SS and Police Leader, directly subordinate to Himmler, and was also a state secretary in the Ministry of the Interior. Following the assassination of Heydrich (q.v.), he was ordered to assume the functions of Protector, and it was in his name that the actions against the Czech people were carried out. He proclaimed martial law, arrested 3188 people and executed 1357, while a further 657 died under police interrogation. He also ordered the destruction of the villages of Lidice and Lezaky. Frank effectively continued to rule Bohemia and Moravia for the rest of the war, although Frick was nominally the protector. At the war's end he was arrested, tried by a Czech court and publicly hanged near Prague on 22 May 1946.

FREEMAN, Benson Railton Metcalf

RANK: SS-Untersturmführer
BORN: 6 October 1903
DIED: unknown
PARTY NUMBER: —
SS NUMBER: —

An Englishman, Freeman was commissioned in August 1924 into the Kings Own Royal Regiment as a second lieutenant. He later qualified as a fighter pilot, transferring to the RAF. In 1931 he retired, taking up farming, which gave him time to develop his political views, and in 1937 he joined the BUF (British Union of Fascists), remaining a member until September 1939.

Despite the conflict of loyalties produced by his political beliefs, Freeman returned to the RAF, assuming that he would hold a non-combatant position. On 22 May 1940, however, he was ordered to fly to Merville in France, where on landing the planes were destroyed by enemy air action. Freeman, accompanied by other RAF personnel, ordered a DC3 for England, only to be forced down by ground fire and

taken prisoner. He moved to a special camp established to extract information from newly captured air crew. However, it seems that his incarceration was due to his pro-Nazi views, and his position in the camp became increasingly uneasy; he was concerned to discover that air crews were being informed in briefings by MI9 that he was 'a German informer'. Eventually, after a number of heated disagreements with his fellow prisoners, he and a few others were asked to sign a document requesting their removal from the camp. He was eventually taken to Berlin to meet Rudolf Hess (q.v.), who asked him if he was prepared to help in the 'promotion of peace and the frustration of Bolshevist plans'. Freeman agreed.

In June 1942 he became a propagandist and the next two years were a disaster for him and his employers. In September 1944 a chance meeting with d'Alquen (q.v.) at a social function in Berlin changed his resolve. Taking a liking to Freeman and holding similar views on the likelihood of the German defeat in the East, d'Alquen offered him a commission in the 'Kurt Eggers Regiment'. Freeman joined the Waffen-SS in October 1944, where he made a declaration that he was 'an Englishman of Aryan descent and has never, neither now nor previously, been a member of a freemasons lodge nor any other secret society.' He was not required to command troops, but to vet propaganda material.

By the end of April 1945 d'Alquen decided to evacuate his remaining staff from Berlin. With his deputy, Sturmbannführer Anton Kriegbaum, American SS-Hauptsturmführer Ackermann and Freeman, he commandeered three Storch planes and flew to Lenggries in southwest Germany. Pressurised to fly to Switzerland, Freeman refused and subsequently surrendered to American forces on 9 May. He was court-martialled, receiving a sentence of 10 years.

G

GLOBOCNIK, Odilo

RANK: SS-Gruppenführer
BORN: 21 April 1904
DIED: 31 May 1945 (S)
PARTY NUMBER: 442939
SS NUMBER: 292776
AWARDS: Golden Party Badge; 1939 Iron Cross Second Class; 1939 Iron Cross First Class; War Merit Cross Second Class with Swords; War Merit Cross First Class with Swords; SS Honour Ring; SS Honour Sword.

A vicious character, Globocnik was born in Trieste, Italy, and emigrated to Austria in 1918. In 1922 he joined the NSDAP, holding a number of posts in the Austrian party. He joined the SS in 1933 and later that year was promoted to Deputy Gauleiter of Austria, despite his involvement in a murderous jewellery robbery in the suburbs of Favoriten. He contributed to the Anschluss and after Austria's absorption into the Reich, was rewarded by being appointed State Secretary. For a short time from 24 May 1938, he was Gauleiter of Vienna, but this position was short-lived: he was dismissed in January 1939 for personal corruption and illegal speculations in foreign exchange.

This blight on his character curtailed Globocnik's career in the NSDAP, but the SS seemed totally unconcerned, and in September 1939 he became SS and Police Leader in Lublin. Himmler (q.v.) selected him for the job of liquidator of the Polish Jews. He became, by default, head of the death camp organisation, Abteilung Reinhard, and founded the line of extermination camps along the Bug river. Unstable to the point that he terrorised his own camp commanders, he publicly plundered his victims, and Frank's (q.v.) civil administration had to put up with this drunken sadist for four years. Himmler transferred him to Trieste as SS and Police Leader for the Adriatic coast. After the war he was taken prisoner by the British and he committed suicide in Weissensee in Corinthia.

GLÜCKS, Richard
RANK: SS-Gruppenführer
BORN: 22 April 1889
DIED: unknown
PARTY NUMBER: 214805
SS NUMBER: 58706
AWARDS: 1914 Iron Cross Second Class; 1914 Iron Cross First Class; Cross of Honour 1914-1918 Combatants; War Merit Cross Second Class with Swords; War Merit Cross First Class with Swords; SS Honour Ring; SS Honour Sword.

Glücks joined Theodor Eicke's (q.v.) staff in 1936 and was appointed to succeed him as inspector of concentration camps in 1939, a position he held until the war's end. He was last seen near the Danish border in May 1945 and thereafter vanished without trace. There is a story that Glücks ended up in a naval hospital working under a false name after the surrender.

GRAF, Ulrich
RANK: SS-Brigadeführer
BORN: 6 July 1878
DIED: 3 March 1950 (D)
PARTY NUMBER: 8
SS NUMBER: 26
AWARDS: Golden Party Badge; Coburg Badge 14 October 1932; Blood Order No 21; SS Honour Ring; SS Honour Sword.

Graf was born in Pachhagel, Dillingen-Donau, the son of a small farmer. He joined the army before his 18th birthday and served for several years. A roughneck and amateur wrestler, he held several jobs including one for the Munich council. He left his job as a butcher to become Hitler's personal bodyguard, afterwards forming the Stosstrupp with eight others. He was on the Coburg expedition that broke the communist hold on the city, which provided the impetus for the 1923 Putsch. He was at Hitler's side when the police opened fire, and he jumped in front of him, stopping five bullets that left him critically wounded, but undoubtedly saving Hitler's life. From 1 January 1925 until it was dissolved in 1933, he was a Munich town councillor. He was made a freeman of his home town in 1934, and in 1935 Hitler appointed him Munich Alderman. In 1936 he was elected to the Reichstag.

After the war he served five years in a labour camp, a sentence his daughter thought unfair, blaming it for his death in 1950.

GRAWITZ, Prof Dr Ernst-Robert
RANK: SS-Obergruppenführer
BORN: 8 June 1899
DIED: April 1945 (S)
PARTY NUMBER: 1102844
SS NUMBER: 27483
AWARDS: 1914 Iron Cross Second Class; Cross of Honour 1914-1918 Combatants; 1939 Iron Cross Second Class Bar; War Merit Cross Second Class with Swords; War Merit Cross First Class with Swords; SS Honour Ring; SS Honour Sword.

Head of the SS medical services from 1936 until the end of the war, and controller of the German Red Cross, Grawitz worked with Dr Herbert Linden of the health ministry, and under Brandt (q.v.) and Bouhler (q.v.), to choose doctors for leadership roles. Their criteria included the closeness of these doctors to the regime, high recognition in the profession and known sympathy for euthanasia or a radical approach to it.

Despite a rift with Himmler (q.v.), when his favourite general Bach-Zelewski (q.v.) suffered a nervous breakdown after his experience with the killings in Russia, Grawitz remained a trusted adviser. He recommended the use of gas chambers as the most efficient method of mass killing. The methods of selection for work or death in the camps were largely laid down by Grawitz, who held the view that only those Jews completely fit and able to work should be selected for employment. The weak, the old and those who were only relatively robust would quickly become incapable, causing a further deterioration in their health and an unnecessary need for an increase in hospital accommodation. Further medical personnel and medicines would be required, all for no purpose, since the Jews would have to be killed in the end. Grawitz committed suicide in April 1945.

GREISER, Arthur
RANK: SS-Obergruppenführer, Gauleiter of Warthegau 1939-45
BORN: 22 January 1897
DIED: 21 July 1946 (E.A.)
PARTY NUMBER: 166635
SS NUMBER: 10795
AWARDS: 1914 Iron Cross Second Class; 1914 Iron Cross First Class; Cross of Honour 1914-1918 Combatants; 1914 Wound Badge Black Class; Golden Party Badge; SS Honour Ring; SS Honour Sword.

Greiser was a pilot during World War I and co-founded the Stahlhem, the war veterans' organisation in Danzig. In 1929, he joined the NSDAP and became president of the Danzig senate. With the absorption of Danzig into Greater Germany in September 1939, and the invasion of Poland, he was rewarded by being appointed Gauleiter of the new Gau Warthegau, which was renamed Wartheland in 1940. He held this position until the war's end. On the 25 May 1945, SS-Obergruppenführer Heinz Reinefarth and Arthur Greiser surrendered to the Americans in Austria, probably thinking they would be treated less harshly. He was extradited to Poland, where he was tried, found guilty of war crimes and hanged at Poznan.

GRESE, Irma
RANK: SS-Helferinnen
BORN: 7 October 1923
DIED: 13 December 1945 (E.A.)

Having joined the SS when she was 18, Grese's first appointment was to supervise women prisoners at the Auschwitz concentration camp. A 19-year-old sadist, she was promoted to control blocks of women prisoners. She was known there as the 'angel of Birkenau'. It has been reported that she was lover to both Mengele and SS-Sturmbannfuhrer Karl Mummenthey. When Auschwitz closed, she was transferred to Bergen-Belsen to oversee the female quarters. When the camp was liberated in April 1945 she was captured and charged with war crimes. A British military court sat between 17 September and 17 November, trying 45 former staff members; 14 were acquitted, 19 sentenced to varying terms of imprisonment and 11 executed. Grese was numbered nine during the trial and found guilty. She fervently denied up to the end that she had ever ill-treated detainees, all to no avail. She was hanged on the 12 December 1945.

GRIMMINGER, Jakob

RANK: SS-Standartenführer
BORN: 25 April 1892
DIED: 28 January 1969 (D)
PARTY NUMBER: 759
SS NUMBER: 135
AWARDS: 1914 Iron Cross Second Class; Cross of Honour 1914-1918
Combatants; Golden Party Badge; Coburg Badge 14 October 1932;
Blood Order No 714, 9 November 1923; Turkey Iron Half Moon
First Class; SS Honour Ring; SS Honour Sword.

Grimminger served honourably in World War I and joined the NSDAP
soon after, becoming an early party member. He took part in the 1923
Putsch and was in 10 Company, SA Regiment Munich. He was appointed
standard-bearer of the hallowed blood flag which had been carried on
the march and was spattered with the blood of the fallen. About 2000
took part in the march to the centre of Munich, but they were stopped
by police, who blocked their path. The police opened fire and both Hitler
and Göring were wounded. All in all it was a rather feeble and ill-planned
attempt to take control in Bavaria and Germany. However, it did provide
the Nazis with publicity. The flag became the spiritual icon of the Nazi
Party, and each new standard was consecrated by being ritually touched
by the blood flag at the presentation ceremony. Grimminger became a
Munich city councillor, but after the war he faded into obscurity and
died in Munich in poverty.

GROTHMANN, Werner

RANK: SS Obersturmbannführer
BORN: 23 August 1915
DIED: unknown
PARTY NUMBER: —
SS NUMBER: 181334
AWARDS: 1939 Iron Cross Second Class; 1939 Iron Cross First Class;
SS Honour Ring; SS Honour Sword.

Grothmann succeeded Karl Wolff (q.v.) as Himmler's (q.v.) military
adjutant in 1943. Grothmann could best be described as an 'old hand at
court'. He was with Himmler when he tried to escape in an ill-conceived
disguise, and was apprehended on 23 May 1945 by the British authorities. Why Himmler revealed himself to the British is still a mystery,
but one theory is that Grothmann and Himmler's secretary, perceiving
the futility of Himmler's plans, were going to turn him in anyway.

GRÜNEWALD, Adam

RANK: SS-Sturmbannführer
BORN: 20 October 1902
DIED: January 1945 (K.I.A.)
PARTY NUMBER: 536404
SS NUMBER: 253631
AWARDS: SS Honour Ring; SS Honour Sword.

Before the war Grünewald served as commander of the Dachau detention centre and was an administrative officer in the *Totenkopfverbande*.
He was transferred to the new SS-TK at the beginning of the war and
was appointed to command the bakery company. He executed this assignment well enough to be promoted to command the division's procurement service, and remained with the *Totenkopf* Division from November
1939 until October 1942. He was reassigned to camp duty as commander
of the detention centre at Oranienburg, a post he held until January 1943,
when he was moved up to the larger assignment of commandant of the
huge concentration camp and deportation centre in Vught in occupied
Holland.

Grünewald's stewardship of Vught became unusually notorious,
and in early 1944 an SS investigation revealed that he had sanctioned
especially brutal treatment of prisoners, allowing such overcrowding
in the camp's detention cells that the unsanitary conditions killed a
number of women political detainees. Grünewald was removed from his
command and court-martialled at Himmler's express order. As punish-

ment he was demoted to the rank of SS private and sentenced in April
1944 to an indefinite term of combat with the *Totenkopf* Division. While
fighting with the division in Hungary in January 1945, Grünewald was
killed in action fighting the Russians.

GÜNSCHE, Otto

RANK: SS-Sturmbannführer
BORN: 1917
DIED: 2 March 2003
PARTY NUMBER: —
SS NUMBER: 257773
AWARDS: 1939 Iron Cross Second Class; 1939 Iron Cross First Class;
War Merit Cross Second Class with Swords; Wound Badge '20 July
1944' Black Class; Army Long Service Medal 4 Years' Service;
Golden Hitler Youth Honour Badge; Commemorative Medal of 13
March 1938; Commemorative Medal of 1 October 1938; Prague
Castle Bar; Commemorative Medal For The Return Of The Memel
Region; German Defence Medal; Infantry Assault Badge.

Günsche joined the SS Begleit-
Kommando on 1 May 1936, the unit
tasked with protecting Hitler. From 1940
until 1941, he was employed as an SS
ordnance officer, followed by training
and active service. In January 1943, he
was appointed personal adjutant and
served with Fritz Darges (q.v.) until
August of that year, when he returned
to active service. Appointed as Hitler's
personal adjutant in March 1944, he was
injured in the 20 July Bomb Plot, suffer-
ing lacerations to his head and seared eyebrows. Notwithstanding his own
state, he helped Hitler to stumble from the shattered building.

Günsche remained in this job until the end of the war, and one of
his last duties was, on Hitler's express orders, to see to the destruction
of the couple's bodies. Hitler had informed him that he and Eva were
committing suicide and told him to 'be sure to burn our bodies. I don't
want to be put on display in some Russian waxworks.' Günsche was
the first person to see his body and helped to incinerate it. He attempted
to escape Berlin, but was arrested by the Soviets and imprisoned for 10
years. He died of heart failure at his home in Lohmar, Germany, on
2 March 2003.

H

HANKE, Karl

RANK: SS-Obergruppenführer, Gauleiter of Lower Silesia 1940–45
BORN: 24 August 1903
DIED: 1945 (M)
PARTY NUMBER: 102606
SS NUMBER: 203013
AWARDS: German Order, 12 April 1945; SS Honour Ring; SS
Honour Sword.

Hanke's first key position in the NSDAP was as personal adjutant to
Göbbels in the Propaganda Ministry. He paid court to Magda, Göbbels'
wife, while his boss was having a liaison with Lida Baarova, a Czech
film star, although both affairs were broken off at Hitler's insistence.
Promoted to State Secretary in the Propaganda Ministry, Hanke joined
the army at the beginning of the war.

He was attached to Erwin Rommel's staff in the French campaign
of 1940, and although not a career soldier, fought courageously enough.
He was recommended for the Knight's Cross of the Iron Cross by
Rommel himself, but this recommendation was subsequently withdrawn
because of some unpleasant remarks Hanke had made. He was released
from military service at the end of 1940.

Still not in favour in Berlin, Hanke was appointed Gauleiter of
Niedersachsen, Lower Silesia, a position he held until the end of the

war. In the closing weeks of the war he conducted the defence of Breslau, and on 12 April 1945 was awarded the party's and state's highest decoration, the German Order, referred to in the announcement as the 'Golden Cross of the German Order'. Soon after he flew from besieged Breslau, ostensibly to take up his appointment with Dönitz in Flensburg, as he had been nominated in Hitler's will to succeed Himmler (q.v.) as Reichsführer-SS and head of the police. In fact, he flew by helicopter to find refuge at Field Marshal Schörner's headquarters at Kronenberg, and there to disguise himself. Three ends have been promulgated for him: first, that he was shot by Czech partisans while escaping from arrest soon after the capitulation in May 1945; second, that he was beaten to death by them; third, that he was executed by the Poles. No one knows for certain.

HARTJENSTEIN, Friedrich
RANK: SS-Sturmbannführer
BORN: 3 July 1905
DIED: 1954 (D)
PARTY NUMBER: —
SS NUMBER: 327350
AWARDS: 1939 Iron Cross Second Class; 1939 Iron Cross First Class; SS Honour Ring; SS Honour Sword.

Having seen extensive duty in the reserve *Totenkopf* regiments, Hartjenstein was transferred in March 1940 to the *Totenkopf* Division where, by October 1941, he had served successively as a company commander and staff officer. The *Totenkopf* Division's officer corps was depleted during the first summer of the Russian campaign, leading Eicke (q.v.) to give Hartjenstein command of the 1st Battalion of Infantry Regiment 3. The results were disastrous, and Hartjenstein proved totally unfit to command an infantry battalion. His incompetence led to the severe mauling of his unit during the spring of 1942. Eicke had no option but to relieve him of his command in late August and transfer him to camp duties.

Hartjenstein was given command of the SS guard detachment at Auschwitz, where he evidently redeemed himself, as on 10 March 1943 he was promoted to commandant of Birkenau extermination camp, the main liquidation centre within the Auschwitz complex. Birkenau had a railway siding disguised as a railway station – though in every sense it was the end of the line. It started operations in 1941 as a speedily built camp for the extermination of Russian prisoners of war. Hartjenstein held this position until May 1944, when Himmler (q.v.) transferred him to command the large slave labour camp of Natzweiler in Alsace in recognition of his outstanding service. He was captured by the French in 1945 and a military tribunal found him guilty of mass murder of prisoners in Natzweiler. He was condemned to death, but while this sentence was under appeal in 1954 he died of a heart attack in prison in Metz.

HAUSSER, Paul
RANK: SS-Oberstgruppenführer und Generaloberst der Waffen-SS
BORN: 7 October 1880
DIED: 21 December 1972 (D)
PARTY NUMBER: 4158779
SS NUMBER: 239795
AWARDS: 1914 Iron Cross Second Class; 1914 Iron Cross First Class; Cross of Honour 1914-1918 Combatants; 1939 Iron Cross Second Class Bar, September 1939; 1939 Iron Cross First Class Bar, 17 May 1940; Knight's Cross, 8 August 1941; Oakleaves, 28 July 1943; Oakleaves with Swords, 26 August 1944; 1939 Wound Badge Silver; SS Honour Ring; SS Honour Sword.

Hausser entered military service as a cadet, and was commissioned prior to the outbreak of World War I, when he served as a line and staff officer. In 1932 he retired from the Reichswehr as a major -general, only to be reactivated in 1934 when he joined the SS-*Verfügungstruppe*. He was made inspector of that organisation in 1936, bringing outstanding qualities of leadership to the job, and formulating the directives and codes of practice it was to use. Known as 'Papa' Hausser by his men,

Paul Hausser made a remarkable impact on the SS. Hausser was engaged in combat from the start in Poland and France. The *Das Reich* Division was transferred to the Russian Front where, as a Generalleutnant of the Waffen-SS attached to Army Group Centre, he earned the Knight's Cross of the Iron Cross. He was severely wounded two months later, losing his eye; the black eye patch he sported afterwards became his trademark on and off the battlefield.

His military endeavours were remarkable. The Russian offensive of early 1943 took Kursk and threatened Kharkov. Hitler ordered Hausser, in command of II SS Panzer Corps, to hold the city at all costs. However, Hausser realised that to get trapped inside the city would mean annihilation. On 15 February, therefore, he abandoned the city, but in a brilliant counterattack he retook it in March. His actions undoubtedly saved the Waffen-SS corps and inflicted a massive defeat on the Red Army. It was also a badly needed morale booster following the debacle at Stalingrad. For actions such as these on the Russian Front, and while serving as II SS Panzer Corps commander, he was awarded the Oakleaves, becoming the 216th recipient (though Hitler did delay four months before eventually including him in the Kharkov medal winners).

When German forces were threatened with encirclement by the Allies in the Falaise Gap in 1944, Hausser effectively led the breakout, and he was again severely wounded. His bravery earned him the Oakleaves with Swords, of which he was the 90th recipient. During the closing months of the war he commanded Army Group G until his capture in April 1945. He died at Ludwigsburg in December 1972.

HENLEIN, Konrad
RANK: SS-Obergruppenführer
BORN: 6 May 1898
DIED: 10 May 1945 (S)
PARTY NUMBER: 6600001
SS NUMBER: 310307
AWARDS: Golden Party Badge; Cross of Honour 1914-1918 Combatants; 1914 Wound Badge Black Class; War Merit Cross Second Class without Swords; War Merit Cross First Class without Swords; SS Honour Ring; SS Honour Sword.

A Bohemian who served in the Austrian Army during World War I, Henlein began his career as a bank clerk. In 1919 he became a gymnastics teacher in the recently formed Deutsche Turnerbund in the Sudetenland. It was to be as much a political and nationalist force as a physical training group, and he became its head in 1923. The Treaty of Versailles had reconstructed Europe creating new states and realigned borders, among which was Czechoslovakia. However, considerable numbers of ethnic Germans were left within the confines of the new country. These minorities were not always happy to accept their new national status, and their reluctance turned to militancy within neighbouring Germany during Hitler's rise to power. Discontent was deliberately encouraged as part of long-term Nazi strategy. Hitler saw the chance to expand into the region, enlarging his Empire and enriching it with all the important armaments and vehicle works that the region held. By 1933, Henlein had founded the Sudeten-German Party with an ideology and organisation based on that of the NSDAP.

Funded by the German Foreign Office, Henlein was used to ferment the crisis of 1938, visiting Germany between March and September for instructions. From July 1938, the German Army ran weekly, five-day courses Monday to Saturday at Neuhammer for *Freiwilliger Schutzdienst* men who secretly slipped out of and back into Czechoslovakia under the guise of holiday makers or travelling businessmen. In Germany they were instructed in the military arts. Each course comprised some 50 trainees, who at its conclusion took an oath of loyalty to Hitler. When the Czech Government offered to accede to all Sudeten German demands, Henlein broke off negotiations with them on a minor pretext (his group was used to foment the Sudeten crisis). Hitler made speeches threatening violence (a peaceful solution would not suit his aims), Sudeten leaders rose against the Czech Government, martial law was declared and Henlein fled to Germany. A Sudeten Freikorps was raised and supported by SS detachments, who occupied two frontier towns: the Sudeten uprising had begun. This was prevented only by the shameful 'Munich Agreement', by which Britain and France, without consulting or even informing the Czechs, turned over the entire Sudetenland to Hitler. Henlein was rewarded with the post of gauleiter after Hitler marched into Czechoslovakia in March 1939.

In early May 1945, he was captured by the US Seventh Army, and later committed suicide in an Allied internment camp at Pilsen, by slashing his wrists with a concealed razor blade.

HESS, Rudolf
RANK: SS-Obergruppenführer
BORN: 26 April 1894
DIED: 17 August 1987 (S)
PARTY NUMBER: 16
AWARDS: 1914 Iron Cross Second Class; Cross of Honour 1914-1918 Combatants; 1914 Wound Badge Black Class, 12 June 1916; Blood Order No 29, November 1923; SS Honour Ring.

Hess was born in Alexandria, Egypt, the son of a German merchant, and was educated in Switzerland and Hamburg. He served in the same regiment as Hitler during World War I. Later, he transferred to the Imperial Air Force as a lieutenant. With the end of the war he served in der Ritter von Epp in the Freikorps. Hess came under the influence of the geopolitical Professor Karl Haushofer while at university at Munich. His right-wing views, already formed, were seduced by the oratory of Hitler and he joined the NSDAP in 1920. He marched with Hitler in the 1923 Putsch and was imprisoned at Landsberg. The closeness of the two men occurred during this period, with Hitler dictating Mein Kampf to Hess.

On his release, Hess played a leading part in the reformation of the NSDAP. By 1932 he had been appointed chairman of the central political commission of the party. When Hitler assumed power Hess became Deputy Leader, and in June 1933 Reich Minister without Portfolio. In 1935 Hess was a selector of all senior Nazi officials. He was appointed a ministerial member for the defence of the Reich in 1939. For a man of very modest intellectual ability it was a meteoric rise in power.

By 1939, however, Hess had been eclipsed by the generals and admirals on one hand, and Göring and Himmler on the other. Hess felt himself estranged from Hitler and excluded from the centre of power.

His loyalty to Hitler prompted his flight to Britain on 10 May 1941, and he hoped, ultimately, to recover his position with the Führer. Hess believed a diplomatic coup was possible if he could have an audience with George VI, whom he might persuade to dismiss Churchill. Peace could then be made between the two countries and they could act in concert against a common enemy: Russia. Hess flew himself to Britain. On landing he gave his name as Captain Horn and asked to be escorted to the Duke of Hamilton, whom he had met at the 1936 Berlin Olympic Games.

He was incarcerated until 1945 and then tried at Nuremberg. Sentenced to life at Spandau, Hess committed suicide in 1987.

HEWEL, Walther
RANK: SS-Brigadeführer
BORN: 25 March 1904
DIED: 2 May 1945 (K.I.A.)
PARTY NUMBER: 3280789
SS NUMBER: 283985
AWARDS: Golden Party Badge; Blood Order No 90; Stosstrupp Adolf Hitler; 20 July Wound Badge Black Class; SS Honour Ring; SS Honour Sword.

Hewel's father was a wealthy conserves manufacturer whose business was ruined in the currency collapse after World War I. Hewel was an early Nazi member, taking part in the 1923 Putsch, after which he was jailed in Landsberg, where he is reputed to have corrected the final text of Mein Kampf. His part as a young student in the Putsch was conveniently forgotten for many years and he settled down as a planter in Sumatra, but he eventually succumbed to Hitler's appeals for his return.

By the beginning of the war Hewel's popularity with Hitler as a court entertainer had induced Ribbentrop (q.v.) to negotiate for his services, and he became Ribbentrop's foreign ministry representative at the Führer's headquarters. Although Hewel was far too timid to use his intimacy with the Führer to become another Bormann (q.v.), he had no scruples about advising Hitler without Ribbentrop's approval and Ribbentrop had to accept this unsatisfactory situation.

Hewel discovered that Himmler's *Abwehr* advisers had a better knowledge of Eastern European affairs than the foreign office. Hewel's recommendation for autonomy in the Baltic states, which had Himmler's (q.v.) approval, was rejected by Hitler. A right-wing coup had put Hungary under the quasi-fascist rule of Admiral Nicholas Horthy. In 1920, when he was appointed Regent, he had taken the Hungarians, albeit without great popular enthusiasm, into Hitler's 'crusade' against communism. His enthusiasm for the cause was wavering in 1944. Undaunted, Hewel put forward another SS proposal, this time with success, luring Admiral Horthy to Hitler's guest castle at Klessheim and there, with the threat of kidnapping, forcing him to accept a German occupational force in Hungary, consisting of Plenipotentiary Edmund Veesenmayer, (q.v.) a Higher SS Police Leader, a police force and garrison in the capital. The elderly regent agreed, appointing a pro-German cabinet and dismissing a number of generals.

Hewel was wounded with Hitler in the 20 July Bomb Plot. He probably died trying to escape from the bunker in May 1945, a fact confirmed by his wife, but his death is unsubstantiated.

HEYDE, Dr Werner
RANK: SS-Obersturmbannführer
BORN: 25 April 1902
DIED: 1961 (S)
PARTY NUMBER: 3068165
SS NUMBER: 276656
AWARDS: SS Honour Ring

Born in Lausitz, the son of a textile manufacturer, Heyde enlisted in the army at sixteen during the last months of World War I. At 18 he participated in the Kapp Putsch and then in a long series of organisations and events connected with radical nationalism and National Socialism. His early scholastic achievements did not continue when he attended Hoche's psychiatric lectures as a medical student during the early 1920s, but he developed into a competent, though unremarkable, psychiatrist.

Originally a ward physician, and eventually a clinical chief doctor in a psychiatric hospital, he joined the NSDAP on 1 May 1933. In 1935, he became leader of the Würzburg Office of Racial Politics and was appointed a full professor at Würzburg in 1939. His SS career really began when he formed a close relationship with one of his patients, Theodore Eicke (q.v.), who persuaded Heyde to join the party and, in 1936, to join the SS.

One of Heyde's assignments was the establishment of neuropsychiatric research and supervising psychiatric, neurological and heredity research on concentration camp prisoners. He was also a consulting neuropsychiatric expert for the Gestapo. In this capacity he was involved in secret activities, which probably included advice on torture methods used to induce prisoners to provide information, as well as psychiatric evaluations useful to the Gestapo. He was a central figure in the extermination programme, the structure of the deception of prisoners and the overall killing procedures.

After the war he was arrested but escaped, obtaining false papers, and had a number of jobs. Finally, using the alias 'Sawade', he obtained a position as a sports physician in a school near Kiel. He lived a flamboyant lifestyle and was subsequently exposed. He was arrested, but committed suicide in his cell in 1961 before the trial began.

HEYDRICH, Reinhard

RANK: SS-Obergruppenführer
BORN: 7 March 1904
DIED: 4 June 1942 (K.I.A.)
PARTY NUMBER: 544916
SS NUMBER: 10120
AWARDS: German Order (Posthumous), 9 June 1942; Blood Order No ? (Posthumous), 4 June 1942; Golden Party Badge; German Olympic Games Decoration First Class; German Social Welfare Decoration First Class; 1939 Iron Cross Second Class; 1939 Iron Cross First Class; Danzig Cross First Class; Pilot's Badge; Luftwaffe Reconnaissance, Air, Sea Rescue & Meteorological Clasp; Police Long Service Cross 18 years' service; NSDAP Long Service Medal 10 Years; Commemorative Medal of 13 March 1938; Commemorative Medal of 1 October 1938; Prague Castle Bar; Commemorative Medal for the Return of the Memel Region; German Defence Medal; Wound Badge; SS Honour Ring; SS Honour Sword.

A man of exceptional skills and talents, Heydrich was born in Halle, Saxony, the son of the founder of the Halle Conservatory. He inherited his musical ability from his father and could play the violin to concert pitch. With singular intellectual ability, he was also an accomplished sportsman, especially in the fields of fencing, sailing and swimming. In 1922, he joined the navy as a cadet and was under the orders and tutelage of Admiral Canaris. In April 1931, however, after allegations of dishonourable conduct towards a young lady who declared that he had impregnated her, he was brought before an honour-court, presided over by Canaris, which found him guilty and dismissed him from the service. Heydrich became engaged to Lina von Osten, who was to convert him to Nazism and he joined the NSDAP in 1931. Lina enlisted the help of Friedrich Karl von Eberstein (q.v.) to bring him to Himmler's (q.v.) notice. Himmler found him appealing; the interview on 14 June 1931 was short and he came straight to the point: 'I want to set up a security and information service within the SS and I need a specialist. If you think you can do this management job, will you please write down on paper how you think you would tackle it, I'll give you 20 minutes.'

Heydrich's considerable organisational abilities, his total ruthlessness, the intensity of his anti-Semitism and his Nordic appearance were self-evident or were soon to be so. Himmler perhaps perceived the perverse view that Heydrich's fear of being considered Jewish, or partly Jewish, would be a means of controlling his talented associate. Heydrich's ancestry was, in SS terms, questionable; in the Lexicon of Music and Musicians, Heydrich's father's real name was described as Süss, a name with distinctly Jewish connotations. Later investigations tended to indicate that the family was not, in fact, Jewish, but Heydrich was rather sensitive about the issue and had gone so far as to erase the name Sarah from his mother's gravestone.

On 5 October 1931 Heydrich became a member of the SS, and after a short spell at the Brown House decided to set up the SD in another location, away from enquiring eyes. Certainly from this time Heydrich experienced a meteoric rise, becoming the second most powerful man in the RSHA. By 1941 he was head of the SD, he had contrived numerous espionage plans, become head of the SS security police and organised the Einsatzgruppen. In July 1941 Göring ordered Heydrich to submit a comprehensive draft for the achievement of the 'final solution of the Jewish problem'. It was his hand which drafted the protocol, endorsed by the Wannsee Conference in January 1942, and led to the systematic murder of European Jews in the extermination camps in the East from 1942 to 1944 (the conference was held in the SS RSHA at Wannsee in Berlin; Heydrich chaired the conference).

Perhaps in reward for his efforts, certainly in recognition of his considerable talents, he was appointed to succeed von Neurath as Protector of Bohemia and Moravia in September 1941. His administration of the territory was masterful. It began in brutality, but within months adroitly combined stick and carrot. Czech industrial production began to rise. Fuelled with this success, he issued additional ration cards on a productivity basis. The message was unequivocal: collaborate and prosper, or resist and perish. Heydrich was shown the crown jewels of Czechoslovakia by President Hacha, who told him of an intriguing legend that surrounded them: any person who was not the true heir who put the crown on his head is sure to die. It seems that Heydrich laughed and tried it on.

A plan was implemented in London for the assassination of Heydrich. This decision has always caused speculation, as he was the only Nazi leader thus targeted. The decision to assassinate Heydrich was taken by the British Government because of his policies in Czechoslovakia. London knew subsequent reprisals would shatter any cooperation between the Czechs and their German rulers, a cooperation which London feared could be transferred to other conquered countries.

In late spring 1942, a section of Czech soldiers flew from England and were dropped outside Prague. The assassination team struck on 27 May 1942. Heydrich, possibly through bravado, rode in an open-topped, unprotected car on his way from his residence to the palace. It was machine-gunned on the Kirchmayer Boulevard. He was injured and drew his pistol. The assassin's Sten gun jammed. Heydrich was about to pursue him when a grenade, thrown by another member, Kubis, exploded, impregnating him with horsehair stuffing and pieces of metal springs from the car seat. He died painfully from septicaemia on 4 June in a Prague hospital.

Heydrich's coffin lay in state in the main courtyard of Hradcany Castle and the people of Prague filed by in resemblance of homage, some giving the Nazi salute. At 1500 hours on 8 June 1942, Heydrich's coffin was carried into the courtyard of the Reich Chancellery for the state funeral. Hitler bestowed upon him the German Order, the highest party and state award. Heydrich was the archetypal Nazi: cold, ruthless and cunning. It was well known, for example, that he kept files on all the leading Nazis, even on Hitler himself, and many inside and outside the party were secretly relieved to see him dead. Himmler's first act after he had recovered from the shock of hearing about Heydrich's death, was to locate the key to the safe in which Reinhard Heydrich kept all his 'personal' files.

HIMMLER, Heinrich

RANK: Reichsführer-SS und Chef der Deutschen Polizei
BORN: 7 October 1900
DIED: 23 May 1945 (S)
PARTY NUMBER: 14303
SS NUMBER: 168
AWARDS: Combined Pilot and Observer Badge in Gold with Diamonds July 1942; Blood Order No 3, 9 November 1923; Golden Party Badge; Golden Hitler Youth Honour Badge with Oakleaves; German Olympic Games Decoration, First Class; Gau General Commemorative Badge 1923 or 1925; Nuremberg Party Day Badge of 1929, 15 August 1929; SS Long Service Cross 12 Years' Service; NSDAP Long Service Medal 15 Years; NSDAP Long Service Medal 10 Years; Commemorative Medal of 13 March 1938; Commemorative Medal of 1 October 1938; Prague Castle Bar; Commemorative Medal For The Return Of The Memel Region; German Defence Medal; SS Honour Ring; SS Honour Sword.

Himmler was born in Landshut, Bavaria, into a solid respectable middle-class family. His father was a headmaster, who was conservative in outlook and staunchly monarchist. Heinrich was named after his godfather, Prince Heinrich of Bavaria, to whom his father was tutor. As well as being a sickly child, young Heinrich had to endure the discomfiture of attending his father's school.

Heinrich welcomed the outbreak of World War I enthusiastically, but it was not until January 1918 that he was able to report for duty as an officer cadet in the 11th Bavarian Infantry Regiment. He was discharged on 17 December 1918, and returned to school in Landshut. He attended the Munich Technical High School where he studied for a degree in agriculture. He became embroiled in right-wing politics, first joining the Freikorps Oberland and then the Reichskriegsflagge. He joined the NSDAP in August 1923 and carried the imperial war flag during the Beer Hall Putsch, leading the column as it marched through the streets of Munich. The coup ended in a complete fiasco: the rank and file surrendered their weapons, identified themselves to the police and returned home, while the leaders were arrested. He returned to Landshut where he sold advertising space in the Völkischer Beobachter. He acted as general secretary to Gregor Strasser, who, in February 1925, agreed to disband his party and assimilate it into the reformed NSDAP.

Himmler now found himself a local party official with command over the tiny SS in his district. Strasser was appointed Reich Propaganda Leader of the NSDAP in September 1926, and Himmler accompanied him to party headquarters as his secretary. However, his party career still allowed him time to run a chicken smallholding where he carried out breeding experiments. He married Margarete Bodern, the daughter of a German landowner from Conerzewo, west Prussia, on 3 July 1928. Known as Marge, she was eight years older than Himmler and specialised in homeopathy and herbs. It was in fact her money that enabled Himmler to buy the smallholding.

Himmler's organisational ability did not go unnoticed and he was appointed Deputy SS Leader and then National Leader in January 1929

when he commanded approximately 1000 men, while the SS was still part of the SA. He gradually asserted the separation of the SS from the SA, and quickly won approval for a recruiting system designed to create a truly elite body. The army, which perceived Röhm and the SA as a rival, took a fairly favourable view of the SS as a force, regarding it simply as a bodyguard.

Himmler devoted his life to the expansion of the SS. By 1934, it was 200,000 strong and Himmler had added many refinements to the recruiting process, such as biological criteria and the concept of racial purity in order to select the finest troops from the large number of applicants who ranged from ex-Freikorps to unemployed bourgeois volunteers. Himmler became Polizeipräsident of Munich after Hitler became Chancellor in January 1933. This modest post enabled him to gradually gain control of the German police network except in Prussia, where Göring was Minister of the Interior. But he finally achieved complete control in 1936.

Himmler expanded the SS far beyond the bounds of any other military force; he was responsible for the ideological and mystical ceremonies, and for acquiring funding for the socio-historical research organisation, the Ahnenerbe. The castle of Wewelsburg was rebuilt at immense expense as a shrine to Germanic civilisation. Here, the Hold Order of the SS was founded and, from 1934, ceremonies were held several times a year. Karl Wolff (q.v.) ushered each SS leader into a monastic cell, where he steeped himself in Germanic mysticism surrounded by treasures from ancient Germany. Beneath their mock medieval coats of arms, the leading 12 'High' SS officers were assigned places around an Arthurian table.

Himmler also started the Allach ceramics works in Dachau which produced fine porcelain and earthenware. A Damascus smithy was also established. Himmler concerned himself with the perfecting of a future German elite through the SS. Not only would they be of guaranteed Aryan stock, but would be encouraged to form the new 'master race' through the large Lebensborn network of maternity homes.

Himmler took over the Gestapo and made it a Europe-wide organisation. Through Heydrich and the SD he formed an intelligence service that covered internal and external German operations. His involvement in the 'Night of the Long Knives' eliminated the power of the SA and closed their 'wild man camps', leading to the formation of the concentration camp system. In 1943, he became Minister of the Interior as well.

Himmler was appointed Chief of the Home Army in 1944, and a week before Hitler's suicide he made an effort to negotiate the surrender of Germany. Hitler, having heard of Himmler's treachery, dismissed him from all posts. The final Dönitz government saw him as a liability. He tried to escape at 1700 hours on 22 May 1945, a miserable-looking and shabbily dressed man with two rather more military looking companions, and was stopped by a British bridge control detail at Bremervorde in northern Germany. The identity papers in the name of Heinrich Hizinger and the black eye patch could not conceal his true identity. Himmler revealed himself. As a doctor made an oral inspection, he bit on a cyanide phial and was dead within seconds.

HIRT, Professor Dr August

RANK: SS-Sturmbannführer
BORN: 29 April 1898
DIED: unknown
PARTY NUMBER: 4012784
SS NUMBER: 100414
AWARDS: 1914 Iron Cross Second Class; Cross of Honour 1914-1918 Combatants; 1914 Wound Badge Silver Class.

Professor Hirt occupied the chair of anatomy at the University of Strasbourg, where SS students were particularly numerous. He was a member of the Ahnenerbe, which was set up with the object of studying and researching Germanic antiquity for the purpose of supporting National Socialist beliefs with scientific proof. Himmler was willingly seduced by the fascination of an idea that lay so close to his preoccupation, and the society was accordingly set up in 1935, with the status of a learned society. Hirt was one of the most alarming individuals among the researchers. With Himmler's support he brought together at the concentration camp in Auschwitz a collection of skulls for the purpose of making anthropomorphic measurements.

Hirt had 'far-reaching perspectives', and he stated: 'we have large collections of skulls of almost all races and peoples at our disposal. Of the Jewish race, however, only very few specimens of skulls are available. The war in the East now presents us with the opportunity to overcome this deficiency. By procuring the skulls of the Jewish-Bolshevik Commissars, who represent the prototype of the repulsive, but characteristic, subhuman, we have the chance now to obtain scientific material.' He did not want the heads of the already dead. He proposed that the heads of person's first be measured while alive. Then following the induced death of the victim, taking care not to damage it, the doctor would sever the head from the body and would forward it in a hermetically sealed tin can to Strasbourg.

He went personally to the front to study the behaviour of combatants in relation to their racial category. Hirt wished to study skeletons, and by June 1943 SS-Standartenführer Wolfram Sievers had collected at Auschwitz the men and women who were to furnish the skeletons for the 'scientific measurements'. A total of 115 victims – 79 Jews, 30 Jewesses, four Asiatics and two Poles – were processed. Joseph Krammer undertook the killings with gas supplied by Hirt. The bodies were sent to Strasbourg, where he assembled the skeleton collection which was previously non-existent. But time was fast running out for him. The advancing American and French troops were approaching Strasbourg and Hirt asked for a directive as to what was to be done with the collection. The order was obtained to dispose of the evidence. But the Allies found evidence both physical and written of the enterprise. Hirt disappeared and as he left Strasbourg he was heard boasting that no one would ever take him alive. It seems no one has, alive or dead.

HUBER, Franz Josef

RANK: SS-Brigadeführer
BORN: 22 January 1902
DIED: unknown
PARTY NUMBER: 4583151
SS NUMBER: 107099
AWARDS: War Merit Cross Second Class with Swords; War Merit Cross First Class with Swords; SS Honour Ring; SS Honour Sword.

Huber was the Vienna Gestapo chief and was engaged in top-level security meetings with Himmler (q.v.). One such occasion was in November 1939 at the Burgerbrau Bierkeller, where he was in the company of Artur Nebe (q.v.), Chief of Criminal Police, Heinrich Himmler, Reinhard Heydrich (q.v.) and Heinrich Müller (q.v.), chief of the Gestapo.

Müller spent practically all his time in his office, on account of his unpleasant conditions at home. Most of his social life was spent with officials such as Huber.

HUPPENKOTHEN, Walter

RANK: SS-Standartenführer
BORN: 31 December 1907
DIED: 1979 (D)
PARTY NUMBER: 1950150
SS NUMBER: 126785
AWARDS: 1939 Iron Cross Second Class; War Merit Cross Second Class without Swords; SS Honour Ring; SS Honour Sword.

The Criminal Commissar of the Gestapo, Huppenkothen was ordered by Himmler (q.v.) to investigate Göring's connection with the resistance circle that was responsible for the attempt on Hitler's life in the 20 July Bomb Plot. No evidence of any collusion on Göring's part was discovered. The conspirators were ill-prepared and were apprehended or chose to commit suicide. One of the main conspirators was Admiral Canaris, who headed the *Abwehr*. It seems that Keitel, who was always singularly loyal to him, contrived to halt the Volksgericht trial where he was to be arraigned for his involvement in the plot. This was to have followed Canaris's expulsion from the *Wehrmacht*. Hitler immediately

ordered Himmler to convene a summary court with the former inspector of the SS judicial section, SS-Sturmbannführer Dr Otto Thorbeck, as judge and Huppenkothen acting as the Gestapo prosecutor.

This secret trial was somehow delayed until 9 April 1945, when it took place in Flossenbürg concentration camp. Canaris was tried along with Hans Oster, Pastor Bonhöffer, Judge Advocate Carl Sack and the *Abwehr* officers Strünck and Gehre, all being the last indicted conspirators. They were all found guilty and condemned to death. All the condemned men were led to the gallows naked. It could be argued that they were the 'lucky' ones. Those executed in early August 1944 were hanged with a wire noose, the hangman laughing and joking as he went about his grisly work. The victims' death throes were recorded on camera, the film then being speedily developed and rushed over to Hitler's residence for his amusement and private satisfaction.

Neither Huppenkothen or Thorbeck supposedly attended the executions held in April 1945; they claimed, rather dubiously, that they did not even know whether Hitler had confirmed their findings or whether the sentences had been carried out.

Huppenkothen was tried in Munich in February 1951 for being an accessory to the murder of the five men. The charges were dismissed, but he was found guilty of 'extorting evidence and causing bodily harm' and sentenced to three and a half years of imprisonment. This case was reviewed by the West German Federal Supreme Court in Karlsruhe, which quashed the sentence but ordered a second trial. In November 1952 the Munich court upheld the original verdict, but indicted Thorbeck as a second defendant. The case continued to drag on.

In October 1955 a third trial was held at Augsburg; new witnesses stated that they had seen Walter Huppenkothen attend the executions which took place on 9 April 1945. Thorbeck was sentenced to four years' and Huppenkothen to seven years' imprisonment. Another trial on 19 June 1956 in Karlsruhe dismissed Huppenkothen's appeal; Thorbeck's, on the other hand, was allowed without hearing any fresh evidence.

J

JECKELN, Friedrich

RANK: SS-Obergruppenführer und General der Polizei
BORN: 2 February 1895
DIED: 3 February 1946 (E.A)
PARTY NUMBER: 163348
SS NUMBER: 4367
AWARDS: 1914 Iron Cross Second Class; 1939 Iron Cross Second Class Bar, October 1941; German Cross in Gold, 19 December 1943; Knight's Cross of the Iron Cross, 27 August 1944; Oakleaves, 8 March 1945; SS Honour Ring; SS Honour Sword.

A resolute member of the SS, Jeckeln was born in Hormberg, Baden. After serving in the 76th Field Artillery Regiment during World War I, he joined the Border Protection Force East, and subsequently the police. With the invasion of Russia in 1941, Jeckeln was appointed Higher SS and Police Leader with his headquarters in Riga, Latvia. Officially he had responsibility for the protection of German installations against partisan attacks; in reality, he headed an Einsatzgruppe designated to exterminate Jews in Kiev. In 1941, with great zeal, he performed his task of liquidation, reporting 44,125 executions, mainly of Jews, in the month of August alone. In February and March 1942 he initiated an operation entitled 'Action March Fever'; when completed he reported 8350 Jews liquidated, 1274 persons shot on suspicion and 389 partisans killed.

In mid-August 1944, strong Soviet forces attempted a breakthrough southwest of Lake Plesaku, which posed a grave threat to Latvian territory. Jeckeln commanded a combined battle group of poorly armed German and Latvian police forces in the 18th Army, Army Group North, and won the Knight's Cross of the Iron Cross for his efforts.

After the war he was tried by the Russians as a major war criminal. His responsibility for security, together with his cooperation with the Latvian puppet government, were used as his indictment. He was found guilty and executed in Riga in 1946.

JOST, Heinz

RANK: SS-Brigadeführer
BORN: 9 July 1904
DIED: 12 November 1964 (D)
PARTY NUMBER: 75946
SS NUMBER: 36243
AWARDS: Golden Party Badge; SS Honour Ring; SS Honour Sword.

Jost joined the NSDAP in 1928 and was a member of the SD from 1934. Having worked in Spain during the Civil War, he was made head of the foreign intelligence section of the SS in 1938.

This intelligence service, later known as Amt VI SD-Ausland, was responsible for investigations abroad and included Heydrich's (q.v.) military intelligence service. It was successfully led by Jost until 1941 when Schellenberg (q.v.) took over, although he was nominally Jost's deputy, until the beginning of 1942.

Jost worked with the occupying forces in Czechoslovakia. When Heydrich planned an elaborate subterfuge to give credence to the German invasion of Poland in 1939 by staging a mock Polish invasion on the German radio station at Gleiwitz, it fell to Jost to inform Admiral Canaris (head of the army intelligence service, the *Abwehr*), that Hitler had ordered the *Abwehr* to assist the SD. Jost gave him a list of requirements that included 150 Polish Army uniforms, side-arms, pay books and 364 men to be placed on temporary duty with the SD.

Heydrich got rid of Jost by giving him command of an Einsatzgruppe in Russia, an offer which he dared not refuse. He was the original commander of Einsatzgruppe A, but managed to discover a loophole in the assignment and found another position prior to the start of the killings. He entered the Ostministerium under Alfred Rosenberg, as liaison officer at Ewald von Kleist's Southern Army Group headquarters in South Russia. Himmler did not discover him until May 1944, when he succeeded in transferring him to the Waffen-SS as a lowly SS-Untersturmführer. After the war Jost was tried as a war criminal and sentenced to life imprisonment, although the sentence was commuted and he was released in December 1951. Another report, however, suggested that he was one of the last war criminals to be hanged at Landsberg in 1951 by the American forces.

JURY, Dr Hugo

RANK: SS-Obergruppenführer, Gauleiter of Lower Danube 1938-45
BORN: 13 July 1887
DIED: 8 May 1945 (S)
PARTY NUMBER: 410338
SS NUMBER: 292777
AWARDS: Golden Party Badge; SS Honour Ring; SS Honour Sword.

A doctor specialising in tuberculosis, Jury was a key member of the Austrian Nazi Party, becoming deputy leader to Seyss-Inquart (q.v.). In 1934, Austrian Nazis had murdered Chancellor Dollfuss in an attempted coup. However, government forces led by Kurt Schuschnigg defeated the Nazis. He was also a prime mover in the Austrian Anschluss of 1938, and held the post of Minister of Social Administration in Seyss-Inquart's extremely short-lived government. He was appointed Gauleiter of Lower Danube in 1938, a post he held until he committed suicide on the day Germany surrendered.

K

KAINDLE, Anton

RANK: SS-Standartenführer
BORN: 14 July 1902
DIED: 1951 (D)

PARTY NUMBER: 4390500
SS NUMBER: 241248
AWARDS: 1939 Iron Cross Second Class; War Merit Cross Second Class with Swords; War Merit Cross First Class with Swords; SS Honour Ring; SS Honour Sword.

A competent administrative officer, Kaindle served on the staff of the inspectorate of concentration camps before the war, moving with Eicke (q.v.) to the *Totenkopf* Division in October 1939 as the division's personnel officer. He remained a member of Eicke's staff until October 1941, when Himmler moved him back to the inspectorate of concentration camps, as chief paymaster of the camp guard units.

Kaindle was transferred from the *Totenkopf* Division because of his obvious administrative qualifications at a time when the casualties of the SS field divisions were draining personnel from the camp administrative system (the war in Russia was consuming human and material resources at an alarming rate). However, Heinrich Himmler desperately needed SS officers with Kaindle's competence and experience nearer to home. His second term with the camp inspectorate, however, was brief. In August 1942, Kaindle was appointed to untangle a complicated financial scandal involving the commandant at Sachsenhausen. Himmler sent the honest and reliable Kaindle to serve as commandant of Sachsenhausen until the end of the war, where he gained a reputation among his superiors as a scrupulously correct, thoroughly reliable camp commander.

Kaindle was tried as a war criminal by the Russians in 1947 and sentenced to life imprisonment, where he died in 1951.

KALTENBRUNNER, Dr Ernst

RANK: SS-Obergruppenführer und General der Polizei
BORN: 4 October 1903
DIED: 16 October 1946 (E.A.)
PARTY NUMBER: 300179
SS NUMBER: 13039
AWARDS: Golden Party Badge; Blood Order, 6 May 1942; Knight's Cross of the War Merit Cross with Swords, 15 November 1944; War Merit Cross with Swords Second Class; War Merit Cross First Class with Swords; SS Honour Ring; SS Honour Sword.

Kaltenbrunner was born in Ried in Innkreis, not far from Branau am Inn, Hitler's birthplace. After receiving his law doctorate at the early age of 23, Kaltenbrunner spent two years with a lawyer in Salzburg, before setting himself up in practice in Linz in 1928.

During this time he began his political activities as a member of the Independent Movement for a Free Austria. He joined the Austrian National Socialists in 1932 and a year later he entered the SS, where he founded the Sturmbann with Adolf Eichmann (q.v.) and was a party speaker in north Austria. Still in the first year of his membership, Kaltenbrunner was commissioned as the leader of the SS-Standarte 37, and in April 1935 as the leader of the whole Austrian SS. In January 1936, he was arrested and committed to the Dollfuss concentration camp at Kaisersteinbruch for being involved in anti-government activities; he was released in 1937.

Through the Austrian Bundeskanzler, Dr Seyss-Inquart (q.v.), Kaltenbrunner was appointed State Secretary of Security on 11 March 1938 and a day later was promoted to SS-Brigadeführer and appointed to the deployment of the SS-Oberabschnitts Österreich. Kaltenbrunner advised Himmler on the legal grounds for the reunification of Austria with Germany. In September 1938 Kaltenbrunner was promoted to SS-Gruppenführer and appointed to higher SS and Police Chief of Vienna, Upper and Lower Donau. One month earlier he had joined the Grossdeutschen Reichstag. In April 1942, he was promoted to Generalleutnant der Polizei, on 21 June 1943 to SS-Obergruppenführer and General der Polizei. After Heydrich's (q.v.) death, Himmler appointed Kaltenbrunner as his successor, after eight months of doing the job himself. Later on Himmler said of Kaltenbrunner: 'Presumably he is only in a drunk state to be able to think clearly.' This clearly illustrates Himmler's views on Kaltenbrunner's typical state.

The bestowal of the Knight's Cross of the War Merit Cross with Swords followed Kaltenbrunner's completion of the preliminary proceedings against the chief of the *Abwehr*, Canaris, with the proof of his involvement in the 20 July Bomb Plot. He received the Golden Party Badge (Honour Award) on 20 July 1944, having become an honourary holder of the Blood Order in May 1942. At Nuremberg he was charged by the International Military Tribunal and condemned to death on 1 October 1946. He was executed 15 days later.

KAMINSKI, Bronislav Vladislavovich

RANK: SS-Brigadeführer
BORN: unknown
DIED: September 1944 (E.R.)
PARTY NUMBER: —
SS NUMBER: —
AWARDS: 1939 Iron Cross Second Class; 1939 Iron Cross First Class.

Born in St Petersburg, the son of a Polish father and German mother, Kaminski was a chemical engineer who had no reason to love the Soviets. Under suspicion as a 'foreigner', bourgeois intellectual and potential dissident, he spent five years in one of Stalin's labour camps, and was released only a few months prior to the German invasion. He was a brilliant if autocratic organiser, spoke German fluently and threw himself wholeheartedly behind the German cause. He tried, unsuccessfully, to form a Russian Nazi Party, but apart from this one failure his record was one of unqualified success.

In January 1942, the town of Lokot fell under the jurisdiction of the Second Panzer Army. It stood on the edge of the Bryanask Forest, about halfway between Orec and Kursk in central Russia. It became a model of self-sufficiency under his guidance, having its own newspapers, hospitals, banks and even its own tax system devised by Kaminski. The stipulated food supplies never failed to be delivered to the *Wehrmacht* on time, and the Germans found it necessary to maintain only a minimum liaison staff.

The original defence force of 500 men was expanded into a small private army, which by September 1943 had grown into a brigade of some 10,000 men organised in five infantry regiments, supported by its own artillery of 36 field guns, and armour comprising 24 captured Soviet T-34 tanks, as well as various engineer, signals and medical units. This force went under the grandiose title of the 'Russian People's Liberation Army', or RONA.

RONA fought several successful actions against the partisans of Bryanask and even induced some of them to change sides. Kaminski was dubbed, 'the War Lord of the Bryanask Forest'. By the autumn of 1943, the Germans were in continuous retreat in Russia, and it was not long before Lokot had to be evacuated in the face of the Red Army's relentless advance. Kaminski and his RONA, which now comprised some 15,000 men, were removed to Ratibor on the Polish-Czech border, prompting an exodus accompanied by 10,500 civilians and 1500 cows.

In March 1944 the RONA was renamed a 'Volksheer Brigade' (People's Brigade). In July it was accepted into the Waffen-SS as SS Assault Brigade RONA. Kaminski was granted a commission as a Waffen-Brigadeführer. His men were not, as yet, deemed fit for frontline service and were sent for further training to Hungary. When the Polish Home Army began its abortive uprising in Warsaw in August 1944, one regiment of around 1700 men under Vrolov was detached from the brigade and sent to the Polish capital to assist in the suppression of the revolt. It arrived on 5 August, but was withdrawn three weeks later on the orders of Erich von dem Bach-Zelewski (q.v.) because of its

atrocious conduct and general lack of discipline. Kaminski himself was in Warsaw for only about 10 days. Later, he was arrested by the SS in Lodz and charged with looting, an offence punishable by death. He was shot by an SS firing squad on being found guilty. His death was officially attributed to a Polish partisan ambush on the road to Lodz.

KAMMLER, Dr Hans

RANK: SS-Gruppenführer
BORN: 26 August 1901
DIED: May 1945 (K.I.A.)
PARTY NUMBER: 1011855
SS NUMBER: 113619
AWARDS: 1939 Iron Cross Second Class; 1939 Iron Cross First Class; War Merit Cross Second Class with Swords; War Merit Cross First Class with Swords; Knight's Cross of the War Merit Cross with Swords 1945; SS Honour Ring; SS Honour Sword.

Kammler worked in the Reich Aeronautical Ministry until the end of 1941. He joined the Allgemeine-SS in 1938, transferring to the SS Economic Administration Department in the autumn of 1941. He was appointed chief of Amtsgruppe C, overseeing the Reich's building and construction industry, as well as that the SS. Under his leadership the SS-Baustäbe was created, which employed thousands of concentration camp prisoners as builders between 1943 and 1943, on military projects such as the Atlantic Wall, as well as in clearance operations in bombed-out German towns and cities. He may have been in charge of the construction of the gas chambers at Auschwitz, although this has never been proved.

Kammler's ascent into the administrative hierarchy of the Reich began on 26 August 1943, when the SS succeeded in establishing production of the V-bombs. An agreement between Kammler, Armaments Minister Speer and General Dornberger proposed the installation and operation of the 'A4' underground factory by the SS. Two days later, the first prisoner transport arrived at Camp Dora, 5km (three miles) northwest of Nordhausen. Kammler was then set up, carrying out all subsequent building work for the Armaments Ministry. Approximately 60,000 prisoners arrived and cleared away an underground surface area of eight million square metres; 13,000 of them did not survive. In January 1944 the first A4 (renamed the Vergeltungswaffe 2 or V-2) left the production line, and from August the plant was producing about 600 missiles a month. In 15 months about 6000 missiles were produced, of which 3500 were shot down.

From 1943 Sonderstab Kammler employed skilled workers from all sections of the *Wehrmacht*, being assigned increasing numbers of special weapon projects. Himmler (q.v.) personally appointed Kammler to run the 'Jägerprogram', the scheme implementing the transfer of the aeroplane industry into underground plants: he led 15 projects and also started the production of the 'Volksjäger' He 162 jet fighter shortly before the 'ultimate victory'. From May 1944 he was involved with the Geilenberg Programme, transferring fuel production into underground factories.

In August 1944 Hitler appointed Kammler Plenipotentiary for the V-2 project, involving him with the preparation for their launching, and in September he took command of the division. In December 1944 he was promoted to commander general of the AK, in this capacity receiving orders directly from Hitler for the employment of the V-2. On 31

January 1945, all sections involved in the deployment of the V-1 and V-2, personnel and materials, were put under the control of the Waffen-SS under Kammler's command. Shortly before this Reichsmarschall Göring had appointed him special emissary for ensuring advancement of development and testing of rocket-propelled weapons, answerable to the Reichsmarschall, as well as inspector of the equipment of all Luftwaffe units equipped with rocket-propelled weapons.

On 27 March 1945, as the Reich collapsed, Kammler was designated the

Führer's Plenipotentiary for jet planes. All sections of the *Wehrmacht*, the NSDAP and the Reich would be affected by Kammler's orders from this day. A truly incredible career of a man who had not served a single day in the army!

Kammler's indisputable successes were made possible by strictly following his motto, as expressed to SS leaders: 'Don't concern yourselves with the human victims. The work must be done, and in the shortest possible time.' A few weeks before the end of the war he was transferred to the defence of Harz against the advancing Allies. His ultimate fate is unclear, but he probably died in the Battle of Berlin.

KÄMPFE, Helmut

RANK: SS-Obersturmbannführer der Reserve
BORN: 31 July 1909
DIED: 10 June 1944 (K.I.A.)
PARTY NUMBER: —
SS NUMBER: —
AWARDS: 1939 Iron Cross Second Class, 26 August 1941; 1939 Iron Cross First Class, 7 November 1941; German Cross in Gold, 11 March 1943; Knight's Cross of the Iron Cross, 10 December 1943; Medal for the Winter Campaign in Russia 1941-1942; Commemorative Medal of 13 March 1938; Prague Castle Bar; Close Combat Clasp Silver Class; General Assault Badge; 1939 Wound Badge Silver Class.

Kämpfe was born in Jena, Thüringen. He saw service on the Russian Front and was the commanding officer of the 3rd Battalion, 4th SS-Panzergrenadier Regiment *Der Führer*, *Das Reich* Division. Kämpfe was awarded the Knight's Cross of the Iron Cross for bravery demonstrated by himself and his battalion during the fighting east of Zhitomir, Russia.

Most of the division was withdrawn from Russia at the beginning of March 1944 for refitting with men and materials in southern France, near Montauban. In June 1944 it was transferred via Brives, Tulle, Limoges, Poitiers, Tours and Laval to the area around Chaumont and Villedien. There were bloody encounters with the French Resistance during the transfer, and individual units suffered heavy casualties in the battle against the 'invisible enemy'. In one of these attacks on 9 June 1944, Kämpfe was kidnapped with his driver. He was apparently executed by his captors on 10 June 1944 near Limoges. This triggered a reprisal action against the village of Oradour-sur-Glane; the entire village of 642 inhabitants were murdered. The women were separated from the men and were mown down with 207 children by machine guns in the church. Two days later, the bodies of 15 children were found packed behind the altar.

KAPPLER, Herbert

RANK: SS-Obersturmbannführer
BORN: 29 September 1907
DIED: 9 February 1978 (D)
PARTY NUMBER: 594899
SS NUMBER: 55211
AWARDS: SS Honour Ring; SS Honour Sword.

Heydrich (q.v.) chose to appoint Herbert Kappler, a typical Gestapo man. as security police commander for Rome. Höttl described his colleague as 'an intelligent Schwabian'. Kappler held the position from 1941 until 1944, during which time he was expected to be an intelligence officer as well as a butcher, the normal combination of skills expected by Heydrich. This was in contradiction to Hitler's edicts, for he forbade the use of secret agents on Italy's friendly soil.

In March 1944, in retaliation for the killing of German soldiers by the partisans, Kappler ordered 335 Italian civilians into the Ardeatine tunnel, where they were executed. After the war he was sentenced in 1947 in Rome to life imprisonment for this action.

In 1977, 30 years later, having been in hospital for several months undergoing treatment for stomach cancer, he appealed for release on humanitarian grounds, but this was denied by the Italian High Court. The fraternity of ex-SS men decided to rectify the matter and a bizarre plan was devised. Kappler was held on the fourth floor of the military hospital in Rome. His wife Annelies visited him almost daily, and on 15 August she visited with a large suitcase, explaining to the guards that it was to take his dirty clothes away in. She stayed until 01:00 hours the following morning, and when she left she was dragging the heavy case. One of the guards generously offered to help but she refused, saying that she had help outside. The case containing Kappler, who now weighed only 100 pounds, was placed in a Fiat and his escape was not discovered until the following day. He died the following year, aged 70.

KEMPKA, Erich

RANK: SS-Sturmbannführer
BORN: 16 October 1910
DIED: 24 January 1975 (D)
PARTY NUMBER: 225639
SS NUMBER: 2803
AWARDS: Golden Party Badge; SS Honour Ring; SS Honour Sword.

Kempka became Josef Turboven's chauffeur, transferring on 1 March 1932 to Hitler's staff as a member of his bodyguard, and acting as his chauffeur after the death of Julius Schreck (q.v.) in 1936.

Kempka's position gave him an intimate perception of Hitler's inner circle. He described Eva Braun as 'the unhappiest woman in Germany'. In the last days of the war, Hitler told Günsche (q.v.) that he and Eva were going to commit suicide and that he was to be sure that he burned their bodies so that they did not fall into Russian hands. Günsche ordered Kempka to forage for the fuel necessary to incinerate the corpses.

Finding only 160 litres (42.21 gallons US) in the Reich Chancellery garage, Kempka 'borrowed' another 20 litres (5.27 gallons US) from the Chancellery's chief technician, Hentschel. It fell to Kempka, after the suicide pact, to carry Eva's body out to the garden; he carried her halfway up the stairs leading from the bunker to the garden, only to be relieved by Günsche, who carried her the rest of the way, placing her body next to Hitler's. The corpses were doused with the fuel and ignited by Bormann (q.v.) in a Viking-like funeral pyre, in accordance with Adolf Hitler's last orders.

KEPPLER, Wilhelm

RANK: SS-Obergruppenführer
BORN: 14 December 1882
DIED: 13 June 1960 (D)
PARTY NUMBER: 62424
SS NUMBER: 50816
AWARDS: Golden Party Badge; War Merit Cross Second Class without Swords; War Merit Cross First Class without Swords; SS Honour Ring; SS Honour Sword.

Keppler became a member of the NSDAP in the 1920s. He was an engineer and industrialist who was a useful intermediary with the bankers and anti-Schleicher conservatives. In 1931 he brought together a group known as the 'Keppler circle' to support and fund the party. He was elected to the Reichstag, becoming a Commissioner for Economic Affairs in 1933. He was Hitler's economic adviser from 1932 to 1936, after which he was appointed adviser to Göring on the Four Year Plan.

Attached to the German Embassy in Vienna as embassy secretary, Keppler helped to engineer the Anschluss, and subsequently became Reich Commissioner to Austria from March until June 1938. During the war he was employed in the Ministry of Foreign Affairs and became chairman of many SS businesses. He continued to run the Keppler

Bureau in the Ministry of Economics and liaised with Himmler (q.v.). After the war he was sentenced to 10 years' imprisonment for his part in war crimes. He was released from Landsberg Prison in January 1951. Keppler was heavily involved before the war in trying to reduce the amount of imports to Germany by increasing the production of synthetic products.

KLINGENBERG, Fritz
RANK: SS Obersturmbannführer
BORN: 17 December 1912
DIED: 22 March 1945 (K.I.A.)
PARTY NUMBER: 851328
SS NUMBER: 51487
AWARDS: 1939 Iron Cross Second Class, 23 June 1940;1939 Iron Cross First Class, 24 June 1940; German Cross in Gold, 28 April 1944; Knight's Cross of the Iron Cross, 14 May 1941; SS Honour Sword; SS Honour Ring.

Klingenberg volunteered for the SS-*Verfügungstruppe* in 1934, and went to the officers' training school at Bad Tölz in 1935. He was a company commander in the SS-Standarte *Germania* and subsequently served on the staff of the inspectorate of the SS-*Verfügungstruppe*. After the fall of France he assumed command of a newly-raised motorcycle battalion of *Das Reich*.

On 11 April 1941, determined to reach Belgrade before any other German troops, Klingenberg crossed the River Danube at Belgrade with barely a dozen men, and marched unopposed into the Yugoslav capital to accept the mayor's surrender. At the conclusion of the campaign Klingenberg was received by Hitler, who personally awarded him the Knight's Cross of the Iron Cross.

In 1942 he joined the staff of the SS-Officers' school Bad Tölz and specialised in the instruction of non-German officer candidates. In January 1945 he took command of the 17th SS Panzergrenadier Division *Götz von Berlichingen*. He was killed in action not far from Herxheim in the Palatinate in March 1945. His remains have never been located.

KNOCHEN, Dr Helmut
RANK: SS-Standartenführer
BORN: 14 March 1910
DIED: July 1956 (E.A)
PARTY NUMBER: 1430331
SS NUMBER: 280350
AWARDS: 1914 Iron Cross Second Class;1914 Iron Cross First Class; Cross of Honour 1914-1918 Combatants; SS Honour Ring; SS Honour Sword.

Knochen was commander of the security police in Paris from 1940 to 1944. He was an appointee of Heydrich (q.v.), who wanted to dictate his own procedure and could countenance no other secret police but his own in any part of Europe.

Heydrich's new campaign opened with a farcical incident to blow up two Paris synagogues. Knochen reported to Stülpnagel, the military

governor of France, that Eugé Delonche, the former leader of the ultra-right fascist 'Cagoulards', was suspected by the French police of the bombings. Knochen had conveniently overlooked the fact that he had arrested a member of his own staff, SS-Obersturmführer Sommer. Stülpnagel discovered, quite by accident, that Sommer, during a court of enquiry, had admitted that he had provided the explosives on Knochen's order. It is unclear if Sommer was arrested in order to conceal Knochen's involvement in the bombings, or if he had been arrested for other infringements, and his providing of the bombs had been coincidentally discovered during the course of his enquiries. Stülpnagel was incensed and complained to Keitel that the Gestapo were intensifying his difficulties with the French, which the 'necessary shooting of hostages had already made bad enough'.

Keitel wrote to Heydrich on 22 October, requesting the recall of Max Thomas (q.v.) and Knochen from France. Thomas was transferred to an Einsatzgruppe in Russia, but Knochen remained. Stülpnagel withdrew his complaint against Knochen on 5 February because he expressed his willingness to cooperate.

Knochen was responsible for the execution of captured Allied airmen, and after the war he was tried by the British court at Wuppertal and sentenced in June 1946 to life imprisonment. He was subsequently sentenced to death, but this was commuted to 20 years' forced labour. He died during his prison term.

KNÖCHLEIN, Franz
RANK: SS-Obersturmbannführer
BORN: 27 May 1911
DIED: 21 January 1949 (E.A).
PARTY NUMBER: 157016
SS NUMBER: 87881
AWARDS: 1939 Iron Cross Second Class, 31 May 1940; 1939 Iron Cross First Class, 15 June 1940; German Cross in Gold, 12 November 1941; Knight's Cross of the Iron Cross, 16 November 1944; SS Honour Ring; SS Honour Sword.

Knöchlein was the officer responsible for the infamous murder of 100 British prisoners of war during the Allied retreat to Dunkirk in 1940. On 27 May 1940, during the French campaign near the village of Le Paradis, some 100 men of the Second Royal Norfolk Regiment barricaded themselves inside a farmhouse to slow the advance of the *Totenkopf* soldiers. They pinned down Knöchlein's company for nearly an hour with accurate rifle and machine-gun fire, killing and wounding several of his men. The defenders ran out of ammunition and decided to surrender. They showed a white flag, laid their weapons down and marched out, hands raised.

Knöchlein had them searched, then marched them across the road into a barnyard, lined them up against a wall and cut them down in a withering crossfire from two heavy machine guns. The gunners continued until all cries were extinguished. Knöchlein then detailed a squad to bayonet and shoot in the head any who still showed signs of life. After an hour he was satisfied all were dead and ordered his company onward. Miraculously, Privates Albert Pooley and William O'Callaghan survived. They evaded capture until the severity of Pooley's wounds forced them to give themselves up. Pooley was eventually repatriated to England in 1943, where he made a full report. Once the incident became known, both the *Totenkopf* Division and the German Army, to which it was subordinated, instituted investigations. It was claimed that the fighting had been particularly bitter and 'evidence' was presented that the Norfolks had used 'Dumm-Dumm' rounds. After the war the graves were discovered, and autopsies and the testimony of French witnesses clarified the situation. Knöchlein was tried by a British court, found guilty and sentenced to death. He was hanged in 1949 in Hameln, Weser, a British-controlled penitentiary.

KOCH, Karl-Otto
RANK: SS-Standartenführer
BORN: 2 August 1897
DIED: 1945 (E.R.)
PARTY NUMBER: 475586
SS NUMBER: 14830
AWARDS: 1914 Iron Cross Second Class; Cross of Honour 1914-1918 Combatants; 1914 Wound Badge Black Class; Badge of the SA Rally at Brunswick 1931; SS Honour Sword.

Koch became commandant of Esterwegen concentration camp. In an open-air wedding ceremony in 1936 he married Ilse and they both went to Buchenwald in 1939, he as camp commandant and she as an SS assistant. Despite Himmler's (q.v.) continuous preaching about SS honour and integrity, Koch and others like him grew exceedingly rich from the concentration camp system, but he went too far, even by the apppalling standards of the time. While commandant of the camp at Lublin, by an irony of SS practice, Koch was judged to be criminally involved by his SS peers. The investigation of an SS court conducted by Dr Morgen (q.v.) found him guilty of embezzlement and the illegal killing of two prisoners, Krämer and Peix. The SS court sentenced him to death and he was hanged by his SS colleagues.

KOCH, Ilse
RANK: SS-Helferinnen
BORN: 22 September 1906
DIED: 2 September 1967 (S)

Having married Karl Koch (q.v.), whom she referred to as 'Karli', in 1936, Ilse Koch accompanied her husband to Buchenwald as an SS-Helferinnen in 1939. She soon gained a reputation of having an unrestrained sexual appetite, and her extreme sadism is undoubtedly best illustrated by her collection of lampshades, gloves and wallets made from the tattooed skin of camp inmates, whom she had personally selected for execution. When the supply of prisoners bearing artistic tattoos was low, she had others decorated. She became known as the 'bitch of Buchenwald'. While her husband was hanged by the SS, she continued her work at the camp until it was liberated in 1945 by US forces. Himmler took a curious attitude towards his concentration camp personnel. He believed corruption destroyed the SS's ideology and sadism undermined discipline. Surprisingly, sadists and criminals formed only a small percentage of the personnel involved in the mass extermination programme. Chillingly, most of those who took part were 'normal' people who were just 'doing their job'.

In 1947, at her first trial, Ilse was found guilty of murder and sentenced to life imprisonment. General Lucius Clay, reviewing the case, reduced her sentence to four years. On 17 October 1949 she was released from American captivity only to be immediately re-arrested for incitement to murder. A Senate investigation committee in 1948 had also reviewed her practices. She was brought to trial again in 1951, where she was once more sentenced to life imprisonment and judged to be a 'perverted, nymphomaniacal, power-mad demon'. While in prison she seduced an American Army warder and had his baby. She hanged herself in her cell in Aibach prison in September 1967.

KRAMER, Josef
RANK: SS-Hauptsturmführer
BORN: 10 November 1906
DIED: 13 December 1945 (E.A.)
PARTY NUMBER: 32217
SS NUMBER: 733597
AWARDS: War Merit Cross Second Class, spring 1943; War Merit Cross First Class, January 1945.

Kramer was an early participant in the concentration camp service, from 1934. He served in Natzweiler camp, where he was rewarded with the War Merit Cross First Class in the spring of 1943 for his efficiency in running the camp. He commanded the extermination centre at Auschwitz in the last months of its existence, before being transferred in November 1944 to Bergen-Belsen.

Bergen-Belsen was established in 1943 as an 'exchange camp' for Jews living in Germany and was originally perceived as a special 'privileged transit camp' for Jews with relatives in Palestine, Paraguay and Honduras, Jewish diamond workers and those decorated with the Iron Cross. By a grisly irony it was also classified as a 'Krankenlager' – a reception centre for sick prisoners. Jews who had paid an individual ransom were forwarded from Strasshof to the camp. Meanwhile, Jewish international charities found 20 million Swiss francs to 'buy' Jews, and 1684, mainly from the former Romanian town of Cluj, were moved from Bergen-Belsen and released in Switzerland in two train loads on 21 August and 6 December 1944. But during late 1944 they were replaced by prisoners from camps evacuated from Eastern Europe, mere disease-ridden skeletons who were dying at the rate of 2-300 a day from spotted typhus.

From November 1944 conditions in Belsen deteriorated rapidly, ironically coincidental with Kramer's appointment. Evidence offered at his trial suggested he was responsible for selling off food supplies, but it is more likely that the desperate food shortage was the result of the increase in prisoner numbers from 15,000 to almost 50,000.

The horrific newsreels showed him to the world in 1945 as being stocky and well-fed among the dying inmates, a man neither shocked nor stricken by conscience, a man simply awaiting new orders. Kramer was found guilty of war crimes and executed on 13 December 1945.

KRAUSE, Karl Wilhelm
RANK: SS-Hauptsturmführer
BORN: 5 March 1911
DIED: unknown
PARTY NUMBER: —
SS NUMBER: —
AWARDS: German Cross in Gold; 1939 Iron Cross Second Class; 1939 Iron Cross First Class; Commemorative Medal of 13 March 1938; Commemorative Medal of 1 October 1938; Prague Castle Bar; Commemorative Medal for the return of the Memel Region; Destroyer's War Badge; Narvik Shield in Gold; DRL Sports Badge.

Born in Michelau, West Prussia, near Danzig, Krause studied cabinet making and architecture, before joining the navy in 1931. Hitler chose Krause to be his personal orderly in 1934, impressed by his tall, 'Nordic' appearance. Although he was not a Nazi, Krause was entrusted with the most important role of protecting the Führer from assault or assassination, which involved walking directly behind him on tours and at public appearances. Hitler often jokingly referred to him as 'shadow', as he had the ability of appearing to blend with Hitler's shadow, becoming unseen.

Krause was constantly with Hitler between 1934 and 1939. On Christmas Eve 1937, Hitler managed to elude the SS guards, and crept out, accompanied by Krause, on an incognito jaunt through Berlin, where they had an exciting midnight stroll. Himmler (q.v.) reprimanded Krause the next day for allowing Hitler to expose himself to nocturnal dangers. In September 1939, after a petty squabble over some 'spring water', Hitler dismissed Krause. He served in the navy, then as an ordnance aide in the Reich Chancellery. Finally, he joined the Waffen-SS and served in a flak unit, which was credited with shooting down 45 aircraft. He escaped from the Soviets and went into American custody. After various interrogations he was fined seven marks and released.

KRYSSING, P. C.
RANK: Legions-Obersturmbannführer
PARTY NUMBER: —
SS NUMBER: —

Freikorps *Danmark* was an officially sponsored body, and on 3 July 1941 Lieutenant-Colonel P. C. Kryssing of the 5th Artillery Regiment of the Danish Army was to be given command of the new unit. The Freikorps was part of the Waffen-SS from the start, but Himmler (q.v.) was displeased by the slow progress in training. The Danes, it transpired, suffered from inefficient leadership and poor coordination with their German instructors. Furthermore, Kryssing disliked what he considered to be German interference with his handling of the corps. He deliberately allowed the training programme to fall behind schedule, with the result that Himmler dismissed him from his command on 8 February 1942. Kryssing was then moved to an administration post on the grounds that an artillery man could not be expected to command an infantry battalion. He recommended as his replacement Captain Schock, but, as he was a freemason, he was deemed unacceptable to the SS.

KUBE, Wilhelm-Richard Paul
RANK: SS-Gruppenführer Gauleiter of Ostmark 1928-33; Gauleiter of Kurmark 1933-6
BORN: 13 November 1887
DIED: 22 September 1943 (K.I.A.)
PARTY NUMBER: 71682
SS NUMBER: 114771
AWARDS: War Merit Cross Second Class with Swords; War Merit Cross First Class with Swords; Knight's Cross of the War Merit Cross with Swords (Posthumous), 27 September 1943.

Wilhelm Kube was born in Glogau, the son of a Prussian sergeant. In 1928 he joined the NSDAP and the members of the DNVP enrolled in the NSDAP.

In recognition he was appointed, in 1928, Gauleiter of Ostmark and in 1933 Kurmark. A particularly nasty character, he was removed from office in 1936 on the grounds that he had apparently attributed Jewish ancestry to Major Walter Buch. The real basis for his dismissal, however, was undoubtedly corruption; considering who he had supposedly slandered, it is remarkable that he was still permitted to use the title Gauleiter (he was lucky to retain his freedom).

On 16 July 1941 Hitler proposed him for the position of Kommissar of Moscow (in expectation of another easy Blitzkrieg victory), but Göring and Rosenberg strongly opposed this posting and Kube was made the generalkommissariat of Belorussia. Although not hostile to the population of his territory and protesting against anti-Jewish measures, he was ineffective in resisting the atrocities, strangely taking the credit for 50,000 Jewish deaths in 1942. The real hallmark of Kube's regime was the introduction of corruption on a grand scale. He did argue that the Belorussians should be treated better and permitted self-government of some type, though no doubt he hoped to profit out of any such situation. He met a strange and grisly end, having a bomb planted under his bed by a servant girl, which blew him to pieces on 22 September 1943.

L

LAMMERDING, Heinz
RANK: SS-Gruppenführer und Generalleutnant der Waffen-SS
BORN: 27 August 1905
DIED: 13 January 1971 (D)
PARTY NUMBER: 722395
SS NUMBER: 247062
AWARDS: 1939 Iron Cross Second Class, 23 May 1940; 1939 Iron Cross First Class, 22 June 1940; German Cross in Gold, 25 April 1943; Knight's Cross, 11 April 1943; Demjansk Shield; General Assault Badge, Badge of the SA rally at Brunswick 1931, SS Honour Ring; SS Honour Sword.

An engineer who served with the head office of the Training Department of the Reichswehr, Lammerding joined the SS-*Verfügungstruppe* as an engineering officer and then served during the 1940 French campaign in the engineer battalion of the Totenkopf Division.

Transferred to the Eastern Front, in the summer of 1941 he was successful in breaking through the Stalin Line near Sebesh, and was the first staff officer of the *Totenkopf* Division in the Demjansk Pocket. In 1942 he commanded the Motorcycle Regiment Thule, subsequently he commanded the armoured Battle Group *Das Reich*. In March 1944 most of the division was transferred for refit to Montauban in southern France. In June, it was moved to the area around Chaumont and Viliedien. During this transfer the French Resistance inflicted heavy casualties on individual units, angering the Waffen-SS soldiers. After the Allied landings on 6 June, the number of attacks intensified and SS-Obersturmbannführer Kämpfe was captured and executed by the Resistance on 9 June (his body was not found until after the war; Kämpfe's companion, SS-Obersturmführer Gerlach, reported the incident). In reprisal the men of Oradour-sur-Glane were shot, and the women and children locked in the church. The town was then put to the torch. The fire spread quickly to the church and all inside perished (the location has never been rebuilt; it stands in mute testimony to the ruthlessness of National Socialist ideology and Waffen-SS brutality).

Lammerding went on to become Himmler's chief of staff, Vistula Army Group, from January to March 1945. After the war Lammerding was tried in absentia in Bordeaux for the Oradour-sur-Glane massacre and sentenced to death. He never suffered this penalty or imprisonment; even though the French Government requested that the Bundesrepublik extradite him on several occasions, but the German Government steadfastly refused. It can thus be said that Lammerding, like so many in the SS as a whole, escaped lightly. He died of cancer in Bad Tölz in 1971 and was buried in Düsseldorf.

LAMMERS, Dr Hans
RANK: SS-Obergruppenführer
BORN: 27 May 1879
DIED: 4 January 1962 (D)
PARTY NUMBER: 1010255
SS NUMBER: 118404
AWARDS: Golden Party Badge; 1914 Iron Cross Second Class; 1914 Iron Cross First Class; Cross of Honour 1914-1918 Combatants; SS Honour Ring; SS Honour Sword.

Born at Lublinitz, Upper Silesia, Lammers was a brilliant lawyer who acted for the Nazi Party and distinguished himself by interpreting legal tangles for it. He was State Secretary from 1933 to 1945, becoming minister and head of the Chancellery. Hitler ordered his arrest for high treason on 23 April 1945, but the war ended before this order could be implemented.

Lammers was tried at Nuremberg in April 1949 for his part in drafting anti-Jewish decrees. In his defence he pleaded he was unaware of 'the Final Solution of the Jewish problem'. He was sentenced to 20 years' imprisonment for his part, but was released on 15 December 1951. He died in Düsseldorf 11 years later.

LEISTER, John

RANK: SS-Schütze
BORN: 19 June 1922
PARTY NUMBER: —
SS NUMBER: —

Born in London, Leister was the son of a north London baker who had served in World War I in the Middlesex Regiment, despite his German birth. In the interwar years he made frequent visits to his family in Germany, who were NSDAP members and took some delight in dressing their small English relation in party uniform. From 1935 to 1936 he lived with his great-aunt in Germany, attending school and learning to speak the native language fluently.

The outbreak of war in 1939 caused a conflict of loyalties and he decided to join the Peace Pledge Union Scheme, providing agricultural workers for the Channel Islands. The invasion of the Channel Islands in July 1940 put him in a difficult position. He became an interpreter for the Germans, while his friend Pleasants (q.v.) teamed up with Eddie Chapman, the notorious triple spy. Leister and Pleasants decided to escape to England, but were caught and sentenced to six months in prison. They were sent to France, and afterwards Leister was sent to a civilian internment camp where he attempted to escape again. He was apprehended and served a further six weeks in a Gestapo prison.

Finally, he and Pleasants were interned at Marlag-Milage, where they decided to join the British Freikorps. Leister also worked for the broadcasting service and subsequently joined the Kurt Eggers Regiment, and on a false pass, provided by his girlfriend Lena Jurgens, escaped to Italy in her company. They surrendered to the American authorities, who returned him to England, where he was tried at the Old Bailey, found guilty and sentenced to three years' penal servitude.

LEROY, Jaques

RANK: SS-Untersturmführer
BORN: 10 September 1924
DIED: 5 August 1996 (D)
PARTY NUMBER: —
SS NUMBER: —
AWARDS: 1939 Iron Cross Second Class, 11 November 1943; 1939 Iron Cross First Class, 8 July 1944; Knight's Cross of the Iron Cross, 20 April 1945;
Close Combat Clasp Silver Class.

Leroy was born in Binche, Belgium, and volunteered for service in the Waffen-SS as a foreigner. He was the commanding NCO of the First Company SS-Panzergrenadier Regiment 69 in the 28th SS Freiwilligen-Panzergrenadier Division *Wallonien*, serving on the Eastern Front. He was awarded the Knight's Cross of the Iron Cross for his bravery in an action where he lost his eye and his arm. He was recovering in hospital when the award was made. He re-mustered with his unit, terribly wounded, to continue the fight, but the prestigious award was never actually bestowed upon him, nor did he receive the preliminary citation; worst of all, his name had not been entered on the role of winners. It was not until 20 May 1957 that his entitlement was proved by the division adjutant Roger Wastian, and it was confirmed on 8 December 1973 by Leroy's commander, Léon Degrelle (q.v.).

LIE, Jonas

RANK: SS-Oberführer
BORN: 31 December 1899
DIED: 1945 (D)
PARTY number: —
SS NUMBER: 401276
AWARD: 1939 Iron Cross Second Class; 1939 Iron Cross First Class; SS Honour Ring.

A Norwegian, Lie was a professional police officer and amateur author who used the pseudonym of Max Mauser. In 1934 he was chosen by the League of Nations to lead the peacekeeping force sent to the Saar to supervise the plebiscite held to determine the territory's future. By a strange turn of fate Lie met and struck up a friendship with Josef Terboven, the Gauleiter of Essen and later Reichskommissar of Norway. Later, Terboven was to make no secret of the fact that he would have preferred Lie, rather than Quisling, to have been the leader of the Nasjonal Samling (the Norwegian Nazi Party). Although a sympathiser, Lie never joined the party (in Germany membership of the SS also did not necessarily mean membership of the NSDAP), a state of affairs pertinent to many who enlisted in the Waffen-SS in Norway and other occupied countries. Lie, as with the majority of those responsible for recruiting, as well as the majority of the volunteers that joined the Waffen-SS to fight in Russia, was not by nature a sympathiser to the Nazi cause, but can be best described as a fervent anti-communist, who joined Hitler's 'crusade against communism' out of a fear of a communist takeover in his country. In the case of Norway it must be seen that the Russian war with Finland directly endangered it. Likewise Danish volunteers felt threatened, and hence the fervour for volunteering to fight in this campaign can be easily understood. Equally it must be noted that the British Government allowed serving British military personnel to stand down, appear in mufti and volunteer for service with the Finnish forces against the Soviet Union. This led to a number of Britons in fact serving in Russia with the Finns, supporting SS units. Of course these men were never brought to trial for serving in this manner and have only relatively recently been allowed to receive the Finnish Winter War Medal.

A patriot, in April 1940 Lie ignored Quisling's 'demobilisation order' and continued to fight against the Germans until the end of the campaign; he was a patriotic Norwegian and therefore considered it his duty to uphold the integrity of his country against the invasion. His anti-communist views led to him having the position of responsibility in the police, plus the fact that due to his friendship with Terboven, which was formed in the 1930s, meant that when Terboven became commissioner for Norway he trusted Lie more than Quisling. Lie was altogether a more ruthless and unscrupulous character than Quisling. Enmity and jealousy soon sprang up between the two. Quisling had proposed a cabinet in which Lie was to be the minister of justice, but this was quashed. On 25 September 1941 Terboven dismissed the administrative council and replaced it by a Committee of Commissarial State Councillors, in which Lie was made responsible for the police.

SS recruiting propaganda in Norway was considered in rather nebulous National Socialist terms, but did claim that German intervention had foiled a British plot to occupy Norway. Quisling broadcast an appeal for volunteers for Regiment *Nordland* to participate in 'the war of freedom and independence against English despotism' on 13 January 1941. Recruitment was very slow to begin with; only around 300 volunteers came forward in the first year. Even after the commando raids on the Lofoten Islands, few Norwegians were concerned about this so-called threat to their homeland. Jonas Lie spoke of ancient claims to the Orkney and Shetland Isles and the Outer Hebrides. Few listened.

In the summer of 1942 Jonas Lie commanded the First Police Company, and in September it joined the rest of the legion outside Leningrad on the Eastern Front. The Norwegians did not take part in any major battles as such, but rather undertook patrols and reconnaissances. However, their attrition rate was high and their morale suffered as a result. Lie retained his position until its return to Norway on 6 April 1943.

In July 1942 the SS made a move calculated to weaken Quisling's grip on his own party. On the 21st Himmler let it be known that *Norges SS* had been transformed into the *Germanske SS Norge* and was now part of a new complex: non-Germanic Nordic Allgemeine-SS units, which were under the general leadership of the Germanic SS. This was directly responsible to Himmler and he confirmed Lie as leader of the new formation in Norway.

Lie survived the war and was arrested. The former chief of the Norwegian police and the police company died of a heart attack while awaiting trial in prison.

LINGE, Heinz

RANK: SS-Sturmbannführer
BORN: 22 March 1913
DIED: 9 March 1981 (D)
PARTY NUMBER: —
SS NUMBER: —

A bricklayer by profession, Linge joined the SS in 1933 and was subsequently posted to the SS-Begleitkommando which was charged with Hitler's protection. In July 1935, he undertook the task of Hitler's ordnance officer, and with the dismissal of Hitler's head valet, Karl Krause (q.v.), in September 1939 Linge was appointed to the post. During his tenure Hitler became fond of him. After Hitler's suicide, it fell to Linge to help wrap the corpse in an army blanket and carry it into the Chancellery garden to be cremated alongside Eva Braun. He helped inter the charred remains in a shell hole. He was in the 'bunker breakout' but was subsequently captured and spent 10 years in Soviet captivity. After his release he became a successful businessman in Hamburg where he eventually died in 1981.

LORENZ, Werner

RANK: SS-Obergruppenführer
BORN: 2 October 1891
DIED: 13 May 1974 (D)
PARTY NUMBER: 397994
SS NUMBER: 6636
AWARDS: SS Honour Ring; SS Honour Sword.

Born in Grünhof, Lorenz saw service in World War I as a pilot. He owned an estate in Danzig and became a zealous early party member, joining the SS in 1931. He headed the VOMI, the office charged with responsibility for the welfare of German nationals residing in other countries. From 1933 until the war's end he was the driving force in Himmler's (q.v.) ambitions to absorb racial Germans into the Reich, thus being able to control and use the extra manpower this afforded in the occupied territories.

The stewardship he exercised over his office never resorted to brutality, but epitomised skill and dexterity. Lorenz was captured at Flensburg on 10 May 1945, brought to trial and sentenced on 10 March 1948 to 20 years' imprisonment, although he was released in 1955.

LORITZ, Hans

RANK: SS-Oberführer
BORN: 21 December 1895
DIED: February 1946 (S)
PARTY NUMBER: 298668
SS NUMBER: 4165
AWARDS: 1914 Iron Cross Second Class, Cross of Honour 1914-1918 Combatants, 1914 Wound Badge Silver Class, War Merit Cross Second Class with Swords, War Merit Cross First Class with Swords, SS Honour Ring, SS Honour Sword.

Loritz served in World War I and afterwards joined the SS, becoming one of its early members. He was one of Dachau's most sadistic commanders and was responsible, with the connivance of the politische Abteilung, for introducing one of the most appalling tortures known in Dachau, the Baum or Pfahl experience.

Twice a week, selected prisoners had their hands tied behind their backs, forced on to a stool and were then hung to hooks on a post by their

wrists. The stool was kicked away and the victim remained suspended with his feet clear of the ground for up to two hours. The pain was excruciating. An added refinement was to make the body swing and flog it. The sudden drop caused broken joints, and even when there were no permanent effects, a victim could not use his arms for weeks afterwards.

After the war, he was arrested as a war criminal and imprisoned at the internment camp in Neumünster to await trial by the Soviets. However he committed suicide in February 1946.

M

MACHER, Heinz

RANK: SS-Sturmbannführer
BORN: 31 December 1919
DIED: 21 December 2001 (D)
PARTY NUMBER: —
SS NUMBER: —
AWARDS: 1939 Iron Cross Second Class, 24 September 1941; 1939 Iron Cross First Class, 15 March 1942; German Cross in Gold, 7 August 1944; Knight's Cross of the Iron Cross, 3 April 1943; Oakleaves, 19 August 1944; Close Combat Clasp Gold Class, 23 October 1944; Tank Destruction Strip Silver Class; Medal for the Winter Campaign in Russia 1941-1942; 1939 Wound Badge Gold Class, July 1943.

Born in Chemnitz, Saxony, Macher served in the RAD before joining the Waffen-SS as a pioneer on 3 April 1939. He was posted to the Second Company of the SS-Pioneer Battalion at Dresden, and his unit was engaged in the Polish campaign. Macher's outstanding leadership qualities led to his selection for the SS-Junkerschule at Bad-Tölz from October 1939 to August 1940. On completion of the course, he was transferred to the SS-Junkerschule at Brünswick. In March 1941 he remustered with his old unit, now the pioneer battalion of the 2nd SS Panzer Division *Das Reich*.

Macher led his platoon on the Russian Front and was wounded during Operation 'Barbarossa'. He discharged himself from hospital and continued in various capacities. During the night of the 11/12 March 1943, Macher formed an assault group from his company and undertook a daring attack against Soviet positions on the outskirts of Kharkov. After infiltrating the Soviet lines the detachment took the Russian defenders completely by surprise. In fierce hand-to-hand fighting, Macher secured a substantial bridgehead within the Soviet positions, killing 90 or more of the Russian defenders and capturing 28, as well as substantial amounts of small arms, mortars and anti-tank weapons. Accomplished without loss of life, the bridgehead facilitated the German armoured units' drive deep into the Soviets' rear areas. Macher was awarded the Knight's Cross of the Iron Cross.

Macher's unit was transferred to France for a refit in March 1944, and after the Normandy landings it was positioned near St Lo. Here it suffered continual aerial bombardment and sustained ground attacks, repulsing 38 different assaults and engaging in equal numbers of counterattacks. Macher became the 554th recipient of the Oakleaves. He was critically wounded and evacuated through the rapidly closing Falaise Gap.

In January 1945 he was assigned as a staff officer at Army Group Weichs, then transferred to Pomerania and assigned to the Second Division under General Bleckwendt. Due to the severity of his wounds, he was transferred to WASAG, a company involved in the production of explosives, and was engaged in research on grenades and anti-tank mines. Macher was summoned to Himmler's (q.v.) headquarters on 30

March 1945 and was entrusted with the task of destroying Wewelsburg Castle, Himmler's SS shrine. Macher remained as part of Himmler's headquarters staff. The final and most bizarre escapade came when, in the company of SS-Obersturmbannführer Grothmann (q.v.), he accompanied Himmler in his attempt to escape disguised as an army sergeant. He and his comrades were captured.

MARTINSEN, Knud Borge

RANK: Legions-Obersturmbannführer
BORN: unknown
DIED: 25 June 1949 (E.A.)
PARTY NUMBER: —
SS NUMBER: —
AWARDS: 1939 Iron Cross Second Class; 1939 Iron Cross First Class.

When the commander of the Freikorps *Danmark*, von Schalburg (q.v.), was wounded in the leg during an attack on 2 June 1942, and then killed by an artillery salvo, Martinsen, his second-in-command, took over and ordered a withdrawal. The assault company pulled back leaving the bodies of von Schalburg and 24 comrades buried beside the road near Biakovo. On 10 June 1942 Martinsen was replaced as commander by SS-Obersturmbannführer Hans-Albert von Lettow-Vorbeck, an appointment bitterly resented by the Danes, as they believed it broke the agreement that the Freikorps was essentially a Danish unit with Danish officers. What was more, Martinsen had proved himself to be more than a capable commander in the short time he had been in command. Lettow-Vorbeck only commanded the unit for nine days, however, when he was killed in action on 11 June 1942.

Martinsen took over once again and succeeded in extricating the Freikorps from a dangerous situation imposed by a surprise Soviet attack on Bolshoi Dubovitsky. Following this, Martinsen was promoted and confirmed as the Freikorps' commander. Having suffered 121 killed, the Freikorps was given home leave in September for four weeks. It returned to the front in October 1942 and was finally withdrawn in April 1943, being officially disbanded the following month.

On his return home, Martinsen set up, with German connivance, a Danish branch of the Germanic SS. It was formed in April 1943 and Martinsen called it *Germansk* Korps, which he quickly renamed *Schalburg* Korps, in memory of the Freikorps' most popular commander. The corps opened its ranks to 'all young men of Nordic blood' without, theoretically, regard to their political affiliation. After the general strike in Denmark in June and July 1944, the corps was withdrawn from Copenhagen and moved outside the city to Ringstad and absorbed into the SS. In October 1944, ostensibly for criticising the Germans, Martinsen was relieved of his command.

After the war he was sentenced to death. The death penalty had been abolished in 1895 in Denmark, but was restored on 1 June 1945 for extreme cases of collaboration or crimes against humanity. Martinsen was executed on 25 June 1949.

MAURICE, Emil

RANK: SS-Oberführer
BORN: 19 January 1897
DIED: 6 February 1972 (D)
PARTY NUMBER: 39
SS NUMBER: 2
AWARDS: Golden Party Badge; Coburg Badge, 14 October 1932; Blood Order No 495; War Merit Cross Second Class without Swords; SS Honour Ring; SS Honour Sword.

A watchmaker by trade, Maurice was born in Westmoor. In 1919 he joined the German Workers' Party, the forerunner of the NSDAP, becoming Hitler's bodyguard and chauffeur. He took part in the 1923 Putsch

and joined the fugitives on its failure, but was captured and imprisoned in Landsberg. He become an intimate of Hitler and acted as secretary, noting down Mein Kampf until Hess took over.

Following his release, he remained in Hitler's inner circle, continuing in his previous role. Tension broke out between them in 1927 because of Maurice's unwanted liaison with Hitler's niece, Geli Raubal. This ultimately ousted him from the inner circle. Nevertheless, in June 1934 Maurice was with Hitler when he raided Röhm and his associates, shooting the homosexual Edmund Heinz and the boy found in his bed. He is also credited with the murder of Father Stempfle.

By 1935 the tension between Hitler and Maurice had begun to subside, due in part to Maurice's application to marry; since he was in the SS, the couple both had to submit proof of Aryan purity. When Himmler announced that 'without question SS-Standartenführer Emil Maurice is, according to his ancestral table, not of Aryan descent', Hitler refused to expel him from either the party or the SS. Himmler was outraged, but promotion followed, with Maurice becoming SS-Brigadeführer. From 1940 to 1942 he served as an officer in the Luftwaffe. He also headed a Munich handicraft works guild. In 1948 a de-Nazification court sentenced him to four years in a labour camp. He died in Munich on 6 February 1972.

MEISSNER, Otto

BORN: 1880
DIED: 27 May 1953 (D)

State Secretary and chief of the President's Chancellery from 1920 to 1933 under President Hindenburg, Meissner retained this position when Hitler assumed power and held it until 1945. In 1937 he was elevated to the higher position of Reichsminister.

Meissner was a functionary with little real power, but on the occasion of Heydrich's (q.v.) state funeral, Hitler told President Hacha and his Czech delegation that if he had any more trouble, he would deport the entire population. Thereupon, Meissner, who never had anything to do but arrange the seating at the dinner, took Dr Hacha for a walk in the garden and told him Hitler meant it. The result was a mass rally in Prague declaring the loyalty of the Czech nation. Hitler was deeply impressed. Meissner was arrested and tried at Nuremberg for war crimes on 11 April 1949 but was acquitted. He died in Munich in 1953.

MEYER, Kurt

RANK: SS-Brigadeführer und Generalmajor der Waffen-SS
BORN: 23 December 1910
DIED: 23 December 1960 (D)
PARTY NUMBER: 316714
SS NUMBER: 17559
AWARDS: 1939 Iron Cross Second Class, 20 September 1939; 1939 Iron Cross First Class, 8 June 1940; German Cross in Gold, 8 February 1942; Knight's Cross, 18 May 1941; Oakleaves, 23 May 1943; Oakleaves with Swords, 27 August 1944; Wound Badge Black Class; SS Honour Ring; SS Honour Sword; (Bulgaria: Military Order for Bravery).

One of the youngest generals in the Waffen-SS, Meyer was born in Jerxheim and originally served with the Mecklenburg Police, joining the *Leibstandarte* in Berlin in 1934. He saw service during the campaigns in Poland and France.

The LSSAH marched through Yugoslavia on its way to Greece in early 1941, where his impressive leadership was largely responsible for the defeat of Greek resistance near Lake Castoria. Always at the front of his reconnaissance unit and later his division, Meyer's daring actions earned him the nicknames 'Panzermeyer' and 'Schnell Meyer' during the early days of the war. He won the Knight's Cross of the Iron Cross.

Meyer was in charge of the Reconnaissance Detachment during

the Russian campaign, and led his men to Uman, Cherson, Perikop, Taganrog and Rostov. In recognition of his achievements, he became the 195th recipient of the Oakleaves.

In 1943 'Panzermeyer', as he was now known, left the *Leibstandarte*, taking command of his own regiment in the 12th SS-Panzer Division *Hitlerjugend*. When the commander, SS-Brigadeführer Fritz Witt, was killed in action on 16 June 1944 by Allied naval gunfire, Meyer assumed command of the division, and led it in an unsuccessful effort to counter the advancing Allied invasion. His leadership earned him the Oakleaves and Swords.

By now a major-general in the Waffen-SS, he was severely wounded on 6 September and captured at Amiens on 17 November 1944, falling into the hands of Belgian partisans. He would have preferred to have been killed on the spot, but the Americans intervened and turned him over to the British. After he had made a limited recovery he was transferred to England.

After the war he was brought before a Canadian military court at Aurich, tried for war crimes (the murder of Canadian prisoners in Normandy by troops under his command) and convicted with a sentence of execution by firing squad. However, this sentence was commuted to life imprisonment and he was taken to Canada. Several years later he was transferred to West Germany, and finally released on 6 September 1954 after a number of appeals. As a result of his war wounds, his health deteriorated. While celebrating his 50th birthday he suffered a fatal heart attack, from which he died on 23 December 1960 in Hagen, Westphalia.

MODER, Paul
RANK: SS-Gruppenführer
BORN: 1 October 1896
DIED: 8 February 1942 (K.I.A.)
PARTY NUMBER: 9425
SS NUMBER: 11716

Moder was SS and police commander in Warsaw from October 1939 to June 1940. He then served as a staff officer with SS-Oberabschnitt Ost until 19 July 1941. Awaiting Himmler's (q.v.) decision on a new police assignment for him in the East, he joined the *Totenkopf* Division. With a combat rank of SS-Sturmbannführer, Moder was attached to the motorcycle battalion in Russia. At his own request he was given an extension of his stay, and in the autumn of 1941 became involved in the extremely bitter fighting south of Lake Ilmen. At the height of the Soviet winter counteroffensive in the Demjansk sector, he was killed in action on 8 February 1942.

MOHNKE, Wilhelm
RANK: SS-Oberführer
BORN: 15 March 1911
DIED: 6 August 2001 (D)
PARTY NUMBER: 649684
SS NUMBER: 15541
AWARDS: 1939 Iron Cross, 21 September 1939; 1939 Iron Cross First Class, 8 November 1939; German Cross in Gold, 26 December 1941; Knight's Cross of the Iron Cross, 11 July 1944; SS Honour Ring; SS Honour Sword.

Born in Lübeck, Mohnke was a fervent Nazi, an original member of the *Leibstandarte* who commanded Hitler's bodyguard during the 1930s.

Mohnke fought in France in 1940 and is notorious for shooting prisoners of war. On 28 May 1940 his commanding officer, 'Sepp' Dietrich, (q.v) ordered him to attack and secure the village of Wormhoudt, which lay between Kassel and Dunkirk. It was held by men of the British 48th Division with troops from the Second Royal Warwicks and machine gunners of the 4th Cheshire Regiment. Resistance was determined and the *Leibstandarte* lost 23 men killed and many more were wounded.

Many prisoners were taken and some appear to have been reasonably treated. One group of between 80 and 90 Royal Warwicks, Cheshires and a few artillery men were seen late in the afternoon by the new

commander of the second battalion, Mohnke. He was in an angry mood. Completely losing his temper, he accused the NCO in charge of the escort of disobeying orders by taking prisoners instead of shooting them. Mohnke ordered them to be escorted to a nearby barn and killed. First, a salvo of grenades was thrown into the small, crowded barn. This was followed by small-arms fire. The survivors were ordered out in groups of five, and the first two were immediately executed, although one badly wounded private feigned death and later managed to crawl into the barn and lie among the dead. Only 15 men survived the massacre, and when four of the survivors were repatriated in 1943, they reported the atrocity to the British authorities.

In 1941 Mohnke served with the *Leibstandarte* in the Balkans and was badly wounded in the foot by a Yugoslav air strike. Later, he rejoined the *Leibstandarte* in Russia, but in mid-1943 was transferred to the newly formed 12th SS Panzer Division *Hitlerjugend* and was given command of the 26th SS-Panzergrenadier Regiment.

In June 1944, Mohnke's regiment was on the Normandy invasion front, where it was locked in battle with elements of the Canadian 3rd Infantry Division. Three Canadian soldiers, riflemen A. R. Owens of the Royal Winnipeg Rifles, Sapper Jionel and G. A. Benner of the Royal Canadian Engineers, were captured and escorted to the HQ of the 26th SS-Panzergrenadier Regiment. Mohnke interrogated them for 20 minutes. After its conclusion two Feldgendarmerie marched the prisoners to a nearby bomb crater and shot them, while Mohnke watched impassively. Mohnke was also implicated in four other separate similar incidents, involving another nine Canadian prisoners.

Mohnke assumed command of the *Leibstandarte* after its commander, Theodor Wisch, had been badly wounded. He led it in the Ardennes counteroffensive of December 1944 and he was implicated in the Malmédy Massacre. After the failure in the Ardennes, 6th SS Panzer Army was withdrawn for refitting and sent to Hungary. Mohnke was transferred to Berlin as Commandant of the Reich Chancellery. He was in the Führer bunker when Hitler committed suicide and an eyewitness reported that he wept openly. It was Mohnke who set fire to the bunker on the following day, 1 May, and he joined one of the escape groups that night. He was captured by the Russians while hiding in a cellar in the Schönhauser Allee. In October 1955 he was one of the first Germans to be released from Soviet captivity. Mohnke died in 2001 in Hamburg.

MOOYMAN, Gerardus
RANK: SS-Untersturmführer
BORN: 23 September 1923
DIED: 21 June 1987 (D)
PARTY NUMBER: —
SS NUMBER: —
AWARDS: 1939 Iron Cross Second Class, 4 February 1943; 1939 Iron Cross First Class, 10 February 1943; Knight's Cross of the Iron Cross, 20 February 1943; Medal for the Winter Campaign in Russia 1941-1942.

Mooyman was born in Apeldoorn in Holland and was one of the first 'Germanic' volunteers in the Waffen-SS, joining the SS-Volunteer Legion *Nederland* as a gunner in the 14th anti-tank company. During the fierce fighting on the northeastern front in February 1943, he destroyed more than 15 Russian tanks south of Lake Ladoga with his anti-tank gun.

He became the first Germanic volunteer to be awarded the Knight's Cross, on 20 February 1943, and General Major Fritz von Scholz decorated him personally on 17 March 1943. Subsequently, he was paraded for propaganda purposes, first in Berlin, where he met Dutch journalists on 23 March, and notably by being welcomed in April in Holland by SS-Gruppenführer Reuter and Seyss-Inquart (q.v.). He made further photo calls in Belgium.

After the war he was sentenced to six years' imprisonment for his involvement in the Waffen-SS, but was released after only two years. He was involved in a road accident and died from his injuries in 1987.

MORGEN, Konrad

RANK: SS-Obersturmbannführer
BORN: 1909
DIED: 1976 (D)
PARTY NUMBER: —
SS NUMBER: —

An assistant SS judge, Morgen's function was to investigate irregularities in the administration of the concentration camps. His brief, astonishingly, was to ensure that no brutality took place. Considering the transportations to Auschwitz and Treblinka, the gassing and cremations, it depicts an extraordinary ambivalence in SS attitudes towards its purpose as exterminator.

Morgen was also instructed to investigate theft by guards or SS officers. In both functions he acted scrupulously. In camp after camp he obtained sentences against SS personnel for brutality. In 1943 he discovered the camp commandant of Buchenwald, Karl Koch (q.v), had concealed murders, falsified documents and embezzled over 100,000 Marks. Morgen presented his report to SS headquarters, where it was directed to Kaltenbrunner (q.v) who passed it to the legal department, both authorities preferring not to handle it. Himmler (q.v) acted on it, and Koch was found guilty and executed. Belzec, Majdanek, Sobibor and Treblinka extermination camps built by Wirth (q.v) were subsequently inspected and Morgen found not less than 800 cases of corruption and murder. After the war he was a Nuremberg witness. he practiced law in West Germany until his death in 1976.

MRUGOWSKY, Prof Dr Joachim

RANK: SS-Oberführer
BORN: 15 August 1905
DIED: 2 June 1948 (E.A.)
PARTY NUMBER: 210049
SS NUMBER: 25811
AWARDS: 1939 Iron Cross Second Class; War Merit Cross Second Class with Swords; War Merit Cross First Class with Swords; SS Honour Ring; SS Honour Sword.

A professor of bacteriology, Mrugowsky joined the SS in 1931 and became head of the SS health department Hygiene Institute in Berlin in 1939, a post he held until the end of the war. He believed in the doctor's function as 'the priest of the holy flame of life' and wrote of the 'art of healing' as the doctor's 'divine mission'.

In March 1942, Himmler (q.v) was greatly impressed with Zyklon B because it offered no possibility of a mechanical breakdown and in August commissioned Mrugowsky to send a demonstrator to Wirth, (q.v) the commander in Poland. From then on the distribution of Zyklon B within the SS became centrally regulated by the SS Hygiene Institute in Berlin. Mrugowsky also ordered experimentation with phenol in Buchenwald after it had been noted that tiny percentages of carbolic acid preservative in serum had contributed to the accidental death of several German soldiers. He also observed the effect of poison bullets on inmates. Tried in the doctors' trials, Mrugowsky was found guilty of extensive involvement in fatal medical experiments. He was hanged at Landsberg Prison on 2 June 1948.

MÜLLER, Heinrich

RANK: SS-Gruppenführer und Generalleutnant der Polizei
BORN: 28 April 1900
DIED: May 1945 (M.I.A.)
PARTY NUMBER: 4583199
SS NUMBER: 107043
AWARDS: 1914 Iron Cross Second Class; 1914 Iron Cross First Class; Cross of Honour 1914-1918 Combatants; 1939 Iron Cross Second Class Bar, 29 October 1940; 1939 Iron Cross First Class Bar, 29 October 1940; War Merit Cross Second Class with Swords; War Merit Cross First Class with Swords; Knight's Cross to the War Merit Cross with Swords, 5 October 1944; SS Honour Ring; SS Honour Sword.

Born in Munich, Müller served as an NCO and pilot in the Fliegerabteilung 287A on the Western Front in World War I. From 1919 to 1934, he served in the Bavarian Police as an official of the Munich political police, employed as an expert on politics and the surveillance of communists. In 1931, when Hitler's niece, Geli Raubal, was shot, Bormann (q.v), using the 'Adolf Hitler Fund', allegedly paid Müller, the investigating police inspector, to ensure that no whiff of scandal tainted Hitler. Müller proved himself reliable, and Bormann recruited him to the party. Heydrich (q.v) selected him to take over the Gestapo from Diels (q.v), who was Göring's man.

As head of the SS-RSHA Amt IV, the bureaucratic office that was Gestapo headquarters, 'Gestapo' Müller directed the department run by Eichmann (q.v), and his position remained unchanged for the remainder of the war. The promotions and changes that followed Heydrich's assassination in 1942 did not affect him and he continued to serve under Kaltenbrunner (q.v). He headed the investigation committee that sought out the 20th July conspirators and was awarded the Knight's Cross of the War Merit Cross with Swords for its success. He shunned publicity and is believed to have planned an escape well in advance of the inevitable defeat. He was last seen in Berlin in the closing weeks of the war, but then vanished. The mystery of his disappearance remains, but it has been reported in a recent publication that he was recruited into the CIA and thus made his way to America.

N

NAUJOCKS, Alfred

RANK: SS-Sturmbannführer
BORN: 20 September 1911
DIED: 4 April 1960 (D)
PARTY NUMBER: 26240
SS NUMBER: 624279

An engineering student at Kiel University, Naujocks spent more time brawling than studying. He joined the SS in 1931, and became an official of the Amt VI of the SS security service in 1934 and was one of the most audacious commanders of the SD. He was not an intelligent leader and lacked the mental capacity for creating intricate plans such as those conceived by Heydrich (q.v). However, he was expert at carrying out an operation once it was explained clearly to him.

A trusted associate of Heydrich, Naujocks was involved in a number of shady but important operations. He helped Heydrich with the Tukhachedsky affair and staged some bombings in Slovakia, which were blamed on Slovak nationalists. Heydrich chose him to lead the simulated attack on the Gleiwitz radio stations in Poland on 10 August 1939, which provided Germany with justification for invasion. He was also involved in the Venlo incident, abducting two British intelligence officers, Captain S. Payne-Best and Major R. H. Stephens, in the Netherlands in order to accuse them of involvement in the 1939 Munich bomb plot. The Venlo incident provided the excuse for invading the Low Countries.

Naujocks worked on Operation 'Bernhard', the operation of faking British bank notes by inmates of the Sachsenhausen concentration camp. The escapade gives a prime example of the bizarre nature of the Third Reich's leaders. The Nazi authorities were so pleased with the results that 12 prisoners, three of whom were Jews, were awarded the War Merit Medal, and six of the SS guards the War Merit Cross Second

Class without Swords. One wonders what the Jewish medal winners thought of their awards.

Dismissed by the SD for disobedience, Naujocks joined the Waffen SS in 1943 and was responsible for the murder of members of the Danish Resistance. In November 1944 he deserted to the Americans and at the war's end he escaped from a US internment camp, suspected of organising the ODESSA operation that provided ex-SS members with an escape route. He died in 1960 in Germany. Naujocks has been described as being an 'intellectual gangster'. He was certainly one of Heydrich's most ruthless assassination squad leaders. During the attack on the Gleiwitz radio station, for example, he had no qualms about shooting a dozen concentration camp inmates in Polish uniforms and leaving their bodies scattered around the site. He was very fortunate to have escaped a death sentence in 1945.

NEBE, Artur

RANK: SS-Gruppenführer
BORN: 13 November 1894
DIED: 3 March 1945 (unverified)
PARTY NUMBER: 280152
SS NUMBER: 574307
AWARDS: 1914 Iron Cross Second Class; 1914 Iron Cross First Class; Cross of Honour 1914-1918 Combatants; 1939 Iron Cross Second Class Bar; War Merit Cross Second Class with Swords; Police Long Service Cross, 18 Years; Army Long Service Medal, NSDAP Long Service Cross, 10 Years; Commemorative Medal of 13 March 1938; Commemorative Medal of 1 October 1938; Prague Castle Bar.

The director of Kripo led something of a double life; he was a survivor who obeyed his instincts. In February 1934 he and Gisevius were summoned by 'Sepp' Dietrich (q.v) to Lichterfelde barracks and asked to compile a report for Himmler (q.v) and Heydrich (q.v) stating all known excesses committed by the Gestapo and SA. In typical character during 1933-34, Nebe sided with Himmler against Göring over Gestapo control, and later became a very questionable member of the Resistance Circle before the 20 July Bomb Plot. Principally, he was an old-style police officer who, since 1934, had seen his criminal police department infiltrated by amateur Gestapo officers and finally absorbed by Heydrich in 1939.

Nebe's retention of office was due to the five months he spent in Russia heading Einsatzgruppe B, which worked with Army Group Centre in the Soviet Union in the area between the Baltic states and the Ukraine. Nebe's headquarters were at Minsk and later Smolensk where he was in touch with Hans Oster, an old friend and an opponent of Hitler's war aims. Nebe supposedly fought against Heydrich's orders, disclosing them to the Oster circle, who had used him as an information post for four years. This may explain why Heydrich's reports credit Nebe with a quite modest score of 46,000 liquidations compared to Stahlecker's (q.v) 221,000.

The winter of 1941-42 had taken a toll on the Einsatzgruppen leaders, who were feeling the effects of the murders. Nebe was a mere shadow of himself and on the verge of a nervous breakdown. One of his associates had described him as being 'a mere shadow of his former self, nerves on edge and depressed'. Nebe's driver, a man called Köhn, had shot himself in horror at the actions being taken against the Jews, which must have depressed and shaken Nebe even further.

Himmler travelled to Minsk to encourage his executioners, asking to witness a liquidation, and obligingly supplying 100 partisans from the city jail, all but two being men. According to one account, Himmler ordered Nebe to seduce the two women before shooting them, thinking it a useful way of obtaining information regarding partisan activities. Himmler became hysterical and nearly collapsed on witnessing the shootings (he was splattered with victims' brains) and ordered Nebe to develop a method of killing less distressing to the executioners! Nebe readily agreed, for the psychological effect on those who had to carry out the executions was very great.

Nebe began experimenting with killing people, using exhaust gases from his car, an eight-cylinder Horch. A keen amateur film maker, he enthusiastically filmed his work. After the war footage showing a gas chamber, worked by the exhaust of a lorry, was found in his Berlin flat.

On the dismissal of Diels (q.v), Himmler rearranged the police organisations. Nebe controlled the Kripo, the frontier police and counter-espionage police. His brinkmanship foundered with the 1944 Bomb Plot. He supported the plotters and with the failure of the early stages of the revolt, Nebe played the tireless policeman rooting out the guilty. The arrest of his colleague Helldorf brought the Gestapo too close for comfort. Nebe had not even been suspected at the time of his colleague's arrest and he might not have been pulled in at all had he not chosen to hide.

On 23 August 1944, SS-Standartenführer Werner of the RSHA issued a description and offered a reward of 50,000 Reichsmarks for Nebe. Himmler expelled Nebe from the SS on 30 November, adding, 'It has been proved by documents found and investigations carried out by the state police, that for years Nebe had maintained close relations with people directly involved in the Putsch of 20 July. His betrayal had been to support the Putschists, breaking his allegiance to the Führer.' The latter was certainly true, for as early as 1941, when he was involved in Einsatzgruppe activities, he had secretly urged the murder of Hitler as the only way of ending the Nazi regime. However, he was appalled by the poor security measures taken by his fellow conspirators. He himself was always careful to cover his tracks and avoid any danger.

Nebe was arrested on 16 January 1945, evidently betrayed by a girlfriend, and sentenced by the People's Court to death. There is no official mention of a Volksgericht trial, however, and Nebe is not on Pechel's list of Plötzensee executions. The author Gregory Douglas suggests in his book that Müller became a CIA agent. Could Nebe have followed the same route?

NEUMANN, Eggert

RANK: SS-Sturmbannführer
BORN: 30 December 1912
DIED: 28 May 1970 (D)
PARTY NUMBER: 1162622
SS NUMBER: 45654
AWARDS: 1939 Iron Cross Second Class; 1939 Iron Cross First Class; Knight's Cross of the Iron Cross; SS Honour Ring.

Neumann was the commander of SS Gebirge Aufklärungsabteilung 7 of the 7th SS Freiwilligen-Gebirgs Division *Prinz Eugen*, where he distinguished himself through his personal courage and initiative. For this he was awarded the Knight's Cross of the Iron Cross. employed in actions against Tito's partisans in Yugoslavia, in October 1944, the division was transferred to Belgrade to cover the flank of the German retreat through Yugoslavia after the Romanian and Bulgarian defections to the Allies. Here, the division suffered appalling losses at the hands of the Soviet forces. Reconstructed and redeployed against the partisans, the division was held responsible for some of the worst atrocities carried out in the war, although the partisan fighting was particularly brutal. In one incident, an NCO had placed some young recruits in a house and paid the lady of the house for their keep. After half an hour he returned to find the young soldiers being emasculated by a group of women. He felt he had little option but to throw two grenades into the house, to save his recruits further agony and to punish the women.

When the division surrendered to the Soviet forces in May 1945 it numbered only a few hundred troops, who were brutally treated by their captors. The division, which had contained Serbs, Romanians and Hungarians, had always been viewed as a unit for anti-partisan duties. As such, it had never been allocated first-rate weapons and equipment to fight with. Neumann died in Hamburg in 1970.

O

OBERG, Carl-Albrecht

Rank: SS-Obergruppenführer
Born: 27 January 1897
Died: 3 June 1965 (D)
Party Number: 575205
SS Number: 36075
Awards: 1914 Iron Cross Second Class; 1914 Iron Cross First Class; Cross of Honour 1914-1918 Combatants; War Merit Cross Second Class with Swords; War Merit Cross First Class with Swords; SS Honour Ring; SS Honour Sword.

Oberg, along with millions of others, had been thrown on the streets in the Depression, where he had been an executive with a firm of banana importers. His motive in joining the SS had been partly monetary: it had meant an end to financial problems. Oberg trailed Heydrich (q.v.) to Munich within months of the Nazis coming to power, feeling that he held the key to his future. His rate of promotion in the intervening nine years was impressive: on 1 July 1933 he was a mere SS-Untersturmführer, but by September 1941 he was SD and Polizeiführer at Radom in Poland, where he had been most assiduous in his pursuit of Jews.

Escorted by Heydrich, Oberg departed for Paris on 7 May 1942 to reorganise the regional branches of the SS and Gestapo in France in an attempt to quash the French Resistance. The SD took over surveillance of the French police, and the head office of the German police service in Paris was modelled on RSHA in Berlin, with regional offices established throughout occupied France. The actual Gestapo was controlled by Sonderkommando IV, later IV B4, engaged in the anti-Jewish campaign and under the control of Theo Dannecker.

Many members of the staff of Heinrich von Stülpnagel, the military governor of France, were part of the 1944 Bomb Plot conspiracy, and Oberg and Helmuth Knochen (q.v), the Paris commander of the security police, were arrested with the entire staff of the Gestapo and the SD, although they only spent three hours in captivity. At 0130 hours in the morning, on the threat of armed intervention, Stülpnagel released his captives and the affair ended with an all-night drinking party in the Hotel Raphael, where ambassador Abtez made Stülpnagel and Oberg shake hands.

On Oberg's suggestion, the troops who had conducted the arrests and who had got the sand ready for the executions in the Ecole Militaire, were thanked at morning parade for carrying out a practical exercise with the higher SS police leader. At the end of the war Oberg went into hiding. As Albrecht Heintze he had a fleeting period of anonymity in Kirchberg, a small Tyrolean village near Kitzbühel. However, his real identity was soon established and in August he was handed over to the French authorities at Wildbad. Oberg was sentenced by a British court in 1946 for the illegal execution of captured airmen in his capacity as SS police commander in France. He was further sentenced to death in Paris in October 1954 and was imprisoned in Cherche-Midi Prison, where he remained until December 1959 when his sentence was commuted to 20 years' forced labour.

OHLENDORF, Otto

Rank: SS-Gruppenführer
Born: 4 February 1907
Died: 8 June 1951 (E.A.)
Party Number: 6531
SS Number: 880
Awards: Golden Party Badge; War Merit Cross Second Class with Swords; War Merit Cross First Class with Swords; SS Honour Ring; SS Honour Sword.

A Hanoverian farmer, who was both a lawyer and an economist, Ohlendorf was an early member of the NSDAP, although he soon discov-

ered that he did not agree with all of its policies. While a member of the Institute of World Economics in Kiel, he came to the conclusion that the NSDAP had collective socialist tendencies and spoke out against this flaw. The Gestapo arrested him for his continued lecturing and after the Gestapo's investigators had concluded their work, he had no wish to speak out further against party policies. Ohlendorf thought his party career was ended, but a chance introduction to Professor Reinhard Höhn in Berlin, who headed an SD section, led to his appointment as an economic adviser.

Catapulted to the centre of the Nazi Party movement, Ohlendorf assembled a staff of economists from all over Germany and analysed the economic affairs of the Third Reich. He expanded his activities to include reporting on culture, science, education, law, administration, and even the hallowed ground of the party and the state. Initially these reports found little favour with Hitler and Himmler (q.v), who tended to disregard them, but Himmler began to call him 'Nazism's Knight of the Holy Grail'. However, when Ohlendorf overstepped the mark, Himmler explained to him in no uncertain terms that his reports were illegal and unwanted and he was to concentrate on less critical economic accounts in the future. Ohlendorf tended his resignation; Himmler ignored it. Ohlendorf became chief of the inland (internal) SD and acquired a reputation as an administrator who was intelligent and humane.

The Führer's plan for the invasion of Poland was simple: Himmler was to form Einsatzgruppen which were to follow the German troops and liquidate the upper classes. A month after the invasion Heydrich was able to announce: 'Of the Polish upper classes in the occupied territories only a maximum of three per cent is still present.' With the invasion of Russia and the decision to liquidate the Jews, the SS and OKW came to an agreement in April 1941 stating that 'the Einsatzgruppen are authorised, within the framework of their task and on their own responsibility, to take executive measures affecting the civilian population.' Commander of Einsatzgruppe D in the Ukraine, Ohlendorf immediately became an expert on extermination, keeping exact scores of his achievements. By the winter of 1941–42 his command had murdered 92,000 Jews and was still going strong. The other groups were feeling the psychological strain and replacements were made. Ohlendorf, however, became more fanatical.

On 30 April 1945 he travelled to Flensberg, where Himmler had established his HQ, and advised him to surrender to the Allies. Himmler refused. Ohlendorf accompanied Himmler in his escape from Flensberg, until they were apprehended by the British. Ohlendorf learnt of Himmler's suicide, but suicide was furthest from his own thoughts. He was convinced he could justify all his actions and looked forward to the opportunity to do so. He was tried for war crimes and on 10 April 1948 was found guilty and sentenced to death. After all appeals had been heard, he was hanged at Landsberg Prison on 8 June 1951.

P

PEIPER, Joachim

Rank: SS-Standartenführer
Born: 30 January 1915
Died: 14 July 1976 (M)
Party Number:
SS Number: 132496
Awards: 1939 Iron Cross Second Class, 31 May 1940; 1939 Iron Cross First Class, 1 July 1940; Knight's Cross of the Iron Cross, 9 March 1943; Oakleaves, 27 January 1944; Swords, 11 January 1945; Close Combat Clasp Silver Class, SS Honour Ring; SS Honour Sword.

Peiper was born in Berlin-Wilmersdorf, the son of an army officer. He volunteered for duty with the *Leibstandarte* in October 1934 and attended the SS-Officers' school at Brünswick. He served as Himmler's (q.v.) adjutant from 1938 to 1939, and when war broke out served with the motorised regiment *Leibstandarte* in the Western campaign. He was transferred to the Eastern Front, and while serving as commanding officer of the 3rd Battalion, SS-Panzergrenadier Regiment 2, LSSAH, was awarded the Knight's Cross of the Iron Cross for his bravery in action near Kharkov.

In autumn 1943 Peiper took command of the panzer regiment of the *Leibstandarte*, and as commanding officer of the 1st Regiment was awarded the Oakleaves, becoming the 277th recipient. His command was transferred to the Western Front and during the defensive withdrawal following the Allied invasion in 1944 he was awarded the Swords, becoming the 119th recipient.

During the Ardennes Offensive men of Peiper's unit took a number of American prisoners at a small crossroads in Malmédy, Belgium. The events that surrounded the incident are confused, but 74 Americans were murdered, and after the war the senior commanders were tried at Dachau for war crimes as a result of this massacre. On 16 July 1946, 43 death sentences were handed down to the 74 defendants on trial. Thanks

to the energetic efforts of the American prosecution council, Major Everett, none of the controversial sentences were ever carried out. Peiper was one of those condemned, and his sentence was commuted to life imprisonment in 1951.

He was released from Landsberg Prison on 22 December 1956. He changed his name and settled in France, but on 13 July 1976 he was brutally murdered, probably by former French Resistance members.

PISTER, Hermann
RANK: SS-Standartenführer
BORN: 21 February 1885
DIED: 11 April 1947 (E.A.)
PARTY NUMBER: 918391
SS NUMBER: 29892
AWARDS: 1914 Iron Cross Second Class; Cross of Honour 1914-1918 Combatants; War Merit Cross Second Class with Swords; War Merit Cross First Class with Swords; SS Honour Ring; SS Honour Sword.

Pister was in command of concentration camps in the south and commandant of Buchenwald, which supplied prisoners on 12-hour shifts to local armaments factories. In the closing weeks of the war Hitler told Pister that Dachau, Mauthausen and Theresienstadt were to be blown up, together with their inhabitants if they could not be evacuated before the arrival of the Allies. But in fact there was little will left to carry out the order. One view was that Pister only carried out the terrible evacuations from Buchenwald under direct pressure from Erbprinz Waldeck-Pirmont, who had persistently sheltered the worst Buchenwald criminals. Liberated by the US 80th Division in April 1945, Pister was tried at Dachau on 11 April 1947 and sentenced to death. The sentence was carried out without any delay.

PLEASANTS, Eric
RANK: SS-Schütze
BORN: 1911
DIED: unknown
PARTY NUMBER: —
SS NUMBER: —

Pleasants was born in Norfolk, the son of a gamekeeper. As a youngster he became interested in body building, physical fitness and sport, taking up amateur boxing and wrestling. He attended Loughborough College under the patronage of the Bowes-Lyon family. He there obtained a diploma in physical education and physiotherapy.

The Norwich branch of the BUF (British Union of Fascists) asked him to become a member of their protection squad in the mid-1930s. He held pacifist views, and when war broke out was offered the opportunity, through the Peace Pledge Union, to work as an agricultural labourer

in Jersey. He arrived in May 1940, one month before the Germans invaded. Pleasants stole a motor boat and attempted to escape to Britain with Leister (q.v.) and Keith Barnes. They were caught, and Pleasants and Leister were given six months' imprisonment which they served in Dijon. Being of military age they were then sent to Kreuzberg, a civilian internment camp. They claimed to be merchant seamen and demanded transfer to a POW camp, thinking the rations were better.

Pleasants decided to volunteer for the British Freikorps, becoming the Korps' physical training instructor. His time in the Korps was uneventful. He married a German girl, Annelise, and together they escaped from Berlin in 1945, taking first to the underground and then through the sewers with the hope of reaching her parents' home near Dresden. On the way, despite his pacifist leanings, he had to kill two Russian soldiers with his bare hands. Despite the countryside being filled with Red Army patrols, they got to Dresden. Reaching her parents' home, they hid for some months, and Pleasants even earned a modest living doing a strong man act to entertain the occupying Russian soldiers until they were both arrested in early 1946 on suspicion of spying. He received a quick trial and was sent to the 'Inter' camp in the Russian Arctic. He was released seven years later and was the subject of a German newsreel. As for Annelise, she was never heard of again.

POHL, Oswald
RANK: SS-Obergruppenführer und General der Waffen-SS und Polizei
BORN: 30 June 1892
DIED: 8 June 1951 (E.A).
PARTY NUMBER: 30842
SS NUMBER: 147614
AWARDS: 1914 Iron Cross Second Class; 1914 Iron Cross First Class; Cross of Honour 1914-1918 Combatants; 1914 Wound Badge Silver Class; War Merit Cross Second Class with Swords; War Merit Cross First Class with Swords; Knight's Cross of the War Merit Cross with Swords, 10 October 1944 (16 November 1944); German Cross in Silver; Gold Sports Badge; SS Honour Ring; SS Honour Sword.

In 1912 Pohl joined the navy to follow an administrative career. His training ended in April 1918 with his promotion to naval paymaster. After World War I he completed a law degree at Kiel University. Until taking charge of the Reichs-marine in 1920, he was with the Loewenfeld Freikorps in Oberschlesien and in the Ruhr, and in the summer of 1923 he joined the Uwe Jens Lornsen Volksbund, a disguised NSDAP organisation. In 1929 became a full member of the NSDAP, running for election to Kiel council. From 1929 to 1931 Pohl was the Ortsgruppenleiter and SA-Führer in Swinemünde, returning to Kiel in 1932, where he founded the town parliament and the Marine-SA.

In May 1933 Pohl met Himmler (q.v.), and after some initial hesitation took up his offer to construct an SS administration office. His rise was meteoric. From 1 February 1934 he belonged to the SS with the rank of Standartenführer. After the extension of his powers to include the SS-*Verfügungstruppen* and SS-*Totenkopfverbände* (KL-Wacheinheiten), Pohl was raised to the post of Verwaltungschef and Reichskassenverwalter of the SS (SS Chief of Administration and Reich Treasurer) on 1 June 1935, and on 20 April 1939 he was made head of an independent Hauptamt. In June he accepted the appointment of Ministerialdirektor und Leiter vom Hauptamt Haushalt und Bauten im Reichsministerium des Innern – permanent secretary and leader of the main Amt economy and construction.

Pohl was an administrative schemer who developed a number of economic projects for the SS, the full details of which are still not known over 50 years later. By 1945 the SS was the owner of over 40 enterprises with around 150 firms and factories. They included very different areas of business, among them food and drink (Apollinaris), textiles, agriculture and forestry, distribution, stone and soil.

The WVHA also controlled the administration of all concentration camps. Because of this, Pohl was indicted by the American Military Tribunal IV in Nuremberg, condemned to death and hanged on 8 June 1951 in Landsberg.

PRIESS, Hermann

RANK: SS-Gruppenführer
BORN: 24 May 1901
DIED: 2 February 1985 (D)
PARTY NUMBER: 1472296
SS NUMBER: 113258
AWARDS: 1939 Iron Cross Second Class, 22 September 1939; 1939 Iron Cross First Class ,15 October 1939; German Cross in Gold, 6 January 1942; Knight's Cross of the Iron Cross, 28 April 1943; Oakleaves, 9 September 1943; Oakleaves with Swords, 29 April 1944; SS Honour Ring; SS Honour Sword.

Preiss joined the 18th Volunteer-Dragoon Regiment on 12 January 1919 and was engaged in the fighting on Germany's eastern border, subsequently serving in the Reichswehr. He joined the SS-*Verfügungstruppe* in 1934 and went on to serve in the SS-Standarte *Germania* in 1939. As a qualified artillery man, he developed artillery use within the Waffen-SS and the unit became part of the *Totenkopf* Division. He commanded this regiment in 1941 when it proved its worth as an infantry unit. He was awarded the Knight's Cross of the Iron Cross for actions on the Russian Front while leading Artillery Regiment 3 of the *Totenkopf* Division.

On Eicke's (q.v.) death Priess took command of the *Totenkopf* Division. He was largely responsible for the achievements of the division during the bitter fighting of 1943-44, and was awarded the Oakleaves, becoming the 297th recipient. Six months later he became the 65th recipient of the Swords.

In late 1944 Priess assumed command of I SS Panzer Corps and led it during the Battle of the Bulge, and later in Hungary and Austria. After the war he was tried at Dachau in the Malmédy trial. He was found guilty and sentenced on 16 July 1946 to 20 years' imprisonment, but was released from Landsberg prison in 1954. He died in Ahrensburg in 1985.

PRÜTZMANN, Hans

RANK: SS-Obergruppenführer und General der Waffen-SS und der Polizei
BORN: 31 August 1901
DIED: 21 May 1945 (S)
PARTY NUMBER: 142290
SS NUMBER: 3002
AWARDS: Golden Party Badge; German Cross in Gold; 1939 Iron Cross Second Class; 1939 Iron Cross First Class; War Merit Cross Second Class with Swords; War Merit Cross First Class with Swords; SS Honour Ring; SS Honour Sword.

Prützmann was the higher SS police chief in the Ukraine from 1942 until 1944 when he was made head of the 'Werewolf' organisation, a body invented by Himmler (q.v.) for last-ditch resistance. The Werewolf organisation was the very embodiment of Himmler's muddled thinking after the 20 July Bomb Plot, when he was catapulted into military prominence out of his depth. If Himmler believed that within a few months the Western Allies would ask him to restore order in Europe and would require his SS to combat the menace of communism, what purpose could Himmler or the SS achieve by sabotaging the Western Allies, in

an attempt to slow the advance on the Western and Eastern Fronts? They had few achievements in this area, but claimed some small successes behind the Allied lines, such as the American appointed mayor of Aachen and in April an American divisional commander being shot in March 1945.

Dönitz learned from General Kinzel that the personnel of a Luftwaffe squadron were following Himmler's orders and forming themselves into a 'Werewolf' unit. Dönitz sent for Prützmann, who had, for the last six months, been in charge of these daydreams, and warned him that he had forbidden 'Werewolf' activities for the end of resistance by regular troops had rendered it obsolete. The only achievement of the 'Werewolves' was to make Allied soldiers more suspicious of the German population as a whole, which ultimately harmed only the Germans. Prützmann committed suicide at Lüneburg.

Q

QUIST, Arthur

RANK: SS-Sturmbannführer
PARTY NUMBER: —
SS NUMBER: —
AWARDS: 1939 Iron Cross Second Class; 1939 Iron Cross First Class.

Quist commanded the Norwegian Freiwillige Legion from 1942. Quisling's exhortations to his Norwegian brethren to join the fight against 'English despotism' fell on deaf ears, although Hitler's 'crusade against Bolshevism' was a more effective propaganda weapon. Stalin's unprovoked attack on Finland had already angered Norwegians, causing some to volunteer for a legion of Scandinavians to fight the 'Red Menace'. On 29 June 1941, the formation of a Norwegian Legion was announced, with Quisling declaring on 4 July that it would comprise two battalions. They were named after the two Oslo district regiments of

the Rikshird Viken Viking, and commanded by career officers of the Norwegian Army, Major Jorgen Bakke and Major Kjellsturp. The legion was officially christened Freiwillige Legion Norwegen on 1 August and came under the command of Arthur Quist on 1 February 1942. He held this position until 5 May 1943 when the legion was brought home from Russia and disbanded. After the war he was captured, subsequently found guilty of treason and given 10 years' imprisonment.

R

RASCHER, Sigmund

RANK: SS-Sturmbannführer
BORN: 1909
DIED: May 1945 (E.R)
PARTY NUMBER: —
SS NUMBER: —

A particularly unpleasant character, Sigmund Rascher was urged to join the Allgemeine-SS when he demonstrated considerable Nazi spirit by denouncing his own father. He married a woman 15 years his senior, and as mother worship formed an essential part of Heinrich Himmler's (q.v.) folklore, he became very interested in the young man.

Rascher was engaged on a boring medical course with the Luftwaffe in Munich in May 1941 when he wrote to Himmler, asking if he could have human guinea pigs for high-altitude experiments using a pressure chamber which involved the death of the victims. Himmler agreed, and Rascher undertook the experiment at Dachau. Luftwaffe Colonel-General Milch had some misgivings a year later, and wrote to Karl Wolff (q.v.), requesting that the apparatus be returned to the Luftwaffe and suggesting that Rascher should undertake freezing experiments. Himmler visited him at Dachau in November 1941, and Rascher discussed the use of animal heat in reviving frozen airmen. Himmler found this fascinating, although Rascher's report showed that the experiment had been useless. Himmler ordered Pohl (q.v.) to have four prostitutes sent to Dachau for further experiments in reviving the frozen bodies, although he later protested that Pohl should not have selected girls of German blood.

Himmler had Rascher transferred to the Waffen-SS and permanently situated at Dachau, where he worked until May 1945, when Karl von Eberstein (q.v.) came to arrest him, not for his experiments, but because his wife had kidnapped children from orphanages. The camp commandant and the chief medical officer seized their chance, emitting a flood of complaints against Rascher, whom they described as a 'dangerous, incredible person' who had Himmler's patronage in performing 'unspeakable horrors'. Himmler would not countenance a trial of the Raschers, but they were confined in the political bunkers of Dachau and Ravensbrück, the fate of people who knew too much. It is believed they both perished at the beginning of May 1945.

RATTENHUBER, Hans

RANK: SS-Brigadeführer
BORN: 30 April 1897
DIED: 30 JUNE 1957 (D)
PARTY NUMBER: 3212449
SS NUMBER: 52877
AWARDS: Golden Party Badge; 1914 Iron Cross Second Class; 1914 Iron Cross First Class; Cross of Honour 1914-1918 Combatants; SS Honour Ring; SS Honour Sword.

Head of the Reich security service and Hitler's personal safety, Rattenhuber held this position from the beginning of the war until Hitler's suicide. During this time he was also Hitler's personal security officer. After Hitler's death it should have been Rattenhuber who bargained for the lives of those left in the bunker, but it fell on the shoulders of Hans Krebs, the last Chief of Staff of the German Army, who hoped to bargain the lives of Hitler's court against the surrender of Berlin.

Russian General Vassili Chuikov demanded nothing less than the unconditional surrender of all those in the bunker. When Krebs returned with the terms, Göbbels, Burgdorf and Krebs chose suicide; Bormann (q.v.), Hewel (q.v.) and Rattenhuber, together with a group of minor officials and officers, chose escape. In the general panic, the fate of the men fighting in Berlin was totally disregarded. Most of the Waffen-SS troops fighting in the city in the defence of Hitler were actually non-Germans. They comprised men of the *Nordland* and *Charlemagne* Divisions, a battalion of Latvians from the 15th Waffen-Grenadier Division der SS and 600 men of Himmler's Escort Battalion, who fought much better than their commander.

The arrangements for a ceasefire were undertaken by a mere civilian, Hans Fritsche, the head of the broadcasting service. Rattenhuber was captured by the Russians while escaping from the Reich Chancellery on 2 May 1945. After serving a prison term he was repatriated to Germany on 10 October 1955. He died in Munich in 1957.

RAUTER, Hanns Albert

RANK: SS-Obergruppenführer
BORN: 4 February 1895
DIED: 25 March 1949 (E.A.)
PARTY NUMBER: —
SS NUMBER: 262958
AWARDS: Cross of Honour 1914-1918 Combatants; 1914 Wound Badge Black Class; 1939 Iron Cross Second Class; 1939 Iron Cross First Class; War Merit Cross Second Class with Swords; War Merit Cross First Class with Swords; SS Honour Ring; SS Honour Sword.

Born in Klagenfurt in Austria, Rauter joined the Styrian Home Guard, a pan-German, fanatically anti-Semitic paramilitary organisation during the 1920s. This group formed links with the newly emergent NSDAP, and Hanns Rauter, a crude street fighter, was drawn to the potential of a powerful police formation within the Third Reich.

With the outbreak of war, Rauter became Higher SS and Police

Chief of the Netherlands, a position he held until the end of the war. In addition to detecting and repressing political crimes, he undertook wider activities, particularly informing a network of Dutch informers, called 'V men,' who had the job of infiltrating the underground organisations. Rauter ruthlessly suppressed the Jews and undertook their deportation to the concentration camps. Hitler's *Niedermachungsbefehl*, the instructions to the police to publicly execute any *Todeskandidaten* (death candidates) who were Resistance members, was also strictly enforced.

By the end of the first few months of 1945, the Dutch hoped that they had endured the worst of the terror. However, a single incident brought about a blood bath on an unprecedented scale. Members of the Resistance shot and badly wounded Rauter on the night of 6/7 March, an unintentional attack, as they really only wanted to hijack an army vehicle to seize food destined for the *Wehrmacht*. Retribution was swift and decisive: the definition of Todeskandidaten was expanded to include not only Resistance members, but also looters and curfew breakers.

After the war, Rauter was tried by the Dutch for war crimes. In his defence he declared that he had begged Seyss-Inquart (q.v.) and Schoengarth to refrain from the reprisals. His protestations were not believed and he was found guilty and sentenced to death. He mounted the gallows on 25 March 1945.

REBANE, Alfons

RANK: Standartenführer der Waffen-SS
BORN: 24 June 1908
DIED: 3 March 1976 (D)
PARTY NUMBER: —
SS NUMBER: —
AWARDS: 1939 Iron Cross Second Class; 1939 Iron Cross First Class; Knight's Cross of the Iron Cross, 23 February 1944, Oakleaves, 9 May 1945; Close Combat Clasp Bronze Class, Infantry Assault Badge in Silver.

Born in Walk, Estonia, Rebane volunteered for service in an Estonian legion to fight alongside the Germans in the common struggle against Bolshevism. This was launched on 28 August 1942, the first anniversary of the liberation of the Estonian capital Tallinn, by Generalkommissar Litzman. The 1st battalion of the new regiment was despatched in March 1943 for active service with the 5th SS Panzer Division *Wiking*. It was popularly called the Estonian Volunteer Battalion *Narwa* while it served with the division. At the beginning of 1944 Himmler (q.v.) decided to increase the Estonian contribution to the Waffen-SS by absorbing the existing German Army's Estonian battalions and the Estonian police formations and combining these with the brigades, creating an Estonian division. The brigade's two existing regiments, SS-Freiwilligen Grenadier Regiments 45 and 46, were supplemented by a new regiment, 47. This was formed by the amalgamation of two Estonian battalions, 658 and 659, serving with the German Army.

Major Alfons Rebane, a distinguished Estonian officer, commanded 658 Battalion and was the country's first recipient of the Knight's Cross of the Iron Cross. To celebrate, he was a guest of honour at a grand reception held in Kadriorg Palace in Tallin. On 19 March 1945, the commanding officer, Augsberger, was killed in action and Rebane was promoted to deputy divisional commander. His superb leadership and bravery earned him the Oakleaves; he became the 875th recipient; a rare distinction for a foreigner. He survived the war and died in Augsburg, Bavaria in 1976.

RIBBENTROP, Joachim von

RANK: SS-Obergruppenführer, Foreign Minister
BORN: 30 April 1893
DIED: 16 October 1946 (E.A.)
PARTY NUMBER: 1199927
SS NUMBER: 63083
AWARDS: Golden Party Badge; Meritorious Order of the German Eagle; Grand Cross in Gold; 1939 Decoration of the Red Cross; Grand Cross Special Grade 1934; SS Honour Ring; SS Honour Sword; Japan – Order of the Rising Sun with Pavlovnia-Flowers Grand Cross Badge and Breast Star.

Handsome, humourless and arrogant, von Ribbentrop was the son of an artillery officer, born in Wesel and raised in Kassel. His mother died when he was 15 and two years later he left for Canada, where he remained for four years until 1914, when he joined the Torgauer Husarenregeiment Nr. 12 as an officer. He served with bravery and was transferred to the intelligence service where he was tutored by von Papen.

He became a vintner after the war and in 1920 married Annalies Henkel of the wine and champagne family. He travelled extensively as a salesman for the firm, and this elevated position and wealth made him eager to join society; he added von to his name by grace of an aunt who adopted him.

Von Ribbentrop joined the NSDAP in 1932, and was immediately useful. Von Papen and Hitler used his house in Berlin-Dahlem on 22 January 1933 to plot their secret plan to make Hitler Chancellor-designate. Under Hess's secretariat, the Ribbentrop Bureau was established in 1933 in the Wilhelm Strasse, (provocatively just across the street from the Foreign Office). Staffed by careerists and journalists of dubious qualifications, it operated in direct opposition to the foreign ministry, with the objective of proving Nazi methods more effective than the foreign ministry's traditional policies. Having served in 1934 as special commissioner for disarmament, von Ribbentrop's career took off when he was able to conclude the Anglo-German naval treaty in May 1935, unaided by foreign ministry officials. The following year he cajoled Japan into joining an anti-Comintern pact, which Mussolini signed in 1937 (this was designed to combat the worldwide spread of communism; it talked of the blood of Japan containing Nordic virtues).

In 1936 Hitler appointed him ambassador to Great Britain. Von Ribbentrop's ambition was to replace von Neurath as Foreign Minister and he accepted the appointment with reluctance, fully believing that von Neurath was trying to sideline him. His reluctance was illustrated by the fact that he didn't take up the post for three months. Once ensconced, he shuttled between the two capitals. Diplomat he was not, for he greeted the King of England at a court reception at St James's in 1937, with 'Heil Hitler!' As a result British society rejected him, deeply offending his sensibilities, and causing a deeply held hatred of everything British, a situation that certainly contributed to the reports he sent Hitler, and thus Hitler's beliefs of British intentions in the pre-war years.

In February 1938 Hitler dismissed von Neurath and appointed von Ribbentrop as Foreign Minister. Himmler (q.v.) considered it a major victory for SS prestige, with the SS uniform to be seen in that bastion of conservatism, the Foreign Office. In August 1939 von Ribbentrop negotiated the agreement between Russia and Germany by which the two countries agreed to divide Poland. With the coming of the war in September 1939, von Ribbentrop's career as a diplomat effectively ceased. He was arrested on 14 June 1945 in Hamburg by Sergeant R. C. Holloway, accompanied by two British and one Belgian soldier. He was tried at Nuremberg, found guilty and hanged.

RÜHLE VON LILIENSTERN, Hans-Joachim

RANK: SS-Hauptsturmführer der Reserve
BORN: 9 January 1915
DIED: 1983 (D)
PARTY NUMBER: 3287913
SS NUMBER: 151372
AWARDS: 1939 Iron Cross Second Class, 9 November 1940; 1939 Iron Cross First Class, 22 January 1944; Knight's Cross of the Iron Cross, 12 February 1944.

The son of a Hessian doctor Rühle served as a platoon commander in the French campaign of 1940. Transferred to the Russian Front as commander of I Battalion, SS-Freiwilligen Panzergrenadier Regiment 48 General Seyffardt, he was part of the 23rd Freiwilligen Panzergrenadier Division *Nederland*. The division was composed of Dutch volunteers and in June 1944 had a strength of 6713 men. He was heavily involved in the actions on the Leningrad Front.

In February 1944 Rühle was rewarded with the Knight's Cross of the Iron Cross, but by June the division was in full retreat before the bludgeoning Red Army. In July it took part in the 'Battle of the European SS' at Narva, which lasted six months and held up the Red Army. In February 1945 they were evacuated by sea from Libau on the Baltic coast to Stetin. After only a brief respite they joined battle in Pomerania, moving south later to Fürstenwalde, where they surrendered. He died in Frankfurt in 1983.

S

SAUCKEL, Fritz

RANK: SS-Obergruppenführer, Gauleiter of Thüringia 1927-45 and Governor of Anhalt and Brunswick
BORN: 27 October 1894
DIED: 16 October 1946 (E.A.)
PARTY NUMBER: 1395
SS NUMBER: 254890
AWARDS: Golden Party Badge; Coburg Badge, 14 October 1932; Gau Thüringen Badge; SS Honour Ring; SS Honour Sword.

Responsible for the Reich's labour procurement from 1942, Sauckel succeeded in deporting some five million people to Germany. Born in Lower Franconia, Sauckel became a seaman in 1910. His ship was captured in 1914 by the French and he was interned as a prisoner of war until 1919. On his return he joined the People's Defence Union and worked in a factory while attending engineering school. In 1921 he joined the NSDAP, and after holding a variety of posts he was appointed Gauleiter of Thüringia in 1927, a position he held until the war's end. He was made governor in 1933.

Sauckel was described by Göbbels as 'the dullest of the dull'. He was also perceived as quasi-literate, leading the life of an ordinary high-ranking Nazi political functionary until March 1942, when he was appointed Plenipotentiary General for Mobilisation to meet the labour demands of Speer's armament and munitions production programme. Speer found the flow of workers too slow and suggested that a tough Gauleiter be found to undertake the job. Sauckel was proposed. This prosaic little man, who in another time and place would have been a complete cipher, was entrusted with labour recruiting in the countries and territories overrun by Germany. He became the most notorious 'slave driver' in the history of man.

More than two million people came from the conquered East, about half of them women, but unlike those who came from the West, the

Ostarbeiter (Eastern workers) were treated more as slaves than as fellow labourers in the German cause.

Their presence was a constant anxiety to the German authorities, who felt that the aliens would have to be marked in some way, just as the Jews were, to ensure that they did not stray outside the strict prescribed confines of their life in the Reich. They were, for example, banned from all places of public entertainment, relaxation and refreshment. The first workers to be marked thus were the Poles. A second Ostabzeichen (Eastern Badge) was introduced in February 1942 which was to be worn by all other workers from the East.

The workers found wearing the patch deeply offensive, and Sauckel asked Himmler (q.v.) that the Ukranians, 80 per cent of whom were volunteers, be allowed to wear a Ukrainian emblem instead. Himmler forcibly refused. Various German labour agencies, worried by the declining morale of these workers, contributed to pressure for an abolition of the detested badges, appreciating that low morale meant a decline in production. This morale decline, together with the Nazis' love of ritual, led in April 1943 to the granting of the medal of the Order of the German Eagle in Bronze without Swords to be awarded to outstanding foreign workers from countries without diplomatic representation in the Reich. The normal requirements for this dubious 'honour' was at least two years' good work connected with the German war effort, or a single act of merit.

Sauckel's teams went out on the streets all over Europe, even in Italy, to round up men and women, taking them from their homes, from shops and cinemas, by false arrest or by getting them drunk before signing them up. Sauckel recruited more than five million workers, thousands of whom died of malnutrition or disease in the labour camps and factories where they were subject to brutal treatment. Sauckel regarded himself as an agent supplying workers for factories. He was shocked when arrested in 1945 by the British, who put him on trial at Nuremberg. He claimed to have known nothing about the concentration camps and protested his innocence until the moment he was hanged in October 1946.

SCHALBURG, Count Christian Frederik von

RANK: SS-Obersturmbannführer
BORN: 1906
DIED: 2 June 1942 (K.I.A.)
PARTY NUMBER: —
SS NUMBER: —
AWARDS: 1939 Iron Cross Second Class; 1939 Iron Cross First Class; Demjansk Shield; Cross of the Danish Volunteer Battalion in Finland.

Born at Poltava in the Ukraine, the son of wealthy parents of Baltic German stock, Schalburg's family emigrated to Denmark after the Russian Revolution and he became a naturalised Dane.

He served as a lieutenant in the Royal Danish Life Guards and was also National Youth Leader of Clausen's DNSAP. Schalburg served in the Danish battalion during the 'Winter War' in Finland and later he was among the first to volunteer for the newly raised SS-Regiment *Nordland*. He went on to serve in the *Wiking* Division. In March 1942 he took command of the Freikorps *Danmark*, and by May it was ready for service. It went into battle as part of the *Totenkopf* Division in the Demjansk Pocket, but von Schalburg was killed in the first action on 2 June 1942.

The body of this very popular commander was brought back to Denmark and interred with full military honours. In April 1943 Martinsen (q.v.) set up what he called a 'Germanic' corps, which he renamed the Schalburg Corps in memory of the Freikorps' most popular commander. He also has the dubious honour of having a decoration created in his memory: the Cross of Merit of the Schalburg Corps.

SCHAUB, Julius

RANK: SS-Obergruppenführer
BORN: 20 August 1898
DIED: 27 December 1967 (D)
PARTY NUMBER: 81
SS NUMBER: 7
AWARDS: Golden Party Badge; Coburg Badge 14 October 1932; Blood Order No 296; SS Honour Ring; SS Honour Sword.

Born in Munich, Schaub (left in picture) was one of the first members of the NSDAP. He became a member of the Stosstrupp which was formed under Julius Schreck (q.v.), took part in the 1923 Putsch and was imprisoned with Hitler, soon becoming a member of Hitler's inner circle. After their release, he became a member of the 1925-26 Schutzkommando which was the forerunner of the SS. Hitler made him number two adjutant and when Wilhelm Brückner was dismissed Schaub became Hitler's chief personal adjutant.

Schaub was influential because he controlled access to Hitler, who became increasingly isolated as the war progressed, and made him his confidante. He mentioned his secret dislike of Himmler, saying: 'I need such policemen, but I don't like them.' Schaub was sent to destroy Hitler's personal papers in Berchtesgaden and Munich just prior to the Führer's suicide in April 1945. At the end of the war he was caught in Bavaria. Subsequently he became a pharmacist and died in Munich.

SCHELLENBERG, Walter

RANK: SS-Brigadeführer
BORN: 16 January 1910
DIED: 1952 (D)
PARTY NUMBER: 3504508
SS NUMBER: 124817
AWARDS: 1939 Iron Cross Second Class; 1939 Iron Cross First Class; War Merit Cross Second Class with Swords; War Merit Cross First Class with Swords; SS Honour Ring; SS Honour Sword.

Schellenberg was a secret service agent who became Head of Combined Secret Services in 1944. A law graduate of Bonn with a strong interest and command of several languages, Schellenberg joined the SS in 1934. His intelligence and culture won him the patronage of the head of the SD, Heydrich (q.v.).

Schellenberg was involved in a number of plots, notably investigating British intelligence operations in 1939, when he posed as a Resistance agent to gain the confidence of two MI5 agents in Holland. This led to their kidnap by SS troops on neutral territory. He is also believed to have been involved in the plot to abduct the Duke of Windsor. In 1938 he organised the notorious Einsatzguppen (which by March 1943 had

murdered 633,000 Jews) under Heydrich's orders. He was one of the first to enter both Austria and Poland after their annexation, to carry out Himmler's (q.v.) secretive objectives. In 1944, after the arrest of Canaris and the dismantling of the *Abwehr*, he became head of all the secret services.

In 1945 he assumed a leading role in Himmler's attempt to arrange an armistice with the Western Allies. Schellenberg arranged meetings in April 1945 between Count Bernadotte and Himmler, and when the German surrender came he was in Denmark, still apparently negotiating.

He was released from prison in December 1950 and died two years later. Schellenburg's memoirs provide a detailed account of life in the higher reaches of the Third Reich.

SCHRECK, Julius

RANK: SS-Brigadeführer
BORN: 13 July 1898
DIED: 16 May 1936 (D)
PARTY NUMBER: 53
SS NUMBER: 5
AWARDS: Golden Party Badge; Blood Order No 349; Coburg Badge 14 October 1932.

Born in Munich, he was an early member of the party and one of the first members of the SA. He was well liked and apparently on very good terms with Hitler. A founder of the Stosstrupp, he participated in the 1923 Putsch and was incarcerated in Landsberg. In 1925, with the reformation of the party, he founded the Schutzkommando, which was charged with Hitler's safety and subsequently became the embryonic SS. From this time he was constantly at Hitler's side and succeeded Emil Maurice (q.v.) as his personal chauffeur. Hitler considered him to be the best driver imaginable. In 1936 he contracted meningitis and died. Hitler was deeply distressed and gave him the honour of a state funeral.

SCHULZE, Richard

RANK: SS-Obersturmbannführer
BORN: 2 October 1914
DIED: 3 July 1988 (D)
PARTY NUMBER: —
SS NUMBER: 264059
AWARDS: German Cross in Gold; 1939 Iron Cross Second Class; 1939 Iron Cross First Class; 1939 Wound Badge Black Class; SS Honour Ring; SS Honour Sword.

Having begun his career as Ribbentrop's adjutant, a position he held from April 1939 until January 1941, Richard Schulze replaced his younger brother Hans-Georg as Hitler's SS ordnance officer on 3 October 1941. During this assignment he had short intervals of combat duty. From October 1942 he was a personal adjutant to Hitler, who grew extremely fond of him and paid him great attention. Schulze was also made responsible for all SS men serving in the SS-Begleitskommando. He held this position with periods of combat duty and service at the SS training school, until he became the last commander of Bad Tölz in December 1944.

SEYSS-INQUART, Dr Arthur

RANK: SS-Obergruppenführer
BORN: 22 July 1892
DIED: 16 October 1946 (E.A.)
PARTY NUMBER: 6270392
SS NUMBER: 292771
AWARDS: Golden Party Badge; Cross of Honour 1914-1918 Combatants; 1914 Wound Badge Black Class; War Merit Cross Second Class without Swords; War Merit Cross First Class without Swords; SS Honour Ring; SS Honour Sword.

Seyss-Inquart was an Austrian Nazi who prepared the way for the Anschluss. Born in Iglow, Moravia, he attended read law at Vienna University. During World War I he served in the Tyrol Kaiser Jägers with distinction. In 1921 he set up in practice and devoted himself, according to his own testimony, to working for the Anschluss through political means via the Austrian Volksbund.

As early as 1930 the SS Frauenfeld introduced black uniforms into Austria and recruited and equipped assault squads. Later, the SD infiltrated the Austrian police. SS officers entered Austria to conduct a campaign of intimidation, setting up an Austrian legion, controlled by them. In spite of the suppression of the SA and SS in Austria, and the closure of the Brown House, the Austrian Nazi organisation was never dismantled. Its spearhead was the SS Standarte 89, a clandestine unit meeting under the guise of an athletics association; 154 of its men took part in the attack on Chancellor Dollfuss on 25 July 1934. His successor, Schuschnigg, concluded an agreement with Hitler which included secret clauses permitting the establishment of Nazi organisations in Austria.

Acting as secret representative for the Nazis while the party was still illegal, Seyss-Inquart finally came to power in 1938 when Hitler demanded, on threat of invasion, the legalisation of the Nazi Party and the appointment of Seyss-Inquart as Minister of the Interior, with control over the police. By February this was accomplished and he began taking his orders directly from Berlin, acting independently of the chancellor. On 11 March, with Hitler's troops at the border, he was appointed Chancellor. He forced a law through parliament making Austria a province of Greater Germany. He was subsequently appointed president, a title that eventually changed to governor.

In October 1939 he was made the Deputy Governor General, under Frank, of the Polish General Government. In May 1940, he became Reich Commissioner of the Netherlands with complete control of the entire country's resources, which were directed exclusively to the demands of the German war machine. He ruled authoritatively, answering only to Hitler. He generally followed the 'carrot and stick' method of rule but did cooperate with Himmler in the deportation of 500 Jewish youths to Mauthausen in February 1941. By March 1941 he had powers of summary justice in any case pertaining to dissension or suspected resistance. He forced five million Dutch to work for the Germans and deported 117,000 Jews. In early 1945, he did join with Speer in preventing the application of Hitler's scorched earth policy.

Canadian forces arrested him in May 1945 and he was sent for trial at Nuremberg, being indicted on four charges. As with regard to his defence, an interchange with American prosecutor Robert Dodd pretty well sums it up. Seyss-Inquart: "I have done many things in Holland that have been good". Dodd: "And you have done many things in Holland that have been bad". Seyss-Inquart: "Perhaps only harsh". Dodd: "It is easy to tell you are a lawyer". During the deliberations Seyss-Inquart's defence was brushed off with the comment that it is no defence that he was less oppressive than Himmler. He was convicted on three counts and there were no dissenting votes among the judges that he should receive the death penalty. This took place in the execution chamber of the Nuremberg Prison on 16 October 1946, when the first prisoner, von Ribbentrop, mounted the gallows at 11 minutes past 01:00 hours. Seyss-Inquart followed as the 9th candidate.

SIEBKEN, Bernhard

RANK: SS-Obersturmbannführer
BORN: 5 April 1910
DIED: 20 January 1949 (E.A.)
PARTY NUMBER: 558752
SS NUMBER: 44894
AWARDS: 1939 Iron Cross Second Class; 1939 Iron Cross First Class; War Merit Cross Second Class without Swords; War Merit Cross First Class without Swords; Knight's Cross of the Iron Cross, 17 April 1945; Medal for the Winter Campaign in Russia 1941-1942; SS Honour Ring,; SS Honour Sword.

Siebken commanded the 2nd Battalion, 26th SS-Panzergrenadier Regiment, *Hitlerjugend* Division, during the Normandy invasion, when a British armoured assault group broke through and captured a German regiment's HQ on 8 June. The British used several German officers as hostages in an attempt to regain their own lines. Colonel Luzemburger was fatally wounded after being tied to a British armoured vehicle, dying a few days later. British and Canadian troops were alleged to have killed and wounded German soldiers. The fighting was particularly brutal, and there were also numerous cases of British and Canadian prisoners being summarily executed. Two British prisoners were found shot in Siebken's battle area and he was placed on the British wanted list. Found in a POW camp after the war, he was tried before a military court for war crimes and hanged in the Hamlyn military penitentiary in 1949.

SIMON, Max

RANK: SS-Gruppenführer
BORN: 6 January 1899
DIED: 1 February 1961 (D)
PARTY NUMBER: 1359576
SS NUMBER: 83086
AWARDS: 1914 Iron Cross Second Class; 1914 Iron Cross First Class; Cross of Honour 1914-1918 Combatants; 1939 Iron Cross Second Class Bar, 13 September 1939; 1939 Iron Cross First Class Bar, 2 October 1939; Knight's Cross of the Iron Cross, 20 October 1941; Oakleaves, 28 October 1944; German Cross in Gold, 9 October 1944; Wound Badge 1939 Black Class; Medal for the Winter Campaign in Russia 1941-1942; Demjansk Shield, 31 December 1943; Danzig Cross First Class, 24 October 1939; Italian Order of the Crown Officers Cross, 19 December 1941; SS Honour Ring; SS Honour Sword.

Born in Breslau, Silesia, Simon served in World War I and afterwards joined the Reichswehr. Simon was one of Eicke's (q.v.) most devoted protégés and having earned his complete confidence and trust, helped to form the SS-*Totenkopf Standarte Oberbayern*. This unit became a regiment of the newly formed *Totenkopf* Division.

Simon served in the Polish and French campaigns. Eicke chose him to command the first SS-TK Infantry Regiment in the Russian campaign and he performed with the measure of ruthlessness and bravery that Eicke expected, winning the Knight's Cross of the Iron Cross. His long association with Eicke and the SS-TK, coupled with his outstanding combat reports, prompted Himmler (q.v.) to give Simon command of the *Totenkopf* Division for a period.

On 16 October 1943 he was given command of the 16th SS Panzergrenadier Division *Reichsführer-SS*, a position he held until 24 October 1944; in recognition of his service, he was awarded the Oakleaves, becoming the 639th recipient. He then became commanding officer of XIII SS Army Corps, fighting on the Western and Southwestern Fronts in Germany.

After the war he was tried for war crimes, earning the special distinction of being condemned to death by both the Russians and the British. The unsubstantiated Russian charges stemmed from atrocities allegedly ordered during the German withdrawal from Kharkov (having said that, Simon is on record for urging his men to be ruthless, stating the Russians were 'bandits who must be slaughtered without pity').

The British sentenced him for the massacre of 2700 Italian civilians in reprisal for the activities of a partisan brigade in the Apennines. The sentence was commuted and he was freed in 1954. After his release he was tried twice by German courts for committing war crimes in Germany and was acquitted. He faced a third trial on the same charges, but before it began, he died, in 1961. Max Simon was lucky that he did not fall into Russian hands, for if he had have done his sentence would have been much harsher.

SIX, Prof Dr Franz

RANK: SS-Oberführer
BORN: 12 August 1909
DIED: 9 July 1975
PARTY NUMBER: 245670
SS NUMBER: 107480
AWARDS: War Merit Cross Second Class with Swords; War Merit Cross First Class with Swords; SS Honour Ring; SS Honour Sword.

Six joined the SD in the 1930s as a pupil of the economics expert, Professor Höhn. Himmler (q.v.) was acutely aware of the lack of competent professional men in the large bureaucracy. He constantly tried to recruit intellectuals, but in the main was unsuccessful with them, and both Höhn and Six tried to leave.

Six served in an Einsatzgruppe in Russia in 1941. Ribbentrop (q.v.) seconded him from the cultural activities section of RSHA to the cultural division of the Foreign Office as an expert on anti-Semitic matters. He was sentenced to life imprisonment after the war. This was commuted; he was released on 30 September 1952.

SKORZENY, Otto

RANK: SS-Sturmbannführer
BORN: 12 June 1908
DIED: 8 July 1975 (D)
PARTY NUMBER: 1083671
SS NUMBER: 295979
AWARDS: 1939 Iron Cross Second Class, 27 July 1941; 1939 Iron Cross First Class; German Cross in Gold, 16 January 1945; Knight's Cross of the Iron Cross, 13 September 1943; Oakleaves, 8 March 1945; Combined Pilot and Observer Badge in Gold with Diamonds; SS Honour Ring.

One of the Reich's most successful maverick soldiers, Skorzeny was born in Vienna. He joined the NSDAP in 1930 and was later accepted into the Waffen-SS and served with a field unit until he had a serious accident. After meeting him, Kaltenbrunner (q.v.) gave orders that he should form a special forces unit, as he was technically skilled and a linguist. He formed the commando unit Oranienburg in Amt II of the RuSHA in April 1943. On Hitler's orders, Skorzeny rescued Mussolini from his Italian captors at the Gran Sasso Hotel in a daredevil paratroop raid on 12 September 1943. He helped stop a possible mutiny among the tank troops in Berlin after the 20 July Bomb Plot, and halted the indiscriminate execution of suspected conspirators. He kidnapped the son of the Hungarian premier, Admiral Horthy, thus forestalling Hungary's defection to the Allies. During the Battle of the Bulge, a brigade of English-speaking Germans led by Skorzeny masqueraded as American troops, causing havoc behind American lines. The Americans tried him for conducting illegal practices in the Ardennes Offensive, but acquitted him. He lived in Spain as a businessman and died in Madrid in 1975.

STAHLECKER, Franz-Walter

RANK: SS-Gruppenführer
BORN: 10 October 1900
DIED: March 1942 (K.I.A.)
PARTY NUMBER: 1069130
SS NUMBER: 73041

Stahlecker was an 'information officer' in the SD in 1938 and went on to become Head of Section VIa of the Reich Main Security Office. In early 1942 Heydrich (q.v.) sidelined Stahlecker by dubiously promoting him to the command of an Einsatzgruppe in the Baltic states. Heydrich's reports claimed that Stahlecker's group liquidated 221,000 victims, although it is possible that such figures were reached carelessly and the same totals were added several times over. Heydrich stood to benefit from this misrepresentation, firstly by demonstrating his success in the 'final solution', and secondly to neutralise Nebe (q.v.), who is said to have opposed Heydrich's orders and to have disclosed them to the Oster Circle. Stahlecker was apparently killed by partisans in March 1942.

STANGL, Franz
RANK: Commandant of Treblinka Konzentrationslager
BORN: 26 March 1908
DIED: 28 June 1971 (D)

Stangl was commandant at Treblinka, an extermination camp located on the Bug River near Warsaw. He was extremely careful, however, to conceal his 'accomplishments' at the camp. This was a Herculean feat given that Treblinka is accredited with the extermination of nearly 700,000 people, second only to Auschwitz in numbers gassed. Himmler (q.v.) was aware Treblinka was operating very efficiently: during its operational life it contributed to the SS bank accounts $2,800,000, £400,000, 12,000,000 roubles, 145 kilograms of gold from rings and teeth, 4000 carats of diamonds, as well as hair and used clothing for SS factories. Himmler failed to bestow on Stangl the praise he deserved because of the latter's reluctance for publicity. The Nazi authorities deemed it prudent to destroy the evidence that Treblinka would yield to the advancing Russians, by demolishing the camp and removing possible witnesses. They exterminated the inmates (only 40 people survived when the camp was demolished), and transferred the SS guards to fight the partisans in Yugoslavia, a virtual death sentence for them as well.

Stangl himself was among those who survived the war, however, and in 1945 returned to his wife and family in Austria. The destruction of the camp, coupled with his reluctance for publicity in part hid his identity, and he was arrested, not for his involvement, but on account of his SS rank. Consequently, those responsible for his arrest were in ignorance of his role in the Treblinka camp. When his career was uncovered he was sent to Linz to await trial by the Austrian courts. At this stage the Allied control commission was still ignorant of his full involvement, and when he escaped from an outside working party, he was not considered important enough to pursue. He slipped away a few weeks later through Italy to Syria, where he was joined by his family, who had been assisted by Skorzeny (q.v.). Stangl reached Brazil and then worked in the Volkswagen factory in São Paulo. Life was uneventful for 16 years, and then the Wiesenthal investigations caught up with him. In 1967 a disaffected cousin informed Wiesenthal of Stangl's whereabouts, and a former Gestapo man gave him the precise location. After much legal wrangling, he was returned to Germany for trial on 2 June 1969. He was tried three years later, where he stated: 'my conscience is clear. I was simply doing my duty.' Sentenced to life imprisonment, he died in 1971.

STEINER, Felix
RANK: SS Obergruppenführer und General der Waffen-SS
BORN: 23 May 1896
DIED: 12 May 1966 (D)
PARTY NUMBER: 4264295
SS NUMBER: 253351
AWARDS: 1914 Iron Cross Second Class; 1914 Iron Cross First Class; Cross of Honour 1914-1918 Combatants; 1914 Wound Badge Black; 1939 Iron Cross Second Class Bar, 17 September 1939; 1939 Iron Cross First Class Bar, 26 September 1939; German Cross in Gold, 22 April 1942; Knight's Cross, 15 August 1940; Oakleaves, 23 December 1942; Oakleaves with Swords, 10 August 1944; SS Honour Ring and Sword; Finnish Freedom Cross with Swords.

A career soldier from East Prussia who saw frontline service during World War I, Steiner joined the Freikorps and subsequently the Reichswehr. In 1933 he left the Reichswehr, enabling him to undertake special assignments with the *Wehrmacht* training department. In 1935

he joined the SS-*Verfügungstruppe* and helped to develop the 3rd Battalion of the SS-Standarte *Deutschland*, stationed in Munich and the SS training camp at Dachau. He applied his military training to the men, instituting training schedules in application of his motto 'sweat saves blood'.

While serving as commanding officer of the SS-Standarte *Deutschland*, attached to Army Group B on the Russian Front, he was awarded the Knight's Cross of the Iron Cross; as commanding general of the *Wiking* Division, he won the Oakleaves, becoming the 159th recipient. In 1943, using German and European volunteers including Latvians, he formed III (Germanic) SS Panzer Corps, which served on the Russian Front. He was awarded the Swords for his decisive leadership, becoming the 86th recipient. As the war drew to a close, Hitler ordered his army group and the forces of General Wenck to break the encirclement of Berlin. Realising they had insufficient strength to accomplish the mission, Steiner directed his men to avoid Soviet capture. He was taken prisoner at Lüneburg on 3 May 1945. He died in Munich in 1966.

STRECKENBACH, Bruno
RANK: SS-Gruppenführer und Generalleutnant der Polizei und Waffen-SS
BORN: 7 February 1902
DIED: 28 October 1977 (D)
PARTY NUMBER: 489972
SS NUMBER: 14713
AWARDS: 1939 Iron Cross Second Class (Polish Campaign); 1939 Iron Cross First Class, 15 July 1943; German Cross in Gold, 15 December 1943; Knight's Cross of the Iron Cross, 27 August 1944; Oakleaves, 21 January 1945; Close Combat Clasp Silver Class; SS Honour Ring; SS Honour Sword.

A particularly brutal commander, Streckenbach was born in Hamburg, the son of a customs official. He joined the Hamburg police in 1933 and was appointed to lead it when the Gestapo absorbed it. He was an early member of the SS and commanded the first Stürm in Hamburg.

Streckenbach joined the RSHA and was Heydrich's (q.v.) deputy in Amt 1, the personnel office. He selected personnel for the various executive units of the security police and SD, as well as being responsible for their discipline. After the fall of Poland and the establishment of the General Government, he was appointed commander of its security police. He directed the mass arrests of Polish intelligentsia, in Operation 'Action AB' in May 1940, and most of the Einsatzgruppen officers took their instructions from him. In May 1941, he held a course at the frontier police school at Pretzsch on the Elbe near Leipzig for over 100 candidates from the Gestapo or SD. Apart from lectures on the sub-human enemy, there were terrain exercises which one candidate described as games of hide-and-seek.

Streckenbach retained his position after Heydrich's death, but on 15 April 1944 he took over the command of the Latvian 19th Waffen-Grenadier Division der SS (Lettische Nr. 2). He was awarded the Knight's Cross of the Iron Cross and the Oakleaves, becoming the 701st recipient, for his leadership of the poorly equipped division during the heavy fighting in the Baltic area. He was taken prisoner by the Russians. He was not surrendered to the Nuremberg Tribunal to face the charges which were brought against Ohlendorf (q.v.) and his associates, nor was he hanged in Russia. He returned from the Soviet Union on 10 October 1955. He lived in Hamburg where he died in 1977.

STROOP, Jürgen
RANK: SS-Gruppenführer
BORN: 26 September 1895
DIED: 9 July 1952 (E.A.)
PARTY NUMBER: 1292297
SS NUMBER: 44611

AWARDS: 1914 Iron Cross Second Class; Cross of Honour 1914-1918 Combatants; 1914 Wound Badge Black Class; 1939 Iron Cross Second Class; 1939 Iron Cross First Class; 1939 Iron Cross Second Class Bar; War Merit Cross Second Class with Swords; Infantry Assault Badge, 21 January 1943; SS Honour Ring; SS Honour Sword.

Stroop was the SS and Police Chief of Warsaw in the spring of 1943 when Himmler (q.v.) decided to remove the remaining 56,000 Jews from the Warsaw Ghetto.

As an anti-partisan commander he was empowered to call on all troops in the Warsaw area, as well as the security police, and his force included two training battalions, some *Wehrmacht* units and numbered 2096 men in total. The first Warsaw rebellion was treated as a military campaign. Himmler was at Zhitomir and did not personally visit Warsaw, but sent the police leaders Krüger and von Herff, to act as observers, and personally dispatched orders to Stroop.

Stroop sent situation reports to Himmler, dispassionate records of the numbers killed daily. They were bound as a sumptuous illustrated album entitled There are no more Jews in Poland for presentation to Himmler. Himmler reported on the action to Hitler at Rastenberg and tried, by means of photographs, to convince the high command that military emplacements had been built in the ghetto. Himmler was determined that this desperate resistance and the fag-end of the extermination of two million Polish Jews should figure as a genuine campaign and battle honour for the SS and police. Stroop personally supervised the deportation or summary execution of those Jews who surrendered, and blew up the venerated Tlomacki synagogue to celebrate the victory.

As a reward for his Warsaw successes, Himmler appointed Stroop as the Higher Police Leader in Greece on 13 September 1943, a post then

critically important in the wake of the surrender of Marshal Badoglio's Italian Government. Stroop established his headquarters in Athens, and for the next two months busied himself with directing the deportation of Jews from the Greek mainland to Auschwitz.

After the war Stroop was apprehended in the American zone and tried for war crimes by an American court at Dachau. The book he had submitted to Himmler convicted him, and he was condemned to death on 22 March 1947. He was then turned over to the Poles who tried him on 8 September 1951; he was publicly executed on 9 July 1952 on the site of the former ghetto.

STUCKART, Dr Wilhelm
RANK: SS-Obergruppenführer
BORN: 16 November 1902
DIED: December 1953 (D)
PARTY NUMBER: 378144
SS NUMBER: 280042
AWARDS: Golden Party Badge; War Merit Cross Second Class without Swords; War Merit Cross First Class without Swords; SS Honour Ring; SS Honour Sword.

Born in Wiesbaden, Stuckhart was a lawyer and a devoted supporter of Hitler. He drew up the Nuremberg laws, which were made public at the 1935 Nuremberg Rally and enforced from September of that year.

The first Reich law of citizenship recognised two degrees of humanity: the Reichsbürger, described as the citizens of pure German blood, and Staatsangehörige for all other categories of person who were the subjects of the state. The law for protection of German blood and honour forbade intermarriage between the two groups.

Stuckart replaced Hans Pfundtner as Chief State Secretary in Frick's Ministry of the Interior, and Himmler controlled it through him from 1935. After the death of the Minister of Justice, Gürtner, on 22 January 1941, Himmler wanted the administration of civil law to be handled by the Ministry of the Interior, which he also would control through Stuckart. Stuckart was appalled by the 'final solution' and he tried to persuade

Eichmann (q.v.) to spare the fringe categories of Jews, half-castes and those born of mixed marriages. Eichmann remained adamant. Stuckart appealed directly to Himmler, suggesting sterilisation, although having secretly ascertained from Dr Conti (q.v.) that this was impractical.

Himmler was convinced by his appeal and issued an edict to spare the lives of Jews born of mixed marriages, saving 28,000 people. After the 20 July Bomb Plot, Stuckart interrogated one of the leading conspirators, Paul Kanstein, and released him. Kaltenbrunner (q.v.), convinced of his guilt, was furious with Stuckart and never forgave him for his meddling and leniency.

After the war Stuckart was tried in the Wilhelmstrasse Case in 1949. The humane acts he carried out during the war at considerable personal risk brought a sentence of three years and 10 months' imprisonment. He was released the day after his sentence. He was killed near Hanover in a car accident in December 1953.

T

THOMAS, Dr Max
RANK: SS-Gruppenführer
BORN: 4 August 1891
DIED: 1944 (K.I.A.)
PARTY NUMBER: 1848453
SS NUMBER: 141341
AWARDS: 1914 Iron Cross Second Class; 1914 Iron Cross First Class; Cross of Honour 1914-1918 Combatants; 1939 Iron Cross First Class Bar; War Merit Cross Second Class with Swords; War Merit Cross First Class with Swords; 1939 Wound Badge Black Class; SS Honour Ring; SS Honour Sword.

Thomas was the SS Police Chief in France from 1940 until 1942, when one of Heydrich's (q.v.) plots to bomb two of Paris's synagogues went farcically wrong. Stülpnagel, the military governor of France, discovered accidentally the involvement of Knochen (q.v) and the implied involvement of Thomas.

Highly incensed, Stülpnagel complained to Keitel, commander of the High Command of the Armed Forces, that the Gestapo was intensifying his difficulties with the French. In response, Keitel politely wrote to Heydrich on 22 October requesting the recall of Thomas and Knochen from France. Heydrich answered Keitel from Prague with a letter to Quartermaster-General Wagner, which he worded in the most insulting terms: 'My director of services in Paris did not think it necessary to tell Stülpnagel because our experience gave little hope of his comprehension. I was well aware of the political consequences of these measures, the more so since I have been entrusted for years with the final solution of the Jewish problem.'

However, Thomas was transferred to Russia, where Heydrich saddled him with an Einsatzgruppe. He went on to become the SS Police Chief for the Ukraine, and it is thought he was killed in action sometime in 1944, though his ultimate fate is unknown.

V

VEESENMAYER, Dr Edmund
RANK: SS-Brigadeführer
BORN: 12 November 1904
DIED: November 1977 (D)
PARTY NUMBER: 873780
SS NUMBER: 202122
AWARDS: War Merit Cross Second Class with Swords; War Merit Cross First Class with Swords; Knight's Cross of the War Merit Cross with Swords, 29 October 1944; SS Honour Ring; SS Honour Sword.

Rabidly anti-Semitic, Veesenmayer joined the Allgemeine-SS and became a protégé of Wilhelm Keppler (q.v.). Keppler's failure to become minister of economic affairs channelled his ambitions towards diplomacy. During the plotting which preceded the Austrian Anschluss, Himmler (q.v.) secured his appointment as Secretary of the Vienna Embassy. Keppler fulfilled similar missions in Slovakia and Danzig on the eve of their digestion, and Veesenmayer accompanied him. Veesenmayer became a recognised member of the Foreign Office at the beginning of the war, with the post of Plenipotentiary for Ireland, and with Admiral Canaris, he concocted schemes for using Irish nationalist terrorists against England in early 1940.

Veesenmayer's professional home was not the Foreign Office, but the SS, and he had to serve two masters: his immediate chief, von Ribbentrop, and Kaltenbrunner (q.v.) at the Reich's main security office. His position was often tricky, because Kaltenbrunner, having swallowed Canaris's *Abwehr*, was trying to absorb the Foreign Office too. However, there could never be any quarrel between Kaltenbrunner and Ribbentrop over the extermination of European Jewry. For this purpose Veesenmayer was not ill-chosen. He composed long reports to Ribbentrop on Hungary's failure to deport Jews in May 1943 and on Slovakia's failure to renew the deportations in December.

On the strength of these cold, inhumane and ill-informed documents (which Veesenmayer insisted later were amended by Ribbentrop before he signed them), this insignificant person became Plenipotentiary to Hungary, a position he held from March to October 1944 due to Hewel's forcing Admiral Horthy, Hungary's Regent, with the threat of kidnapping, to accept a German occupational force. He was really appointed for little other purpose than to provide Eichmann (q.v.) with diplomatic cover to continue deporting Jews from Hungary.

After the war Veesenmayer was tried for war crimes and sentenced to 25 years' imprisonment. This sentence was commuted to 10 years; he was released from Landsberg in December 1951, having played a part in the murder of at least 300,000 persons.

VEISS, Woldemars

RANK: Waffen-Standartenführer der SS
BORN: 7 November 1899
DIED: 16 April 1944 (K.I.A.)
PARTY NUMBER: —
SS NUMBER: —
AWARDS: 1939 Iron Cross Second Class; 1939 Iron Cross First Class; Knight's Cross of the Iron Cross, 9 February 1944.

Born in Riga, Latvia, Veiss joined the Latvian anti-Soviet forces under Colonel Kalpak when he was a student in 1918, and was quickly made an officer. He went on to join the Latvian regular army, holding many commands and serving as military attaché in Finland and Estonia in 1939. The three independent Baltic states were occupied in June 1940 by the Soviets as a result of the Russo-German Pact of 1939, when Stalin announced their 'voluntary incorporation' into the Union of Soviet Socialist Republics.

There followed a year of terror and repression when Veiss had no alternative than to go underground until the German invasion of June 1941. To the Baltic people, everyone who took up arms against the Stalinist regime had to be regarded as a protester, if not as a friend.

Veiss assisted in the formation of security forces which attempted to rid the country of Soviet soldiers and communist partisans who had banded together. Hitler and the SS main office in 1943 ordered the expansion of the Latvian forces, and Veiss was instrumental in forming the new unit.

He became the commanding officer of the new 40th Volunteer Brigade of the SS, and fought for several months against advancing Soviet forces in the Wolchov area. Veiss and his men displayed considerable heroism in both offensive and defensive actions, and for this he was awarded the Knight's Cross of the Iron Cross.

Later, he was seriously wounded and died of his wounds in a military hospital in Riga. He was given a formal funeral which was attended by several high-ranking German officers, including the army commanding general, Georg Lindemann.

W

WÄCHTER, Dr Otto

RANK: SS-Gruppenführer
BORN: 8 July 1901
DIED: unknown
PARTY NUMBER: 301093
SS NUMBER: 235368
AWARDS: Commemorative Medal of 13 March 1938; Commemorative Medal of 1 October 1938; Prague Castle Bar; SS Honour Ring; SS Honour Sword.

Dr Otto Wächter was a key figure in the formation of the Ukrainian SS divisions after the invasion of Russia.

The Stalin-Hitler 'Pact of Friendship' in August 1939 put Galicia in the Russian sphere of influence. With Poland's partition in September, Galicia was among the territories ceded to the USSR and for the next 21 months was subject to Stalinist rule. It was therefore with something akin to relief that the Galicians welcomed the arrival, in June 1941, of Hitler's armies. In August 1941 Galicia was made a fourth district of the General Government. Dr Otto Wächter, who was attached to the staff of the SS-Oberabschnitt Ost, had been promoted to the purely SS rank of SS-Brigadeführer on 9 November 1939, and was made Governor of Galicia in 1941, a position he held until 1944. Under his governorship it enjoyed a fair degree of autonomy.

Wächter was one of the more enlightened German administrators of the eastern territories, seeking to win the local population's cooperation rather than bludgeoning them into submission. As a result, Galicia was one of the most peaceful regions of the occupied Ostgebiete. Wächter had been in Lvov since 1941 and knew and understood the people; he was anxious to obtain from his fellow countrymen a better understanding of the Ukrainians and a closer collaboration between the Ukraine and Germany. He believed that raising a Ukrainian division to fight Bolshevism alongside the Germans was a step in the right direction. He suggested the idea to Himmler (q.v.), and in March 1943 obtained approval for the raising of a 'police regiment Galicia'.

Disaster at Stalingrad in January 1943 made Himmler more receptive to the idea of recruiting slaves for the Waffen-SS, and he proposed that the police regiment be transferred into a combat division. Wächter's ultimate fate is unknown.

WAGNER, Jürgen

RANK: SS-Gruppenführer und Generalleutnant der Waffen-SS
BORN: 9 September 1901
DIED: August 1947 (E.A.)
PARTY NUMBER: 707279
SS NUMBER: 23692
AWARDS: 1939 Iron Cross Second Class, 16 May 1940; Iron Cross First Class,
7 July 1940; German Cross in Gold, 14 December 1942; Knight's Cross, 24 July 1943; Oakleaves, 29 December 1944; 1939 Wound Badge Black Class; SS Honour Ring; SS Honour Sword.

Born in Strassburg-Neudorf, Alsace, Wagner joined the *Leibstandarte* in July 1933, and was transferred to the SS-Standarte *Deutschland* in 1939. He became regimental commander of Panzergrenadier Regiment *Germania*, 5th SS Panzer Division *Wiking*, on the Russian Front, where he was awarded the Knight's Cross of the Iron Cross.

Wagner assumed command of the 23rd Freiwilligen Panzergrenadier Division *Nederland* when Himmler (q.v.) wanted to pool all 'Nordic' volunteers into a single division. Mussert, the Dutch Nazi leader, was outraged by this suggestion and complained that since the Dutch outnumbered all the rest, they were entitled to an ethnic unit of their own. Hitler supported this and ordered Himmler to withdraw the Dutch complement from the projected *Nordland* Division. Eventually sufficient numbers – some 5500 men – were obtained, to advance the unit as a battalion.

It was raised in Croatia in 1943, where it first saw action against Tito's partisans. Wagner was awarded the Oakleaves, becoming the 580th recipient. The unit acquired an excellent combat reputation and Wagner went on to lead his unit with considerable success against the advancing Russian forces. He surrendered the remnants of his unit to the American forces at Tangermünde on the River Elbe on 1 May 1945. He was handed over to the British military authorities, who then sent him on to Belgrade after a request from the Yugoslav Government to have him extradited as a war criminal. He was tried by a military tribunal for war crimes, found guilty and sentenced to death. He was executed in 1947.

WEBER, Christian
RANK: SS-Brigadeführer
BORN: 25 August 1883
DIED: April 1945 (K.I.A)
PARTY NUMBER: 15
SS NUMBER: 265902
AWARDS: Stosstrupp Cuff Band; Blood Order No 84; Coburg Badge, 14 October 1932; SS Honour Ring; SS Honour Sword.

Born in Polsingen, Weber was a lifelong horse fancier, becoming a bookmaker and publican. He was one of the first members of Hitler's Stosstrupp, whose headquarters were established in the Torbräu public house. The formation was commanded by Berchtold and Schreck (q.v.), accompanied by Ulrich Graf (q.v.), Emil Maurice (q.v.), 'Sepp' Dietrich (q.v.) and Weber himself. All were linked by a strong sense of camaraderie and by an absolute commitment to protect Hitler, even at the risk of losing their own lives. In this privileged position Weber became part of Hitler's inner circle and was involved in the Röhm Purge of 1934. The sanctity of the Blood Order, its award and the social benefits conferred upon its holders was carefully scrutinised by the office of '9 November'. It also looked after the participants of the 1923 Putsch. Although he faded from prominence, Hitler entrusted him with his safety during the 'old guard's' annual gathering on 8 November in Munich.

Had the police or SS been responsible for security on these occasions, the bomb that exploded on 8 November 1939, nearly killing Hitler, would probably have been detected. In the event, Weber was compromised. He was killed in April 1945 during the Bavarian separatist uprising.

WEIDINGER, Otto
RANK: SS-Obersturmbannführer
BORN: 27 May 1914
DIED: 10 January 1990 (D)
AWARDS: 1939 Iron Cross Second Class, 15 July 1939; 1939 Iron Cross First Class, 25 July 1940; German Cross in Gold, 26 November 1943; Knight's Cross of the Iron Cross, 21 April 1944; Oakleaves, 26 December 1944; Swords, 6 May 1945; War Merit Cross Second Class with Swords; Commemorative Medal of 13 March 1938; Commemorative Medal of 1 October 1938; Close Combat Clasp Bronze Class; 1939 Wound Badge Black Class; SS Honour Ring; SS Honour Sword.

Weidinger was born in Würzburg on the Main river and volunteered for the SS-*Verfügungstruppe* in 1934. He attended the SS officers' school in Brünswick, graduating in 1935. He was the adjutant of a reconnaissance unit that was the eyes and ears of the Standarte *Deutschland* in the campaigns in Poland and France.

Having served in Yugoslavia and then on the Russian Front, he returned to the SS officers' school at Brünswick in October 1943, this time as an instructor in tactics. Later that year he was transferred to the *Das Reich* Division in Russia. There he was awarded the Knight's Cross of the Iron Cross for actions on the Russian Front.

In 1944 he took command of the Battle Group *Das Reich*. His unit was transferred to France, where he commanded the 4th SS-Panzergrenadier Regiment Der Führer. With the American advance into northern France, thousands of German troops were threatened with encirclement but Weidinger's leadership enabled the German forces to escape north. In recognition of his leadership and bravery he was awarded the Oakleaves, becoming the 688th recipient. His unit was transferred to Hungary where it fought a rearguard action and Weidinger was awarded the Swords, becoming the 150th recipient. He surrendered his unit on 9 May 1945.

Weidinger and some of his men were tried by the French for war crimes, but were acquitted. He later died in Aalen in April 1990.

WINKELMANN, Otto
RANK: SS-Obergruppenführer und General der Polizei
BORN: 4 September 1894
DIED: 24 September 1977 (D)
PARTY NUMBER: 1373131
SS NUMBER: 308238
AWARDS: War Merit Cross with Swords Second Class, 20 April 1941; War Merit Cross with Swords First Class, 30 January 1942; German Cross in Silver, 5 November 1943; Knight's Cross of the War Merit Cross with Swords, 21 December 1944; Silesian Eagle First Class; Wound Badge; SS Honour Ring; SS Honour Sword.

Born in Otterndorf near Bordesholm Hrlothew, Winkelmann joined the army as a cadet in 1912, was commissioned as a lieutenant in 1913 and fought through World War I. In 1919, he joined the Prussian Schutzpolizei, and from 1933 to 1937 he was the State Police Director in Göritz. In November 1937, he was transferred to the headquarters of the *Ordnungspolizei*, and in March 1944 he was appointed Higher SS and Police Leader in Hungary by Hitler himself.

Winkelmann was a colourless individual who had been Daluege's (q.v.) successor as the head of the German regular police. He was not a violently indoctrinated SS man; he was good-natured and lazy, and left his nasty responsibilities in the hands of Edmund Veesenmayer (q.v.) and the two Hungarian special commissioners, Endre and Baky. An Einsatzgruppe of the security police had been assembled in Mauthausen concentration camp for use in the Hungarian region.

The real purpose of it was to remove all Jews from Hungary when the country became a combat area. Hitler's brief to Winkelmann was 'to perform tasks of the SS and police concerning Hungary and especially duties in connection with the Jewish problem'. By December 1944 Winkelmann had become combat commander of Budapest, and he was awarded the Knight's Cross of the War Merit Cross for his services. Himmler (q.v.) proposed treating Budapest like Warsaw, smashing all resistance and making the defence of the city against the Russians a purely German matter.

Finally he declared it an area of partisan warfare and sent in von dem Bach-Zelewski (q.v.). The position in Budapest and with Horthy became very fraught and Bach-Zelewski was recalled by Himmler for more important tasks. Winkelmann was again in control. He survived the war and died in Kiel in 1977.

WIRTH, Christian

RANK: SS-Oberführer
DIED: 1945 (K.I.A.)
PARTY NUMBER: —
SS NUMBER: —

A former Stuttgart police officer, Wirth was recommended to Himmler's (q.v.) euthanasia programme by Nebe (q.v). He was an expert in all three phases of the programme: incurables, direct extermination by special treatment, and experiments in mass sterilisation. When Himmler complained that a better method had to be found to liquidate Polish Jews, Grawitz (q.v.) suggested Wirth for the task. Wirth was immediately assigned to Poland to work under Odilo Globocnik (q.v.), with the brief to find a method of dispatching one million Polish Jews more efficiently than the gas vans and firing squads. He selected an area along the Lublin-Lwow railway for his first experimental camp and went on to head an organisation of four extermination camps.

Wirth decided he wanted nothing to do with gas vans or mobile death units, using instead a stationary unit with three 'shower rooms', constructed at the centre of the camp. He camouflaged them by planting geraniums and trimming the surrounding grass. The victims were pacified by the thought of a shower, but inside were killed by exhaust gas from diesel engines. Wirth fitted wide doors on both front and back walls to make the removal of gassed victims easier. He was so pleased with the killing centre that he added three more to allow the camp to deal with 1500 Jews daily. In a particularly sick touch, he hung a sign over the gate that read, 'Entrance to the Jewish State'. Above the entrance to the gas chamber was a banner made from a synagogue curtain which stated in Hebrew, 'This is the gate of the Lord into which the righteous shall enter'.

Wirth was an egotist without conscience. An eyewitness remembers him striking a woman across the face with five lashes of a whip to encourage her into the chamber. Worse, the engines failed to work and the victims were crammed in for two hours and 49 minutes before they started. A further 35 minutes passed before all were dead. Then, the workers prised open the victims' mouths with iron bars, searching for gold teeth, and checked their private parts for hidden valuables.

Wirth was dubbed, 'the death camp king' but this title aroused the jealousy of others determined to topple him, in particular Höss (q.v.), who eventually succeeded him. Wirth accompanied Globocnik to Trieste in September 1943 and it is said that he was ultimately killed by Tito's partisans.

WISLICENY, Dieter

RANK: Sturmbannführer
BORN: 1899
DIED: July 1948 (E.A.)
PARTY NUMBER: —
SS NUMBER: —

Born in East Prussia, Wisliceny joined the SS and became an official in Eichmann's (q.v.) Jewish resettlement office, part of the Gestapo Büro IV A,4b. He became a key figure in devising schemes and making collective bargains for Jewish lives in Slovakia, Hungary and Greece. In 1942, Himmler (q.v.) received a proposal through him, from the Bratislava Zionist Relief Committee, that two million Dollars' worth of foreign currency would be available for Jewish lives. Ultimately this money did not materialise, but the offer was a bridge not only to immense international funds which might be extracted from world Jewry, but also towards peace discussions with the West.

Wisliceny was transferred to Budapest and his first proposals to the head of the Hungarian Jewish community were modest, but on 5 May 1944 a staggering offer was made by Eichmann to Joel Brand of the Budapest Joint Distribution Committee. The author of this plan is unclear: Becher (q.v.), Schellenberg (q.v.) or Himmler (q.v.) himself. Brand was to go to Istanbul and offer the lives of 700,000 Jews of Greater Hungary in exchange for 10,000 lorries from the Allies which would be delivered to the port of Salonika.

Eichmann promised that the Jews, who had already been deported to Germany, would be kept alive for a fortnight, but if he heard nothing, he would 'let the Auschwitz mills grind'. On 14 June Eichmann made the Budapest Jews a new proposal – 20 million Swiss Francs would save the lives of 30,000 Jews who were to be deported from old Hungarian communities west of the River Theisses. Meanwhile, Jewish international charity found the 20 million Francs and 1684 Jews were taken from Belsen and released in Switzerland in two trains on 21 August and 6 December 1944. However, only five million Swiss Francs were transferred to Himmler, and this only after a further 1100 Jews were released in Switzerland in February 1945.

After the war, Wisliceny was arrested and became a prosecution witness at Nuremberg. He was returned to Czechoslovakia where he was tried, and hanged at Bratislava in July 1948.

WITTMANN, Michael

RANK: SS-Hauptsturmführer
BORN: 22 April 1914
DIED: 8 August 1944 (K.I.A.)
PARTY NUMBER: —
SS NUMBER: —
AWARDS: 1939 Iron Cross Second Class, 12 July 1941; 1939 Iron Cross First Class, 8 September 1941; Knight's Cross of the Iron Cross, 14 January 1944; Oakleaves, 30 January 1944; Swords, 22 June 1944.

Wittmann was one of the most successful tank killers in World War II. He was born in Vogenthal, Upper Palatinate, and joined the *Leibstandarte*, remaining with this unit until his death. He saw action in the Polish campaign followed by Holland, France, Greece, Russia and then returning to France.

In early 1943, Wittmann received his first Tiger tank on the Eastern Front. The secret of his success was patience and steady nerves – he often waited for his victim to come within close range. By the end of the Kursk Offensive, Wittmann had destroyed some 38 enemy tanks and 45 artillery pieces. He was awarded the Knight's Cross of the Iron Cross as a platoon leader on the Russian Front, where he achieved the majority of his kills. Two weeks later he won the Oakleaves, becoming the 380th recipient. When the D-Day invasion came, I SS Panzer Corps, to which the LSSAH was attached, quickly engaged the invading force. During the fierce counterattacks against the Allies in the area of Caen and Villers-Bocage, Wittmann and his crew performed almost superhuman feats. When total chaos reigned among the British, Wittmann suddenly appeared in the middle of a column of tanks and motorised units, wreaking havoc. He was awarded the Swords for his actions, being the 71st recipient. At this time he was accredited with 138 tanks and 132 vehicles destroyed. Wittmann was killed with his crew on 8 August 1944 by either a bomb or tank shell, near Gaumesnil, just south of Caen.

WOLFF, Karl

RANK: SS-Obergruppenführer
BORN: 13 May 1900
DIED: July 1984 (D)
PARTY NUMBER: 695131
SS NUMBER: 14235
AWARDS: 1914 Iron Cross Second Class; 1914 Iron Cross First Class; Cross of Honour 1914-1918 Combatants; 1914 Wound Badge Black Class; German Olympic Games Decoration First Class, 29 October 1936; 1939 Iron Cross Second Class Bar; 1939 Iron Cross First Class Bar; NSDAP Long Service Medal 10 Years, 30 January 1941; Commemorative Medal of 13 March 1938; Commemorative Medal of 1 October 1938; Prague Castle Bar, 19 December 1939; Commemorative Medal for the return of the Memel Region, 19 December 1939; SS Honour Ring; SS Honour Sword; Italy: Grand Cross of the Order of the Crown.

Having served in World War I, Wolff subsequently joined the Hessian Freikorps. He joined both the NSDAP and SS in 1931 and served briefly as Ritter von Epp's personal adjutant in 1933. Himmler (q.v.) noticed him and in 1935 appointed him as his own adjutant. Wolff headed Himmler's personal staff and was liaison officer for the Reichsführer with Hitler from 1939 until 1943, when Himmler dismissed him because of his insistence on divorcing his wife, against Himmler's wishes. Throughout this period, he was a close confidant of Himmler's and shared in the development of the SS and its Teutonic mystique.

Wolff was transferred to Italy as military governor of northern Italy and Plenipotentiary General of the *Wehrmacht* in 1943, helping Mussolini to re-establish a Fascist regime under German domination. By February 1945 he was convinced that the war was lost, but real power in the region lay with Kesselring, commander of the German armed forces. Wolff attempted to make peace with the Allies in Italy, making contact with Allen Dulles, the American head of the capital's OSS (Office of Strategic Services). Although forbidden by Hitler to negotiate peace in Italy, he went ahead and a surrender was signed on the day of Hitler's suicide.

After the war Wolff was sentenced by a de-Nazification court to four years, but only served one week of his sentence before being released. He was living quietly as a successful public relations man when, during the Eichmann trial (q.v.), he wrote an article on Himmler. He was then tried in July 1964 and eventually charged with organising additional rolling stock to transport Jews to extermination camps. This rather flimsy charge resulted in a 10-year prison sentence.

WOYRSCH, Udo von

RANK: SS-Obergruppenführer
BORN: 24 July 1895
DIED: unknown
PARTY NUMBER: 162349
SS NUMBER: 3689
AWARDS: Golden Party Badge; 1914 Iron Cross Second Class; 1914 Iron Cross First Class; Cross of Honour 1914-1918 Combatants; War Merit Cross Second Class with Swords; War Merit Cross First Class with Swords; SS Honour Ring; SS Honour Sword.

Von Woyrsch served as a first lieutenant during World War I and joined the frontier protection service afterwards. He organised the SS in Silesia on Himmler's (q.v.) direction. During the Röhm Putsch of 30 June 1934 he took command in Silesia, and on the orders of Göring arrested a number of SA leaders, disarmed all SA headquarters' guards and occupied the Breslau police headquarters. Von Woyrsch's men murdered some of the SA officers as a result of an on-going private feud.

A particularly barbaric man, Woyrsch headed an Einsatzgruppe in September 1939 that was to operate in the Katowice area to liquidate the Jews and Poles. The plan was to transport 50,000 Jews from West Prussia and Danzig into Poland's interior. However, German officers in the area strongly objected, so brutal were his troops and so frequent were the mass murders. These officers also called for Woyrsch's men to be transferred to the front and face real fighting rather than rounding up and murdering defenceless civilians.

On their insistence, particularly that of General Gerd von Rundstedt, Commander-in-Chief East, Himmler withdrew Woyrsch's special task force and called a halt to the massacres, albeit very grudgingly. From 20 April 1940, he was Higher SS and Police Leader in military IV and district leader in Dresden until February 1944. Like many others, Von Woyrsch's ultimate fate is unknown.

Z

ZIEGLER, Joachim

RANK: SS-Brigadeführer und Generalmajor der Waffen-SS
BORN: 18 October 1904

DIED: 1 May 1945 (K.I.A.)
PARTY NUMBER: —
SS NUMBER: 491403
AWARDS: Iron Cross Second Class, 23 September 1939; Iron Cross First Class, 28 June 1940; German Cross in Gold, 15 March 1943; Knight's Cross of the Iron Cross, 5 September 1944; Oakleaves, 28 April 1945.

Ziegler was born in Hanau, Main. He saw service in Poland and then in the Low Countries and France in 1940. On 28 July 1944, he became the commanding officer of the 11th SS Freiwilligen-Panzer-grenadier Division *Nordland*, III (Germ.) SS Panzer Corps, Army Group North, and was awarded the Knight's Cross of the Iron Cross two months later. *Nordland* joined a variety of elements under Army Group Steiner in a desperate offensive in Pomerania on 16 February 1945. The aim was to thrust to the northwest against the northern flank of Marshal Zhukov's First Russian Front. In two days the offensive ground to a halt.

Fighting followed around Storgard, but *Nordland* was forced to leave on 3 March. Defensive battles followed around the Altdamm Bridgehead until the division was withdrawn on 20 March and sent to the Schwedt-Angermünde area, some 44 miles (70km) northwest of Berlin. Ziegler established his staff quarters at Angermünde. It was here that a number of Britons were added to the division's ranks: members of the British Freikorps. The *Nordland* Division was now desperately trying to hold the Russian drive to Berlin.

The final Soviet offensive against the city opened on 16 April, and two days later the division was ordered into the city. In the face of vastly superior numbers it fell back towards the government quarter. Plans had been made for *Nordland* to escort Hitler in a desperate breakout through Grunewald, but even Hitler realised that this was impossible. An enraged Führer relieved Ziegler of his command on 26 April and placed him under arrest in the bunker, although strangely he bestowed the Oakleaves on him two days later, making him the 848th recipient.

After Hitler's suicide Ziegler was freed, and while he was trying to negotiate a truce was killed near the Friedrichstrasse railway station in Berlin on 1 May 1945.

ZIEREIS, Franz

RANK: SS-Standartenführer
BORN: 13 August 1905
DIED: May 1945 (K.I.A.)
PARTY NUMBER: 5716146
SS NUMBER: 276998
AWARDS: War Merit Cross Second Class with Swords; War Merit Cross First Class with Swords; German Horseman's Badge Bronze; SS Honour Ring; SS Honour Sword.

Ziereis was commandant of Mauthausen concentration camp. In the closing days of the war Hitler ordered Pister (q.v.), who was in command of the camps in the south, that Dachau, Mauthausen and Theresienstadt were to be blown up, with their inmates if they could not be evacuated before the arrival of the Allies. It would have fallen to Kaltenbrunner (q.v.) to implement Hitler's murderous order, but he had no motive for doing so. An affidavit from an assistant to the Gauleiter of Munich reported that he was going to bomb Dachau from the air, while a Swiss Red Cross observer, who was allowed into Mauthausen, learned that Ziereis planned to blow up all the inmates in an aircraft construction hangar at Gusen. However, he never attempted to put the plan into action, preferring to disguise himself and hide in the camp. After the liberation he was shot by a US Army patrol while resisting capture. In a dying testimony taken down by a camp inmate in the presence of American officers who spoke no German, Ziereis denounced Kaltenbrunner as the author of the Gusen plan, whereas Kaltenbrunner had in fact signed an order that the camp should be handed over to Patten's troops intact.

WAFFEN-SS DIVISIONS 1939–45

TITLE (AND NOMINAL DIVISIONAL STRENGTH AT THE BEGINNING OF 1945)	GRANTED DIVISIONAL STATUS	KNIGHT'S CROSSES AWARDED
1st SS-Panzer Division *Leibstandarte*-SS Adolf Hitler (22,000)	1942	58
2nd SS-Panzer Division *Das Reich* (18,000)	1939	69
3rd SS-Panzer Division *Totenkopf* (15,400)	1939	47
4th SS-Panzergrenadier Division *Polizei* (9,000)	1939	25
5th SS-Panzer Division *Wiking* (14,800)	1940	55
6th SS-Gebirgs Division *Nord* (15,000)	1941	4
7th SS-Freiwilligen Gebirgs Division *Prinz Eugen* (20,000)	1942	6
8th SS-Kavallerie Division *Florian Geyer* (13,000)	1942	22
9th SS-Panzer Division *Hohenstaufen* (19,000)	1943	12
10th SS-Panzer Division *Frundsberg* (15,500)	1943	13
11th SS-Freiwilligen Panzergrenadier Division *Nordland* (9,000)	1943	25
12th SS-Panzer Division Hitlerjugend (19,500)	1943	14
13th Waffen Gebirgs Division der SS *Handschar* (12,700)	1943	4
14th Waffen Grenadier Division der SS (22,000)	1943	1
15th Waffen Grenadier Division der SS (16,800)	1943	3
16th SS-Panzergrenadier Division *Reichsführer-SS* (14,000)	1943	1
17th SS-Panzergrenadier Division *Götz von Berlichingen* (3500)	1943	4
18th SS-Freiwilligen Panzergrenadier Division *Horst Wessel* (11,000)	1944	2
19th Waffen Grenadier Division der SS (9000)	1944	12
20th Waffen Grenadier Division der SS (15,500)	1944	5
21st Waffen Gebirgs Division der SS *Skanderbeg* (5000)	1944	0
22nd SS-Freiwilligen Kavallerie Division *Maria Theresa* (8000)	1944	6
23rd Waffen Gebirgs Division der SS *Kama* (disbanded late 1944, number '23' given to next division)	1944	0
23rd SS-Freiwilligen Panzergrenadier Division *Nederland* (6000)	1945	19
24th Waffen Gebirgskarstjäger Division der SS (3000)	1944	0
25th Waffen Grenadier Division der SS *Hunyadi* (15,000)	1944	0
26th Waffen Grenadier Division der SS (13,000)	1945	0
27th SS-Freiwilligen Grenadier Division *Langemarck* (7000)	1944	1
28th SS-Freiwilligen Grenadier Division *Wallonien* (4000)	1944	3
29th Waffen Grenadier Division der SS (disbanded late 1944, number '29' given to next division)	1944	0
29th Waffen Grenadier Division der SS (15,000)	1945	0
30th Waffen Grenadier Division der SS (4500)	1945	0
31st SS-Freiwilligen Grenadier Division *Böhmen-Mähren* (11,000)	1945	0
32nd SS-Freiwilligen Grenadier Division *30 Januar* (2000)	1945	0
33rd Waffen Kavallerie Division der SS (destroyed soon after formation, number '33' given to next division)	1945	0
33rd Waffen Grenadier Division der SS *Charlemagne* (7000)	1945	2
34th SS-Freiwilligen Grenadier Division *Landstorm Nederland* (7000)	1945	3
35th SS-Polizei Grenadier Division (5000)	1945	0
36th Waffen Grenadier Division der SS (6000)	1945	1
37th SS-Freiwilligen Kavallerie Division *Lützow* (1000)	1945	0
38th SS-Grenadier Division *Nibelungen* (1000)	1945	0

ORIGINS OF *WAFFEN-SS* HONOUR TITLES

Readers will have become familiar in the course of reading this book with the widespread practice in the Waffen-SS of awarding honour titles to various units. Although a few units of the Army were given titles as opposed to, or as well as, numbers, such as *Grossdeutschland*, *Feldherrnhalle*, etc., the use of titles was far more common in the Waffen-SS than in other branches of Germany's armed forces during World War II.

Honour titles fall into three basic categories. First, those which identify the ethnic or geographic origins of the unit and are self-explanatory: *Deutschland*, *Nederland*, *Danmark*, *Wallonien*, etc. Second, a number of units, particularly at regimental level, were named after contemporary German political and military figures, for example Adolf Hitler, Reinhard Heydrich and Theodor Eicke. Third, those named after historical characters. A number of Waffen-SS Divisions were named after politically acceptable characters from German and European history. Among the most important were:

Prinz Eugen: named after Prince Eugene of Savoy (1663–1736), who did much to improve the quality and reputation of the armies of Austria.

Florian Geyer: named after a Franconian Knight who led the peasant armies in the 'Bauernkrieg' of 1522–1525.

Hohenstaufen: almost certainly named after Friedrich Barbarossa (1194–1250), one of the most important of the Hohenstaufen family of German kings.

Frundsberg: named after Georg von Frundsberg (1473–1528), a German knight who had fought in the service of the Hapsburg Monarchy in several wars.

Götz von Berlichingen: named after a famous German Landsknecht (1480–1562), whose hand had been shot off in battle and replaced with a false fist made of iron, hence the mailed fist emblem of the division.

Inexplicably, some Waffen-SS units of extremely dubious military value were awarded honour titles, for example *Handschar* and *Skanderbeg*. The latter was even given the right to wear a cuffband bearing the name, while other divisions of excellent fighting quality, such as the 19th Waffen-Grenadier Division, received neither cuff title nor name. The bearing of an honour title by a Waffen-SS unit was therefore no real indication of elite status.

In the years since the end of World War II, original examples of Waffen-SS cuffbands have become highly prized collectors items commanding very high prices, so much so that fakes abound, not only of cuff titles which did exist, but for units which were never authorised a cuff title.

WAFFEN-SS RANKS AND THEIR ENGLISH EQUIVALENTS

WAFFEN-SS	ENGLISH EQUIVALENT	WAFFEN-SS	ENGLISH EQUIVALENT
SS-Schütze	Private	SS-Hauptsturmführer	Captain
SS-Oberschütze	Senior Private, attained after six months' service	SS-Sturmbannführer	Major
		SS-Oberbannsturmführer	Lieutenant-Colonel
SS-Sturmmann	Lance-Corporal	SS-Standartenführer	Colonel
SS-Rottenführer	Corporal	SS-Oberführer	Senior Colonel
SS-Unterscharführer	Senior Corporal /Lance-Sergeant	SS-Brigadeführer und Generalmajor der Waffen-SS	Major-General
SS-Scharführer	Sergeant	SS-Gruppenführer und Generalleutnant der Waffen-SS	Lieutenant-General
SS-Oberscharführer	Staff Sergeant		
SS-Hauptscharführer	Warrant Officer	SS-Obergruppenführer und General der Waffen-SS	General
SS-Sturmscharführer	Senior Warrant Officer after 15 years' service	SS-Oberstgruppenführer und Generaloberst der Waffen-SS	Colonel-General
SS-Untersturmführer	Second Lieutenant		
SS-Obersturmführer	First Lieutenant	Reichsführer-SS	(no English equivalent)

ORDER OF BATTLE OF THE WAFFEN- SS

The following list gives the final order of battle of the 38 divisions of the Waffen-SS, together with each division's principal component units (the numerical strength of a Waffen-SS division was around 19,000 men, though the later divisions never approached this level of manpower):

1ST SS PANZER DIVISION *LEIBSTANDARTE SS ADOLF HITLER*
SS-Panzergrenadier Regiment 1
SS-Panzergrenadier Regiment 2
SS-Panzer Regiment 1
SS-Panzer Artillerie Regiment

2ND SS PANZER DIVISION *DAS REICH*
SS-Panzergrenadier Regiment 3 *Deutschland*
SS-Panzergrenadier Regiment 4 *Der Führer*
SS-Panzer Regiment 2
SS-Panzer Artillerie Regiment 2

3RD SS PANZER DIVISION *TOTENKOPF*
SS-Panzergrenadier Regiment 5 *Thule*
SS-Panzergrenadier Regiment 6 *Theodor Eicke*
SS-Panzer Regiment 3
SS-Panzer Artillerie Regiment 3

4TH SS PANZERGRENADIER DIVISION *SS-POLIZEI*
SS-Panzergrenadier Regiment 7
SS-Panzergrenadier Regiment 8
SS-Artillerie Regiment 4
SS-Sturmgeschutz Abteilung 4

5TH SS PANZER DIVISION *WIKING*
SS-Panzergrenadier Regiment 9 *Germania*
SS-Panzergrenadier Regiment 10 *Westland*
SS-Panzer Regiment 5
SS-Panzer Artillerie Regiment 5

6TH SS GEBIRGS DIVISION *NORD*
SS-Gebirgsjäger Regiment 11 *Reinhard Heydrich*
SS-Gebirgsjäger Regiment 12 *Michael Gaissmair*
SS-Gebirgs Artillerie Regiment 6
SS-Sturmgeschutz Batterie 6

7TH SS FREIWILLIGEN-GEBIRGS DIVISION *PRINZ EUGEN*
SS-Freiwilligen Gebirgsjäger Regiment 13 *Artur Phleps*
SS-Freiwilligen Gebirgsjäger Regiment 14 *Skanderbeg*
SS-Freiwilligen Gebirgs Artillerie Regiment 7
SS-Sturmgeschutz Abteilung 7

8TH SS KAVALLERIE DIVISION *FLORIAN GEYER*
SS-Kavallerie Regiment 15
SS-Kavallerie Regiment 16
SS-Kavallerie Regiment 18
SS-Artillerie Regiment (mot) 8
SS-Panzerjäger Abteilung 8

9TH SS PANZER DIVISION *HOHENSTAUFEN*
SS-Panzergrenadier Regiment 19
SS-Panzergrenadier Regiment 20
SS-Panzer Regiment 9
SS-Panzer Artillerie Regiment 9

10TH SS PANZER DIVISION *FRUNDSBERG*
SS-Panzergrenadier Regiment 21
SS-Panzergrenadier Regiment 22
SS-Panzer Regiment 10
SS-Panzer Artillerie Regiment 10

11TH SS FREIWILLIGEN-PANZERGRENADIER DIVISION *NORDLAND*
SS-Panzergrenadier Regiment 23 *Norge*
SS-Panzergrenadier Regiment 24 *Danmark*
SS-Panzer Abteilung 11 *Herman von Salza*
SS-Panzer Artillerie Regiment 11

12TH SS PANZER DIVISION *HITLERJUGEND*
SS-Panzergrenadier Regiment 25
SS-Panzergrenadier Regiment 26
SS-Panzer Regiment 12
SS-Panzer Artillerie Regiment 12

13TH WAFFEN-GEBIRGS DIVISION DER SS (KROATISCHE NR 1) *HANDSCHAR*
SS-Waffen Gebirgsjäger Regiment 27
SS-Waffen Gebirgsjäger Regiment 28
SS-Waffen Artillerie Regiment 13
SS-Panzerjager Abteilung 13

14TH WAFFEN-GRENADIER DIVISION DER SS (UKRAINISCHE NR 1)
Waffen-Grenadier Regiment der SS 29
Waffen-Grenadier Regiment der SS 30
Waffen-Grenadier Regiment der SS 31
Waffen-Artillerie Regiment der SS 14

15TH WAFFEN-GRENADIER DIVISION DER SS (LETTISCHE NR 1)

Waffen-Grenadier Regiment der SS 32
Waffen-Grenadier Regiment der SS 33
Waffen-Grenadier Regiment der SS 34
Waffen-Artillerie Regiment der SS 15

16TH SS PANZERGRENADIER DIVISION *REICHSFÜHRER-SS*

SS-Panzergrenadier Regiment 35
SS-Panzergrenadier Regiment 36
SS-Artillerie Regiment 16
SS-Panzer Abteilung 16

17TH SS PANZERGRENADIER DIVISION *GÖTZ VON BERLICHINGEN*

SS-Panzergrenadier Regiment 37
SS-Panzergrenadier Regiment 38
SS-Panzer Artillerie Regiment 17
SS-Panzerjäger Abteilung 17

18TH SS FREIWILLIGEN-PANZERGRENADIER DIVISION *HORST WESSEL*

SS-Panzergrenadier Regiment 39
SS-Panzergrenadier Regiment 40
SS-Artillerie Regiment 18
SS Panzerjäger Abteilung 18

19TH WAFFEN-GRENADIER DIVISION DER SS (LETTISCHES NR 2)

Waffen-Grenadier Regiment der SS 42
Voldemars Veiss
Waffen-Grenadier Regiment der SS 43
Heinrich Schuldt
Waffen-Grenadier Regiment der SS 44
Waffen-Artillerie Regiment 19

20TH WAFFEN-GRENADIER DIVISION DER SS (ESTNISCHE NR 1)

Waffen-Grenadier Division der SS 45
Waffen-Grenadier Division der SS 46
Waffen-Grenadier Division der SS 47
Waffen-Artillerie Regiment 20

21ST WAFFEN-GEBIRGS DIVISION DER SS (ALBANISCHE NR 1) *SKANDERBEG*

Waffen-Gebirgs Division der SS 50
Waffen-Gebirgs Division der SS 51
Waffen-Gebirgs Artillerie Regiment 21

22ND FREIWILLIGEN-KAVALLERIE DIVISION DER SS *MARIA THERESIA*

Freiwilligen-Kavallerie Regiment der SS 52
Freiwilligen-Kavallerie Regiment der SS 53
Freiwilligen-Kavallerie Regiment der SS 54
Freiwilligen-Kavallerie Regiment der SS 55

23RD WAFFEN-GEBIRGS DIVISION DER SS *KAMA*

Waffen-Gebirgsjäger Regiment der SS 56
Waffen-Gebirgsjäger Regiment der SS 57
Waffen-Gebirgsjäger Regiment der SS 58
Waffen-Gebirgs Artillerie Regiment der SS 23

This division was disbanded in late 1944 and its remnants allocated to the 23rd Freiwilligen Panzergrenadier Division *Nederland*, though the latter never exceeded regimental strength. *Nederland* comprised the remains of two existing regiments, SS Freiwilligen Panzergrenadier Regiments 48 (*General Seyffardt*) and 49 (*De Ruiter*).

24TH SS GEBIRGS DIVISION *KARSTJÄGER*

Waffen-Gebirgsjäger Regiment der SS 59
Waffen-Gebirgsjäger Regiment der SS 60
Waffen-Gebirgs Artillerie Regiment 24

25TH WAFFEN-GRENADIER DIVISION DER SS (UNGARISCHE NR 1) *HUNYADI*

Waffen-Grenadier Regiment der SS 61
Waffen-Grenadier Regiment der SS 62
Waffen-Grenadier Regiment der SS 63
Waffen-Artillerie Regiment der SS 25

26TH WAFFEN-GRENADIER DIVISION DER SS (UNGARISCHE NR 2) *HUNGARIA*

Waffen-Grenadier Regiment der SS 64
Waffen-Grenadier Regiment der SS 65
Waffen-Grenadier Regiment der SS 66
SS-Panzer Bataillon 26

This division never reached full divisional status.

27TH SS FREIWILLIGEN-PANZERGRENADIER DIVISION (FLÄMISCHE NR 1) *LANGEMARCK*

This was a division in name only, and never exceeded regimental strength.

28TH SS FREIWILLIGEN-PANZERGRENADIER DIVISION *WALLONIEN*

This 'division' never exceeded regimental strength.

29TH WAFFEN-GRENADIER DIVISION DER SS (RUSSISCHE NR 1)

This unit was formed from Kaminski's infamous brigade. It was never a true division, and was subsequently absorbed into the Free Russian Army.

29TH WAFFEN-GRENADIER DIVISION DER SS (ITALIENISCHE NR 1)

This unit is not thought to have exceeded regimental strength. It received its number when the other 29th Division was absorbed into Vlassov's Army.

30TH WAFFEN-GRENADIER DIVISION DER SS (WEISSRUTHENISCHE NR 1)

Waffen-Grenadier Regiment der SS 75
Waffen-Grenadier Regiment der SS 76
Waffen-Grenadier Regiment der SS 77
Waffen-Artillerie Regiment der SS 30

31ST SS FREIWILLIGEN GRENADIER DIVISION

SS-Freiwilligen Grenadier Regiment 78
SS-Freiwilligen Grenadier Regiment 79
SS-Freiwilligen Grenadier Regiment 80
SS-Artillerie Regiment 31

32ND SS FREIWILLIGEN GRENADIER DIVISION *30 JANUAR*

This division was formed very late in the war and never reached full strength.

33RD WAFFEN-KAVALLERIE DIVISION DER SS (UNGARISCHE NR 3)

This division was never fully formed and was overrun by the Soviets when Hungary fell in 1945.

33RD WAFFEN-GRENADIER DIVISION DER SS (FRANZÖSISCHE NR 1) *CHARLEMAGNE*

This unit was formed from a Waffen-SS volunteer brigade, which in turn had originated from volunteers from the Army's *Legion Volontaire Français*. It never reached full divisional strength.

34TH WAFFEN-GRENADIER DIVISION DER SS *LANDSTORM NEDERLAND*

SS Freiwilligen Grenadier Regiment 48

This unit originated from the home guard Landwacht *Nederland*, being taken into the SS in 1943. Between November 1944 and March 1945 it was expanded and reformed as a division, but saw little action.

35TH SS POLIZEI GRENADIER DIVISION

Formed from policemen in the closing months of the war, this unit never reached divisional strength.

36TH WAFFEN-GRENADIER DIVISION DER SS

The infamous *Dirlewanger* Brigade, this unit thankfully never reached divisional strength. It was of extremely dubious military value.

37TH SS FREIWILLIGEN-KAVALLERIE DIVISION *LÜTZOW*

Little is known of the composition of the unit, which was formed in the closing days of the war and committed to action around Vienna.

38TH SS GRENADIER DIVISION *NIBELUNGEN*

Formed from staff and cadets of the Bad Tölz officer training school, this unit never exceeded regimental strength.

By the time the war ended, most of the Waffen-SS foreign volunteer units had been disbanded or amalgamated with newly formed divisions in the above order of battle.

Those which were not included in the order of battle of the Waffen-SS divisions, but which still existed by 1945, included such oddities as the Indische Freiwilligen-Legion der Waffen-SS, with its Indian volunteers; the Kaukasicher Waffenverband der SS, comprised of Azerbaidzhanis, Armenians, Georgians and volunteers from the Caucasus region; and the principally Moslem Osttürkische Waffenverband der SS. None of these units proved of great military value to the Waffen-SS.

ORGANISATION OF
AN SS PANZER DIVISION

The most effective, and certainly the most successful, of the Waffen-SS units were the elite panzer divisions. While, in the latter part of the war especially, few Waffen-SS divisions reached their full nominal strength, and several never even reached regimental strength, the panzer divisions of the Waffen-SS remained powerful and effective fighting forces throughout the war.

The following chart lists the main constituent units of a typical Waffen-SS panzer division at the time of the 1944 **Normandy battles:**

Divisions Stab (divisional staff)
Divisional Commander
General Staff Officers
Cartography Unit
Signals Element
Divisional Escort Unit
Military Police Element

Quartiermeister (divisional quartermaster)
Weapons Platoon
Mechanics
Staff Doctor
Staff Dentist

Panzer Regiment (tank regiment)
I Abteilung (detachment) – Four Companies (1-4)
                     Workshop Company
II Abteilung   Five Companies (5-9)
                     Workshop Company

Panzerjäger Abteilung (tank destroyer detachment)
Three companies of self-propelled guns

Panzergrenadier Regiment (armoured infantry regiment)
I Bataillon – Four Companies (1-4)
II Bataillon – Four Companies (5-8)
III Bataillon – Four Companies (9-12)
           Heavy Gun Company (13)
           Flak Company (14)
           Recce Company (15)
           Pioneer Company (16)

Panzergrenadier Regiment (as above)
(Waffen-SS panzer divisions fielded two panzer-grenadier regiments)

Panzer Aufklärungs Abteilung (armoured recce detachment)
Two Companies of Armoured Cars
Two Recce Companies
One Heavy Company

Panzer Artillerie Regiment (armoured artillery regiment)
I Abteilung – Three Batteries
II Abteilung – Three Batteries
III Abteilung – Three Batteries

Werfer Abteilung (mortar detachment)
Four Batteries

Flak Abteilung (anti-aircraft detachment)
Five Batteries

Panzer Pioniere Abteilung (armoured engineer detachment)
One Armoured Company
Three Pioneer Companies
One Bridging Company

Panzer Nachrichten Abteilung (armoured signals detachment)
One Telephone Company
One Radio Company

Divisions Nachschubtruppe (divisional supply troop)
Six Companies of Lorries
One Supply Company

Panzer Instandsetzungsabteilung (armoured maintenance detachment)
Three Workshop Companies
One Weapons Company
One Spares Company

Wirtschafts Bataillon (literally 'housekeeping' battalion)
Bakery Company
Butchery Company
Cooks
Field Post Office

No two Waffen-SS panzer divisions were absolutely identical in their composition, but the above, based on the 12th SS Panzer Division *Hitlerjugend*, is fairly typical.

CONCENTRATION CAMP STAFF

As the war in Europe drew to a close, few of the staff of Himmler's concentration camps harboured any illusions as to their fate if they fell into Allied hands. As enemy troops neared the sites of the concentration camps, the inmates were evacuated and force-marched to alternative camps still in German hands. In the last few days of the war, most of these unfortunates were simply abandoned or shot by their guards, who then made good their escape, hoping to assume false identities and thus avoid capture. Many were successful in this, and either avoided detection or remained at large for many years before being apprehended or killed.

Eventually, over 50,000 war criminals were tracked down, tried and punished for their deeds by courts in Germany and abroad.

The following list indicates the fate of some of the more notorious SS officers who served on the staff of the concentration camps:

Aumeier, Hans: served at Grini in Norway. Extradited to Poland, found guilty of war crimes and executed.

Baer, Richard: served at Auschwitz. Arrested but died in 1960 before being brought to trial.

Endreis, Friedrich Karl Hermann: served at Mauthausen. Found guilty of war crimes and executed in 1947.

Grabner, Max: served at Auschwitz. Captured after the war and hanged.

Göth, Amon: served at Plascow. Captured by the Americans, extradited to Poland and hanged.

Hasselbroek, Johannes: served at Auschwitz. Captured, served 15 years in prison.

Hoffmann, Franz Johann: served at Dachau. Sentenced to life imprisonment. On his release he was tried again for crimes committed at Auschwitz and received a further life sentence.

Hoppe, Paul Werner: served at Stutthof. Arrested but escaped to Switzerland; returned to Germany in the 1950s and was re-arrested. Served nine years in prison.

Hössler, Franz: served at Belsen. Executed in 1945.

Höss, Rudolf: commandant of Auschwitz. Executed.

Hüttig, Hans: served at Nazweiler. Captured, tried and sentenced to death. Commuted to 11 years in prison.

Kitt, Bruno: served at Neuengamme. Executed in 1946.

Koch, Karl: served at Buchenwald. Shot by the SS in 1945 for corruption.

Kögel, Max: served at Flossenbürg. Captured; committed suicide in 1946.

Kramer, Josef: commandant of Belsen. The 'Beast of Belsen' was captured by the British and executed.

Liebhenscher, Arthur: served at Auschwitz. Tried by the Poles and executed.

Moll, Otto: served at Auschwitz. Captured by the Americans. Tried and executed in 1946.

Muhsfeldt, Erich: served at Auschwitz. Tried by the Poles and executed.

Pauly, Max: served at Neuengamme. Executed.

Schwarz, Heinrich: served at Natzweiler. Tried by the French and executed in 1947.

Schwarzhuber, Johan: served at Ravensbrück. Tried in Hamburg in 1947 and sentenced to death.

Stangl, Franz: served at Treblinka. Escaped to South America but was subsequently discovered and extradited to Germany in 1967. Died awaiting trial.

Vetter, Helmuth: served at Mauthausen. Tried by the Americans in 1947; convicted and hanged in 1949.

Wirths, Eduard: served at Neuengamme. Captured and committed suicide in prison.

Ziereis, Franz: served at Mauthausen. Shot during his capture and died of his wounds.

Zill, Egon: served at Flossenbürg. Tried by a German court and given a life sentence. Served 15 years.

Also sought by the Allies were personnel of the Gestapo and SD. In many cases, however, there was little intent to prosecute these men. Rather, Allied intelligence services wished to make use of their talents. In the new communist East Germany, for example, many SD and Gestapo men found work with the Stasi – the Staatssicherheitsdienst – while in the West it is estimated that as much as five per cent of the personnel of the West German Bundesnachrichtendienst (BND) were former members of Hitler's security services. In addition, the American intelligence services also helped Nazi fugitives whom they considered useful.

Many German civil policemen served with police regiments on the Eastern Front during the war, often in conjunction with the notorious Einsatzgruppen. Little effort was made to punish the majority of these men, and many simply returned to their jobs in the civil police after the war.

The preparation of a book such as this requires, of necessity, the study of both published and unpublished works. The following list includes not only those works which were consulted in the preparation of this book, but those which are recommended for further reading:

Angolia, John R, *Cloth Insignia of the SS*, published by Bender Publishing, San Jose, Calif. (1983)

Bender, Roger J & Taylor, Hugh P, *Uniforms, Organisation and History of the Waffen-SS*, volumes 1-5, published by Bender Publishing, San Jose, Calif. (1969-83)

Browning, Christopher R, *Ordinary Men*, published by HarperCollins Publishing, New York (1992)

Bruce, George, *The Warsaw Uprising*, published by Rupert Hart-Davis Ltd, London (1972)

Buss, Phillip H & Mollo A, *Hitler's Germanic Legions*, published by McDonald & James, London (1978)

Butler, Rupert, *An Illustrated History of the Gestapo*, published by Ian Allan, Shepperton (1992)

Cross, Robin, *Citadel, The Battle of Kursk*, published by Michael O'Mara Books (1993)

Davis, Brian L, *Waffen-SS*, published by Blandford, Poole (1985)

Gilbert, Martin, *Final Journey: The Fate of the Jews in Europe*, published by George Allen & Unwin, London (1979)

Gilbert, Martin, *The Holocaust*, published by Collins, London (1986)

Höhne, Heinz, *The Order of the Death's Head*, published by Verlag Der Spiegel, Hamburg (1966)

Littlejohn, David, *Foreign Legions of the Third Reich*, vols 1-4, published by Bender Publishing, San Jose, Calif. (1979-87)

Lucas, James, *Das Reich*, published by Arms & Armour Press, London (1991)

Lucas, James, *Hitler's Mountain Troops*, published by Arms & Armour Press, London (1992)

Lumsden, Robin, *The Black Corps*, published by Ian Allan, Shepperton (1992)

Mackness, Robin, *Oradour, Massacre and Aftermath*, published by Bloomsbury Publishing Ltd (1988)

Mollo, Andrew, *Uniforms of the SS*, vols 1-7, published by the Historical Research Unit (1969-76)

Padfield, Peter, *Himmler: Reichsführer-SS*, published by Macmillan, London (1990)

Quarrie, Bruce, *Weapons of the Waffen-SS*, published by PSL, Cambridge (1988)

Quarrie, Bruce, *Lightning Death*, published by PSL, Cambridge (1991)

Read, Anthony & Fisher, David, *The Fall of Berlin*, published by Pimlico, London (1993)

Reitlinger, Gerald, *The SS: Alibi of a Nation*, published by Heinemann, London (1956)

Schoenberner, Gerhard, *The Yellow Star*, published by Corgi, London (1969)

Segev, Tom, *Soldiers of Evil: The Commandants of the Nazi Concentration Camps*, published by Collins, London (1969)

Stein, George H, *The Waffen-SS: Hitler's Elite Guard at War 1939-45*, published by Cornell, New York (1966)

Taylor, Simon, *Germany 1918-1933*, published by Duckworth, London (1983)

Additionally, the following divisional and regimental histories of the Waffen-SS combat units, published by Munin-Verlag of Osnabrück, contain information on the units and the personnel who served with them:

Lehman, Rudolf, *Leibstandarte*

Meyer, Hubert, *Die Kriegsgeschichte der 12 SS Panzer Division*

Proschek, Rolf, *Verweht sind die Spuren*

Schulze-Kossens, Richard & Ertel, Karl-Heinz, *Europaische Freiwilligen*

Stöber, Hans, *Die Sturmflut und das Ende*

Truppenkameradschaft der 4 SS-Polizei Division, *Die guten Glaubens waren*

Ullrich, Karl, *Wie ein Fels im Meer*

Weidinger, Otto, *Division Das Reich*

Also of importance to any study of the SS are the captured files held at the US Document Center in Berlin. A huge number of the original SS-Personalakte (personnel files) still exist, and many of these were consulted for this book, for both general information and information specific to individual characters.

INDEX

PHOTOGRAPHIC CREDITS

b = bottom, c = centre, l = left, r = right, t = top

Christopher Ailsby Historical Archives: 109, 112, 118, 210, 212t, 244 both, 246–289
Amber Books: 126, 127
Josef Charita: 19, 21, 50b, 95, 108, 110, 111, 129 both, 133, 135, 137, 172, 173
Robert Hunt Picture Library: 29, 31, 45, 46/47, 48, 50t, 52, 56, 57, 72b, 82/83, 85–92, 96/97, 99, 103, 107, 166, 168, 178, 182/3, 194, 198–201, 209, 224/5, 227–233, 236, 239, 242
Imperial War Museum: 187, 190, 235
Hans Heinrich Karck: 174r
Peter Newark's Pictures: 2/3, 6/7, 11, 49, 53tl, 53tc, 59t, 62, 63 both, 72t, 74, 76b, 156r, 158 both, 161t
Private Collection: 114, 115, 125
Popperfoto: 245
Bruce Quarrie Collection: 8, 9, 12–16, 22/23, 25–28, 30, 34, 37–44, 54, 55, 59b, 60 both, 61 both, 64/65, 67, 68, 70, 71t, 73 both, 76t, 77, 79–81, 84, 101, 116, 117, 120–123, 130, 136, 138–154, 156l, 157, 159, 160/161, 162–165, 169, 171, 174l, 175, 177, 180, 181, 185, 188, 189, 197, 202–207, 211, 212b, 213–223, 226, 240, 241, 243
Heinrich Springer: 66, 75
TRH Pictures: 71b, 186, 192 both, 193, 195, 196
John White: 32, 33, 35, 105, 134
Gordon Williamson: 24, 175

ARTWORK CREDITS

Graham Bingham: 194
Orbis Publishing Ltd: All other artworks